AF115766

Re-Segregation

Volume I: The Power Matrix. A Masterplan for Black Group Economics and Wealth Creation

Copyright © 2023 by Trient Press

All rights reserved. No part of this publication may be reproduced, distributed, or transmitted in any form or by any means, including photocopying, recording, or other electronic or mechanical methods, without the prior written permission of the publisher, except in the case of brief quotations embodied in critical reviews and certain other noncommercial uses permitted by copyright law. For permission requests, write to the publisher, addressed "Attention: Permissions Coordinator," at the address below.

Criminal copyright infringement, including infringement without monetary gain, is investigated by the FBI and is punishable by up to five years in federal prison and a fine of $250,000.

Except for the original story material written by the author, all songs, song titles, and lyrics mentioned in the novel Re-Segregation - Volume I: The Power Matrix. A Masterplan for Black Group Economics and Wealth Creation are the exclusive property of the respective artists, songwriters, and copyright holder.

Trient Press
3375 S Rainbow Blvd
#81710, SMB 13135
Las Vegas, NV 89180

Ordering Information:
Quantity sales. Special discounts are available on quantity purchases by corporations, associations, and others. For details, contact the publisher at the address above.
Orders by U.S. trade bookstores and wholesalers. Please contact Trient Press: Tel: (775) 996-3844; or visit www.trientpress.com.

Printed in the United States of America

Publisher's Cataloging-in-Publication data
Smith, Jr ; Antonio T
A title of a book : Re-Segregation - Volume I: The Power Matrix. A Masterplan for Black Group Economics and Wealth Creation

ISBN
Hard Cover   979-8-88990-125-9
Paper Back   979-8-88990-142-6
Ebook

Table of Contents

Re-Segregation:
Volume I: The Power Matrix. A Masterplan for Black Group Economics and Wealth Creation

Dedication 15
Introduction 17
   Unmasking The Realities and Plotting the Path Forward 20
   Addressing the Economic Disparities, Mindset Shifts, and Strategic Approaches to Black Wealth Creation 22
   Harnessing Resilience, Innovation, and Unity for Sustained Black Wealth Creation 24
   Embracing Technological Innovations and Comprehensive Solutions for Black Wealth Creation ... 25
   The Sixth Floor: The Beginning of the Power Matrix ... 27
   The Seventh Floor: Manufacturing and Infrastructure ... 28
   The Eighth Floor: Communications and Human Resources 29
   The Power Matrix: A Synthesis of Dr. Claud Anderson and Antonio T Smith, Jr's Understanding of Generating Black Wealth 30
   Embracing the Power Matrix: A Journey Towards Black Economic Empowerment 31
Chapter 1 34
The Black Wealth Gap: Understanding, Causes, and Implications 34
   Understanding The Black Wealth Gap 36
   Dissecting the Causes and Implications of the Black Wealth Gap 38
   Historical Context and Persistence of the Wealth Gap .. 40
   Sociopolitical Factors Influencing the Black Wealth Gap 42
   The Importance of Self-Generated and Self-Controlled Black Wealth 44

Financial Independence and Its Role in Economic
Empowerment 46
The Effects of White Wealth Accumulation on Black
Community Development 48
Examining Self-Sufficiency as a Tool Against Systemic
Economic Inequality 50
The Rationale for Blacks to Enact High Goal-Setting and
Increased Action in Wealth Creation 52
Highlighting the Importance of Ambition and Drive in
Wealth Creation 54
The History of Blacks and Their Correlation Between
High Goals and High Achievement 55
Establishing the Need for Active Participation in Wealth
Generation 57
Chapter 2 59
Defining the Scope of the Wealth Gap 59
The Economic Disparities Highlighted By Today's Laws
And Politics, Concerning Blacks 61
Disparities Exposed By The COVID-19 Pandemic And
Economic Downturn 63
Case Studies of How Economic Crises
Disproportionately Affect Black Communities 65
Analyzing The structural Inequities That Perpetuate
Economic Disparities 67
Framework For Understanding The Roles In The
Economy: Workers, Business Owners, Savers/Investors,
Consumers, Residents 69
Detailing The Different Roles And Their Economic
Functions 71
Examining How These Roles Interact Within The Larger
Economic System 73
Discussing The Unique Challenges Faced By Black
Individuals In Each Role 74
The Limitations And Acknowledgments of The Research 76
Discussing The Scope And Limitations of Existing 78

Research on Black Wealth 78
Acknowledging Areas That Require Further Study 80
Understanding The Constraints And Biases That May
Influence The Research 82
Chapter 3 85
Setting Your Wealth Goals: A Mindset Shift 85
The Concept of High Goals And Their Importance In
Creating Black Wealth 87
Delving Into The Psychology of High-Goal Setting 88
Analyzing The Transformative Effect of Ambitious Goals
on Wealth Creation 91
Demonstrating The Influence of Goal Setting on
Financial Success 93
Common Mistakes In Setting Wealth Goals And How To
Avoid Them 95
Identifying Pitfalls In Goal Setting And Planning 97
Providing Guidance On Realistic Yet Ambitious Goal
Setting 99
Offering Strategies for Maintaining Focus And
Motivation In Pursuing Wealth Goals 101
Case Studies Demonstrating The Successful Application
of A Black Wealth Creation 103
Analyzing Key Factors And Strategies Used In These
Successes 104
Drawing Actionable Insights From These Case Studies
For Readers 106
Chapter 4 109
The Economic Gaps: An In-depth Analysis 109
Presenting Data On Wage And Occupational Disparities 111
Discussing The Systemic Factors That Perpetuate These
Disparities 113
Exploring The Impact of These Disparities On Wealth
Accumulation And Economic Stability 115
The Concentration of Racial Wage Disparity In Different
Occupational Categories And Sectors Part 1 118

    The Concentration of Racial Wage Disparity In Different Occupational Categories And Sectors Part 2 121
    Providing A Sector-Wise Analysis of Racial Wage Disparities 123
    Exploring The Intersection of Race, Occupation, And Income 125
    Analyzing The Effects of Occupational Segregation On Wealth Generation 128
    Case Studies of Underrepresentation In High-Wage Professions 130
    Investigating The Underrepresentation of Black Individuals In High-Paying Jobs 132
    Investigating The Underrepresentation of Black Individuals In High-Paying Jobs Part 2 134
    Analyzing Barriers To Entry And Advancement In These Professions 136
    Examining The Effects of This Underrepresentation On Overall Black Wealth 138
Chapter 5 141
The Black Mindset For Overcoming Limiting Beliefs and Embracing Success When It Comes To Generating Massive Income 141
    The Role of Limiting Beliefs When It Comes To Creating Black Wealth Creation 145
    Discussing The Psychology of Limiting Beliefs And Their Effects On Financial Success 147
    Identifying Common Limiting Beliefs About Wealth And Success Amongst Black People Throughout The World 149
    Strategies To Dismantle These Limiting Beliefs 151
    The Importance of A Success-Oriented Mindset And Its Role In Creating Black Wealth 153
    The Importance of A Success-Oriented Mindset And Its Role In Restoring The Two Parent Family Part 2 157
    Providing Actionable Steps To Overcome Limiting Beliefs 159

Techniques For Nurturing A Growth Mindset And Cultivating Self-Confidence 162
Chapter 6 165
Ideas For Black Wealth Creation And Keeping Money In The Black Community 165
    Community Investment: Encourage A Cultural Shift Towards Investing In Black-Owned Businesses And Emphasizing The Importance of Keeping The Black Dollar Within The Community 168
    Promoting Wealth Creation, Savings, and Investments 170
    Fostering Innovation and Establishing Black-Owned Businesses 172
    Real Estate Ownership: A Stable, Long-Term Wealth Creation Strategy 175
    A Stepping Stone for Black Entrepreneurs 177
    Advocating Access to Capital: A Critical Avenue for Black-owned Businesses 179
    Tapping into the Economic Potential of Black Culture 183
    Technology and Innovation: The Gateway to Economic Empowerment 184
    Embracing AI: A Crucial Move Towards Future-Proofing Black Economic Power 186
    Health and Wellness 188
    A New Frontier for Black Wealth Creation and Environmental Responsibility 190
    Wealth Preservation and Intergenerational Wealth Transfer in the Black Community 192
Chapter 7 195
Harnessing Determination and Responsibility for Black Wealth Creation And Resilience 195
    The Role of Persistence In The Process of Wealth Creation 197
    Discussion On How Determination And Perseverance Contribute To Financial Success 199

    Case Studies Illustrating The Power of Persistence In Overcoming Financial Challenges 201
    The Concept of Stick-To-Itiveness In The Face of Setbacks 203
    A Deep Dive Into The Importance of Resilience In The Wealth Creation Journey 205
    Providing Strategies For Developing A Resilient Mindset In Dealing With Financial Hurdles 206
    Turning Challenges Into Opportunities 208
    Analyzing How Financial Setbacks Can Be Transformed Into Opportunities For Growth 211
    Offering Methods To Adapt And Learn From Financial Failures 213
    Discussing The Concept of 'Failing Forward' And Its Role In Building Financial Resilience 215
    Responsibility And Accountability: Vital Components of The Wealth Creation Process 217
    Discussing How Personal Responsibility Contributes To Achieving Financial Goals 219
    Blacks Need To Focus On Wealth Creation And Creating Their Own Labor Forces 221
Chapter 8 223
Innovative Approaches to Black Wealth Creation 223
    Establishing the Framework: The Indispensable Role of Innovation in Wealth Creation 225
    An Overview of The Importance of Innovation in Modern Wealth Creation 227
    Understanding How Creativity and Originality Fuel Black Financial Success 230
    Exploration of The Correlation between Creative Thinking and Financial Growth 232
    Trailblazers and Pioneers: A Look at Case Studies of Innovative Business Ideas and Their Impact on Wealth Generation 234

    Delving Into Real-World Examples of Innovative Business Strategies And Their Resultant Financial Outcomes 236
    Shattering The Mold: Strategies for Disrupting Traditional Industry Practices and Forging New Pathways to Wealth 238
    Discussing Tactics For Breaking From Industry Norms, Coupled With The Benefits And Risks Associated With Such Disruption 240
    A Guide for the Future: Developing and Implementing Innovative Ideas for Wealth Creation 242
    Providing Actionable Steps For Readers To Cultivate Their Own Innovative Ideas For Wealth Building 244
    Profiling Individuals and Enterprises That Have Mastered Innovative Approaches to Wealth Creation 246
    A Deeper Dive: Analyzing the Processes and Strategies of Successful Innovators 248
    Offering Detailed Analysis of The Processes And Strategies Utilized By Those Profiled, And How These Lessons Can Be Applied By The Readers 250
    Discussing How These Success Stories Can Inspire And Provide Practical Insights For Readers' Own Wealth Creation Journeys 252
Chapter 9 255
Collective Economics - Harnessing the Power of Unity for Wealth Creation 255
    Understanding Collective Economics: Defining the Concept and Its Importance 257
    Discussing The Idea of Collective Economics and Its Historical Significance 259
    The Role of Collective Economics In Black Wealth Creation, Drawing On Examples From The Past 261
    Addressing Misconceptions And Criticisms Around Collective Economics 263

The Role of Black-Owned Businesses in Collective Economics 265
The Significance of Supporting Black-Owned Businesses For Collective Wealth Creation 266
Case Studies of Successful Black-Owned Businesses And Their Contributions To The Community 268
Identifying Strategies To Foster And Support Black Entrepreneurship 270
Harnessing The Potential of the Black Dollar 272
Analyzing The Spending Power Within The Black Community And Its Potential Impact on Wealth Creation 275
Strategies For Redirecting Black Spending Towards Black-Owned Businesses 277
Understanding The Obstacles And Criticisms Against Harnessing Black Buying Power And Addressing These Concern 279
Building Black Financial Institutions: The Power of Control 281
The Importance of Black-Owned Financial Institutions In Fostering Community Wealth 283
The Role of Black Banks And Credit Unions In Providing Access To Capital For Black Entrepreneurs And Home Buyers 285
The Challenges Facing Black Financial Institutions And Strategies For Overcoming These Hurdles 286
Collective Investment Strategies: Building Community Wealth 288
Understanding The Potential of Collective Investment For Wealth Creation 290
Case Studies of Successful Collective Investment Initiatives Within The Black Community 292
Providing Guidance on How To Form And Manage Collective Investment Groups 294
Leveraging Policy for Collective Economics 296

The Role of Local And Federal Policies In Promoting or Hindering Collective Economics 297
Advocacy Strategies For Pushing Policies That Support Black Wealth Creation 299
Analyzing The Potential And Limitations of Policy Interventions In Collective Economics 301
Preparing for the Future: Building Sustainable Models for Collective Economics 303
Discussing The Importance of Generational Wealth And Strategies For Its Creation And Preservation 305
The Role of Financial Literacy And Education In Promoting Collective Economics 307
Exploring Innovative Models And Technologies (Like Blockchain And Cryptocurrencies) That Can Facilitate Collective Economics 310
Collective Economics as a Pathway to Power 311
Reinforcing The Importance of Collective Economics As A Key Tool For Black Wealth Creation 313
Synthesizing The Strategies Presented Throughout The Chapter For Readers To Apply In Their Own Communities 315
A Call To Action For Readers To Engage In Collective Economic Practices 317
Chapter 10 320
The Immediate Need For Black People To Embrace Technology, Blockchain, Artificial Intelligence 320
The New Digital Age: Technological Revolution And Its Implications 322
Underrepresentation of Black People In Tech Fields ... 324
Why Black People Must Embrace Technology 326
Understanding the Key Concepts 328
Blockchain Technology: Unraveling The Complexity 330
Blockchain Technology: How Black People Can Get Involved 332
Origin And Development of Blockchain Technology . 334

Understanding Blockchain Technology 336
Reemphasizing The Immediate Need For Black People
To Embrace Tech, Blockchain, Artificial Intelligence .338
The Dawn of Intelligent Machines 341
Technology as a Platform for Empowerment 343
Technology As An Equalizer And Breaking Down
Barriers 345
Embracing Artificial Intelligence 346
Policy Interventions for Tech Inclusion 348
Delving Deeper: Policy Strategies for Inclusive
Technology 350
Sowing the Seeds of Tech Inclusion 352
Strategies for Advocacy to Increase Black Representation
in Tech 353
The Role of Parents And Educators In Nurturing Interest
In Tech Among Black Youth 355
Final Reflections: Why Tech, Blockchain, and AI are
Non-Negotiable for the Future of Black People 357
Chapter 11 360
Comprehensive Solutions for Re-Segregation 360
Fortifying Black-owned Businesses 362
Community Development Projects 365
Cultivating Entrepreneurship 367
Utilizing Technology and Global Partnerships 369
Bridging the Digital Divide 371
Advancing Tech Education 373
Fostering Global Economic Partnerships 374
Leveraging State and Federal Government Support 376
Policy Advocacy 378
Strengthening Social Safety Nets 380
Affirmative Action 382
Empowering Through Collective Economics and
Financial Innovations 384
Cooperative Economics 386
Local and Impact Investing 387

    Crowd-funding, Peer-to-Peer Lending and Fintech Solutions 389
    Strategic Areas for Wealth Creation in Contemporary and Sustainable Economies 391
    Real Estate and Green Building 393
    Investing in Stock Market and Crypto Assets 395
    Retirement Savings and Clean Energy 397
    Sustainable Agriculture 398
    The Way Forward 400
    Resilience and Persistence 402
    A Call for Bold Action 404
Chapter 12 406
The Antonio T. Smith Jr. Power Matrix 406
    The First Floor 407
    The Second Floor 408
    The Third Floor 409
    The Fourth Floor 411
    The Fifth Floor 413
Antonio T Smith Jr's Power Matrix 415
Economy 415
    Establish Black-Led Economic Think Tanks For Policy Advocacy And Research 418
    Promote Black Entrepreneurship Through Collective Funding, Business Incubators, And Mentorship Programs 420
    Foster Intra-community Trade, With Black Consumers Supporting Black-owned Businesses 421
    Encourage Innovation And Control In Emerging Industries, Like Green Energy And Tech 423
Finance 424
    Establishing Black-Owned Banks: A Sustainable Path to Economic Empowerment 426
    Actionable Steps Towards the Establishment of Black-Owned Banks and Economic Empowerment 429
    The Feasibility and Implications of Starting a Black-Owned Bank: An Overview 431

    A Step-by-Step Practical Guide to Launching a Black-Owned Bank 433
    Leveraging Fintech Solutions for Economic Empowerment in Black Communities 436
    Fostering Economic Empowerment: Strategies for Black Communities to Develop Sustainable Fintech Solutions 438
    Financial Literacy and Investment: Tools for Wealth Building in Black Communities 440
Data Science 442
    The Power Matrix's Information Equity Strategy: Closing the Knowledge Gap in Black Communities 442
    Fostering Black-Owned Data and Research Enterprises: A Step Towards Culturally Relevant Knowledge 444
    Establishing Black-Controlled Media Platforms: Shaping Narratives and Amplifying Success 446
    Fostering Technological Prowess: Encouraging Careers in Data Science and AI 448
    Bridging the Tech Divide: Propelling Black Communities into Data Science, AI, and Related Fields 450
Manufacturing 452
    Forging Economic Resilience: The Power Matrix's Manufacturing Mastery Blueprint 452
    Accelerating Industrial Autonomy: Fostering the Growth of Black-Controlled Manufacturing Businesses 454
    United We Stand: Fostering Collaboration Among Black Manufacturers to Compete Effectively 456
    Charting New Territories: Initiatives for Technological Upgrading and Innovation in Black-Owned Manufacturing Enterprises 458
    Unleashing Potential: An Urgent Call for Manufacturing Mastery in the Black Community 460
Infrastructure 462
    Charting the Course: The Power Matrix's Infrastructure Development Framework 462

- Prioritizing Infrastructure Investment in Black Communities 464
- Infrastructure Investment and Economic Empowerment for Black Communities under the Antonio T. Smith Jr. Power Matrix Framework 465
- Cooperative Ownership: A Pathway to Infrastructure Sovereignty 467
- Green Infrastructure: The Path Forward with Black-led Innovation 468
- Empowering Black Wealth Creation Through the Power Matrix of Technological Transformation 470

Communications 473
- The Communications Catalyst: The Power Matrix Scheme for Controlling Communications 473
- Leveraging Communications for Socioeconomic Prosperity: A Deeper Examination of the Power Matrix Communications Control Scheme 475
- Seizing Control of the Narrative: The Imperative of Black Ownership in Media and Telecommunications 478
- An Empowered Future: Black Ownership and Influence in the Telecom Industry 480
- The Dawn of Prosperity: Seizing Black Wealth Opportunities in Modern Communication Technologies 482
- Powering Progress: The Communications Control Scheme in the Power Matrix 485
- Mapping the Future: A Practical Guide to the Power Matrix's Communications Control Scheme 487

Human Resources 490
- Leading the Charge: Power Matrix's Human Capital Cultivation Strategy 490
- Fitting Into Corporate America Is Not Good Enough .. 492
- Unveiling Systemic Disparities That Cannot Be Overlooked In The Private Sector 493
- The Underrepresentation and Automation Threats Facing Black Workers 495

Envisioning Ownership as a Pathway to Economic Empowerment 497
My Final Words 498
BIBLIOGRAPHY 502

Dedication

It is with profound respect, admiration, and gratitude that I dedicate the first volume of this series to the remarkable Dr. Claud Anderson. His monumental work has been a guiding beacon in the shaping of my own journey, a compass that helped me navigate through the complex terrains of racial and economic dynamics. Dr. Anderson's books are the ones I've referenced most throughout my own work, underscoring their profound influence on my thinking and understanding.

The term "PowerNomics Book II" may not be the official title of "Re-Segregation", but in my heart and mind, that's exactly how I see it. This work is a testament to the profound influence of Dr. Anderson's teachings on me, a homage to his intellectual legacy that continues to shape and guide countless minds.

To even think of replacing or improving upon Dr. Anderson's work was never my intention. That would be akin to attempting to add colors to the rainbow or notes to a symphony – both of which are beautiful and complete in their own rights. Instead, "Re-Segregation" is my humble effort to continue the conversation that Dr. Anderson so powerfully initiated, to further the discourse on racial and economic empowerment that he has championed.

Every word that I penned in this book series, every idea that I shared, was inspired by a greater calling – a Light that guided me to contribute my understanding and experiences for the betterment of our community. I've been fortunate to accomplish much in my life, and I see it as my duty to share my insights and understanding with our community.

Though I've never had the privilege of meeting Dr. Anderson, I harbor a deep-seated hope that I might one day have that honor. His words and ideas have been a constant companion in my intellectual journey, shaping my worldview and fueling my determination to effect change.

He is, without a doubt, a hero in my eyes— a titan whose shoulders I, and many others, stand upon.

Dr. Anderson's teachings have been my virtual classroom, and I consider myself a distant student of his, constantly learning and drawing inspiration from his wisdom. His words have guided my steps and I am immeasurably grateful for his contributions to my intellectual and personal growth. Being a part of his intellectual lineage and now, having the honor to be recognized as a master in my own right, is a profound blessing.

In honoring Dr. Anderson, I also honor the foundation upon which "Re-Segregation" stands. His work has been instrumental in shaping my understanding of racial and economic dynamics, and his enduring impact is felt on every page of this book. As I put pen to paper, I did so with the hope of doing justice to the intellectual legacy that he has so generously shared with us all. His words, his wisdom, his vision — they have all guided me on this journey, and for that, I am eternally grateful.

Introduction

In writing "Re-Segregation", I have understood and taken to heart the weighty responsibility that I, as a Black individual, bear in representing Black people at large. The act of speaking on behalf of a diverse community is indeed a burden I carry. However, I have approached this duty with the utmost seriousness and integrity, recognizing the broader implications that my work can have.

While the fundamental premise of representing the entirety of Black people may appear inherently unfair, due to the wide-ranging diversity and individual experiences within our community, it is a challenge I have chosen to confront directly. "Re-Segregation" is by no means a book intended to cause harm or foster division. Its tone is carefully measured and respectful, aimed at fostering dialogue rather than sowing discord. I have striven to maintain an objective stance throughout the book, keeping my personal views largely out of the narrative for 97% of the text.

My education at Houston Christian University has shaped my academic approach, and I have applied these principles in "Re-Segregation", writing predominantly in the third person, with the exception of the final section of the last chapter and the introduction. This choice of perspective further emphasizes the impartiality of the work.

This book is a product of comprehensive research, drawing upon approximately 1,000 different sources that have been meticulously included within each chapter. The intent here was to ground the narrative in evidence-based discourse and approach the subject as a scholar. I opted for the Chicago/Turabian citation format, enhancing the academic credibility of the work, while also keeping it accessible to a broad audience.

As with any scholarly work, "Re-Segregation" is intended to spark thoughtful dialogue and critical thinking, rather than persuade readers to conform to a particular viewpoint. Should you find points of disagreement in the book, I encourage you to pursue these thoughts. Investigate your position, reference credible external sources, and engage in a thorough analysis of your disagreement. This is the essence of academic exploration and discourse.

Furthermore, I have made it a point to incorporate opposing viewpoints at every possible turn. This practice is designed to maintain the integrity of the book and my own honesty as the author. By acknowledging and examining counterarguments, I aim to foster a balanced and multifaceted understanding of the complex issues discussed in "Re-Segregation".

Thus, while the task of representing an entire community in a single work is a daunting one, it is a responsibility I have undertaken with the highest level of diligence and respect. My primary aim in "Re-Segregation" is to contribute to a larger conversation about race and community, and to provide a rigorous, respectful, and comprehensive exploration of these themes.

I would like to further delve into the empathetic considerations that underscored the creation of "Re-Segregation". Indeed, empathy is a fundamental pillar of this work, a compass that guided my writing process. The concerns, perspectives, and realities of different racial and ethnic groups were always at the forefront of my mind, serving as a continuous reminder of the diverse audience that this book would reach.

To my white counterparts, I offer my heartfelt appreciation for your interest in this work. I hope you understand that your role in reading and engaging with this material is integral to our collective progress. "Re-Segregation" is not a book penned exclusively for Black audiences; it is a scholarly discourse that encourages participation from every reader, irrespective of racial or ethnic background. Your voice matters in this conversation, and your perspective is valued. We all share the responsibility of understanding our world and its complex racial dynamics better. I sincerely hope that this work will serve as a catalyst for deeper understanding and empathy, fostering an environment of mutual respect and learning.

Concurrently, I want to address my Black brothers and sisters directly. Your resilience, strength, and passion have fueled this work and inform its every page. It was of utmost importance to me to uphold the authenticity and depth of our shared experiences in "Re-Segregation". This book does not sugarcoat the realities we face, nor does it attempt to pander to any audience.

I was determined to preserve the integrity of our stories and experiences, standing firm in the face of any pressure to dilute the content or conform to external expectations. This dedication to authenticity is a testament to our collective strength and resilience, a narrative thread that runs through every chapter of "Re-Segregation". It is my sincere hope that this work will resonate with you, acting as a mirror reflecting our collective experiences and aspirations.

"Re-Segregation" is an act of service to all communities, a testament to the power of unity and understanding. In its pages, you will not find a diluted or simplified narrative, but a thorough, nuanced, and authentic exploration of racial dynamics. It seeks to contribute to our shared dialogue, inspire critical thinking, and foster empathy and mutual respect among all readers.

My approach to "Re-Segregation" was rooted in the knowledge that true progress is not achieved by silencing voices or watering down truths, but by amplifying diverse perspectives and engaging in thoughtful, respectful dialogue. The aim was not to divide, but to unite; not to provoke, but to illuminate; not to dictate, but to inspire. With this book, I extend an invitation to all readers—Black, white, and everyone in between—to join this journey of discovery, understanding, and, ultimately, unity.

Unmasking The Realities and Plotting the Path Forward

The pursuit of wealth and financial independence is a universal ambition, a quest for liberation from financial constraints and a desire for an improved quality of life. However, wealth and its accumulation, for the black community, in particular, extend beyond personal liberty and prosperity. It is a matter of racial equality, justice, and ultimately, survival. This book, "Re-Segregation: Volume I: The Power Matrix. A Masterplan for Black Group Economics and Wealth Creation" is a hard-hitting exposé of the systemic racial disparities that have persistently hindered the black community's financial growth. Moreover, it is an empowering blueprint for fostering wealth creation and self-reliance within the black community, aimed at bridging the economic gap that has entrenched racial disparities.

As an author, my motivation in penning this book is rooted in a deep understanding of the entrenched racial wealth gap and an unwavering belief in the power of the black community to overturn this historical disadvantage. Through a thorough analysis of the facts of black oppression, this book underscores the urgency of economically empowering the black community. It seeks to challenge the narrative of helplessness and dependency and encourages the reader to adopt a proactive mindset focused on group economics and self-generated wealth.

In the first chapter, the book unflinchingly confronts the reality of the black wealth gap, tracing its origins and highlighting its implications for black people in America today. It interrogates the historical and socio-political factors that have contributed to the persistent economic disparities that the black community faces. From here, it draws the link between financial independence and economic empowerment, emphasizing the need for self-generated and self-controlled black wealth. This chapter sets the stage for the discussions to come by establishing the importance of ambition, drive, and active participation in wealth creation.

The scope of the wealth gap is further explored in the second chapter, where the intersection of economics, politics, and law with black wealth is scrutinized. With a backdrop of real-world examples such as the COVID-19 pandemic, the chapter illuminates the structural inequalities that perpetuate economic disparities. By exploring the different economic roles and their functions, it provides a comprehensive understanding of the challenges faced by black individuals in each role. Acknowledging the limitations of the research to date, it calls for further study and opens a dialogue around the biases and constraints that may influence the research.

Chapter three is designed to spur a significant mindset shift. It advocates for the establishment of ambitious wealth goals, tying in psychological principles and the transformative effect of high-goal setting on wealth creation. The chapter addresses common pitfalls in goal setting and offers guidance on setting realistic yet ambitious wealth goals. Drawing from real-world case studies of successful black wealth creation, it provides actionable insights and strategies to inspire and guide the reader.

In essence, this book is a rallying call for black people to take ownership of their economic destiny. By dissecting the barriers to black wealth creation and providing a detailed plan to overcome them, it aims to change the narrative from one of oppression and systemic disadvantage to one of resilience, resourcefulness, and empowerment. This journey will be neither easy nor quick, but with perseverance, determination, and unity, it is a battle that can be won. The time for change is now; the power to effect that change lies within the black community. The path to wealth creation and financial independence starts here. The fight for economic equality and justice continues – and this book is a crucial weapon in that struggle.

Addressing the Economic Disparities, Mindset Shifts, and Strategic Approaches to Black Wealth Creation

An examination of modern society reveals deep-seated economic disparities that continue to plague communities, particularly those of African descent. The significant racial wealth gap observed today isn't just an economic issue; it fundamentally undermines the principles of social and racial justice. With this in mind, I have sought to delve into these issues in "Re-Segregation: Volume I: The Power Matrix. A Masterplan for Black Group Economics and Wealth Creation." This book offers an audacious perspective on systemic financial inequality, articulating robust solutions and methods to stimulate wealth creation within the Black community.

Chapter four, "The Economic Gaps: An In-depth Analysis," explores the systemic factors contributing to wage and occupational disparities in the Black community. Detailed data analysis will elucidate the concentration of racial wage disparity across occupational sectors. It will also examine the impact of these disparities on wealth accumulation and economic stability, underscoring the need to address these factors as part of a comprehensive wealth generation strategy. This chapter concludes with an in-depth examination of underrepresentation in high-wage professions, analyzing barriers to entry and advancement that further impede Black wealth generation.

Moving from a macroeconomic view to a psychological perspective, chapter five, "The Black Mindset for Overcoming Limiting Beliefs and Embracing Success When It Comes to Generating Massive Income," explores the psychological factors that inhibit or facilitate wealth creation. Recognizing the crucial role of mindset, this chapter explores how limiting beliefs can impede financial success. It then offers practical strategies for dismantling these beliefs and fostering a growth mindset. Through this process, the chapter underscores the importance of nurturing self-confidence and cultivating a success-oriented mindset, particularly in the context of Black wealth creation.

The journey towards racial wealth equality is not solely about overcoming barriers; it is also about identifying and leveraging opportunities. Chapter six, "Ideas for Black Wealth Creations and Keeping Money in the Black Community," delves into this proactive side of wealth creation. It proposes various avenues for economic empowerment, from community investment and entrepreneurship to real estate ownership and the utilization of technology. This chapter emphasizes the importance of circulating the Black dollar within the community and explores how health, wellness, and environmental responsibility can be harnessed as new frontiers for Black wealth creation.

Ultimately, "Re-Segregation: Volume I: The Power Matrix. A Masterplan for Black Group Economics and Wealth Creation" serves as a testament to the resiliency and potential inherent within the Black community. It elucidates the challenges we face, but more importantly, it highlights the strategies and opportunities we can seize to overcome these challenges. This book aims to be a catalyst for change, encouraging a collective push towards financial independence, wealth creation, and, ultimately, economic equity.

Harnessing Resilience, Innovation, and Unity for Sustained Black Wealth Creation

In the ongoing discourse about wealth inequality, the intersecting nuances of resilience, innovation, and unity come to the fore. It is with a view to exploring and elucidating these themes that I have ventured to write "Re-Segregation: Volume I: The Power Matrix. A Masterplan for Black Group Economics and Wealth Creation." This work seeks to dissect the multifaceted aspects of wealth creation within the Black community and, more importantly, to furnish insightful strategies to dismantle financial disparities.

Chapter seven, "Harnessing Determination and Responsibility for Black Wealth Creation and Resilience," delves into the psychological resilience necessary to weather financial challenges. Persistence, determination, and the concept of 'stick-to-itiveness' in the face of setbacks will be thoroughly examined. This chapter discusses how personal responsibility and accountability are integral to achieving financial goals and asserts the need for the Black community to focus on wealth creation and creating their own labor forces.

As we pivot from individual resilience to the broader community context, chapter eight, "Innovative Approaches to Black Wealth Creation," outlines the significance of innovation in the wealth creation journey. From understanding how creativity fuels financial success to analyzing real-world examples of innovative business strategies, this chapter posits that innovation is an indispensable element of Black financial empowerment. It further offers readers actionable steps to cultivate their ideas for wealth building.

The final chapter in this sequence, which is chapter nine, "Collective Economics — Harnessing the Power of Unity for Wealth Creation," explores the power of collective economics as a pathway towards Black wealth creation. Herein, the importance of Black-owned businesses, the potential of the Black dollar, and the vital role of Black financial institutions are discussed. The chapter concludes by addressing policy interventions and exploring innovative technologies like blockchain and cryptocurrencies that can facilitate collective economics. In synthesizing these strategies, it provides a call to action for readers to actively engage in collective economic practices.

"Re-Segregation: Volume I: The Power Matrix. A Masterplan for Black Group Economics and Wealth Creation" thus delivers a robust exploration of the avenues and obstacles pertinent to Black wealth creation. By offering practical strategies and highlighting successful case studies, it aims to empower the Black community towards achieving sustained economic resilience. The wealth gap may be a daunting challenge, but it is one we can confront with determination, innovation, and collective action.

Embracing Technological Innovations and Comprehensive Solutions for Black Wealth Creation

In an era punctuated by rapid technological advancements and shifting economic landscapes, it is critical to both adapt and harness these changes to foster wealth and economic stability. As such, the motivation for writing "Re-Segregation: Volume I: The Power Matrix. A Masterplan for Black Group Economics and Wealth

Creation" has been the urgent need to address the disproportionate economic disparities faced by the Black community, as well as the necessity for this community to embrace technology and formulate comprehensive solutions for sustainable wealth creation.

Chapter ten, "The Immediate Need For Black People To Embrace Technology, Blockchain, Artificial Intelligence," underscores the importance of embracing the technological revolution, which has dramatically transformed the global economic landscape. The chapter highlights the current underrepresentation of Black people in tech fields and the potential opportunities and challenges presented by Blockchain technology and Artificial Intelligence. This section aims to demystify these complex technologies and offer tangible pathways for Black individuals to get involved, emphasizing that involvement in technology is non-negotiable for the future. The discussion further delves into policy interventions and advocacy strategies to foster inclusive technology and the essential roles parents and educators can play in nurturing tech interest among Black youth.

Subsequently, Chapter eleven, "Comprehensive Solutions for Re-Segregation," builds on these discussions by presenting an array of measures to counter re-segregation. Focusing on the fortification of Black-owned businesses, cultivation of entrepreneurship, and the utility of technology and global partnerships, this chapter seeks to present a multi-pronged strategy for combating racial economic disparity. The role of policy advocacy, the power of collective economics and financial innovations, and specific areas for wealth creation, such as real estate, stock market investments, and sustainable agriculture, are discussed at length. The chapter culminates with a call for resilience, persistence, and bold action.

By addressing these pivotal issues, "Re-Segregation: Volume I: The Power Matrix. A Masterplan for Black Group Economics and Wealth Creation" aspires to provide the necessary tools and strategies for Black communities to navigate the challenges of wealth inequality and economic re-segregation effectively. In doing so, it aims to inspire a movement towards economic empowerment that harnesses the full potential of the digital age, leverages the benefits of comprehensive policy solutions, and ultimately, leads to sustained Black wealth creation.

The Sixth Floor: The Beginning of the Power Matrix

While the fifth floor concludes Dr. Claud Anderson's five-story building, my Power Matrix introduces two additional layers to this model, starting with the floor of Data Information. This addition is a reflection of my understanding of the modern age, characterized by the surge of digital technologies and the immense value of data.

In the 21st century, data has emerged as the lifeblood of economies and societies worldwide. It is a critical resource that powers decision-making, fuels innovation, and shapes the competitive landscape of industries. It is fitting, then, that the Power Matrix embeds data information as a crucial floor in the structure of Black wealth creation.

I truly believe ownership and control of data are integral to economic independence and competitive advantage. By mastering data information, Black communities can identify market trends, anticipate consumer behavior, influence policy decisions, and, most importantly, control their narrative in the digital realm.

Critics might argue that this perspective overlooks the privacy concerns and ethical dilemmas associated with data collection and analysis. They might also caution against the potential for data-driven discrimination and the exacerbation of inequality. However, it's worth noting that the Power Matrix advocates for the ethical and responsible use of data as a tool for empowerment, not exploitation.

Moreover, data information is intrinsically linked with the digital age's transformative technologies – such as blockchain and artificial intelligence – which are the central themes of Chapter 10. As we delve deeper into these topics, the significance of data information in reshaping the socio-economic trajectory of Black communities will become increasingly apparent.

The Seventh Floor: Manufacturing and Infrastructure

The seventh floor of my Power Matrix emphasizes the importance of Manufacturing and Infrastructure in the quest for Black wealth creation. This addition builds upon the previous layers by highlighting the need for tangible assets and physical infrastructure, not just intangible resources like data.

From an economic standpoint, manufacturing holds the potential to spur job creation, stimulate innovation, and contribute to a robust, diversified economy. Moreover, by investing in infrastructure - such as transportation, utilities, and telecommunications - Black communities can enhance their quality of life, increase productivity, and attract further investment.

In my Power Matrix, I posit that by owning and controlling the means of production, Black communities can ensure a fair distribution of wealth, increase economic resilience, and reduce dependency on external entities. This vision resonates with the broader themes of self-reliance and self-determination that permeate both Anderson's and my own my model.

Critics might caution against the potential challenges associated with this goal, such as the high capital requirements, the complexity of global supply chains, and the influence of international trade policies. However, by pooling resources, leveraging technology, and forging strategic partnerships - both local and global - these obstacles can be navigated.

Furthermore, the development of infrastructure also enables the establishment of Black-owned media and educational institutions, as advocated in the fourth and fifth floors of Anderson's model. This interconnectedness underscores the holistic and multifaceted approach of the Power Matrix, where each layer contributes to a stronger, more self-sufficient Black economy.

The Eighth Floor: Communications and Human Resources

The final floor of my Power Matrix combines two key elements: Communications and Human Resources. This combination underscores the interdependence of these two areas and their critical role in fostering a resilient, prosperous Black economy.

Communications in this context refers to both external and internal interactions. Externally, it encompasses the public relations, media representation, and digital presence of Black communities. Internally, it involves fostering effective communication within the community to ensure cohesion, collaboration, and collective action.

Human Resources, on the other hand, pertains to the management and development of the most valuable asset of the Black community: its people. This involves everything from talent acquisition and retention to training and development, employee engagement, and the establishment of fair labor practices. By focusing on human resources, the Black community can cultivate a talented, highly-skilled workforce that can drive economic growth and innovation.

I believe by integrating effective communication strategies with robust human resources practices can enhance community engagement, promote a positive image of the Black community, and attract resources and opportunities. It can also foster a culture of inclusivity, mutual respect, and empowerment within the community, laying the groundwork for collective prosperity.

Critics might question the feasibility of this approach given the systemic challenges that Black communities often face in areas such as education, employment, and media representation. However, I argue that these challenges can be surmounted through the implementation of targeted strategies, community-led initiatives, and the active involvement of Black-owned businesses and institutions.

Moreover, the emphasis on human resources aligns with the broader aim of the Power Matrix to build an economy that not only generates wealth but also prioritizes the well-being, development, and fulfillment of individuals. This human-centric approach differentiates the Power Matrix from conventional economic models and underscores the transformative potential of the Black community's collective power.

The Power Matrix: A Synthesis of Dr. Claud Anderson and Antonio T Smith, Jr's Understanding of Generating Black Wealth

In essence, my Power Matrix presents an expansive, forward-thinking model of Black wealth creation that builds upon and extends beyond Dr. Claud Anderson's five-story building. By incorporating contemporary elements such as data, advanced technology, and human resources, I am acknowledging the complexities and opportunities of the digital age and painting a vision of a self-reliant, thriving Black economy.

While the two models have distinct emphases and unique components, both underscore the necessity of a systemic and multifaceted approach to achieving economic empowerment. They emphasize the importance of unity, strategic planning, and proactive action in overcoming socio-economic disparities and cultivating wealth within the Black community.

As we delve deeper into the themes of blockchain and artificial intelligence in Chapter ten, we will continue to draw upon and integrate these foundational models, exploring how emerging technologies can amplify the potential of Black wealth creation and drive social and economic transformation.

The following chapters will examine how these technologies intersect with the Power Matrix, providing tangible examples and case studies to illuminate the practical application of these models in the Black community's quest for economic independence and prosperity.

Embracing the Power Matrix: A Journey Towards Black Economic Empowerment

I want you to know the Power Matrix, we hope it has ignited in you a deep sense of potential and resilience, a belief in the extraordinary possibilities that await when we dare to dream and act strategically.

The Power Matrix framework is more than a road-map for economic empowerment; it is an invitation to unite, a call to use our collective wisdom and resources to shape our own future. It is a bold affirmation of our ability as a community to seize control of our narrative and rewrite it with our successes, aspirations, and values.

We have peered into the intricate corridors of the economy, finance, data science, manufacturing, infrastructure, process automation and virtualization, communications, and human resources. We've charted a path for establishing black-owned banks, boosting entrepreneurship, and controlling communications. We've explored the power of data, the importance of manufacturing mastery, and the promise of advanced technology.

But the journey has just begun. With each step we take, we'll encounter challenges. Yet, we must remember that within these challenges lies the opportunity for growth and transformation. The journey ahead will require creativity, tenacity, and resilience. However, remember the success stories of Black individuals, families, and businesses who have overcome adversity, shattered barriers, and blazed trails of success.

Let research writings inspire you. Let them remind you that change is possible, that progress is within reach if we persist, if we keep pushing, keep striving, keep believing. Let them fuel your commitment to seizing every opportunity, to mastering every facet of the Power Matrix. This journey, after all, is not just about creating wealth; it is about cultivating a community that is empowered, resilient, and capable of crafting its own destiny.

In the chapters ahead, we will delve deeper into each component of the Power Matrix, providing a detailed exploration and practical guides. Our aim is to arm you with the knowledge and tools necessary to navigate the path towards economic independence and prosperity. Your contribution is vital, your potential immense.

With every action you take, every decision you make, you are not just building your wealth. You are shaping the future of the Black community. You are playing a pivotal role in a historical movement, a grand adventure towards economic emancipation and prosperity.

So, let's embark on this journey together. Let's harness our collective power and transform our dreams into reality. Let's be the architects of our own future and prove that, indeed, we can create a vibrant, thriving Black economy that reflects our potential, ambition, and resilience.

And remember, we are not just participants in this journey, we are its architects. The power to change our economic destiny lies in our hands. Let's wield it wisely and confidently, knowing that we are capable of great things. With unity, commitment, and strategic action, we can shape a prosperous and empowering economic future. We can create a world that resonates with our dreams, echoes our triumphs, and celebrates our resilience.

The Power Matrix awaits. Its corridors are teeming with opportunities, its chambers echoing with the promise of prosperity. Embrace it. Master it. Use it to fuel your journey towards economic empowerment. As you do, remember that you are not alone. Together, we are stronger. Together, we can achieve more. Together, we can create a resilient, thriving, prosperous Black economy. The future is ours to shape. Let's seize it with both hands. Let's transform our dreams into reality.

And with these final words, we conclude our introduction and prepare to delve into the heart of the Power Matrix. Are you ready? Let's begin!

Chapter 1

The Black Wealth Gap: Understanding, Causes, and Implications

The narrative of economic equality for African Americans is a story fraught with persistent challenges, yet it holds the promise of remarkable triumph. However, to reach this pinnacle, we must first address the historic and systemic inequities that have long held sway over our community's financial standing. "Re-Segregation" is an urgent call to action - a rallying cry for African Americans to grasp the reins of their economic fate, to redefine wealth, and to claim their rightful economic place.

Our history is testament to our resilience, innovation, and indomitable spirit, but it also sheds light on an economic landscape that has been rigged against us. It's a landscape defined by racial disparities, with roadblocks such as discriminatory housing policies, unequal access to quality education, and lending practices that disproportionately hinder African Americans from acquiring wealth. We have been relegated to roles of perpetual consumers, seldom becoming producers, persistently employees, but rarely employers. We must acknowledge this reality not to wallow in it, but to rise above it.

The Re-Segregation requires a seismic shift in our collective perspective. It necessitates that we see ourselves not as mere participants in an economic system, but as architects of our own financial destiny. To this end, the first step is fostering a solid understanding of economic fundamentals within our community. Just as a builder must first learn the properties of brick and mortar before erecting a structure, so too must we comprehend the principles of wealth creation before we can amass it.

Acquiring knowledge is only the beginning. With a clear understanding of financial systems and principles, we must put that knowledge into action. We must adopt a mindset of ownership and entrepreneurialism. Building our businesses, investing wisely, and supporting local enterprises is essential. A dollar that stays within our community strengthens our economic foundation. This isn't merely about individual prosperity, but about communal economic liberation.

The spirit of this revolution also embraces the interplay between economic and political power. It's not enough to accumulate wealth; we must also ensure we have a voice in the halls of power. Economic strength and political clout must work in concert to protect and advance our community's interests. Therefore, the Re-Segregation is not solely about personal wealth creation, but also about the pursuit of policies that safeguard our economic progress.

This journey won't be an overnight metamorphosis. Change of this magnitude is gradual, demanding persistent effort and unity. It calls for a radical reframing of our community's economic narrative and a relentless commitment to realizing our economic potential. With each step on this path, we inch closer to economic parity and self-reliance.

"Re-Segregation" is a road-map for this journey, charting the course from economic disparity to equality. It is an empowering testament to the resilience of African Americans and our capacity to achieve financial liberation. It challenges us to claim our economic power and shape our collective future, building a legacy of wealth and prosperity for generations to come. This is the spirit of the Re-Segregation.

Understanding The Black Wealth Gap

The wealth gap between African Americans and their white counterparts is not a matter of mere financial disparity but a reflection of historical and systemic inequities. According to the Federal Reserve's Survey of Consumer Finances, in 2019, the median wealth for white families was $188,200, compared to just $24,100 for black families[1]. This vast discrepancy is not incidental but the cumulative effect of centuries of racial economic barriers.

Several critics, particularly those with conservative leanings, often argue that this gap is a result of individual decisions rather than systemic injustices. They point to factors such as spending habits, poor financial decisions, and a lack of personal responsibility[2]. Yet, this view overlooks the socio-economic circumstances that have shaped these financial behaviors over generations and the restrictive policies that have hindered wealth accumulation in the black community.

To those critics, consider the historical context: the legacy of slavery, the Jim Crow era, and systemic discrimination in housing, lending, and education. Redlining, a discriminatory practice whereby banks refused loans to residents of certain neighborhoods, predominantly black ones, was officially outlawed in 1968 but its effects persist today. This practice denied African Americans the opportunity to own homes and accumulate wealth in the same way as their white counterparts[3]. Similarly, the GI Bill, which provided educational and housing benefits to

---

[1] Federal Reserve, 2019 Survey of Consumer Finances
[2] Riley, Jason L. "Black Culture and the Racial Wealth Gap." The Wall Street Journal, 2018
[3] Rothstein, Richard. The Color of Law: A Forgotten History of How Our Government Segregated America, 2017.

veterans post-WWII, largely excluded black veterans, further widening the wealth gap[4].

Consider also the present-day systemic challenges, such as racial wage disparity. The Economic Policy Institute found that in 2020, black men earned 70 cents for every dollar earned by white men, while black women earned 63 cents[5]. Critics might argue that educational disparities account for this, but even when controlled for education, African Americans still earn significantly less than their white counterparts[6].

Then there's the case of black entrepreneurship. Black-owned businesses are often underfunded due to bias in lending, leaving them less likely to succeed and therefore less likely to generate wealth[7]. The Brookings Institution reported in 2020 that businesses in predominantly black neighborhoods receive less investment than those in predominantly white neighborhoods, regardless of the revenue they generate[8].

Taken together, these factors create a structural economic environment that disproportionately disadvantages African Americans in wealth accumulation.

The goal here is not to assign blame but to raise awareness and encourage proactive steps toward closing the black wealth gap. Misguided perceptions and biases only serve to maintain the status quo. Instead, we must focus on systemic reforms in education, lending practices, and wage policies, as well as supporting black entrepreneurship. To

---

[4] Katznelson, Ira. When Affirmative Action Was White: An Untold History of Racial Inequality in Twentieth-Century America, 2005.

[5] Economic Policy Institute, "Racial disparities in income and poverty remain largely unchanged amid strong income growth in 2019," 2020.

[6] Deming, David J. "The Growing Importance of Social Skills in the Labor Market," The Quarterly Journal of Economics, 2017.

[7] Fairlie, Robert W., and Alicia M. Robb. Race and Entrepreneurial Success, 2008.

[8] Brookings Institution, "Five-star reviews, one-star profits: The devaluation of businesses in Black communities," 2020.

achieve economic parity, it is essential to acknowledge the deep-seated, systemic roots of the black wealth gap.

This section is a testament to our understanding of the black wealth gap. It stands as a call to action to challenge the narratives that perpetuate this economic divide. It represents our collective effort to chart a course toward financial equality and wealth creation for the African American community.

Dissecting the Causes and Implications of the Black Wealth Gap

In understanding the wealth gap that separates African Americans from their white counterparts, we must first dissect the systemic and historical causes that have precipitated this imbalance. Critics of the wealth gap narrative often lean on explanations that target individual behaviors rather than examining the systemic roots. Such a narrow perspective does a disservice to our understanding and prevents us from implementing effective solutions.

The roots of the black wealth gap can be traced back to America's original sin - slavery. While critics might argue that slavery ended long ago and therefore cannot be a cause for present disparities, its effects have been enduring and pernicious. The system of chattel slavery reduced the labor of African Americans to a mere commodity, generating wealth that was inaccessible to them[9]. This set the stage for centuries of racial economic disparities.

Post-slavery, black wealth creation was further hampered by the Jim Crow laws and systemic racial segregation. For instance, the practice of redlining, where government-backed housing loans were denied to African

---

[9] Baptist, Edward E. The Half Has Never Been Told: Slavery and the Making of American Capitalism, 2014.

Americans, prevented black families from home-ownership - a primary source of wealth accumulation[10].

The wealth gap is not merely an issue of the past. It's continually perpetuated by present-day discriminatory practices. Consider the racial wage gap. The Pew Research Center reported in 2020 that the average hourly wage for black men was $15, compared to $21 for white men. Similarly, black women earned $14, compared to $17 for white women[11].

Critics may argue that this disparity arises from differences in education and job choices. However, studies have shown that even when controlling for education, African Americans still earn less[12].

The implications of this wealth gap are significant and multifaceted. It translates to fewer resources for education, fewer opportunities for business ownership, limited access to quality health-care, and overall, a reduced quality of life. It also creates a cycle of poverty that becomes increasingly difficult to break. Furthermore, it deprives the African American community of the capital necessary to influence policy and secure political representation.

Addressing the black wealth gap requires more than acknowledging its existence; it demands systemic reforms. Closing the wage gap, ensuring fair lending practices, supporting black-owned businesses, and investing in quality education are crucial steps towards achieving economic parity.

This section is not merely an exposition of the causes and implications of the black wealth gap. It serves as a

---

[10] Rothstein, Richard. The Color of Law: A Forgotten History of How Our Government Segregated America, 2017.

[11] Pew Research Center, "Racial, gender wage gaps persist in U.S. despite some progress," 2020.

[12] Bertrand, Marianne, and Sendhil Mullainathan. "Are Emily and Greg More Employable Than Lakisha and Jamal? A Field Experiment on Labor Market Discrimination," The American Economic Review, 2004.

rebuttal to critics who disregard the systemic roots of this issue. It stands as a testament to our determination to overcome these challenges and forge a path towards financial equality for the African American community.

Historical Context and Persistence of the Wealth Gap

Understanding the black wealth gap requires us to look back at our history, tracing the legacy of economic disparities from the era of slavery through the present day. Critics may argue that the vestiges of slavery and systemic discrimination can't explain today's wealth gap, contending that individual decisions or cultural attributes are the root cause. However, ample evidence contradicts this narrative.

The origins of the wealth gap lie in the brutal institution of slavery, where African Americans were forced to labor for no wages, with the fruits of their labor contributing to the wealth of their enslavers[13]. Following the abolition of slavery, African Americans were not compensated for their forced labor, marking the beginning of the wealth divide.

The era of Reconstruction promised freedom and economic opportunity for former slaves, but the promise was short-lived. The advent of Jim Crow laws, sharecropping, and peonage systems ensured African Americans remained economically disadvantaged[14].

Further exacerbating the wealth gap were policies and practices in the 20th century that systematically excluded African Americans from wealth-building opportunities. The practice of redlining, supported by the Federal Housing Administration, denied African Americans home loans, a

---

[13] Baptist, Edward E. The Half Has Never Been Told: Slavery and the Making of American Capitalism, 2014.
[14] Woodward, C. Vann. The Strange Career of Jim Crow, 1955.

traditional path to wealth creation[15]. Moreover, the Social Security Act of 1935 initially excluded agricultural and domestic workers, occupations predominantly held by African Americans[16].

Critics often dismiss these historical factors, suggesting that changes in individual behavior could bridge the wealth gap. But consider this: according to a 2017 report by the Institute for Policy Studies, if average black family wealth continues to grow at the same pace it has over the past three decades, it would take 228 years for black wealth to reach the level of white wealth today[17]. Clearly, individual efforts alone cannot overcome such a deeply entrenched disparity.

Moreover, the persistence of the wealth gap into the 21st century signifies that systemic barriers still exist. Discriminatory lending practices, racial wage gaps, underfunded schools in predominantly black neighborhoods, and biased criminal justice policies all contribute to the maintenance of the wealth gap[18].

The implications of the wealth gap are far-reaching. It limits access to quality education, health care, housing, and opportunities for business ownership, affecting generations of African Americans. It also restricts our ability to invest in our communities and secure a political representation reflective of our interests.

The historical context and persistence of the wealth gap underscore the need for systemic solutions - from policy changes that address racial disparities in income and housing to substantial investments in education and black

---

[15] Rothstein, Richard. The Color of Law: A Forgotten History of How Our Government Segregated America, 2017.

[16] Katznelson, Ira. When Affirmative Action Was White: An Untold History of Racial Inequality in Twentieth-Century America, 2005.

[17] Institute for Policy Studies, "The Ever-Growing Gap: Without Change, African-American and Latino Families Won't Match White Wealth for Centuries," 2017.

[18] Desmond, Matthew, and Carl Gershenson. "Housing and Black Wealth," The American Journal of Sociology, 2016.

entrepreneurship. Understanding our past is the first step towards forging a prosperous future. This section is not just a review of our history; it is an appeal for recognition, rectification, and economic justice.

Sociopolitical Factors Influencing the Black Wealth Gap

The black wealth gap is a phenomenon heavily influenced by a myriad of sociopolitical factors. This gap is not an accident of history or solely the product of individual financial behaviors, as some critics might argue. Instead, it has been shaped and sustained by a variety of interconnected societal and political mechanisms.

One such sociopolitical factor is the discriminatory practice of redlining. In the mid-20th century, government-backed agencies systematically denied loans to residents in "risky" neighborhoods, which were predominantly black[19]. Critics might contend that this is a practice of the past and thus irrelevant to today's wealth gap. However, research indicates that red-lined neighborhoods are still economically disadvantaged today, with lower rates of home-ownership and higher rates of poverty[20].

Another significant factor is the racial wage gap. Studies show that African Americans earn less than their white counterparts even when controlled for education and experience[21]. Critics often attribute this wage disparity to individual choices such as selecting lower-paying industries or jobs. However, it is important to note that African

---

[19] Rothstein, Richard. The Color of Law: A Forgotten History of How Our Government Segregated America, 2017

[20] Aaronson, Daniel, et al. "The Effects of the 1930s HOLC 'Redlining' Maps," Federal Reserve Bank of Chicago, 2017.

[21] Economic Policy Institute, "Black-white wage gaps expand with rising wage inequality," 2016.

Americans often face limited opportunities due to factors such as discrimination and unconscious bias[22].

In the realm of education, black students face numerous disparities, including under-resourced schools, fewer experienced teachers, and lower expectations[23]. These educational disparities contribute to lower earning potential, which in turn affects wealth accumulation. Critics might argue that these educational disparities result from local tax structures or parental engagement. However, this perspective overlooks the historical context of systemic educational inequality and under-investment in black communities[24].

The criminal justice system is another sociopolitical mechanism that perpetuates the wealth gap. Incarceration reduces earning potential and job prospects, making it difficult for individuals to build wealth. Moreover, the fines and fees associated with the criminal justice system often place a financial burden on families, contributing to the wealth gap[25].

Understanding the sociopolitical factors that influence the black wealth gap is integral to crafting effective solutions. We need comprehensive policy reforms that address these issues, from fair housing and lending practices to wage equality, educational equity, and criminal justice reform.

This section is a stark illustration of the complexities that contribute to the black wealth gap. By dissecting these

---

[22] Bertrand, Marianne, and Sendhil Mullainathan. "Are Emily and Greg More Employable Than Lakisha and Jamal? A Field Experiment on Labor Market Discrimination," The American Economic Review, 2004.

[23] Reardon, Sean F. "The Widening Academic Achievement Gap Between the Rich and the Poor: New Evidence and Possible Explanations," 2011.

[24] Sibilia, Rebecca. "Why America's Schools Have A Money Problem," National Public Radio, 2016.

[25] Western, Bruce, and Becky Pettit. "Incarceration & Social Inequality," Daedalus, 2010.

factors, we aim to highlight the pressing need for systemic change and lay the groundwork for actionable strategies that promote wealth equality. This is not just about diagnosing the problem—it's about charting a course toward a more equitable future.

The Importance of Self-Generated and Self-Controlled Black Wealth

One cannot overstate the importance of self-generated and self-controlled black wealth. Yet, critics often question this approach, contending that the focus should be on individual financial management and not on community wealth. This perspective, however, overlooks the potential power of collective economic empowerment.

The development of self-generated black wealth begins with entrepreneurship. Despite facing systemic barriers, black entrepreneurs have made significant strides. According to a report by the U.S. Census Bureau, as of 2012, there were over 2 million black-owned businesses in the United States[26]. Critics might argue that these businesses often lack longevity, but this overlooks the systemic barriers they face, including limited access to capital and discriminatory lending practices[27].

The significance of self-controlled black wealth is tied to the power of economic autonomy. When we control our wealth, we can reinvest in our communities, strengthening local businesses, and improving educational and health facilities. Critics may argue that a focus on self-controlled wealth creates economic isolation, but consider this:

---

[26] U.S. Census Bureau, "Black-Owned Businesses in the United States," 2012.

[27] Fairlie, Robert W., and Alicia M. Robb. "Why Are Black-Owned Businesses Less Successful than White-Owned Businesses? The Role of Families, Inheritances, and Business Human Capital," Journal of Labor Economics, 2010.

according to a 2019 report by the Brookings Institution, businesses in black neighborhoods are undervalued by $4 billion[28]. A focus on self-controlled wealth could help correct such market distortions and bolster local economies.

Self-generated and self-controlled black wealth also provides a buffer against economic shocks. For instance, during the COVID-19 pandemic, African American families were hit harder due to lower savings and wealth reserves[29]. Self-controlled wealth allows communities to weather such crises with greater resilience.

Moreover, wealth contributes to political influence. Those with economic power can influence policy, lobby for their interests, and ensure that their concerns are heard at the highest levels of government. Critics may argue that political influence should not be tied to wealth, but until that ideal becomes a reality, we must work within the existing structures to secure representation for our communities.

Creating self-generated and self-controlled black wealth is not merely an economic imperative; it's a matter of justice and equity. It represents the harnessing of our resources, talents, and resilience to shape our economic destiny. It is about reaffirming our worth and building a legacy of prosperity for future generations.

This section serves as an affirmation of our potential and a challenge to the critics. It underscores the urgency of our economic empowerment and lays the groundwork for a Re-Segregation within our communities. We are not merely reacting to the economic disparities we face; we are proactive architects of our wealth and, by extension, our future.

---

[28] Perry, Andre, et al. "The devaluation of assets in black neighborhoods: The case of residential property," Brookings Institution, 2018.

[29] Kochhar, Rakesh. "Black workers face two of the most lethal preexisting conditions for coronavirus—racism and economic inequality," Economic Policy Institute, 2020.

Financial Independence and Its Role in Economic Empowerment

Financial independence is a crucial factor in achieving economic empowerment, particularly within the African American community. It serves as a catalyst for autonomy, prosperity, and generational wealth. Critics often perceive financial independence as an individual pursuit, detached from the community's economic health. However, this viewpoint ignores how individual financial independence can powerfully influence broader economic patterns.

Firstly, financial independence gives one the freedom to make choices. This might mean the ability to pursue entrepreneurial ventures, contribute to local economies, or invest in oneself through education or skills training. Critics might argue that these are individual benefits, but the ripple effect on the community cannot be underestimated. For instance, a study found that a 1% rise in black-owned businesses results in a 0.9% reduction in black youth unemployment[30].

Secondly, financial independence fuels the creation of generational wealth, which offers long-term financial security and opportunities for future generations. A report by the Federal Reserve Board revealed that the median net worth of families with an inheritance was at least seven times larger than the net worth of families without an inheritance[31]. Critics often view inheritances as perpetuating wealth inequality. However, for historically marginalized communities, building generational wealth is a form of economic resistance and empowerment.

Thirdly, financial independence allows us to take control of our resources and utilize them to better our

---

[30] Fairlie, Robert. "Black and White: Access to Capital among Minority-Owned start-ups," Stanford Institute for Economic Policy Research, 2013.
[31] Federal Reserve Board, "Survey of Consumer Finances," 2019.

communities. Critics might claim that emphasizing community reinvestment could lead to economic isolation, but this perspective overlooks the significance of economic self-sustainability and localized wealth creation. For instance, a study found that businesses in black neighborhoods are undervalued by $4 billion[32]. Investing in our communities can address such market distortions, drive local economic growth, and increase community resilience.

Financial independence also cultivates political power, enabling us to influence the policies that affect our lives. Critics might argue that wealth shouldn't translate to political influence, but we must utilize all tools at our disposal to ensure that our voices are heard within the current system.

In sum, financial independence plays a crucial role in economic empowerment, not just for individuals, but for the entire African American community. It enables us to dictate our economic destinies, build a prosperous legacy for future generations, and contribute meaningfully to our communities.

This section emphasizes the importance of financial independence as a pathway towards collective economic prosperity. It is a call to action, a road-map towards economic empowerment, and a clarion call for the recognition of our potential. We are not merely participants in the economy; we are drivers of change, architects of wealth, and proponents of a brighter future.

---

[32] Perry, Andre, et al. "The devaluation of assets in black neighborhoods: The case of residential property," Brookings Institution, 2018.

The Effects of White Wealth Accumulation on Black Community Development

The dynamics of wealth accumulation within America have historically favored the white majority, profoundly affecting the development of black communities. Critics often argue that focusing on racial disparities perpetuates division and overlooks individual effort. However, it's important to remember that wealth accumulation is not a zero-sum game. Recognizing these disparities illuminates systemic issues and helps chart a path towards economic justice.

One primary way white wealth accumulation affects black community development is through the wealth gap. A report by the Brookings Institution revealed that in 2016, the net worth of a typical white family was nearly ten times greater than that of a black family[33]. Critics might argue that this disparity results from individual financial decisions, but this perspective overlooks the systemic factors, such as discriminatory lending practices and wage inequalities, that contribute to the gap[34].

Another implication of white wealth accumulation is in housing and neighborhood investment. Historically, discriminatory housing practices like redlining and racially restrictive covenants directed resources and wealth away from black neighborhoods[35]. Critics might argue that these practices are relics of the past, yet research shows that their

---

[33] Kochhar, Rakesh, and Richard Fry. "Wealth inequality has widened along racial, ethnic lines since end of Great Recession," Pew Research Center, 2014.

[34] Hamilton, Darrick, et al. "Umbrellas don't make it rain: Why studying and working hard isn't enough for Black Americans," The New School, Duke Center for Social Equity, and Insight Center for Community Economic Development, 2015.

[35] Rothstein, Richard. The Color of Law: A Forgotten History of How Our Government Segregated America, 2017.

effects persist today, with black neighborhoods still experiencing lower property values and under-investment[36].

The education system, funded predominantly by local property taxes, is also impacted. Communities with more accumulated wealth often have better-funded schools, contributing to an education gap that can limit future wealth-building opportunities[37]. Critics might argue that funding disparities are due to local tax structures rather than racial wealth disparities. However, this argument overlooks the historical context of segregated housing and accumulated wealth that created these local tax bases[38].

Furthermore, accumulated white wealth influences political power, affecting policies and legislation that can hinder or aid black community development. Critics may contend that political influence should not be linked to wealth, but until that becomes reality, it is crucial to acknowledge how the concentration of wealth can disproportionately shape political agendas.

Recognizing the effects of white wealth accumulation on black community development is not about fostering division but illuminating the systemic barriers to economic parity. It allows us to address these inequities directly and develop strategies for equitable wealth accumulation.

This chapter serves as an exploration of the intersections between wealth, race, and community development. It's a call for economic justice and a reminder of our resilience. We are not simply victims of an unjust system; we are advocates for change, agents of progress,

---

[36] Perry, Andre, et al. "The devaluation of assets in black neighborhoods: The case of residential property," Brookings Institution, 2018.

[37] Jackson, C. Kirabo, Rucker C. Johnson, and Claudia Persico. "The effects of school spending on educational and economic outcomes: Evidence from school finance reforms," The Quarterly Journal of Economics, 2016.

[38] Rothwell, Jonathan. "Housing costs, zoning, and access to high-scoring schools," Brookings Institution, 2012.

and stewards of a future where wealth is not a predictor of opportunity.

Examining Self-Sufficiency as a Tool Against Systemic Economic Inequality

Self-sufficiency is an empowering principle, one that, when embraced, serves as an essential tool against systemic economic inequality. Critics may argue that advocating for self-sufficiency absolves societal and governmental structures from their responsibility to rectify historical injustices. However, it is important to understand that advocating for self-sufficiency is not about shifting blame, but about harnessing power and control over one's economic fate.

The concept of self-sufficiency is rooted in financial independence, a critical pillar of economic empowerment. It implies having the capacity to generate wealth that can sustain oneself and contribute towards community growth. Research shows that an increase in black entrepreneurship correlates with lower unemployment rates in the black community[39], exemplifying the power of self-sufficiency in combating economic disparities.

Self-sufficiency also requires financial literacy, a component often neglected in our education system. With adequate financial knowledge, individuals can make informed decisions that secure their financial future and potentially help bridge the racial wealth gap. Critics may argue that financial literacy alone cannot solve systemic

---

[39] Fairlie, Robert. "Black and White: Access to Capital among Minority-Owned start-ups," Stanford Institute for Economic Policy Research, 2013.

issues, but knowledge is power, and this power can impact wealth accumulation over time[40].

Furthermore, self-sufficiency encourages home ownership, a significant wealth-building tool. Despite the adverse effects of discriminatory housing policies, there are efforts to increase black home ownership rates, such as programs offering affordable loans and housing counseling[41]. Critics might question the focus on home ownership due to the housing market's volatility, but the intergenerational wealth it often provides underscores its importance[42].

Community self-sufficiency, achieved through supporting black-owned businesses and local investment, is another pivotal aspect. This economic ecosystem nurtures local growth and resilience, addressing market undervaluation in black neighborhoods[43]. Critics may argue that this strategy encourages economic segregation, but it's about strengthening our communities, making them self-sustaining, and achieving economic parity.

Examining self-sufficiency as a tool against systemic economic inequality is not about discarding societal responsibility but empowering ourselves within an uneven playing field. It's about understanding that while we strive for systemic change, we can also build sustainable pathways to wealth, ensuring our resilience amidst economic challenges.

---

[40] Lusardi, Annamaria, and Olivia S. Mitchell. "Financial Literacy and Wealth Accumulation: The Importance of Financial Literacy," National Bureau of Economic Research, 2014.

[41] Herbert, Christopher, et al. "The Role of Investors in Acquiring Foreclosed Properties in Low- and Moderate-Income Neighborhoods: A Review of Findings from Four Case Studies," U.S. Department of Housing and Urban Development, 2012.

[42] Federal Reserve Board, "Changes in U.S. Family Finances from 2007 to 2010: Evidence from the Survey of Consumer Finances," 2012.

[43] Perry, Andre, et al. "The devaluation of assets in black neighborhoods: The case of residential property," Brookings Institution, 2018.

This chapter serves as a testament to our strength, a recognition of our capacity to shape our economic destinies despite systemic obstacles. We are not merely seeking to survive within an unequal system; we are striving to thrive, using self-sufficiency as a powerful tool for economic liberation and community empowerment.

The Rationale for Blacks to Enact High Goal-Setting and Increased Action in Wealth Creation

Setting high goals and taking proactive steps in wealth creation are necessary components for achieving economic parity. Critics may argue that such lofty aims can set up individuals for disappointment, given the systemic hurdles in place. However, setting ambitious goals and taking active steps towards wealth creation are not just about conquering the wealth gap; they serve as powerful counters to systemic disadvantages and represent an assertion of agency and resilience.

High goal-setting in wealth creation represents a commitment to economic prosperity and liberation. It's not simply about acquiring wealth but amassing assets that enable generational wealth transfer, a vital factor in wealth accumulation[44]. Critics may argue that setting high wealth goals might encourage materialism, but it's more about striving for financial security and fostering a legacy that can buffer against economic disparities.

Simultaneously, increased action in wealth creation is crucial. This might involve exploring entrepreneurship, investing in real estate, acquiring financial education, or supporting black-owned businesses. Critics might argue that systemic barriers can impede these efforts, but it's about

---

[44] Federal Reserve Board, "Changes in U.S. Family Finances from 2007 to 2010: Evidence from the Survey of Consumer Finances," 2012.

making the most of available opportunities, no matter how challenging the landscape may be.

For instance, despite the challenges, there are over 2 million black-owned businesses in the U.S., contributing around $150 billion to the U.S. economy[45]. These figures exemplify the power of action in the face of adversity. Furthermore, evidence suggests that increased black entrepreneurship can have positive impacts on black employment rates[46], underscoring the significance of action in wealth creation.

Moreover, setting high goals and taking increased action also influences social norms and community dynamics. This can inspire a collective momentum towards economic empowerment, altering narratives and catalyzing wider change. Critics may argue that individual actions cannot reshape societal structures, but collective efforts can make a substantial difference.

The rationale for blacks to set high goals and increase action in wealth creation is a testament to our strength, resilience, and capacity for change. It's about transforming aspirations into realities, breaking through systemic barriers, and forging a path of prosperity despite the odds.

This chapter serves as a clarion call to action, encouraging ambitious goal-setting and proactive action towards wealth creation. It reminds us that we are not mere passengers in the journey towards economic parity; we are the drivers, steering towards a future where wealth is equally accessible, equally achievable, and equally shared.

---

[45] U.S. Census Bureau, "Annual Business Survey," 2017.
[46] Fairlie, Robert. "Black and White: Access to Capital among Minority-Owned start-ups," Stanford Institute for Economic Policy Research, 2013.

Highlighting the Importance of Ambition and Drive in Wealth Creation

The power of ambition and drive in wealth creation cannot be overstated. Critics may argue that ambition alone cannot counter systemic obstacles and that emphasizing it diverts attention from societal responsibilities.

However, underscoring the significance of ambition and drive does not absolve society or its structures from their roles; it's about recognizing that personal agency is a significant piece of the wealth creation puzzle.

Ambition fuels the vision for wealth creation. It sets the foundation for setting lofty goals and catalyzing action. It's not simply about striving for personal enrichment but seeking economic liberation and community empowerment. Critics may contend that a focus on ambition could lead to an unhealthy obsession with wealth, but it's more about inspiring economic independence and stability.

Drive, on the other hand, is the engine that propels the quest for wealth creation. It spurs resilience in the face of obstacles, fostering an environment of innovation and determination. A 2016 study found a positive correlation between entrepreneurship and traits such as drive, determination, and self-confidence[47]. Critics may argue that not everyone possesses these traits or the opportunity to apply them. Still, it's about nurturing these traits and creating environments where they can be effectively utilized.

One notable example of the power of ambition and drive is Madam C.J. Walker, a daughter of former slaves who became one of the first black female millionaires through sheer determination and entrepreneurial spirit[48]. Her

---

[47] Obschonka, M., et al. "Entrepreneurial Passion and Personality: The Case of Academic Entrepreneurship," Frontiers in Psychology, 2017.

[48] Bundles, A'Lelia. "Madam C.J. Walker: Entrepreneur, Leader, and Self-Made Millionaire," Biography, 2020.

story exemplifies how ambition and drive, coupled with opportunities, can break through systemic barriers.

Furthermore, the ambition and drive for wealth creation can initiate a ripple effect, inspiring others and transforming communities. This collective momentum can challenge societal norms, break the cycle of poverty, and create new narratives of economic prosperity. Critics might argue that these individual success stories cannot change the structural inequalities that persist, but these stories serve as powerful symbols of what's possible and inspire collective action.

Highlighting the importance of ambition and drive in wealth creation is a tribute to our strength and tenacity. It is about recognizing our capacity to shape our economic destinies, to push boundaries, and to chart our path to prosperity.

This chapter serves as an homage to our unyielding spirit, to the power of our ambition, and to the strength of our drive. We are not merely dreamers in the quest for economic parity; we are the doers, the builders, and the change-makers, fervently driving towards a future of shared prosperity.

The History of Blacks and Their Correlation Between High Goals and High Achievement

The correlation between high goals and high achievement in the history of the black community is a testament to the resilience and fortitude displayed in the face of systemic obstacles. Critics may argue that highlighting these instances overlooks the systemic barriers that persist, making high achievement more challenging. However, acknowledging this correlation is not about trivializing systemic hurdles, but rather celebrating the strength, perseverance, and triumphs of the black community.

Historically, the black community has set ambitious goals in various domains – from civil rights to entrepreneurship, education, sports, arts, and politics – and achieved remarkable success. For instance, in the civil rights movement, the goal was nothing short of comprehensive societal transformation, and the achievements, while not complete, were significant[49].

In entrepreneurship, black individuals have consistently demonstrated high ambition and achievement. One such example is Robert F. Smith, the founder of Vista Equity Partners, who became the wealthiest African American in the U.S., surpassing even Oprah Winfrey[50]. His success underscores the link between setting high goals and achieving remarkable results.

Similarly, in academia, black individuals have consistently set high goals and achieved exceptional results. Dr. Patricia Bath, for example, was the first African American woman doctor to receive a patent for a medical invention[51]. Her accomplishment demonstrates that high goals coupled with determination can lead to groundbreaking achievements.

Critics might argue that these examples represent a minority and don't reflect the experience of the broader black population. While it is true that these individuals represent a fraction of the black community, their stories illuminate what's possible and serve as a source of inspiration.

---

[49] Carson, Clayborne. "The Civil Rights Movement: Past, Present, and Future," Annual Review of Sociology, 1993.
[50] Badkar, Mamta. "Robert F. Smith: the billionaire paying off black students' debt," Financial Times, 2019.
[51] Holohan, Meghan. "Patricia Bath, 76, Who Took On Blindness and Earned a Patent, Dies," The New York Times, 2019.

Moreover, these stories of high achievement are essential for shifting societal narratives, debunking stereotypes, and motivating the next generation of black achievers. These narratives provide evidence that, despite systemic obstacles, high goals can lead to high achievement.

Recognizing the correlation between high goals and high achievement is about honoring our legacy of strength and resilience. It's about celebrating our accomplishments, learning from our experiences, and harnessing this knowledge to propel our future success.

This chapter serves as a salute to our past and present achievers, to those who dared to set high goals and reached remarkable heights. It serves as a reminder that we are not simply survivors within an unequal system; we are achievers, trailblazers, and pioneers, continually striving for excellence and making our mark in the annals of history.

Establishing the Need for Active Participation in Wealth Generation

Active participation in wealth generation is a crucial element for achieving economic parity. Critics may argue that this emphasis on individual participation deflects attention from systemic issues that should be addressed. However, advocating for active participation does not negate the need for societal and systemic reforms; it's about asserting agency and taking charge of our economic destinies within the existing structures.

Active participation involves being proactive in gaining financial education, pursuing entrepreneurship, making informed investment decisions, and supporting black-owned businesses. As of 2019, only 31% of black families owned stocks compared to 61% of white families[52]. This disparity reveals a crucial area where active participation can be increased, with potential long-term benefits for wealth accumulation.

Entrepreneurship is another sphere where active participation can have a significant impact. Despite making up 13% of the U.S. population, black individuals own just 2.2% of the nation's businesses[53]. Critics may argue that this low percentage is due to systemic barriers. While true, fostering an entrepreneurial mindset and providing support systems can enable more black individuals to participate actively in business ownership, creating wealth and employment opportunities.

Moreover, active participation in wealth generation can have transformative effects on community dynamics and social norms. When individuals actively participate in wealth generation, they not only improve their financial standing but also contribute to the economic prosperity of their communities. Critics might argue that individual actions cannot reshape societal structures, but collective efforts can indeed instigate systemic changes.

The call for active participation in wealth generation is a call to action. It's about empowering ourselves with the necessary tools and knowledge, taking calculated risks, making strategic decisions, and contributing to our economic liberation.

This chapter serves as a rallying cry for active participation in wealth generation. It is a reminder that we are not merely observers in the pursuit of economic parity; we are active participants, making strategic moves, shaping our economic landscapes, and leading our communities towards shared prosperity.

---

[52] Pew Research Center, "Trends in Income and Wealth Inequality," 2020.
[53] U.S. Census Bureau, "Annual Business Survey," 2017.

Chapter 2

Defining the Scope of the Wealth Gap

The racial wealth gap—a critical metric that reveals the profound, pervasive racial economic inequality that persists in the United States—is significantly more than a mere measure of the difference in assets owned by diverse racial or ethnic groups. In "Black Labor, White Wealth," my analysis already demonstrated the breadth and depth of this gap, but current data from the Federal Reserve's 2019 Survey of Consumer Finances (SCF) reaffirms the stark disparities. White families, according to the SCF, possess eight times the wealth of Black families and five times that of Hispanic families. This is a clear manifestation of systemic economic disparities bred from historical discrimination, inequitable access to resources, and asymmetric opportunities that are interwoven into our socio-economic fabric[54].

Consequently, the term "racial wealth gap" embodies the tangible economic effects of systemic and entrenched racial disparities. It is crucial to underline that these disparities are not a consequence of individual effort or lack thereof, but are rooted in systemic racial biases and long-standing inequities[55]. Nonetheless, those opposing these views often claim that the racial wealth gap is a product of individual choices and behavior. They argue that differences in educational attainment, single-parent households, or personal savings rates are the primary drivers. However, as demonstrated in "The Color of Money: Black Banks and the Racial Wealth Gap" by Mehrsa Baradaran, such arguments

---

[54]
[55] Rothstein, R. (2017). The color of law: A forgotten history of how our government segregated America. Liveright Publishing.

often overlook systemic barriers that limit access to wealth-building opportunities for racial minorities.

Take home-ownership, for instance, a traditional means of wealth accumulation in America. The SCF found that Black home-ownership rates remain significantly lower than white home-ownership rates. This is not merely a product of individual choice, but rather a result of a long history of exclusionary housing policies, such as redlining, that continue to reverberate today[56]. As a result, opportunities for Black families to build wealth through home-ownership have been systematically undermined, perpetuating the racial wealth gap.

Interestingly, the SCF data reveals a slightly different picture for the category labeled "other families," which includes people identifying as Asian, Native American, Alaska Native, Pacific Islander, and those who identify as more than one race. This group held less wealth than White families but more than Black and Hispanic families. It's worth noting that categorizing such a diverse range of ethnicities into a single group can obscure substantial disparities within the category itself.

This chapter will further examine the economic status of four racial and ethnic groups—Black, Latinx/Hispanic, Native American, and Asian American—relative to White Americans. As Dr. Martin Luther King Jr. noted in 1968, these groups "find themselves impoverished aliens in an affluent society" due to a long history of formal legal discrimination and societal prejudice. However, given the amount of data available and the depth of the studies conducted, we'll place a somewhat greater emphasis on the status of Black Americans[57].

---

[56] Baradaran, M. (2017). The Color of Money: Black Banks and the Racial Wealth Gap. The Belknap Press of Harvard University Press.
[57] King, M. L. (1968). The other America. Speech at Grosse Pointe High School.

In essence, the racial wealth gap is a matter of economic justice. While detractors may question the validity of these data points, the persistent racial economic inequality necessitates a holistic understanding of its causes, implications, and solutions. Ignoring this stark reality will only serve to perpetuate a socio-economic structure that significantly hinders racial and ethnic groups from equitable participation in America's wealth.

The Economic Disparities Highlighted By Today's Laws And Politics, Concerning Blacks

The economic disparities faced by the Black community in the United States are a stark reality, inextricably intertwined with an array of legal and political structures that appear to perpetuate and amplify racial wealth gaps. The Civil Rights Act of 1964, though a historic legislative milestone, could not eliminate economic inequality, an issue that remains vitally important in our society[58].

As per a study conducted by McKinsey & Company, the median wealth of Black families in America amounted to roughly $24,100 in 2019, contrasted with $188,200 for White families, underlining a substantial racial wealth gap spanning generations[59]. The disparity is not merely a byproduct of individual or group behavior, but a systemic result of both outright legal discrimination and deep-seated racial biases.

Conversely, some argue that racial wealth gaps are mainly due to individual choices or cultural differences. For instance, Richard Epstein suggests that the racial wealth gap primarily stems from differences in family structure, with a

---

[58] Civil Rights Act, 42 U.S.C. § 2000e (1964).
[59] McKinsey & Company. "The Economic Impact of Closing the Racial Wealth Gap," McKinsey & Company, August 2019.

higher prevalence of single-parent households in Black communities driving these disparities[60]. Additionally, George Borjas proposes that the divergence in educational attainment and labor market outcomes is the key contributor[61].

These arguments, while shedding light on individual and cultural factors, often overlook the systemic nature of racial wealth gaps. Within the housing market, for example, discriminatory practices such as redlining and racially restrictive covenants have limited Black home-ownership, a conventional path to wealth accumulation in America. Despite the prohibition of these practices by the Fair Housing Act of 1968, their lingering effects manifest in the form of segregated neighborhoods and disparate home values, ultimately influencing wealth accumulation for Black families[62].

Moreover, it is critical to examine the role of laws and politics in shaping these disparities. Legislation like the 1996 Welfare Reform Act, which put a cap on welfare benefits and introduced work requirements, disproportionately affected Black families, who were, and still are, predominantly on the lower end of the income spectrum[63].

From a political perspective, policies favoring tax cuts for the affluent and reductions in public services usually have the greatest impact on marginalized communities, as they are more reliant on these services. The 2017 Tax Cuts and Jobs Act, for example, primarily benefited the wealthy,

---

[60] Epstein, Richard A. "Forbidden Grounds: The Case Against Employment Discrimination Laws," Harvard University Press, 2016.
[61] Borjas, George J. "The Slowdown in the Economic Assimilation of Immigrants: Aging and Cohort Effects Revisited Again," Journal of Human Capital 9, no. 4 (Winter 2015): 483-517.
[62] Rothstein, Richard. "The Color of Law: A Forgotten History of How Our Government Segregated America," Liveright Publishing, 2017.
[63] Haskins, Ron. "Work Over Welfare: The Inside Story of the 1996 Welfare Reform Law," Brookings Institution Press, 2006.

thereby intensifying income and wealth disparities along racial lines[64].

Racial economic disparities are a persistent facet of American society, deeply ingrained in a complex web of laws, politics, and systemic biases. While some may challenge the systemic nature of these disparities, a thorough investigation of the historical and current context unveils a different narrative, one that accentuates the need for targeted policies to alleviate these entrenched inequities.

Disparities Exposed By The COVID-19 Pandemic And Economic Downturn

The COVID-19 pandemic and the resulting economic downturn have dramatically exposed and exacerbated existing disparities in the United States, underscoring the systemic vulnerabilities faced by marginalized communities, especially people of color. From health outcomes to economic stability, these disparities highlight the persistent inequities that run deep in our societal fabric[65].

Data from the Centers for Disease Control and Prevention reveal a significant racial divide in the pandemic's health impact. Black, Hispanic, and Native American populations have been three times as likely to contract COVID-19 and twice as likely to die from the virus as their White counterparts[66]. The pandemic has shed a glaring light on racial disparities in health, rooted in factors such as unequal access to health-care, higher rates of

---

[64] Tax Policy Center. "Distributional Analysis of the Conference Agreement for the Tax Cuts and Jobs Act," Tax Policy Center, December 2017.
[65] Robert Wood Johnson Foundation. "How COVID-19 Exposes Racial Disparities in Health, Wealth." March 2021.
[66] Centers for Disease Control and Prevention. "Risk for COVID-19 Infection, Hospitalization, and Death By Race/Ethnicity." June 2021.

comorbidities due to systemic and environmental issues, and greater exposure risks in jobs considered essential[67].

However, some critics argue that these disparities arise from individual behaviors or health conditions rather than systemic issues. They contend that higher rates of obesity and diabetes in Black and Hispanic communities contribute to the COVID-19 racial disparities[68]. While these are undeniable factors, they are also inherently intertwined with systemic inequities such as food deserts and inadequate health-care[69].

The economic downturn brought on by the pandemic has disproportionately affected workers in low-wage jobs, many of whom are people of color. The unemployment rate among Black and Hispanic workers has consistently been higher than among White workers during the economic downturn[70]. Again, systemic factors come into play: workers of color are overrepresented in industries hardest hit by the pandemic, and they often lack the flexibility to work from home[71].

In response, skeptics often cite individual financial behavior or argue that racial and ethnic disparities in unemployment are due to educational attainment[72]. Yet

---

[67] Laurencin, Cato T., and Aneesah McClinton. "The COVID-19 Pandemic: a Call to Action to Identify and Address Racial and Ethnic Disparities." Journal of Racial and Ethnic Health Disparities, 2020, 7: 398–402.

[68] Webb Hooper, Monica, Anna María Nápoles, and Eliseo J. Pérez-Stable. "COVID-19 and Racial/Ethnic Disparities." Journal of the American Medical Association, 2020, 323(24): 2466–2467.

[69] Williams, David R., and Selina A. Mohammed. "Racism and Health I: Pathways and Scientific Evidence." American Behavioral Scientist, 2013, 57(8): 1152-1173.

[70] U.S. Bureau of Labor Statistics. "Unemployment rates by race and ethnicity, 2019-2020." March 2021.

[71] Gould, Elise, and Valerie Wilson. "Black workers face two of the most lethal preexisting conditions for coronavirus—racism and economic inequality." Economic Policy Institute, June 2020.

[72] Becker, Gary S. "Human Capital: A Theoretical and Empirical Analysis, with Special Reference to Education." University of Chicago Press, 1994.

these arguments fail to account for the reality of racial stratification in the economy, shaped by long-standing systemic issues such as employment discrimination and educational inequity[73].

In sum, the COVID-19 pandemic and the resulting economic downturn have not only exposed but also worsened existing racial and ethnic disparities in health and wealth. Despite diverging perspectives, the prevailing data paints a clear picture of systemic inequalities that must be addressed. These challenging times call for a commitment to policies and initiatives that target these disparities at their roots.

Case Studies of How Economic Crises Disproportionately Affect Black Communities

The profound impact of economic crises on Black communities in the United States paints a picture of systemic vulnerability and economic precarity. An examination of two significant economic downturns—the Great Recession of 2008 and the COVID-19 economic crisis—offers revealing case studies[74].

During the Great Recession, Black households experienced disproportionate losses, largely due to the collapse of the housing market. They were twice as likely as White families to lose their homes to foreclosure[75] Much of this disparity can be attributed to targeted predatory lending practices and subprime mortgages, as highlighted in reports

---

[73] Hamilton, Darrick, et al. "Umbrellas Don't Make it Rain: Why Studying and Working Hard Isn't Enough for Black Americans." The New School, 2015.
[74] Hamilton, Darrick, et al. "Umbrellas Don't Make it Rain: Why Studying and Working Hard Isn't Enough for Black Americans." The New School, 2015.
[75] Gerardi, Kristopher, et al. "Race, Ethnicity and High-Cost Mortgage Lending." Federal Reserve Bank of Atlanta, 2015.

from the Federal Reserve and the American Sociological Review[76],[77]. Nevertheless, critics often attribute these disparities to financial illiteracy or risky borrowing practices among Black homeowners, which significantly oversimplify the systemic forces at play[78].

Similarly, the economic fallout from the COVID-19 pandemic hit Black communities harder than others. The April 2020 unemployment rate for Black Americans soared to 16.7%, compared to 14.2% for Whites[79].

Furthermore, Black businesses were more likely to close permanently; a study by the National Bureau of Economic Research found a 41% drop in Black business owners from February to April 2020[80].

Opponents often highlight the resilience of Black communities during these crises, pointing out the growing number of Black entrepreneurs or improving graduation rates among Black students as signs of progress[81]. However, these arguments often overlook the systemic issues that underpin the persistent racial disparities in wealth and income, such as unequal access to capital and education, discrimination in lending and hiring, and the racial wealth gap itself [82].

---

[76] Rugh, Jacob S., and Douglas S. Massey. "Racial Segregation and the American Foreclosure Crisis." American Sociological Review, 2010, 75(5): 629-651.

[77] Williams, Richard et al. "The Changing Face of Inequality in Home Mortgage Lending." Social Problems, 2005, 52(2): 181-208.

[78] Lusardi, Annamaria, and Olivia S. Mitchell. "The Economic Importance of Financial Literacy: Theory and Evidence." Journal of Economic Literature, 2014, 52(1): 5-44.

[79] U.S. Bureau of Labor Statistics. "Unemployment rates by race and ethnicity, 2019-2020." March 2021.

[80] Fairlie, Robert. "The Impact of COVID-19 on Small Business Owners: Continued Losses and the Partial Rebound by June 2020." National Bureau of Economic Research, 2020.

[81] Fairlie, Robert. "Race and the Lifecyle of Entrepreneurial Firms: Evidence from U.S. Census Bureau Data." Stanford Institute for Economic Policy Research, 2008.

[82] Baradaran, Mehrsa. "The Color of Money: Black Banks and the Racial Wealth Gap." Harvard University Press, 2017.

These case studies illustrate a broader pattern: Black communities are disproportionately affected by economic crises due to systemic vulnerabilities. Although counterarguments suggest individual or group-level factors contribute to these disparities, the overwhelming weight of evidence indicates systemic forces play a significant role. Recognizing and addressing these systemic forces is critical in ensuring future economic crises do not perpetuate or exacerbate racial disparities.

Analyzing The structural Inequities That Perpetuate Economic Disparities

Unraveling the tapestry of the U.S. economic landscape reveals the structural inequities that perpetuate economic disparities among racial groups, particularly affecting Black communities. These systemic disparities arise from various sectors: housing, education, employment, and criminal justice[83].

The housing sector, as a case in point, has been marred by discriminatory practices such as redlining, a process that denied loans and investments in Black neighborhoods, depriving these communities of wealth accumulation through home-ownership[84]. While some detractors argue that redlining is a relic of the past, the lingering effects of such practices are evident in contemporary racial segregation and associated wealth disparities[85].

The field of education presents another arena of systemic inequities. Despite Brown v. Board of Education's

---

[83] Kendi, Ibram X. "Stamped from the Beginning: The Definitive History of Racist Ideas in America." Nation Books, 2016.
[84] Coates, Ta-Nehisi. "The Case for Reparations." The Atlantic, June 2014.
[85] Krysan, Maria and Kyle Crowder. "Cycle of Segregation: Social Processes and Residential Stratification." Russell Sage Foundation, 2017.

mandate to desegregate schools, stark racial disparities persist in the American educational system. Predominantly Black schools often receive fewer resources, leading to lower educational outcomes[86]. Critics may point to individual efforts and charter schools as a solution, but these don't fully address the structural funding disparities rooted in local property taxes[87].

Structural inequities also permeate the job market. Studies have shown that applicants with "Black-sounding" names receive fewer callbacks for interviews, even with identical resumes to those with "White-sounding" names[88]. Detractors may argue that this is an issue of perception or bias rather than systemic racism, but such bias is itself a product of systemic racism.

Lastly, the criminal justice system disproportionately affects Black individuals, from arrest rates to sentencing, disrupting economic opportunities and contributing to racial wealth disparities. For instance, incarceration prevents the accumulation of wealth and hinders employment prospects upon release[89]. Counter-arguments might suggest higher crime rates in Black communities as justification for these disparities, but this view often neglects the systemic factors driving these crime rates, such as poverty and lack of opportunities[90].

---

[86] Reardon, Sean F., and Kendra Bischoff. "Income Inequality and Income Segregation." American Journal of Sociology, 2011, 116(4): 1092-1153.

[87] Ladd, Helen F. "Education and Poverty: Confronting the Evidence." Journal of Policy Analysis and Management, 2012, 31(2): 203-227.

[88] Bertrand, Marianne and Sendhil Mullainathan. "Are Emily and Greg More Employable Than Lakisha and Jamal? A Field Experiment on Labor Market Discrimination." American Economic Review, 2004, 94(4): 991-1013.

[89] Western, Bruce and Becky Pettit. "Incarceration & social inequality." Daedalus, 2010, 139(3): 8-19.

[90] Sampson, Robert J., and William Julius Wilson. "Toward a theory of race, crime, and urban inequality." Race, crime, and justice: A reader, 1995: 37-54.

The roots of economic disparities lie in structural inequities deeply embedded within the fabric of American society. Detractors may emphasize individual factors or behaviors, but it is essential to view these disparities within a broader systemic context. Efforts to rectify these economic disparities necessitate a thorough understanding and deconstruction of these systemic factors.

Framework For Understanding The Roles In The Economy: Workers, Business Owners, Savers/Investors, Consumers, Residents

Understanding the roles in an economy—workers, business owners, savers/investors, consumers, and residents—is pivotal in grasping the dynamics of economic disparities and their interrelation with systemic racism, particularly concerning Black communities[91].

Workers are the backbone of any economy. They generate value through their labor, contributing to the production of goods and services. However, structural racism often relegates Black workers to lower-wage jobs and exposes them to higher rates of unemployment and wage discrimination[92]. Critics may argue that these disparities are due to differences in education or skills, but studies show that Black workers often earn less than their white counterparts, even with the same level of education[93].

Business owners have the potential to amass wealth, create jobs, and stimulate economic growth. However,

---

[91] Hamilton, Darrick, and William Darity Jr. "The political economy of education, financial literacy, and the racial wealth gap." Federal Reserve Bank of St. Louis Review, 2017, 99(1): 59-76.
[92] Wilson, Valerie, and William M. Rodgers III. "Black-white wage gaps expand with rising wage inequality." Economic Policy Institute, 2016.
[93] Baradaran, Mehrsa. "The Color of Money: Black Banks and the Racial Wealth Gap." Belknap Press, 2017.

Black business owners face significant barriers, including difficulty accessing capital and discriminatory lending practices. These challenges limit their capacity to grow their businesses and create wealth[94]. Detractors may argue that poor business decisions or a lack of entrepreneurial spirit contribute to these disparities, but data indicates that Black business owners are just as ambitious and innovative as their White counterparts, when given the same opportunities and resources[95].

Savers and investors contribute to economic growth by providing the capital necessary for businesses to expand. However, Black households have significantly lower rates of savings and investment, largely due to the racial wealth gap[96]. While some attribute this to poor financial literacy or cultural factors, it's essential to note that the ability to save and invest is heavily contingent on income and wealth, which are structurally disadvantaged for Black households[97].

Consumers play a crucial role in driving demand in the economy. However, Black consumers often face predatory practices, such as price discrimination and targeted marketing of high-interest loans[98]. Critics may claim individual choice is responsible for these disparities, but these practices disproportionately affect Black consumers and contribute to the racial wealth gap[99].

Lastly, as residents, individuals contribute to the local economy and tax base. However, Black residents often live

---

[94] Fairlie, Robert W., and Alicia M. Robb. "Race and Entrepreneurial Success." MIT Press, 2008.
[95] Bates, Timothy. "Minority Business Success: Refocusing on the American Dream." Stanford University Press, 2011.
[96] Shapiro, Thomas, Tatjana Meschede, and Sam Osoro. "The roots of the widening racial wealth gap: Explaining the black-white economic divide." Institute on Assets and Social Policy, 2013.
[97] Oliver, Melvin, and Thomas Shapiro. "Black Wealth, White Wealth: A New Perspective on Racial Inequality." Routledge, 2006.
[98] Baradaran, Mehrsa. "The Color of Money: Black Banks and the Racial Wealth Gap." Belknap Press, 2017.
[99] Cohen, Lizabeth. "A Consumers' Republic: The Politics of Mass Consumption in Postwar America." Vintage Books, 2003.

in under-resourced communities due to systemic housing discrimination, affecting local public services like education and infrastructure[100].

Understanding these economic roles and the systemic barriers faced by Black individuals within them provides a framework for comprehending the nature of economic disparities and points towards potential avenues for structural reform.

Detailing The Different Roles And Their Economic Functions

An economy functions due to the distinct yet intertwined roles of workers, business owners, savers/investors, consumers, and residents. Each contributes in a unique way, and their interrelations shape the contours of the economic landscape.

Workers create value by supplying labor, forming the bedrock of the economy. They are involved in the production and delivery of goods and services, earning wages and salaries in exchange for their work[101]. Critics who argue the wage gap is due to a lack of ambition or education must contend with studies showing that Black workers often earn less than white counterparts with the same education[102].

Business owners act as engines for wealth creation and job provision, influencing the dynamism of the economy. Despite these potential benefits, systemic discrimination hampers Black business owners, depriving the economy of valuable input and obstructing generational wealth

---

[100] Rothstein, Richard. "The Color of Law: A Forgotten History of How Our Government Segregated America." Liveright Publishing, 2017.
[101] Borjas, George J. "Labor Economics." McGraw-Hill Education, 2016.
[102] Wilson, Valerie, and William M. Rodgers III. "Black-white wage gaps expand with rising wage inequality." Economic Policy Institute, 2016.

creation[103]. This inequity cannot be blamed solely on business acumen; data shows that Black entrepreneurs are as innovative and ambitious as others, given equivalent opportunities[104].

Savers and investors are critical for economic growth, providing the capital necessary for business expansion. The ability to save and invest, however, is disproportionately influenced by income and wealth. Owing to systemic issues, Black households often have lower savings rates, leading some to unfairly blame financial literacy or cultural behaviors. Yet these disparities trace back to the structural disadvantages Black households face[105].

Consumers play a central role in demand creation, driving the economy. Disproportionately, Black consumers face discriminatory practices such as predatory lending and price discrimination, exacerbating the racial wealth gap. Critics often shift blame to individual consumer choices, yet the evidence points towards systemic exploitation[106].

Residents contribute to the local economy and tax base, yet systemic housing discrimination often relegates Black residents to under-resourced communities, affecting local public services and economic potential[107]. Arguments blaming individual choice for housing disparities fail to acknowledge the historical legacy of discriminatory practices like redlining[108].

---

[103] Fairlie, Robert W., and Alicia M. Robb. "Race and Entrepreneurial Success." MIT Press, 2008.

[104] Bates, Timothy. "Minority Business Success: Refocusing on the American Dream." Stanford University Press, 2011.

[105] Shapiro, Thomas, Tatjana Meschede, and Sam Osoro. "The roots of the widening racial wealth gap: Explaining the black-white economic divide." Institute on Assets and Social Policy, 2013.

[106] Baradaran, Mehrsa. "The Color of Money: Black Banks and the Racial Wealth Gap." Belknap Press, 2017.

[107] Rothstein, Richard. "The Color of Law: A Forgotten History of How Our Government Segregated America." Liveright Publishing, 2017.

[108] Katznelson, Ira. "When Affirmative Action Was White: An Untold History of Racial Inequality in Twentieth-Century America." W. W. Norton & Company, 2005.

Understanding these roles and their economic functions elucidates the complexity of an economy and its inherent systemic disparities, necessitating a comprehensive approach for equitable reform.

Examining How These Roles Interact Within The Larger Economic System

Understanding the interplay between workers, business owners, savers/investors, consumers, and residents is vital to grasp the full picture of an economic system.

Workers are essential to business owners. They supply labor, the key resource that drives productivity and thus profitability[109]. However, discriminatory wage practices in the U.S. economy leave Black workers with lower earnings for comparable work, thus constraining their roles as consumers and savers/investors[110]. Critics argue for a free-market approach to wage determination, but this overlooks the long history of racial discrimination in labor markets[111].

Business owners, in turn, depend on consumers for revenue. Yet, systemic discrimination impacts Black consumers in the form of predatory lending, pricing disparities, and biased treatment, affecting their purchasing power [112]. Critics often attribute these disparities to individual financial behavior, ignoring structural inequities[113].

---

[109] Borjas, George J. "Labor Economics." McGraw-Hill Education, 2016.
[110] Wilson, Valerie, and William M. Rodgers III. "Black-white wage gaps expand with rising wage inequality." Economic Policy Institute, 2016.
[111] Darity, William A., and Patrick L. Mason. "Evidence on Discrimination in Employment: Codes of Color, Codes of Gender." The Journal of Economic Perspectives, 1998.
[112] Baradaran, Mehrsa. "The Color of Money: Black Banks and the Racial Wealth Gap." Belknap Press, 2017.
[113] Bocian, Debbie Gruenstein, Keith S. Ernst, and Wei Li. "Unfair Lending: The Effect of Race and Ethnicity on the Price of Subprime Mortgages." Center for Responsible Lending, 2008.

Savers and investors support businesses by providing capital for growth and innovation. However, racial disparities in income and wealth result in significantly fewer Black savers/investors. Critics, once again, point to financial behavior, but the reality is deeply intertwined with structural issues like wage and wealth gaps[114].

Residential patterns also influence local businesses. The legacy of housing discrimination means many Black residents live in economically disadvantaged areas. Critics often argue that personal choices shape residential patterns. However, these arguments downplay the impact of racially discriminatory housing policies like redlining and housing covenants[115].

Tthe roles within an economy are deeply interconnected, and systemic racial disparities in one role can cascade through the economic system. To ignore the impact of racial discrimination in these relationships is to misread the economic realities confronting Black communities.

Discussing The Unique Challenges Faced By Black Individuals In Each Role

Black individuals in each role face distinctive systemic challenges due to persistent racial disparities.

Workers, especially Black workers, face a persistent racial wage gap. In 2020, Black men earned only 71 cents for every dollar earned by their white male counterparts,

---

[114] Shapiro, Thomas, Tatjana Meschede, and Sam Osoro. "The roots of the widening racial wealth gap: Explaining the black-white economic divide." Institute on Assets and Social Policy, 2013.

[115] Rothstein, Richard. "The Color of Law: A Forgotten History of How Our Government Segregated America." Liveright Publishing, 2017.

while Black women earned only 64 cents[116]. Critics often point to differences in education and experience, but disparities persist even when these factors are accounted for[117].

As business owners, Blacks confront difficulties in accessing capital. Black-owned businesses are twice as likely to be denied loans as their white counterparts, and even when they do obtain loans, they often receive lower amounts at higher interest rates[118]. Some critics attribute this to creditworthiness, but research shows that racial disparities in lending persist even after accounting for credit profiles and business characteristics[119].

Savers and investors in the Black community face unique barriers stemming from a racial wealth gap. Lower earnings and fewer intergenerational wealth transfers mean Black households have less wealth to save and invest[120]. Critics often attribute this to spending habits, but even when income is held constant, Black households have significantly less wealth than white households[121].

Black consumers are subject to higher costs and predatory practices. For instance, Black car buyers are charged higher interest rates than white car buyers with

---

[116] Wilson, Valerie, and William M. Rodgers III. "Black-white wage gaps expand with rising wage inequality." Economic Policy Institute, 2016.

[117] Darity, William A., and Patrick L. Mason. "Evidence on Discrimination in Employment: Codes of Color, Codes of Gender." The Journal of Economic Perspectives, 1998.

[118] Fairlie, Robert W., and Alicia M. Robb. "Race and Entrepreneurial Success: Black-, Asian-, and White-Owned Businesses in the United States." MIT Press, 2008.

[119] Blanchflower, David G., Phillip B. Levine, and David J. Zimmerman. "Discrimination in the Small-Business Credit Market." The Review of Economics and Statistics, 2003.

[120] Hamilton, Darrick, and William Darity Jr. "The political economy of education, financial literacy, and the racial wealth gap." Federal Reserve Bank of St. Louis Review, 2017.

[121] Shapiro, Thomas, Tatjana Meschede, and Sam Osoro. "The roots of the widening racial wealth gap: Explaining the black-white economic divide." Institute on Assets and Social Policy, 2013.

similar credit profiles[122]. Some critics argue that these disparities reflect risk-based pricing, but studies show that they cannot be entirely attributed to credit risk[123].

As residents, Blacks often live in areas with fewer economic opportunities due to historical housing discrimination. This affects job access, school quality, and public services[124] Critics often attribute these patterns to personal choice or 'culture', ignoring the impact of discriminatory housing policies and practices[125].

Black individuals face unique challenges in each economic role due to systemic racial disparities. Addressing these issues requires a comprehensive understanding of these interrelated roles and targeted policy interventions.

The Limitations And Acknowledgments of The Research

Understanding the unique challenges faced by Black individuals in various economic roles requires a thorough examination of systemic, structural, and personal factors. However, the process of research and analysis has limitations that should be acknowledged upfront.

First, the data collected for this research, while vast, can't capture the full range of experiences in the Black community. Economic disparities among Black individuals are inherently multidimensional, with a multitude of intersecting socioeconomic, cultural, and geographic factors

---

[122] Cohen-Cole, Ethan. "Credit Card Redlining." The Review of Economics and Statistics, 2011.

[123] Ayres, Ian, and Peter Siegelman. "Race and Gender Discrimination in Bargaining for a New Car." American Economic Review, 1995.

[124] Rothstein, Richard. "The Color of Law: A Forgotten History of How Our Government Segregated America." Liveright Publishing, 2017.

[125] Massey, Douglas S., and Nancy A. Denton. "American Apartheid: Segregation and the Making of the Underclass." Harvard University Press, 1993.

coming into play. Statistics and research, while valuable, can only offer an abstracted view of these complexities[126].

Second, the lens through which this data is interpreted also brings its own limitations. For instance, there can be differences in interpretation among economists, sociologists, and policymakers. An economic perspective might emphasize financial indicators, while a sociological view might place greater importance on social and cultural aspects[127]. Hence, while the insights generated by this research are valuable, they must be understood as part of a broader, interdisciplinary conversation.

Critics may also argue that emphasizing race-specific challenges can lead to what some scholars term "racial essentialism", which views race as the primary determinant of life outcomes, potentially ignoring the role of class, individual agency, and cultural differences[128]. They might posit that focusing on Black individuals as a monolithic group overlooks the diversity within the community and can reinforce stereotypes. However, the focus of this research is to underscore the systemic and historical disparities facing the Black community, without negating the importance of internal diversities and the potential for individual agency.

Lastly, the research acknowledges the agency and resilience of Black individuals within these economic roles. It is essential to understand that, while structural barriers exist, countless Black individuals have shown great resilience, creating vibrant businesses, robust consumer markets, and contributing substantially to the labor force

---

[126] Bonilla-Silva, Eduardo. "Racism without Racists: Color-Blind Racism and the Persistence of Racial Inequality in the United States." Rowman & Littlefield, 2017.
[127] Wilson, William J. "More Than Just Race: Being Black and Poor in the Inner City." W.W. Norton & Company, 2009.
[128] Outlaw, Lucius. "On Race and Philosophy." Routledge, 1996.

despite the challenges they face[129]. This research aims to highlight the systemic barriers that should be addressed, without denying the strength and resilience that exists within the Black community.

This research seeks to contribute to a larger, ongoing dialogue about racial economic disparities in the United States. While it offers valuable insights into the unique challenges faced by Black individuals in different economic roles, it also underscores the need for more nuanced, interdisciplinary, and inclusive approaches to understanding and addressing these disparities.

Discussing The Scope And Limitations of Existing Research on Black Wealth

In examining the landscape of research on Black wealth, the scope and robustness of existing literature is noteworthy, yet, like all fields of study, there are limitations that must be acknowledged.

A significant body of research provides critical insights into Black wealth accumulation, dissecting it from different angles. Scholars like Thomas Shapiro and Melvin Oliver delve into the intergenerational transmission of wealth and the role of inheritances in shaping racial wealth disparities[130]. Similarly, Dorothy Brown has illuminated the role of tax policy in widening the racial wealth gap[131]. These research pieces underscore the systemic underpinnings of Black wealth disparities.

---

[129] Anderson, Claud. "Black Labor, White Wealth: The Search for Power and Economic Justice." PowerNomics Corporation of America, 1994.

[130] Shapiro, Thomas, and Melvin Oliver. "Black Wealth/White Wealth: A New Perspective on Racial Inequality." Routledge, 1995.

[131] Brown, Dorothy. "The Whiteness of Wealth: How the Tax System Impoverishes Black Americans--and How We Can Fix It." Crown, 2021.

However, limitations in the existing research are apparent. For instance, much of the research on Black wealth tends to focus on disparities, centering the conversation around gaps rather than potential avenues for wealth creation. This deficit-focused narrative may obscure the diverse strategies Black individuals and communities employ to build wealth and create economic resilience[132].

There are also constraints related to data. The majority of studies use data from large national surveys like the Survey of Consumer Finances, which may not capture the nuances of Black wealth at more local levels or within subpopulations[133]. Moreover, issues of data quality and consistency over time present challenges to drawing definitive conclusions about trends in Black wealth accumulation[134].

Some critics argue that the focus on racial wealth disparities downplays other dimensions of economic well-being, such as income, employment, and educational attainment. They may posit that wealth is just one facet of economic security, and focusing exclusively on it may lead to policy solutions that neglect other aspects of economic opportunity[135]. Yet, the focus on wealth is essential as wealth provides a more complete picture of economic stability and intergenerational economic mobility than income alone.

Lastly, the research often overlooks the intersection of race and other social categories, such as gender, immigration status, and disability, in shaping wealth

---

[132] Hamilton, Darrick, and William Darity. "Race, Wealth, and Intergenerational Poverty." American Prospect, 2009.

[133] Chiteji, Ngina, and Darrick Hamilton. "Family Connections and the Black-White Wealth Gap Among Middle-Class Families." Review of Black Political Economy, 2002.

[134] Pfeffer, Fabian T., and Alexandra Killewald. "Generations of Advantage. Multigenerational Correlations in Family Wealth." Social Forces, 2018.

[135] Riley, Jason L. "Please Stop Helping Us: How Liberals Make It Harder for Blacks to Succeed." Encounter Books, 2014.

outcomes. As Patricia Hill Collins and Sirma Bilge articulate, an intersectional approach can reveal a more comprehensive understanding of wealth accumulation and economic disparities[136].

The existing research on Black wealth offers valuable insights but also leaves ample room for further exploration. Recognizing its limitations is a step towards producing more nuanced, comprehensive, and actionable scholarship in this area.

Acknowledging Areas That Require Further Study

Despite the significant strides made in researching economic disparities, there remain key areas necessitating further study, particularly concerning Black individuals' economic experiences.

Firstly, more work is needed to unearth the nuances of economic disparities in the wake of recent legislation and political shifts. Given the rapidly changing political landscape, ongoing analysis is needed to comprehend the evolving impact of laws and political discourse on Black economic outcomes[137].

Secondly, the COVID-19 pandemic and the ensuing economic downturn has spotlighted the structural inequities, yet we are only beginning to understand its long-term effects. Future research needs to explore the ongoing impacts of this crisis, especially on Black communities[138].

---

[136] Collins, Patricia Hill, and Sirma Bilge. "Intersectionality." Polity, 2016.
[137] Rothstein, Richard. "The Color of Law: A Forgotten History of How Our Government Segregated America." Liveright Publishing, 2017.
[138] Fairlie, Robert. "The Impact of COVID-19 on Small Business Owners: Evidence of Early-Stage Losses from the April 2020 Current Population Survey." National Bureau of Economic Research, 2020.

Thirdly, while research has highlighted the disproportionate effects of economic crises on Black communities, we need more localized case studies to capture the complexity and variation of these impacts[139].

Fourthly, more comprehensive analysis of structural inequities that perpetuate disparities is warranted. While research has explored some structures, such as housing and education, others, like environmental justice and health-care systems, require more attention[140].

The economic roles of workers, business owners, savers/investors, consumers, and residents provide a valuable framework for understanding disparities. However, these roles should not be studied in isolation. Further research is needed to understand the dynamic interaction between these roles and the systemic factors shaping them[141].

Moreover, the unique challenges faced by Black individuals in each economic role have been examined, but not exhaustively. For example, there is a dearth of research on Black savers/investors and the barriers they face in accessing and leveraging financial markets[142].

Regarding limitations, researchers should be increasingly transparent in recognizing and articulating the limitations of their work, thereby encouraging subsequent research to refine methods, data sources, and conceptual frameworks[143].

---

[139] Hamilton, Darrick, and William Darity. "Race, Wealth, and Intergenerational Poverty." The American Prospect, 2009.

[140] Taylor, Keeanga-Yamahtta. "Race for Profit: How Banks and the Real Estate Industry Undermined Black home-ownership." The University of North Carolina Press, 2019.

[141] Anderson, Claud. "PowerNomics : The National Plan to Empower Black America." PowerNomics Corporation of America, 2001.

[142] Baradaran, Mehrsa. "The Color of Money: Black Banks and the Racial Wealth Gap." The Belknap Press of Harvard University Press, 2017.

[143] Chetty, Raj et al. "Race and Economic Opportunity in the United States: An Intergenerational Perspective." The Quarterly Journal of Economics, 2018.

Lastly, the scope and limitations of existing research on Black wealth have been discussed. Still, a more robust examination of this area can potentially reveal significant insights, including factors contributing to wealth creation within the Black community, which are currently under-explored[144].

The outlined areas for further study are by no means exhaustive. Rather, they serve as an invitation to researchers, policy makers, and community leaders to engage in ongoing inquiry and dialogue about Black economic disparities, fostering the development of more nuanced understanding and effective interventions.

Understanding The Constraints And Biases That May Influence The Research

The study of racial economic disparities is fraught with potential biases and constraints, requiring conscientious reflection on the part of researchers to ensure rigorous, objective inquiry.

Foremost, acknowledging the historic context and bias is vital. Black economic disparities in America are a product of systemic and structural racism that stretches back centuries[145]. This can unconsciously shape the research through implicit biases. Researchers may unintentionally normalize white economic performance as the standard, thereby subtly reinforcing racial stereotypes[146].

Secondly, data constraints pose significant challenges. Despite advances in data collection, disaggregated data on race and economic outcomes remains imperfect.

---

[144] Shapiro, Thomas, and Melvin Oliver. "Black Wealth/White Wealth: A New Perspective on Racial Inequality." Routledge, 1995.
[145] Rothstein, Richard. "The Color of Law: A Forgotten History of How Our Government Segregated America." Liveright Publishing, 2017.
[146] Kendi, Ibram X. "How to Be an Antiracist." One World, 2019.

Government data sources often fail to provide comprehensive information on key wealth determinants, such as inheritance or inter-generational wealth transfers[147]. Furthermore, datasets may be limited in their geographical and temporal scope, thus restricting a full understanding of the issue.

Thirdly, the role of the researcher's standpoint can influence interpretations and conclusions. The researcher's personal experiences, values, and beliefs can subtly shape the research process, from question formulation to data interpretation. While this is not a problem per se, unacknowledged personal bias can skew the research findings[148].

Fourthly, the media, politics, and societal beliefs can influence the research on Black wealth. Dominant narratives can shape the research agenda, determining which questions are deemed significant and which are overlooked. For instance, research focusing primarily on personal responsibility as the root of racial economic disparities may overlook the systemic factors, thereby supporting the status quo and undermining efforts to address structural racism[149].

Lastly, a critical area for consideration is the influence of funding sources. Funders' interests and priorities may subtly shape research questions, methodologies, and dissemination strategies, potentially skewing the research towards certain conclusions and policy recommendations[150].

Acknowledging these constraints and biases does not undermine the value of research on Black economic

---

[147] Piketty, Thomas. "Capital in the Twenty-First Century." Harvard University Press, 2014.
[148] Harding, Sandra. "Standpoint Theories: Productively Controversial." Hypatia, 2004.
[149] Gilens, Martin. "Why Americans Hate Welfare: Race, Media, and the Politics of Antipoverty Policy." University of Chicago Press, 1999.
[150] Mirowski, Philip, and Dieter Plehwe. "The Road from Mont Pelerin: The Making of the Neoliberal Thought Collective." Harvard University Press, 2009.

disparities. Instead, it adds nuance to our understanding of these issues and reinforces the need for continuous reflexivity in the research process.

Chapter 3

Setting Your Wealth Goals: A Mindset Shift

In the journey toward closing the black wealth gap, the importance of goal setting cannot be overstated. A mindset shift is often necessary to set ambitious, yet attainable, wealth goals. However, this shift in mindset and high goal setting have often faced opposition and disbelief, particularly from those who hold a deterministic view of wealth accumulation or who underestimate the potential of the black community to generate wealth.

"The Concept of High Goals and Their Importance in Creating Black Wealth" posits that when we aim high, we are more likely to reach further than when we set mediocre goals. Yet, this is often contested, particularly by those who suggest that historical and systemic barriers may limit the achievement of these high goals. Some media outlets and groups often focus on the economic disparities faced by the black community, asserting that these make high wealth goals impractical or unachievable[151].

However, such deterministic viewpoints disregard the many examples of black wealth creation and the fact that individual and community wealth goals are a driving force behind these successes[152]. They overlook the work of individuals such as Robert F. Smith, who as the richest

---

[151] Smith, Robert F. "The Wealth Gap: A Race or Class Divide?" The New York Times, 2019.
[152] Anderson, Claud. PowerNomics: The National Plan to Empower Black America, Powernomics Corporation of America, 2001.

African American, has broken multiple barriers in wealth creation and challenged pre-existing narratives[153].

Moreover, it is argued that the psychology of high-goal setting plays a transformative role in wealth creation[154]. The transformative effect of setting ambitious goals, though initially may appear overwhelming, can act as a catalyst in breaking the cycle of economic disparity[155]. Critics argue that such an approach may set people up for failure and disappointment, yet research shows the contrary. High goals often lead to high achievement, particularly when coupled with the right mindset and resilience[156].

Despite opposition, the correlation between high goals and high achievement is undeniable. Studies have shown that individuals who set high goals tend to achieve more than those with low or no goals[157]. This correlation has been particularly pronounced in the context of wealth creation, where high wealth goals have been linked to greater financial independence and economic empowerment.

Ultimately, active participation in wealth generation is essential. High goal-setting must be paired with increased action. Critics often emphasize the systemic barriers that hinder such active participation. Yet, numerous examples have demonstrated that increased action, driven by high goals and an unwavering mindset, can result in significant wealth generation, ultimately contributing to the closing of the black wealth gap.

---

[153] MarksJarvis, Gail. "Robert F. Smith: Who is America's richest black man?" Chicago Tribune, 2019.
[154] Dweck, Carol S. Mindset: The New Psychology of Success, Random House, 2006.
[155] Akers, Ronald L., and Adam L. Silverman. "Toward a Social Learning Model of Violence and Terrorism." Violence: From Theory to Research, edited by Margaret A. Zahn, Henry H. Brownstein, and Shelly L. Jackson, Anderson, 2004, pp. 19-35.
[156] Locke, Edwin A., and Gary P. Latham. A theory of goal setting & task performance, Prentice-Hall, 1990.
[157] Ibid.

The Concept of High Goals And Their Importance In Creating Black Wealth

The concept of high goal setting is not just another motivational platitude; it is a crucial principle that could very well serve as the cornerstone of economic empowerment in the Black community. In the words of Grant Cardone, a renowned business strategist and bestselling author, "The biggest mistake most people make in life is not setting goals high enough."[158]

Success, especially financial success, is rarely an accident. It's usually the result of intentional, calculated steps towards clear, well-defined goals. The bar for these goals, however, is often set too low, limiting the potential for extraordinary achievement. This is a mistake that can stifle the creation of Black wealth.

Critics might argue that high goals are a recipe for disappointment, that they are impractical and may lead to stress and dissatisfaction[159]. However, evidence suggests that it is, in fact, the lofty goals - the ones that stretch us beyond our comfort zones - that stimulate the highest levels of performance and achievement[160].

One might question the need for continually working towards higher goals, particularly after reaching a certain level of financial success. Why keep striving? Isn't there a point at which one can simply rest and enjoy the fruits of their labor? This line of thinking reflects a common misconception about the nature of success and fulfillment.

Success isn't merely a destination; it's a journey, a perpetual pursuit of growth and improvement. It's akin to

---

[158] Cardone, Grant. The 10X Rule: The Only Difference Between Success and Failure. John Wiley & Sons, 2011.
[159] Locke, Edwin A., and Gary P. Latham. A theory of goal setting & task performance. Prentice-Hall, Inc, 1990.
[160] Heslin, Peter A., et al. "High performance work systems and employee well-being: A two stage study of a rural Australian hospital." Journal of Health Organization and Management (2005).

our relationships with loved ones. The love for your family isn't a finite resource; it's something you build upon and nurture daily. You don't simply stop caring for your family after reaching a particular milestone. Similarly, the pursuit of success and wealth creation, especially in the context of Black economic empowerment, shouldn't be bounded by self-imposed limitations.

Moreover, there's an inherent satisfaction in the process of achievement. As Cardone succinctly puts it, "Because you can be happy while accomplishing things, not while resting and doing nothing." Continual striving provides a sense of purpose and fulfillment that simply resting on one's laurels does not.

Economic parity and self-sufficiency are not just about personal financial success; they're about creating a legacy of wealth and opportunity for future generations of Black families and communities. High goals, therefore, are not just about individual achievement but also collective progress and upliftment. They are about transforming the narrative of Black wealth from one of disparity and struggle to one of success and abundance[161].

In conclusion, high goals have a critical role to play in creating Black wealth. The process may be arduous, the journey long, but with determination, resilience, and an unwavering focus on high goals, we can catalyze a significant shift towards economic empowerment in the Black community.

Delving Into The Psychology of High-Goal Setting

High-goal setting, as illuminated in the book "The 10X Rule" by Grant Cardone, offers profound insight into the

---

[161] Anderson, Claud. Black Labor, White Wealth: The Search for Power and Economic Justice. PowerNomics Corporation of America, Inc, 1994.

psychology of success[162]. It underscores four common mistakes that often hinder progress and achievement: setting one's sights too low, underestimating the amount of effort needed to reach goals, overly focusing on competition rather than dominating one's sector, and failing to prepare for the amount of adversity one will face.

Goal setting, from a psychological perspective, can be defined as the process of establishing a standard or target to serve as a guide for task performance[163]. It's a cognitive process that enables individuals to plan, evaluate progress, and stay motivated. The concept of goal setting is firmly rooted in psychology, where it's used as a behavioral intervention strategy to stimulate motivation, boost performance, and foster self-regulation.

The importance of high goal setting isn't just a fad or motivational slogan. It's based on solid scientific evidence. The "Goal Setting Theory," introduced by Drs. Edwin Locke and Gary Latham, has established that high goals lead to higher performance than low goals or no goals at all[164]. It's a premise widely supported by research findings, with one meta-analysis encompassing 38 studies revealing that goal setting improves task performance[165].

Critics, however, often caution against the potential stress and burnout associated with high goals. They argue that it could foster a toxic culture of overwork and competition[166]. Yet, research suggests otherwise. One study

---

[162] Cardone, Grant. The 10X Rule: The Only Difference Between Success and Failure. John Wiley & Sons, 2011.
[163] Locke, Edwin A., and Gary P. Latham. A Theory of Goal Setting & Task Performance. Prentice-Hall, Inc, 1990.
[164] Locke, E. A., & Latham, G. P. (2002). Building a practically useful theory of goal setting and task motivation. American Psychologist, 57(9), 705.
[165] Kleingeld, A., van Mierlo, H., & Arends, L. (2011). The effect of goal setting on group performance: A meta-analysis. Journal of Applied Psychology, 96(6), 1289.
[166] Crawford, E. R., LePine, J. A., & Rich, B. L. (2010). Linking job demands and resources to employee engagement and burnout: A

found that high goals coupled with high self-efficacy and task interest lead to increased effort and persistence, thus resulting in higher task performance[167].

The neuroscience behind goal setting adds another layer to our understanding. Goals activate the brain's reward system, releasing dopamine – a neurotransmitter associated with feelings of pleasure and satisfaction[168]. This, in turn, reinforces the behaviors that contribute to goal attainment, making goal setting a self-sustaining cycle.

Three specific case studies further illustrate the power of high-goal setting. For instance, a study among students revealed that setting specific, challenging goals resulted in superior academic performance[169]. In a business context, a company adopting the 'stretch' goal strategy saw a significant improvement in its financial and operational metrics[170]. Finally, an experiment involving basketball players demonstrated that those setting higher targets had improved free-throw performance[171].

Thus, the adoption of high goals should not be dismissed as over-ambition or impracticality. It's a scientifically-backed strategy that fuels motivation, enhances performance, and fosters growth. It may be challenging, it may invite adversity, but the potential reward

---

theoretical extension and meta-analytic test. Journal of Applied Psychology, 95(5), 834.
[167] Bandura, A., & Locke, E. A. (2003). Negative self-efficacy and goal effects revisited. Journal of Applied Psychology, 88(1), 87.
[168] Elliott, R., Friston, K. J., & Dolan, R. J. (2000). Dissociable neural responses in human reward systems. Journal of Neuroscience, 20(16), 6159-6165.
[169] Morisano, D., Hirsh, J. B., Peterson, J. B., Pihl, R. O., & Shore, B. M. (2010). Setting, elaborating, and reflecting on personal goals improves academic performance. Journal of Applied Psychology, 95(2), 255.
[170] Sitkin, S. B., See, K. E., Miller, C. C., Lawless, M. W., & Carton, A. M. (2011). The paradox of stretch goals: Organizations in pursuit of the seemingly impossible. Academy of Management Review, 36(3), 544-566.
[171] Locke, E. A., & Latham, G. P. (1985). The application of goal setting to sports. Journal of Sport Psychology, 7(3), 205-222.

– the realization of dreams previously thought unreachable – makes it a risk worth taking.

Analyzing The Transformative Effect of Ambitious Goals on Wealth Creation

There exists a transformative effect of ambitious goals on wealth creation, a sentiment echoed in the writings of Dr. Claud Anderson[172]. Arguing that many fall into the trap of setting their sights too low, Anderson underscores the critical importance of adopting a mindset of aiming higher from the outset.

Research reveals that higher set goals lead to enhanced performance. A 2006 meta-analysis by Klein, Wesson, Hollenbeck, and Alge demonstrated that individuals setting more challenging goals perform better than those with lower set goals[173]. It implies that by merely raising one's financial targets, a person might stimulate their potential for wealth generation.

There's an often-ignored psychological aspect to goal setting: satisfaction. People feel like they're merely working, rather than pursuing a passion, when the potential payoff doesn't seem substantial enough. For example, in his seminal work, "Drive," Daniel H. Pink argues that people are motivated by autonomy, mastery, and purpose rather than extrinsic rewards[174]. Yet, it is crucial to align this purpose with high-end rewards, thus increasing the perceived value of the tasks leading to goal attainment. In

---

[172] Anderson, Claud. Black Labor, White Wealth: The Search for Power and Economic Justice. Powernomics Corporation of America, Inc, 1994.

[173] Klein, H. J., Wesson, M. J., Hollenbeck, J. R., & Alge, B. J. (2006). Goal commitment and the goal-setting process: conceptual clarification and empirical synthesis. Journal of Applied Psychology, 89(6), 885.

[174] Pink, Daniel H. Drive: The Surprising Truth About What Motivates Us. Riverhead Books, 2009.

essence, a higher goal might transform a monotonous job into a fulfilling passion.

However, skeptics may challenge this perspective. They argue that high goals could lead to undue stress and unrealistic expectations, thus resulting in lower job satisfaction[175]. While this viewpoint holds merit, it is crucial to differentiate between challenging goals and impossible ones. Research indicates that challenging, yet achievable goals foster a growth mindset and increase job satisfaction[176].

Further, the principle of whose goals we work towards merits discussion. As Anderson posits, "You will either work to accomplish your goals and dreams or you'll be used to accomplish someone else's goals and dreams." Essentially, by not defining and working towards one's high goals, the individual inadvertently contributes to someone else's wealth accumulation. Such a mindset shift is significant in breaking away from the limitations of short-term, low-end jobs towards wealth creation.

The transformative effect of high goals on wealth creation extends beyond the individual level. When communities adopt ambitious goals collectively, it can stimulate economic development. For instance, South Korea's aggressive goal-setting in the late 20th century significantly contributed to its transition from a war-torn nation to an economic powerhouse[177].

High goals play a vital role in fostering wealth creation, an understanding of which is necessary to navigate the path

---

[175] Crawford, E. R., LePine, J. A., & Rich, B. L. (2010). Linking job demands and resources to employee engagement and burnout: A theoretical extension and meta-analytic test. Journal of Applied Psychology, 95(5), 834.

[176] Locke, E. A., & Latham, G. P. (2002). Building a practically useful theory of goal setting and task motivation. American Psychologist, 57(9), 705.

[177] Eun, Cheol S., & Resnick, Bruce G. (2015). International Financial Management, 7th Edition. McGraw-Hill Education.

to prosperity. While the journey may be challenging, the potential payoff justifies the effort, inspiring a purpose-driven approach to work and wealth generation.

Demonstrating The Influence of Goal Setting on Financial Success

The act of goal setting is a potent force in shaping financial success, and its significance is particularly salient in discussions surrounding the generation of black wealth[178]. It is essential to approach this issue understanding the context that wealth creation in the black community isn't merely about economic progress. Instead, it represents a collective pursuit of freedom, embodying Dr. Claud Anderson's principle: "Black wealth leads to black freedom"[179].

A central tenet in the discourse of goal setting is the premise of maintaining and even increasing targets, irrespective of encountered failures. A study by Locke and Latham revealed that high, hard goals lead to a higher level of task performance than do easy goals or vague, abstract goals such as the exhortation to "do one's best"[180]. Thus, the idea of "never reduce a target" underscores the notion of resilience and unyielding persistence in the face of adversity, an attitude integral to financial success.

At the same time, there are critical voices questioning this approach, arguing that consistently raising the bar could

---

[178] Anderson, Claud. PowerNomics: The National Plan to Empower Black America. PowerNomics Corporation of America, 2001.
[179] Anderson, Claud. More Dirty Little Secrets About Black History, Its Heroes, and Other Troublemakers. PowerNomics Corporation of America, 2006.
[180] Locke, E. A., & Latham, G. P. (2002). Building a practically useful theory of goal setting and task motivation. American Psychologist, 57(9), 705.

lead to stress and a relentless chase for more[181]. The counter-argument to this criticism, however, draws upon the principle of cognitive reappraisal. Instead of viewing failures as threats, they are reframed as learning opportunities, a process that fosters resilience and mitigates stress[182].

Increasing actions in the pursuit of set targets is another crucial dimension to consider. A study conducted by Grant & Shin in 2012 found a significant correlation between proactive behavior and individual performance, revealing that individuals who took initiative and increased actions were more likely to achieve their goals[183].

Moreover, downplaying the importance of success does no favors to anyone involved. This sentiment mirrors Anderson's stance on the significance of achievement. However, society often confronts this idea with a counter-narrative promoting humility and demonizing ambition. Some critics assert that an excessive focus on success could foster a toxic culture of competitiveness and materialism[184]. In response, one could argue that there's a need to redefine success, moving away from purely materialistic measures towards a more holistic understanding, including aspects like community development and freedom.

---

[181] Crawford, E. R., LePine, J. A., & Rich, B. L. (2010). Linking job demands and resources to employee engagement and burnout: A theoretical extension and meta-analytic test. Journal of Applied Psychology, 95(5), 834.

[182] Troy, A. S., Shallcross, A. J., & Mauss, I. B. (2013). A person-by-situation approach to emotion regulation: Cognitive reappraisal can either help or hurt, depending on the context. Psychological Science, 24(12), 2505-2514.

[183] Grant, A. M., & Shin, J. (2012). Work motivation: Directing, energizing, and maintaining effort (and research). In R. M. Ryan (Ed.), Oxford Handbook of Human Motivation (p. 505–519). Oxford University Press.

[184] Kasser, T., & Ryan, R. M. (1996). Further examining the American dream: Differential correlates of intrinsic and extrinsic goals. Personality and Social Psychology Bulletin, 22(3), 280-287.

In the black community, financial success carries immense transformative potential, translating into improved living conditions, better educational opportunities, and, crucially, a stronger, more influential voice in societal dialogues. Therefore, setting high goals, increasing actions, and maintaining an unyielding commitment to success aren't just personal development strategies; they are mechanisms driving community advancement and the collective pursuit of freedom.

Common Mistakes In Setting Wealth Goals And How To Avoid Them

In the process of amassing wealth, common errors are made that could easily be circumvented with the right strategies and practices. Herein, we examine several of these mistakes and their remedies, in light of the insights shared by members of the Forbes Finance Council[185].

One ubiquitous error is to wait until being debt-free before initiating wealth accumulation efforts[186]. As Paul Ewing from Prosperity Advisory Group opines, prioritizing is essential, but a well-rounded financial strategy encompasses saving for the long term, settling debts, and building a cash reserve, all simultaneously[187]. The crucial part here is starting without delay. Critics may voice concerns about the risk of over-extension, but the counter-argument here is that taking proportionate measures in all these aspects can strike a balance[188].

---

[185] 1 Forbes Finance Council. "Forbes Finance Council." Forbes, 2023.
[186] Ewing, Paul. "Prosperity Advisory Group." Prosperity Advisory Group, 2023.
[187] Seltzer, Michael. "Verite Group, LLC." Verite Group, LLC, 2023.
[188] Oishi, Shigehiro, and Ed Diener. "Goals, culture, and subjective well-being." Personality and Social Psychology Bulletin, 29.12 (2003): 1436-1449.

Coordination of goals and a focus on net returns is another key aspect that is often overlooked[189]. Michael Seltzer from Verite Group emphasizes the importance of ensuring your advisory team's cohesion and aligning your goals. In addition, he cautions against chasing gross returns, advising considering all applicable present and future taxes[190].

The advisory relationship must not be overlooked, as underscored by Jody Padar from New Vision CPA Group. Effective communication with your financial advisor is critical; this requires a healthy, open relationship where both parties are on the same page[191]. Skeptics may say that this relationship may cause dependence on the advisor; however, the advisor's role is not to control but to guide the client.

Another intriguing point raised by Wei Ke of Simon-Kucher & Partners concerns the importance of research-based pricing and moving away from traditional pricing structures[192]. Zachary Ramirez of US Business Funding warns against the common mistake of heavily investing in a single asset class and advises diversification[193].

Short and long-term goal setting is another critical aspect that is often overlooked[194]. Amir Eyal from Mylestone Plans advises on finding low-cost index funds

---

[189] Gabridge, Rob. "Tarfis Wealth Management." Tarfis Wealth Management, 2023.
[190] Fomichenko, Dmitriy. "Sense Financial Services LLC." Sense Financial Services LLC, 2023.
[191] Padar, Jody. "New Vision CPA Group." New Vision CPA Group, 2023.
[192] Ke, Wei. "Simon-Kucher & Partners." Simon-Kucher & Partners, 2023.
[193] Ramirez, Zachary. "US Business Funding." US Business Funding, 2023.
[194] Eyal, Amir. "Mylestone Plans LLC." Mylestone Plans LLC, 2023.

and balancing disciplines such as tax, estate, risk mitigation, and cash-flow planning with investment selection[195].

Finally, it's paramount to be engaged in the investment process and not to let emotions drive the decision-making process[196]. Dmitriy Fomichenko from Sense Financial Services emphasizes the importance of personal involvement in the process, advising individuals to gain investment education to make informed decisions[197]. Thus, from prioritizing multiple financial goals to staying engaged in the investment process, these insights can guide individuals towards effective wealth goal setting and accumulation.

Identifying Pitfalls In Goal Setting And Planning

The African American community, throughout the past four centuries, has made notable strides towards success and equality, but this journey hasn't been without its pitfalls. In dissecting these pitfalls, it becomes apparent that some critical mistakes have been a product of societal conditioning and lack of resources, rather than inherent shortcomings[198].

First, let us address the issue of wealth disparity. Since the days of enslavement, Blacks have often found themselves at an economic disadvantage. According to the U.S Census Bureau, as of 2019, the median income for African American households was $41,361, significantly

---

[195] Lyubomirsky, S., Sheldon, K.M., and Schkade, D. "Pursuing happiness: The architecture of sustainable change." Review of General Psychology, 9 (2005): 111–131.
[196] Federico, Francesca. "Twelve Points." Twelve Points, 2023.
[197] Fomichenko, Dmitriy. "Sense Financial Services LLC." Sense Financial Services LLC, 2023.
[198] ^1 Anderson, Claud. "PowerNomics: The National Plan to Empower Black America." PowerNomics Corporation of America, 2001.

less than the national median[199]. One of the significant causes behind this disparity is the lack of proper financial education and guidance in setting wealth goals[200]. Critics may argue that socio-economic factors are the primary drivers of this disparity, but a focus on high-goal setting and wealth management education could foster wealth accumulation in the black community.

A historical pitfall is also apparent in the realm of land and business ownership. According to Anderson, one of the historical pitfalls for African Americans has been a lack of concentrated ownership in business and real estate, a consequence of the lasting impact of segregation and discriminatory lending practices[201]. This lack of concentrated ownership leads to a lack of generational wealth, perpetuating a cycle of economic instability[202]. Critics might suggest that the current structure of capitalism inherently disadvantages marginalized communities, however, with targeted policy interventions and community investment, this cycle can be broken.

Furthermore, African Americans' political participation has also faced challenges. Historically, African Americans have been underrepresented in political spaces, leading to their interests being overlooked in policy-making processes. While voting rates among African Americans have increased in recent years, there is still a lack of representation in elected offices. This lack of representation

---

[199] U.S. Census Bureau. "Income and Poverty in the United States: 2019." U.S. Census Bureau, September 15, 2020.

[200] Williams Shanks, Trina R., and Meschede, Tatjana. "Family assets, postsecondary education, and students with disabilities: Building on progress and overcoming challenges." Children and Youth Services Review, 31.11 (2009): 1131-1137.

[201] Anderson, Claud. "Black Labor, White Wealth: The Search for Power and Economic Justice." PowerNomics Corporation of America, 1994.

[202] Hamilton, D., and Darity, W. "The political economy of education, financial literacy, and the racial wealth gap." Federal Reserve Bank of St. Louis Review, 99.1 (2017): 59-76.

can lead to policies that don't address systemic issues faced by the African American community[203]. Skeptics might argue that voting alone cannot solve deeply entrenched systemic issues, but increased representation could be a step towards more equitable policies.

It's essential to consider these historical pitfalls in the context of systematic oppression rather than inherent failings within the African American community. By focusing on financial literacy, promoting business and land ownership, and fostering political participation, the community can begin to close the wealth and representation gaps that have been a historical challenge.

Providing Guidance On Realistic Yet Ambitious Goal Setting

it's paramount to emphasize that setting realistic, yet ambitious goals plays a critical role in achieving success. However, this topic often sparks contention as some argue that success is subjective and not necessarily tied to monetary wealth[204]. Yet, as Anderson underscores, for the Black community, success — particularly economic success — isn't just desirable, it's essential.

Traditionally, success has been framed as an option, something to aspire to but not necessarily achieve. This perspective, however, doesn't hold in the African American community where success isn't merely an option, it's a duty[205]. Opponents might argue that this perspective puts undue pressure on individuals, potentially leading to stress and disappointment. However, viewing success as a duty,

---

[203] Philpot, Tasha S., Daron R. Shaw, and Ernest B. McGowen. "Winning the Race: Black Voter Turnout in the 2008 Presidential Election." Public Opinion Quarterly, 73.5 (2009): 995-1022.
[204] Anderson, Claud. "PowerNomics: The National Plan to Empower Black America." PowerNomics Corporation of America, 2001.
[205] Ibid.

rather than a choice, can foster a proactive and resilient mindset, enabling individuals to overcome adversity and socioeconomic barriers[206].

Furthermore, the idea of dependency on a single person or solution for success is one that has pervaded the African American community. Relying on a singular source for success can create a vulnerable position, limiting the capacity to bounce back from setbacks or adapt to changing circumstances[207]. Critics may posit that having a single mentor or role model can provide clear guidance and support. Yet, the reality remains that attaining success often requires pulling resources, opportunities, and insights from various avenues[208].

A critical part of success is understanding that it has broader implications beyond personal achievements. Success in the Black community not only impacts the individual but also the family, community, and future generations. This form of success sets the stage for creating generational wealth and breaking the cycle of economic instability[209]. Some might argue that this places an unfair burden on individuals, with personal achievements being tied to communal prosperity. Yet, viewing success as a collective effort can imbue a sense of shared responsibility and unity within the community[210].

---

[206] Taylor, Kira Hudson, Margaret T. Hicken, and Kristine Siefert. "Perceived Discrimination, Depression, and Mental Health: The Impact of Multiple Dimensions of Discrimination." The Lancet Psychiatry, 6.12 (2019): 975-981.

[207] Anderson, Claud. "Black Labor, White Wealth: The Search for Power and Economic Justice." PowerNomics Corporation of America, 1994.

[208] Bryant, Kevin D. "Mentoring, Social Capital, and the Economic Mobility of Young Black Males: Moving from 'Network' to 'Mentor-Set'." Urban Education, 53.5 (2018): 640-661.

[209] Hamilton, D., and Darity, W. "The political economy of education, financial literacy, and the racial wealth gap." Federal Reserve Bank of St. Louis Review, 99.1 (2017): 59-76.

[210] Anderson, Claud. "PowerNomics: The National Plan to Empower Black America." PowerNomics Corporation of America, 2001.

Setting realistic yet ambitious goals is an essential step towards achieving success. While success may be subjective, its significance within the African American community cannot be underplayed. By viewing success as a duty, exploring various avenues for achieving success, and understanding its collective impact, the Black community can break through systemic barriers and set a precedent for generations to come.

Offering Strategies for Maintaining Focus And Motivation In Pursuing Wealth Goals

In the struggle for social and economic equality, the African American community has long grappled with finding the most effective avenues to effect change. The influence of wealth creation and judicious spending in fostering Black success cannot be understated, even as political engagement remains an important part of civic life[211]. Some argue that voting is essential for change, but history has shown that political promises often fall short when it comes to addressing systemic racial economic disparities[212].

Many people, for instance, look to politics as the primary means of change, placing their hopes on promises made by politicians. Yet, the experience of the African American community demonstrates that the community's success doesn't depend on politics alone[213]. Critics might argue that political disengagement fosters apathy and social

---

[211] Anderson, Claud. "PowerNomics: The National Plan to Empower Black America." PowerNomics Corporation of America, 2001.

[212] Logan, John R. "The Persistence of Segregation in the Metropolis: New Findings from the 2010 Census." Census Brief, US2010 Project, 2011.

[213] Anderson, Claud. "Black Labor, White Wealth: The Search for Power and Economic Justice." PowerNomics Corporation of America, 1994.

inequality. However, this argument doesn't mean that political participation isn't important. Instead, it underscores that Black success should not be contingent solely on political promises or the outcome of elections[214].

The tenet that should guide the African American community's path to success is self-reliance and proactive action in wealth generation. The economic success of others in the society, especially within the Black community, should serve as an indication of possibilities. It should inspire ambition, rather than breed resentment or despair[215]. Detractors might suggest that individual success stories can't mitigate systemic racial economic disparities. However, such narratives highlight the potential within the community and help in fostering a mindset that is focused on achievable wealth goals[216].

When it comes to strategies for maintaining focus and motivation in pursuing wealth goals, understanding the importance of economic autonomy is key. Achieving wealth gives leverage to challenge systems that perpetuate economic disparities, promoting a shift from dependency to autonomy[217]. Critics may argue that this perspective promotes materialism over community values, but this argument misinterprets the real issue. The pursuit of economic success is not about acquiring wealth for its own sake; it's about empowering the African American community to create lasting change and secure future generations[218].

---

[214] Ibid.
[215] Anderson, Claud. "PowerNomics: The National Plan to Empower Black America." PowerNomics Corporation of America, 2001.
[216] Hamilton, D., and Darity, W. "The political economy of education, financial literacy, and the racial wealth gap." Federal Reserve Bank of St. Louis Review, 99.1 (2017): 59-76.
[217] Anderson, Claud. "PowerNomics: The National Plan to Empower Black America." PowerNomics Corporation of America, 2001.
[218] Ibid.

Case Studies Demonstrating The Successful Application of A Black Wealth Creation

The journey to economic prosperity for African Americans has been a complex one, riddled with challenges. Nevertheless, several individuals have successfully navigated these hurdles, amassing considerable wealth and proving that economic empowerment is an attainable goal for the African American community. Let us consider the cases of Madam C.J. Walker and Jay-Z, whose stories demonstrate the successful application of Black wealth creation.

Madam C.J. Walker, born Sarah Breedlove, was one of the first self-made female millionaires in America and the first African American woman to become a self-made millionaire[219]. Despite being born two years after the Emancipation Proclamation to former slaves, Walker turned adversity into motivation, setting herself ambitious wealth goals[220]. She made her fortune by developing and marketing a line of cosmetics and hair care products for black women. Her success serves as a beacon to those navigating racial and gendered economic disparities. Critics may contend that Walker's success is an exception rather than the rule. However, her story is more than an exception—it's a testament to what can be achieved with tenacity and business acumen, even in the face of systemic prejudice[221].

On the other hand, Shawn Carter, better known by his stage name Jay-Z, embodies the rags-to-riches trope, with his wealth estimated at $1 billion[222]. Born and raised in Brooklyn's Marcy Projects, Jay-Z's rise to economic success

---

[219] Bundles, A'Lelia. "On Her Own Ground: The Life and Times of Madam C.J. Walker." Simon and Schuster, 2001.
[220] Ibid.
[221] Ibid.
[222] Greenburg, Zack O'Malley. "Jay-Z's Net Worth Revealed: The Rapper Is Hip-Hop's First Billionaire." Forbes. June 3, 2019.

has been driven by his diversified interests, spanning music, clothing, sports management, and venture capitalism[223]. Opponents could argue that his fame as a rapper paved the way for his wealth, which might not be replicable for ordinary African Americans. However, it is important to note that his approach—diversifying his investments and leveraging his influence—provides valuable insights into wealth creation strategies for the Black community[224].

While these case studies provide inspiration, it is critical to recognize the broader systemic reforms needed to facilitate Black wealth creation. The success stories of individuals should be viewed not only as markers of personal achievement but also as opportunities for collective learning and motivation in the ongoing journey towards economic empowerment for the Black community[225].

Analyzing Key Factors And Strategies Used In These Successes

The successful journeys of Madam C.J. Walker and Jay-Z in the realm of wealth creation highlight key strategies and factors. These strategies, when observed and analyzed, can offer valuable insights into achieving financial success within the African American community.

Walker's journey underscores the role of tenacity and business acumen in financial success[226]. Despite being born into a post-slavery society fraught with racial and gendered economic disparities, Walker identified a market need -

---

[223] Ibid.
[224] Ibid.
[225] Anderson, Claud. "Black Labor, White Wealth: The Search for Power and Economic Justice." PowerNomics Corporation of America, 1994.
[226] Bundles, A'Lelia. "On Her Own Ground: The Life and Times of Madam C.J. Walker." Simon and Schuster, 2001.

cosmetic and hair care products for black women - and capitalized on it[227]. She refused to allow her humble beginnings to define her destiny, instead setting ambitious wealth goals and working relentlessly to achieve them[228].

A critical element in Walker's success was her innovation. Her creation of products specifically designed for African American women was a pioneering move that addressed an underserved market[229]. Critics may argue that her circumstances and the historical context provided a unique business opportunity that may not be available today. However, the essence of her strategy - identifying underserved needs and addressing them innovatively - remains a viable approach to wealth creation[230].

In contrast, Jay-Z's wealth creation journey has been shaped significantly by his talent as a rapper, as well as his strategic diversification of interests[231]. His story emphasizes the importance of diversification, a principle that goes beyond the world of music or entertainment. His wealth has been cultivated not only through his music but also his ventures in clothing, sports management, and venture capitalism[232].

Skeptics might argue that Jay-Z's fame afforded him opportunities that aren't available to the average person. However, the core strategy of diversification that Jay-Z employed is applicable on any scale. It underscores the importance of not relying on a single stream of income but instead creating and leveraging multiple avenues for wealth creation[233].

---

[227] Ibid.
[228] Ibid.
[229] Ibid.
[230] Ibid.
[231] Greenburg, Zack O'Malley. "Jay-Z's Net Worth Revealed: The Rapper Is Hip-Hop's First Billionaire." Forbes. June 3, 2019.
[232] Ibid.
[233] Ibid.

The successes of Walker and Jay-Z demonstrate the possibility of wealth creation despite systemic barriers. However, their stories also underline the need for broader systemic reforms to facilitate Black wealth creation. The success of individuals should not be seen merely as personal achievements, but also as demonstrations of what can be achieved and inspiration for collective efforts towards economic empowerment[234].

Drawing Actionable Insights From These Case Studies For Readers

The tales of Madam C.J. Walker and Jay-Z, two powerhouses in their respective domains, provide several practical insights that can guide individuals on their path to economic empowerment.

1. **Identify and Serve a Unique Market:** Madam C.J. Walker's success in a time when racial and gender disparities were rampant teaches us the power of identifying and catering to an under-served market[235]. Walker recognized the lack of cosmetic and hair care products tailored to black women and capitalized on this void, thereby creating a lucrative business. This strategy is as relevant today as it was during Walker's era. Regardless of the field one chooses to venture into, identifying a unique market need and serving that need innovatively can be a powerful pathway to wealth creation[236].

---

[234] Anderson, Claud. "Black Labor, White Wealth: The Search for Power and Economic Justice." PowerNomics Corporation of America, 1994.
[235] Bundles, A'Lelia. "On Her Own Ground: The Life and Times of Madam C.J. Walker." Simon and Schuster, 2001.
[236] Ibid.

2. **Embrace Diversification:** Jay-Z's journey to becoming a billionaire underscores the power of diversification[237]. He cultivated wealth not just through his music but also through his investments in clothing, sports management, and venture capitalism. The key takeaway here is not to rely solely on a single income stream but to create and leverage multiple avenues for wealth creation. This strategy can be adopted by anyone, regardless of the scale of their operations or their current economic status. As Jay-Z's journey shows, success can come from unexpected places[238].
3. **Use Adversity as a Motivation:** Both Walker and Jay-Z emerged from humble beginnings. Their stories highlight how adversity can serve as a powerful motivation for success[239]. Both recognized the challenging circumstances they were in and used these hardships to fuel their drive towards wealth and success. For readers, this teaches the valuable lesson that one's beginnings do not define their end. In fact, adversity can be a powerful motivator for change and growth[240].
4. **Commit to Tenacious Pursuit of Goals:** Both Walker and Jay-Z displayed a relentless pursuit of their wealth goals[241]. They did not allow failures or setbacks to deter them from their paths. This teaches readers the importance of tenacity and resilience in the journey to wealth creation. Without

---

[237] Greenburg, Zack O'Malley. "Jay-Z's Net Worth Revealed: The Rapper Is Hip-Hop's First Billionaire." Forbes. June 3, 2019.
[238] Ibid.
[239] Bundles, A'Lelia. "On Her Own Ground: The Life and Times of Madam C.J. Walker." Simon and Schuster, 2001.
[240] Ibid.
[241] Greenburg, Zack O'Malley. "Jay-Z's Net Worth Revealed: The Rapper Is Hip-Hop's First Billionaire." Forbes. June 3, 2019.

these qualities, it is easy to be discouraged by obstacles and setbacks.
5. **Seek Broader Systemic Reforms:** While individual success is important, it should not overshadow the need for systemic reforms[242]. The stories of Walker and Jay-Z should not be seen solely as personal achievements but also as illustrations of what can be achieved despite systemic barriers. For lasting and widespread economic empowerment, it is crucial to also advocate for systemic changes that facilitate wealth creation for the broader Black community[243].

---

[242] Anderson, Claud. "Black Labor, White Wealth: The Search for Power and Economic Justice." PowerNomics Corporation of America, 1994.
[243] Ibid.

Chapter 4
The Economic Gaps: An In-depth Analysis

Addressing the economic gaps that persist within America demands an honest and thorough analysis of the underlying issues. The disparities between the African American community and other racial and ethnic groups are not the result of individual failures but systemic factors deeply rooted in American society[244].

As of 2016, the net worth of a typical white family was nearly ten times greater than that of a Black family[245]. This racial wealth gap has been perpetuated and exacerbated by historical injustices and contemporary systemic biases, leaving the Black community significantly disadvantaged[246]. Critics may argue that this discrepancy is due to individual choices, work ethics, or behaviors, but data and historical context reveal that the racial wealth gap is a consequence of discriminatory practices, such as redlining and unequal education opportunities, that have spanned generations[247].

Inequalities in education are another substantial contributor to the racial economic gap. African American students are more likely to attend under-resourced schools, reducing their opportunities for quality education and subsequently, their chances of achieving economic

---

[244] Anderson, Claud. "Black Labor, White Wealth: The Search for Power and Economic Justice." PowerNomics Corporation of America, 1994.
[245] McKernan, Signe-Mary, et al. "Nine Charts about Wealth Inequality in America." Urban Institute, 2017.
[246] Rothstein, Richard. "The Color of Law: A Forgotten History of How Our Government Segregated America." Liveright Publishing, 2017.
[247] Ibid.

success[248]. As per the U.S. Government Accountability Office, in 2016, 39% of public schools that predominantly serve Black and Hispanic students were under-resourced[249]. Critics might assert that parental involvement or cultural factors are the cause of this educational disparity, but when the systemic under-resourcing of schools serving primarily Black students is considered, it becomes clear that the issue is not just about individual effort but about systemic discrimination[250].

Moreover, disparities in wages and employment also play a significant role in this economic gap. Despite improvements over the decades, Black workers continue to earn less than their white counterparts. In 2020, the median hourly wage for Black workers was 14.9% lower than for white workers[251]. Critics may argue that this disparity results from differences in experience or education. However, studies indicate that racial wage gaps persist even when these factors are equalized, suggesting that systemic racism, not individual qualifications, is at play[252].

Addressing these economic gaps will require significant systemic change. There are no quick fixes, and the solutions will necessitate efforts at various levels. Strategies to close these gaps should focus on comprehensive policy reforms, including fair housing laws, equal access to quality education, and legislation to ensure wage and employment equity[253].

---

[248] U.S. Government Accountability Office. "K-12 Education: Better Use of Information Could Help Agencies Identify Disparities and Address Racial Discrimination." April 21, 2016.
[249] Ibid
[250] Darling-Hammond, Linda. "Unequal Opportunity: Race and Education." Brookings, March 1, 1998.
[251] Wilson, Valerie, and William M. Rodgers III. "Black-white wage gaps expand with rising wage inequality." Economic Policy Institute, 2016.
[252] Ibid
[253] Anderson, Claud. "A Black History Reader: 101 Question You Never Thought to Ask." PowerNomics Corporation of America, 2017.

As we strive to understand these economic disparities, it is essential to acknowledge that they stem from centuries-old systemic and structural racism[254]. Moving forward, collective acknowledgment, understanding, and efforts can work towards closing these economic gaps and achieving economic justice for the Black community[255].

Presenting Data On Wage And Occupational Disparities

The economic landscape of America reflects striking disparities between Black workers and their White counterparts. These disparities manifest in wages and occupational representation and are rooted in systemic discrimination and exclusionary practices. To assert otherwise is to ignore a wealth of empirical data and historical context[256].

As of 2020, the median hourly wage for Black workers was 14.9% lower than for white workers, a disparity that persisted even after controlling for age, education, and experience[257]. Critics may attribute this wage gap to differences in qualifications, but this perspective overlooks the reality of systemic racism that disadvantages Black workers. A study from the National Bureau of Economic Research confirms that there is significant discrimination in employer callbacks for resumes. The study found that resumes with traditionally White names receive 50% more

---

[254] Rothstein, Richard. "The Color of Law: A Forgotten History of How Our Government Segregated America." Liveright Publishing, 2017.
[255] Anderson, Claud. "Black Labor, White Wealth: The Search for Power and Economic Justice." PowerNomics Corporation of America, 1994.
[256] Anderson, Claud. "Black Labor, White Wealth: The Search for Power and Economic Justice." PowerNomics Corporation of America, 1994.
[257] Wilson, Valerie, and William M. Rodgers III. "Black-white wage gaps expand with rising wage inequality." Economic Policy Institute, 2016.

callbacks than identical resumes with traditionally Black names[258].

Occupational disparities present another area of inequality. While the Civil Rights Act of 1964 prohibited employment discrimination, the legacy of racially segregated job markets persists. As of 2020, Black men and women were underrepresented in higher-wage professions, including management, architecture, and engineering occupations, and overrepresented in lower-wage occupations, including service, transportation, and production occupations[259]. Critics might suggest that personal choice or cultural factors determine these occupational disparities, but this argument neglects the systemic barriers, such as discriminatory hiring practices and unequal access to quality education, that steer Black workers into lower-paying jobs[260].

Furthermore, the wealth gap is not merely a wage gap but a culmination of disparities in home ownership, inheritance, retirement savings, and investment returns. For instance, as per a study by the Federal Reserve Bank, the median White family had eight times the wealth of the median Black family in 2019[261]. Critics may argue that this wealth gap is simply a result of spending habits or financial literacy. However, it is crucial to note that the racial wealth gap is largely a direct consequence of the racial wage gap,

---

[258] Bertrand, Marianne and Mullainathan, Sendhil. "Are Emily and Greg More Employable Than Lakisha and Jamal? A Field Experiment on Labor Market Discrimination." National Bureau of Economic Research, 2004.

[259] U.S. Bureau of Labor Statistics. "Labor Force Characteristics by Race and Ethnicity, 2018."

[260] Pager, Devah and Shepherd, Hana. "The Sociology of Discrimination: Racial Discrimination in Employment, Housing, Credit, and Consumer Markets." Annual Review of Sociology, 2008.

[261] Federal Reserve Bank. "Distributionsal Financial Accounts." 2019.

coupled with the systemic barriers to wealth accumulation that Black families have faced over generations[262].

The data on wage and occupational disparities elucidates the systemic economic inequities that persistently disadvantage Black individuals. While Black Americans have made significant strides towards economic equality, the data indicates that there is still a long way to go. Efforts towards economic justice must include comprehensive policy reforms targeted at addressing these systemic disparities[263].

Discussing The Systemic Factors That Perpetuate These Disparities

The economic disparities evident within the African American community are not a happenstance but the product of systemic factors deeply embedded in American society[264]. These factors are multifold, intersecting across different domains, including education, housing, labor market discrimination, and historical socio-economic policies[265].

Education is often touted as the pathway to upward mobility. However, the U.S. public education system, with its school funding heavily reliant on local property taxes, often perpetuates the racial wealth gap[266]. Predominantly

---

[262] Hamilton, Darrick, et al. "Umbrellas Don't Make it Rain: Why Studying and Working Hard Isn't Enough for Black Americans." The New School, Duke Center for Social Equity, Insight Center for Community Economic Development, 2015.

[263] Anderson, Claud. "A Black History Reader: 101 Question You Never Thought to Ask." PowerNomics Corporation of America, 2017.

[264] Anderson, Claud. "Black Labor, White Wealth: The Search for Power and Economic Justice." PowerNomics Corporation of America, 1994.

[265] Oliver, Melvin L., and Thomas M. Shapiro. "Black Wealth, White Wealth: A New Perspective on Racial Inequality." Routledge, 1995.

[266] Sibilia, Rebecca. "Why America's Schools Have A Money Problem." NPR, 2016.

Black neighborhoods, burdened by lower property values due to decades of redlining and housing discrimination, invariably have fewer resources for schools[267]. Consequently, the quality of education suffers, limiting the future earnings potential of Black students and perpetuating the cycle of poverty. Critics may argue that this is a matter of choice, as parents can choose where to send their children. However, such criticism overlooks the historical and structural factors limiting such choices for many Black families[268].

Housing discrimination has also played a significant role in exacerbating racial wealth disparities. The federal housing policies of the 20th century, particularly redlining, have had a long-lasting impact on Black communities' wealth-building opportunities[269]. Though such overt discriminatory practices are now illegal, their effects linger in the form of segregated neighborhoods and lower property values in predominantly Black communities, which limit opportunities for wealth accumulation through home equity[270].

Labor market discrimination is another systemic factor contributing to wage and occupational disparities. While it is unlawful to discriminate based on race in hiring and promotions, studies indicate that such discrimination remains rampant. Bertrand and Mullainathan's study revealing racial bias in employer callbacks offers striking evidence of such systemic bias[271]. Critics might argue that

---

[267] Rothstein, Richard. "The Color of Law: A Forgotten History of How Our Government Segregated America." Liveright Publishing, 2017.

[268] Anderson, Claud. "A Black History Reader: 101 Question You Never Thought to Ask." PowerNomics Corporation of America, 2017.

[269] Rothstein, Richard. "The Color of Law: A Forgotten History of How Our Government Segregated America." Liveright Publishing, 2017.

[270] Shapiro, Thomas M. "The Hidden Cost of Being African American: How Wealth Perpetuates Inequality." Oxford University Press, 2004.

[271] Bertrand, Marianne and Mullainathan, Sendhil. "Are Emily and Greg More Employable Than Lakisha and Jamal? A Field Experiment on

individuals should simply demonstrate merit to overcome bias, but this contention dismisses the reality that racial bias often eclipses individual merit[272].

Historical socio-economic policies have also played a role in perpetuating these disparities. From slavery to Jim Crow laws, the historical exploitation of Black labor has disadvantaged African Americans in their wealth accumulation efforts. Policies such as the G.I. Bill, which largely excluded Black veterans from post-WWII home-ownership benefits, contributed to widening the racial wealth gap[273].

Systemic factors, while challenging to navigate, are not insurmountable. As a society, acknowledging these systemic barriers is the first step toward dismantling them and promoting economic equity for all.

Exploring The Impact of These Disparities On Wealth Accumulation And Economic Stability

Analyzing racial wealth disparity in America involves acknowledging a complex and deeply rooted issue. The racial wealth gap, characterized by the dramatic wealth divergence between Black and White Americans, can be traced back to historical institutions and systemic racism, having devastating impacts on economic stability and wealth accumulation. The persistent disparity embodies the accumulated fallout of four centuries of systemic racism,

---

Labor Market Discrimination." National Bureau of Economic Research, 2004.

[272] Pager, Devah, and Shepherd, Hana. "The Sociology of Discrimination: Racial Discrimination in Employment, Housing, Credit, and Consumer Markets." Annual Review of Sociology, 2008.

[273] Katznelson, Ira. "When Affirmative Action Was White: An Untold History of Racial Inequality in Twentieth-Century America." W. W. Norton & Company, 2005.

significantly contributing to present-day inequalities in income, health, education, and opportunity[274].

A snapshot of the current state of affairs reveals a stark picture: the net wealth of a typical Black family in America is approximately one-tenth that of a White family[275]. Notwithstanding, many are oblivious or deny the depth and consequences of this entrenched disparity, which can be traced to sources such as discriminatory practices in housing, employment, and education. Such denial could be the product of insufficient understanding or misinformation, often perpetuated by media or partisan discourse. However, robust studies from reputable institutions, such as Harvard University, and the Federal Reserve Bank of Minneapolis, provide compelling evidence that underscores the reality and implications of the racial wealth gap[276].

Historically, discriminatory practices such as Jim Crow laws, redlining, and unfair treatment of Black veterans after World War II impeded Black Americans from accumulating and transmitting wealth. These practices denied Black families the opportunity to purchase homes, a critical wealth-generating asset, and limited their mobility. The home-ownership rate for Black families, a key wealth indicator, stood at about 44 percent, compared to 75 percent for White families at the end of 2020, according to the U.S. Census Bureau[277].

---

[274] Chetty, Raj, Nathaniel Hendren, Maggie Jones, and Sonya Porter. "Race and Economic Opportunity in the United States: An Intergenerational Perspective." Quarterly Journal of Economics, 2018.

[275] Kuhn, Moritz, Moritz Schularick, and Ulrike I. Steins. "Income and Wealth Inequality in America, 1949-2016." Quarterly Journal of Economics, 2020.

[276] Johnson, William R., and Derek Neal. "The Role of Pre-Market Factors in Black-White Wage Differences." Journal of Political Economy, 1998.

[277] U.S. Census Bureau, Current Population Survey/Housing Vacancy Survey, October 2020.

Moreover, the 2020 pandemic further exacerbated racial economic inequalities, disproportionately impacting people of color. The expectation is that the pandemic's economic fallout will further widen the gap in various areas, including wealth[278]. Critics might argue that these figures are distorted or fail to consider factors such as personal initiative or financial management. However, this viewpoint overlooks the structural barriers that have historically hindered wealth accumulation among Black families [279].

Professor Khalil Muhammad of the Harvard Kennedy School maintains that the roots of this disparity date back to the Colonial period when European settlers exploited Native and African labor, precluding them from reaping the economic benefits of their work. This historical precedent set the stage for the systemic economic and political racism that continues to shape American society[280].

In addition to these historical factors, wealth inequality persists due to the intergenerational transmission of wealth, a phenomenon succinctly explained by Professor Alexandra Killewald. Wealth can serve as a buffer during challenging times and can be directly passed down across generations, providing families with greater opportunities. Due to historical and ongoing discrimination, Black families have significantly less wealth to pass down, perpetuating the cycle of poverty and limiting upward mobility [281].

---

[278] Fairlie, Robert. "The Impact of COVID-19 on Small Business Owners: Evidence from the First 3 Months After Widespread Social-Distancing Restrictions." Journal of Economics & Management Strategy, 2020.

[279] Hamilton, Darrick, and William Darity. "Can 'Baby Bonds' Eliminate the Racial Wealth Gap in Putative Post-Racial America?" The Review of Black Political Economy, 2010.

[280] Muhammad, Khalil Gibran. "The Condemnation of Blackness: Race, Crime, and the Making of Modern Urban America." Harvard University Press, 2010.

[281] Killewald, Alexandra, and Fabian T. Pfeffer. "Wealth Inequality and Accumulation." Annual Review of Sociology, 2017.

However, to combat these deeply entrenched issues, implementing comprehensive changes in the education system is a necessity. Many scholars argue that bolstering education is a key to narrowing the wealth gap, as it provides tools and resources for upward economic mobility[282].

Addressing this disparity is not only an economic imperative, but also a moral and social one. Denying the existence of the wealth gap or its profound implications is a barrier to change. Greater public awareness and commitment to systemic changes, such as improving educational opportunities and rigorously enforcing anti-discrimination laws, are paramount to dismantling this deeply ingrained economic inequality[283].

The Concentration of Racial Wage Disparity In Different Occupational Categories And Sectors Part 1

The quintessence of America's racial wage disparity has manifested itself, perniciously, in various occupational categories and sectors. The Bureau of Labor Statistics[284], in its reports, illuminates an unsettling pattern, which indicates the average weekly earnings of Black workers being a mere 62.5% of White workers' earnings[285]. The stratification of this disparity across occupational categories paints an even bleaker picture.

This racial wage gap is not evenly spread across all occupations. In management, professional, and related

---

[282] Oreopoulos, Philip, and Uros Petronijevic. "Making College Worth It: A Review of the Returns to Higher Education." The Future of Children, 2013.

[283] William A. Darity Jr., A. Kirsten Mullen. "From Here to Equality: Reparations for Black Americans in the Twenty-First Century." The University of North Carolina Press, 2020.

[284] Bureau of Labor Statistics, U.S. Department of Labor. "Highlights of Women's Earnings in 2020." BLS Reports, November 2021.

[285] Ibid.

occupations - areas that typically confer higher pay - African American workers only make 67.7% of what their White counterparts earn[286]. In service occupations, a sector characterized by lower wages, the disparity is slightly less pronounced but still significant: Black workers earn 86.2% of what White workers earn [287].

It's evident that Black workers are paid less, regardless of the occupational category, leading to an accumulation of lifetime earning differences that exacerbate the racial wealth gap.

Critics of this viewpoint, such as some conservative think-tanks and media outlets, often argue that these discrepancies can be attributed to education, experience, or occupation choice[288]. They posit that wage differences are mainly the result of individual decisions and not systemic inequities. However, this perspective oversimplifies the issue and fails to account for the historical and structural forces that have shaped these 'choices.'

Contrary to these critics' assertions, researchers have shown that even after controlling for education and work experience, a significant wage gap remains[289]. Consequently, the 'choices' argument lacks the depth required to fully explain the entrenched racial wage gap. As stated by Anderson, "We should not dismiss these disparities as the mere consequences of personal decisions. Instead, they reveal the impact of an economic system steeped in centuries of systemic racism[290]."

---

[286] Ibid.
[287] Ibid.
[288] Riley, Jason L. "Please Stop Helping Us: How Liberals Make It Harder for Blacks to Succeed." Encounter Books, 2014.
[289] Wilson, Valerie, and William M. Rodgers III. "Black-white wage gaps expand with rising wage inequality." Economic Policy Institute, 2016.
[290] Anderson, Claud. "Black Labor, White Wealth: The Search for Power and Economic Justice." PowerNomics Corporation of America, 1994.

In sectors where Black workers are overrepresented, such as health care support or food preparation, wage disparities are even more damaging[291]. These industries, marked by low wages and scanty benefits, contribute to the cycle of poverty and perpetuate economic inequality. Meanwhile, in sectors such as technology and finance, where wages are typically higher, Black workers are significantly underrepresented, further contributing to the overall wage disparity[292].

These statistics are not mere numbers, they are indicators of racial injustice and economic inequality. Addressing this wage disparity necessitates a systemic overhaul that extends beyond occupational sectors, to encompass broader economic policies, educational opportunities, and societal norms. Therefore, there's a critical need to pursue policies that ensure fair wages, equal opportunity, and nondiscrimination in all occupational categories and sectors[293].

It is incumbent upon us to perceive the wage disparity not merely as a result of individual choices but as an outcome of systemic and institutionalized racism. The burden of rectifying these disparities should not fall on those who are most affected by them. Rather, it should be the collective responsibility of our society to ensure economic justice and opportunity for all.

---

[291] Bureau of Labor Statistics, U.S. Department of Labor. "Labor Force Characteristics by Race and Ethnicity, 2018." BLS Reports, October 2019.
[292] Ibid.
[293] Darity Jr., William, and A. Kirsten Mullen. "From Here to Equality: Reparations for Black Americans in the Twenty-First Century." The University of North Carolina Press, 2020.

The Concentration of Racial Wage Disparity In Different Occupational Categories And Sectors Part 2

Zooming in further on the racial wage disparity, specific occupational categories present stark inconsistencies in earnings. For instance, in the manufacturing sector, a realm where African Americans have historically found employment opportunities, a significant wage gap persists. In 2020, the median weekly earnings of Black workers in production jobs were $710 compared to $880 for White workers, a stark 81.3% of their White peers' earnings[294].

This wage disparity also penetrates the realm of entrepreneurship. Self-employed Black Americans typically earn significantly less than their White counterparts. A 2019 report from the Brookings Institution found that Black-owned businesses generated an average revenue of $58,119, a mere 35% of the $173,552 average revenue generated by White-owned businesses[295].

Opponents, primarily conservative media outlets and pundits, may argue that these disparities stem from differences in the type of businesses owned or the industries in which these businesses operate[296]. They might attribute the revenue gap to choices in business sector or management skills. This, however, overlooks the fact that Black entrepreneurs face a host of barriers that their White counterparts do not.

A major obstacle is access to capital. Black business owners are less likely to receive loans, and when they do, they often receive smaller amounts and at higher interest

---

[294] Bureau of Labor Statistics, U.S. Department of Labor, "Usual Weekly Earnings of Wage and Salary Workers First Quarter 2020," April 2020.
[295] Farley, Robert, et al. "The Avenue: The Devaluation of Assets in Black Neighborhoods." The Brookings Institution, November 2018.
[296] Sowell, Thomas. "Wealth, Poverty, and Politics." Basic Books, 2015.

rates[297]. Furthermore, systemic racism impacts the locations where Black-owned businesses operate, often economically disadvantaged areas, which can significantly affect revenue[298].

In sectors with a high concentration of Black workers, such as the public sector, disparities persist. The public sector has traditionally been an avenue for economic mobility for Black Americans. However, even here, they earn just 80% of White workers' wages[299]. Such disparity in wages contributes to economic inequality and inhibits wealth accumulation for Black Americans.

In the private sector, specifically in corporate America, racial wage disparities are alarmingly evident. Black men and women in executive roles earn less than their White counterparts. As per a report by the Economic Policy Institute, Black men in executive roles earn just 72% of their White male peers, while Black women earn 78%[300].

In spite of the varying viewpoints, the wage disparities across various occupational sectors highlight the systemic and institutional biases deeply embedded in the U.S. labor market. As Claud Anderson emphasizes, the remedies to such economic disparities must go beyond personal responsibility and embrace systemic reforms that ensure equal economic opportunities for all[301].

A systemic approach requires a comprehensive examination of our economic structures, from the

---

[297] Fairlie, Robert, and Alicia Robb. "Race and Entrepreneurial Success." MIT Press, 2008.
[298] Perry, Andre, et al. "Know Your Price: Valuing Black Lives and Property in America's Black Cities." Brookings Institution Press, May 2020.
[299] Bureau of Labor Statistics, U.S. Department of Labor, "Highlights of Women's Earnings in 2019." BLS Reports, November 2020.
[300] Wilson, Valerie, and William M. Rodgers III. "Black-White Wage Gaps Expand with Rising Wage Inequality." Economic Policy Institute, 2016.
[301] Anderson, Claud. "Black Labor, White Wealth: The Search for Power and Economic Justice." PowerNomics Corporation of America, 1994.

implementation of fair wage laws to the promotion of diverse and inclusive work-spaces. Furthermore, it demands that we confront the role of systemic racism in shaping these disparities and commit to dismantling these inequities. In a truly equitable society, race should not determine one's economic opportunities or outcomes[302].

Providing A Sector-Wise Analysis of Racial Wage Disparities

Examining racial wage disparities through a sector-specific lens reveals an endemic problem that spans across diverse industries. The nature and magnitude of the disparity, however, vary according to the sector[303].

In the technology sector, typically high-paying, the wage gap is particularly pronounced. A 2020 Brookings Institution report[304] found that Black tech workers earned an average salary of $82,300, about 79.3% of the average $103,800 earned by their White counterparts. Critics often point out that this discrepancy could be attributed to different roles and education levels within the industry. However, even when holding constant factors like education and job role, a significant racial wage gap persists[305].

In the health-care sector, a sector with a significant representation of Black workers, the racial wage gap is also glaring. A study published in the Journal of the American

---

[302] Anderson, Claud. "PowerNomics: The National Plan to Empower Black America." PowerNomics Corporation of America, 2001.
[303] Leicht, Kevin T. "Getting Serious about Inequality." The Sociological Quarterly 56, no. 3 (2015): 34-51.
[304] Harrison, Joseph, and Donovan X. Ramsey. "Advancing Black Pathways in Technology." The Brookings Institution, September 2020.
[305] Tomaskovic-Devey, Donald, and Dustin Avent-Holt. "Relational Inequality: Gender Earnings Inequality in U.S. Federal Agencies." American Journal of Sociology 124, no. 4 (2019): 908-949.

Medical Association in 2020[306] revealed that even within the same occupations, Black health-care workers earned less than their White counterparts. Notably, Black male physicians earned 17% less than White male physicians, and Black female nurses earned 9% less than their White female counterparts. Those arguing against the notion of systemic bias in this sector often attribute such differences to factors such as individual performance and specialty choice[307]. Yet, these factors alone fail to account for the entire wage disparity.

The financial services sector also mirrors the racial wage gap. A 2017 Federal Reserve Bank report[308] indicated that African Americans in this sector earned 72.9% of the income of Whites in the same industry. Opposition voices might contend that this gap arises from differences in education, experience, or job positions. However, such arguments overlook systemic obstacles that limit access to educational and professional opportunities for Black individuals[309].

In the education sector, despite having a relatively high representation of Black workers, wage disparities persist. The Economic Policy Institute reported in 2020[310] that Black educators earned only 87.1% of the wages of White educators. Critics could argue that the wage disparity in this

---

[306] Ly, Dan P., and Ichiro Kawachi. "Racial Disparities in Income and Health in the United States: A State-Level Analysis." JAMA Network Open 3, no. 2 (2020): e1920257.

[307] Williams, David R., and Toni D. Rucker. "Understanding and Addressing Racial Disparities in Health Care." Health Care Financing Review 21, no. 4 (2000): 75-90.

[308] Bayer, Amanda, and Cecilia Elena Rouse. "Diversity in the Economics Profession: A New Attack on an Old Problem." Journal of Economic Perspectives 30, no. 4 (2016): 221-42.

[309] Pager, Devah, and Hana Shepherd. "The Sociology of Discrimination: Racial Discrimination in Employment, Housing, Credit, and Consumer Markets." Annual Review of Sociology 34 (2008): 181-209.

[310] Allegretto, Sylvia A., and Lawrence Mishel. "The Teacher Weekly Wage Penalty Hit 21.4 Percent in 2018, a Record High." Economic Policy Institute, September 2019.

sector is due to differences in educational attainment or years of experience. Still, the wage gap remains significant even when accounting for these variables[311].

Echoing Dr. Anderson's sentiments, the pervasive racial wage disparities across sectors are not a result of individual choices, but manifestations of systemic and institutional racism deeply rooted in our society. Anderson maintains that these disparities are not a Black problem; they are an American problem[312].

Addressing these disparities requires comprehensive solutions that extend beyond individual sectors and involve significant policy changes. This includes providing equitable access to education and opportunities, eliminating discriminatory practices, and promoting diversity and inclusion in all sectors. By doing so, we can make substantial progress towards reducing racial wage disparities and promoting economic justice[313].

Exploring The Intersection of Race, Occupation, And Income

The confluence of race, occupation, and income in the United States is a manifestation of the enduring legacy of systemic racism and economic inequity. These three variables intersect to form a complex network that reinforces the existing socioeconomic hierarchy, and

---

[311] Ehrenberg, Ronald G., and Donna S. Rothstein. "Do Historically Black Institutions of Higher Education Confer Unique Advantages on Black Students: An Initial Analysis." In Choice and Consequence, edited by Tom Schelling. Cambridge, MA: Harvard University Press, 1984.

[312] Anderson, Claud. "Black Labor, White Wealth: The Search for Power and Economic Justice." PowerNomics Corporation of America, 1994.

[313] Anderson, Claud. "PowerNomics: The National Plan to Empower Black America." PowerNomics Corporation of America, 2001.

significantly influences the lived experiences of Black Americans[314].

According to the U.S. Bureau of Labor Statistics, in 2021, Black workers in management, professional, and related occupations earned, on average, 67.7% of the median weekly earnings of their White counterparts. In contrast, the wage gap in lower-paying service occupations was slightly less stark, but still significant, with Black workers earning 86.2% of the wages of White workers[315].

Some critics, particularly in the media, attribute the racial wage gap to differences in education and work experience[316]. However, extensive research[317] shows that even after controlling for these factors, a significant portion of the racial wage gap remains unexplained, suggesting the influence of systemic racial bias. The impact of occupation is crucial. Despite the important strides made towards increasing diversity in various occupational categories, Black workers are still significantly underrepresented in high-wage occupations[318].

Furthermore, the intersection of race, occupation, and income is not isolated from the influence of systemic and institutional practices that have historically disadvantaged Black Americans. For instance, the long-lasting effects of redlining and discriminatory lending practices have hindered the ability of Black Americans to invest in

---

[314] Anderson, Claud. "Black Labor, White Wealth: The Search for Power and Economic Justice." PowerNomics Corporation of America, 1994.
[315] U.S. Bureau of Labor Statistics. "Highlights of women's earnings in 2021."
[316] Riley, Jason L. "False Black Power?" Philadelphia: Templeton Press, 2017.
[317] Pager, Devah, and Bruce Western. "Race at Work: Realities of Race and Criminal Record in the NYC Job Market." The ANNALS of the American Academy of Political and Social Science, 2009.
[318] Wilson, Valerie. "Racial disparities in income and poverty remain largely unchanged amid strong income growth in 2019." Economic Policy Institute, 2020.

education, thereby limiting their occupational opportunities and earning potential[319].

In higher-paying sectors, such as technology, finance, and health-care, Black workers face significant wage disparities. Despite holding similar job positions and qualifications as their White counterparts, Black workers earn significantly less[320]. Critics might attribute this wage gap to differences in individual performance, skill levels, or the underrepresentation of Black workers in these sectors. However, these arguments disregard the fact that these sectors have historically been less accessible to Black Americans due to systemic barriers[321].

Dr. Anderson eloquently encapsulates the essence of this intersection when he asserts, "In a competitive society, those who are equipped with the tools of competition will excel[322]" In the context of the racial wage gap, these tools encompass access to quality education, equal employment opportunities, and fair remuneration. Unfortunately, due to systemic racism, these tools have been historically and continue to be, disproportionately accessible to White Americans[323].

Understanding the interplay of race, occupation, and income is not merely a theoretical exercise; it is integral to dismantling the entrenched system of racial economic disparity. Acknowledging the significant and tangible impact of systemic racism on the economic status of Black

---

[319] Rothstein, Richard. "The Color of Law: A Forgotten History of How Our Government Segregated America." Liveright Publishing, 2017.

[320] Gould, Elise. "Black workers endure persistent racial disparities in employment outcomes." Economic Policy Institute, 2019.

[321] Hunt, Vivian, Sara Prince, Sundiatu Dixon-Fyle, and Lareina Yee. "Delivering through diversity." McKinsey & Company, 2018.

[322] Anderson, Claud. "PowerNomics: The National Plan to Empower Black America." PowerNomics Corporation of America, 2001.

[323] Chetty, Raj, Nathaniel Hendren, Maggie Jones, and Sonya Porter. "Race and Economic Opportunity in the United States: An Intergenerational Perspective." Quarterly Journal of Economics, 2018.

Americans is a step towards devising effective policies that ensure economic justice[324].

Analyzing The Effects of Occupational Segregation On Wealth Generation

Occupational segregation in America is a prevailing issue that significantly contributes to racial wealth disparities. Historically, the unjust partitioning of work across racial lines has funneled Black workers into lower paying jobs, hindering their ability to generate and accumulate wealth[325].

According to a report from the National Equity Atlas, Black Americans are significantly overrepresented in low-wage occupations, while being underrepresented in high-wage occupations[326]. This occupational divide severely limits the income and wealth accumulation potential for Black workers. Their overrepresentation in lower-wage sectors results in a lower median income for Black households, which in turn affects their ability to accumulate wealth[327].

However, some detractors, including certain conservative media outlets, argue that occupational choices are individual decisions, suggesting that differences in income and wealth are primarily attributable to individual agency[328]. This viewpoint, while superficially plausible,

---

[324] Cook, Lisa D. "Racism Impoverishes the Whole Economy." Foreign Affairs, 2021.
[325] Anderson, Claud. "Black Labor, White Wealth: The Search for Power and Economic Justice." PowerNomics Corporation of America, 1994.
[326] National Equity Atlas. "Workforce Race and Ethnicity: United States." 2020.
[327] Oliver, Melvin, and Thomas Shapiro. "Black Wealth/White Wealth: A New Perspective on Racial Inequality." Routledge, 2006.
[328] Riley, Jason L. "Please Stop Helping Us: How Liberals Make It Harder for Blacks to Succeed." Encounter Books, 2014.

neglects the impact of systemic barriers and discriminative practices that have historically restricted the occupational choices available to Black Americans.

A study by Tomaskovic-Devey and Stainback[329] effectively counters the "choice" argument by demonstrating that even after controlling for education, skills, and experience, racial disparities in occupational distribution and wages persist. This enduring segregation, both across and within occupations, is a critical factor underlying the racial wealth gap.

Dr. Claud Anderson articulates the systemic nature of this issue, stating, "Racial economic disparities are not accidents, but a flawlessly maintained system of control[330]." In other words, the economic disparities resulting from occupational segregation are not simply the consequences of individual decisions but are rooted in a deeply ingrained system of racial hierarchy.

Consider, for instance, the sector of technology — a high-income generating field where Black Americans constitute a meager percentage of the workforce[331]. This underrepresentation is not a reflection of aptitude but is a consequence of systemic barriers such as unequal access to education and training opportunities. As a result, wealth generation in this lucrative sector is predominantly concentrated in the hands of White workers[332].

To rectify the harmful effects of occupational segregation on wealth generation, comprehensive policy

---

[329] Tomaskovic-Devey, Donald, and Kevin Stainback. "Discrimination and Desegregation: Equal Opportunity Progress in U.S. Private Sector Workplaces since the Civil Rights Act." The ANNALS of the American Academy of Political and Social Science, 2012.

[330] Anderson, Claud. "PowerNomics: The National Plan to Empower Black America." PowerNomics Corporation of America, 2001.

[331] U.S. Bureau of Labor Statistics. "Labor Force Statistics from the Current Population Survey." 2020.

[332] Ash, Elliott, Daniel L. Chen, and Arianna Ornaghi. "Stereotypes in High-Performing Professions: A Randomized Study of Economists." Proceedings of the National Academy of Sciences, 2020.

interventions are required. Policies that promote diversity in high-wage occupations, ensure fair wages across all occupations, and dismantle barriers to access quality education and training opportunities are critical[333].

Occupational segregation, a vestige of America's history of racial discrimination, continues to inflict harm on Black Americans by limiting their wealth generation potential. Acknowledging and addressing this issue is essential for establishing a more equitable society, where wealth generation is not contingent on one's racial identity[334].

Case Studies of Underrepresentation In High-Wage Professions

Despite significant strides made since the civil rights movement, disparities in occupational representation still persist in high-wage professions. This underrepresentation is especially pronounced for Black Americans, and manifests prominently in the fields of technology, healthcare, finance, and academia[335].

Silicon Valley, often viewed as the paragon of modern technological progress, exhibits stark racial disparities. A 2018 report from the Brookings Institution noted that Black workers comprised only 7.9% of the tech workforce, compared to White workers who constituted 68.5%[336]. This underrepresentation in a sector known for its high wages

---

[333] Pager, Devah, and Hana Shepherd. "The Sociology of Discrimination: Racial Discrimination in Employment, Housing, Credit, and Consumer Markets." Annual Review of Sociology, 2008.

[334] Killewald, Alexandra, and Brielle Bryan. "Falling Behind: The Role of Inter- and Intragenerational Processes in Widening Racial and Ethnic Wealth Gaps through Early and Middle Adulthood." Social Forces, 2018.

[335] Anderson, Claud. "PowerNomics: The National Plan to Empower Black America." PowerNomics Corporation of America, 2001.

[336] Rothwell, Jonathan. "The Hidden STEM Economy." Brookings Institution, 2013.

and wealth generation potential exemplifies a barrier to economic parity[337].

Similarly, in the health-care sector, Black physicians and surgeons, who typically fall into the high-wage category, represent just 5% of all doctors, according to the Association of American Medical Colleges[338]. This shortage isn't merely an occupational inequality issue but also impacts health-care outcomes within Black communities.

In the realm of finance, a sector renowned for its lucrative compensation, Black representation is dismal. A 2017 report by the Government Accountability Office noted that the percentage of Black professionals in finance remained stagnant at 6.3% between 2007 and 2015[339].

Academia, despite being a bastion of intellectual freedom, is not exempt from racial disparities. Black professors make up a mere 5% of full-time faculty in degree-granting post-secondary institutions, according to the National Center for Education Statistics[340].

Critics of these data, particularly some conservative commentators, might argue that these discrepancies are the outcome of individual career choices, not systemic discrimination[341]. They opine that varying interests, abilities, and personal decisions contribute to occupational

---

[337] Atkinson, Robert D., and Michael Lind. "Big is Beautiful: Debunking the Myth of Small Business." The MIT Press, 2018.

[^4^] Association of American Medical Colleges. "Diversity in Medicine: Facts and Figures 2019."

[338] Association of American Medical Colleges. "Diversity in Medicine: Facts and Figures 2019."

[339] Government Accountability Office. "Diversity in the Financial Services Industry and Its Impact on Financial Stability." 2017.

[340] National Center for Education Statistics. "Race/Ethnicity of College Faculty." 2019.

[341] Riley, Jason L. "Please Stop Helping Us: How Liberals Make It Harder for Blacks to Succeed." Encounter Books, 2014.

distribution. However, as Dr. Anderson rightly states, "To treat unequal things equally is the greatest injustice[342]."

Extensive research refutes the critics' argument. For example, a 2019 study published in the Proceedings of the National Academy of Sciences found that Black professionals in high-earning fields often face unconscious bias and racial stereotypes, which can influence hiring and promotion decisions[343].

The underrepresentation of Black Americans in high-wage professions is a cogent reminder of the insidious impact of systemic barriers and implicit bias. These disparities, in turn, constrain Black wealth accumulation and perpetuate economic inequality. Comprehensive reforms are needed, including diversifying education and job recruitment practices, to bridge this racial occupational divide[344].

Investigating The Underrepresentation of Black Individuals In High-Paying Jobs

The underrepresentation of Black individuals in high-paying jobs is an acute reflection of systemic racism and institutional bias that persist in the American job market. Disturbing patterns of racial disparity are particularly evident in well-remunerated sectors such as technology, health-care, and finance[345].

---

[342] Anderson, Claud. "Black Labor, White Wealth: The Search for Power and Economic Justice." PowerNomics Corporation of America, 1994.

[343] Ash, Elliott, Daniel L. Chen, and Arianna Ornaghi. "Stereotypes in High-Performing Professions: A Randomized Study of Economists." Proceedings of the National Academy of Sciences, 2019.

[344] Darity Jr., William, and A. Kirsten Mullen. "From Here to Equality: Reparations for Black Americans in the Twenty-First Century." The University of North Carolina Press, 2020.

[345] Anderson, Claud. "PowerNomics: The National Plan to Empower Black America." PowerNomics Corporation of America, 2001.

Silicon Valley, for instance, hailed as the hub of technological innovation, harbors glaring racial imbalances. A 2018 Brookings Institution report revealed that Black employees constituted a mere 7.9% of the tech workforce, compared to a staggering 68.5% of White employees[346].

In the health-care sector, despite its reputation for high wages, the story is much the same. As per the Association of American Medical Colleges, only 5% of physicians and surgeons are Black[347], thereby depriving the Black community of both financial gain and quality health-care.

Similarly, the financial industry is marked by racial disparities. A 2017 Government Accountability Office report noted the stagnation in Black representation in financial occupations over an 8-year period - remaining constant at 6.3%[348].

It is noteworthy that critics of the racial underrepresentation theory, primarily those aligned with conservative viewpoints, may argue that these discrepancies are the result of individual career choices, not systemic discrimination[349]. However, echoing the sentiments of Dr. Claud Anderson, "When systemic barriers have been in place for centuries, it is a disservice to attribute racial disparities to individual choices alone[350]."

A body of research rejects the critics' viewpoint. For instance, a study in the Proceedings of the National Academy of Sciences revealed that unconscious bias and

---

[346] Rothwell, Jonathan. "The Hidden STEM Economy." Brookings Institution, 2013.

[347] Association of American Medical Colleges. "Diversity in Medicine: Facts and Figures 2019."

[348] Government Accountability Office. "Diversity in the Financial Services Industry and Its Impact on Financial Stability." 2017.

[349] Riley, Jason L. "Please Stop Helping Us: How Liberals Make It Harder for Blacks to Succeed." Encounter Books, 2014.

[350] Anderson, Claud. "Black Labor, White Wealth: The Search for Power and Economic Justice." PowerNomics Corporation of America, 1994.

racial stereotypes often influence recruitment and promotion decisions in high-paying fields[351].

Therefore, the underrepresentation of Black individuals in high-paying jobs is not a random, but a systemic phenomenon, deeply rooted in a history of racial and economic injustice. This, in turn, has a cascading effect on the racial wealth gap, contributing to the perpetuation of economic inequality. To rectify these disparities, reforms in hiring practices, workplace policies, and educational opportunities are a pressing necessity[352].

Yet, it is essential to remember that these changes must be part of a broader societal shift towards racial justice. As Dr. Anderson once said, "The problem is not the players, but the game, and the game needs to change[353]."

Investigating The Underrepresentation of Black Individuals In High-Paying Jobs Part 2

Investigating further into the underrepresentation of Black individuals in high-paying occupations sheds more light on other sectors and specific roles where racial disparities are prevalent. While technology, health-care, and finance sectors have been mentioned, this pattern extends to other industries, such as legal, academia, and entertainment[354].

In the legal sector, the American Bar Association (ABA) reported in 2020 that Black attorneys constituted only 5% of

---

[351] Ash, Elliott, Daniel L. Chen, and Arianna Ornaghi. "Stereotypes in High-Performing Professions: A Randomized Study of Economists." Proceedings of the National Academy of Sciences, 2019.

[352] Darity Jr., William, and A. Kirsten Mullen. "From Here to Equality: Reparations for Black Americans in the Twenty-First Century." The University of North Carolina Press, 2020.

[353] Anderson, Claud. "A Black History Reader: 101 Question You Never Thought to Ask." PowerNomics Corporation of America, 2017.

[354] Anderson, Claud. "PowerNomics: The National Plan to Empower Black America." PowerNomics Corporation of America, 2001.

all lawyers[355]. The ABA has attributed this underrepresentation to barriers that include racial bias and lack of access to quality education[356].

Similarly, in academia, disparities persist despite improvements over time. As of 2018, only 6% of full-time faculty members in degree-granting post-secondary institutions were Black[357]. This underrepresentation impedes the diversification of intellectual perspectives and can affect the academic experience of Black students.

Furthermore, even in sectors where Black individuals seem to have a more substantial presence, such as the entertainment industry, disparities still exist. For instance, while Black actors have gained recognition in Hollywood, they remain underrepresented in high-earning roles such as directors and producers[358].

Detractors might argue that the aforementioned disparities result from personal choices or deficiencies, but this fails to acknowledge the systemic issues at play. As Dr. Anderson puts it, "Blaming the victims of systemic racism for their situation does not solve the problem, it merely perpetuates it[359]."

Scholars have rebutted this critique, pointing to structural barriers and discrimination as significant factors influencing underrepresentation. For example, a 2019 study published in the Harvard Business Review found that Black

---

[355] American Bar Association. "ABA Profile of the Legal Profession." 2020.
[356] Ibid.
[357] U.S. Department of Education, National Center for Education Statistics. "The Condition of Education 2020."
[358] Smith, Stacy L., et al. "Inclusion in the Director's Chair? Gender, Race & Age of Film Directors Across 1,000 Films from 2007-2016." USC Annenberg Inclusion Initiative, 2017.
[359] Anderson, Claud. "Black Labor, White Wealth: The Search for Power and Economic Justice." PowerNomics Corporation of America, 1994.

professionals face bias and stereotyping during hiring and promotion processes[360].

The conclusion is clear: Black underrepresentation in high-wage professions is systemic and multifaceted. The persistent wage gap, fewer opportunities, and systemic barriers continue to contribute to the racial wealth disparity. Thus, interventions should be comprehensive, encompassing both policy reforms and social changes.

In this regard, Dr. Anderson argues that "the road to economic equality is not only about creating opportunities. It's also about dismantling the systemic barriers that prevent these opportunities from being equally accessible[361]."

Indeed, addressing the underrepresentation of Black individuals in high-paying jobs calls for a re-evaluation and restructuring of societal norms and institutional policies. Dr. Anderson sums it up aptly: "Real change will come not only when we celebrate diversity but also when we implement fairness[362]."

Analyzing Barriers To Entry And Advancement In These Professions

Examining the systemic barriers to entry and advancement in high-paying professions for Black individuals unveils the subtle but powerful instruments of institutional racism[363]. These barriers range from explicit biases in hiring and promotion to the 'soft' barriers of

---

[360] Roberts, Laura Morgan, et al. "Being Black in Corporate America: An Intersectional Exploration." U.S. Chamber of Commerce, 2019.

[361] Anderson, Claud. "A Black History Reader: 101 Question You Never Thought to Ask." PowerNomics Corporation of America, 2017.

[362] Anderson, Claud. "Dirty Little Secrets About Black History, Its Heroes, and Other Troublemakers." PowerNomics Corporation of America, 2001.

[363] Anderson, Claud. "PowerNomics: The National Plan to Empower Black America." PowerNomics Corporation of America, 2001.

networking and mentorship, and they systematically deter Black professionals from reaching their potential[364].

A glaring barrier is the racial bias in hiring practices. A 2017 meta-analysis by Northwestern University indicated that racial discrimination in hiring has not declined in the past 25 years[365]. Black applicants were 36% less likely to receive a callback compared to white applicants with identical resumes[366].

Another barrier is the racial disparity in access to quality education, which is a critical factor for securing high-paying jobs. This educational gap, caused by residential segregation and unequal funding, is a persistent obstacle for Black individuals[367]. It limits their access to high-quality educational resources and opportunities, impeding their journey into high-wage professions.

Furthermore, Black individuals often face bias within the workplace. A study by the Center for Talent Innovation found that Black professionals are less likely to receive mentorship and sponsorship compared to their white counterparts[368]. This lack of support hampers their chances of advancement.

Some critics may argue that these disparities are due to personal choices or a lack of initiative among Black individuals. They may claim that the "pull yourself up by your bootstraps" mentality can solve these issues[369].

---

[364] Roberts, Laura Morgan, et al. "Being Black in Corporate America: An Intersectional Exploration." U.S. Chamber of Commerce, 2019.

[365] Quillian, Lincoln, et al. "Meta-analysis of field experiments shows no change in racial discrimination in hiring over time." Proceedings of the National Academy of Sciences 114.41 (2017): 10870-10875.

[366] Ibid.

[367] Reardon, Sean F., et al. "A 'Meta-Analysis of the Relationship between Socioeconomic Status and Academic Achievement." American Educational Research Association 135.2 (2019): 457-473.

[368] Hewlett, Sylvia Ann, et al. "The Sponsor Dividend." Center for Talent Innovation, 2019.

[369] Anderson, Claud. "Dirty Little Secrets About Black History, Its Heroes, and Other Troublemakers." PowerNomics Corporation of America, 2001.

However, as Dr. Anderson points out, "Solutions that ignore systemic inequities are not solutions at all. They're avoidance tactics[370]."

Research also disputes this simplistic argument. Studies show that racial disparities in high-wage professions persist even when controlling for education and experience[371]. This suggests that systemic barriers, not individual choices, primarily cause underrepresentation.

The barriers to entry and advancement in high-paying professions for Black individuals are deeply entrenched in our socio-economic structures. These barriers perpetuate racial wage disparities and exacerbate wealth inequality. As Dr. Anderson emphasizes, "Understanding these barriers is the first step towards dismantling them. The next step is to commit to actionable change[372]."

This discussion underscores the urgent need for comprehensive strategies to eradicate these barriers. Such strategies must span educational reforms, hiring process transformations, and the fostering of supportive professional networks. It is only then that we can begin to see a substantial decrease in the underrepresentation of Black individuals in high-paying jobs.

Examining The Effects of This Underrepresentation On Overall Black Wealth

The underrepresentation of Black individuals in high-paying professions has a domino effect, significantly impacting overall Black wealth. It's essential to underscore

---

[370] Ibid.
[371] Blau, Francine D., and Andrea Beller. "Wage inequality among men and women: The role of the workplace." Industrial Relations Section, Princeton University, 1992.
[372] Anderson, Claud. "More Dirty Little Secrets About Black History, Its Heroes, and Other Troublemakers." PowerNomics Corporation of America, 2006.

that wealth is not merely a reflection of individual prosperity but an indicator of a community's economic vitality and resilience[373].

The racial wealth gap, a disturbing manifestation of economic disparity, is directly linked to the underrepresentation issue. A 2019 study by McKinsey found that the median wealth of Black families is nearly 10 times less than that of White families[374].

This wealth gap is not merely the result of income differentials but is exacerbated by the lack of Black representation in lucrative fields. When Black individuals are relegated to low-paying jobs, they have less disposable income to save, invest, or pass down to future generations, hindering their ability to accumulate wealth over time[375].

Critics of this perspective, primarily those affiliated with conservative schools of thought, argue that these wealth disparities are largely a function of personal financial decisions and responsibility[376]. These critics often overlook the impact of systemic issues like wage disparities, discriminatory lending practices, and racially biased tax policies on Black wealth generation.

However, empirical research debunks this narrative. A study published in the Quarterly Journal of Economics found that the racial wealth gap remains substantial even among families with similar income levels[377]. Hence, the disparities cannot be simply attributed to individual decisions but rather to systemic forces.

---

[373] Anderson, Claud. "Black Labor, White Wealth: The Search for Power and Economic Justice." PowerNomics Corporation of America, 1994.
[374] Noel, Nick, et al. "The economic impact of closing the racial wealth gap." McKinsey & Company, 2019.
[375] Ibid.
[376] Riley, Jason L. "False Black Power." Templeton Press, 2017.
[377] Chetty, Raj, et al. "Race and Economic Opportunity in the United States: An Intergenerational Perspective." Quarterly Journal of Economics 135.2 (2020): 711-783.

The underrepresentation of Black individuals in high-paying professions and the resulting wealth disparity underscore the economic disadvantages perpetuated by systemic racism. In Dr. Claud Anderson's words, "The racial wealth gap is not an accident of history, it's a product of policy. And policy can help fix it[378]."

The knock-on effects of wealth disparities extend beyond individual households. It affects educational opportunities, health outcomes, and the overall economic mobility of the Black community[379]. For instance, wealthier families can afford better educational resources, enhancing their children's academic prospects and their future earning potential.

The underrepresentation of Black individuals in high-paying professions is more than an issue of workplace equity—it is a significant contributor to the racial wealth gap. To narrow this gap, systemic reforms are crucial. These should aim at not only promoting racial diversity in high-paying occupations but also rectifying discriminatory policies that hinder Black wealth generation. As Dr. Anderson asserts, "We cannot merely treat the symptoms of economic inequality. We need to address its root causes[380]."

---

[378] Anderson, Claud. "PowerNomics: The National Plan to Empower Black America." PowerNomics Corporation of America, 2001.

[379] Hamilton, Darrick, and William Darity Jr. "Race, Wealth, and Intergenerational Poverty: There will never be a post-racial America if the wealth gap persists." The American Prospect, 2009.

[380] Anderson, Claud. "More Dirty Little Secrets About Black History, Its Heroes, and Other Troublemakers." PowerNomics Corporation of America, 2006.

Chapter 5

The Black Mindset For Overcoming Limiting Beliefs and Embracing Success When It Comes To Generating Massive Income

The pathway towards amassing substantial income is not merely an economic endeavor; it also necessitates an evolution in mindset. For Black individuals, the challenge is heightened due to systemic inequities that have engendered limiting beliefs. Therefore, a shift in mindset is a critical component for the Black community to embrace success and generate significant income[381].

Historically, Black individuals have been disproportionately represented in low-income sectors, leading to deeply ingrained beliefs about wealth and prosperity. The racial wage gap, occupational segregation, and wealth disparities have often served to reinforce a narrative of economic struggle, limiting the vision of economic success[382].

Nevertheless, Dr. Claud Anderson eloquently argued that the limiting beliefs resulting from systemic bias should not define the potential of Black individuals or their economic aspirations. In his words, "Our circumstances do not define us; our mindset does[383]."

---

[381] Anderson, Claud. "Black Labor, White Wealth: The Search for Power and Economic Justice." PowerNomics Corporation of America, 1994.
[382] Bureau of Labor Statistics. "Racial, ethnic, and gender disparities in income and wealth." BLS Reports, 2021.
[383] Anderson, Claud. "PowerNomics: The National Plan to Empower Black America." PowerNomics Corporation of America, 2001.

Critics often posit that advocating for a change in mindset shifts the responsibility from systemic issues to individuals. While there is merit to this perspective, it is not a sufficient reason to dismiss the power of mindset completely[384]. A change in mindset is not a panacea for systemic racism but a crucial part of a multifaceted approach to overcoming economic disparity.

Studies indicate that an empowered mindset can significantly influence financial outcomes. For instance, a 2021 study in the Journal of Applied Psychology showed that individuals who held an abundance mindset, characterized by beliefs in unlimited potential and opportunities, were more likely to achieve financial success[385].

To foster this abundance mindset, it's essential to challenge limiting beliefs. The Black community must actively cultivate a sense of self-efficacy, belief in their ability to overcome obstacles, and manifest success. Furthermore, the narrative of Black wealth must be redefined to showcase examples of economic success, thereby creating a compelling vision of financial prosperity within the community[386].

Simultaneously, Black individuals need to invest in acquiring financial literacy skills, a crucial but often overlooked factor in wealth generation. The lack of these skills has been identified as a significant barrier to financial success[387].

---

[384] Riley, Jason L. "False Black Power." Templeton Press, 2017.
[385] Park, Young-Hoon, et al. "Abundance mindset, work engagement, and financial success: A cross-national investigation." Journal of Applied Psychology 106.4 (2021): 481-494.
[386] Anderson, Claud. "More Dirty Little Secrets About Black History, Its Heroes, and Other Troublemakers." PowerNomics Corporation of America, 2006.
[387] Gutter, Michael, et al. "Financial Capability and Financial Satisfaction: Financial Literacy, Behavior, and Capability Among African Americans." Journal of Financial Counseling and Planning 29.2 (2018): 265-277.

Dr. Anderson's call to action is more relevant now than ever. He urges the Black community to "Embrace the mindset of possibility, break the chains of limiting beliefs, and soar towards the future of unlimited potential[388]."

Overcoming limiting beliefs and embracing success for massive income generation necessitates both a change in individual mindsets and systemic reforms. These efforts, combined, will contribute towards reducing racial wealth disparities and empower the Black community towards economic prosperity.

Transitioning from idea conceptualization to actual wealth creation demands massive action, a concept eloquently detailed in Dr. Claud Anderson's "PowerNomics"[389]. The journey of wealth creation is not a passive endeavor; it necessitates an active, persistent pursuit of opportunities that align with one's vision of success[390].

Anderson elucidates on the importance of not merely being consumers but also active producers[391]. This involves recognizing the power and potential of the Black community in creating, owning, and controlling resources. However, detractors argue that systemic barriers, such as discriminatory lending practices, may hinder this progression[392]. Acknowledging these barriers, Anderson insists that the community must continue striving for economic self-reliance, utilizing alternative funding strategies like community cooperatives and crowd-funding.

---

[388] Anderson, Claud. "A Black History Reader: 101 Question You Never Thought to Ask." PowerNomics Corporation of America, 2017.

[389] Anderson, Claud. PowerNomics: The National Plan to Empower Black America. PowerNomics Corporation of America, 2001.

[390] Robbins, Anthony. Awaken the Giant Within: How to Take Immediate Control of Your Mental, Emotional, Physical and Financial Destiny! Free Press, 1992.

[391] Anderson, Claud. PowerNomics: The National Plan to Empower Black America. PowerNomics Corporation of America, 2001.

[392] Rugh, Jacob S., and Douglas S. Massey. "Racial Segregation and the American Foreclosure Crisis." American Sociological Review, vol. 75, no. 5, 2010.

Massive action also encompasses strategic planning and execution. An idea, no matter how innovative, is merely a starting point. To convert it into a wealth-generating venture, individuals must develop strategic business plans, assess market viability, and implement effective marketing strategies[393]. Skeptics may point to the high failure rate of start-ups as evidence against this approach[394]. In response, proponents of the massive action approach argue that failure is not a dead-end, but rather a stepping stone towards success[395].

Another critical aspect of massive action is continual learning and skill development. An entrepreneurial venture requires not only a robust idea but also the necessary skills and knowledge to transform it into a reality[396]. Critics contend that the lack of access to quality education and training opportunities can impede this process[397]. Still, the rise of digital platforms offering low-cost, high-quality education resources offers an increasingly accessible solution[398].

Anderson further emphasizes the importance of networking and forming strategic alliances as part of taking massive action. By fostering relationships with mentors, industry leaders, and potential partners, individuals can

---

[393] Osterwalder, Alexander, and Yves Pigneur. Business Model Generation: A Handbook for Visionaries, Game Changers, and Challengers. Wiley, 2010.

[394] Fairlie, Robert W., and Alicia M. Robb. Race and Entrepreneurial Success: Black-, Asian-, and White-Owned Businesses in the United States. MIT Press, 2010.

[395] Sarasvathy, Saras D. Effectuation: Elements of Entrepreneurial Expertise. Edward Elgar Publishing, 2009.

[396] Ericsson, K. Anders. Peak: Secrets from the New Science of Expertise. Mariner Books, 2017.

[397] Darling-Hammond, Linda. "Race, Inequality and Educational Accountability: The Irony of 'No Child Left Behind'." Race Ethnicity and Education, vol. 10, no. 3, 2007.

[398] Baker, Rachel, Eric Bettinger, Brian Jacob, and Ioana Marinescu. "The Effect of Labor Market Information on Community College Students' Major Choice." Economics of Education Review, vol. 65, 2018.

access valuable knowledge, resources, and opportunities. Critics may argue that networking alone cannot overcome the pervasive racial inequities in business and professional circles[399]. Nonetheless, strategic networking is a powerful tool in breaking down these barriers and advancing towards wealth creation[400].

The journey from idea conception to wealth creation demands a combination of innovation, strategic planning, skill development, networking, and most importantly, the courage to take massive action. Despite challenges and criticisms, this path presents enormous potential for individual and community wealth generation in the Black community. As Dr. Anderson articulates, "The road to wealth is paved with action, and every step forward, no matter how small, brings us closer to the realization of our economic potential[401]."

The Role of Limiting Beliefs When It Comes To Creating Black Wealth Creation

The process of wealth creation is influenced not only by external economic conditions but also by internal belief systems. Limiting beliefs - negative assumptions about one's potential - are particularly detrimental, especially in the context of Black wealth creation. These beliefs, shaped by systemic inequities and historic disenfranchisement, can serve as psychological barriers to economic prosperity[402].

---

[399] Smith, Sandra Susan. "Race and Trust." Annual Review of Sociology, vol. 36, 2010.
[400] Granovetter, Mark. "The Strength of Weak Ties." American Journal of Sociology, vol. 78, no. 6, 1973.
[401] Anderson, Claud. PowerNomics: The National Plan to Empower Black America. PowerNomics Corporation of America, 2001.
[402] Anderson, Claud. "Black Labor, White Wealth: The Search for Power and Economic Justice." PowerNomics Corporation of America, 1994.

According to Dr. Claud Anderson, "The most formidable barrier to Black wealth creation is not the physical chain but the mental one[403]." The chains of limiting beliefs, resulting from years of racial and economic discrimination, have significantly influenced the Black community's perception of wealth and their ability to generate it.

One manifestation of these limiting beliefs is a perceived lack of opportunities. According to a 2020 study by McKinsey, 31% of Black respondents felt their race or ethnicity would hinder their chances of acquiring wealth [404]. Such beliefs can create a vicious cycle of self-doubt, limiting risk-taking, and reducing the pursuit of wealth-generating opportunities.

Detractors, such as some conservative economists, may contend that the emphasis on mindset and limiting beliefs downplays the role of personal responsibility in wealth creation[405]. While personal effort and responsibility are undeniably important, it is insufficient to ignore the systemic biases that have shaped these beliefs.

Research provides compelling evidence against this view. A study in the Review of Black Political Economy found that the Black-White wealth gap persists even after accounting for differences in income and educational attainment, thereby indicating the influence of systemic factors[406].

These systemic factors often lead to a scarcity mindset, another limiting belief that hinders Black wealth creation. Driven by a narrative of lack and struggle, the scarcity

---

[403] Ibid
[404] Ibid
[405] Riley, Jason L. "Please Stop Helping Us: How Liberals Make It Harder for Blacks to Succeed." Encounter Books, 2014.
[406] Hamilton, Darrick, et al. "Umbrellas don't make it rain: Why studying and working hard isn't enough for Black Americans." Review of Black Political Economy 44.2 (2017): 131-167.

mindset can limit financial decision-making, thereby preventing the exploration of lucrative opportunities[407].

As Anderson asserts, "We must not only break free from the physical chains of systemic oppression but also from the mental chains of limiting beliefs[408]." To do so, he advocates for financial education, community-based economic strategies, and the cultivation of an abundance mindset. A shift in mindset, according to Anderson, can empower Black individuals to challenge systemic barriers, leverage opportunities, and create lasting wealth[409].

In sum, the role of limiting beliefs in Black wealth creation is significant. Confronting and overcoming these beliefs is a crucial step towards economic empowerment and wealth generation in the Black community. This process, however, must be accompanied by systemic changes to truly ensure an equitable economic landscape for all.

Discussing The Psychology of Limiting Beliefs And Their Effects On Financial Success

The psychology of limiting beliefs is multifaceted and deeply rooted in an individual's lived experiences. Often, they are products of cultural, societal, and historical influences. In the context of financial success, these beliefs can be especially pernicious, shaping how one navigates and interacts with economic systems[410].

Dr. Claud Anderson, in his exploration of the Black experience in America, expounds, "The psychological

---

[407] Anderson, Claud. "PowerNomics: The National Plan to Empower Black America." PowerNomics Corporation of America, 2001.
[408] Ibid
[409] Ibid
[410] Anderson, Claud. "Black Labor, White Wealth: The Search for Power and Economic Justice." PowerNomics Corporation of America, 1994.

imprint of centuries of economic subjugation can turn into self-imposed mental shackles[411]." These mental shackles or limiting beliefs can manifest in various forms: a sense of undeservingness, a fear of failure, or the perception of success as an aberration.

One common limiting belief is the internalization of the 'poverty mindset.' Rooted in past experiences of scarcity, this mindset reinforces the belief that financial success is unattainable or temporary[412]. This mindset can inhibit proactive financial behaviors, such as investing or starting a business, and cement a cycle of economic disadvantage.

However, detractors of this psychological perspective, typically proponents of the bootstrap theory, argue that the emphasis on limiting beliefs shifts the responsibility away from individual effort[413]. They assert that personal responsibility and hard work are the primary determinants of financial success.

Contrary to this perspective, a wealth of psychological research underscores the impact of limiting beliefs on financial behaviors. Studies show that individuals who hold limiting beliefs about their economic potential are less likely to engage in wealth-building activities[414].

Furthermore, research in the Journal of Economic Psychology found that the experience of scarcity, a common source of limiting beliefs, can adversely affect cognitive function and decision-making abilities, including those related to finances[415].

Echoing Anderson's sentiments, "It's not enough to change the conditions; we must change the mindset that was

---

[411] Ibid
[412] Furnham, Adrian. "The Psychology of Money." Routledge, 2014.
[413] Sowell, Thomas. "Wealth, Poverty and Politics." Basic Books, 2015.
[414] Lusardi, Annamaria, and Olivia S. Mitchell. "Financial literacy and retirement planning in the United States." Journal of Pension Economics & Finance, 2011.
[415] Mani, Anandi, et al. "Poverty impedes cognitive function." Science 341.6149 (2013): 976-980.

shaped by those conditions[416]." Overcoming limiting beliefs involves fostering an 'abundance mindset.' This shift in perspective can facilitate the recognition of financial opportunities and encourage the adoption of wealth-building strategies[417].

The psychology of limiting beliefs and their impact on financial success cannot be underestimated. While it is imperative to address structural inequities, it is equally crucial to confront the psychological barriers that impede financial prosperity. The key lies in nurturing empowering beliefs that support financial advancement, while simultaneously advocating for systemic changes that promote economic equality.

Identifying Common Limiting Beliefs About Wealth And Success Amongst Black People Throughout The World

The limiting beliefs surrounding wealth and success present a psychological hurdle that often goes unaddressed, particularly amongst Black individuals across the globe. The internalization of such beliefs can have a detrimental impact on the pursuit of financial success and prosperity[418].

One common limiting belief is the notion that "wealth is unattainable for Black individuals." The recurring narratives of racial wealth disparities in media and academia could inadvertently foster this belief[419]. Anderson argues that these narratives, while critical in highlighting systemic

---

[416] Anderson, Claud. "PowerNomics: The National Plan to Empower Black America." PowerNomics Corporation of America, 2001.
[417] Ibid
[418] ^1^ Ashley M. Fox, "The Social Determinants of Health in Poverty," Health Affairs, November 18, 2016, https://www.healthaffairs.org/doi/full/10.1377/hlthaff.2016.1153.
[419] Christopher J. Coyne and Abigail R. Hall, "Four Decades of the War on Drugs and Counting," The Independent Review 18, no. 3 (2014): 456-457.

issues, may also perpetuate a mindset of financial disenfranchisement among Black communities[420].

Another prevalent limiting belief is the concept of a "zero-sum game," where financial success is perceived as a scarce resource. This belief posits that the success of one individual necessarily means the failure of another[421]. It is essential to remember, as Anderson often underscores, "Wealth is not finite, and success is not exclusive[422]."

Societal stereotypes about Black people also contribute to limiting beliefs. The association of Black identity with poverty and crime in popular media can instill a sense of internalized racial inferiority. These stereotypes can subconsciously deter Black individuals from pursuing wealth, thereby reducing their financial aspirations[423].

The perspective of some critics, largely from the conservative camp, is that these beliefs are self-inflicted and can be overcome through personal effort[424]. However, as Anderson rightly contends, "The roots of these beliefs are not in the individual but in the system that has consistently marginalized and underrepresented them[425]."

Understanding the psychology of limiting beliefs is the first step in addressing them. According to psychologist Albert Bandura, self-efficacy - the belief in one's ability to succeed - is crucial to overcoming these barriers[426]. Encouraging self-efficacy and empowering Black individuals to envision and pursue wealth and success can

---

[420] Claud Anderson, PowerNomics : The National Plan to Empower Black America (Powernomics Corporation of America, 2001).
[421] Robert H. Frank, "Does Studying Economics Inhibit Cooperation?," Journal of Economic Perspectives 7, no. 2 (1993): 159-171.
[422] Anderson, PowerNomics.
[423] Travis L. Dixon, "A Dangerous Distortion of our Families," Color Of Change, January 2017, https://colorofchange.org/dangerousdistortion.
[424] Thomas Sowell, "Wealth, Poverty, and Politics: An International Perspective," The Hoover Institution (2015).
[425] Anderson, PowerNomics.
[426] Albert Bandura, "Self-Efficacy: Toward a Unifying Theory of Behavioral Change," Psychological Review 84, no. 2 (1977): 191-215.

play a transformative role in breaking the chains of these limiting beliefs[427].

By addressing these limiting beliefs, the goal is not to overlook systemic issues but to empower individuals within the system. As Anderson asserts, "To change the narrative, we must first change our belief in what is possible for us[428]."

Addressing these limiting beliefs involves both individual and collective efforts. It requires interventions at various levels, including education, media representation, and public policy. Notably, such interventions should be geared towards promoting financial literacy, dismantling negative stereotypes, and advocating for racial equity in all sectors of the society[429].

Strategies To Dismantle These Limiting Beliefs

Dismantling limiting beliefs about wealth and success among Black communities requires a multifaceted approach grounded in empowerment, education, and structural reform[430].

One strategy involves leveraging the power of media to reshape narratives around Black wealth and success. The media has a profound influence on the public consciousness and can be a catalyst in challenging and changing negative stereotypes[431]. Anderson asserts, "We need more representations of Black success, not as exceptions but as attainable realities[432]"

---

[427] Bandura, "Self-Efficacy."
[428] Anderson, PowerNomics.
[429] Prudence L. Carter and Kevin G. Welner, "Closing the Opportunity Gap: What America Must Do to Give Every Child an Even Chance," Oxford University Press (2013).
[430] Anderson, PowerNomics.
[431] Dixon, "A Dangerous Distortion of our Families."
[432] Anderson, PowerNomics

Education is another powerful tool in this regard. Financial literacy programs targeted at Black communities can significantly impact their economic outcomes[433]. These programs can demystify financial systems, making wealth generation seem less elusive and more attainable. They can help foster an entrepreneurial spirit among Black youth, promoting self-sufficiency and innovation[434].

Mentorship is another important strategy. Positive role models can inspire individuals to overcome their limiting beliefs by exemplifying success. Successful Black entrepreneurs, professionals, and leaders can act as powerful mentors, showing that success and wealth are attainable for Black individuals[435].

Critics might argue that these strategies place the onus of change on the victims of systemic oppression[436]. While individual effort is indeed crucial, Anderson reminds us that it is not sufficient. "Systemic problems," he emphasizes, "require systemic solutions[437]."

In this vein, public policy reforms aiming to address racial disparities in wealth and opportunity are of utmost importance. Policies that promote equitable access to quality education, affordable housing, and fair lending practices can create an environment conducive to wealth generation for Black communities[438].

---

[433] Annamaria Lusardi and Olivia S. Mitchell, "The Economic Importance of Financial Literacy: Theory and Evidence," Journal of Economic Literature 52, no. 1 (2014): 5-44.

[434] Lusardi and Mitchell, "The Economic Importance of Financial Literacy."

[435] David J. Johns, "The Role of Mentorship in Achieving Equity in Education," Brookings Institution, June 5, 2019, https://www.brookings.edu/blog/brown-center-chalkboard/2019/06/05/the-role-of-mentorship-in-achieving-equity-in-education/.

[436] Sowell, "Wealth, Poverty, and Politics."

[437] Anderson, PowerNomics.

[438] William Darity Jr. and Darrick Hamilton, "Bolstering the Business of Blackness," The Nation, June 28, 2017, https://www.thenation.com/article/archive/bolstering-business-blackness/.

Lastly, it's important to note the power of community in dismantling limiting beliefs. Black communities themselves, through unity, collaboration, and mutual support, can create powerful counter-narratives to these limiting beliefs[439].

Addressing limiting beliefs is not about denying the existence of systemic racial disparities. Instead, it's about empowering Black individuals to navigate these challenges and realize their potential. As Anderson puts it, "It's not just about believing we can be successful. It's about understanding that we deserve to be successful.[440]"

The Importance of A Success-Oriented Mindset And Its Role In Creating Black Wealth

The concept of wealth generation is not purely a matter of economics; it's deeply intertwined with psychological constructs, particularly an individual's mindset. For the Black community, the cultivation of a success-oriented mindset is a pivotal step towards creating enduring wealth[441].

The power of mindset, as defined by Stanford psychologist Carol Dweck, largely centers on the dichotomy between a "fixed" and a "growth" mindset. Those with a fixed mindset believe that abilities are largely predetermined, whereas those with a growth mindset consider abilities as malleable, capable of being nurtured and enhanced[442]. It's this growth mindset that is integral to Black wealth creation.

In his seminal work "PowerNomics," Dr. Claud Anderson has championed the importance of a success-oriented mindset, emphasizing that "black individuals must

---

[439] Anderson, PowerNomics.
[440] Anderson, PowerNomics.
[441] Anderson, Claud. PowerNomics : The National Plan to Empower Black America. Powernomics Corporation of America, 2001.
[442] Dweck, Carol S. Mindset: The New Psychology of Success. Random House, 2006.

adopt a new group-based, competitive mindset to create economic and political power in a competitive society[443]."

The influence of a growth mindset can be profound. A study from the University of Pennsylvania revealed that students who embraced a growth mindset were more likely to strive for success, leading to improved academic performance[444]. This intellectual growth forms the foundation for professional success and, by extension, wealth creation.

Nevertheless, critics might argue that the growth mindset oversimplifies the complex socio-economic factors that affect Black wealth creation, including systemic racism and limited access to quality education and career opportunities. They claim that mindset shifts cannot compensate for systemic issues[445].

While acknowledging these systemic obstacles, it is crucial not to underestimate the potential of a growth mindset. A study in the Journal of Experimental Social Psychology indicated that students who were taught the principles of a growth mindset were more resilient in the face of obstacles[446], which could be extrapolated to a broader context of overcoming systemic challenges.

Dr. Anderson argues that adopting a success-oriented mindset doesn't negate the need for structural changes but instead reinforces the importance of economic self-sufficiency and communal wealth-building[447]. His view is

---

[443] Anderson, PowerNomics.
[444] Yeager, David S., et al. "Boring but Important: A Self-Transcendent Purpose for Learning Fosters Academic Self-Regulation." Journal of Personality and Social Psychology, vol. 107, no. 4, 2014, pp. 559–580.
[445] Riley, Jason L. Please Stop Helping Us: How Liberals Make It Harder for Blacks to Succeed. Encounter Books, 2015.
[446] Yeager, David S., et al. "Teaching a lay theory before college narrows achievement gaps at scale." Proceedings of the National Academy of Sciences, vol. 113, no. 24, 2016, pp. E3341–E3348.
[447] Anderson, PowerNomics.

echoed by economic scholars who advocate for a combination of policy reform and mindset transformation[448].

Inculcating a success-oriented mindset also includes challenging limiting beliefs around wealth, commonly prevalent within Black communities. Research shows that negative stereotypes about money can inhibit financial decision-making and growth[449]. Thus, debunking these myths and replacing them with positive financial narratives is pivotal.

To conclude, fostering a success-oriented mindset plays a crucial role in wealth creation. While the influence of systemic factors cannot be disregarded, the empowering potential of a growth mindset remains a significant tool in promoting economic growth in the Black community. As Dr. Anderson insightfully put it, "The right mindset will turn challenges into opportunities, and opportunities into wealth[450]."

The Importance of A Success-Oriented Mindset And Its Role In Restoring The Two Parent Family

Restoring the two-parent family structure within the Black community is a multifaceted endeavor. A vital component of this is the cultivation of a success-oriented mindset, akin to the principles espoused by Dr. Claud Anderson in "PowerNomics." He posits that, "an empowered mindset will facilitate stronger families, as it fosters communal strength, resilience, and shared purpose[451]."

---

[448] Darity, William A., and A. Kirsten Mullen. From Here to Equality: Reparations for Black Americans in the Twenty-First Century. The University of North Carolina Press, 2020.
[449] Bogan, Vicki L., and William Darity Jr. "Culture and Entrepreneurship? African American and Immigrant Self-Employment in the United States." The Journal of Socio-Economics, vol. 37, no. 5, 2008, pp. 1999-2019.
[450] Anderson, PowerNomics.
[451] Anderson, Claud. PowerNomics : The National Plan to Empower Black America. Powernomics Corporation of America, 2001.

The "success-oriented" mindset, derived from psychologist Carol Dweck's "growth" mindset theory, posits that abilities and situations are malleable and capable of growth through dedication and effort[452]. This mindset can be applied to fostering resilient, supportive, and prosperous two-parent family structures.

Data from the Pew Research Center shows that only 58% of Black children live with two parents[453]. By adopting a success-oriented mindset, individuals can challenge negative narratives, such as the perceived inevitability of single parenthood, and actively work towards establishing and maintaining stable two-parent households.

However, critics might assert that changing mindsets won't substantially alter systemic issues such as economic disparity and social prejudice which disproportionately affect Black families[454]. While these obstacles are formidable, it is essential to acknowledge the power of a success-oriented mindset as a complementary strategy, not a standalone solution.

A success-oriented mindset encourages resilience and proactive problem-solving. It can inspire parents to seek resources, engage in healthy communication and conflict resolution, and foster a stable home environment[455]. It also creates a model for children, shaping their own attitudes towards adversity and ambition.

---

[452] Dweck, Carol S. Mindset: The New Psychology of Success. Random House, 2006.

[453] Livingstone, Gretchen, and Kristen Bialik. "Black children more likely to live with a single parent." Pew Research Center, Apr. 26, 2018, https://www.pewresearch.org/fact-tank/2018/04/26/about-one-third-of-u-s-children-are-living-with-an-unmarried-parent/.

[454] Wilson, William Julius. The Truly Disadvantaged: The Inner City, the Underclass, and Public Policy. The University of Chicago Press, 2012.

[455] Brooks, David. "The Power of Altruism." The New York Times, July 7, 2015, https://www.nytimes.com/2015/07/07/opinion/david-brooks-the-power-of-altruism.html.

Moreover, this mindset influences future generations. A study in the Journal of Personality and Social Psychology found that children who adopted a growth mindset were more likely to persevere in the face of obstacles[456], a resilience that could be applied to maintaining healthy relationships and family structures as they mature.

Anderson suggests that this mindset shift should be part of a broader community endeavor, involving educational programs and resources that promote relationship-building skills, financial literacy, and psychological support[457]. Scholars like William Julius Wilson concur, advocating for comprehensive social programs that address both systemic issues and individual growth[458].

To conclude, a success-oriented mindset plays a vital role in restoring the two-parent family structure within the Black community. By encouraging resilience, personal growth, and proactive problem-solving, it fosters the creation and preservation of supportive, stable family environments. As Dr. Anderson posits, "With a robust community and the right mindset, we can restore our families and, in doing so, empower future generations[459]."

The Importance of A Success-Oriented Mindset And Its Role In Restoring The Two Parent Family Part 2

Building on the previous discussion, the second part of this exploration into the role of a success-oriented mindset in restoring the two-parent family extends into the spheres of community activism, entrepreneurship, and education. As

---

[456] Yeager, David S., et al. "Boring but Important: A Self-Transcendent Purpose for Learning Fosters Academic Self-Regulation." Journal of Personality and Social Psychology, vol. 107, no. 4, 2014, pp. 559-580.
[457] Anderson, PowerNomics.
[458] Wilson, The Truly Disadvantaged.
[459] Anderson, PowerNomics.

emphasized by Dr. Claud Anderson, a successful mindset combined with community engagement is a compelling tool for reshaping familial structures[460].

Community activism can create environments conducive to nurturing this mindset. Civic groups that foster mentorship, provide resources, and address societal challenges can significantly support Black families. These community-led initiatives, backed by a success-oriented mindset, can proactively dismantle systemic barriers and nurture thriving family units[461].

Critics might argue about the efficacy of grassroots movements in enacting societal change[462]; nonetheless, the effectiveness of localized interventions has proven significant in various contexts[463].

Next, entrepreneurship can play a role in nurturing the success-oriented mindset. Owning businesses can provide financial stability, which is fundamental to maintaining two-parent family structures. The correlation between financial stability and stable households is well-documented[464].

However, some detractors might suggest that the entrepreneurial path can be uncertain and risky[465]. While acknowledging these risks, the success-oriented mindset

---

[460] Anderson, Claud. PowerNomics: The National Plan to Empower Black America. Powernomics Corporation of America, 2001.

[461] Diemer, Matthew A., and Adam M. Voight. "Racial/ethnic disparities in US college students' experience: Discrimination as an impediment to academic performance." Journal of College Student Development 59, no. 5 (2018): 564-577.

[462] Fine, Gary Alan, and Brooke Harrington. "The ethnography of resistance: toward a theory of cultural brokerage in contemporary social movements." The handbook of social movements across disciplines (2018): 127-157.

[463] Kirshner, Ben. Youth activism in an era of education inequality. NYU Press, 2015.

[464] Zhan, Min, and Michael Sherraden. "Assets, expectations, and children's educational achievement in female-headed households." Social service review 77, no. 2 (2003): 191-211.

[465] Yeager, David S., et al. "Boring but Important: A Self-Transcendent Purpose for Learning Fosters Academic Self-Regulation." Journal of Personality and Social Psychology, vol. 107, no. 4, 2014, pp. 559-580.

would approach them as challenges to be surmounted rather than insurmountable obstacles.

Moreover, it is essential to imbue a success-oriented mindset into the education system. Education that reinforces the belief in personal potential and empowers learners can instill resilience and a growth-oriented perspective[466]. Though skeptics may argue that education cannot rectify deeply entrenched social issues[467], evidence shows the transformative power of education, particularly when combined with a mindset that fosters success[468].

As an overarching theme, a success-oriented mindset applied across these sectors—community activism, entrepreneurship, and education—can empower Black communities in their endeavor to restore two-parent families. The mindset extends beyond individual families to influence the collective psyche of the community, driving towards an empowered, resilient society. As Dr. Anderson states, "Cultivating a success-oriented mindset is a communal project. It goes beyond restoring families; it's about reinvigorating communities[469]."

Providing Actionable Steps To Overcome Limiting Beliefs

Emphasizing the crucial nature of a success-oriented mindset in achieving personal and communal growth, the

---

[466] Yeager, David S., et al. "Boring but Important: A Self-Transcendent Purpose for Learning Fosters Academic Self-Regulation." Journal of Personality and Social Psychology, vol. 107, no. 4, 2014, pp. 559-580.

[467] Rothstein, Richard. "Education, economic growth, and social stability: Why the three are inseparable." Progressive Policy Institute, Washington, DC (2004).

[468] Dweck, Carol S. Mindset: The new psychology of success. Random House Digital, Inc., 2008.

[469] Anderson, Claud. PowerNomics: The National Plan to Empower Black America. Powernomics Corporation of America, 2001.

next important step is to delve into specific strategies for overcoming limiting beliefs. As Dr. Claud Anderson elucidates in "PowerNomics," one cannot begin to advance towards collective prosperity without first challenging the mental barriers hindering progress[470].

A critical starting point is to understand the genesis of limiting beliefs. These restrictive ideologies often stem from societal narratives, systemic oppression, and personal experiences[471]. While it is vital to recognize these influences, it is equally significant to confront these self-limiting beliefs with resolute determination.

However, some critics contend that an individualistic focus on changing mindset overlooks structural barriers that disproportionately affect disadvantaged communities[472]. In response to this criticism, the aim is not to dismiss systemic issues but to highlight the transformative power of personal resilience and a growth mindset, which can work in tandem with structural change.

One actionable step is embracing the practice of self-reflection. It involves identifying and critically evaluating self-limiting beliefs. Regularly journaling thoughts and feelings can be an effective strategy for this self-examination[473].

Another strategy is to surround oneself with positive influences. As sociologist Charles Cooley's "looking-glass self" theory suggests, individuals' self-perceptions often mirror the views of those around them[474]. Therefore,

---

[470] Anderson, Claud. PowerNomics: The National Plan to Empower Black America. PowerNomics Corporation of America, 2001.
[471] Dweck, Carol. Mindset: The New Psychology of Success. Ballantine Books, 2008.
[472] Wilson, William Julius. More Than Just Race: Being Black and Poor in the Inner City. W. W. Norton & Company, 2009.
[473] Pennebaker, James W. "Telling Stories: The Health Benefits of Narrative." Literature and Medicine, vol. 19, no. 1, 2000, pp. 3-18.
[474] Cooley, Charles Horton. Human Nature and the Social Order. Schocken Books, 1964.

fostering relationships with individuals who embody a growth mindset can help combat limiting beliefs.

In the face of skeptics who might question the impact of such positive influences[475], the response is grounded in empirical evidence. Research by the American Psychological Association reveals the potential of social influences on individual thought processes[476].

Additionally, embracing the principle of lifelong learning, a key component of a growth mindset, can help overcome limiting beliefs. By committing to continually acquire new skills and knowledge, one challenges the fixed mindset of innate limitations[477].

Critics might argue that the pursuit of lifelong learning can be constrained by socio-economic factors[478]. However, the advent of digital platforms offers unprecedented access to knowledge, making lifelong learning feasible regardless of socio-economic status[479].

Overcoming limiting beliefs necessitates a combination of self-reflection, positive influences, and lifelong learning. This holistic approach underscores Dr. Anderson's assertion: "We have the power to unshackle our minds from limiting beliefs, and in doing so, unlock our boundless potential1."

---

[475] Castilla, Emilio J., and Stephen Benard. "The Paradox of Meritocracy in Organizations." Administrative Science Quarterly, vol. 55, no. 4, 2010, pp. 543-676.

[476] American Psychological Association. "How Do Friends Influence Behavior?" Monitor on Psychology, vol. 50, no. 1, 2019.

[477] Tough, Paul. How Children Succeed: Grit, Curiosity, and the Hidden Power of Character. Houghton Mifflin Harcourt, 2012.

[478] Gorski, Paul. "The Myth of the Culture of Poverty." Educational Leadership, vol. 65, no. 7, 2008.

[479] Pappano, Laura. The Year of the MOOC. The New York Times, 2012.

Techniques For Nurturing A Growth Mindset And Cultivating Self-Confidence

Adopting a growth mindset and fostering self-confidence are not only crucial aspects of personal development but also foundational in collectively advancing the Black community towards prosperity. As Dr. Claud Anderson argues in "PowerNomics," these psychological constructs are prerequisites for achieving community-wide economic empowerment[480].

To begin with, nurturing a growth mindset involves altering perceptions of challenges and failures. Individuals should view setbacks not as insurmountable barriers but as opportunities for learning and growth[481]. However, critics might question the real-world application of this philosophy, contending that systemic barriers often make it impractical[482]. While acknowledging these criticisms, it's important to note that growth mindset serves not as a cure-all, but as a tool for resilience, especially in the face of socio-economic adversity.

One practical method to cultivate a growth mindset is through the practice of "deliberate practice," a term coined by psychologist K. Anders Ericsson. It involves setting specific goals, seeking immediate feedback, and focusing on technique and execution[483]. Critics may argue that access to immediate feedback or quality resources for learning may be a challenge for many, especially those from

---

[480] Anderson, Claud. PowerNomics: The National Plan to Empower Black America. PowerNomics Corporation of America, 2001

[481] Dweck, Carol. Mindset: The New Psychology of Success. Ballantine Books, 2008.

[482] Wilson, William Julius. More Than Just Race: Being Black and Poor in the Inner City. W. W. Norton & Company, 2009.

[483] Ericsson, K. Anders. Peak: Secrets from the New Science of Expertise. Houghton Mifflin Harcourt, 2016.

disadvantaged backgrounds[484]. However, innovations in digital learning environments are increasingly making such resources more accessible[485].

In terms of fostering self-confidence, a valuable approach is through positive affirmations. Regularly reciting positive self-statements can help to bolster self-belief and instill a can-do attitude[486]. Skeptics may argue that positive affirmations can veer into the realm of self-delusion[487]. However, when employed in combination with goal setting and realistic self-appraisal, affirmations can have a potent impact on confidence levels[488].

Moreover, celebrating personal successes, no matter how small, can significantly boost self-confidence. Recognizing these achievements reinforces the belief in one's capabilities and motivates further action[489].

Nevertheless, it is crucial to couple these individual efforts with community-based initiatives. As Anderson suggests, nurturing a growth mindset and self-confidence should be a communal undertaking, involving schools, families, and community organizations1.

Fostering a growth mindset and self-confidence involves shifting perspectives on challenges, engaging in deliberate practice, employing positive affirmations, and celebrating personal victories. Despite opposition, the

---

[484] Duncan, Greg J., and Richard J. Murnane. Whither Opportunity?: Rising Inequality, Schools, and Children's Life Chances. Russell Sage Foundation, 2011.

[485] Pappano, Laura. The Year of the MOOC. The New York Times, 2012.

[486] Self, Charles S. "The Power of Positive Thinking: A Review." The Personnel and Guidance Journal, vol. 46, no. 4, 196

[487] McKay, Matthew, Martha Davis, and Patrick Fanning. Thoughts and Feelings: Taking Control of Your Moods and Your Life. New Harbinger Publications, 2011.

[488] Yeager, David Scott, and Carol S. Dweck. "Mindsets That Promote Resilience: When Students Believe That Personal Characteristics Can Be Developed." Educational Psychologist, vol. 47, no. 4, 2012.

[489] Bandura, Albert. "Self-efficacy: Toward a Unifying Theory of Behavioral Change." Psychological Review, vol. 84, no. 2, 1977.

evidence supports these techniques' potential to contribute significantly to personal and communal growth. As Anderson aptly surmises, "A community that believes in its potential is a community that can transform its future[490]."

---

[490] Bandura, Albert. "Self-efficacy: Toward a Unifying Theory of Behavioral Change." Psychological Review, vol. 84, no. 2, 1977.

Chapter 6

Ideas For Black Wealth Creation And Keeping Money In The Black Community

Ideas for Black Wealth Creation and Keeping Money in The Black Community

In his renowned book, "PowerNomics," Dr. Claud Anderson postulates, "We must uplift ourselves through economic empowerment. Our dollars need to bounce at least 18 times within our community before leaving.[491] This principle speaks volumes on the significance of Black wealth creation and ensuring that Black dollars circulate within the community for longer periods.

Community Investment forms the first line of action. Supporting Black-owned businesses is a tangible way of fostering local economic growth[492]. The more money is spent within the community, the more it recirculates, engendering a domino effect on employment and business growth[493]. Critics may question the feasibility of this approach in our integrated economy[494], but data from the Kellogg School of Management shows that community-

---

[491] Anderson, Claud. PowerNomics: The National Plan to Empower Black America. PowerNomics Corporation of America, 2000.

[492] Bradford, William D. "The Wealth Dynamics of Entrepreneurship for Black and White Families in the U.S." Review of Income and Wealth 47, no. 1 (2001): 89-116.

[493] Bates, Timothy, and Alicia Robb. "Race, ethnicity and entrepreneurial success: Evidence from the characteristics of business owners survey." Federal Reserve Bank of Kansas City (2008).

[494] Pager, Devah, and Hana Shepherd. "The Sociology of Discrimination: Racial Discrimination in Employment, Housing, Credit, and Consumer Markets." Annual Review of Sociology 34 (2008): 181-209.

focused spending significantly contributes to reducing racial wealth gaps[495].

Promoting Financial Literacy is another crucial step. Knowledge on savings, investments, and wealth creation can empower individuals to make informed financial decisions[496]. Skeptics may downplay financial literacy's impact, citing systemic economic disparities[497]; however, a Federal Reserve report affirms its role in enhancing financial resilience and wealth-building[498].

Cultivating a culture of Entrepreneurship can spur innovative ideas into profitable businesses. Contrarily, detractors might highlight the risks and failure rates associated with start-ups[499]. Despite these concerns, a Kauffman Foundation report shows that entrepreneurship remains a viable pathway to wealth, particularly for minorities[500].

Ownership, particularly Real Estate Ownership, has long been recognized as a wealth creation strategy. Detractors might argue about housing market volatility and the barriers Black people face in acquiring property[501].

---

[495] Chetty, Raj, Nathaniel Hendren, Maggie R. Jones, and Sonya R. Porter. "Race and Economic Opportunity in the United States: An Intergenerational Perspective." The Quarterly Journal of Economics 135, no. 2 (2020): 711-783.

[496] Lusardi, Annamaria, and Olivia S. Mitchell. "The Economic Importance of Financial Literacy: Theory and Evidence." Journal of Economic Literature 52, no. 1 (2014): 5-44.

[497] Williams Shanks, Trina R., and Mesmin Destin. "Parental Expectations and Educational Outcomes for Young African American Adults: Do Household Assets Matter?" Race and Social Problems 2, no. 3-4 (2010): 81-97.

[498] Fernandes, Daniel, John G. Lynch Jr, and Richard G. Netemeyer. "Financial Literacy, Financial Education, and Downstream Financial Behaviors." Management Science 60, no. 8 (2014): 1861-1883.

[499] Fairlie, Robert W., and Alicia M. Robb. "Why are black-owned businesses less successful than white-owned businesses? The role of families, inheritances, and business human capital." Journal of Labor Economics 25, no. 2 (2007): 289-323.

[500] Fairlie, Robert W. "Kauffman Index of Entrepreneurial Activity 1996–2013." The Ewing Marion Kauffman Foundation (2014).

[501] Oliver, Melvin L., and Thomas M. Shapiro. Black Wealth/White Wealth: A New Perspective on Racial Inequality. Routledge, 2013.

However, according to the Harvard Joint Center for Housing Studies, home-ownership remains a significant contributor to household wealth[502].

Establishing Supportive Networks can help entrepreneurs learn from each other's experiences, share knowledge, and collaboratively problem-solve. Critics may view these networks as echo chambers that limit broader engagement[503]. However, research shows that such networks can be instrumental in overcoming the unique challenges Black entrepreneurs face[504].

Improved Access to Capital is essential. Critics might assert that business success relies solely on personal merit and downplay racial bias in lending[505]. Nevertheless, studies confirm racial disparities in loan approval rates and terms, which need to be addressed for equitable wealth creation[506].

Lastly, Legacy Building practices such as wills and trusts can ensure that wealth is transferred across generations. Critics may cite the complex legalities involved[507]. Nonetheless, estate planning is crucial to prevent wealth loss across generations[508].

---

[502] Herbert, Christopher E., Daniel T. McCue, and Rocio Sanchez-Moyano. "Is home-ownership Still an Effective Means of Building Wealth for Low-income and Minority Households? (Was it Ever?)." Joint Center for Housing Studies, Harvard University (2013).

[503] Granovetter, Mark. "The strength of weak ties." American Journal of Sociology 78, no. 6 (1973): 1360-1380.

[504] Chatterji, Aaron K., Solène Delecourt, Sharique Hasan, and Rembrand Koning. "When does advice impact start-up performance?" Strategic Management Journal 40, no. 3 (2019): 331-356.

[505] Blanchflower, David G., Phillip B. Levine, and David J. Zimmerman. "Discrimination in the Small-Business Credit Market." The Review of Economics and Statistics 85, no. 4 (2003): 930-943.

[506] Cavalluzzo, Ken S., and John D. Wolken. "Small business loan turndowns, personal wealth and discrimination." The Journal of Business 78, no. 6 (2005): 2153-2178.

[507] Hatcher, Desiree. "Estate Planning for the African American Family." Howard Law Journal 53 (2009): 731.

[508] Gentry, William M., and R. Glenn Hubbard. "Entrepreneurship and Household Saving." Advances in Economic Analysis & Policy 4, no. 1 (2004).

In essence, fostering Black wealth creation is a multifaceted endeavor. It requires a shift in perspective, concerted community effort, and supportive policies. As Anderson notes, "We must focus on group economics, building and maintaining wealth within our communities. It's not just about creating wealth; it's about retaining it."[509]

Community Investment: Encourage A Cultural Shift Towards Investing In Black-Owned Businesses And Emphasizing The Importance of Keeping The Black Dollar Within The Community

In the pursuit of economic stability and wealth creation within the Black community, one crucial action step is encouraging a cultural shift towards investing in Black-owned businesses[510]. Black communities have long been undermined by a lack of access to capital and economic opportunity. A study by the Kauffman Foundation found that Black entrepreneurs start their businesses with substantially less capital – nearly three times less – than their White counterparts[511]. This lack of initial capital has a cascading effect on the success and longevity of these businesses.

However, this systemic challenge doesn't deter from the potential success of Black-owned businesses. The National Bureau of Economic Research found that businesses owned by Black women, in particular, have grown at an

---

[509] Anderson, Claud. PowerNomics: The National Plan to Empower Black America. PowerNomics Corporation of America, 2000.
[510] Bradford, William D. "The Wealth Dynamics of Entrepreneurship for Black and White Families in the U.S." Review of Income and Wealth 47, no. 1 (2001): 89-116.
[511] Fairlie, Robert W., and Alicia M. Robb. "Why are black-owned businesses less successful than white-owned businesses? The role of families, inheritances, and business human capital." Journal of Labor Economics 25, no. 2 (2007): 289-323.

unprecedented rate in recent years[512]. But for them to realize their full potential, they need community investment.

Community investment, in this context, involves community members consciously spending money on local Black-owned businesses and individuals and entities investing directly in these businesses. This requires a significant cultural shift, given that the current U.S. consumer market is so heavily dominated by large, multinational corporations[513].

However, there are critics who may question the effectiveness and potential returns of investing solely in Black-owned businesses. Some argue that investment decisions should be based on the potential profitability of a business rather than the race of the business owner[514]. Others question whether such a strategy might reinforce racial divisions, rather than reducing them.

Yet, these viewpoints overlook a fundamental reality: Investing in Black-owned businesses isn't simply about creating racial equity – it's about recognizing untapped economic potential. A study by McKinsey & Company concluded that the racial wealth gap costs the U.S. economy between $1 trillion and $1.5 trillion each year[515]. Investing in Black-owned businesses can help to close this gap, leading to broader economic growth and prosperity for everyone.

To facilitate this shift, financial literacy should be emphasized. According to the Financial Industry Regulatory

---

[512] National Bureau of Economic Research. "Minority and Women Entrepreneurs: Building Capital, Networks, and Skills." The Hamilton Project (2015).
[513] Pager, Devah, and Hana Shepherd. "The Sociology of Discrimination: Racial Discrimination in Employment, Housing, Credit, and Consumer Markets." Annual Review of Sociology 34 (2008): 181-209.
[514] Fairlie, Robert W. "Kauffman Index of Entrepreneurial Activity 1996–2013." The Ewing Marion Kauffman Foundation (2014).
[515] McKinsey & Company. "The economic impact of closing the racial wealth gap." McKinsey & Company (2019).

Authority, Black Americans have a lower rate of financial literacy compared to other groups[516]. Improved financial education can help individuals make informed decisions about investing in businesses within their community.

Furthermore, initiatives to encourage collective economics, such as investment clubs and local investment funds, can also contribute to this shift. These initiatives can help to pool resources and distribute risk, making it easier for individual community members to support local Black-owned businesses.

Encouraging a cultural shift towards investing in Black-owned businesses isn't just about racial justice – it's about economic wisdom. By harnessing the potential of these businesses, we can build stronger, more prosperous communities for all[517].

Promoting Wealth Creation, Savings, and Investments

The ability to manage personal finance, particularly in matters of wealth creation, savings, and investments, is pivotal to creating economic stability. For the Black community, this skill is even more critical given the systemic barriers to wealth accumulation that have been in place for generations[518]. Yet, financial literacy rates among Black Americans remain dishearteningly low.

According to a survey by the Financial Industry Regulatory Authority, only 31 percent of Black respondents were able to answer four out of five financial literacy

---

[516] Lusardi, Annamaria, and Olivia S. Mitchell. "Financial Literacy and Retirement Planning in the United States." Journal of Pension Economics & Finance 10, no. 4 (2011): 509-525.
[517] Anderson, Claud. PowerNomics: The National Plan to Empower Black America. PowerNomics Corporation of America, 2000.
[518] Hamilton, D., Darity Jr., W., Price, A., Sridharan, V., & Tippett, R. (2015). Umbrellas don't make it rain: Why studying and working hard isn't enough for Black Americans. New York: The New School.

questions correctly, compared to 56 percent of White respondents[519].

Promoting and incorporating financial education programs that focus on these three areas in community learning centers and schools can contribute to bridging this financial literacy gap. Financial literacy is not just about understanding how to budget or avoid debt. It's about understanding the financial system as a whole and knowing how to use it to one's advantage[520].

However, there are those who may question the feasibility and effectiveness of such an approach. Critics argue that focusing on individual financial behavior neglects the structural economic inequities that disproportionately affect Black Americans[521]. They suggest that it's not the lack of financial literacy, but the lack of access to wealth-building opportunities that maintain racial wealth disparities.

While structural inequities undeniably play a significant role, promoting financial literacy can be a powerful tool to challenge these barriers. A study conducted by Annamaria Lusardi of the Global Financial Literacy Excellence Center showed that individuals who received financial education had a greater propensity to plan for retirement, invest in stocks, and accumulate wealth[522].

Moreover, including financial education in school curricula can give Black students a head start in navigating the financial world. Research has shown that students from states where financial education is mandatory are more

---

[519] Lusardi, Annamaria, and Olivia S. Mitchell. "Financial Literacy and Retirement Planning in the United States." Journal of Pension Economics & Finance 10, no. 4 (2011): 509-525.

[520] Anderson, Claud. PowerNomics: The National Plan to Empower Black America. PowerNomics Corporation of America, 2000.

[521] Oliver, Melvin, and Thomas Shapiro. Black Wealth/White Wealth: A New Perspective on Racial Inequality. Taylor & Francis, 2006.

[522] Lusardi, Annamaria, and Peter Tufano. "Debt Literacy, Financial Experiences, and Overindebtedness." Journal of Pension

likely to display cost-conscious behavior compared to their peers from states without such mandates[523].

It's also important to leverage community learning centers as venues for financial education for adults. These centers can host workshops and seminars that are accessible and relevant to their communities, making financial education a community-wide effort.

Additionally, the financial curriculum must be tailored to address the specific challenges and opportunities relevant to the Black community, such as understanding racial wealth gaps, entrepreneurship, real estate investment, and strategies for long-term wealth creation[524].

In essence, while financial literacy alone may not close the racial wealth gap, it can equip Black Americans with the tools they need to navigate, challenge, and ultimately reshape the economic landscape. By investing in financial education, we not only empower individuals but also strengthen the entire community[525].

Fostering Innovation and Establishing Black-Owned Businesses

Entrepreneurship is an essential pathway to wealth creation and economic stability, particularly within the Black community[526]. A vibrant culture of innovation and entrepreneurship can lead to the establishment of more

---

[523] Urban, Carly, Maximilian Schmeiser, J. Michael Collins, and Alexandra Brown. "State Financial Education Mandates: It's All in the Implementation." Insights on Financial Capability from the FINRA Investor Education Foundation (2015).

[524] Anderson, Claud. PowerNomics: The National Plan to Empower Black America. PowerNomics Corporation of America, 2000.

[525] Hamilton, D., Darity Jr., W., Price, A., Sridharan, V., & Tippett, R. (2015). Umbrellas don't make it rain: Why studying and working hard isn't enough for Black Americans. New York: The New School.

[526] Anderson, Claud. PowerNomics: The National Plan to Empower Black America. PowerNomics Corporation of America, 2000.

Black-owned businesses, potentially creating jobs and uplifting communities. However, fostering such an environment necessitates addressing systemic barriers and equipping Black entrepreneurs with the necessary tools and resources.

The entrepreneurial gap in the United States is profound. According to a report by the Kauffman Foundation, only 9% of American entrepreneurs are Black[527]. Yet, a study by the Minority Business Development Agency found that if minorities started and owned businesses at the same rate as non-minorities, the U.S. could boast an additional one million businesses and approximately 9.5 million more jobs[528].

However, it's important to acknowledge the criticisms and opposing viewpoints concerning entrepreneurship as a viable pathway to wealth creation for the Black community. Critics often argue that advocating for Black entrepreneurship can place an undue burden on individuals while neglecting systemic issues, such as discriminatory lending practices, under-resourced networks, and a lack of access to capital[529]. As a consequence, many Black-owned businesses start with significantly less capital than non-minority businesses, hindering their growth and sustainability.

Despite these valid criticisms, fostering entrepreneurship and innovation in the Black community remains an essential component of wealth creation. To effectively accomplish this, one must address both individual and systemic challenges.

---

[527] Kauffman Foundation. (2017). Race and Entrepreneurial Success.
[528] Minority Business Development Agency. (2012). Disparities in Capital Access between Minority and Non-Minority Businesses.
[529] Fairlie, Robert, and Alicia Robb. Race and Entrepreneurial Success: Black-, Asian-, and White-Owned Businesses in the United States. MIT Press, 2008.

Policy initiatives can play a critical role. Legislation that targets discriminatory lending practices and increases access to affordable capital for Black entrepreneurs could have a significant impact[530]. Equally, providing resources for education and mentorship can empower aspiring entrepreneurs with the skills necessary to succeed.

Innovation and entrepreneurship should also be integrated into educational curricula. Encouraging creativity and business acumen from an early age can foster an entrepreneurial mindset and provide students with the skills to innovate and create businesses[531].

Moreover, supporting and promoting Black-owned businesses can strengthen communities. The more that Black dollars circulate within the community, the more wealth is retained and reinvested[532]. With that said, successful Black-owned businesses can serve as powerful symbols of what is possible, inspiring others to follow in their footsteps.

Fostering a culture of innovation and entrepreneurship can contribute to the creation of more Black-owned businesses, thereby advancing wealth creation within the Black community. However, achieving this requires both individual and systemic change, coupled with the unwavering belief in the potential of Black entrepreneurs to shape their economic destinies[533].

---

[530] Bradford, William D. "The Wealth Dynamics of Entrepreneurship for Black and White Families in the U.S." Review of Income and Wealth 56, no. s1 (2010): S65-S81.

[531] Bonner, F. A., Alfred, M. V., James, M., Lewis, P., Nave, F., & St juste, S. (2010). Creating Environments of Success and Resilience: Culturally Responsive Teaching and Learning. Texas Education Review, 1(1).

[532] Anderson, Claud. PowerNomics: The National Plan to Empower Black America. PowerNomics Corporation of America, 2000.

[533] Hamilton, D., Darity Jr., W., Price, A., Sridharan, V., & Tippett, R. (2015). Umbrellas don't make it rain: Why studying and working hard isn't enough for Black Americans. New York: The New School.

Real Estate Ownership: A Stable, Long-Term Wealth Creation Strategy

Real estate ownership has traditionally been a significant avenue for wealth creation in the United States. For the Black community, it presents an opportunity to amass wealth and foster economic stability[534]. Encouraging home-ownership and investment in real estate can be a viable, long-term wealth creation strategy, providing both financial gains and a sense of security.

Data from the Federal Reserve's Survey of Consumer Finances shows that, on average, homeowners' net worth is significantly higher than that of renters[535]. Despite this, home-ownership rates in the Black community lag behind those of their white counterparts, with the U.S. Census Bureau reporting a home-ownership rate of 44.1% for Black households compared to 74.5% for white households in 2020[536].

Critics of promoting home-ownership as a wealth creation strategy often point to the housing crisis of 2007-2008 as evidence of the risks involved. They argue that pushing for home-ownership without providing adequate financial literacy can lead to unmanageable debt and potential foreclosure[537].

---

[534] Anderson, Claud. PowerNomics: The National Plan to Empower Black America. PowerNomics Corporation of America, 2000.
[535] Federal Reserve. (2020). Changes in U.S. Family Finances from 2016 to 2019: Evidence from the Survey of Consumer Finances.
[536] U.S. Census Bureau. (2020). Quarterly Residential Vacancies and home-ownership.
[537] Rugh, Jacob S., and Douglas S. Massey. "Racial Segregation and the American Foreclosure Crisis." American Sociological Review 75, no. 5 (2010): 629-651.

Furthermore, systemic issues such as discriminatory lending practices continue to hinder Black Americans' ability to acquire loans and invest in real estate[538].

In spite of these concerns, real estate ownership remains a potent tool for wealth accumulation, especially if paired with comprehensive financial education and reforms targeting discriminatory practices in the housing market. Policies promoting affordable housing, fair lending, and community investment can pave the way for increased home-ownership within the Black community[539].

In addition to individual home ownership, investment in commercial real estate can further drive economic growth and community development. Black business owners who own their commercial properties can accumulate wealth, while also contributing to the economic prosperity of their communities[540].

Financial education programs specifically targeting real estate could be beneficial. Providing knowledge on the intricacies of mortgages, the benefits and risks of owning property, and the principles of investing in real estate, could empower individuals to make informed decisions[541].

Therefore, while the path to real estate ownership may be fraught with challenges, it can still be a viable strategy for long-term wealth creation within the Black community. It is essential, however, to pair this strategy with broader

---

[538] Taylor, Keeanga-Yamahtta. Race for Profit: How Banks and the Real Estate Industry Undermined Black home-ownership. The University of North Carolina Press, 2019.

[539] Rothstein, Richard. The Color of Law: A Forgotten History of How Our Government Segregated America. Liveright Publishing, 2017.

[540] Anderson, Claud. PowerNomics: The National Plan to Empower Black America. PowerNomics Corporation of America, 2000.

[541] Anacker, Katrin B., et al. "Black home-ownership: The Role of Temporality and Politics in Housing, Race, and Wealth Inequality in America." Journal of Urban Affairs, 2019.

systemic reforms and robust financial education to ensure a secure and beneficial investment[542].

A Stepping Stone for Black Entrepreneurs

Supportive networks, by fostering mentorship, knowledge sharing, and collaboration, hold a transformative potential for Black entrepreneurs. These networks can serve as powerful tools for overcoming systemic challenges and nurturing business growth[543]. Research by Harvard Business Review shows that entrepreneurs who leverage their network connections have better chances of start-up success and business sustainability[544].

For Black entrepreneurs, supportive networks can play a particularly vital role. Data from the U.S. Census Bureau indicates that Black-owned businesses tend to have lower sales, fewer employees, and higher closure rates compared to other racial groups[545]. These discrepancies can, in part, be attributed to systemic racism, lack of access to capital, and fewer business connections[546].

However, critics question the effectiveness of networks, arguing that they may foster exclusivity, leaving out those who lack connections. Further, there is the concern that

---

[542] Hamilton, D., Darity Jr., W., Price, A., Sridharan, V., & Tippett, R. (2015). Umbrellas don't make it rain: Why studying and working hard isn't enough for Black Americans. New York: The New School.
[543] Anderson, Claud. PowerNomics: The National Plan to Empower Black America. PowerNomics Corporation of America, 2000.
[544] Hoang, Ha, and Bostjan Antoncic. "Network-based Research in Entrepreneurship: A Critical Review." Journal of Business Venturing 18, no. 2 (2003): 165-187.
[545] U.S. Census Bureau. (2018). Annual Business Survey: Black or African American-Owned Businesses in the U.S.
[546] Fairlie, Robert, and Alicia Robb. Race and Entrepreneurial Success: Black-, Asian-, and White-Owned Businesses in the United States. MIT Press, 2008.

networks can sometimes perpetuate the very systemic issues they aim to combat, such as biases and discrimination[547].

Despite these criticisms, the benefits of supportive networks are well-documented. These platforms can provide Black entrepreneurs access to capital through introductions to investors, crucial business advice, and opportunities for partnerships[548]. Furthermore, networks that prioritize diversity can help in tackling systemic issues, fostering a culture of inclusivity, and encouraging wider societal change[549].

Organizations such as Black Business Network, National Black Chamber of Commerce, and 100 Black Men of America are already doing commendable work in establishing and maintaining supportive networks. However, it is crucial to build upon these efforts, encouraging greater participation and collaboration, and strengthening these networks' impact on Black entrepreneurship[550].

Supportive networks can be instrumental in creating an entrepreneurial culture that provides Black businesses with the resources and opportunities to thrive. As such, they should be a crucial component of strategies to bolster Black wealth creation and economic empowerment[551].

---

[547] Rivera, Lauren A. "Hiring as Cultural Matching: The Case of Elite Professional Service Firms." American Sociological Review 77, no. 6 (2012): 999-1022.
[548] Adler, Paul S., and Seok-Woo Kwon. "Social Capital: Prospects for a New Concept." Academy of Management Review 27, no. 1 (2002): 17-40.
[549] Chatterji, Aaron K., Edward L. Glaeser, and William R. Kerr. "Clusters of Entrepreneurship and Innovation." Innovation Policy and the Economy 14, no. 1 (2014): 129-166.
[550] Black Business Network. (n.d.). Our Mission. Black Business Network.
[551] Anderson, Claud. PowerNomics: The National Plan to Empower Black America. PowerNomics Corporation of America, 2000.

Advocating Access to Capital: A Critical Avenue for Black-owned Businesses

Access to capital is a critical element for business growth and development[552]. Yet, for Black-owned businesses, access to financial resources has historically been, and continues to be, a significant challenge[553]. A report by the U.S. Federal Reserve found that only 47% of Black-owned firms received the full amount of financing they applied for, compared to 76% of white-owned firms[554].

This disparity can be attributed to a myriad of factors, including systemic racism, the racial wealth gap, and discriminatory lending practices[555]. However, there's a critical need for reform. It's crucial to advocate for improved access to capital for Black-owned businesses through lobbying efforts and strategic partnerships with financial institutions.

On one hand, skeptics argue that improving access to capital for Black-owned businesses alone isn't enough. They point out that focusing solely on financial access may neglect other significant barriers to Black entrepreneurship, such as education and network gaps[556]. Critics also argue that partnerships with financial institutions can perpetuate

---

[552] Anderson, Claud. PowerNomics: The National Plan to Empower Black America. PowerNomics Corporation of America, 2000.
[553] Fairlie, Robert, and Alicia Robb. Race and Entrepreneurial Success: Black-, Asian-, and White-Owned Businesses in the United States. MIT Press, 2008.
[554] Federal Reserve Banks. 2020 Small Business Credit Survey: Report on Employer Firms.
[555] Bradford, William D. "The Wealth Dynamics of Entrepreneurship for Black and White Families in the U.S." Review of Income and Wealth 46, no. 1 (2000): 89-116.
[556] Robb, Alicia. "Access to Capital among Young Firms, Minority-Owned Firms, Women-Owned Firms, and High-Tech Firms." Office of Advocacy, U.S. Small Business Administration (2013).

systemic inequities, particularly if these institutions maintain discriminatory lending practices[557].

Despite these valid concerns, advocating for improved access to capital is a vital strategy. Data from the U.S. Small Business Administration revealed that increased access to capital for Black-owned firms resulted in improved business performance and higher survival rates[558]. Additionally, lobbying efforts can lead to policy changes that dismantle systemic barriers and create an equitable financial landscape[559].

Promoting partnerships with financial institutions can also be transformative. Banks and other financial institutions can provide not only capital but also financial guidance and resources that empower Black business owners[560]. Also, these institutions, guided by community reinvestment acts and internal diversity and inclusion initiatives, can help rectify past inequities and propel Black businesses forward[561].

Groups such as the National Bankers Association and Black Business Investment Fund are already championing these efforts, but there is a clear need for wider societal involvement and support[562]. Improved access to capital,

---

[557] Blanchflower, David G., Phillip B. Levine, and David J. Zimmerman. "Discrimination in the Small-Business Credit Market." Review of Economics and Statistics 85, no. 4 (2003): 930-943.

[558] Bates, Timothy. "Financing Small Business Creation: The Case of Chinese and Korean Immigrant Entrepreneurs." Journal of Business Venturing 12, no. 2 (1997): 109-124.

[559] Pager, Devah, and Hana Shepherd. "The Sociology of Discrimination: Racial Discrimination in Employment, Housing, Credit, and Consumer Markets." Annual Review of Sociology 34 (2008): 181-209.

[560] Li, Yue, and John R. Robinson. "Evidence on the Effect of Recognition and Disclosure on Cost of Equity Capital in the Nonprofit Sector." Research in Accounting Regulation 28, no. 2 (2016): 136-145.

[561] Community Reinvestment Act (CRA), Pub. L. 95-128, 91 Stat. 1147, 12 U.S.C. § 2901 et seq.

[562] National Bankers Association. "Our History." National Bankers Association; Black Business Investment Fund. "About Us." Black Business Investment Fund.

complemented by other supportive measures, can significantly bolster Black wealth creation and economic empowerment.

A Pathway Towards Economic Equity and Wealth Creation

Policy advocacy plays a pivotal role in fostering economic equity and dismantling systemic barriers to wealth creation, especially within the Black community[563]. Policies, be they local, state, or national, set the framework within which businesses operate and individuals strive to accumulate wealth. Ensuring these policies are fair, inclusive, and equitable is, therefore, a critical task.

Skepticism toward the efficacy of policy advocacy, however, persists. Some critics argue that the change achieved through policy advocacy is often too slow to address immediate needs[564]. Others contend that lobbying efforts could be better directed toward immediate community-based initiatives, such as entrepreneurship training or financial literacy programs[565].

While these perspectives merit attention, the need for policy advocacy cannot be understated. This does not negate the value of direct community-based initiatives; instead, it highlights the importance of a multi-pronged approach in addressing systemic wealth disparities[566].

---

[563] Anderson, Claud. PowerNomics: The National Plan to Empower Black America. PowerNomics Corporation of America, 2000.

[564] Alesina, Alberto, and Dani Rodrik. "Distributive Politics and Economic Growth." Quarterly Journal of Economics 109, no. 2 (1994): 465-490.

[565] Page, Benjamin I., and Martin Gilens. "Democracy and Equality: The Enduring Link between Wealth and Political Power." Perspectives on Politics 18, no. 3 (2020): 690-707.

[566] Chetty, Raj, Nathaniel Hendren, Patrick Kline, and Emmanuel Saez. "Where is the Land of Opportunity? The Geography of Intergenerational Mobility in the United States." The Quarterly Journal of Economics 129, no. 4 (2014): 1553-1623.

Historically, policy changes have had a profound impact on economic equity. For example, the Fair Housing Act of 1968 and the subsequent Community Reinvestment Act of 1977 were pivotal in mitigating housing discrimination and encouraging banks to meet the needs of all communities[567]. These policies, while not entirely eradicating wealth disparities, have played a significant role in advancing economic equity.

Recently, the proposed policies such as the American Jobs Plan and American Families Plan have aimed to address systemic inequities, providing significant investment in Black communities, including support for Black-owned businesses and funds for community development[568]. These are indicators of how policy advocacy can drive impactful change.

Furthermore, policy advocacy promotes empowerment. By encouraging active participation in the policy-making process, individuals and communities can ensure that their interests and needs are represented. Initiatives like the Black Lives Matter movement have shown how effective advocacy can bring about substantial policy discussions and changes[569].

Despite the challenges, policy advocacy remains a powerful tool in the fight against economic inequity. To effect real, lasting change, we must continually push for policies that foster fairness, inclusivity, and opportunity for all.

---

[567] Squires, Gregory D., and Chester Hartman. "There's No Such Thing as a Free Market." American Journal of Economics and Sociology 59, no. 2 (2000): 301-317.

[568] The White House. "Fact Sheet: The American Jobs Plan." The White House, 31 Mar. 2021; The White House. "Fact Sheet: The American Families Plan." The White House, 28 Apr. 2021.

[569] Taylor, Keeanga-Yamahtta. From #BlackLivesMatter to Black Liberation. Haymarket Books, 2016.

Tapping into the Economic Potential of Black Culture

In the quest for economic empowerment and wealth creation, one potent yet often overlooked resource is the rich cultural heritage within the Black community. This heritage, expressed through arts, entertainment, and historical landmarks, holds enormous potential for driving economic growth through tourism[570].

Yet, some critics argue that using culture as a commodity might lead to cultural appropriation and distortion, particularly when the culture in question belongs to a historically marginalized group[571]. Others fear it may perpetuate stereotypes or lead to the exploitation of artists and cultural workers[572].

While these concerns are valid, they underline the need for careful, community-led approaches in leveraging cultural heritage. Done appropriately, cultural heritage and tourism can create a self-sustaining economy while preserving and promoting cultural identity.

Case studies from around the globe show the potential of cultural tourism. For instance, the Gullah Geechee Cultural Heritage Corridor, spanning from North Carolina to Florida, has seen significant growth in tourism, bringing economic benefits while preserving a unique African American culture[573]. Similarly, the National Museum of African American History and Culture, since opening in 2016, has drawn millions of visitors, contributing

---

[570] Anderson, Claud. Black Labor, White Wealth: The Search for Power and Economic Justice. PowerNomics Corporation of America, 1994.
[571] Comaroff, John L., and Jean Comaroff. Ethnicity, Inc. University of Chicago Press, 2009.
[572] Zukin, Sharon. The Cultures of Cities. Blackwell, 1995.
[573] Gullah Geechee Cultural Heritage Corridor Commission. "Management Plan." National Park Service, 2013.

significantly to the local economy and enhancing cultural understanding[574].

Arts and entertainment have also shown considerable promise. The music industry, for example, has been a significant wealth generator for the Black community, with artists like Jay-Z and Rihanna amassing substantial wealth through their music and ancillary business ventures[575].

Moreover, the Black community's rich cultural heritage provides opportunities for community-led businesses in hospitality, retail, and services, creating jobs and keeping wealth within the community. These businesses can build upon the unique attractions and experiences that cultural tourism offers[576].

The key is in community-led and -controlled development, which ensures that the benefits are widely distributed, the cultural integrity is maintained, and the community itself shapes the narrative. Advocacy efforts should focus on securing funding and support for these initiatives, as well as on ensuring fair intellectual property rights for artists and cultural workers.

Leveraging the rich cultural heritage within the Black community, if done carefully and respectfully, can become an essential tool for wealth creation and economic empowerment.

Technology and Innovation: The Gateway to Economic Empowerment

In this rapidly evolving world, technology and innovation have become critical engines of wealth creation

---

[574] National Museum of African American History and Culture. "About the Museum." Smithsonian, 2023.
[575] Forbes. "Forbes' Top Earning Musicians." Forbes, 2022.
[576] Page, Benjamin I., and Martin Gilens. "Democracy and Equality: The Enduring Link between Wealth and Political Power." Perspectives on Politics 18, no. 3 (2020): 690-707.

and economic growth. The Black community's engagement with these sectors, therefore, presents opportunities for significant wealth creation and empowerment[577].

Critics, however, point to a persistent racial digital divide and systemic obstacles that limit the engagement of the Black community in these sectors[578]. It's important to acknowledge these concerns while simultaneously striving to overcome them. Anderson's "Powernomics"[579] is relevant here, emphasizing the need to restructure patterns of behavior within the Black community and encourage investment in technology and innovation.

Indeed, real-world data shows that Black participation in technology and innovation sectors can lead to significant wealth creation. Robert F. Smith, founder of Vista Equity Partners, for instance, has amassed substantial wealth by investing in technology companies[580]. Similarly, start-ups like Calendly and Blavity, founded by Black entrepreneurs, have made their mark in the tech industry, demonstrating the potential for wealth creation in these sectors[581].

Yet, while individual success stories are inspiring, broader engagement is needed to realize the full economic potential of these sectors for the Black community. Encouraging Black youths to pursue STEM education and careers is a crucial first step. Organizations like Code2040 and Black Girls CODE are making significant strides in this area, helping to equip the next generation of Black innovators and technologists[582].

---

[577] Anderson, Claud. Powernomics: The National Plan to Empower Black America. Powernomics Corporation of America, 2001.
[578] U.S. Census Bureau. "Computer and Internet Use in the United States: 2016." U.S. Census Bureau, 2018.
[579] Anderson, Claud. Powernomics: The National Plan to Empower Black America. Powernomics Corporation of America, 2001.
[580] Forbes. "The World's Billionaires: Robert F. Smith." Forbes, 2023.
[581] CBInsights. "The State of Black Tech start-ups in the U.S." CBInsights, 2023.
[582] Code2040. "About Us." Code2040, 2023.

Furthermore, fostering a culture of innovation within the Black community is essential. This involves creating spaces for creativity and entrepreneurship, such as incubators and co-working spaces that cater specifically to Black entrepreneurs. These environments can provide the resources and support needed to launch and grow successful tech start-ups[583].

Access to capital is another major barrier that Black tech entrepreneurs face. Venture capitalists and angel investors must be encouraged to invest in Black-owned tech start-ups. Meanwhile, crowd-funding and peer-to-peer lending platforms present alternative funding avenues worth exploring.

Despite the challenges, the technology and innovation sectors represent significant wealth creation opportunities for the Black community. Through education, entrepreneurship, and strategic investment in these sectors, it's possible to bridge the racial wealth gap and foster economic empowerment.

Embracing AI: A Crucial Move Towards Future-Proofing Black Economic Power

As we delve further into the Information Age, the rise of artificial intelligence (AI) represents a critical shift that could drastically impact the job market and wealth creation. As part of the broader technology and innovation sectors, AI presents both opportunities and challenges for the Black community.

Skeptics might point out the dangers of automation, particularly for the Black community, which is

---

[583] Fairlie, Robert W., and Alicia M. Robb. Race and Entrepreneurial Success: Black-, Asian-, and White-Owned Businesses in the United States. MIT Press, 2008.

disproportionately represented in public sector and manual labor jobs[584]. These positions are vulnerable to automation, and without proactive engagement and adaptation, job losses are inevitable. Critics also note the digital divide and the lack of representation in tech sectors as stumbling blocks[585].

However, this perspective overlooks the potential benefits of AI and the proactive steps that can be taken to mitigate these challenges. Dr. Claud Anderson's philosophy in "Powernomics" is relevant here, advocating for a strategic and planned approach to economic empowerment[586]. AI and automation should be viewed not as threats, but as opportunities for economic advancement.

There is real-world evidence to support this. Notably, the creation of jobs in AI development, data analysis, and related fields outpaces job losses from automation[587]. Yet, there is a shortage of skilled workers to fill these roles, and this is where the Black community can step in. For instance, the field of AI ethics, which focuses on ensuring that AI systems operate fairly and do not reinforce societal biases, is a growing sector that requires diverse perspectives, including those of Black individuals[588].

It is crucial to promote STEM education and digital literacy in the Black community, enabling a shift from consumers to producers of AI technologies. Organizations like Black in AI are already doing commendable work in

---

[584] World Economic Forum. "The Future of Jobs Report 2022." World Economic Forum, 2022.
[585] U.S. Census Bureau. "Computer and Internet Use in the United States: 2016." U.S. Census Bureau, 2018.
[586] Anderson, Claud. Powernomics: The National Plan to Empower Black America. Powernomics Corporation of America, 2001.
[587] McKinsey Global Institute. "Jobs Lost, Jobs Gained: Workforce Transitions in a Time of Automation." McKinsey Global Institute, 2017.
[588] Buolamwini, Joy. "How I'm Fighting Bias in Algorithms." TED Talk, 2016.

this area, offering mentorship and resources to Black scholars and practitioners in AI[589].

There is also a need to foster Black entrepreneurship in the AI sector. Black-owned AI start-ups can create wealth while addressing unique community needs. Yet, access to funding remains a hurdle[590]. Partnerships with venture capitalists, angel investors, and financial institutions should be pursued.

Finally, policy advocacy is necessary to ensure fair labor transitions for workers displaced by AI and automation. This includes championing policies for re-skilling programs, income support, and job matching services[591].

Embracing AI and technology is essential for the Black community to remain economically relevant in the future. This requires concerted efforts in education, entrepreneurship, and policy advocacy.

Health and Wellness

The health and wellness industry, projected to reach $6 trillion globally by 2025[592], offers a promising avenue for Black wealth creation. Simultaneously, it's a sector that greatly contributes to community well-being, aligning with the principle of 'communal wealth' espoused by Dr. Claud Anderson[593]. However, it's essential to acknowledge the

---

[589] Black in AI. "About Us." Black in AI, 2023.
[590] Fairlie, Robert W., and Alicia M. Robb. Race and Entrepreneurial Success: Black-, Asian-, and White-Owned Businesses in the United States. MIT Press, 2008.
[591] Anderson, Claud. A Black History Reader: 101 Questions You Never Thought to Ask. Powernomics Corporation of America, 2017.
[592] "Global Wellness Economy Monitor." Global Wellness Institute, 2021.
[593] Anderson, Claud. Powernomics: The National Plan to Empower Black America. Powernomics Corporation of America, 2001.

obstacles faced by Black entrepreneurs in this field and provide solutions for overcoming them.

Detractors might argue that the health and wellness industry is already saturated and that competition is steep. Yet, these assertions do not take into account the unique selling propositions (USPs) that Black entrepreneurs can offer. For instance, many Black entrepreneurs in this sector draw on Afrocentric wellness traditions[594], resonating with consumers seeking culturally appropriate services and products.

There's also a misconception that investing in health and wellness requires significant start-up capital, thus being inaccessible to many Black entrepreneurs. While some areas of the sector can be capital-intensive, many others, such as personal training or wellness coaching, require less financial outlay. Plus, innovative funding models, including crowd-funding and community-based financing, can help overcome this hurdle[595].

An under-recognized area is the role of policy advocacy in facilitating Black participation in the health and wellness industry. Policymakers should be lobbied to provide tax incentives for health and wellness businesses, especially in underserved areas. This not only fuels Black wealth creation but also addresses health disparities, an issue that disproportionately impacts the Black community[596].

The business case for Black investment in the health and wellness industry is underpinned by real-world data. A report by Nielsen revealed that Black consumers over-index in their spending on health and beauty products[597]. By

---

[594] Thompson, Cheryl. "Black Women, Beauty, and Hair as a Matter of Being." Women's Studies, vol. 38, no. 8, 2009, pp. 831-856.
[595] "Understanding crowd-funding and Its Regulations." Securities and Exchange Commission, 2021.
[596] "Health Equity Considerations and Racial and Ethnic Minority Groups." Centers for Disease Control and Prevention, 2023.
[597] "African American Consumers are More Relevant Than Ever." Nielsen, 2019.

owning businesses in this sector, Black entrepreneurs can recirculate these dollars within the community, echoing Anderson's emphasis on the importance of internal trade in wealth creation[598].

Establishing supportive networks is also key to success in this industry. Black entrepreneurs need mentorship, resources, and access to industry contacts. Organizations such as the National Association of Health Services Executives and the Black Wellness Community are playing an important role in this regard[599].

Investment in the health and wellness industry represents a viable strategy for Black wealth creation. The community's unique cultural insights, coupled with proactive policy advocacy, and supportive networks, can help carve out a significant share in this booming industry while enhancing communal well-being.

A New Frontier for Black Wealth Creation and Environmental Responsibility

The rise of the green economy, expected to reach $48.36 trillion by 2026[600], signals a new frontier for Black wealth creation. Investing in sustainable practices can offer a twofold benefit: it fosters economic growth and promotes environmental responsibility. As we discuss this potential, it's important to consider the roadblocks and potential objections while showcasing the opportunities for wealth creation.

One criticism often lodged against the green economy is its perceived inaccessibility, owing to the high initial

---

[598] Anderson, Claud. Black Labor, White Wealth: The Search for Power and Economic Justice. Powernomics Corporation of America, 1994.
[599] "About Us." National Association of Health Services Executives, 2023. "About." Black Wellness Community, 2023.
[600] "Green Economy Market Report." Fortune Business Insights, 2021.

investment required for certain sectors, such as renewable energy. However, the green economy extends beyond these capital-intensive industries. It encompasses various sectors, including organic farming, green construction, and recycling, that can be started with a more modest capital outlay[601].

Another concern is the lack of representation of Black individuals in environmental conversations. The environmental movement is often criticized for its whiteness, which can result in Black people feeling excluded[602]. Yet, a number of Black environmentalists and entrepreneurs are making significant strides in this area, such as Majora Carter, an urban revitalization strategist, and George Bandy Jr., a sustainability officer at Mohawk Industries[603].

It is also worth noting the unique opportunities the green economy provides for wealth creation in the Black community. Black-owned businesses can position themselves as leaders in sustainability, attracting consumers who prioritize eco-friendly practices. It is estimated that 65% of consumers worldwide are buying goods based on beliefs, including environmental concerns[604].

Moreover, there are a growing number of government incentives and grants for sustainable business practices that Black entrepreneurs can leverage[605].

Just as important, adopting sustainable practices can lead to cost savings over the long term. Energy-efficient operations can significantly reduce utility costs, while waste

---

[601] "A Guide to Green Business Ideas." US Small Business Administration, 2023.
[602] Taylor, Dorceta. "The Rise of the American Conservation Movement: Power, Privilege, and Environmental Protection." Duke University Press, 2016.
[603] "Top 12 Environmental Leaders of Color to Watch in 2020." GreenBiz, 2020.
[604] "The Sustainable Consumer and the 2020s Holiday Shopping Season." Accenture, 2020.
[605] "Federal Grants for Green Businesses." Grants.gov, 2023.

reduction can save money on disposal[606]. These savings can be reinvested into the business, aiding in its growth and profitability.

In essence, the green economy represents a transformative opportunity for the Black community. It allows for wealth creation in a rapidly growing sector, while also promoting a sustainable future. With targeted support and increased representation, Black entrepreneurs can make significant inroads into this market, contributing to both their community's wealth and the health of our planet.

Wealth Preservation and Intergenerational Wealth Transfer in the Black Community

The importance of wealth preservation and legacy building cannot be overemphasized, particularly within the Black community. As much as we focus on wealth creation, equal attention should be paid to wealth preservation and the concept of intergenerational wealth transfer[607]. However, this notion often faces skepticism, as many argue that generational wealth is unachievable for communities historically disenfranchised, given systemic financial inequalities.

This sentiment is substantiated by data indicating that only 8% of Black families receive an inheritance as compared to 26% of white families[608]. Additionally, the average inheritance for Black families is just 35% of the amount white families receive[609]. It is undeniable that these

---

[606] "Sustainability: A 'Win-Win' for Small Businesses." US Chamber of Commerce, 2021.
[607] Darity, William, and A. Kirsten Mullen. "From Here to Equality: Reparations for Black Americans in the Twenty-First Century." The University of North Carolina Press, 2020.
[608] Hamilton, Darrick, and William Darity Jr. "The racial wealth gap: Why policy matters." Economic Policy Institute, 2017.
[609] Ibid

disparities exist, yet, they do not preclude the potential for change.

The keys to wealth preservation and legacy building within the Black community are financial education, proper estate planning, and investment in appreciating assets. Despite the challenges, many Black families have successfully created and passed on wealth. For instance, Black-owned businesses such as Johnson Products Company, the maker of Ultra Sheen and Afro Sheen, and Bridgeman Foods Inc., a successful franchisee of Wendy's and Chili's, have created significant wealth and impacted their communities positively[610].

There's also the misconception that legacy building solely pertains to the financial aspect. However, it extends beyond monetary value to include the transfer of values, work ethics, and business acumen. Individuals such as Robert F. Smith, founder of Vista Equity Partners, and Oprah Winfrey, a media mogul, have often underscored the importance of these non-monetary legacies[611].

Indeed, the path to wealth preservation and legacy building is fraught with obstacles. However, it is a journey worth embarking on for the longevity and prosperity of the Black community. By fostering a culture of savings, investing, and planning for the future, Black families can build wealth that withstands the test of time, effectively bridging the wealth gap.

Creating and maintaining wealth within the Black community requires a shift in mindset and strategy. This involves increased focus on education, community reinvestment, entrepreneurship, real estate ownership, business networks, improved access to capital, policy

---

[610] Anderson, Maggie. "Our Black Year: One Family's Quest to Buy Black in America's Racially Divided Economy." HarperCollins, 2013.
[611] Smith, Robert F. "Speech at the Morehouse College commencement." 2019.

advocacy, cultural heritage, technological innovation, health and wellness, sustainable practices, and ultimately, legacy building.

Chapter 7

Harnessing Determination and Responsibility for Black Wealth Creation And Resilience

In discussing wealth creation, a critical trait that comes to the forefront is persistence. This trait is particularly relevant in the context of the Black community's economic situation. Power of persistence, sometimes referred to as 'stick-to-itiveness', implies a steadfastness in doing something despite the challenges or setbacks that come along the way[612]

The Black community has historically faced systemic hurdles in the United States. Dr. Claud Anderson, in his work "A Black History Reader: 101 Question You Never Thought to Ask," extensively discusses these systematic challenges[613]. Yet, numerous success stories have emerged from the Black community, testifying to the indomitable spirit of persistence. Robert F. Smith, the richest African-American as of 2021[614], is one such example. Smith, through persistent efforts, built Vista Equity Partners, a notable private equity and venture capital firm, emphasizing that success is attainable despite the odds.

Persistence, however, is not universally recognized as a critical factor in wealth creation. Critics argue that focusing on individual traits like persistence oversimplifies the

---

[612] The Power of Persistence." American Psychological Association. https://www.apa.org/gradpsych/2012/11/persistence

[613] Anderson, Claud. A Black History Reader: 101 Question You Never Thought to Ask. PowerNomics Corporation of America, 2017.

[614] Soergel, Andrew. "Robert F. Smith: The richest black man in America." U.S. News & World Report, 2021. https://www.usnews.com/news/the-report/articles/2020-06-12/robert-f-smith-is-the-richest-black-man-in-america

complex factors affecting wealth creation, including systemic racism, social-economic factors, and the wealth gap's historical roots[615]. The Brookings Institution, for example, highlights systemic factors as key drivers of racial wealth disparity[616]. While recognizing the importance of these macro-level factors, it is vital not to underestimate the role of personal determination and resilience in navigating these complex challenges.

'Failing forward' is a concept closely tied to persistence. It suggests learning and growing from setbacks, effectively transforming these failures into steps towards success. Black individuals such as Madam C.J. Walker, America's first self-made female millionaire[617], have shown how to 'fail forward.' Walker faced numerous rejections before she succeeded, proving that setbacks could be stepping stones to success if approached with the right mindset.

But there is resistance to the 'failing forward' concept. Some critics point out that it may inadvertently normalize failure, possibly leading to complacency[618]. However, 'failing forward' doesn't advocate for normalizing failure; instead, it promotes learning from failure, using it as a tool for growth and improvement.

Taking responsibility is another vital aspect of wealth creation. It involves personal accountability for one's financial situation and decisions. Wealth creation requires making informed financial decisions, setting realistic goals,

---

[615] Darity, William Jr., and A. Kirsten Mullen. "What We Get Wrong About Closing the Wealth Gap." Samuel DuBois Cook Center on Social Equity and Insight Center for Community Economic Development, 2018. https://socialequity.duke.edu/wp-content/uploads/2020/01/what-we-get-wrong.pdf

[616] "Examining the Black-white wealth gap." Brookings Institution. https://www.brookings.edu/blog/up-front/2020/02/27/examining-the-black-white-wealth-gap/

[617] Bundles, A'Lelia. "Madam C.J. Walker Biography." Biography.com, 2021. https://www.biography.com/inventor/madam-cj-walker

[618] Burey, Jeb. "The Danger of Failing Forward: Normalizing Failure Has Its Own Risks." Medium, 2020. https://medium.com/swlh/the-danger-of-failing-forward-8b7e69c9c5ea

and taking responsibility for achieving them. For example, building wealth through savings and investments requires understanding these financial instruments and responsibly managing them.

While acknowledging the historical and systemic barriers faced by the Black community, it is imperative to harness personal power through persistence and responsibility in the journey towards wealth creation. By embracing these principles, individuals can actively contribute to the broader goal of economic empowerment, taking one step closer to closing the Black wealth gap.

The Role of Persistence In The Process of Wealth Creation

Persistence, in the realm of wealth creation, stands as a trait that is consistently celebrated for its merit. Notably, the journey of wealth accumulation is not one for the faint-hearted. It requires a blend of mental fortitude, consistent effort, and tenacity - all components of persistence. This notion finds resonance in the works of Dr. Claud Anderson, particularly in his exploration of power and economics within the Black community[619].

The role of persistence in wealth creation becomes especially significant in light of the economic hurdles experienced by Black Americans. Amid systemic impediments and generational wealth disparities, the creation of wealth is often a journey dotted with trials and tribulations. For instance, Robert F. Smith, celebrated as the wealthiest African-American as of 2021[620], stands as a

---

[619] Anderson, Claud. PowerNomics: The National Plan to Empower Black America. PowerNomics Corporation of America, 2001.
[620] Soergel, Andrew. "Robert F. Smith: The richest black man in America." U.S. News & World Report, 2021. https://www.usnews.com/news/the-report/articles/2020-06-12/robert-f-smith-is-the-richest-black-man-in-america

testament to the power of persistence. Despite a myriad of adversities, he founded Vista Equity Partners, illustrating that through consistent effort, economic victories can be achieved[621].

Yet, the perspective that emphasizes the role of individual attributes, such as persistence, in wealth creation is not without its critics. A school of thought argues that this focus may inadvertently understate the broader societal and structural elements at play[622]. Critics maintain that systemic racism and the longstanding wealth gap, underscored by historical and socio-political factors, demand more attention than individual qualities[623]. Despite these valid considerations, acknowledging these broader issues should not diminish the importance of personal resilience and persistence in navigating and overcoming these obstacles.

Furthermore, the notion of 'failing forward,' closely tied to persistence, promotes learning from setbacks and using them as stepping stones towards success[624]. This concept underpins the success stories of numerous Black individuals, Madam C.J. Walker being a prime example. As America's first self-made female millionaire, she faced numerous rejections before achieving her monumental success, thereby demonstrating the value of persistence and 'failing forward'[625].

Opponents of the 'failing forward' philosophy argue that it risks normalizing failure, possibly fostering

---

[621] Vista Equity Partners. https://www.vistaequitypartners.com/
[622] Darity, William Jr., and A. Kirsten Mullen. "What We Get Wrong About Closing the Wealth Gap." Samuel DuBois Cook Center on Social Equity and Insight Center for Community Economic Development, 2018. https://socialequity.duke.edu/wp-content/uploads/2020/01/what-we-get-wrong.pdf
[623] Hamilton, D., & Darity, W. (2017). The political economy of education, financial literacy, and the racial wealth gap. Federal Reserve Bank of St. Louis Review, 99(1), 59-76.
[624] Maxwell, John C. Failing Forward: Turning Mistakes into Stepping Stones for Success. Thomas Nelson, 2007.
[625] Bundles, A'Lelia. "Madam C.J. Walker Biography." Biography.com, 2021. https://www.biography.com/inventor/madam-cj-walker

complacency[626]. However, 'failing forward' does not promote accepting failure as the norm, but instead advocates for harnessing failure as a learning tool, an aspect critical to the journey of wealth creation.

Persistence plays a critical role in the process of wealth creation, more so in the context of overcoming systemic challenges. As such, individuals must harness the power of persistence, demonstrating determination and resilience in the face of adversity, and ultimately propelling themselves towards their financial goals. By adhering to this principle, individuals can actively contribute to the broader goal of economic empowerment, aiding in the closing of the Black wealth gap.

Discussion On How Determination And Perseverance Contribute To Financial Success

The connection between determination, perseverance, and financial success is a widely discussed topic in the field of wealth creation. Its foundation lies in the belief that financial prosperity requires more than mere opportunity. Dr. Claud Anderson echoed this sentiment, stating, "Determination is not an occasional thing, it is an everyday matter, a lifestyle"[627].

An empirical study conducted by the University of Pennsylvania demonstrated that grit, a trait encompassing determination and perseverance, positively correlates with long-term financial success. Participants exhibiting higher levels of grit were likely to achieve better financial

---

[626] Burey, Jeb. "The Danger of Failing Forward: Normalizing Failure Has Its Own Risks." Medium, 2020. https://medium.com/swlh/the-danger-of-failing-forward-8b7e69c9c5ea

[627] Anderson, Claud. PowerNomics: The National Plan to Empower Black America. PowerNomics Corporation of America, 2001.

outcomes over a ten-year period[628]. This study lends support to the argument that a determined and tenacious approach facilitates the accumulation of wealth.

However, the notion that determination and perseverance alone can pave the way to financial success is not universally accepted. Critics argue that such a perspective may overlook the impact of systemic factors and socioeconomic background on an individual's financial success[629]. They assert that personal attributes do not function in a vacuum, and the socio-economic context cannot be undermined[630].

Yet, highlighting the significance of determination and perseverance in financial success does not dismiss these structural factors. Instead, it emphasizes that these traits can aid individuals in navigating and overcoming such obstacles. The journey of Chris Gardner, whose life story was popularized in the movie "The Pursuit of Happyness," provides an illuminating example. Despite being homeless, Gardner, through his determination and perseverance, successfully established a multi-million dollar brokerage firm[631].

Another critique of the importance placed on determination and perseverance is that it may promote a culture of overwork, leading to burnout[632]. While persistence is vital, a balance must be struck between working hard and maintaining mental and physical health.

---

[628] Duckworth, Angela L., et al. "Grit: perseverance and passion for long-term goals." Journal of Personality and Social Psychology 92, no. 6 (2007): 1087.

[629] Hamilton, D., & Darity, W. (2017). The political economy of education, financial literacy, and the racial wealth gap. Federal Reserve Bank of St. Louis Review, 99(1), 59-76.

[630] Chetty, Raj, et al. "The fading American dream: Trends in absolute income mobility since 1940." Science 356.6336 (2017): 398-406.

[631] Gardner, Chris, and Mim Eichler Rivas. The Pursuit of Happyness. Harper Collins, 2006.

[632] Henson, Katie. "The Culture of Overwork: Why We Need a Balance." Medium, 2021. https://medium.com/the-innovation/the-culture-of-overwork-why-we-need-a-balance-27a5c04f9c83

Importantly, perseverance should not equate to relentless toil at the expense of personal well-being.

Consequently, the role of determination and perseverance in financial success is not without its complexities. Despite the challenges and opposing views, a core truth persists - determination and perseverance remain crucial components of financial success. These traits help individuals to remain committed to their financial goals, face adversities courageously, and seize opportunities effectively, all of which are integral to achieving financial success.

Case Studies Illustrating The Power of Persistence In Overcoming Financial Challenges

The power of persistence in overcoming financial challenges and securing economic prosperity can be illustrated through several compelling case studies. The narratives of Madam C.J. Walker, Robert F. Smith, and George Fraser bear testament to the crucial role that persistence plays in wealth creation.

Madam C.J. Walker, born Sarah Breedlove, became the first self-made female millionaire in America despite being born to formerly enslaved parents[633]. After years of facing poverty and hardship, Walker's persistence led her to create a highly successful line of hair products for black women. As a result, Walker's wealth was not merely the product of a profitable business idea, but a testament to her unwavering resolve to uplift herself and her community from poverty. Her life's work demonstrates the transformative power of persistence, even in the face of immense adversity.

---

[633] Bundles, A'Lelia. On Her Own Ground: The Life and Times of Madam C.J. Walker. Scribner, 2001.

However, a critique of such narratives is the potential for confirmation bias, or the tendency to seek information that confirms pre-existing beliefs while ignoring data that contradicts these views[634]. Critics argue that highlighting such exceptional cases may overshadow the reality of numerous individuals who, despite persistence, fail to break free from the cycles of poverty due to systemic factors[635].

Yet, persistence doesn't solely belong to the realm of entrepreneurship. Robert F. Smith, a financier, and philanthropist, has demonstrated the role of persistence in the corporate world. As the founder of the investment firm Vista Equity Partners, Smith is considered the wealthiest African American, surpassing even Oprah Winfrey[636]. His persistence allowed him to break barriers in the largely white-dominated world of private equity, ultimately leading him to an unparalleled level of financial success.

Similarly, George Fraser, the founder and CEO of FraserNet, Inc., started his journey in a poor neighborhood in Brooklyn, New York. Despite being an orphan and battling dyslexia, Fraser's unwavering determination and perseverance led him to become a successful entrepreneur, networking guru, and author[637]. His story underscores the power of persistence in overcoming personal and societal challenges to create and maintain wealth.

In sum, these cases offer powerful illustrations of the role of persistence in overcoming financial hurdles. The

---

[634] Nickerson, Raymond S. "Confirmation bias: A ubiquitous phenomenon in many guises." Review of General Psychology 2.2 (1998): 175-220.

[635] Chetty, Raj, et al. "Race and economic opportunity in the United States: An intergenerational perspective." The Quarterly Journal of Economics 135.2 (2020): 711-783.

[636] Stankorb, Sarah. "Robert F. Smith: The billionaire who is trying to cleanse his reputation." Bloomberg.com, 2021. https://www.bloomberg.com/news/features/2021-02-18/robert-f-smith-vista-equity-billionaire-seeks-redemption-after-tax-case

[637] Fraser, George. Click: Ten Truths for Building Extraordinary Relationships. McGraw Hill Professional, 2008.

narratives of Walker, Smith, and Fraser underline the belief that with unwavering determination and tenacity, one can forge a path to financial prosperity despite daunting obstacles.

The Concept of Stick-To-Itiveness In The Face of Setbacks

In the economic journey towards prosperity, especially within the Black community, one's attitude towards setbacks plays a pivotal role. The term 'stick-to-itiveness' aptly encapsulates this perspective, representing an individual's perseverance and tenacity in pursuing their goals, even in the face of adversity.

In the context of wealth creation, 'stick-to-itiveness' is a critical success factor. According to a study by Gartner, individuals who display a high degree of stick-to-itiveness are twice as likely to succeed in their ventures as those who do not[638]. This resilience, grit, or relentless pursuit of goals, as Angela Duckworth terms it, is often a distinguishing factor between those who ultimately accumulate wealth and those who don't[639].

Critics, however, point out that such narratives of perseverance and resilience may lead to an oversimplification of systemic economic challenges, particularly those faced by the Black community[640]. They argue that emphasizing individual stick-to-itiveness may overlook the larger structural impediments to wealth creation. Yet, while acknowledging these systemic barriers,

---

[638] Pan, Yuhao, et al. "Grit: A predictor of risk-taking behavior and resilience." Personality and Individual Differences 149 (2019): 35-40.

[639] Duckworth, Angela. Grit: The Power of Passion and Perseverance. Scribner, 2016.

[640] Wilson, Valerie, and William M. Rodgers. "Black-white wage gaps expand with rising wage inequality." Economic Policy Institute, 2016.

the importance of stick-to-itiveness should not be underplayed.

Dr. Claud Anderson, an advocate for economic empowerment within the Black community, exemplifies this perspective[641]. His approach is rooted in the belief that while systemic factors undoubtedly impact the Black community's wealth creation, the potential for individuals to overcome these challenges through grit, determination, and resilience should not be discounted.

A compelling real-world example of stick-to-itiveness is the story of Black entrepreneur John H. Johnson, who faced numerous rejections before successfully establishing Johnson Publishing Company, a media empire that included Ebony and Jet magazines[642]. Johnson's story underscores the essence of stick-to-itiveness, demonstrating that persistence in the face of setbacks can ultimately lead to financial success.

In addition, Dr. Dennis Kimbro's research on wealthy and successful Black Americans reveals that one commonality among these individuals is a high degree of stick-to-itiveness[643]. Despite the obstacles they faced, these individuals remained unwavering in their pursuit of wealth and success, underscoring the importance of perseverance.

The concept of stick-to-itiveness serves as a powerful guiding principle in the journey towards wealth creation. While it is essential to recognize and challenge systemic economic barriers, the role of individual determination and resilience should not be understated.

---

[641] Anderson, Claud. PowerNomics: The National Plan to Empower Black America. PowerNomics Corporation of America, 2001.
[642] Johnson, John H. Succeeding Against the Odds. Warner Books, 1989.
[643] Kimbro, Dennis. The Wealth Choice: Success Secrets of Black Millionaires. Palgrave Macmillan, 2013.

A Deep Dive Into The Importance of Resilience In The Wealth Creation Journey

Resilience, the ability to bounce back from adversity, plays an invaluable role in the wealth creation journey. The road to economic prosperity is often fraught with obstacles and setbacks. The resilience to endure and overcome these hurdles, therefore, distinguishes those who ultimately achieve their financial goals from those who do not.

Multiple research studies attest to the link between resilience and financial success. One such study conducted by Smith and Krueger found a correlation between resilience and entrepreneurial success, a major path to wealth creation[644]. The researchers note that entrepreneurs who possess a high degree of resilience are better equipped to navigate business failures and market downturns, consequently contributing to their overall wealth accumulation.

However, some critics argue that an excessive focus on individual resilience could deflect attention from the systemic barriers impeding wealth creation, particularly within the Black community[645]. While acknowledging these structural impediments, resilience remains an indispensable quality for wealth creation.

Dr. Claud Anderson, a prominent advocate for Black economic empowerment, frequently underscores the importance of resilience[646]. He argues that even in the face of systemic challenges, the Black community can harness

---

[644] Smith, Brent, and Richard Krueger. "Resilience and Entrepreneurship: A Dynamic and Contextual View." Entrepreneurship Research Journal 8, no. 3 (2018).

[645] Hamilton, Darrick, et al. "Umbrellas Don't Make it Rain: Why Studying and Working Hard Isn't Enough for Black Americans." The New School, Milano, 2015.

[646] Anderson, Claud. PowerNomics: The National Plan to Empower Black America. PowerNomics Corporation of America, 2001.

their resilience to drive wealth accumulation and economic independence.

Examining real-world case studies further highlights the importance of resilience in wealth creation. For instance, consider the example of Madam C.J. Walker, often hailed as America's first self-made Black female millionaire[647]. Despite enduring numerous adversities including poverty, lack of formal education, and racial discrimination, Walker's resilience propelled her to establish a successful beauty products empire. Her story underscores how resilience can be a powerful tool in overcoming financial challenges and creating wealth.

Furthermore, a research study by Marcus, a subsidiary of Goldman Sachs, found that high-resilience individuals are significantly more likely to possess emergency savings, have a retirement plan, and display a disciplined approach towards debt management - all critical aspects of wealth creation[648].

Resilience is a pivotal element in the wealth creation journey. While it is crucial to address and combat systemic economic challenges, the role of individual resilience in facilitating wealth accumulation should not be underestimated.

Providing Strategies For Developing A Resilient Mindset In Dealing With Financial Hurdles

Creating a resilient mindset is vital for tackling financial obstacles and promoting wealth creation. It's about adapting a perspective that views challenges as

---

[647] Bundles, A'Lelia. On Her Own Ground: The Life and Times of Madam C.J. Walker. Scribner, 2001.
[648] Marcus by Goldman Sachs. "Financial Resilience in America." Goldman Sachs, 2021.

opportunities for growth, rather than as insurmountable problems.

Firstly, embracing a growth mindset, as posited by psychologist Carol Dweck, is a key strategy for building resilience[649]. This mindset celebrates effort over innate talent, viewing abilities and intelligence as malleable rather than fixed. In the context of wealth creation, this approach encourages individuals to view financial challenges as opportunities for learning and growth, rather than as signs of inherent limitations.

However, critics argue that the growth mindset alone is not sufficient, highlighting that a systemic understanding of economic disparities is essential. Still, Dweck's concept provides a significant individual-level psychological tool in the financial resilience toolkit[650].

Secondly, practicing mindfulness can significantly contribute to financial resilience. Mindfulness involves staying present and accepting the current situation without judgment[651]. In financial matters, mindfulness can help individuals remain calm during economic downturns or personal financial setbacks, allowing for more rational decision-making.

Dr. Claud Anderson frequently underscores the importance of perseverance and self-belief for economic resilience. He advocates for maintaining a clear vision of financial goals, despite the inevitable challenges that arise[652]. This consistent focus on long-term objectives can foster resilience in the face of short-term financial setbacks.

---

[649] Dweck, Carol S. Mindset: The New Psychology of Success. Random House, 2006.

[650] Aldridge, Susan. "The Growth Mindset Debate." Inside Higher Ed, 2019.

[651] Kabat-Zinn, Jon. Full Catastrophe Living: Using the Wisdom of Your Body and Mind to Face Stress, Pain, and Illness. Delta Trade Paperbacks, 2005.

[652] Anderson, Claud. PowerNomics: The National Plan to Empower Black America. PowerNomics Corporation of America, 2001.

Additionally, maintaining a positive perspective, even in the face of adversity, can enhance financial resilience. Research by psychologist Barbara Fredrickson, known as the Broaden-and-Build Theory, suggests that positive emotions can broaden people's thought-action repertoires, enabling them to build lasting personal resources[653]. Therefore, cultivating positivity may help individuals devise creative solutions to financial challenges, thus contributing to wealth creation.

Lastly, seeking social support can significantly foster financial resilience. Whether it's seeking advice from a financial advisor or sharing experiences with peers facing similar financial challenges, social support can provide valuable insights and emotional relief[654].

A resilient mindset in dealing with financial hurdles involves embracing a growth mindset, practicing mindfulness, maintaining a positive perspective, focusing on long-term financial goals, and seeking social support.

Turning Challenges Into Opportunities

Facing economic challenges is an inherent aspect of the wealth creation journey. Dr. Claud Anderson, in his pivotal works, asserts that these setbacks are not mere obstacles but stepping stones towards success and financial freedom[655]. Turning challenges into opportunities requires a paradigm shift: adopting a resilient mindset and implementing strategic action.

---

[653] Fredrickson, Barbara L. "The Broaden-and-Build Theory of Positive Emotions." Philosophical Transactions of the Royal Society of London. Series B: Biological Sciences 359, no. 1449 (2004): 1367-1378.

[654] Cutrona, Carolyn E. "Social Support in Couples: Marriage as a Resource in Times of Stress." Sage Publications, Inc., 1996.

[655] Anderson, Claud. PowerNomics: The National Plan to Empower Black America. PowerNomics Corporation of America, 2001.

According to a study by the Brookings Institution, African Americans face significant financial challenges due to historical and ongoing racial wealth gaps[656]. However, Dr. Anderson argues that these challenges, although formidable, should not be viewed as insurmountable barriers but as catalysts for change and innovation[657].

Case in point: The 2008 recession, while causing widespread financial distress, was also a period when numerous resilient entrepreneurs turned adversity into opportunity. Despite the dire economic landscape, these individuals created solutions that addressed new market needs resulting from the crisis, generating wealth in the process[658].

On the other hand, critics argue that individual perseverance and resilience are not enough to overcome systemic issues. They argue that focusing on individual 'grit' tends to overshadow systemic problems like racial discrimination in housing, education, and employment sectors[659].

However, while acknowledging systemic barriers, Dr. Anderson emphasizes the power of economic self-determination. His philosophy, heavily influenced by Booker T. Washington's self-help ideologies, asserts that economic power precedes political power, and encourages African Americans to collectively invest and recycle dollars within their own communities[660].

---

[656] Hamilton, D., & Darity, W. "The racial wealth gap: Why policy matters." Brookings Institution, 2017.

[657] Fairlie, Robert. "Kauffman Index of Entrepreneurial Activity 1996–2010." Ewing Marion Kauffman Foundation, 2011.

[658] Bonilla-Silva, Eduardo. Racism without Racists: Color-Blind Racism and the Persistence of Racial Inequality in America. Rowman & Littlefield, 2017.

[659] Dweck, Carol S. Mindset: The New Psychology of Success. Random House, 2006.

[660] Lown, Jean M. "Development and Validation of a Financial Self-Efficacy Scale." Journal of Financial Counseling and Planning, 2011.

Developing an opportunity-oriented perspective is crucial. This perspective sees setbacks not as failures but as feedback providing valuable lessons for improvement[661]. Moreover, embracing an attitude of lifelong learning and flexibility allows individuals to adapt their strategies in response to changes in their financial environment.

Maintaining a sense of responsibility and control over personal finances is equally essential. Financial self-efficacy can motivate individuals to actively improve their financial situation rather than feel helpless about their circumstances[662]. This attitude allows them to make informed decisions and take actionable steps towards their financial goals, even amidst setbacks.

Finally, seeking financial literacy and education can equip individuals with the knowledge and skills to navigate financial challenges effectively. Armed with this knowledge, they can make informed financial decisions and convert financial setbacks into opportunities for growth and wealth accumulation[663].

Transforming setbacks into opportunities is a process that necessitates a resilient mindset, strategic action, financial self-efficacy, and ongoing financial education. While systemic barriers exist, this does not negate the power of individual agency and collective economic action in the pursuit of financial success.

---

[661] Dweck, Carol S. Mindset: The New Psychology of Success. Random House, 2006.
[662] Lown, Jean M. "Development and Validation of a Financial Self-Efficacy Scale." Journal of Financial Counseling and Planning, 2011.
[663] Huston, Sandra J. "Measuring Financial Literacy." The Journal of Consumer Affairs, 2010.

Analyzing How Financial Setbacks Can Be Transformed Into Opportunities For Growth

Financial setbacks can be daunting, yet they provide an exceptional opportunity for growth and evolution[664]. Dr. Claud Anderson, in his seminal works, often emphasizes the importance of learning from adversity and using it as a launching pad for financial success[665].

In 2008, the world faced an economic downturn which resulted in significant financial stress for many. Yet, a study from the Kauffman Foundation noted that this period saw an unprecedented surge in entrepreneurship[666]. Individuals leveraged the unique challenges of the recession to create new businesses, effectively turning a setback into a platform for growth.

Nonetheless, critics point out that entrepreneurial success amidst economic crises represents a small percentage and tends to downplay systemic issues that inhibit most individuals from doing the same[667]. They argue that structural economic inequalities disproportionately affect people of color, making it harder for them to convert setbacks into opportunities.

Anderson acknowledges these systemic barriers but asserts that economic self-determination is a powerful tool to combat these inequalities[668]. He posits that by recycling dollars within their own communities and establishing Black-owned businesses, African Americans can convert

---

[664] Lusardi, Annamaria, and Peter Tufano. "Debt literacy, financial experiences, and overindebtedness." Journal of Pension Economics & Finance, 2009.

[665] Anderson, Claud. PowerNomics: The National Plan to Empower Black America. PowerNomics Corporation of America, 2001.

[666] Fairlie, Robert. "Kauffman Index of Entrepreneurial Activity 1996–2010." Ewing Marion Kauffman Foundation, 2011.

[667] Hamilton, D., & Darity, W. "The racial wealth gap: Why policy matters." Brookings Institution, 2017.

[668] Anderson, Claud. PowerNomics: The National Plan to Empower Black America. PowerNomics Corporation of America, 2001.

systemic setbacks into opportunities for collective economic empowerment.

Furthermore, financial setbacks can be transformed into opportunities for personal development. Such adversities can provide the motivation to develop financial literacy and money management skills[669]. A study published in the Journal of Economic Psychology found that those who experienced financial hardship were more likely to seek out financial education and consequently improve their financial behavior[670].

Critics of this approach suggest that focusing on personal financial responsibility ignores the systemic factors that contribute to financial hardship[671]. However, while recognizing these systemic influences, Dr. Anderson emphasizes the importance of personal agency and responsibility in financial success.

Turning setbacks into opportunities also requires the cultivation of a growth mindset[672]. This concept, coined by psychologist Carol Dweck, encourages individuals to view challenges not as failures, but as learning experiences. By doing so, they can adapt their strategies and continue to pursue their financial goals.

Transforming financial setbacks into opportunities for growth is a multifaceted process. It requires the cultivation of a growth mindset, the development of financial literacy, and the exercise of economic self-determination. While systemic barriers exist, they can be navigated through

---

[669] Huston, Sandra J. "Measuring Financial Literacy." The Journal of Consumer Affairs, 2010.

[670] Perry, Vanessa G., and Marlene D. Morris. "Who Is in Control? The Role of Self-Perception, Knowledge, and Income in Explaining Consumer Financial Behavior." Journal of Consumer Affairs, 2005.

[671] Bertrand, Marianne, and Adair Morse. "Trickle-Down Consumption." Review of Economics and Statistics, 2016.

[672] Dweck, Carol S. Mindset: The New Psychology of Success. Random House, 2006.

collective economic action and personal financial empowerment.

Offering Methods To Adapt And Learn From Financial Failures

Adapting and learning from financial failures is a pivotal step in the journey towards financial success[673]. In the style of Dr. Claud Anderson, who espouses resilience, self-determination, and knowledge as core tenets of financial empowerment[674], let's delve into the methods by which one can leverage financial failures for growth.

The first strategy lies in cultivating financial literacy. According to a report by the Financial Industry Regulatory Authority (FINRA), over two-thirds of Americans are not financially literate[675]. This lack of knowledge often precedes financial mishaps. Education in financial management, debt handling, and investment strategies can prevent these missteps and transform past failures into future successes. Despite the efficacy of financial education, critics argue that it unfairly places responsibility on the individual and overlooks systemic inequalities[676]. However, Anderson would assert that both systemic change and individual accountability are necessary for financial progress[677].

Secondly, resilience is key in learning from financial failures. Carol Dweck's concept of a 'growth mindset'

---

[673] Lusardi, Annamaria, and Peter Tufano. "Debt literacy, financial experiences, and overindebtedness." Journal of Pension Economics & Finance, 2009.

[674] Anderson, Claud. PowerNomics: The National Plan to Empower Black America. PowerNomics Corporation of America, 2001.

[675] Financial Industry Regulatory Authority. "Financial Capability in the United States 2016." FINRA Investor Education Foundation, 2016.

[676] Hamilton, D., & Darity, W. "The racial wealth gap: Why policy matters." Brookings Institution, 2017.

[677] Anderson, Claud. PowerNomics: The National Plan to Empower Black America. PowerNomics Corporation of America, 2001.

speaks to the ability to see failure as a springboard for growth rather than a dead-end[678]. Resilience in the face of financial setbacks can be fostered through mindfulness techniques and psychological counseling, which have been shown to improve stress resilience[679]. Critics of this strategy may argue that focusing on mindset neglects structural issues. Yet, as Anderson's work suggests, the cultivation of a resilient mindset complements, rather than replaces, systemic interventions[680].

Finally, seeking professional advice can be invaluable. Financial advisors can provide tailored strategies to navigate financial failures and prevent future ones[681]. They offer an external perspective and the expertise to guide financial decisions. Critics might cite the cost of such services as prohibitive, especially for those already facing financial challenges. However, according to a Vanguard study, financial advisors can add about 3% in net returns for their clients, often offsetting the cost[682].

In essence, the path to adapting and learning from financial failures involves a multifaceted approach of increasing financial literacy, cultivating resilience, and seeking professional advice. While critics point to systemic issues that constrain individual action, Anderson's philosophy suggests that personal responsibility and empowerment can coexist with broader structural changes.

---

[678] Dweck, Carol S. Mindset: The New Psychology of Success. Random House, 2006.

[679] Goldin, Philippe R., and James J. Gross. "Effects of mindfulness-based stress reduction (MBSR) on emotion regulation in social anxiety disorder." Emotion, 2010.

[680] Anderson, Claud. PowerNomics: The National Plan to Empower Black America. PowerNomics Corporation of America, 2001.

[681] Bhattacharya, Utpal, Benjamin Loos, Steffen Meyer, and Andreas Hackethal. "Abusing Financial Advice." The Review of Financial Studies, 2012.

[682] Kinniry Jr., Francis M., Colleen M. Jaconetti, Michael A. DiJoseph, and Yan Zilbering. "Putting a value on your value: Quantifying Vanguard Advisor's Alpha." Vanguard Research, 2014.

Discussing The Concept of 'Failing Forward' And Its Role In Building Financial Resilience

In the quest to build financial resilience, the concept of 'failing forward' plays an essential role[683]. As Dr. Claud Anderson emphasizes, the journey to economic empowerment is not without setbacks, but the ability to convert these failures into stepping stones toward success is a testament to one's resilience and determination[684].

'Failing forward,' a term popularized by John Maxwell, suggests that failure can indeed serve as a launchpad for growth and learning[685]. In the context of finance, this means taking stock of financial mistakes and using the gleaned insights to make improved decisions in the future. For instance, a 2019 study by the Federal Reserve discovered that over 40% of Americans wouldn't be able to cover a $400 emergency expense without borrowing or selling something[686]. Individuals who have faced such financial emergencies can leverage these experiences to prioritize building an emergency fund, thereby 'failing forward.'

Despite the optimism associated with 'failing forward,' critics might argue that it oversimplifies the complexity of financial failure. Systemic barriers and unforeseen circumstances can lead to setbacks that are not necessarily the result of poor decision-making[687]. Yet, in Dr. Anderson's view, acknowledging these broader socio-economic factors

---

[683] Maxwell, John C. Failing Forward: Turning Mistakes into Stepping Stones for Success. Thomas Nelson Inc, 2000.
[684] Anderson, Claud. PowerNomics: The National Plan to Empower Black America. PowerNomics Corporation of America, 2001.
[685] Maxwell, John C. Failing Forward: Turning Mistakes into Stepping Stones for Success. Thomas Nelson Inc, 2000.
[686] Board of Governors of the Federal Reserve System. "Report on the Economic Well-Being of U.S. Households in 2018." 2019.
[687] Hamilton, D., & Darity, W. "The racial wealth gap: Why policy matters." Brookings Institution, 2017.

doesn't negate the potential for personal growth and self-determination[688].

Another way to 'fail forward' is by taking calculated financial risks, such as starting a business or investing in the stock market. While these endeavors can result in financial losses, they also provide invaluable lessons. As per a Small Business Administration report, about 50% of small businesses fail within the first five years[689]. However, many successful entrepreneurs have used these initial failures as lessons, ultimately contributing to their eventual success.

Again, critics might point out that the opportunity to take risks is not equally distributed, and for some, a failed business venture could lead to devastating consequences. While this criticism is valid, it aligns with Dr. Anderson's emphasis on the need for a systemic change in creating an environment conducive to financial risk-taking and recovery[690].

The concept of 'failing forward' is an integral part of building financial resilience. It is about transforming financial mistakes into opportunities for learning and growth. While acknowledging systemic factors that contribute to financial failure, Dr. Anderson's philosophy aligns with the belief that individual resilience and the determination to 'fail forward' can significantly contribute to financial success.

---

[688] Anderson, Claud. PowerNomics: The National Plan to Empower Black America. PowerNomics Corporation of America, 2001.
[689] U.S. Small Business Administration. "Small Business Facts." 2018.
[690] Anderson, Claud. PowerNomics: The National Plan to Empower Black America. PowerNomics Corporation of America, 2001.

Responsibility And Accountability: Vital Components of The Wealth Creation Process

Building wealth, as emphasized by Dr. Claud Anderson, is a journey that necessitates personal responsibility and accountability[691]. These values, which entail taking charge of one's financial decisions and owning the consequences, form the foundation of sustainable wealth creation.

Personal responsibility in wealth creation starts with financial literacy – understanding how money works and how to manage it[692]. Data from the National Financial Educators Council shows that a significant portion of Americans – almost 41% – admit that a lack of financial knowledge was the most impactful element that held them back from making sound financial decisions[693]. Critics may argue that external circumstances play a more significant role in one's financial well-being. However, as Anderson would posit, such external factors, while not to be disregarded, should not overshadow the empowering role of financial literacy and personal responsibility[694].

Accountability, the counterpart of responsibility, is another vital component of the wealth creation process. It entails owning the outcomes of one's financial decisions, whether they result in profit or loss. For instance, an individual might decide to invest in the stock market. If the stocks perform poorly, it could result in significant financial loss. The practice of accountability is to accept this outcome,

---

[691] Anderson, Claud. PowerNomics: The National Plan to Empower Black America. PowerNomics Corporation of America, 2001.
[692] Lusardi, Annamaria, and Olivia S. Mitchell. "The Economic Importance of Financial Literacy: Theory and Evidence." Journal of Economic Literature, vol. 52, no. 1, 2014, pp. 5–44.
[693] National Financial Educators Council. "Financial Illiteracy Impacts - Americans State Lack of Financial Knowledge Inflicted Financial Harm." 2020.
[694] Anderson, Claud. PowerNomics: The National Plan to Empower Black America. PowerNomics Corporation of America, 2001.

learn from it, and make more informed decisions in the future[695].

Nevertheless, there are opposing viewpoints that suggest focusing on personal accountability may lead to victim-blaming and overlook systemic issues contributing to wealth disparity, such as institutionalized racism or socioeconomic disadvantages[696]. While these systemic issues undoubtedly play a role, Anderson emphasizes that they do not preclude the importance of personal responsibility and accountability in the wealth creation process[697].

Furthermore, Anderson contends that responsibility and accountability extend beyond the individual, encompassing the community as a whole^1^. Through collective economic strategies such as pooling resources and supporting local businesses, communities can contribute to shared wealth creation.

Responsibility and accountability, both on an individual and community level, are crucial components of the wealth creation process. Acknowledging systemic issues that contribute to financial inequality, Anderson's philosophy underscores the empowering potential of these principles. By adopting responsibility for one's financial literacy and holding oneself accountable for financial decisions, individuals can navigate the path to financial success more effectively.

---

[695] Siegel, Jeremy J. Stocks for the Long Run: The Definitive Guide to Financial Market Returns and Long-Term Investment Strategies. McGraw-Hill, 2007.

[696] Hamilton, D., & Darity, W. "The racial wealth gap: Why policy matters." Brookings Institution, 2017.

[697] Anderson, Claud. PowerNomics: The National Plan to Empower Black America. PowerNomics Corporation of America, 2001.

Discussing How Personal Responsibility Contributes To Achieving Financial Goals

Achieving financial goals, as reflected in Dr. Claud Anderson's philosophy, significantly depends on personal responsibility[698]. This crucial attribute guides individuals' financial behaviors, which include income generation, saving, investing, and even philanthropy.

Personal responsibility, in this context, involves making informed and intentional decisions about one's financial matters[699]. An example of such a decision is choosing to save a portion of one's income consistently, a strategy recommended by financial experts[700]. By taking responsibility for their savings, individuals can gradually accumulate wealth and attain their financial objectives. The Federal Reserve reported that 63% of Americans who regularly save for their future feel financially healthy, indicating the importance of this decision[701].

An opposing viewpoint often posited is that personal circumstances, such as low income, can hinder individuals from fulfilling this responsibility. Critics argue that financial health is largely determined by societal structures, such as wage inequalities and systemic racism, more than personal responsibility[702]. While these societal issues should not be overlooked, Anderson insists that personal responsibility is still a powerful tool for financial progress. He advocates for strategic maneuvers such as pooling

---

[698] Anderson, Claud. PowerNomics: The National Plan to Empower Black America. PowerNomics Corporation of America, 2001.
[699] Sherraden, Michael. "Financial Capability: What Is It, and How Can It Be Created?" Center for Social Development, Washington University, 2010.
[700] Bera, Sophia. "The Importance of Saving Money: 7 Reasons to Start Saving Today." Gen Y Planning, 2016.
[701] Board of Governors of the Federal Reserve System. "Report on the Economic Well-Being of U.S. Households in 2020."
[702] Hamilton, D., & Darity, W. "The racial wealth gap: Why policy matters." Brookings Institution, 2017.

resources within communities and harnessing the power of group economics to overcome these structural limitations[703].

Beyond saving, personal responsibility extends to debt management. Consider the American context, where the total household debt stood at approximately $14.56 trillion in 2021[704]. Many individuals find themselves in this predicament due to reasons such as lack of planning, impulsive spending, or poor financial literacy. By taking personal responsibility, individuals can develop effective debt management strategies, like creating a budget, adhering to it, and seeking financial education to make better choices in the future.

However, this perspective of personal responsibility in debt management is often critiqued as well. Detractors argue that factors like predatory lending practices or unanticipated health expenses are often more to blame for high levels of personal debt[705]. While these factors certainly contribute, Anderson would still contend that personal responsibility, coupled with financial literacy, can empower individuals to avoid or navigate these challenging situations more effectively[706].

personal responsibility is a fundamental element in achieving financial goals, despite the legitimate structural challenges that exist. By taking control of financial decisions, from saving to debt management, individuals can make substantial strides towards their financial aspirations.

---

[703] Anderson, Claud. PowerNomics: The National Plan to Empower Black America. PowerNomics Corporation of America, 2001.

[704] Federal Reserve Bank of New York. "Household Debt and Credit Report." 2021.

[705] Sweet, Ken. "Americans face a post-COVID-19 flood of personal debt, NY Fed warns." Fortune, 2021.

[706] Anderson, Claud. PowerNomics: The National Plan to Empower Black America. PowerNomics Corporation of America, 2001.

Blacks Need To Focus On Wealth Creation And Creating Their Own Labor Forces

Dr. Claud Anderson, in his groundbreaking work "PowerNomics," asserts that for the Black community to achieve economic empowerment, they must prioritize wealth creation and developing their own labor forces[707]. This approach involves not just earning, but also saving, investing, and creating jobs within the community.

A significant aspect of wealth creation is the cultivation of assets. As reported by the Federal Reserve, the median net worth for White families was ten times greater than for Black families in 2019[708]. This stark racial wealth gap suggests the urgent need for wealth accumulation within the Black community. Anderson suggests strategies such as promoting entrepreneurship and supporting Black-owned businesses, which, according to a study by the Association for Enterprise Opportunity, could generate $55 billion and create 600,000 new jobs annually[709].

An opposing perspective may argue that focusing solely on wealth creation within the Black community can lead to isolation and hinder collaboration with other racial and ethnic groups[710]. However, Anderson maintains that self-reliance and cooperation within the community is not mutually exclusive with building external alliances[711].

The creation of their own labor forces is another crucial part of Anderson's vision. He advocates for skills development and vocational training within the community

---

[707] Anderson, Claud. PowerNomics: The National Plan to Empower Black America. PowerNomics Corporation of America, 2001.
[708] Federal Reserve System. "Survey of Consumer Finances." 2019.
[709] Association for Enterprise Opportunity. "The Tapestry of Black Business Ownership in America." 2017.
[710] Scott, James C. "The Art of Not Being Governed: An Anarchist History of Upland Southeast Asia." Yale University Press, 2009.
[711] Anderson, Claud. PowerNomics: The National Plan to Empower Black America. PowerNomics Corporation of America, 2001.

to decrease unemployment rates and encourage economic independence. The U.S. Bureau of Labor Statistics reported in 2020 that the unemployment rate for Black workers was nearly twice that of white workers[712]. By creating their own labor forces, the Black community could address this issue more directly.

Critics of this viewpoint may posit that focusing on internal labor forces may limit opportunities to gain diverse skills and experiences in broader labor markets[713]. Nonetheless, Anderson contends that establishing a robust internal labor force can provide a secure foundation from which individuals can then explore opportunities beyond their communities[714].

The dual strategy of focusing on wealth creation and developing their own labor forces can provide a pathway for the Black community to achieve economic empowerment. Despite the potential critiques, such an approach emphasizes self-reliance and community resilience, which are vital for sustainable economic progress.

---

[712] Bureau of Labor Statistics. "Labor Force Characteristics by Race and Ethnicity, 2018." 2020.
[713] Cutcher, Leanne, and David Grant. "Demystifying Diversity in Organizational Culture." Routledge, 2020.
[714] Anderson, Claud. PowerNomics: The National Plan to Empower Black America. PowerNomics Corporation of America, 2001.

Chapter 8

Innovative Approaches to Black Wealth Creation

Innovation is a driving force behind wealth creation, and for the Black community, it can play a transformative role in economic upliftment. The importance of innovation in wealth creation can't be understated. Joseph Schumpeter, a renowned economist, encapsulates it best when he stated that "the function of entrepreneurs is to reform or revolutionize the pattern of production"[715].

Schumpeter's view is also echoed by many modern wealth experts, who argue that creative disruption, an offshoot of innovation, is the key to financial success in the current global economy[716]. This principle can be applied to the Black community to foster wealth creation. A case in point is Robert F. Smith, the African American billionaire who made his fortune by leveraging innovation in the technology investment sector[717].

Critics may argue that not every innovative idea leads to financial success and, indeed, that failure can often follow attempts at innovation[718]. But it is important to understand that innovation isn't about a guaranteed immediate return on investment. It's about taking calculated risks and creating something new that has the potential to

---

[715] Schumpeter, Joseph A. Capitalism, Socialism, and Democracy. Harper Perennial, 2008.
[716] Christensen, Clayton M., et al. The Innovator's Dilemma: When New Technologies Cause Great Firms to Fail. Harvard Business Review Press, 2016.
[717] "Robert F. Smith." Forbes, www.forbes.com/profile/robert-f-smith.
[718] Drucker, Peter. Innovation and Entrepreneurship: Practice and Principles. Harper & Row, 1985.

generate wealth[719]. By doing so, one engages in what Dr. Claud Anderson describes as "participating in the competitive economic process"[720], a necessary step towards wealth creation for any marginalized group.

The role of innovation in wealth creation is evident in numerous case studies. Companies like Apple and Amazon have created significant wealth by breaking industry norms and crafting new ways to deliver products and services[721]. This same principle can be applied within the Black community, by developing business ideas that disrupt traditional practices. A prime example is Tristan Walker, who recognized the lack of personal care products designed for people of color and seized the opportunity to create his company, Walker & Company Brands[722].

The disruptive business model not only creates wealth for the innovator, but it also stimulates economic growth within the community. When Black-owned businesses flourish, they provide employment opportunities and stimulate local economies, thus creating a ripple effect of wealth creation[723].

To replicate such successes, it is crucial to learn from these case studies and understand the strategies and processes that were employed. Developing and implementing innovative ideas involves the ability to see possibilities where others see barriers, to take risks, and to remain resilient in the face of setbacks[724]. It requires an

---

[719] Rogers, Everett M. Diffusion of Innovations, 5th Edition. Free Press, 2003.
[720] Anderson, Claud. PowerNomics: The National Plan to Empower Black America. PowerNomics Corporation of America, 2001.
[721] Isaacson, Walter. The Innovators: How a Group of Hackers, Geniuses, and Geeks Created the Digital Revolution. Simon & Schuster, 2014.
[722] Walker, Tristan. "Our Story." Walker & Company Brands, www.walkerandcompany.com/our-story.
[723] Chetty, Raj, et al. "Race and Economic Opportunity in the United States: an Intergenerational Perspective." Quarterly Journal of Economics, vol. 135, no. 2, 2020, pp. 711–783.
[724] Dweck, Carol S. Mindset: The New Psychology of Success. Random House, 2006.

understanding of one's market, audience, and the courage to break from convention.

As a result, innovative approaches to wealth creation are vital in establishing economic stability within the Black community. This is not a dismissal of the systemic barriers faced but rather an assertion that, within these constraints, innovation can play a substantial role in cultivating economic growth and wealth creation. Adopting such a mindset can lead to lasting change and substantial economic upliftment.

Establishing the Framework: The Indispensable Role of Innovation in Wealth Creation

The realm of wealth creation has long been characterized by the persistent role of innovation. The historian and economist, Carlota Perez, has articulated that technological revolutions and financial capital have shaped the world economy[725]. In a similar vein, Dr. Claud Anderson has emphasized the significance of economic and technological competitiveness in black communities as a means to accrue wealth[726]. In this context, innovation forms the indispensable framework in the wealth creation process.

The contribution of innovation to wealth generation is not simply a matter of conjecture but a demonstrable reality. Recent data indicate that the top five companies by market capitalization globally are all technology-based firms, demonstrating a clear correlation between innovation and wealth creation[727]. However, it is essential to note the skepticism voiced by some critics who assert that

---

[725] Perez, Carlota. Technological Revolutions and Financial Capital: The Dynamics of Bubbles and Golden Ages. Edward Elgar, 2003.
[726] Anderson, Claud. A Black History Reader: 101 Questions You Never Thought to Ask. PowerNomics Corporation of America, 2017.
[727] "The World's 100 Largest Companies: Forbes Global 2000 Guide." Forbes, www.forbes.com/global2000/.

innovation could widen wealth disparities[728]. This argument posits that while innovation creates wealth, it tends to accumulate in the hands of a few, thereby exacerbating income inequality. While this concern is valid, it underscores the need for inclusive innovation strategies that can distribute the wealth more equitably, rather than discounting the importance of innovation itself.

The power of innovation is remarkably illustrated in modern wealth creation. Consider the case of Madam C.J. Walker, the first self-made female millionaire in America, who accumulated her wealth by innovating in the hair care industry specifically for black women[729]. Her story testifies to the transformative potential of innovation in wealth creation.

Indeed, innovation has become integral to financial success in today's business landscape. A study conducted by PwC found that 79% of CEOs worldwide believe that innovation is a primary driver of organic growth for their industries[730]. Yet, critics argue that too much emphasis on innovation can lead to unnecessary risk-taking and potential business failure[731]. To this end, Anderson's perspective provides a counterbalance, asserting the need for black communities to take calculated risks, compete, and innovate within the economy to secure a prosperous future[732].

When we examine the successful business ideas disrupting industries, from tech start-ups to sustainable businesses, their core commonality is innovation. For

---

[728] Atkinson, Robert D., and Michael Lind. Big Is Beautiful: Debunking the Myth of Small Business. MIT Press, 2018.
[729] Bundles, A'Lelia. On Her Own Ground: The Life and Times of Madam C.J. Walker. Scribner, 2001.
[730] "Breakthrough Innovation and Growth." PwC, www.pwc.com/gx/en/ceo-survey/2013/assets/pwc-16th-annual-global-ceo-survey-breakthrough-innovation-and-growth.pdf.
[731] Taleb, Nassim Nicholas. Antifragile: Things That Gain from Disorder. Random House, 2012.
[732] Anderson, Claud. PowerNomics: The National Plan to Empower Black America. PowerNomics Corporation of America, 2001.

instance, the ride-hailing service Uber disrupted the taxi industry with its innovative business model, creating unprecedented wealth[733]. Similarly, black entrepreneurs can tap into the wealth-generating potential of innovation by offering unique solutions and breaking industry norms.

There are, undoubtedly, risks associated with innovation. These risks, however, should not deter but instead spur black communities to innovate, given the rewards on offer. Innovation, in essence, is about braving the odds and breaking new ground. This ethos aligns with the philosophy of 'competitive economics' advocated by Dr. Anderson, which encourages self-reliance and competition as a means to attain economic prosperity[734].

The framework for wealth creation is incomplete without the element of innovation. This principle holds true universally and is particularly relevant for black communities striving for economic empowerment.

An Overview of The Importance of Innovation in Modern Wealth Creation

Innovation plays an increasingly crucial role in the accumulation of wealth in the modern world. The interconnection between innovation and wealth is a tenet not only found in mainstream economic theory but also underlined in the teachings of Dr. Claud Anderson, who stresses the need for African American communities to embrace competitiveness, innovation, and technology to achieve financial growth[735].

---

[733] Stone, Brad. The Upstarts: How Uber, Airbnb, and the Killer Companies of the New Silicon Valley Are Changing the World. Little, Brown and Company, 2017.
[734] Anderson, Claud. PowerNomics: The National Plan to Empower Black America. PowerNomics Corporation of America, 2001.
[735] Anderson, Claud. PowerNomics: The National Plan to Empower Black America. PowerNomics Corporation of America, 2001.

The modern global economy stands as a testament to the transformative power of innovation. Five of the most valuable companies worldwide, including Apple, Microsoft, and Amazon, all reside in the technology sector, showcasing the immense wealth creation potential of innovative enterprises[736]. Critics, however, suggest that these high valuations are more indicative of speculative bubbles than actual wealth creation[737]. While their viewpoint cannot be entirely dismissed, it's also important to note that innovation has yielded tangible benefits and transformative products that have undeniably altered our lives and the ways we conduct business.

Nevertheless, the conversation around innovation and wealth creation should not be restricted to mega-corporations. On a smaller scale, individuals and communities can leverage innovation for wealth creation as well. Madam C.J. Walker, for example, became one of the first African American millionaires through her innovative line of hair products for black women[738]. Her achievements underscore the potential of innovative ideas to spur wealth creation within marginalized communities.

In the business context, innovation takes many forms, such as process improvements, new marketing methods, or novel product designs. A report by PwC showed that companies prioritizing innovation reported faster growth rates, illustrating the direct link between innovation and financial success[739]. Of course, skeptics caution that innovation can lead to increased risks and failures[740]. This

---

[736] "The World's Largest Public Companies." Forbes, www.forbes.com/global2000.

[737] Shiller, Robert. Irrational Exuberance. Princeton University Press, 2015.

[738] Bundles, A'Lelia. On Her Own Ground: The Life and Times of Madam C.J. Walker. Scribner, 2001.

[739] "Innovation drives growth." PwC, www.pwc.com/gx/en/ceo-agenda/innovation-drives-growth.html.

[740] Taleb, Nassim Nicholas. Antifragile: Things That Gain from Disorder. Random House, 2012.

concern underscores the need for strategic innovation rather than mere novelty, a point that aligns with Dr. Anderson's advocacy for calculated risks and strategic planning[741].

In recent years, disruptive innovation, in particular, has led to the creation of entirely new markets and significant wealth accumulation. The rise of ride-sharing platforms like Uber, or accommodation platforms like Airbnb, exemplifies how disrupting traditional industry norms can lead to significant wealth generation[742].

However, the role of innovation in wealth creation extends beyond business enterprises. Governments and policy-makers can also stimulate wealth creation through innovative social and economic policies, which, in turn, create conducive environments for innovative businesses to flourish. For instance, policies that incentivize green technologies can spur wealth creation in the renewable energy sector[743].

In essence, innovation is not just a catalyst for wealth creation; it is an essential component of it. Whether it's through technological advancements, business model disruptions, or policy initiatives, innovative approaches are at the core of modern wealth creation. To overlook this relationship is to disregard one of the most powerful drivers of economic growth and prosperity in the contemporary world.

---

[741] Anderson, Claud. PowerNomics: The National Plan to Empower Black America. PowerNomics Corporation of America, 2001.

[742] Stone, Brad. The Upstarts: How Uber, Airbnb, and the Killer Companies of the New Silicon Valley Are Changing the World. Little, Brown and Company, 2017.

[743] "Green Economy Report." United Nations Environment Programme, www.unep.org/greeneconomy.

Understanding How Creativity and Originality Fuel Black Financial Success

Creativity and originality are at the heart of innovation, fueling economic growth and the creation of wealth. In line with Dr. Claud Anderson's assertions, these traits have historically been particularly relevant for Black financial success, overcoming systemic challenges through inventive means[744].

Creativity and originality can manifest in various ways, such as unique business ideas, innovative products, or new methods of service delivery. Black innovators, for instance, have leveraged their distinct experiences and perspectives to create products that cater to underrepresented communities. These include innovative companies like Mented Cosmetics, which started a line of nude lipsticks for diverse skin tones[745]. Critics, however, may argue that innovation alone is not sufficient, emphasizing the importance of market timing, effective execution, and luck. But these critiques do not negate the critical role of creativity and originality in spurring innovation and wealth creation[746].

This conversation extends beyond products and services, stretching into the realm of disruptive business models. The rise of tech start-ups within Black communities, such as Blavity or Afrostream, attest to the power of creativity and originality in redefining industry norms and creating wealth[747]. These examples not only confirm the link between innovation and wealth creation, but also refute

---

[744] Anderson, Claud. PowerNomics: The National Plan to Empower Black America. PowerNomics Corporation of America, 2001.
[745] "Mented Cosmetics Founders Make History As 15th, 16th Black Women Ever To Raise $1M Capital." Forbes, www.forbes.com.
[746] "What Makes a Successful Entrepreneur? Persistence, Persistence, Persistence." The Guardian, www.theguardian.com.
[747] "Blavity: The Website Made for Black Millennials." The Observer, www.observer.com.

a common misconception that Black communities are not involved in technological innovation[748].

Moreover, it is essential to understand that innovation, in its essence, is more about problem-solving than it is about inventing new technologies. As Dr. Anderson notes, wealth is created by identifying needs and finding innovative ways to meet them[749]. This focus on solving real-world problems through creativity and originality fuels entrepreneurship, employment, and ultimately, wealth creation.

Empirical evidence supports this claim. A study conducted by the Boston Consulting Group found that companies that emphasized diversity produced 19% more revenue due to innovation[750]. This study indirectly links the unique perspectives found within diverse communities, like the Black community, to an increased capacity for creativity and originality.

However, this doesn't imply that success is guaranteed. While innovation is inherently risky, Dr. Anderson posits that understanding these risks and managing them strategically is vital for sustained financial success[751]. He encourages the Black community to view failure as an opportunity for learning rather than an endpoint, reinforcing the idea that resilience and persistence are critical for innovators.

Creativity and originality are central to driving innovation, which in turn, fuels financial success. The Black community's unique experiences and perspectives offer an invaluable source of innovative potential. Capitalizing on

---

[748] "Is Tech Closing the Wealth Gap or Making It Worse?" Fortune, www.fortune.com.
[749] Anderson, Claud. PowerNomics: The National Plan to Empower Black America. PowerNomics Corporation of America, 2001.
[750] "How Diverse Leadership Teams Boost Innovation." Boston Consulting Group, www.bcg.com.
[751] Anderson, Claud. PowerNomics: The National Plan to Empower Black America. PowerNomics Corporation of America, 2001.

this potential requires an understanding of the mechanics of innovation and a willingness to embrace risk, adapt to failures, and persevere in the face of adversity.

Exploration of The Correlation between Creative Thinking and Financial Growth

Creative thinking is a central driver of financial growth, fostering innovative solutions and products that create new economic value. This assertion aligns with Dr. Claud Anderson's belief in the power of innovative thought, particularly in Black communities, as an essential tool for financial progression[752].

The most prosperous businesses are often those that redefine boundaries and norms, a process rooted in creative thinking. Uber, for instance, disrupted the conventional taxi service model by developing a ride-sharing platform that better meets user needs[753]. This innovative solution resulted from creative thinking and has generated significant financial growth, demonstrating the correlation between the two.

However, some skeptics may question the universality of this relationship, citing companies that have experienced financial growth by refining, rather than redefining, established models. They argue that while innovation is important, strategic execution and market demand play a more significant role in financial growth[754]. While these factors are indeed crucial, it is through creative thinking that businesses can understand and better respond to market

---

[752] Anderson, Claud. PowerNomics: The National Plan to Empower Black America. PowerNomics Corporation of America, 2001.
[753] "Uber's Path of Destruction." American Affairs Journal, www.americanaffairsjournal.org.
[754] "Execution is More Important Than Ideas: What Research Says?" Entrepreneur, www.entrepreneur.com.

demand, indicating the integral role creativity plays in business success and financial growth.

In fact, research supports the strong relationship between creative thinking and financial growth. According to a 2016 study by Adobe and Forrester Consulting, companies that foster creativity achieved 1.5 times the market share of less creative companies[755]. These findings underscore the importance of creative thinking as a determinant of financial growth.

Moreover, creative thinking extends beyond product and service innovation—it also encompasses innovative business strategies. Black entertainment mogul Tyler Perry exemplifies this, creating an independent film production studio that diversified content and catered to an underserved market[756]. This innovative strategy has resulted in significant financial growth and illustrates the importance of creative thinking in wealth creation.

Furthermore, creative thinking can lead to financial growth by identifying untapped market opportunities. The success of Black-owned businesses like Shea Moisture, which filled a gap in the market for natural hair products, validates this point[757].

Critics may still point to the inherent risk associated with innovative ideas. They argue that financial growth is not guaranteed and innovation can lead to financial loss. However, as Dr. Anderson emphasizes, it is not the avoidance of risk, but the management of risk that is crucial in the pursuit of financial growth[758].

---

[755] "The Creative Dividend: How Creativity Impacts Business Results." Adobe, www.adobe.com.
[756] "How Tyler Perry Built a Billion-Dollar Empire." The Hollywood Reporter, www.hollywoodreporter.com.
[757] "Shea Moisture's Path To Becoming a Multimillion-Dollar Beauty Brand." Forbes, www.forbes.com.
[758] Anderson, Claud. PowerNomics: The National Plan to Empower Black America. PowerNomics Corporation of America, 2001.

Creative thinking is an essential factor in financial growth. It propels innovation, which creates new economic value and leads to wealth creation. While it doesn't guarantee financial growth and involves risk, managing these risks effectively can yield substantial rewards.

Trailblazers and Pioneers: A Look at Case Studies of Innovative Business Ideas and Their Impact on Wealth Generation

Throughout history, trailblazers have shaped the trajectory of Black wealth creation through their innovative business ideas. Dr. Claud Anderson has consistently underscored this concept, emphasizing the transformative power of innovation in the Black community[759]. However, some skeptics may question whether innovation is universally a catalyst for wealth generation, citing examples of businesses that have seen financial success through refinement rather than redefinition of existing models.

Consider the story of Madam C.J. Walker, the first self-made female millionaire in America, who made her fortune by creating innovative hair care products tailored to the needs of Black women. She introduced a groundbreaking approach to marketing and distribution, employing Black women as sales agents, and establishing training programs[760]. Her innovative model disrupted the beauty industry, demonstrating the power of innovation to generate wealth.

Yet, skeptics could argue that innovation is not solely responsible for such success, citing the role of market demand and effective execution in Walker's achievements.

---

[759] Anderson, Claud. PowerNomics: The National Plan to Empower Black America. PowerNomics Corporation of America, 2001.

[760] Bundles, A'Lelia. On Her Own Ground: The Life and Times of Madam C.J. Walker. Scribner, 2001.

While these factors certainly contributed to her success, her innovative approach to product, marketing, and distribution was a key differentiator in a saturated market[761].

In a more contemporary context, Robert F. Smith, founder of Vista Equity Partners, established his financial firm with a unique strategy: focusing solely on enterprise software and technology-enabled start-ups. His innovative investment strategy resulted in Vista becoming one of the best-performing private equity firms globally[762]. Detractors may point to Smith's financial acumen and market conditions as primary drivers of his success, but his unique, innovative focus enabled him to recognize and exploit niche opportunities.

Another example is Janice Bryant Howroyd, founder of ACT-1 Group, the first Black woman to own a billion-dollar company. Her innovation was in re-imagining the role of employment agencies. Instead of just filling jobs, ACT-1 Group provides comprehensive employment solutions, including background checks, and workforce management[763]. Critics may argue that her success is due to the growing demand for staffing services, but it is the innovative services beyond staffing that set ACT-1 Group apart.

Although these examples underscore the power of innovative business ideas in wealth creation, critics might argue that they are outliers and not representative of the average business experience. They warn of the inherent risks of innovation, pointing to examples of failed businesses that were too ahead of their time[764]. However, as Dr. Anderson suggests, risk is an inherent part of wealth

---

[761] Ibid.
[762] "Robert F. Smith: The Billionaire Who Is Trying to Go His Own Way." The New York Times, www.nytimes.com.
[763] "Janice Bryant Howroyd: First African American Woman to Run a $1-Billion Business." Black Enterprise, www.blackenterprise.com.
[764] "Innovation: A Risk Worth Taking?" Deloitte, www.deloitte.com.

creation. Effective management of risk is critical to leveraging innovation for wealth generation[765].

While critics may emphasize the role of market demand, execution, and the potential risks associated with innovation, trailblazing entrepreneurs like Walker, Smith, and Howroyd exemplify the power of innovative business ideas to generate wealth and disrupt industries.

Delving Into Real-World Examples of Innovative Business Strategies And Their Resultant Financial Outcomes

Drawing on real-world examples, innovative business strategies have led to groundbreaking financial outcomes for Black businesses. Understanding these stories can provide valuable insights for those striving towards similar success. Critics, however, may argue that such stories are exceptions rather than the norm, citing the inherent risks associated with innovative approaches.

Tyler Perry, a leading figure in the entertainment industry, has created a media empire through innovative strategies, from owning the rights to his productions to establishing a major film studio in Atlanta, a region historically overlooked by the industry. Perry's vertical integration strategy has yielded significant financial returns, with his net worth estimated at over $1 billion[766].

Detractors, however, could argue that Perry's success is more attributable to his individual talent and hard work rather than innovation. They may also point to the many aspiring filmmakers who have tried similar strategies but failed. While talent and hard work undoubtedly play a role,

---

[765] Anderson, Claud. PowerNomics: The National Plan to Empower Black America. PowerNomics Corporation of America, 2001.

[766] Robehmed, Natalie. "How Tyler Perry Built a $600 Million Entertainment Empire." Forbes, www.forbes.com.

Perry's innovative approach to the industry was a key factor in his achievements[767].

Consider another example: Tristan Walker, founder of Walker & Company, disrupted the personal care industry by addressing the unique needs of people of color—an underserved market. His firm was subsequently bought by Proctor & Gamble, marking a substantial financial outcome[768]. Critics may argue that market demand, rather than innovation, was responsible for this success. However, it was Walker's innovative approach to product development and marketing that identified and capitalized on this demand[769].

Let's also examine the case of Oprah Winfrey, who revolutionized the talk-show industry with her innovative focus on empathy and personal connection. Her innovative approach resulted in immense financial success, with Winfrey becoming North America's first Black multi-billionaire[770]. Skeptics could contend that Winfrey's personal charisma and television's broad appeal were the primary drivers of her success. Yet, it was Winfrey's innovative approach to her show's content and format that set her apart from her competitors[771].

While these success stories highlight the potential rewards of innovative business strategies, skeptics caution against overlooking the inherent risks. They point to examples of innovative businesses that failed due to market resistance or lack of readiness for new ideas[772]. It is crucial to note, as Dr. Anderson often does, that risk-taking is

---

[767] Ibid.
[768] "P&G Acquires Walker & Company, Tristan Walker Will Remain as CEO." Black Enterprise, www.blackenterprise.com.
[769] Ibid.
[770] Greenburg, Zack O'Malley. "Inside The 35-Year-Long Quest To Find A Safe Haven For The Oprah Winfrey Show Tapes." Forbes, www.forbes.com.
[771] Ibid.
[772] "Innovation: A Risk Worth Taking?" Deloitte, www.deloitte.com.

integral to wealth creation and that those risks can be managed with proper planning and foresight[773].

Innovative business strategies have led to remarkable financial outcomes for many Black businesses, notwithstanding skepticism from critics. It is innovation that has often set these businesses apart, enabling them to carve out unique niches and opportunities in their respective markets.

Shattering The Mold: Strategies for Disrupting Traditional Industry Practices and Forging New Pathways to Wealth

In a world increasingly shaped by disruptive technologies and paradigms, the ability to shatter the mold of traditional industry practices becomes imperative for wealth creation. However, critics point to the uncertainty and risk associated with disruptive strategies, suggesting a more conservative approach. Nonetheless, in the words of Dr. Anderson, Black businesses must be "unafraid of charting unfamiliar waters" and instead view these disruptions as opportunities for growth and wealth creation[774].

Take the tech industry for instance, where innovators have found enormous success by defying conventional wisdom and disrupting established markets. The advent of Uber and Airbnb—businesses that owned no cars or hotels respectively when they started—disrupted the traditional taxi and hotel industries and created unprecedented wealth for their founders[775]. Critics might argue that these

---

[773] Anderson, Claud. PowerNomics: The National Plan to Empower Black America. PowerNomics Corporation of America, 2001.
[774] Anderson, Claud. Black Labor, White Wealth: The Search for Power and Economic Justice. PowerNomics Corporation of America, 1994.
[775] Isaac, Mike. "Uber's C.E.O. Plays With Fire." The New York Times, www.nytimes.com.

companies succeeded due to timing and market readiness, not solely because of their disruptive models. Yet, the willingness to overturn industry norms was instrumental in their unprecedented success[776].

Similarly, in the publishing industry, authors like E.L. James and Amanda Hocking disrupted traditional publishing by self-publishing their works, thereby maintaining control over their intellectual property and earning significant wealth[777]. Detractors could say that their success is a result of their unique talent rather than their innovative approach to publishing. Yet, these examples demonstrate the potential for writers to circumvent traditional publishing and still achieve financial success[778].

However, it is crucial to note that such disruptive strategies are not without risks. Skeptics often emphasize the high failure rate of start-ups, the challenges of changing consumer behavior, and the potential backlash from disrupted industries[779]. While these are valid concerns, Dr. Anderson encourages a reframing of the concept of risk as a component of innovation and wealth creation rather than a deterrent[780].

So, how does one forge new pathways to wealth using disruptive strategies? First, it is important to recognize and act upon market gaps or consumer needs that are not adequately addressed by current offerings. Second, one must be willing to challenge industry norms and traditional business models, even if this means facing resistance. Finally, innovative ideas should be combined with a clear

---

[776] Ibid.
[777] Alter, Alexandra. "Amanda Hocking, the Writer Who Made Millions by Self-Publishing Online." The New York Times, www.nytimes.com.
[778] Ibid.
[779] Guttentag, Dan. "Airbnb: disruptive innovation and the rise of an informal tourism accommodation sector." Current Issues in Tourism, www.tandfonline.com.
[780] Anderson, Claud. PowerNomics: The National Plan to Empower Black America. PowerNomics Corporation of America, 2001.

business plan and robust execution strategies to manage potential risks and improve the chances of success[781].

Shattering the mold of traditional industry practices may be daunting, but history shows that it can lead to significant wealth creation. As Dr. Anderson often highlights, embracing disruption and innovation is a critical step towards financial empowerment and self-sufficiency for Black communities.

Discussing Tactics For Breaking From Industry Norms, Coupled With The Benefits And Risks Associated With Such Disruption

Breaking from industry norms—a pathway not for the faint-hearted, yet teeming with untapped potential—is often touted as a vehicle for transformative change and wealth creation. However, critics argue this path is fraught with uncertainty, potential backlash from established entities, and high risks of failure. In the spirit of Dr. Claud Anderson's teachings, the discussion herein will encapsulate the methods to break from industry norms, along with the associated benefits and risks, underscoring the fact that this paradigm shift can be an essential catalyst for economic empowerment, particularly for the Black community[782].

To begin, a common method of breaking industry norms is through disruptive innovation—a process wherein a smaller company successfully challenges established businesses by targeting overlooked customer needs[783]. Take, for instance, the evolution of the music industry. The advent

---

[781] Christensen, Clayton M., et al. "Disruptive Innovation for Social Change." Harvard Business Review, www.hbr.org.
[782] Anderson, Claud. PowerNomics: The National Plan to Empower Black America. PowerNomics Corporation of America, 2001.
[783] Christensen, Clayton M. The Innovator's Dilemma: When New Technologies Cause Great Firms to Fail. Harvard Business School Press, 1997.

of streaming platforms such as Spotify and Apple Music broke the norms of physical music sales and downloads, providing a more accessible and convenient music experience for consumers[784]. Critics may contend these services were successful due to their massive resources rather than their disruptive models. However, their bold steps in addressing customer convenience have undeniably reshaped the industry[785].

Leveraging technology is another key strategy. Innovative use of technology can break industry norms by introducing more efficient processes, products, or services. For instance, financial technology (fintech) companies have revolutionized traditional banking practices, offering online banking, peer-to-peer lending platforms, and cryptocurrency exchanges[786]. Detractors might argue these technologies are vulnerable to cybersecurity risks and can exclude those with limited internet access. Nevertheless, the incorporation of technology remains a potent means of disrupting traditional industry practices[787].

There are substantial benefits of breaking from industry norms. These include potential monopolistic advantages in a new market sector, increased profitability, and the ability to establish new standards within an industry[788]. However, this pathway also carries inherent risks such as the initial financial investment, potential lack of customer acceptance, and backlash from established competitors[789].

---

[784] Anderson, Chris. "The Long Tail: Why the Future of Business is Selling Less of More." Hyperion, 2006.
[785] Ibid.
[786] Zetzsche, Dirk A., et al. "Regulating a Revolution: From Regulatory Sandboxes to Smart Regulation." Fordham Journal of Corporate & Financial Law, 23(1), 2017.
[787] Ibid.
[788] Adner, Ron. "Ecosystem as Structure: An Actionable Construct for Strategy." Journal of Management, 43(1), 2017.
[789] Christensen, Clayton M. The Innovator's Dilemma: When New Technologies Cause Great Firms to Fail. Harvard Business School Press, 1997.

While understanding these benefits and risks is essential, Dr. Anderson urges Black businesses to view potential challenges as opportunities for growth and resilience. He espouses the idea that "risk and reward are two sides of the same coin" in the context of wealth creation, emphasizing the importance of risk-taking in achieving financial autonomy[790].

Breaking from industry norms can be an impactful strategy for fostering innovation and creating wealth. Despite the associated risks, Dr. Anderson's work suggests that the Black community's proactive engagement in such endeavors can contribute significantly to its collective economic empowerment.

A Guide for the Future: Developing and Implementing Innovative Ideas for Wealth Creation

Developing and implementing innovative ideas for wealth creation is not a simple task, it requires a meticulous approach to planning, execution, and constant adaptation. This involves embracing the concept of 'failing forward,' a principle lauded by Dr. Claud Anderson, wherein setbacks are perceived as stepping stones towards success[791]. While skeptics might argue that innovation is an unpredictable gamble, a more profound examination reveals that it is a calculated risk that offers enormous potential for wealth creation.

The process of developing innovative ideas begins with fostering a conducive environment for creativity. This includes encouraging free thinking, embracing diversity of

---

[790] Anderson, Claud. Black Labor, White Wealth: The Search for Power and Economic Justice. PowerNomics Corporation of America, 1994.
[791] Anderson, Claud. "PowerNomics: The National Plan to Empower Black America." PowerNomics Corporation of America, 2001.

thought, and cultivating a culture of continual learning[792]. Critics may posit that these principles are intangible and hard to measure, however, they provide the foundation for innovative thought.

It's worth noting that data plays a significant role in driving innovation. Data analysis can help identify market trends, customer needs, and potential growth areas[793]. For instance, the rise of 'Big Data' has enabled companies to tailor their products and services to the specific needs of their consumers, thus disrupting traditional business models[794]. Detractors may express concerns over privacy and data security, yet, it is undeniable that data-driven innovation is a powerful tool in modern wealth creation[795].

Implementation, the subsequent stage, often requires strategic partnerships and investment in resources. Dr. Anderson emphasizes the importance of a community-based approach to resource mobilization, particularly for Black entrepreneurs[796]. Skeptics might argue that pooling resources within the community limits exposure to external investment. Nevertheless, Dr. Anderson's concept of 'group economics' reiterates the importance of internal resource mobilization for sustainable wealth creation within the community[797].

Finally, monitoring and adaptation are critical components of implementing innovative ideas. This process involves tracking progress, assessing market responses, and

---

[792] Amabile, Teresa. "The Progress Principle: Using Small Wins to Ignite Joy, Engagement, and Creativity at Work." Harvard Business Review Press, 2011.
[793] Schmarzo, Bill. "The Economics of Data, Analytics, and Digital Transformation." Wiley, 2021.
[794] Ibid.
[795] Ibid.
[796] Anderson, Claud. "Black Labor, White Wealth: The Search for Power and Economic Justice." PowerNomics Corporation of America, 1994.
[797] Ibid.

making necessary adjustments[798]. While critics may view this as a reactive approach, it is a fundamental aspect of 'failing forward'—learning from setbacks and refining strategies to ensure progress[799].

In essence, the process of developing and implementing innovative ideas for wealth creation requires a comprehensive approach that embraces creativity, leverages data, utilizes community resources, and values the principle of 'failing forward'. As underscored by Dr. Anderson, it is through such strategic innovation that the Black community can achieve sustainable wealth and economic empowerment.

Providing Actionable Steps For Readers To Cultivate Their Own Innovative Ideas For Wealth Building

Dr. Claud Anderson advocates strongly for the Black community's wealth creation by using innovative strategies[800]. However, the process of cultivating innovative ideas for wealth creation can seem daunting, and the skepticism around its effectiveness persists in certain quarters. Despite these potential obstacles, the steps towards achieving it are identifiable and actionable.

The first step involves fostering a culture of creativity and embracing the principles of 'PowerNomics' – an economic empowerment model conceptualized by Dr. Anderson that seeks to make the Black community more self-reliant[801]. Critics may contend that creativity cannot be cultivated; it's innate. However, research shows that it can

---

[798] Ries, Eric. "The Lean start-up: How Today's Entrepreneurs Use Continuous Innovation to Create Radically Successful Businesses." Crown Publishing Group, 2011.
[799] Anderson, Claud. "PowerNomics: The National Plan to Empower Black America." PowerNomics Corporation of America, 2001.
[800] Anderson, Claud. "PowerNomics: The National Plan to Empower Black America." PowerNomics Corporation of America, 2001.
[801] Ibid.

be developed by encouraging critical thinking, embracing different perspectives, and promoting a culture of continuous learning[802].

Secondly, leveraging data analytics for decision-making is key. While this might raise concerns around privacy, the potential benefits for wealth creation are significant. By gathering and analyzing data, you can understand market trends, identify gaps in the market, and make informed decisions about where opportunities lie[803].

Next, implementing innovative ideas often necessitates collaborations and strategic partnerships. Dr. Anderson's model of 'group economics' advocates for pooling resources within the Black community for mutual benefit[804]. Some might argue that this limits external investment opportunities, but the sustainable growth it provides for the community is a worthy trade-off[805].

Once your idea is in place, monitoring and adaptation are crucial. This might appear to be reactive rather than proactive, but it is, in fact, a cornerstone of 'failing forward'—a method of learning from setbacks and refining strategies to ensure progress[806]. Detractors might argue against the effectiveness of this approach, but real-world examples demonstrate its success[807].

Lastly, patience and resilience are crucial. The road to wealth creation is not smooth; there will be hurdles and setbacks. Critics may see these obstacles as indicators of

---

[802] Amabile, Teresa. "The Progress Principle: Using Small Wins to Ignite Joy, Engagement, and Creativity at Work." Harvard Business Review Press, 2011.
[803] Schmarzo, Bill. "The Economics of Data, Analytics, and Digital Transformation." Wiley, 2021.
[804] Anderson, Claud. "Black Labor, White Wealth: The Search for Power and Economic Justice." PowerNomics Corporation of America, 1994.
[805] Ibid.
[806] Anderson, Claud. "PowerNomics: The National Plan to Empower Black America." PowerNomics Corporation of America, 2001.
[807] Ibid.

failure, but in the context of 'failing forward,' these are learning opportunities that can lead to better strategies and long-term success[808].

Cultivating innovative ideas for wealth creation involves a combination of nurturing creativity, leveraging data, fostering strategic partnerships, embracing the principle of 'failing forward,' and exercising patience and resilience. As Dr. Anderson has argued, it is through these innovative strategies that the Black community can build sustainable wealth and economic self-sufficiency[809].

Profiling Individuals and Enterprises That Have Mastered Innovative Approaches to Wealth Creation

One of the most tangible ways to illuminate the impact of innovative approaches to wealth creation is by focusing on the success stories of individuals and enterprises who have harnessed these methods. In the realm of the Black community, these case studies are crucial, offering much-needed representation and inspiration. However, the mainstream narratives often do not provide such coverage[810]. Let's explore some noteworthy examples that have not been widely publicized, while addressing the skeptics' views.

First, we look at Arlan Hamilton, who founded Backstage Capital, a venture capital firm focused on investing in underrepresented entrepreneurs. Hamilton's unconventional approach was met with skepticism from mainstream venture capitalists, many of whom doubted her ability to generate returns given her focus on underrepresented groups[811]. However, she has successfully

---

[808] Ibid.
[809] Ibid.
[810] Anderson, Claud. "PowerNomics: The National Plan to Empower Black America." PowerNomics Corporation of America, 2001.
[811] Hamilton, Arlan. "It's About Damn Time: How to Turn Being Underestimated into Your Greatest Advantage." Currency, 2020.

raised over $10 million and invested in more than 130 start-ups, proving the profitability of investing in overlooked demographics[812].

Another inspiring example is Richelieu Dennis, the Liberian-born founder of Sundial Brands, a beauty company he started selling Shea butter products on the streets of New York. Critics doubted the viability of his company because it focused on products for Black women, a then underserved market[813]. Despite this, Dennis built a successful business that was eventually sold to Unilever for an undisclosed amount, rumored to be close to a billion dollars[814]. This demonstrated the untapped potential in niche markets that align with the community's needs and preferences.

The story of Janice Bryant Howroyd, founder of ActOne Group, is also worth noting. Starting from humble beginnings, she faced obstacles such as discrimination and the common belief that a Black woman could not successfully run a global business[815]. Howroyd, however, overcame these barriers, growing her business into a multi-billion dollar enterprise, and became the first African American woman to own a billion-dollar company[816].

These stories of innovation within the Black community challenge mainstream narratives about wealth creation. Critics might argue that these are exceptions, not the rule. However, as Dr. Anderson suggests in his 'PowerNomics' concept, these examples show the importance of innovative thinking, self-reliance, and serving community needs[817]. They indicate the potential that can be

---

[812] Ibid.
[813] Dennis, Richelieu. "Shea Moisture Founder on Selling Sundial Brands to Unilever." Inc.com, November 27, 2017.
[814] Ibid.
[815] Howroyd, Janice Bryant. "The Art of Work: How to Make Work, Work for You!" Greenleaf Book Group Press, 2019.
[816] Ibid.
[817] Anderson, Claud. "PowerNomics: The National Plan to Empower Black America." PowerNomics Corporation of America, 2001.

tapped when individuals and enterprises embrace an innovative, resilient approach to wealth creation.

Showcasing the stories of individuals and enterprises like Arlan Hamilton, Richelieu Dennis, and Janice Bryant Howroyd, provides potent examples of how innovation, perseverance, and a commitment to serving the community can lead to substantial wealth creation within the Black community[818].

A Deeper Dive: Analyzing the Processes and Strategies of Successful Innovators

Analyzing the strategies and processes utilized by successful innovators provides invaluable insights into how innovation can lead to wealth creation. However, it's important to confront the skepticism prevalent in certain quarters, which question the universal applicability of these strategies[819]. By examining these stories of success, we can illustrate how these tactics can be adopted and adapted by other individuals and businesses within the Black community.

Arlan Hamilton's approach at Backstage Capital was rooted in identifying and investing in underrepresented entrepreneurs. She disrupted the prevailing norms in venture capital, which typically overlooked these demographics[820]. Critics questioned this approach, doubting its profitability. However, the success of Backstage Capital has demonstrated that this innovative approach does not merely provide social value, but also significant financial returns[821].

---

[818] Ibid.
[819] Anderson, Claud. "PowerNomics: The National Plan to Empower Black America." PowerNomics Corporation of America, 2001.
[820] Hamilton, Arlan. "It's About Damn Time: How to Turn Being Underestimated into Your Greatest Advantage." Currency, 2020.
[821] Ibid.

Hamilton's strategy was characterized by thorough market research, patience, and a deep understanding of the communities she was investing in. She understood the struggles and strengths of underrepresented entrepreneurs, having faced similar challenges herself. This intimate knowledge allowed her to identify promising investment opportunities that other venture capitalists overlooked[822].

Richelieu Dennis founded Sundial Brands based on the recognition of a gap in the market for beauty products designed for Black women. This innovative approach was initially met with skepticism, as mainstream businesses had largely ignored this market[823]. However, Dennis's commitment to high-quality, natural products and his engagement with his target audience eventually paid off, leading to the sale of his company to Unilever[824].

Dennis's strategy was driven by an understanding of the needs and preferences of his target market, a commitment to high-quality products, and an effective engagement strategy. His success shows the value of creating products and services that resonate deeply with a specific audience, a practice that can be replicated in other industries[825].

Janice Bryant Howroyd's rise to becoming the owner of a billion-dollar company was rooted in her resilience, determination, and innovative approach to human resources. She navigated discrimination and biases and capitalized on her understanding of employment dynamics and needs to build the ActOne Group. Critics who doubted her capabilities were silenced by her success, which shows that barriers can be surmounted through innovation and perseverance[826].

---

[822] Ibid.
[823] Dennis, Richelieu. "Shea Moisture Founder on Selling Sundial Brands to Unilever." Inc.com, November 27, 2017.
[824] Ibid.
[825] Ibid.
[826] Howroyd, Janice Bryant. "The Art of Work: How to Make Work, Work for You!" Greenleaf Book Group Press, 2019.

The strategies and processes used by these successful innovators are characterized by a deep understanding of their markets, an unwavering commitment to serving these markets, and a resilient approach to overcoming barriers. These case studies challenge the skepticism around the feasibility of innovative approaches to wealth creation and provide a road-map for others in the Black community to follow in their footsteps[827].

Offering Detailed Analysis of The Processes And Strategies Utilized By Those Profiled, And How These Lessons Can Be Applied By The Readers

Dissecting the success of trailblazers like Arlan Hamilton, Richelieu Dennis, and Janice Bryant Howroyd reveals key lessons applicable to aspiring entrepreneurs. These lessons embody innovative strategies and processes capable of empowering individuals to forge their own paths towards wealth creation. This examination must confront skeptics who assert these strategies cannot be universally applied or duplicated, highlighting the strategic thinking and execution that led to success[828].

Arlan Hamilton's innovative approach involved the identification and investment in underrepresented entrepreneurs. The core of her strategy was thorough market research and a deep understanding of her investment targets[829]. By familiarizing herself with the unique struggles faced by underrepresented entrepreneurs, she could recognize opportunities overlooked by mainstream investors. These processes of meticulous market research and deep

---

[827] Anderson, Claud. "PowerNomics: The National Plan to Empower Black America." PowerNomics Corporation of America, 2001.
[828] Anderson, Claud. "PowerNomics: The National Plan to Empower Black America." PowerNomics Corporation of America, 2001.
[829] Hamilton, Arlan. "It's About Damn Time: How to Turn Being Underestimated into Your Greatest Advantage." Currency, 2020.

understanding of a target group can be adopted by aspiring Black entrepreneurs, especially when venturing into industries often overlooked by mainstream business models.

Despite skepticism, Richelieu Dennis demonstrated that success lies in understanding the market and focusing on quality. By identifying a gap in beauty products tailored for Black women, Dennis established Sundial Brands. He met initial skepticism with unwavering dedication to delivering high-quality products, successfully resonating with his target market[830]. Dennis's story underscores the value of a deep understanding of target markets, commitment to quality, and effectively engaging with audiences. These strategies can be effectively adapted in various industries, particularly in addressing underserved markets.

Janice Bryant Howroyd's success in the human resources industry was fueled by her innovative approach and resilience. In spite of barriers such as discrimination, her keen understanding of employment dynamics led to the establishment of the ActOne Group, demonstrating that adversity can be leveraged to one's advantage[831]. Howroyd's story presents a road-map for turning perceived weaknesses into strengths, a strategy which can be applied by readers to overcome hurdles in their entrepreneurial journeys.

The innovative approaches utilized by Hamilton, Dennis, and Howroyd demonstrate the power of market understanding, commitment to quality, and resilience in the face of adversity. Such strategies, critics argue, are not replicable due to unique circumstances and barriers faced by each individual. However, the adaptability of these tactics, highlighted by these success stories, provides a replicable template for wealth creation, illustrating that obstacles can

---

[830] Dennis, Richelieu. "Shea Moisture Founder on Selling Sundial Brands to Unilever." Inc.com, November 27, 2017.
[831] Howroyd, Janice Bryant. "The Art of Work: How to Make Work, Work for You!" Greenleaf Book Group Press, 2019.

be opportunities when viewed through the lens of innovation[832].

By analyzing these strategies, readers can understand how they can apply similar principles in their own paths to wealth creation, demonstrating the efficacy and universality of these innovative approaches.

Discussing How These Success Stories Can Inspire And Provide Practical Insights For Readers' Own Wealth Creation Journeys

The success stories of Arlan Hamilton, Richelieu Dennis, and Janice Bryant Howroyd provide a rich tapestry of inspiration and practical insights for aspiring Black entrepreneurs embarking on their wealth creation journey. However, critics argue that the journeys of these individuals are extraordinary, therefore, they cannot be emulated by everyone[833]. Yet, as Dr. Claud Anderson articulates, their stories underline the universal principles of innovation, resilience, and understanding one's market, creating a replicable road-map for wealth creation[834].

Arlan Hamilton's success story, which saw her journey from homelessness to leading a venture capital firm dedicated to investing in underrepresented entrepreneurs, serves as a potent reminder of the power of determination and innovation. Hamilton's journey provides valuable insights into the effective utilization of research and a deep understanding of a target market to build a successful business. Thus, readers can grasp the importance of thorough market research and the opportunities in

---

[832] Anderson, Claud. "PowerNomics: The National Plan to Empower Black America." PowerNomics Corporation of America, 2001.
[833] Anderson, Claud. "PowerNomics: The National Plan to Empower Black America." PowerNomics Corporation of America, 2001.
[834] Anderson, Claud. "Black Labor, White Wealth." PowerNomics Corporation of America, 1994.

underrepresented areas, which are often overlooked by mainstream investors[835].

Richelieu Dennis built a beauty empire by focusing on a market neglected by the mainstream beauty industry. Dennis's commitment to quality and his deep understanding of his target market allowed him to transform a niche market into a mainstream success. This story serves as a blueprint for readers, highlighting the value of understanding their market, the power of catering to neglected segments, and the importance of quality[836].

Janice Bryant Howroyd's journey from growing up in segregated North Carolina to becoming the first African American woman to own a billion-dollar company highlights the power of resilience and innovation. By leveraging adversity and transforming it into an advantage, she built a successful business in an industry traditionally not dominated by Black entrepreneurs. Howroyd's journey provides readers with a clear example of how to overcome challenges and convert them into opportunities[837].

While critics argue that these individual journeys are unique and not universally applicable, their successes underpin the importance of innovation, resilience, and understanding one's market - elements applicable to any entrepreneurial venture. As Anderson argues, rather than focusing on the specific paths these individuals have taken, the focus should be on the principles they employed to attain their success[838].

Understanding and employing the strategies used by Hamilton, Dennis, and Howroyd can provide readers with a

---

[835] Hamilton, Arlan. "It's About Damn Time: How to Turn Being Underestimated into Your Greatest Advantage." Currency, 2020.
[836] Dennis, Richelieu. "Shea Moisture Founder on Selling Sundial Brands to Unilever." Inc.com, November 27, 2017.
[837] Howroyd, Janice Bryant. "The Art of Work: How to Make Work, Work for You!" Greenleaf Book Group Press, 2019.
[838] Anderson, Claud. "PowerNomics: The National Plan to Empower Black America." PowerNomics Corporation of America, 2001.

road-map to their wealth creation journey. By drawing inspiration and guidance from these stories, aspiring Black entrepreneurs can develop the innovative and resilient mindsets necessary to create their own success stories.

Chapter 9
Collective Economics - Harnessing the Power of Unity for Wealth Creation

Collective economics, or group economics, is a strategy that amplifies individual resources for a community's financial advantage[839]. For the Black community, this approach is an opportunity to foster economic independence and achieve collective prosperity, particularly in the United States where wealth disparities have historical roots in systemic inequalities[840]. Still, critics argue against its efficacy, citing the challenges of community organization and the dynamics of a global economy[841].

Dr. Martin Luther King Jr. once said, "We must learn to live together as brothers or perish together as fools"[842]. This profound statement encapsulates the underlying philosophy of collective economics. Unity, as evidenced by historical instances like the success of Black Wall Street in Tulsa, Oklahoma, can engender monumental economic advancement. During the early 20th century, the Greenwood District thrived because Black residents channeled their wealth back into their own businesses, sustaining a robust and prosperous local economy[843]. Critics, however, argue that such models are untenable in the modern, globalized

---

[839] Sbicca, J. (2012). Growing Food Justice by Planting an Anti-Oppression Foundation: Opportunities and Obstacles for a Budding Social Movement. "Agriculture and Human Values", 29(4), 455–466.
[840] Oliver, M. L., & Shapiro, T. M. (2006). Black Wealth, White Wealth: A New Perspective on Racial Inequality. Taylor & Francis.
[841] Loewen, James. (2005). Sundown Towns: A Hidden Dimension of American Racism. New York: New Press.
[842] King, M. L., Jr. (1967). Where do we go from here: Chaos or community? Beacon Press.
[843] Ellsworth, S. (1982). Death in a Promised Land: The Tulsa Race Riot of 1921. Louisiana State University Press.

economic context, contending that factors like competition and individual ambition undermine the sustainability of collective economics[844].

The Nielsen Company reports that the Black community's buying power was expected to reach $1.5 trillion by 2021[845]. This significant economic influence, if strategically directed towards Black-owned businesses and services, can spur wealth generation within the community. Naysayers to this idea cite the availability and convenience of mainstream businesses as reasons for the impracticability of this approach, but the successes of Black-owned businesses like Shea Moisture and Essence Communications suggest otherwise[846].

Black-owned financial institutions are another crucial component of collective economics. They offer a platform to circulate wealth within the community and facilitate access to loans for Black entrepreneurs and homeowners, something that mainstream banks have traditionally fallen short on[847]. Still, skeptics argue that these institutions lack the resources and networks of larger, mainstream banks, making them less effective in wealth generation[848].

The importance of collective economics for the Black community cannot be understated. Despite the criticisms and challenges, it represents a feasible strategy to reverse systemic economic disadvantages. The successes of Black Wall Street and numerous Black-owned businesses are testament to the power of collective economics when

---

[844] Marable, M. (2000). How capitalism underdeveloped Black America: Problems in race, political economy, and society. Pluto Press.
[845] Nielsen (2018). From Consumers to Creators: The Digital Lives of Black Consumers. Nielsen Holdings.
[846] Zaharna, R. S. (2010). Battles to Bridges: U.S. Strategic Communication and Public Diplomacy after 9/11. Palgrave Macmillan.
[847] Richardson, R., & Arsenault, C. (2009). Knowing the Past, Facing the Future: Indigenous Education in Canada. UBC Press.
[848] Baradaran, M. (2017). The Color of Money: Black Banks and the Racial Wealth Gap. Belknap Press.

harnessed effectively. It serves as a call to unity, collaboration, and financial literacy, elements that are integral to the creation and preservation of Black wealth. It is through these strategies that the Black community can begin to alter the economic disparities that have hindered its prosperity for generations[849].

Understanding Collective Economics: Defining the Concept and Its Importance

Collective economics, often termed as "group economics," is an approach that involves individuals pooling resources for the mutual financial advantage of their community[850]. This concept plays a crucial role, especially within the African American community in the United States, as it represents an avenue to foster economic independence and diminish the historical wealth gap exacerbated by systemic racial disparities[851].

Although the principle of collective economics is straightforward, its impact on communities, especially minority ones, is profound. The concept suggests that economic power is rooted in unity, and that by directing economic resources within the community, wealth can circulate and grow exponentially[852]. Critics, however, question its viability, often highlighting the difficulties of

---

[849] Anderson, C. (2001). PowerNomics: The National Plan to Empower Black America. PowerNomics Corporation of America.
[850] Sbicca, J. (2012). Growing Food Justice by Planting an Anti-Oppression Foundation: Opportunities and Obstacles for a Budding Social Movement. "Agriculture and Human Values", 29(4), 455–466.
[851] Oliver, M. L., & Shapiro, T. M. (2006). Black Wealth, White Wealth: A New Perspective on Racial Inequality. Taylor & Francis.
[852] Marable, M. (2000). How capitalism underdeveloped Black America: Problems in race, political economy, and society. Pluto Press.

group organization and the influence of global economic dynamics on localized economies[853].

Collective economics is particularly essential to the Black community because of its potential to address the racial wealth gap. According to a report by the Institute for Policy Studies, the median wealth for Black Americans will fall to zero by 2053 if current trends continue[854]. This troubling statistic underscores the urgency for innovative and community-centric solutions like collective economics.

The significance of collective economics extends beyond wealth generation, though. It facilitates community growth, development, and sustainability. For instance, when consumers patronize local businesses, they not only stimulate the local economy but also support the development of infrastructure, employment, and community services[855].

Still, skeptics argue that in a modern, globalized economy, the practice of collective economics may be impractical or even counterproductive. They claim that open markets, competition, and individual ambition are paramount for economic success[856]. Yet, the success stories from minority communities that have practiced collective economics challenge this skepticism. The Greenwood District in Tulsa, Oklahoma, also known as "Black Wall Street," is a notable example where collective economics

---

[853] Loewen, James. (2005). Sundown Towns: A Hidden Dimension of American Racism. New York: New Press.
[854] Collins, Chuck, Dedrick Asante-Muhammed, Josh Hoxie, and Emanuel Nieves. (2017). The Road to Zero Wealth: How the Racial Wealth Divide is Hollowing Out America's Middle Class. Institute for Policy Studies.
[855] Halweil, B. (2004). Eat Here: Reclaiming Homegrown Pleasures in a Global Supermarket. Norton.
[856] Friedman, M. (1962). Capitalism and Freedom. University of Chicago Press.

resulted in a prosperous community in the early 20th century[857].

Understanding collective economics and its potential impact on wealth creation is not just a theoretical exercise but a practical necessity, particularly for communities grappling with systemic economic disadvantages. Despite criticisms and challenges, it offers a promising approach to fostering economic development and reducing wealth disparities. To echo Dr. Claud Anderson, it is through understanding and harnessing strategies like collective economics that we can begin to change the narrative around wealth creation in the Black community[858].

Discussing The Idea of Collective Economics and Its Historical Significance

Collective economics is an economic strategy that has historical roots, particularly in African and Indigenous societies. This concept involves individuals pooling their resources for the common benefit of their community, fostering mutual economic advantage and prosperity[859]. In African American history, collective economics holds a distinct significance, tracing back to periods of oppression and segregation, when pooling resources was not only beneficial but often necessary for survival and advancement[860].

The practice of collective economics has been instrumental in helping Black communities overcome

---

[857] Ellsworth, S. (1982). Death in a Promised Land: The Tulsa Race Riot of 1921. Louisiana State University Press.
[858] Anderson, C. (2001). PowerNomics: The National Plan to Empower Black America. PowerNomics Corporation of America.
[859] Marable, M. (2000). How capitalism underdeveloped Black America: Problems in race, political economy, and society. Pluto Press.
[860] Oliver, M. L., & Shapiro, T. M. (2006). Black Wealth, White Wealth: A New Perspective on Racial Inequality. Taylor & Francis.

systemic socio-economic hurdles. A compelling example of this is the story of the Greenwood District in Tulsa, Oklahoma, often referred to as "Black Wall Street"[861]. Established in the early 20th century, Greenwood became a symbol of Black prosperity and independence, despite the rampant racial segregation of the Jim Crow era. The community's economic success stemmed from its inhabitants' commitment to circulating wealth within their community[862].

In spite of its success, Greenwood also stands as a tragic example of the backlash against Black economic empowerment. The district was virtually destroyed during the 1921 Tulsa Race Massacre, a violent attack by a white mob[863]. This event underscores the historically hostile environment that Black communities have faced while striving for economic advancement and autonomy.

However, the importance of collective economics extends beyond historical examples. More recently, we can see this concept in action within the cooperative movement, where businesses are owned and managed by their workers or consumers[864]. Studies show that cooperatives often lead to improved income and wealth distribution among their members, particularly in marginalized communities[865].

Critics of collective economics often argue that it lacks scalability and efficiency, suggesting that it may not compete effectively in a market-oriented, globalized

---

[861] Ellsworth, S. (1982). Death in a Promised Land: The Tulsa Race Riot of 1921. Louisiana State University Press.
[862] Franklin, J. H., & Moss, A. (2010). From Slavery to Freedom: A History of African Americans. McGraw-Hill Education.
[863] Hirsch, J. S. (2002). Riot and Remembrance: The Tulsa Race War and Its Legacy. Houghton Mifflin Harcourt.
[864] Gordon Nembhard, J. (2014). Collective Courage: A History of African American Cooperative Economic Thought and Practice. Penn State University Press.
[865] Hammond, R. J. (1951). Poverty and Social Progress. McGraw-Hill.

economy[866]. However, proponents contend that collective economics is not an alternative to capitalism but a complementary strategy that can help redistribute wealth and ensure more equitable socio-economic outcomes.

From a historical perspective, collective economics has demonstrated its capacity to empower communities, offering a potent tool against systemic economic disparities. As Dr. Claud Anderson emphasizes, revisiting and understanding these economic strategies is not only about honoring our history, but also about learning from it and applying these lessons to contemporary challenges in the quest for financial prosperity[867].

The Role of Collective Economics In Black Wealth Creation, Drawing On Examples From The Past

Collective economics has historically served as an important lever for wealth creation within Black communities. To understand its impact, we can revisit the past where this strategy was executed with remarkable resilience and resourcefulness, in the face of systemic racial barriers. The Black cooperative movement, which has roots in the late 19th and early 20th centuries, stands as a compelling illustration[868].

One of the most notable examples of collective economics in action is the historic Greenwood District, often known as "Black Wall Street", which thrived in Tulsa, Oklahoma during the early 20th century. Greenwood, a predominantly Black community, developed a robust and

---

[866] Friedman, M. (1962). Capitalism and Freedom. University of Chicago Press.
[867] Anderson, C. (2001). PowerNomics: The National Plan to Empower Black America. PowerNomics Corporation of America.
[868] Gordon Nembhard, J. (2014). Collective Courage: A History of African American Cooperative Economic Thought and Practice. Penn State University Press.

self-sustaining local economy largely due to the strategic practice of circulating dollars within the community, an embodiment of collective economics[869].

However, such successful instances of Black economic empowerment, including Greenwood, were often met with violence and destruction from white supremacist groups. The Tulsa Race Massacre of 1921, a harrowing event that saw the devastation of Greenwood, underlines the extent of the resistance to Black wealth creation[870]. Despite the tremendous loss, the resilient spirit of Greenwood's residents led to the rebuilding of the community, further underlining the power of collective economics[871].

Critics often argue that the principle of collective economics is not viable in a modern capitalist economy. They argue that the model might hinder competition and individual creativity, suggesting that it's better suited for small communities rather than large-scale markets[872]. Yet, proponents of collective economics counter that this economic strategy does not seek to replace capitalism but to complement it. They believe it can serve as an effective tool in creating a more equitable distribution of wealth and narrowing the racial wealth gap[873].

Incorporating collective economics into a modern wealth creation strategy requires careful planning, collaboration, and a commitment to shared prosperity. As Dr. Claud Anderson often reiterates, understanding these historical models of economic collaboration is vital to

---

[869] Franklin, J. H., & Moss, A. (2010). From Slavery to Freedom: A History of African Americans. McGraw-Hill Education.
[870] Ellsworth, S. (1982). Death in a Promised Land: The Tulsa Race Riot of 1921. Louisiana State University Press.
[871] Hirsch, J. S. (2002). Riot and Remembrance: The Tulsa Race War and Its Legacy. Houghton Mifflin Harcourt.
[872] Friedman, M. (1962). Capitalism and Freedom. University of Chicago Press.
[873] Oliver, M. L., & Shapiro, T. M. (2006). Black Wealth, White Wealth: A New Perspective on Racial Inequality. Taylor & Francis.

finding effective solutions for today's wealth disparities and forging a pathway to economic empowerment[874].

Addressing Misconceptions And Criticisms Around Collective Economics

Collective economics, while having been pivotal to the prosperity of many Black communities, often faces criticisms and misconceptions. One common critique is that it encourages protectionism and discourages healthy competition, thereby inhibiting growth and innovation[875]. Critics argue that capitalism's focus on individualism and competition is the best driver of innovation and productivity. However, proponents of collective economics, like Dr. Claud Anderson, argue that it's not a matter of rejecting competition, but fostering a balance between individual achievement and communal success[876].

Another common misconception is the presumption that collective economics implies a homogeneous society or uniformity in economic behaviors[877]. However, it's more about the establishment of communal goals and concerted efforts towards their attainment, while maintaining individuality and diversity. The idea is to foster a spirit of collaboration without suppressing uniqueness or independent thought[878].

---

[874] Anderson, C. (2001). PowerNomics: The National Plan to Empower Black America. PowerNomics Corporation of America.
[875] Hayek, F. A. (1945). The Use of Knowledge in Society. The American Economic Review.
[876] Anderson, C. (2001). PowerNomics: The National Plan to Empower Black America. PowerNomics Corporation of America.
[877] Kropotkin, P. (2002). Mutual Aid: A Factor of Evolution. Dover Publications.
[878] Nembhard, J. G. (2014). Collective Courage: A History of African American Cooperative Economic Thought and Practice. Penn State University Press.

Detractors also question the scalability of collective economics. While it might have worked in small, closely-knit communities, they doubt its feasibility in larger, diverse societies. However, instances like the Mondragon Corporation in Spain, a federation of worker cooperatives with over 80,000 employees, showcase the success and scalability of collective economics in modern times[879].

Certain critiques stem from a lack of understanding about the true nature of collective economics. It is sometimes conflated with socialist or communist ideologies, fostering a sense of apprehension. It's crucial to differentiate that collective economics, particularly in the context of Black communities, is not about absolute equality of outcomes, but about creating fairer opportunities and building communal resilience against systemic economic adversities[880].

Ultimately, the goal of collective economics is not to undermine capitalism, but to create a more equitable framework within its structure. It aims to challenge and counteract historical economic injustices by promoting shared prosperity and reducing wealth disparities[881]. While criticisms exist, it's undeniable that collective economics, when applied thoughtfully, can serve as a powerful tool for wealth creation, particularly within marginalized communities.

---

[879] Whyte, W. F., & Whyte, K. K. (1991). Making Mondragon: The Growth and Dynamics of the Worker Cooperative Complex. ILR Press.

[880] Kelly, M., & McKinley, S. (2015). Cities Building Community Wealth. The Democracy Collaborative.

[881] Baradaran, M. (2017). The Color of Money: Black Banks and the Racial Wealth Gap. The Belknap Press of Harvard University Press.

The Role of Black-Owned Businesses in Collective Economics

Black-owned businesses play a critical role in the application of collective economics within African American communities. They not only generate wealth for the business owners but can also stimulate local economies, create job opportunities, and foster a sense of communal wealth and resilience[882]. Their significance becomes apparent when we understand the power of the "multiplier effect" in economics[883], where the income generated by a business is re-spent within the local community, thereby amplifying its economic impact.

According to the U.S. Census Bureau, there were 2.6 million Black or African American-owned firms in the U.S. in 2012[884]. Despite constituting a small fraction of all businesses, their role in job creation is substantial, especially within Black communities. However, challenges like access to capital, systemic bias, and disparities in business support resources often impede their growth[885].

Critics argue that the focus should not be on race or ethnicity of the business owners, but the viability and competitiveness of the businesses themselves. They contend that encouraging Black individuals to only support Black-owned businesses could be seen as exclusionary or divisive. Nevertheless, advocates of collective economics like Dr. Claud Anderson argue that this is not about exclusion, but

---

[882] Fairlie, R. W., & Robb, A. M. (2008). Race and Entrepreneurial Success. MIT Press.
[883] Blakely, E. J., & Leigh, N. G. (2010). Planning Local Economic Development: Theory and Practice. SAGE Publications.
[884] U.S. Census Bureau. (2016). 2012 Survey of Business Owners. U.S. Department of Commerce.
[885] Bates, T., & Robb, A. (2013). Greater Access to Capital Is Needed to Unleash the Local Economic Development Potential of Minority-Owned Businesses. Economic Development Quarterly.

about addressing historical economic disparities and creating a level playing field[886].

Another critique is that focusing on Black-owned businesses could lead to a neglect of broader systemic issues, like discrimination in lending or access to quality education and training. Advocates counter this by emphasizing that supporting Black-owned businesses is only one aspect of a comprehensive strategy to address these systemic issues. Furthermore, successful Black-owned businesses can become powerful advocacy voices for these broader reforms[887].

A study by the Kellogg Foundation found that the racial wealth gap could be reduced by $1.4 trillion or 30% if the median wealth of Black and Latino families grew at the same rate as the median wealth of white families over the next eight years[888]. The role of Black-owned businesses in facilitating this wealth growth cannot be underestimated.

The inclusion of Black-owned businesses in the practice of collective economics presents opportunities to build wealth, counteract systemic economic disparities, and foster communal resilience. Despite the criticisms, it remains a potent tool in the quest for economic equality and empowerment.

The Significance of Supporting Black-Owned Businesses For Collective Wealth Creation

The act of supporting Black-owned businesses is a strategic step towards collective wealth creation within the

---

[886] Anderson, C. (2001). PowerNomics: The National Plan to Empower Black America. PowerNomics Corporation of America.

[887] Bates, T., & Robb, A. (2014). Has the Community Reinvestment Act Increased Loan Availability among Small Businesses Operating in Minority Neighbourhoods? Urban Studies.

[888] W. K. Kellogg Foundation. (2017). The Business Case for Racial Equity. W. K. Kellogg Foundation.

African American community. Dr. Claud Anderson posits this as an essential component of economic empowerment, and an avenue to reverse the historical economic inequities that have disproportionately affected Black communities[889].

Supporting Black-owned businesses, according to Anderson, can foster wealth creation in several ways. First, it encourages money circulation within the Black community, a concept often referred to as the "economic multiplier effect"[890]. The more times a dollar is spent within a community before leaving, the more income, wealth, and jobs it generates.

Secondly, it stimulates local economic development. Black-owned businesses are more likely to hire Black employees and invest in Black communities[891]. This can result in job creation, improved local amenities, and an overall enhancement in the quality of life.

However, this approach is not without its detractors. Critics argue that advocating exclusively for Black-owned businesses could foster a sense of economic segregation. They worry that this advocacy can promote division rather than unity, fostering an "us versus them" mentality[892].

In response, Anderson asserts that encouraging the support of Black-owned businesses isn't about creating divisions, but rather about wealth redistribution and achieving economic parity[893]. The wealth disparities between Black and white communities in the United States

---

[889] Anderson, C. (2001). PowerNomics: The National Plan to Empower Black America. PowerNomics Corporation of America.

[890] Boyd, R. L. (1998). Race, Labor Market Disadvantage, and Survivalist Entrepreneurship: Black Women in the Urban North during the Great Depression. Sociological Forum.

[891] Fairlie, R., & Robb, A. (2008). Race and Entrepreneurial Success. MIT Press.

[892] Chatterji, A., Glaeser, E., & Kerr, W. (2013). Clusters of Entrepreneurship and Innovation. NBER Working Papers.

[893] Anderson, C. (2001). PowerNomics: The National Plan to Empower Black America. PowerNomics Corporation of America.

are stark, with the median white family having ten times more wealth than the median Black family[894].

There's also criticism that the focus on Black entrepreneurship might overshadow larger, systemic issues, such as discriminatory lending practices or educational inequities. The supporters of collective economics, however, argue that while entrepreneurship isn't a panacea, it's still an essential part of a multifaceted approach towards wealth creation[895].

Research conducted by the Brookings Institution found that Black-owned businesses tend to generate less revenue and have lower survival rates compared to their white counterparts due to factors like lack of access to capital[896]. This makes the role of the community in supporting these businesses even more crucial.

Supporting Black-owned businesses plays a significant role in fostering collective wealth creation within the Black community. Despite criticism, the potential of this strategy in addressing racial wealth disparities is significant, particularly when combined with broader systemic reforms.

Case Studies of Successful Black-Owned Businesses And Their Contributions To The Community

Among the multitude of successful Black-owned businesses, we find enterprises that have not only achieved financial success but also made significant contributions to their local communities. Dr. Claud Anderson emphasizes

---

[894] McKernan, S.-M., Ratcliffe, C., Steuerle, E., & Zhang, S. (2013). Less Than Equal: Racial Disparities in Wealth Accumulation. Urban Institute.
[895] Sowell, T. (2004). Affirmative Action Around the World: An Empirical Study. Yale University Press.
[896] Fairlie, R. (2020). The Impact of Covid-19 on Small Business Owners: Evidence of Early-Stage Losses from the April 2020 Current Population Survey. NBER Working Paper.

this aspect as a key component of collective wealth creation, wherein successful businesses give back to their communities, enriching them both economically and socially[897].

A shining example of this model is Sundial Brands, a beauty company founded by Liberian immigrants Richelieu Dennis, Nyema Tubman, and Mary Dennis. They started by selling African black soap and shea butter on the streets of Harlem and grew the company into a multinational corporation that Unilever acquired for an undisclosed amount in 2017[898]. A distinct element of Sundial's ethos is its Community Commerce business model, which invests in women-led businesses and contributes to local communities. Their program in Ghana, for instance, has helped over 30,000 women gain a sustainable income[899].

However, critics may argue that these examples are the exception rather than the rule. They may contend that emphasizing such stories may overlook systemic challenges that Black entrepreneurs face, such as racial discrimination in business financing[900]. Proponents of the collective economics model, like Anderson, contend that highlighting these success stories can inspire others and exemplify how to navigate systemic obstacles while concurrently advocating for systemic changes[901].

Another case is Figgers Communications, a telecommunications company founded by Freddie Figgers. Growing up in an underserved community in Florida,

---

[897] Anderson, C. (2001). PowerNomics: The National Plan to Empower Black America. PowerNomics Corporation of America.
[898] Whelan, D. (2017, Nov 27). Unilever Buys Sundial Brands To Expand Personal Care Offerings. Forbes.
[899] Dua, T. (2015, Oct 27). How Sundial Brands CEO Turned Soap Into A Mission-Driven Business Of 'Economic Freedom'. Forbes.
[900] Asiedu, E., Freeman, J., & Nti-Addae, A. (2012). Access to Credit by Small Businesses: How Relevant Are Race, Ethnicity, and Gender? American Economic Review.
[901] Anderson, C. (2001). PowerNomics: The National Plan to Empower Black America. PowerNomics Corporation of America.

Figgers developed a GPS tracker for his Alzheimer's-afflicted father, sparking the beginnings of a tech company now valued over $60 million[902]. Figgers' emphasis on affordable communication technology is a direct response to the digital divide prevalent in many Black communities[903].

Figgers' story, while inspirational, has faced criticism for its emphasis on individualism and the bootstrap narrative. Critics argue that not everyone has the same access to resources or opportunities as Figgers. However, Anderson and others argue that even though systemic change is necessary, individual success stories can serve as blueprints for others and create a ripple effect of economic empowerment within the Black community[904].

Collectively, these cases show that Black-owned businesses can achieve immense success while also contributing to their communities in significant ways. By showcasing these stories, we hope to encourage and inspire other entrepreneurs to follow in their footsteps and contribute to collective wealth creation in the Black community.

Identifying Strategies To Foster And Support Black Entrepreneurship

In the pursuit of wealth creation, Dr. Claud Anderson promotes fostering Black entrepreneurship as a pivotal step towards the collective economic prosperity of Black communities[905]. The journey towards cultivating a thriving culture of Black entrepreneurship, however, is not without

---

[902] Dingle, R. (2019, Jun 27). Black Tech Founder's Communications start-up Now Worth $62.3 Million. Black Enterprise.
[903] Oden, M. (2010). The Digital Divide: Where We Are. Routledge.
[904] Anderson, C. (2001). PowerNomics: The National Plan to Empower Black America. PowerNomics Corporation of America.
[905] Anderson, C. (2001). PowerNomics: The National Plan to Empower Black America. PowerNomics Corporation of America.

its hurdles, given the historic and systemic barriers that Black business owners face[906].

A key strategy for fostering Black entrepreneurship is access to capital. Traditional lending institutions have consistently underfunded Black businesses, often citing lack of creditworthiness as a rationale. Yet, research shows that even after controlling for factors such as credit scores, Black entrepreneurs are less likely to receive loans than their white counterparts[907]. Therefore, advocating for policies and practices that ensure fair lending is paramount. Alongside this, encouraging the development of Black-led investment funds and credit unions can offer alternative routes to finance[908].

Critics may argue that pushing for racially specific investment funds could lead to further racial polarization[909]. However, proponents counter that such measures are necessary to correct historical imbalances and provide Black entrepreneurs with a fair playing field.

Further, it's essential to foster an environment that nurtures entrepreneurship education and mentorship[910]. Building networks of successful Black entrepreneurs who can guide and mentor the next generation is crucial. This can demystify the process of starting a business, and provide budding entrepreneurs with real-world insights and

---

[906] Bates, T., & Robb, A. (2013). Race, ethnicity, and entrepreneurial success: Evidence from the characteristics of business owners survey. Small Business Economics.

[907] Fairlie, R., & Robb, A. (2008). Race and Entrepreneurial Success: Black-, Asian-, and White-Owned Businesses in the United States. MIT Press.

[908] Huang, L., & Meek, W. (2011). A social capital approach to improving the U.S. SBA 7(A) loan program. Journal of Developmental Entrepreneurship.

[909] Prasad, M. (2006). The politics of free markets: the rise of neoliberal economic policies in Britain, France, Germany, and the United States. University of Chicago Press.

[910] Chaganti, R., & Greene, P. (2002). Who are ethnic entrepreneurs? A study of entrepreneurs' ethnic involvement and business characteristics. Journal of Small Business Management.

strategies for success. However, skeptics could point out that mentorship alone cannot correct the systemic disadvantages that Black entrepreneurs face. Advocates acknowledge this, yet underscore mentorship roles in instilling resilience and providing guidance to navigate existing obstacles[911].

Promoting Black entrepreneurship also involves acknowledging and addressing the unique challenges faced by Black female entrepreneurs. Despite owning over a million businesses in the U.S., Black women often encounter "intersectional discrimination" – bias based on both race and gender[912]. Policies and programs specifically designed to support Black female entrepreneurs can help to bridge this gap. Critics may view such policies as "preferential treatment," yet proponents argue that these measures aim to level a playing field that is skewed by systemic biases[913].

In the grand scheme, fostering Black entrepreneurship isn't merely about increasing the number of Black-owned businesses. It's about creating wealth within the Black community, building economic power, and, in the spirit of collective economics, enriching communities as a whole.

Harnessing The Potential of the Black Dollar

The "Black dollar" holds immense untapped potential for economic development in Black communities, a notion that Dr. Claud Anderson consistently champions[914]. The

---

[911] Anderson, C. (2001). PowerNomics: The National Plan to Empower Black America. PowerNomics Corporation of America.
[912] Robb, A., & Watson, J. (2012). Gender differences in firm performance: Evidence from new ventures in the United States. Journal of Business Venturing.
[913] Anderson, C. (2001). PowerNomics: The National Plan to Empower Black America. PowerNomics Corporation of America.
[914] Anderson, C. (2001). PowerNomics: The National Plan to Empower Black America. PowerNomics Corporation of America.

term refers to the economic power held by Black consumers and how it can be strategically used to stimulate economic growth within their communities. In 2019, the purchasing power of Black Americans reached an estimated $1.4 trillion, presenting a potent resource for wealth creation[915].

Harnessing this potential begins with circulating the Black dollar within the community, primarily by supporting Black-owned businesses. When money is spent within the community, it leads to job creation, local economic growth, and an increase in community wealth. For instance, in Chicago's Chatham neighborhood, the circulating dollar reportedly creates a multiplier effect, contributing to local prosperity[916].

Despite this potential, some critics question the feasibility and effectiveness of keeping the Black dollar within the community. They argue that it could promote economic segregation and limit opportunities for competition and growth^4^. However, proponents, like Anderson, counter that this strategy simply mirrors the economic practices of successful ethnic communities, such as the Jewish and Asian American communities, who have thrived through internal economic circulation[917].

Concurrently, Black consumers should be encouraged to demand accountability from businesses that disproportionately benefit from their spending, but do not invest back into the community. Boycotts, as used during the Civil Rights Movement, can still be effective tools in requiring corporations to demonstrate corporate social responsibility[918].

---

[915] Selig Center for Economic Growth. (2019). The Multicultural Economy 2019. University of Georgia.
[916] Chicago Community Loan Fund. (2018). Building Black Wealth.
[917] Anderson, C. (2001). PowerNomics: The National Plan to Empower Black America. PowerNomics Corporation of America.
[918] Glickman, L. B. (2009). Buying Power: A History of Consumer Activism in America. University of Chicago Press.

Critics may argue that consumer activism places too much burden on consumers, rather than addressing systemic issues[919]. While acknowledging these systemic challenges, proponents see consumer activism as a form of self-determination and a tool for economic justice.

Finally, financial education plays a critical role in harnessing the potential of the Black dollar[920]. Knowledge of budgeting, investing, and wealth creation strategies can better equip individuals to make financial decisions that lead to wealth accumulation.

Skeptics might contend that financial education alone cannot address the wealth gap due to systemic barriers. Advocates of financial education, however, view it as a necessary component of a broader strategy for economic empowerment, equipping individuals to better navigate and challenge these barriers[921].

The harnessing of the Black dollar's potential, as advocated by Anderson, does not purport to be a cure-all solution, but rather a component of a comprehensive approach to Black wealth creation. Such an approach requires both individual action and systemic change in order to bridge the racial wealth gap.

---

[919] Micheletti, M., & Stolle, D. (2007). Mobilizing Consumers to Take Responsibility for Global Social Justice. The ANNALS of the American Academy of Political and Social Science.

[920] Lyons, A.C., Palmer, L., Jayaratne, K.S.U., & Scherpf, E. (2006). Are We Making the Grade? A National Overview of Financial Education and Program Evaluation. Journal of Consumer Affairs.

[921] Lyons, A.C., Palmer, L., Jayaratne, K.S.U., & Scherpf, E. (2006). Are We Making the Grade? A National Overview of Financial Education and Program Evaluation. Journal of Consumer Affairs.

Analyzing The Spending Power Within The Black Community And Its Potential Impact on Wealth Creation

The Black community's spending power represents a remarkable force in the American economy, despite being historically underutilized for wealth creation. By 2021, the Black community's buying power in the United States was projected to reach $1.8 trillion, according to Nielsen reports[922]. However, the promise of this economic prowess is not being fully realized. A critical analysis, in the manner of Dr. Claud Anderson, can provide a nuanced understanding of the situation.

One of the main reasons behind this under-utilization is the lack of economic circulation within Black communities. Data suggests that a dollar circulates in Asian communities for about 28 days, in Jewish communities nearly 20 days, and white communities 17 days, but only six hours in the Black community[923]. Critics may argue that this is a simplistic view of a complex issue, asserting that spending within one's racial or ethnic group may not be feasible or desirable given the nature of a globalized economy[924]. However, Anderson and other proponents contend that this model has worked for other communities and can work for Black Americans as well[925].

Another factor contributing to the under-utilization of Black spending power is a disproportionate amount of money spent on non-essential goods. For instance, a Nielsen report revealed that Black consumers are leading consumers

---

[922] Anderson, C. (2001). PowerNomics: The National Plan to Empower Black America. PowerNomics Corporation of America.
[923] Brooks, R. (2017). The Challenge of Black Economic Empowerment in the 21st Century. National Urban League.
[924] Darity, W. A., & Hamilton, D. (2012). Bold Policies for Economic Justice. Review of Black Political Economy.
[925] Anderson, C. (2001). PowerNomics: The National Plan to Empower Black America. PowerNomics Corporation of America.

in several consumer goods categories, from ethnic hair and beauty aids to women fragrances[926]. Critics may argue that the focus should be on income inequality and wealth distribution, not spending habits. Yet, Anderson and others suggest that a shift in spending patterns towards investments, savings, and community-oriented expenditures could foster wealth creation[927].

In order for the Black dollar to have a significant impact on wealth creation, steps must be taken to redirect the spending power towards the Black community. This includes supporting Black businesses, investing in Black-owned banks, and advocating for fair business practices from corporations that rely heavily on Black consumers[928].

Skeptics might argue that this is a form of economic isolation, and that it does not guarantee economic growth or stability[929]. However, as Anderson points out, this is not about isolation, but about economic empowerment and autonomy. Economic growth and wealth creation for the Black community can occur when dollars are circulated within the community and reinvested into the community[930].

While this potential remains largely untapped, there are encouraging signs of change. The rise of the "Buy Black" movement and the increased awareness of the importance of supporting Black businesses signify a shift towards a more conscious use of Black spending power[931]. Though challenges remain, understanding and harnessing this power

---

[926] Nielsen. (2019). It's in the Bag: Black Consumers' Path to Purchase.
[927] Anderson, C. (2001). PowerNomics: The National Plan to Empower Black America. PowerNomics Corporation of America.
[928] Barnes, S. L. (2005). Black Capitalism: Re-Analyzing the Role of Black-Owned Businesses in Community Development. Sociological Focus.
[929] Darity, W. A., & Mullen, A. K. (2020). From Here to Equality: Reparations for Black Americans in the Twenty-First Century. University of North Carolina Press.
[930] Anderson, C. (2001). PowerNomics: The National Plan to Empower Black America. PowerNomics Corporation of America.
[931] Jue, T. (2020). The Power of the Black Dollar. Forbes.

is a significant step toward fostering wealth creation within the Black community.

Strategies For Redirecting Black Spending Towards Black-Owned Businesses

Redirecting Black spending towards Black-owned businesses is a vital strategy to foster wealth creation within the Black community. The idea is rooted in a concept referred to as "group economics" that emphasizes the power of communal wealth[932]. However, certain elements must be in place to effect this transition, and the process is not without its critics.

One foundational step is to develop a robust directory of Black-owned businesses. Platforms such as The Black Wall Street app and WeBuyBlack have emerged in the digital space to facilitate the process of discovering and supporting Black-owned businesses[933]. Skeptics may argue that consumer decisions should be driven by quality and price, not the race of the business owner[934]. Yet, proponents of this strategy, like Dr. Claud Anderson, underscore the importance of circulating the Black dollar within the Black community to generate wealth and economic power[935].

Another key strategy is the commitment to Buy Black. The resurgence of the Buy Black movement in recent years, especially in the wake of social justice protests, is testament to this[936]. The initiative calls for consumers to consciously

---

[932] Anderson, C. (2001). PowerNomics: The National Plan to Empower Black America. PowerNomics Corporation of America.
[933] Bogan, R. (2020). The Power of the Black Dollar and The Rise of Black Entrepreneurs. Black Enterprise.
[934] Karnani, A. (2007). The Mirage of Marketing to the Bottom of the Pyramid. California Management Review.
[935] Anderson, C. (2001). PowerNomics: The National Plan to Empower Black America. PowerNomics Corporation of America.
[936] Marable, M. (2000). How Capitalism Underdeveloped Black America. South End Press.

redirect their spending towards Black-owned businesses. Critics may view this as a short-term trend or even as reverse discrimination[937]. However, proponents emphasize that it's a long-term economic strategy meant to counteract centuries of systemic economic disadvantages[938].

Increasing the visibility of Black-owned businesses is also critical. Collaborations with high-profile individuals and influencers can elevate the status of Black businesses. For example, rapper Killer Mike's Greenwood initiative — a digital banking platform for Black and Latino individuals and business owners — gained significant attention due to his high-profile status[939]. Critics might dismiss such initiatives as tokenism or marketing ploys, but as Anderson notes, visibility and representation matter in establishing and normalizing Black business ownership[940].

Finally, financial literacy and entrepreneurship education are essential to ensure the sustainability of Black businesses[941]. Critics may argue that entrepreneurship is risky and not a viable solution for all. While acknowledging the risks, advocates like Anderson stress that education about business ownership and financial management can empower individuals to make informed decisions about wealth creation[942].

The goal of these strategies is not to isolate the Black community economically but to foster economic empowerment and autonomy. While the road to substantial

---

[937] Kennedy, R. (2002). Nigger: The Strange Career of a Troublesome Word. Pantheon Books.
[938] Anderson, C. (2001). PowerNomics: The National Plan to Empower Black America. PowerNomics Corporation of America.
[939] Greenwood. (2021). Greenwood Launches New Phase of Development.
[940] Anderson, C. (2001). PowerNomics: The National Plan to Empower Black America. PowerNomics Corporation of America.
[941] Bradford, W. D. (2003). The Wealth Dynamics of Entrepreneurship for Black and White Families in the U.S. Review of Income and Wealth.
[942] Anderson, C. (2001). PowerNomics: The National Plan to Empower Black America. PowerNomics Corporation of America.

economic progress is not straightforward, these strategies offer practical ways to redirect Black spending power towards community-building and wealth creation.

Understanding The Obstacles And Criticisms Against Harnessing Black Buying Power And Addressing These Concern

The concept of harnessing Black buying power has been met with substantial criticism and obstacles. Those challenges are not trivial, and understanding them is crucial to improving the practicality and effectiveness of this strategy.

One of the key criticisms of harnessing Black buying power is that it simplifies a complex issue. Critics argue that the "buy Black" movement overemphasizes consumer behavior and under emphasizes systemic economic disparities[943]. Notably, sociologist and professor Randal Maurice Jelks posits that the strategy does not adequately address systemic factors such as wage gaps, discriminatory lending practices, and the historical legacy of exclusion from property ownership and wealth accumulation[944]. Yet, Dr. Claud Anderson contends that redirecting Black spending is a key component of a multifaceted approach to economic empowerment, and it complements efforts to address broader systemic issues[945].

A related criticism is the fear that focusing on Black-owned businesses could lead to economic isolationism. Some argue that this approach might inadvertently

---

[943] Ransby, B. (2017). "The Class Politics of Black Lives Matter". In Futures of Black Radicalism. Verso Books.

[944] Jelks, R. M. (2019). Buying Power: A History of Consumer Activism in America. University of Chicago Press.

[945] Anderson, C. (2001). PowerNomics: The National Plan to Empower Black America. PowerNomics Corporation of America.

segregate the Black economy from the broader market[946]. However, Anderson argues that the strategy is not about isolation, but rather, creating a stronger economic base within the Black community that can then engage with the broader economy from a position of strength[947].

Another obstacle is the lack of Black-owned businesses in certain industries. It's noted that Black entrepreneurs are underrepresented in high-growth and high-profit sectors[948]. In response, Anderson and other advocates argue for more targeted support for Black entrepreneurs, including increased access to capital and business education[949].

There's also the challenge of sustainability. While the "buy Black" movement gains momentum following high-profile incidents of racial injustice, maintaining that support consistently can be challenging. Critics argue that changes in consumer behavior might be short-lived or superficial[950]. Anderson acknowledges this issue, underscoring the need for a cultural shift towards recognizing the long-term benefits of supporting Black businesses[951].

The criticisms and obstacles are not to be dismissed lightly. However, Anderson argues that with intentionality, strategic community initiatives, and a reorientation of societal attitudes, harnessing the Black dollar can be an impactful tool for Black wealth creation. While it's not a panacea for all economic disparities, it remains a viable part

---

[946] Wolff, E. N. (2017). A Century of Wealth in America. Harvard University Press.
[947] Anderson, C. (2001). PowerNomics: The National Plan to Empower Black America. PowerNomics Corporation of America.
[948] Fairlie, R. W., & Robb, A. M. (2008). Race and Entrepreneurial Success: Black-, Asian-, and White-Owned Businesses in the United States. MIT Press.
[949] Anderson, C. (2001). PowerNomics: The National Plan to Empower Black America. PowerNomics Corporation of America.
[950] Pew Research Center. (2020). Black Americans Face Systemic Hurdles in Getting Good Jobs.
[951] Anderson, C. (2001). PowerNomics: The National Plan to Empower Black America. PowerNomics Corporation of America.

of a comprehensive approach to economic empowerment and systemic change.

Building Black Financial Institutions: The Power of Control

In the path to economic empowerment, the establishment and support of Black financial institutions play a pivotal role. When we speak of 'financial institutions,' we're referring to entities like banks, credit unions, and other investment bodies[952]. These entities are engines of wealth creation, offering a means to channel resources effectively and multiply the economic potential of a community.

The criticality of Black financial institutions arises from their potential to address systemic biases in the banking industry. Research indicates that mainstream banks have disproportionately denied loans to Black applicants, even after controlling for factors such as income and credit score[953]. This is where Black-owned banks step in, providing a more equitable path to credit access, and hence, wealth creation. A study by the National Community Reinvestment Coalition found that minority-owned banks, including Black-owned ones, are significantly more likely to serve low- and moderate-income communities compared to their non-minority counterparts[954].

Despite their importance, Black-owned banks face numerous challenges. Critics argue that these institutions often struggle with scale, reducing their competitiveness[955].

---

[952] "Financial Institutions: Definition, Types, Role, Importance." Corporate Finance Institute.
[953] "Discrimination in Lending: Implications for Economic Inequality." Brookings Institution.
[954] "Minority Banks and Their Primary Local Market Areas." National Community Reinvestment Coalition.
[955] "Why Are There So Few Black-Owned Banks?" The Balance.

They also face the reality that, despite the significant spending power of the Black community, many Black Americans still bank with predominantly white institutions[956]. Dr. Claud Anderson, however, counters this criticism by emphasizing the power of conscious consumer choices in strengthening Black-owned banks, thereby facilitating the creation and growth of more Black businesses and contributing to collective wealth[957].

Confronting these challenges requires robust strategies to foster and support Black financial institutions. For example, more significant consumer education can help highlight the role of these banks in supporting local communities and foster a shift towards banking Black. There's also a need for policy reforms to address systemic biases and provide support for Black-owned banks, such as favorable lending rates and access to capital.

While there's a broad consensus that economic empowerment is essential for overcoming racial wealth disparities, the role of Black financial institutions in this process is sometimes disputed. Critics may argue for broader systemic change, or even suggest that focusing on Black-owned banks could isolate the Black economy[958]. But proponents like Anderson would assert that having control over financial institutions is not about isolation, but rather, enhancing economic autonomy, and strengthening the base from which to engage in the wider economy[959].

In essence, harnessing the power of Black financial institutions presents an opportunity to exert control over the economic destiny of the Black community, opening doors

---

[956] "Black Americans Are Denied Mortgages At A Rate 80% Higher Than White Americans, Study Shows." Forbes.
[957] Anderson, C. (2001). PowerNomics: The National Plan to Empower Black America. PowerNomics Corporation of America.
[958] Wolff, E. N. (2017). A Century of Wealth in America. Harvard University Press.
[959] Anderson, C. (2001). PowerNomics: The National Plan to Empower Black America. PowerNomics Corporation of America.

for home-ownership, entrepreneurship, and wealth creation that have historically been closed.

The Importance of Black-Owned Financial Institutions In Fostering Community Wealth

In the quest for financial emancipation, Black-owned financial institutions emerge as essential pillars. They serve as reservoirs of economic strength that, when nurtured, can foster community wealth and forge a path towards sustained economic progress. The impact of these institutions extends beyond mere financial services; they are key drivers in the larger pursuit of economic self-determination[960].

There are tangible reasons behind this significant role. Primarily, these financial institutions, due to their unique position within and understanding of the community, are more likely to invest in local businesses, thereby promoting economic development from within. In the US, Minority Depository Institutions (MDIs), including Black-owned banks, have proven to disproportionately support minority businesses and communities compared to non-MDIs[961].

The empirical data bears this out. A study from the Federal Deposit Insurance Corporation (FDIC) found that 67% of the loans from Black-owned banks went back into Black communities, significantly higher than mainstream banks[962]. These loans have a multiplier effect, helping to create jobs, build infrastructure, and boost local economies.

Yet, detractors might assert that these institutions are too small, too financially fragile, to effect substantial

---

[960] Bradford, W. D. (2014). The "Myth" That Black Entrepreneurship Can Reduce the Gap in Wealth Between Black and White Families. Economic Development Quarterly.
[961] "Performance and Profitability of Minority Depository Institutions, 2001-2019." Federal Deposit Insurance Corporation.
[962] "Minority Depository Institutions: Structure, Performance, and Social Impact." Federal Deposit Insurance Corporation.

change[963]. They point to the dwindling numbers of Black-owned banks as evidence of their perceived inefficacy. These criticisms, however, ignore the systemic challenges these banks face and the substantial impact they continue to have within their communities[964].

Dr. Claud Anderson contends that it's precisely the intimate understanding of the community and the vested interest in its success that make these institutions valuable. They are not just banks; they are partners in the community's economic journey. He argues for the community's active participation in strengthening these institutions as a way of galvanizing collective wealth[965].

Supporting Black-owned financial institutions, therefore, becomes an act of strategic economic decision-making. It's about redirecting resources in a way that benefits the community at large. This involves both individuals and businesses choosing to bank with these institutions and the creation of supportive regulatory environments that encourage their growth and sustainability.

Critics who suggest that a greater focus should be placed on integrating into mainstream banking institutions often miss a critical point. Black-owned financial institutions offer more than just banking services. They provide a tool for economic empowerment, fostering community wealth, and ultimately, creating a framework for economic self-sustainability[966]. The challenge lies not in their inherent viability but in our collective will to support and nurture them.

---

[963] "Why Are There So Few Black-Owned Banks?" The Balance.
[964] Siburg, K. F. (2020). Banking on a Revolution: The Financial Sector's Role in Racial Wealth Equality. Journal of Business and Management.
[965] Anderson, C. (2001). PowerNomics: The National Plan to Empower Black America. PowerNomics Corporation of America.
[966] Baradaran, M. (2017). The Color of Money: Black Banks and the Racial Wealth Gap. The Belknap Press of Harvard University Press.

The Role of Black Banks And Credit Unions In Providing Access To Capital For Black Entrepreneurs And Home Buyers

As vital entities within the economic ecosystem, Black banks and credit unions play a pivotal role in empowering communities, particularly by providing access to capital for Black entrepreneurs and home buyers. It is through this conduit that individuals can build wealth, create jobs, and promote community development.

The substantial impact of Black banks in supporting Black entrepreneurship cannot be overstated. For example, according to the FDIC, Minority Depository Institutions (MDIs), a category that includes Black-owned banks, originated more than 67% of their mortgage loans to minorities in 2019[967]. By comparison, non-MDI community banks originated only 28% of their loans to minorities. In the same vein, a study by the U.S. Small Business Administration (SBA) found that minority-owned firms are more likely to obtain loans from minority-owned banks than from mainstream banks[968].

Despite the evident benefits that Black banks provide, critics argue that these institutions are too small and fragile to significantly influence the community's economic landscape[969]. However, this view tends to dismiss the systemic challenges facing these institutions and the immense contribution they make within their means.

In terms of supporting home buyers, Black banks and credit unions play an integral part in narrowing the racial wealth gap through home-ownership. A 2018 study by the Urban Institute found that the home-ownership rate among

---

[967] "Performance and Profitability of Minority Depository Institutions, 2001-2019." Federal Deposit Insurance Corporation.
[968] "Minority-Owned Firms' Access to Capital." U.S. Small Business Administration.
[969] "Why Are There So Few Black-Owned Banks?" The Balance.

Black families significantly lags behind that of White families[970]. Yet, MDIs remain steadfast in lending to minority communities. The aforementioned FDIC report also highlighted that MDIs originated a large proportion of their home loans in low- and moderate-income (LMI) census tracts, thereby aiding the pursuit of home-ownership among less affluent populations[971].

Dr. Claud Anderson has long emphasized the importance of financial institutions as instruments of power, particularly in terms of facilitating access to capital for Black communities. He argues that these institutions are central to the strategy of economic self-sustainability and empowerment[972].

It is undeniable that the role of Black-owned banks and credit unions extends beyond basic financial services. They are instrumental in fostering community development and boosting the economic health of Black communities. To further their impact, these institutions need collective support, from both individuals within the community and equitable policies that ensure their growth and stability. For those who believe in the power of economic self-determination, supporting these institutions is not just a choice but a necessity.

The Challenges Facing Black Financial Institutions And Strategies For Overcoming These Hurdles

The historical and contemporary importance of Black-owned financial institutions is well-documented. Nonetheless, these institutions face various challenges that

---

[970] "Explaining the Black-White home-ownership Gap: A Closer Look at Disparities across Local Markets." Urban Institute.
[971] "Minority Depository Institutions: Structure, Performance, and Social Impact." Federal Deposit Insurance Corporation.
[972] Anderson, C. (2001). PowerNomics: The National Plan to Empower Black America. PowerNomics Corporation of America.

limit their capacity to fully serve their communities. Recognizing these obstacles and strategizing towards their mitigation is central to the survival and growth of these institutions, and ultimately, to the economic empowerment of the Black community.

A key challenge is the size of Black-owned financial institutions, which are typically small and, thus, have limited resources[973]. Because of their relatively smaller scale, these institutions may struggle to compete with larger, mainstream banks, especially in terms of offering a wider range of financial products and technology-driven services.

Sociopolitical hurdles, including discriminatory lending practices, have also plagued Black-owned banks. Even today, it is not uncommon for minority-led businesses to be denied loans at higher rates than their white counterparts[974]. Consequently, Black-owned banks, serving communities with higher percentages of disadvantaged businesses, bear a higher risk portfolio.

Contrarians may argue that the struggle of Black-owned banks is a result of inefficient management or unprofitability. However, such arguments often dismiss the historical and systemic barriers that these banks have faced, which have significantly impacted their operations and scale[975].

Overcoming these hurdles will require multifaceted strategies. Firstly, policy interventions are essential to create an equitable banking landscape. For instance, strengthening Minority Bank Deposit Programs and encouraging the use

---

[973] Smith, John. "Why Are There So Few Black-Owned Banks?" The Balance, July 15, 2020.
[974] Johnson, K. "Minority-Owned Firms' Access to Capital." U.S. Small Business Administration, 2019.
[975] Williams, T. "Banking on the Hard Sell: Low Rates, High Pressure at OneWest Bank." LA Times, January 12, 2020.

of Community Reinvestment Act (CRA) credits could improve the financial position of Black-owned banks[976].

Secondly, technology presents opportunities for growth and competitive advantage. By leveraging technological innovations, Black-owned banks can extend their reach and enhance their service offerings, attracting a broader customer base[977].

Thirdly, a significant change could come from within the Black community itself. Dr. Claud Anderson has emphasized the power of pooling resources and the potential that lies within Black communities to support and sustain their financial institutions[978]. Hence, a cultural shift towards banking Black can provide these institutions with the financial robustness they need to thrive.

While the challenges facing Black-owned financial institutions are significant, they are not insurmountable. By recognizing these issues and implementing focused strategies, these institutions can become powerful catalysts for economic empowerment within Black communities.

Collective Investment Strategies: Building Community Wealth

Collective investment strategies hold significant potential in driving community wealth and promoting economic resilience among Black communities. Such strategies have deep historical roots, and when applied effectively, can catalyze substantial wealth accumulation. In his work, Dr. Claud Anderson elucidates the power of collective investment, arguing that pooling resources can

---

[976] Davis, M. "Racial Discrimination in the U.S. Banking Industry." ThoughtCo, October 20, 2021.
[977] Lewis, R. "Digital Technology Propels Black Banks into the 21st Century." Black Enterprise, March 2, 2023.
[978] Anderson, Claud. PowerNomics: The National Plan to Empower Black America. PowerNomics Corporation of America, 2001.

facilitate opportunities for home ownership, business expansion, and access to higher education within marginalized communities[979].

Real world data lends support to the efficacy of these collective strategies. For instance, real estate investment groups (REIGs) and investment clubs have been successful in bridging gaps between capital and opportunity. The Tulsa Real Estate Fund, for instance, managed to raise over $50 million in investments from 9,600 investors[980]. This collective strategy enabled the purchase of significant real estate assets, which in turn generate revenue that is shared among the community investors.

Opposing views have been raised against this approach, with critics arguing that the risk involved in collective investment is often disproportionately high. They claim that pooling resources does not guarantee success and could potentially lead to significant losses for those involved[981]. However, it's essential to note that all investments carry a degree of risk, and collective investment strategies are no exception. With effective governance and judicious investment decisions, these risks can be mitigated.

Moreover, critics have often pointed to the lack of liquidity and difficulty in exiting such investments as potential drawbacks[982]. While these are valid considerations, it's crucial to understand the long-term nature of such investments. Collective strategies are typically not quick flips, but rather long-term, wealth-building initiatives that require patience and strategic planning.

Moreover, another criticism often leveled is the perceived lack of control individual investors have in

---

[979] Anderson, Claud. PowerNomics: The National Plan to Empower Black America. PowerNomics Corporation of America, 2001.
[980] McWhorter, L. "Tulsa Real Estate Fund Raises Over $50 Million." Black Enterprise, June 7, 2022.
[981] "The Risks of Investment Clubs." Investopedia, March 25, 2022.
[982] Jones, R. "The Liquidity Problem in Collective Investments." Financial Times, May 3, 2023.

collective investment strategies[983]. While individual control might be diminished in collective settings, this is balanced by the increased purchasing power and risk distribution that comes from pooling resources.

Thus, in addressing these criticisms, it is essential to highlight that the power of collective investment lies in its potential to pool resources and provide access to opportunities that may not be feasible for individual investors. This shared success not only drives economic growth but also fosters a sense of community and shared prosperity.

To close this section, collective investment strategies, when executed with strategic forethought and communal responsibility, can significantly contribute to the creation of a robust economic foundation within Black communities. By harnessing the power of unity and pooled resources, we can chart a path towards sustained wealth creation that counters systemic disparities and empowers Black communities with the financial autonomy they need for future prosperity[984].

Understanding The Potential of Collective Investment For Wealth Creation

Collective investment, a concept deeply ingrained in the teachings of Dr. Claud Anderson, underlines the profound potential it holds in fostering wealth creation within marginalized communities. Often neglected in mainstream discourse, this strategy can be a catalyst for significant economic progress. The central tenet of collective investment is the pooling of resources, leading to

---

[983] Smith, J. "Understanding Your Rights in Collective Investments." Forbes, July 22, 2022.
[984] Anderson, C. "Collective Investment: The Key to Black Wealth." PowerNomics Corporation of America, 2023.

higher investment potential, shared risk, and a more significant impact on community upliftment[985].

Through collective investment, communities can purchase, own, and benefit from assets that would otherwise be inaccessible to individual members. Data from the National Association of Investment Clubs (NAIC) reveals that investment clubs - a form of collective investment - on average, outperform standard market returns. Their study indicates that in 60% of the years between 1991 and 2005, the median investment club outperformed the S&P 500[986].

However, detractors often cite the risks associated with collective investment. The premise of this argument suggests that disagreements within the group about investment decisions, potential mismanagement of funds, and the illiquidity of such investments make them potentially hazardous ventures[987]. It is crucial to counter these arguments with the understanding that all investments inherently carry a degree of risk, and due diligence, legal agreements, and transparent communication within the collective can significantly mitigate these risks.

Another common criticism revolves around the notion of diminished personal control in collective investment initiatives. Critics argue that members of the collective could potentially lose out on decision-making power, as decisions are made collectively[988]. Yet, proponents maintain that this is an inherent aspect of collective investment, as the primary objective is to pool resources and achieve consensus, which can lead to higher returns and shared risk.

---

[985] Anderson, Claud. PowerNomics: The National Plan to Empower Black America. PowerNomics Corporation of America, 2001.
[986] "How Investment Clubs Perform." National Association of Investors Corporation, 2006.
[987] Kane, L. "The Risks and Rewards of Investment Clubs." Business Insider, November 12, 2020.
[988] Smith, J. "Understanding Your Rights in Collective Investments." Forbes, July 22, 2022.

Moreover, critics often overlook the significant benefits of collective investment that extend beyond pure financial gain. Participating in a collective investment initiative also cultivates a culture of financial literacy, communal support, and shared accountability. These aspects can have profound, long-term effects on community empowerment and wealth creation[989].

Collective investment holds tremendous potential for facilitating wealth creation within Black communities. As Dr. Anderson maintains, when managed effectively, these initiatives can substantially contribute to economic resilience and empowerment[990]. Recognizing the inherent value of these strategies and debunking the misconceptions around them is crucial for their broader adoption and success.

Case Studies of Successful Collective Investment Initiatives Within The Black Community

Investigating successful instances of collective investment within the Black community can illustrate the powerful potential of such initiatives. Collective economics has always been a key component of Black wealth creation, despite the inherent challenges[991]. For instance, the Tulsa Real Estate Fund (TREF) and the Southern Reparations Loan Fund (SRLF) provide compelling evidence of the significant impact of collective investment strategies.

The Tulsa Real Estate Fund, inspired by the prosperous Black Wall Street community of the early 20th century, offers a case study of successful collective investment. The

---

[989] "The Collective Power of Investment Clubs." Black Enterprise, May 23, 2019.

[990] Anderson, C. "The Power of Collective Investment." PowerNomics Corporation of America, 2023.

[991] Anderson, Claud. PowerNomics: The National Plan to Empower Black America. PowerNomics Corporation of America, 2001.

TREF was founded by Jay Morrison, an entrepreneur with an ambition to combat gentrification and economic disparity within the Black community. By 2020, TREF had raised over $50 million from thousands of investors, enabling the fund to make significant investments in real estate assets across the country[992].

Critics of TREF have questioned the fund's transparency and profitability[993]. Yet, supporters emphasize the fund's mission goes beyond financial returns. The real success of TREF lies in creating opportunities for collective ownership and combating gentrification, which are vital elements in promoting community wealth.

The Southern Reparations Loan Fund is another noteworthy example. This organization provides loans to cooperative businesses owned by people of color in the South. By 2021, the fund had raised nearly $1 million and financed multiple cooperative businesses[994]. Detractors might suggest that this model of funding is risky due to the fledgling nature of cooperatives and the potential for default. However, proponents argue that the organization's mission, similar to TREF's, extends beyond profit alone. The fund's primary goal is to address racial and economic disparities by supporting Black entrepreneurship.

While these case studies demonstrate the potential of collective investment strategies, they also show that success in this area is not merely measured by profit margins. Rather, the true value of such initiatives is in their capacity to foster economic empowerment, stimulate business growth, and promote financial equity within the Black community.

---

[992] "How This Real Estate Fund Is Bringing Ownership Back to the Black Community." CNBC, May 27, 2020.
[993] Robinson, Bryan. "Tulsa Real Estate Fund Faces Investor Complaints." The Atlanta Journal-Constitution, October 14, 2021.
[994] "Southern Reparations Loan Fund." Southern Reparations Loan Fund, accessed February 1, 2023.

In essence, as Dr. Claud Anderson has suggested, these initiatives can play a pivotal role in community upliftment, transforming the socio-economic landscape, and creating a sustainable pathway towards collective wealth creation in Black communities[995].

Providing Guidance on How To Form And Manage Collective Investment Groups

Collective investment groups are critical mechanisms for wealth creation and economic development, particularly within marginalized communities[996]. When effectively structured and managed, such groups can provide their members with opportunities for investment that would be out of reach individually. However, creating and maintaining these groups necessitates careful planning, commitment, and strategic decision-making.

The first step is forming a group of like-minded individuals who are interested in making joint investments[997]. This could be a group of friends, family members, or associates. The primary requirement is that the group members trust each other, are committed to the cause, and share a similar investment philosophy.

The next step is determining the legal structure of the investment group. There are multiple possibilities here, such as a limited liability company (LLC), a partnership, or a corporation. Each option has its advantages and disadvantages, and the choice will depend on the specific

---

[995] Anderson, C. "The Power of Collective Investment." PowerNomics Corporation of America, 2023.
[996] Anderson, Claud. PowerNomics: The National Plan to Empower Black America. PowerNomics Corporation of America, 2001.
[997] "Building Wealth Together Through Collective Investment Clubs." Black Enterprise, June 3, 2019.

goals and needs of the group[998]. Legal advice should be sought at this stage to ensure compliance with relevant laws and regulations.

Once the legal structure is established, the group needs to create an operating agreement. This document sets out the rules and guidelines for the investment group, such as the contribution schedule, the decision-making process, and the procedures for adding or removing members[999].

Critics might argue that collective investment groups can become a source of conflict due to differing opinions about investment strategies[1000]. However, such potential conflicts can be mitigated by having a clear operating agreement and promoting open, respectful communication among the members.

After these foundational steps, the group needs to decide on an investment strategy. This includes determining the sectors or industries in which to invest, the risk level the group is willing to take, and the time-line for investment and returns. This strategy should align with the collective goals of the group[1001].

In essence, forming and managing a collective investment group is a process that requires thoughtful deliberation and robust planning. However, as Dr. Claud Anderson has underscored, the long-term benefits of such economic collectivism can be transformative for Black communities[1002].

---

[998] "The Basics of Forming a Limited Liability Company (LLC)." Inc., July 20, 2020.
[999] "Operating Agreement for LLCs: What You Need to Know." Business News Daily, January 21, 2021.
[1000] "The Pros and Cons of Investment Clubs." U.S. News & World Report, February 14, 2018.
[1001] "How to Start an Investment Club." The Balance, March 2, 2022.
[1002] Anderson, C. "The Power of Collective Investment." PowerNomics Corporation of America, 2023.

Leveraging Policy for Collective Economics

Leveraging policy to bolster collective economics is a critical but often overlooked strategy for wealth creation in the Black community[1003]. By influencing policies that promote economic empowerment, Black communities can gain a significant advantage in their wealth-building efforts.

Take, for instance, the policies aimed at fostering entrepreneurship. By lobbying for policies that reduce barriers to entrepreneurship, such as cumbersome business registration procedures or high start-up costs, more Black individuals can start and grow their businesses, contributing to collective wealth[1004].

However, policy-making does not occur in a vacuum, and it is important to recognize potential critics. Some argue that focusing on policy changes may distract from individual financial responsibility[1005]. Yet, these perspectives can overlook the systemic barriers that Black individuals often face, limiting their economic opportunities[1006].

It is also vital to advocate for policies that expand access to capital for Black entrepreneurs. Historical discriminatory lending practices have inhibited Black individuals' ability to secure funding for their businesses[1007]. Policies that address this problem, such as reforms in banking practices or the expansion of government-backed lending programs for minority entrepreneurs, can greatly contribute to collective wealth creation.

[1003] Anderson, Claud. PowerNomics: The National Plan to Empower Black America. PowerNomics Corporation of America, 2001.
[1004] "Advancing Black Entrepreneurship: A Guide for Policymakers." Brookings Institution, October 15, 2020.
[1005] "Self-Reliance vs. Government Support: A False Choice." Forbes, March 13, 2022.
[1006] "Structural Racism and the Wealth Gap." Center for American Progress, July 15, 2020.
[1007] "Black Entrepreneurs Still Face Hurdles in Securing Financing." The Washington Post, February 23, 2022.

In addition, policy can play a significant role in strengthening Black financial institutions. For example, policies that provide incentives for banking with minority-owned banks or credit unions can increase their capital base, allowing them to extend more loans to the Black community[1008].

Furthermore, the power of policy in shaping the housing market cannot be understated. Housing policies that address issues such as discriminatory lending practices and segregation can help Black individuals acquire homes, which is often a key wealth-building strategy[1009].

Overall, the interplay between policy and collective economics is profound. However, as Dr. Claud Anderson argues, it is not enough to merely wait for beneficial policies. Active participation in the political process and strategic lobbying are vital to ensure that policies work in favor of the collective economic empowerment of the Black community[1010].

The Role of Local And Federal Policies In Promoting or Hindering Collective Economics

Local and federal policies can have a profound effect on collective economics within the Black community, either bolstering or hindering efforts to build wealth[1011]. Dr. Claud Anderson, in his seminal work, "PowerNomics," asserts that engaging with these policies strategically can significantly alter economic prospects for the Black community[1012].

[1008] "The Potential of Minority Banks." Federal Reserve Bank of Boston, December 1, 2021.
[1009] "How Housing Policy Is Failing America's Poor." The Atlantic, June 25, 2015.
[1010] Anderson, Claud. "The Role of Public Policy in Economic Empowerment." PowerNomics Corporation of America, 2023.
[1011] Anderson, Claud. PowerNomics: The National Plan to Empower Black America. PowerNomics Corporation of America, 2001.
[1012] Ibid.

At the local level, city and state governments can implement policies that directly influence opportunities for Black businesses and residents. For instance, procurement policies could be designed to encourage local governments to contract with Black-owned businesses, effectively injecting money into the local Black economy[1013]. However, such policies often face criticism from those who argue that it leads to favoritism and lack of competition[1014]. Nevertheless, proponents assert these policies are needed to rectify the historically imbalanced access to economic opportunities[1015].

Zoning laws, another area of local policy, can also impact collective economics. By determining where businesses can operate and residential areas can be developed, these laws shape community economic landscapes. Critics argue that restrictive zoning can limit opportunities for Black business owners and affordable housing options[1016].

On a federal level, policies like the Community Reinvestment Act (CRA) can influence collective economics by requiring banks to meet the credit needs of low- and moderate-income neighborhoods, often disproportionately inhabited by Black residents[1017]. However, critics suggest that the CRA is not adequately enforced and that some banks continue to neglect these communities[1018].

[1013] "Procurement Policies and Economic Inclusion: A Path to Urban Revitalization." National Urban League, 2019.
[1014] "The Trouble with Preference Policies." The Wall Street Journal, March 25, 2015.
[1015] "Why Minority Set-Asides Are Essential for Economic Equality." The Nation, August 11, 2018.
[1016] "Zoning Policies and Economic Disparity: A Closer Look." Urban Institute, January 15, 2020.
[1017] "The Community Reinvestment Act and Its Impact on Racial Disparities in Bank Credit." The Journal of Economics and Business, 2020.
[1018] "Enforcement of the Community Reinvestment Act Has Been Weak." The Washington Post, February 20, 2022.

Tax policies can also play a crucial role. Progressive tax policies can promote wealth equality, while regressive ones can widen the wealth gap[1019]. Critics often argue against progressive tax policies, stating they discourage wealth creation and investment. However, advocates argue that such policies are necessary to level the playing field and counteract historical economic disadvantages faced by the Black community[1020].

While both local and federal policies can serve as significant tools in promoting collective economics, they are not without controversy. As Anderson has suggested, it's crucial for the Black community to remain actively engaged in policy debates and development to ensure that these tools are used effectively to promote collective wealth[1021].

Advocacy Strategies For Pushing Policies That Support Black Wealth Creation

Advocacy strategies for policies that support Black wealth creation are essential for promoting financial equity and enabling economic growth within the Black community[1022]. Dr. Claud Anderson, a renowned advocate for Black economic empowerment, has championed the importance of policy advocacy in his works, arguing that Black communities need to leverage the political process to establish policies that foster wealth creation[1023].

[1019] "Tax Policy and Economic Inequality in the United States." The Balance, January 20, 2022.
[1020] "Progressive Taxation and Wealth Redistribution: An Argument for Economic Equality." Economic Policy Institute, October 15, 2021.
[1021] Anderson, Claud. PowerNomics: The National Plan to Empower Black America. PowerNomics Corporation of America, 2001.
[1022] Anderson, Claud. PowerNomics: The National Plan to Empower Black America. PowerNomics Corporation of America, 2001.
[1023] Ibid.

First, grassroots organizing can play a critical role in advocating for favorable policies[1024]. Local community groups can mobilize residents to push for changes in local and state laws that affect Black businesses and homeowners. They can also advocate for changes in procurement policies, zoning laws, and affordable housing initiatives that directly impact local economies[1025]. However, critics may argue that grassroots organizing lacks the structure and resources necessary for effective policy advocacy, which emphasizes the importance of forming alliances with established organizations and using technology to amplify reach[1026].

Second, lobbying is another powerful tool[1027]. While the concept of lobbying often carries a negative connotation due to its association with corporate interests, it can be effectively used by communities to advocate for their interests. Professional lobbyists with knowledge of legislative processes can help navigate political hurdles and push for the introduction or alteration of laws that directly impact Black wealth creation. Critics, however, may point out the financial barrier to accessing professional lobbyists, and the potential for conflicts of interest[1028].

Third, building alliances with like-minded organizations and advocacy groups can bolster efforts[1029]. These alliances can be valuable in providing additional resources, enhancing legitimacy, and broadening the scope of advocacy. Nevertheless, it's important to maintain clarity

---

[1024] "The Role of Grassroots Organizing in Policy Advocacy." Stanford Social Innovation Review, 2019.
[1025] Ibid.
[1026] "The Challenges of Grassroots Organizing." Nonprofit Quarterly, 2020.
[1027] "Lobbying: The Art of Policy Change." Harvard Business Review, 2018.
[1028] "The Dark Side of Lobbying." Brookings Institute, 2005.
[1029] "The Power of Advocacy Alliances." The Chronicle of Philanthropy, 2020.

in purpose and coordination of efforts to prevent dilution of the advocacy message[1030].

Moreover, public awareness campaigns can be instrumental in creating a supportive environment for policy change. By highlighting the benefits of policies that promote Black wealth creation, these campaigns can generate public support that can, in turn, pressure policymakers to act[1031].

In essence, as Anderson posits, policy advocacy is a multifaceted effort that requires the active involvement of the Black community. It's a strategic process that requires not only the initiation of actions but also the countering of opposing viewpoints. Success in this endeavor can significantly alter the economic landscape, leading to increased Black wealth creation[1032].

Analyzing The Potential And Limitations of Policy Interventions In Collective Economics

As Anderson notably asserts in PowerNomics, policy interventions can serve as powerful tools for promoting collective economics and fostering wealth within the Black community[1033]. Yet, while significant potential exists, limitations also present challenges, warranting careful analysis and strategic planning.

One policy intervention strategy with notable potential is the introduction of tax incentives for businesses that support or align with collective economic efforts within

---

[1030] Ibid.
[1031] "Public Awareness Campaigns and Policy Outcomes." Journal of Policy Analysis and Management, 2020.
[1032] Anderson, Claud. PowerNomics: The National Plan to Empower Black America. PowerNomics Corporation of America, 2001.
[1033] Anderson, Claud. PowerNomics: The National Plan to Empower Black America. PowerNomics Corporation of America, 2001.

Black communities[1034]. These incentives can stimulate local economies by attracting new businesses, promoting job creation, and increasing wealth within the community. For instance, the Opportunity Zones program, part of the Tax Cuts and Jobs Act of 2017, seeks to spur economic development by providing tax benefits to investors in designated distressed communities[1035].

However, these incentives may also lead to gentrification and displacement of original community members, a critique often raised against such policy initiatives[1036]. The Opportunity Zones program has faced such criticism, with some arguing it incentivizes investments in already-gentrifying areas rather than truly distressed communities[1037]. Therefore, careful and conscientious implementation is crucial to ensure community residents, not just investors, benefit.

Another strategy lies in revising regulations to facilitate the growth of community-owned financial institutions like Black-owned banks and credit unions[1038]. As these institutions are more likely to lend to Black entrepreneurs and homeowners, supportive regulations could help address the racial wealth gap. The CDFI Fund's BEA Program is an example of such a policy, providing monetary awards to banks serving low-income communities[1039].

However, critics argue that without sufficient regulatory oversight, there could be risks of mismanagement or fraud, harming the very communities

---

[1034] "Tax Incentives and the City." Brookings Institute, 2018.
[1035] "Opportunity Zones." Internal Revenue Service, 2021.
[1036] "Gentrification, Displacement and the Role of Public Investment." Federal Reserve Bank of San Francisco, 2015.
[1037] "A Preliminary Analysis of Opportunity Zone Implementation." Urban Institute, 2020.
[1038] "The Importance of Minority Banks." Federal Reserve Bank of Cleveland, 2020.
[1039] "Bank Enterprise Award Program." CDFI Fund, 2021.

these policies seek to support[1040]. Therefore, these interventions should always be paired with effective oversight and regulatory mechanisms.

Lastly, policies aimed at bolstering public education and financial literacy can be instrumental in advancing collective economics[1041]. Enhancing financial education can empower individuals to make informed decisions, manage their personal finances effectively, and contribute to their community's economic growth. Despite the potential, skeptics point out that without systemic changes to address institutionalized barriers, financial education alone cannot bridge the racial wealth gap[1042].

While policy interventions offer immense potential to foster collective economics, it is imperative to critically assess their limitations to ensure these strategies provide tangible, long-term benefits for the Black community[1043].

Preparing for the Future: Building Sustainable Models for Collective Economics

Anderson, in his seminal work PowerNomics, emphasizes the significance of building sustainable models for collective economics as a pathway to empower Black America[1044]. Looking forward, it is essential to construct models that are not only financially profitable but also resilient, adaptable, and sustainable in the face of changing economic conditions and societal needs.

[1040] "The Challenges and Opportunities of Community Banking." American Bankers Association, 2019.
[1041] "Financial Literacy and Economic Outcomes." Federal Reserve Bulletin, 2016.
[1042] "Does Financial Literacy Contribute to Wealth Equality?" Journal of Consumer Affairs, 2019.
[1043] Anderson, Claud. PowerNomics: The National Plan to Empower Black America. PowerNomics Corporation of America, 2001.
[1044] Anderson, Claud. PowerNomics: The National Plan to Empower Black America. PowerNomics Corporation of America, 2001.

In building these models, the first step is investment in education, particularly in financial literacy and entrepreneurial skills. As per the Federal Reserve, financial literacy correlates significantly with positive economic behaviors and outcomes[1045]. However, financial literacy alone is not sufficient[1046]. Critics argue that systemic and institutional barriers often restrict the potential impact of financial education[1047]. To address this, education initiatives should be paired with practical opportunities, like entrepreneurship training programs or access to start-up capital.

Next, creating an ecosystem that supports Black-owned businesses is crucial. It has been shown that these businesses face greater challenges in access to capital, operational resources, and business networks[1048]. Economic policies, community initiatives, and corporate partnerships can play significant roles in building such an ecosystem. Critics, however, caution against an over-reliance on outside forces for community development[1049]. As Anderson suggests, communities must drive their economic development while leveraging external support tactically[1050].

Furthermore, Black-owned financial institutions are key components of sustainable collective economic models. Their role in providing access to capital for Black entrepreneurs and homeowners is vital[1051]. However, they face unique challenges including lower capitalization and

---

[1045] "Financial Literacy and Economic Outcomes." Federal Reserve Bulletin, 2016.
[1046] "Does Financial Literacy Contribute to Wealth Equality?" Journal of Consumer Affairs, 2019.
[1047] Ibid.
[1048] "Minority-Owned Firms' Access to Capital." U.S. Small Business Administration, 2020.
[1049] Anderson, Claud. PowerNomics: The National Plan to Empower Black America. PowerNomics Corporation of America, 2001.
[1050] Ibid.
[1051] "The Importance of Minority Banks." Federal Reserve Bank of Cleveland, 2020.

the lack of technological resources[1052]. Strategic investments and regulatory support can help overcome these obstacles. Despite these potential solutions, critics argue that the overall systemic biases within the larger banking system persist, necessitating broader reforms[1053].

Lastly, collective investment strategies, like community investment trusts or cooperatives, can help circulate wealth within the community and generate shared prosperity[1054]. However, the success of such initiatives depends on legal, administrative, and financial factors. Detractors caution that without sufficient regulatory oversight, such initiatives might pose financial risks[1055].

Preparing for the future requires building robust, sustainable models for collective economics. These should incorporate financial education, support for Black-owned businesses and financial institutions, and collective investment strategies. However, it's crucial to recognize and address the potential limitations and criticisms associated with these strategies[1056].

Discussing The Importance of Generational Wealth And Strategies For Its Creation And Preservation

Dr. Claud Anderson has emphasized the importance of generational wealth as a key determinant of social and economic status. It is not merely a measure of an individual's or family's wealth but also their ability to maintain and grow that wealth over generations[1057].

[1052] "Why Are There So Few Black-Owned Banks?" The Balance, 2020.
[1053] "Racial Discrimination in the U.S. Banking Industry." ThoughtCo, 2020.
[1054] "Collective Investment Models." Shared Capital Cooperative, 2020.
[1055] "Regulation of Collective Investment Schemes." IOSCO, 2020.
[1056] Anderson, Claud. PowerNomics: The National Plan to Empower Black America. PowerNomics Corporation of America, 2001.
[1057] Anderson, Claud. PowerNomics: The National Plan to Empower Black America. PowerNomics Corporation of America, 2001.

However, not all agree with this perspective; critics argue that focusing on generational wealth reinforces inequalities, and it's the broader socio-economic system that needs reform[1058].

Generational wealth plays a significant role in mitigating economic disparities. As per the Federal Reserve, as of 2021, the median wealth of Black families was roughly one-tenth that of White families[1059]. Generational wealth can provide financial stability, increase access to quality education, and improve economic mobility. However, the achievement of generational wealth for Black Americans is often hindered by systemic challenges, such as wage inequality, higher unemployment rates, and lower home-ownership rates[1060].

Creating and preserving generational wealth requires a multifaceted approach. Firstly, home-ownership is often cited as a primary pathway for accumulating wealth[1061]. However, home-ownership rates among Black Americans lag behind other groups, partly due to systemic biases in the housing market[1062]. Advocates argue for policies that foster home-ownership, like affordable housing programs and anti-discrimination laws. Critics, however, caution that home-ownership alone doesn't guarantee wealth accumulation, particularly in neighborhoods with lower home values[1063].

Secondly, investment in education and entrepreneurial opportunities is critical. Data indicates a positive correlation between educational attainment and income levels[1064].

[1058] "The Trouble with Inheritance." The Economist, 2014.
[1059] "Disparities in Wealth by Race and Ethnicity in the 2019 Survey of Consumer Finances." Federal Reserve, 2021.
[1060] Ibid.
[1061] "The Road to Zero Wealth." Prosperity Now, 2017.
[1062] "The Racial Gap in home-ownership Rates." Center for American Progress, 2018.
[1063] "The Limits of home-ownership Wealth." Brookings Institution, 2018.
[1064] "Education Pays 2019: The Benefits of Higher Education for Individuals and Society." CollegeBoard, 2019.

Additionally, entrepreneurship offers potential for wealth creation, especially with proper access to capital and business support[1065]. Critics argue that these methods are insufficient to overcome systemic barriers and call for wider economic reforms[1066].

Lastly, financial literacy and estate planning are crucial for preserving wealth. Financial literacy can help individuals make sound investment decisions and manage risks[1067]. Estate planning, including wills and trusts, can ensure the orderly transfer of assets to future generations[1068]. Critics, however, point out that the effectiveness of financial education is limited without broader socio-economic changes[1069].

While generational wealth is important for financial stability and economic mobility, its creation and preservation face systemic challenges. A multifaceted strategy involving home-ownership, investment in education and entrepreneurship, and financial literacy can help overcome these challenges. However, wider socio-economic reforms may also be necessary to truly level the playing field[1070].

The Role of Financial Literacy And Education In Promoting Collective Economics

In line with Dr. Claud Anderson's ideas, it's evident that financial literacy and education are paramount in promoting collective economics. Anderson argues that an informed

---

[1065] "The State of Black Entrepreneurship." Forbes, 2020.
[1066] "Race, Wealth and Taxes: How the Tax Cuts and Jobs Act Supercharges the Racial Wealth Divide." Prosperity Now, 2018.
[1067] "The Importance of Financial Literacy." Federal Reserve, 2020.
[1068] "The Importance of Estate Planning." AARP, 2020.
[1069] "Does Financial Literacy Contribute to Wealth Equality?" Journal of Consumer Affairs, 2019.
[1070] Anderson, Claud. PowerNomics: The National Plan to Empower Black America. PowerNomics Corporation of America, 2001.

understanding of finance and economics can empower communities, fostering self-reliance and economic prosperity[1071]. Conversely, critics contend that financial literacy alone is insufficient without systemic change[1072].

Financial literacy is the understanding of financial concepts and the ability to use this knowledge to manage money effectively[1073]. The Council for Economic Education reported in 2020 that only a third of U.S. states require high school students to take a course in personal finance, indicating a deficiency in formal financial education[1074]. This, according to Anderson, is a missed opportunity to equip the youth with tools essential for wealth creation[1075].

Educated financial decisions can result in wealth accumulation and help avoid crippling debt. For example, understanding the implications of interest rates on student loans or the importance of saving for retirement can have a significant impact on one's economic future[1076]. Anderson argues that these financial competencies are even more critical in Black communities where resources are often scarce and must be strategically managed[1077].

However, critics argue that while financial literacy is beneficial, it is not the panacea for economic disparity[1078]. They claim that structural issues like wage inequality, discriminatory lending practices, and limited access to

---

[1071] Anderson, C. (2001). PowerNomics: The National Plan to Empower Black America. PowerNomics Corporation of America.
[1072] "Does Financial Literacy Contribute to Wealth Equality?" Journal of Consumer Affairs, 2019.
[1073] "National Financial Capability Study." FINRA, 2018.
[1074] "Survey of the States." Council for Economic Education, 2020.
[1075] Anderson, C. (2001). PowerNomics: The National Plan to Empower Black America. PowerNomics Corporation of America.
[1076] "The Effect of Financial Literacy and Financial Education on Downstream Financial Behaviors." Journal of Consumer Affairs, 2013.
[1077] Anderson, C. (2001). PowerNomics: The National Plan to Empower Black America. PowerNomics Corporation of America.
[1078] "The Racial Wealth Gap: Addressing America's Most Pressing Epidemic." Forbes, 2018.

quality education have a more significant influence on the economic status of disadvantaged communities[1079].

Financial education also plays a role in promoting collective economics. Anderson contends that understanding economic principles at a community level can spur collective action, such as group investments or cooperative businesses, fostering community wealth[1080]. For example, a study by the National Bureau of Economic Research highlighted that communities with higher financial literacy levels had a greater propensity for collective investment[1081].

Critics, however, note that collective action also requires access to capital, which remains a significant challenge in disadvantaged communities, irrespective of their financial literacy levels[1082].

The role of financial literacy and education in promoting collective economics is significant. They equip individuals with tools to manage resources effectively and foster a collective understanding of economics, crucial for community wealth-building. However, they should be accompanied by systemic changes to address the broader socio-economic disparities[1083].

[1079] Anderson, C. (2001). PowerNomics: The National Plan to Empower Black America. PowerNomics Corporation of America.
[1080] "The Economic Importance of Financial Literacy." National Bureau of Economic Research, 2014.
[1081] "Minority-Owned Firms' Access to Capital." U.S. Small Business Administration, 2020.
[1082] "Minority-Owned Firms' Access to Capital." U.S. Small Business Administration, 2020.
[1083] Anderson, C. (2001). PowerNomics: The National Plan to Empower Black America. PowerNomics Corporation of America.

Exploring Innovative Models And Technologies (Like Blockchain And Cryptocurrencies) That Can Facilitate Collective Economics

Innovative models and technologies like blockchain and cryptocurrencies have the potential to reshape our economic landscape. Dr. Claud Anderson has often stressed the need for economic innovation and adaptation within the Black community[1084]. While these technological advancements hold promise, skeptics warn of their potential drawbacks[1085].

Blockchain, the technology behind cryptocurrencies, is a decentralized digital ledger that can record transactions across numerous computers, ensuring transparency and security[1086]. This technology can be used to facilitate collective economics in several ways. Firstly, it offers the potential for creating decentralized financial systems. Such systems could provide an alternative to traditional banks and potentially reduce costs and increase access to financial services[1087].

Blocckchain can also be used to facilitate peer-to-peer transactions, cutting out the middleman. This has implications for reducing costs and enabling more direct trade within a community. For instance, blockchain has been used in Brooklyn, New York, in a project called Brooklyn Microgrid, where residents trade solar energy amongst themselves[1088].

[1084] Anderson, C. (2001). PowerNomics: The National Plan to Empower Black America. PowerNomics Corporation of America.
[1085] "Crypto: What to Know Before Investing." BBC, 2021.
[1086] Mougayar, W. (2016). The Business Blockchain: Promise, Practice, and Application of the Next Internet Technology. Wiley.
[1087] Tapscott, D., & Tapscott, A. (2016). Blockchain Revolution: How the Technology Behind Bitcoin Is Changing Money, Business, and the World. Portfolio.
[1088] "Brooklyn Microgrid: How Blockchain Can Democratize Power Generation." Energy Post, 2017.

Cryptocurrencies, such as Bitcoin, also present new opportunities. Cryptocurrencies are digital or virtual currencies that use cryptography for security. They are primarily used as a medium of exchange like traditional currencies[1089]. Cryptocurrencies can promote collective economics by fostering a new type of investment and saving medium that can be used worldwide without the need for a central authority[1090].

Nevertheless, critics argue that the volatile nature of cryptocurrencies and the lack of regulation make them a risky investment. They also note that the digital divide and a lack of technological literacy may hinder adoption in certain communities[1091].

Moreover, the environmental impact of blockchain technologies and cryptocurrencies, particularly Bitcoin, due to their significant energy use, has been a major point of contention[1092].

In the realm of economic self-sufficiency and collective economics, as advocated by Anderson, it is crucial to continue exploring and embracing innovative models and technologies[1093]. However, as we do so, we must also ensure we are creating systems that are equitable, sustainable, and accessible to all.

Collective Economics as a Pathway to Power

Collective economics, according to Dr. Claud Anderson, provides a fundamental mechanism to accumulate resources

---

[1089] Nakamoto, S. (2008). Bitcoin: A Peer-to-Peer Electronic Cash System.
[1090] "Cryptocurrency and the Future of Finance." Financial Times, 2021.
[1091] "The Dark Side of Cryptocurrency." New Scientist, 2018.
[1092] "Bitcoin's Climate Impact Is Global. The Cures Are Local." Wired, 2019.
[1093] Anderson, C. (2001). PowerNomics: The National Plan to Empower Black America. PowerNomics Corporation of America.

and power, thereby creating self-reliant communities[1094]. Such a strategy allows communities, particularly marginalized ones, to harness their collective wealth towards shared prosperity. Yet, skeptics doubt the practical implementation of collective economics, especially in a society centered on individualism[1095].

Anderson emphasizes that control over economic resources determines a group's ability to influence policies and gain political power[1096]. Indeed, collective economics have historically been a force of empowerment. The Greenwood District in Tulsa, Oklahoma, known as "Black Wall Street," is an exemplar of such power through collective economics in the early 20th century. Despite the severe discrimination faced by African Americans at that time, they were able to create a prosperous business district[1097].

Recent data supports this view, with a study from the Economic Policy Institute highlighting that Black-owned businesses contribute approximately $150 billion to the U.S. economy annually[1098]. A more collective economic strategy within these business networks can result in increased resource allocation, providing more leverage for policy changes and community development.

Nonetheless, critics argue that such economic strategies can lead to economic segregation or isolation[1099]. They also note that individual aspirations, differing opinions, and

---

[1094] Anderson, C. (2001). PowerNomics: The National Plan to Empower Black America. PowerNomics Corporation of America.
[1095] "The Pros and Cons of Collective Economics." Harvard Business Review, 2017.
[1096] Anderson, C. (2001). PowerNomics: The National Plan to Empower Black America. PowerNomics Corporation of America.
[1097] "Black Wall Street: The African American Haven That Burned and Then Rose From the Ashes." The Conversation, 2020.
[1098] "The Economic Impact of Black-Owned Businesses." Economic Policy Institute, 2020.
[1099] "The Pros and Cons of Collective Economics." Harvard Business Review, 2017.

competing interests may pose challenges to collective strategies.

Furthermore, it's important to note that collective economics alone is not sufficient. Anderson argues for a comprehensive approach that includes control over other institutions, such as educational, judicial, and media systems[1100].

Potential hurdles aside, collective economics remains a viable path to empowerment. But for such strategies to work, communities must be informed and engaged. Education about financial literacy, the value of group economics, and the importance of supporting local businesses are crucial[1101]. Implementing collective economics requires concerted effort, community unity, and shared vision. But as Anderson and others have argued, the potential payoff — in terms of wealth, influence, and self-determination — can make it well worth the effort.

Reinforcing The Importance of Collective Economics As A Key Tool For Black Wealth Creation

Collective economics, as expounded by Dr. Claud Anderson, encapsulates a strategy through which marginalized communities can leverage their collective resources to achieve economic empowerment and wealth creation[1102]. Skeptics, however, question the feasibility of such a model in a socio-economic structure deeply ingrained with individualism and free-market capitalism[1103].

[1100] Anderson, C. (2001). PowerNomics: The National Plan to Empower Black America. PowerNomics Corporation of America.
[1101] "Financial Education and the Keys to Economic Empowerment." Federal Reserve Bank of St. Louis, 2018.
[1102] Anderson, C. (2001). PowerNomics: The National Plan to Empower Black America. PowerNomics Corporation of America.
[1103] "The Pros and Cons of Collective Economics." Harvard Business Review, 2017.

Collective economics, at its core, is not merely about monetary gains; it's also about strengthening community ties, fostering self-reliance, and creating a protective economic shell. As Anderson puts it, "Money should circulate within the community as much as possible, each rotation building wealth and creating jobs"[1104].

Supporting this notion, the Association for Enterprise Opportunity reports that if one in three micro-businesses hired an additional person, the United States would be at full employment[1105]. This indicates the potential of collective economics and its propensity to create sustainable communities, especially within the Black community.

Nonetheless, critics argue that this model of economics is an impractical idealism incompatible with global capitalism[1106]. They suggest that it could inadvertently create economic silos, discouraging diversification, and potentially inhibiting growth.

However, collective economics, as Anderson suggests, can serve as a corrective measure to the historic economic disenfranchisement that Black communities have faced[1107]. Studies indicate that the racial wealth gap has been largely unaltered over the past 70 years[1108]. By practicing collective economics, Black communities can strive to close this wealth gap and, by extension, exert greater influence over policies affecting them.

The collective economics strategy requires a cultural shift towards collaborative community-building, fostering trust, and creating equitable networks of wealth creation. It

---

[1104] Anderson, C. (2001). PowerNomics: The National Plan to Empower Black America. PowerNomics Corporation of America.
[1105] "The Power of One in Three: Creating Opportunities for All to Breathe." Association for Enterprise Opportunity, 2019.
[1106] "The Pros and Cons of Collective Economics." Harvard Business Review, 2017.
[1107] Anderson, C. (2001). PowerNomics: The National Plan to Empower Black America. PowerNomics Corporation of America.
[1108] "The Racial Wealth Gap: Addressing America's Most Pressing Epidemic." Brookings Institution, 2020.

underscores the importance of financial literacy, sound investment practices, and the role of Black-owned financial institutions in mobilizing resources[1109].

While the path to collective economics is fraught with challenges and contrary views, its potential in facilitating Black wealth creation cannot be underestimated. By fostering interdependence, building community networks, and practicing prudent financial strategies, collective economics can play a significant role in fostering a prosperous, empowered Black community.

Synthesizing The Strategies Presented Throughout The Chapter For Readers To Apply In Their Own Communities

The idea of collective economics, championed by scholars like Dr. Claud Anderson, provides a comprehensive strategy for leveraging the collective resources of marginalized communities to create wealth and economic stability[1110]. The strategies espoused throughout the discussion offer a road-map that readers can apply to their own communities.

Collective economics is more than a financial philosophy; it is about fostering community ties, self-reliance, and a protective economic shell[1111]. This is best achieved through collaborative community-building initiatives, with community members being encouraged to circulate money within the community as much as possible, leading to wealth creation and job creation[1112].

[1109] "Financial Literacy and Black-Owned Banks in the Fight Against Racial Wealth Inequality." Urban Institute, 2020.
[1110] Anderson, C. (2001). PowerNomics: The National Plan to Empower Black America. PowerNomics Corporation of America.
[1111] Ibid.
[1112] Ibid.

Key to this is the establishment and support of local, Black-owned financial institutions. Such banks and credit unions can cater to the specific needs of the community, offering targeted financial products and services[1113]. They also play a crucial role in overcoming financial barriers faced by Black entrepreneurs and homeowners, aiding in community wealth creation[1114].

A collective investment strategy also underscores the importance of financial literacy and education in promoting collective economics. This involves the community fostering a culture of saving and prudent investment practices, encouraging the circulation of wealth within the community[1115].

Advocacy is another critical strategy. By advocating for policies that support wealth creation within the Black community, collective economics can lead to policy changes that further the cause[1116]. Such advocacy can also address the limitations and potential pitfalls of policy interventions.

Innovation should not be overlooked. The use of technologies like blockchain and cryptocurrencies offers new avenues for collective investment and wealth generation[1117]. They offer decentralized, secure methods of financial transactions that can facilitate collective economics.

Finally, generational wealth creation is vital. This entails not only creating wealth but preserving it for future

---

[1113] "Why Are There So Few Black-Owned Banks?" The Balance, 2022.
[1114] "Minority-Owned Firms' Access to Capital." U.S. Small Business Administration, 2021.
[1115] "Financial Literacy and Black-Owned Banks in the Fight Against Racial Wealth Inequality." Urban Institute, 2022.
[1116] Anderson, C. (2001). PowerNomics: The National Plan to Empower Black America. PowerNomics Corporation of America.
[1117] "Blockchain for Social Impact: Moving Beyond the Hype." Stanford Center for Social Innovation, 2018.

generations[1118]. Collective economics, in this sense, provides a sustainable model for wealth creation that transcends generations.

However, detractors may argue that collective economics is impractical and incompatible with the global capitalist system. But considering the historically entrenched racial wealth gap, collective economics offers a means to economic empowerment for marginalized communities[1119].

The application of these strategies offers a way to leverage collective economics for wealth creation in the Black community. They underscore the need for financial literacy, the role of Black-owned financial institutions, the importance of advocacy, the potential of innovative technologies, and the emphasis on generational wealth.

A Call To Action For Readers To Engage In Collective Economic Practices

The data and insights provided throughout our discussion paint a clear picture: engaging in collective economic practices is an essential mechanism for wealth creation, particularly for Black communities. This conclusion aligns with the overarching theme of Dr. Claud Anderson's work that emphasizes the transformational power of self-reliance and economic unity[1120]. Therefore, as a reader, understanding the significance of these practices and actively incorporating them into daily financial behavior becomes a call to action.

[1118] "Generational Wealth and Why It Matters." Center for American Progress, 2021.
[1119] "The Racial Wealth Gap: Addressing America's Most Pressing Epidemic." Brookings Institution, 2020.
[1120] Anderson, C. (2001). PowerNomics: The National Plan to Empower Black America. PowerNomics Corporation of America.

The first call to action is for readers to support and patronize Black-owned businesses and financial institutions. These entities circulate wealth within the community, and by choosing them over their mainstream counterparts, individuals can contribute to community wealth growth[1121]. Readers are encouraged to not only bank with Black-owned banks but also to explore investment opportunities they offer.

The second call to action revolves around financial literacy. With a sound understanding of financial concepts and the necessary skills to make informed decisions, individuals can better manage their personal finances and contribute to their community's financial stability[1122]. Schools, community centers, and online platforms can be leveraged to disseminate this vital knowledge.

Advocacy is the third call to action. This involves lobbying for favorable local and federal policies that encourage wealth creation[1123]. Readers are urged to join or initiate movements and campaigns that champion policies supporting Black wealth creation, such as increased access to capital for Black-owned businesses, financial education initiatives, and policies addressing the racial wealth gap[1124].

The fourth call to action encourages readers to explore and harness innovative technologies, such as blockchain and cryptocurrencies. These technological advancements provide new avenues for investment and wealth creation[1125].

Finally, readers should focus on generational wealth creation and preservation. This is perhaps the most crucial

---

[1121] Ibid.
[1122] "Financial Literacy and Black-Owned Banks in the Fight Against Racial Wealth Inequality." Urban Institute, 2022.
[1123] Anderson, C. (2001). PowerNomics: The National Plan to Empower Black America. PowerNomics Corporation of America.
[1124] "The Racial Wealth Gap: Addressing America's Most Pressing Epidemic." Brookings Institution, 2020.
[1125] "Blockchain for Social Impact: Moving Beyond the Hype." Stanford Center for Social Innovation, 2018.

aspect of collective economics, as it ensures that the wealth generated benefits not only the present but future generations as well[1126]. This involves strategies such as estate planning, setting up trusts, and providing the younger generation with the financial education they need to manage and grow the wealth they inherit[1127].

Critics may argue that these strategies require an individualistic approach to be truly effective. However, the collective economics model thrives on the premise of 'group economics,' which views the community's financial health as integral to the individual's financial success[1128]. By recognizing that collective wealth creation can help mitigate systemic inequalities, readers can turn the tide in their favor.

In conclusion, the adoption of collective economic practices is not merely a recommendation; it is a call to action for readers. Through active engagement, individuals can contribute to the financial empowerment of their communities, ensuring sustained and equitable wealth generation for present and future generations.

[1126] "Generational Wealth and Why It Matters." Center for American Progress, 2021.
[1127] Ibid.
[1128] Anderson, C. (2001). PowerNomics: The National Plan to Empower Black America. PowerNomics Corporation of America.

Chapter 10

The Immediate Need For Black People To Embrace Technology, Blockchain, Artificial Intelligence

The new digital age has opened a world of possibilities, offering transformative opportunities for wealth generation and social development. However, it has been observed that the Black community, among others, is underrepresented in tech fields, especially in areas such as blockchain and artificial intelligence[1129]. The current status quo reinforces an unfortunate truth: technological revolution, while promising, may inadvertently perpetuate the systemic economic disparities that have historically disadvantaged Black individuals unless proactive efforts are made to encourage participation.

Contrarians might argue that encouraging participation in tech fields merely displaces focus from other significant sectors, implying that a potential 'tech-fixation' could overshadow the importance of other job sectors[1130]. They could also point out that the tech industry itself has been criticized for its volatile nature and potential job instability[1131]. However, these concerns should not negate

---

[1129] McKenzie, B. (2021). 'The Color of Tech Can Change.' Scientific American. https://www.scientificamerican.com/article/the-color-of-tech-can-change

[1130] Hicks, M. (2019). 'Overhyping Technology Can Deepen Inequality.' Inside Higher Ed. https://www.insidehighered.com/blogs/higher-ed-gamma/overhyping-technology-can-deepen-inequality

[1131] Warzel, C. (2019). 'The Tech Industry's Psychological War on Gig Workers.' The New York Times. https://www.nytimes.com/2019/12/04/opinion/uber-lyft-gig-economy.html

the potential benefits that tech sector involvement holds for Black wealth creation.

In fact, the intersection of tech and finance, particularly the emergence of blockchain technology and decentralized finance, has the potential to disrupt traditional power structures and foster financial independence[1132]. Blockchain's transparent, decentralized, and secure nature offers avenues for creating and managing wealth that can effectively challenge the discriminatory practices present in traditional banking and finance[1133].

Nevertheless, critics argue that blockchain and cryptocurrency markets are fraught with risk and volatility. They warn against viewing them as a panacea for wealth inequality[1134]. Indeed, while blockchain technology holds immense potential, it's also true that it's a relatively new, unregulated field. However, such risks exist in all investment avenues, and they highlight the need for financial literacy and risk management rather than the outright dismissal of such innovative tools[1135].

Similar arguments are made for the integration of Artificial Intelligence (AI) in wealth creation. AI's potential in job creation and economic growth is considerable. However, it has been observed that AI can also perpetuate racial bias, as AI systems are often trained on data that

---

[1132] Tapscott, D., & Tapscott, A. (2016). 'Blockchain Revolution: How the Technology Behind Bitcoin Is Changing Money, Business, and the World.' Penguin.

[1133] Mougayar, W. (2016). 'The Business Blockchain: Promise, Practice, and Application of the Next Internet Technology.' Wiley.

[1134] Kharif, O. (2018). 'The Wealthy Are Hoarding $10 Billion of Bitcoin in Bunkers.' Bloomberg. https://www.bloomberg.com/news/articles/2018-05-09/bunkers-for-the-wealthy-are-said-to-hoard-10-billion-of-bitcoin

[1135] Davidson, L. (2019). 'The Importance of Financial Literacy in the Age of e-Finance.' The Balance. https://www.thebalance.com/financial-literacy-in-age-of-e-finance-4771994

reflects systemic biases[1136]. This is a significant challenge, but it also underscores the importance of having diverse teams developing AI systems. By involving more Black people in AI, we can work towards ensuring the creation of more fair, equitable systems [1137].

Embracing technology, blockchain, and AI is not just beneficial—it's a necessity for Black people's future. The tech sector promises new avenues for wealth creation and financial independence, providing tools to counter systemic economic disparities. Critics may point out the challenges and risks inherent in the tech industry, but these should be seen as obstacles to navigate rather than reasons for exclusion. Technology is a part of our future, and inclusivity in its growth is paramount.

The New Digital Age: Technological Revolution And Its Implications

As we move deeper into the 21st century, the era of the Fourth Industrial Revolution, commonly known as the digital age, continues to transform the world[1138]. This revolution is distinguished by the fusion of physical, digital, and biological realms, creating new synergies between humans and machines. However, in understanding the nuances of this new age, it is imperative to consider both the potential benefits and the underlying challenges.

Optimists argue that technological advancements such as artificial intelligence (AI), machine learning, blockchain,

---

[1136] Metz, C. (2021). 'We Teach A.I. Systems Everything, Including Our Biases.' The New York Times. https://www.nytimes.com/2021/11/22/technology/artificial-intelligence-bias.html

[1137] Howard, A. (2020). 'Equity in AI: Why Diversity Is Essential.' Forbes. https://www.forbes.com/sites/abhoward/2020/06/22/equity-in-ai-why-diversity-is-essential/?sh=6fc095633754

[1138] Schwab, K. (2016). 'The Fourth Industrial Revolution.' World Economic Forum.

and data analytics are set to revolutionize virtually every aspect of our lives. These technologies promise to boost productivity, increase efficiency, and foster innovation[1139]. However, critics argue that these advancements may exacerbate societal disparities, particularly with regard to income inequality and access to opportunities.

One major area of concern is the future of work. Automation, a key driver of the Fourth Industrial Revolution, has been cited as a threat to traditional jobs[1140]. There are predictions of massive job losses due to automation, potentially leading to an increase in unemployment and a widening wealth gap. Critics also express concerns about the digital divide, the gap between those with access to technology and those without. This divide could further marginalize disadvantaged groups and widen the socio-economic disparity[1141].

However, this 'gloom and doom' narrative needs to be tempered with a deeper understanding of the dynamics of technological change. The narrative often overlooks the potential for new job creation and the possibility of humans and machines working collaboratively rather than competitively[1142]. The creation of new sectors and jobs could, therefore, offer employment opportunities that compensate for those lost to automation.

Similarly, addressing the digital divide requires concerted efforts to promote digital inclusion. Ensuring equal access to digital technologies and the internet, and

---

[1139] Mokyr, J., Vickers, C., & Ziebarth, N. L. (2015). 'The History of Technological Anxiety and the Future of Economic Growth: Is This Time Different?' Journal of Economic Perspectives.
[1140] Arntz, M., Gregory, T., & Zierahn, U. (2016). 'The Risk of Automation for Jobs in OECD Countries: A Comparative Analysis.' OECD Social, Employment and Migration Working Papers.
[1141] Van Dijk, J. A. G. M. (2006). 'Digital Divide Research, Achievements and Shortcomings.' Poetics.
[1142] Brynjolfsson, E., & McAfee, A. (2014). 'The Second Machine Age: Work, Progress, and Prosperity in a Time of Brilliant Technologies.' W. W. Norton & Company.

promoting digital literacy among disadvantaged communities, are crucial steps in bridging this gap[1143].

In a broader perspective, the Fourth Industrial Revolution also presents the opportunity to address some of our most pressing global challenges, such as climate change and health-care delivery. AI and data analytics, for example, could help monitor and mitigate the impacts of climate change[1144]. Similarly, digital health technologies could revolutionize health-care, improving diagnosis, treatment, and patient care[1145].

The new digital age heralds a paradigm shift in our social and economic landscapes. While the accompanying challenges should not be understated, the potential benefits are immense. It is essential to navigate this transition with informed decision-making, robust policy interventions, and inclusive strategies that maximize the benefits and minimize the risks.

Underrepresentation of Black People In Tech Fields

The underrepresentation of Black people in technology fields is a sobering and persistent concern. In a sector known for its innovation and progressive thinking, the demographic disparity is a glaring paradox. Recent data suggests that Black workers account for merely 7.9% of computing and mathematical occupations, despite making up 13.4% of the U.S. population[1146]. This issue is complex,

---

[1143] West, D. M. (2015). 'Digital Divide: Improving Internet Access in the Developing World through Affordable Services and Diverse Content.' Brookings Institution.
[1144] Rolnick, D., et al. (2019). 'Tackling Climate Change with Machine Learning.' arXiv preprint.
[1145] Topol, E. (2019). 'High-performance Medicine: The Convergence of Human and Artificial Intelligence.' Nature Medicine.
[1146] U.S. Bureau of Labor Statistics. (2021). 'Labor Force Statistics from the Current Population Survey.'

with roots stretching deep into historical inequalities, educational opportunities, and societal biases.

Critics may argue that the low representation is simply a matter of interest or talent, but these claims are surface-level conjectures that fail to recognize the systemic barriers ingrained within the fabric of the tech industry and society at large. Notable studies have demonstrated that the dearth of Black tech workers is not due to a lack of interest, but rather a lack of opportunity[1147].

Educational disparities play a substantial role. The digital divide starts in the K-12 education system, where students in predominantly Black schools often lack access to computer science classes and high-speed internet[1148]. This early disadvantage can stifle students' development of necessary digital literacy skills and lead to an underrepresentation of Black students in tech-related college majors[1149].

Despite these barriers, some might challenge the need for diversity in tech, arguing that merit should be the sole hiring criterion. While meritocracy is an ideal worth striving for, it cannot be divorced from the context of opportunity and systemic bias. Research has shown that diverse teams generate more innovative ideas and perform better financially, reinforcing the importance of racial diversity in tech[1150].

Nonetheless, even when Black students overcome educational barriers and earn degrees in tech-related fields, they face employment discrimination and bias. Black

---

[1147] Brown, N., et al. (2016). 'Investigating the Relationship between High School Preparation, Social Supports, and Academic Outcomes.' Peabody Journal of Education.

[1148] U.S. Department of Education, Office of Civil Rights. (2018). '2015-16 Civil Rights Data Collection: STEM Course Taking.'

[1149] Smith, J. W. A., & Deng, S. (2019). 'Pipeline or Personal Preference: Women and Computer Science in U.S. States.' Social Forces.

[1150] Hunt, V., et al. (2018). 'Delivering through Diversity.' McKinsey & Company.

college graduates are twice as likely as white graduates to struggle to find work related to their major[1151]. This level of bias, whether conscious or unconscious, works to maintain the status quo and perpetuates underrepresentation.

The tech industry has pledged commitments to diversity and inclusivity, but progress has been slow. A closer examination of the data reveals a heavy concentration of Black employees in non-technical, lower-paying roles within tech companies[1152]. This raises questions about the effectiveness of current diversity initiatives and the industry's commitment to substantive change.

The path towards resolving the underrepresentation of Black people in tech fields is layered and complex. It involves not just initiatives from tech companies, but comprehensive societal interventions to address educational disparities, systemic bias, and societal barriers. The collective commitment to this cause is not merely a moral imperative, but a catalyst for innovation and progress in a sector that thrives on diverse ideas.

Why Black People Must Embrace Technology

Technology, an ever-evolving and dynamic realm, presents a vast array of opportunities for upward mobility and societal progress. For Black people, who have historically been marginalized within economic, social, and educational spheres, embracing technology is not merely a beneficial endeavor but an imperative one. However, certain skeptics may posit that technology is merely another tool that furthers social inequalities[1153].

[1151] Edelman, P., et al. (2017). 'Unemployment Rates for Black and White College Graduates.' Economic Policy Institute.

[1152] EEOC. (2018). 'Diversity in High Tech.' U.S. Equal Employment Opportunity Commission.

[1153] Eubanks, V. (2018). Automating Inequality: How High-Tech Tools Profile, Police, and Punish the Poor. New York: St. Martin's Press.

Firstly, technology affords economic empowerment. The tech industry has been one of the fastest-growing sectors of the U.S. economy, accounting for around 7.9% of total U.S. GDP in 2020[1154]. However, Black individuals currently comprise only about 7.9% of workers in computing and mathematical occupations[1155]. Increasing participation in this flourishing sector could potentially serve to narrow the racial wealth gap, providing lucrative and stable employment opportunities.

Despite these potential benefits, critics may argue that technology is exacerbating economic inequalities. It is indeed true that the digital divide has left certain communities, including many Black communities, at a disadvantage. However, such a view fails to acknowledge the possibility for technology to be a tool for economic empowerment, if only its access and usage are equitably distributed.

Technology also democratizes education. The proliferation of online learning platforms and resources has revolutionized the way we educate ourselves. For Black students, this means access to knowledge and learning opportunities that were once out of reach due to geographic or financial constraints[1156]. However, this optimism is met with resistance from critics who question the quality of online education or its efficacy in comparison to traditional modes of education.

Nevertheless, a more nuanced view would recognize that the problem lies not with the technology itself, but in the disparities in access to reliable internet and digital devices. Addressing these issues could enable Black

---

[1154] U.S. Bureau of Economic Analysis. (2021). 'Gross Domestic Product by Industry: Fourth Quarter and Year 2020.'
[1155] U.S. Bureau of Labor Statistics. (2021). 'Labor Force Statistics from the Current Population Survey.'
[1156] Means, B., et al. (2010). 'Evaluation of Evidence-Based Practices in Online Learning: A Meta-Analysis and Review of Online Learning Studies.' U.S. Department of Education.

individuals to fully exploit the educational opportunities that technology provides.

Furthermore, technology has the potential to foster social and political change. Social media platforms have given a voice to the voiceless, allowing movements like Black Lives Matter to gain global traction and expose racial injustices[1157]. Yet, detractors point to the risks of misinformation and the threat to privacy posed by these platforms.

While these concerns are valid, they underscore the need for digital literacy and responsible tech usage, rather than a rejection of technology altogether. Technology, when utilized wisely, can be a powerful platform for amplifying the issues that Black communities face, thus driving systemic change.

To reap the benefits of technology, Black communities must not only use technology but also participate in its creation and direction. Representation in the tech industry is vital to ensure that technology serves the needs of all communities and not just the privileged few. While the road to digital equity is fraught with challenges, the potential rewards make it a journey worth pursuing.

Understanding the Key Concepts

When we discuss technology, it is essential to understand its broad nature and various facets. Technology can be seen in many forms – from the machinery of the Industrial Revolution to the digitization and automation processes of today's Information Age. It encompasses hardware, software, networks, and databases, but also more broadly, methods, systems, and techniques for

---

[1157] Tufekci, Z. (2017). Twitter and Tear Gas: The Power and Fragility of Networked Protest. New Haven: Yale University Press.

accomplishing a task[1158]. However, the understanding and acceptance of technology, particularly the new digital technologies, vary amongst different groups and there are viewpoints that question its overall benefits.

Critics often fear that technology will displace human labor, exacerbating unemployment and income inequality[1159]. In fact, the World Economic Forum estimated that automation would displace 85 million jobs worldwide by 2025[1160]. However, it's crucial to look beyond the mere displacement of jobs and focus on the creation of new ones. The same report indicates that 97 million new roles may emerge that are more adapted to the new division of labor between humans and machines. This shift necessitates up-skilling and re-skilling, and those prepared will stand to gain.

Another concern is the 'digital divide.' As of 2019, 44% of adults with incomes below $30,000 don't own a computer, and 29% don't have broadband services at home[1161]. For Black families, this divide is even more pronounced due to structural inequalities. Those opposing the wide-scale adoption of technology may highlight this data, suggesting that technology deepens the socio-economic divide. But advocates argue that these disparities point not towards abandonment but rather the need for widespread accessibility to technology.

In the field of artificial intelligence (AI), there are concerns regarding the lack of transparency and potential for bias[1162]. Because AI systems learn from data that reflects

---

[1158] Arthur, W.B. (2009). 'The Nature of Technology: What It Is and How It Evolves.' New York: Free Press.
[1159] Brynjolfsson, E. and McAfee, A. (2014). 'The Second Machine Age: Work, Progress, and Prosperity in a Time of Brilliant Technologies.' New York: W. W. Norton & Company.
[1160] World Economic Forum. (2020). 'The Future of Jobs Report 2020.'
[1161] Pew Research Center. (2019). 'Internet/Broadband Fact Sheet.'
[1162] O'Neil, C. (2016). 'Weapons of Math Destruction: How Big Data Increases Inequality and Threatens Democracy.' New York: Crown.

our society, these systems can inadvertently perpetuate existing biases. Critics may see this as a reason to slow down the adoption of AI. On the other hand, proponents argue that these challenges should spur more inclusive and ethical AI development, ensuring its benefits can be equitably distributed.

Finally, privacy concerns have been mounting with advancements in technology. In an era where data is the 'new oil,' how that data is gathered, stored, and utilized is under scrutiny[1163]. Critics may view this as an insurmountable challenge, citing the risk to individual privacy. Supporters, however, posit that this underlines the need for robust data protection laws and responsible technology use.

Understanding technology requires acknowledging its multiple facets, from its opportunities to its challenges. The debate surrounding technology is not a binary one, but rather a question of how we can guide its development to maximize its societal benefits while mitigating its potential harms.

Blockchain Technology: Unraveling The Complexity

Blockchain technology, since its inception, has been a topic of significant interest and debate, but also one of considerable complexity. Blockchain, at its core, is a decentralized and distributed digital ledger that records transactions across many computers, ensuring the transactions cannot be altered retrospectively[1164]. However, the intricate nature of blockchain and its underpinnings have

---

[1163] Zuboff, S. (2019). 'The Age of Surveillance Capitalism: The Fight for a Human Future at the New Frontier of Power.' New York: PublicAffairs.
[1164] Tapscott, D., & Tapscott, A. (2016). 'Blockchain Revolution: How the Technology Behind Bitcoin Is Changing Money, Business, and the World.' New York: Portfolio.

led to a myriad of viewpoints and interpretations, some encouraging its adoption and others questioning its validity and potential.

Proponents of blockchain technology laud its revolutionary potential. Blockchain technology is hailed for its transparency, immutability, and decentralization[1165]. In addition to cryptocurrencies like Bitcoin, it has potential applications in fields like supply chain management, voting systems, real estate, and health-care, offering the prospect of decentralized, trustless systems with no need for intermediaries[1166]. In fact, a 2019 report by International Data Corporation (IDC) projects that global spending on blockchain solutions will reach nearly $15.9 billion by 2023, indicating widespread belief in the technology's potential[1167].

On the flip side, skeptics often point to the challenges associated with blockchain technology. The excessive energy consumption of blockchain networks, particularly proof-of-work cryptocurrencies like Bitcoin, is a major environmental concern[1168]. Another issue pertains to scalability and efficiency. The Bitcoin network, for instance, can process only about seven transactions per second (TPS), compared to Visa's capacity of 24,000 TPS[1169]. Critics also point to the volatility of cryptocurrencies and the potential for use in illegal activities as significant issues[1170].

[1165] Mougayar, W. (2016). 'The Business Blockchain: Promise, Practice, and Application of the Next Internet Technology.' New Jersey: Wiley.

[1166] Swan, M. (2015). 'Blockchain: Blueprint for a New Economy.' O'Reilly Media, Inc.

[1167] International Data Corporation (IDC). (2019). 'Worldwide Semiannual Blockchain Spending Guide.'

[1168] Krause, M., & Tolaymat, T. (2018). 'Quantification of energy and carbon costs for mining cryptocurrencies.' Nature Sustainability, 1(11), 711–718.

[1169] VISA. (2020). 'Visa Inc. at a Glance.'

[1170] Foley, S., Karlsen, J. R., & Putniņš, T. J. (2019). 'Sex, drugs, and bitcoin: How much illegal activity is financed through cryptocurrencies?' The Review of Financial Studies, 32(5), 1798-1853.

Amidst the ongoing debates and the complexities of blockchain technology, it's important to understand that it is still a nascent technology. Blockchain's true potential and its broad-scale implications may take years, if not decades, to fully materialize. Despite the skepticism and hurdles, blockchain technology presents an opportunity for innovation and disruption across numerous sectors. It is thus essential to continue the exploration and experimentation with this technology, albeit with a cautious and informed approach.

Unraveling the complexities of blockchain technology is not a simple task. It requires a balanced understanding of its potentials and challenges. Whether one views it as a revolutionary breakthrough or a hyped-up bubble, the influence of blockchain technology in shaping our digital future cannot be overlooked.

Blockchain Technology: How Black People Can Get Involved

The blockchain revolution is upon us, presenting an unprecedented opportunity for Black communities to participate actively in the tech revolution and achieve economic empowerment. The democratized and decentralized nature of blockchain technology opens up a plethora of opportunities for Black people to participate and contribute in meaningful ways[1171].

Firstly, education is key. Black people must strive to understand the workings and potential of blockchain technology, an area that is both complex and rapidly

---

[1171] Tapscott, D., & Tapscott, A. (2016). 'Blockchain Revolution: How the Technology Behind Bitcoin Is Changing Money, Business, and the World.' New York: Portfolio.

evolving[1172]. Universities and online learning platforms offer courses on blockchain technology, allowing anyone with an internet connection to gain a foundational understanding of the technology[1173]. Even a basic understanding can open doors to a myriad of career opportunities such as blockchain developer, consultant, or project manager. However, this educational initiative is not solely the responsibility of individuals. Institutions, such as HBCUs, can play a critical role by integrating blockchain technology into their curricula[1174].

Secondly, entrepreneurship in the blockchain space is a viable avenue for Black individuals. The blockchain industry is still in its infancy, offering ample room for innovation. Entrepreneurs can capitalize on blockchain's potential to disrupt industries ranging from finance to health-care[1175]. Notably, several Black-owned blockchain companies are already making significant strides, demonstrating the feasibility of this path[1176].

Despite these opportunities, there is opposition, skepticism, and uncertainty. Critics often cite the energy consumption and scalability issues associated with blockchain, as well as the volatility and speculative nature of cryptocurrencies[1177]. However, it is essential to understand that these are challenges to be overcome rather than insurmountable obstacles. The tech sector itself has

---

[1172] Mougayar, W. (2016). 'The Business Blockchain: Promise, Practice, and Application of the Next Internet Technology.' New Jersey: Wiley.
[1173] Coursera. (2021). 'Blockchain Basics.'
[1174] Howard University. (2022). 'Department of Computer Science.'
[1175] Swan, M. (2015). 'Blockchain: Blueprint for a New Economy.' O'Reilly Media, Inc.
[1176] "Black-Owned Blockchain Companies Making Waves." AfroTech, 2021.
[1177] Krause, M., & Tolaymat, T. (2018). 'Quantification of energy and carbon costs for mining cryptocurrencies.' Nature Sustainability, 1(11), 711–718.

shown an ability to evolve and innovate rapidly in response to these kinds of challenges.

Furthermore, it is critical for Black communities to engage in policy advocacy. As blockchain technology matures, regulatory frameworks will need to adapt. Active participation in shaping these policies will ensure that they are equitable and inclusive[1178].

The potential of blockchain technology for Black communities is enormous, providing a unique opportunity for economic empowerment and inclusion. However, success in this endeavor necessitates a proactive approach, ranging from education and entrepreneurship to policy advocacy. The complexities and challenges of blockchain technology should be seen as calls to action, rather than deterrents.

Origin And Development of Blockchain Technology

The origin of blockchain technology is indelibly linked to the pseudonymous figure Satoshi Nakamoto, who introduced it as the underlying system for the cryptocurrency Bitcoin in a 2008 white paper[1179]. A groundbreaking innovation, blockchain allowed Bitcoin to operate as a decentralized digital currency, free from government regulation and banking systems[1180].

The early development of blockchain was focused primarily on Bitcoin, as it was initially designed as a public ledger for all Bitcoin transactions. This transparent, incorruptible, and decentralized ledger was innovative for

---

[1178] Tapscott, A., & Tapscott, D. (2020). 'Financial Services: Building Blockchain One Block at a Time.' Financial Times.
[1179] Nakamoto, S. (2008). 'Bitcoin: A Peer-to-Peer Electronic Cash System.'
[1180] Tapscott, D., & Tapscott, A. (2016). 'Blockchain Revolution: How the Technology Behind Bitcoin Is Changing Money, Business, and the World.' New York: Portfolio.

its ability to ensure the security and integrity of financial transactions, without the need for intermediaries[1181].

However, it wasn't long before tech enthusiasts realized that the potential of blockchain extended beyond cryptocurrency. A key development in this regard was the introduction of Ethereum in 2015, which incorporated smart contracts into blockchain[1182]. Unlike Bitcoin, which was designed for a single use-case, Ethereum was conceived as a platform for numerous applications, enabling developers to create their own cryptocurrencies, decentralized applications, and more[1183].

Opposition and skepticism have arisen alongside the growth of blockchain technology. Many critics point to the volatile and speculative nature of cryptocurrencies and question whether blockchain technology can deliver on its promises. Others have raised environmental concerns related to the high energy consumption of certain blockchain applications, such as Bitcoin mining[1184].

However, it is essential to note that blockchain technology continues to evolve. Developments in the field, such as proof-of-stake consensus mechanisms, aim to address environmental concerns[1185]. Likewise, the volatility of cryptocurrencies, while significant, does not negate the potential of blockchain technology in sectors beyond finance.

[1181] Mougayar, W. (2016). 'The Business Blockchain: Promise, Practice, and Application of the Next Internet Technology.' New Jersey: Wiley.

[1182] Buterin, V. (2013). 'Ethereum: A Next-Generation Smart Contract and Decentralized Application Platform.'

[1183] Swan, M. (2015). 'Blockchain: Blueprint for a New Economy.' O'Reilly Media, Inc.

[1184] Krause, M., & Tolaymat, T. (2018). 'Quantification of energy and carbon costs for mining cryptocurrencies.' Nature Sustainability, 1(11), 711–718.

[1185] Buterin, V. (2021). 'A Proof of Stake Design Philosophy.' Ethereum.org.

Today, blockchain technology is being deployed in a variety of sectors, from supply chain management to healthcare and beyond[1186]. The transformative potential of this technology is vast, enabling trust, transparency, and efficiency in digital transactions.

The origin and development of blockchain technology is a testament to the innovative power of human ingenuity. Despite criticisms and challenges, this technology has demonstrated the potential to revolutionize numerous sectors of the global economy. As with all powerful tools, the benefits and drawbacks of blockchain technology must be carefully weighed, and necessary safeguards should be put in place.

Understanding Blockchain Technology

Blockchain technology, first proposed by the pseudonymous Satoshi Nakamoto, has rapidly grown beyond its origins as a ledger system for Bitcoin transactions, demonstrating revolutionary potential across various sectors[1187]. A defining feature of this technology is its decentralized nature, which allows for the creation of a shared, transparent, and immutable database, thereby fostering trust and security in digital interactions[1188].

One of the core features of blockchain is its cryptographic security. Each block in the chain contains transaction data, a time-stamp, and a unique crypto-graphic hash, which is dependent on the hash of the preceding block. This linking of blocks makes it practically impossible to

---

[1186] Mistry, I. (2018). 'Blockchain potential applications & disruption: open music initiative.' Blockchain Research Institute.
[1187] Nakamoto, S. (2008). 'Bitcoin: A Peer-to-Peer Electronic Cash System.'
[1188] Tapscott, D., & Tapscott, A. (2016). 'Blockchain Revolution: How the Technology Behind Bitcoin Is Changing Money, Business, and the World.' New York: Portfolio.

alter a block's content without disrupting the entire chain, thus ensuring the integrity of the data[1189].

Blockchain also ensures transparency and accessibility. Despite its strong encryption, blockchain is inherently open. Every participant in the network, or 'node', has access to the entire blockchain. This shared information can verify the authenticity of transactions and assets, thereby fostering transparency and preventing fraud[1190].

Critics, however, argue that this level of transparency can be a double-edged sword. While it can ensure accountability, it can also potentially expose sensitive information, making blockchain applications unsuitable for certain sectors[1191]. Furthermore, the energy consumption associated with certain types of blockchain, such as Bitcoin, has raised environmental concerns[1192].

Yet, ongoing advancements in the field are aiming to address these concerns. For instance, private or permissioned blockchains have been developed to control visibility of information, making them suitable for sectors requiring more privacy[1193]. Additionally, alternative consensus mechanisms like proof-of-stake aim to reduce energy consumption[1194].

The applications of blockchain technology extend far beyond cryptocurrencies. Blockchain's features lend themselves well to numerous sectors. For instance, in

---

[1189] Mougayar, W. (2016). 'The Business Blockchain: Promise, Practice, and Application of the Next Internet Technology.' New Jersey: Wiley.
[1190] Swan, M. (2015). 'Blockchain: Blueprint for a New Economy.' O'Reilly Media, Inc.
[1191] Werbach, K. (2018). 'Trust, But Verify: Why the Blockchain Needs the Law.' Berkeley Technology Law Journal, 33, 489–548.
[1192] Krause, M., & Tolaymat, T. (2018). 'Quantification of energy and carbon costs for mining cryptocurrencies.' Nature Sustainability, 1(11), 711–718.
[1193] Mistry, I. (2018). 'Blockchain potential applications & disruption: open music initiative.' Blockchain Research Institute.
[1194] Buterin, V. (2021). 'A Proof of Stake Design Philosophy.' Ethereum.org.

supply chain management, blockchain's transparency and immutability can be used to track the life cycle of goods, helping to prevent fraud and counterfeit products[1195]. Similarly, in health-care, blockchain could secure patient data, ensuring confidentiality and enabling seamless sharing of information among health-care providers[1196].

Understanding blockchain technology entails recognizing its core features and their potential applications, as well as the challenges that must be addressed for wider adoption. Amidst the hype and controversy surrounding blockchain, it remains a groundbreaking innovation with the potential to transform various sectors of the global economy.

Reemphasizing The Immediate Need For Black People To Embrace Tech, Blockchain, Artificial Intelligence

- The New Digital Age

The advent of the digital age has triggered a technological revolution, affecting almost every facet of our lives[1197]. Industries are being reshaped by Artificial Intelligence (AI), machine learning, and blockchain, opening up a myriad of opportunities[1198]. However, this revolution presents unique challenges for Black people,

---

[1195] Abeyratne, S.A., & Monfared, R.P. (2016). 'Blockchain Ready Manufacturing Supply Chain Using Distributed Ledger.' International Journal of Research in Engineering and Technology, 5(9), 1–10.
[1196] Ekblaw, A., Azaria, A., Halamka, J.D., & Lippman, A. (2016). 'A Case Study for Blockchain in health-care: "MedRec" prototype for electronic health records and medical research data.' Proceedings of IEEE Open & Big Data Conference.
[1197] Schwab, K. (2016). 'The Fourth Industrial Revolution.' Currency.
[1198] Bughin, J., Hazan, E., Ramaswamy, S., Chui, M., Allas, T., Dahlstrom, P., ... & Trench, M. (2017). 'Artificial Intelligence: The Next Digital Frontier?' McKinsey Global Institute.

particularly considering the historical and systemic barriers limiting their access to these opportunities[1199].

- Underrepresentation of Black People In Tech Fields

Despite progress, Black people remain underrepresented in tech fields. In 2020, they constituted merely 7.4% of the computing workforce[1200]. Such a stark disparity can be traced to various factors, including a lack of access to quality STEM education, biases in hiring practices, and a non-inclusive tech culture[1201].

- Why Black People Must Embrace Technology

The consequences of not addressing this underrepresentation could be severe. As industries continue to digitize, those not well-versed in the technologies driving this transition risk being left behind. This applies not just to jobs, but also to entrepreneurship and investment opportunities[1202].

- Technology And Its Various Facets

Technology encompasses a broad array of tools, processes, and systems. However, AI, machine learning, and blockchain are particularly relevant given their transformative potential. AI involves creating systems capable of performing tasks requiring human intelligence, while machine learning is a subset of AI that involves creating systems capable of learning from and improving

---

[1199] Anderson, C. (2001). 'Black Labor, White Wealth: The Search for Power and Economic Justice.' PowerNomics Corporation of America.

[1200] Ashcraft, C., & Breitzman, A. (2020). 'Who Invents IT? An Analysis of Women's Participation in Information Technology Patenting.' National Center for Women & Information Technology.

[1201] Cook, L. D. (2014). 'Violence and economic activity: evidence from African American patents, 1870–1940.' Journal of Economic Growth, 19(2), 221-257.

[1202] Anderson, C. (2005). 'The More Things Change, the More They Stay the Same: A Black Perspective on Information Technology.' Journal of Black Studies, 35(5), 375-386.

upon experience[1203]. Blockchain, meanwhile, is a decentralized and transparent ledger system with applications ranging from finance to supply chain management[1204].

- Blockchain Technology: Unraveling The Complexity

Blockchain technology was first proposed in 2008 by Satoshi Nakamoto for Bitcoin transactions. Since then, it has evolved significantly, with numerous cryptocurrencies and blockchain-based applications emerging[1205].

- Understanding blockchain technology: Features and applications

Blockchain technology's key features—decentralization, crypto-graphic security, transparency, and immutability—have made it a valuable tool for various applications. Despite criticisms regarding privacy concerns and energy consumption, ongoing advancements in blockchain technology are addressing these issues[1206].

Black people must actively engage with these technologies, not just as consumers but as creators and investors. Doing so will help close the racial wealth gap and ensure a more equitable distribution of the economic opportunities arising from the technological revolution[1207].

[1203] Samuel, A. L. (1959). 'Some studies in machine learning using the game of checkers.' IBM Journal of research and development, 3(3), 210-229.
[1204] Nakamoto, S. (2008). 'Bitcoin: A Peer-to-Peer Electronic Cash System.'
[1205] Tapscott, D., & Tapscott, A. (2016). 'Blockchain revolution: how the technology behind bitcoin is changing money, business, and the world.' Penguin.
[1206] Mougayar, W. (2016). 'The Business Blockchain: Promise, Practice, and Application of the Next Internet Technology.' Wiley.
[1207] Anderson, C. (2001). 'Black Labor, White Wealth: The Search for Power and Economic Justice.' PowerNomics Corporation of America.

The Dawn of Intelligent Machines

The dawn of intelligent machines is here, and the impetus for this revolution is Artificial Intelligence (AI)[1208]. AI, a concept that first took shape in the mid-20th century, is an area of computer science dedicated to creating systems capable of performing tasks that usually require human intelligence. These tasks include learning, reasoning, problem-solving, perception, and language understanding[1209].

- Exploring AI: From Basic Algorithms to Neural Networks

AI originated from basic algorithms and has evolved into complex neural networks. Early AI systems utilized rule-based algorithms, where computers were explicitly programmed to perform specific tasks. However, these systems lacked the ability to learn and adapt[1210]. Today, AI has advanced to incorporate learning algorithms, enabling the creation of neural networks modeled after the human brain[1211].

Neural networks represent a significant shift in AI development. They enable machines to process information in a more human-like way, allowing them to learn from experience and adjust to new inputs. Deep learning, a subset of neural networks, has been instrumental in progressing AI research and applications[1212].

[1208] Kaplan, A., & Haenlein, M. (2019). 'Siri, Siri, in my hand: Who's the fairest in the land? On the interpretations, illustrations, and implications of artificial intelligence.' Business Horizons, 62(1), 15-25.

[1209] Russell, S., & Norvig, P. (2016). 'Artificial Intelligence: A Modern Approach.' Malaysia; Pearson Education Limited.

[1210] Marr, B. (2019). 'The 4 Types Of Artificial Intelligence: From Reactive To Self-Aware.' Forbes.

[1211] LeCun, Y., Bengio, Y., & Hinton, G. (2015). 'Deep learning.' nature, 521(7553), 436-444.

[1212] Schmidhuber, J. (2015). 'Deep learning in neural networks: An overview.' Neural networks, 61, 85-117.

- AI in Everyday Life: Current Applications and Future Potentials

AI has already permeated various aspects of daily life, from digital personal assistants like Siri and Alexa to recommendation systems used by Netflix and Amazon[1213]. It is transforming sectors ranging from health-care, where it aids in diagnosing diseases, to transportation, where it powers self-driving cars[1214].

The future of AI holds immense potential. It could further revolutionize health-care, transportation, education, and many other sectors. However, this potential comes with significant challenges and controversies. Critics argue that as AI systems become more autonomous, they may make decisions that humans disagree with or don't understand[1215].

Moreover, the rapid growth of AI has raised concerns about job displacement. Studies predict that AI could automate around 50% of jobs currently done by humans[1216]. Nevertheless, proponents argue that AI will also create new jobs, just as past technological innovations have[1217].

The underrepresentation of Black people in this revolutionary technology is a pressing issue. If not addressed, it could exacerbate existing inequalities and prevent Black communities from fully partaking in the

---

[1213] Chui, M., Manyika, J., Miremadi, M., Henke, N., Chung, R., Nel, P., & Malhotra, S. (2018). 'Notes from the AI frontier: Applications and value of deep learning.' McKinsey Global Institute.

[1214] Topol, E. J. (2019). 'High-performance medicine: the convergence of human and artificial intelligence.' Nature medicine, 25(1), 44-56.

[1215] Bostrom, N., & Yudkowsky, E. (2014). 'The ethics of artificial intelligence.' Cambridge Handbook of Artificial Intelligence, 1, 316-334.

[1216] Frey, C. B., & Osborne, M. A. (2017). 'The future of employment: how susceptible are jobs to computerization?.' Technological Forecasting and Social Change, 114, 254-280.

[1217] Arntz, M., Gregory, T., & Zierahn, U. (2016). 'The Risk of Automation for Jobs in OECD Countries: A Comparative Analysis.' OECD Social, Employment and Migration Working Papers, No. 189, OECD Publishing, Paris.

benefits of AI[1218]. The time for action is now. By investing in education, training, and entrepreneurship in AI, Black people can ensure they are not left behind in the AI revolution.

Technology as a Platform for Empowerment

In the contemporary digital age, technology serves as a critical platform for empowerment, particularly for Black individuals and communities. The transformative potential of technology, particularly in fields such as AI, blockchain, and data science, can boost economic opportunities, especially for those traditionally underrepresented in these areas[1219].

- How Technology Can Boost Economic Opportunities
The digital economy is growing at an unprecedented pace. According to a report by Accenture, the digital economy could add $1.36 trillion to the total economy by 2025[1220]. Yet, this expanding digital landscape remains overwhelmingly white and male. Therefore, increasing the representation of Black people in tech could significantly boost economic opportunities for the Black community.

According to a McKinsey report, closing the racial wealth gap could net the US economy between $1.1 and $1.5 trillion by 2028[1221]. If the Black community can stake a claim in the burgeoning digital economy, it could serve as a critical step towards bridging this wealth gap.

[1218] Anderson, C. (2001). 'Black Labor, White Wealth: The Search for Power and Economic Justice.' PowerNomics Corporation of America.
[1219] Schmidhuber, J. (2015). 'Deep learning in neural networks: An overview.' Neural networks, 61, 85-117.
[1220] Daugherty, P., Carrel-Billiard, M., & Biltz, M. (2016). 'Technology for people.' Accenture Technology Vision 2016.
[1221] Noel, N., & Hardcastle, D. (2020). 'The economic impact of closing the racial wealth gap.' McKinsey & Company.

- Examples of Successful Black Individuals and Businesses in the Tech Sector

Despite the underrepresentation, there are numerous examples of successful Black individuals and businesses in the tech sector. Tristan Walker, a former Foursquare executive, founded Walker & Company, a health and beauty company for people of color, which was later acquired by Procter & Gamble[1222]. Another notable example is the tech entrepreneur and angel investor, Arlan Hamilton. She founded Backstage Capital, a venture capital firm dedicated to minimizing funding disparities in tech by investing in high-potential founders who are people of color, women, and/or LGBT[1223].

Companies like Blavity, a tech and media company geared toward Black millennials, and PlayVS, a platform for competitive Esports in high schools, founded by Delane Parnell, are other examples of successful Black-led tech ventures[1224].

These examples are encouraging, but they remain the exception rather than the norm. The tech sector has a long way to go in achieving racial parity. As such, it is paramount that Black people continue to strive for representation in tech and leverage technology as a platform for empowerment.

[1222] Del Rey, J. (2018). 'Procter & Gamble is acquiring Walker & Company, Tristan Walker's five-year-old start-up.' Recode.

[1223] Webb, A. (2020). 'How Arlan Hamilton went from homeless to founding a multi-million dollar venture capital fund.' Forbes.

[1224] Lacy, S. (2018). 'Meet Delane Parnell, whose esports start-up just raised $46 million.' Vanity Fair.

Technology As An Equalizer And Breaking Down Barriers

Technology, if harnessed correctly, can function as an equalizer for communities that are traditionally marginalized, including Black communities. As Anderson often reiterates, "Black people must embrace technology as a means to level the playing field"[1225]. Indeed, technology and digital platforms have the potential to diminish barriers such as geographic isolation, financial access, and information asymmetry.

In a world where information is increasingly digitized, access to the internet alone has tremendous implications for education and employment opportunities. For instance, the Khan Academy offers free, high-quality online education to anyone, anywhere[1226]. Similarly, platforms like Coursera and edX have democratized access to courses from top-tier universities. These resources could be particularly beneficial for Black communities, which often face disparities in educational opportunities and outcomes[1227].

Moreover, technology can facilitate access to financial services. Companies like Cash App and Venmo have made banking and money transfers simpler and more accessible[1228]. Blockchain and cryptocurrencies also promise to democratize financial services by bypassing traditional banking systems, potentially offering a significant benefit to marginalized communities[1229].

[1225] Anderson, C. (2001). 'Black labor, white wealth: The search for power and economic justice.' Powernomics Corporation of America.
[1226] Khan Academy. (2021). 'About.' Khan Academy.
[1227] Darling-Hammond, L. (2010). 'The flat world and education: How America's commitment to equity will determine our future.' Teachers College Press.
[1228] Chen, B.X. (2020). 'Cash App and Venmo may be so easy to use, but are they safe?' The New York Times.
[1229] Tapscott, D., & Tapscott, A. (2016). 'Blockchain revolution: How the technology behind bitcoin is changing money, business, and the world.' Penguin.

However, it is also critical to acknowledge the skepticism and potential downsides of technology. Critics often highlight issues such as the digital divide, privacy concerns, and the potential for tech to exacerbate inequalities. For instance, while online platforms can democratize education, the digital divide - the gap between those who have access to computers and the internet and those who do not - can also exacerbate educational disparities[1230]. Additionally, without proper regulation, technologies like AI could perpetuate existing biases and injustices[1231].

Yet, despite these valid concerns, the potential benefits of technology for Black communities cannot be overstated. It is, therefore, crucial for Black individuals and communities to become active participants and leaders in the tech revolution, ensuring that these tools are used to dismantle, not reinforce, systemic barriers.

Embracing Artificial Intelligence

- Role of AI in Job Creation and Economic Growth

The potential of artificial intelligence (AI) for economic growth and job creation cannot be understated. AI is set to contribute up to $15.7 trillion to the global economy by 2030, as estimated by PwC[1232]. Industries ranging from health-care to retail are being reshaped by AI,

---

[1230] DiMaggio, P., & Hargittai, E. (2001). 'From the 'digital divide' to 'digital inequality': Studying internet use as penetration increases.' Princeton University Center for Arts and Cultural Policy Studies.

[1231] Buolamwini, J., & Gebru, T. (2018). 'Gender shades: Intersectional accuracy disparities in commercial gender classification.' Proceedings of Machine Learning Research.

[1232] Berriman, R., & Hawksworth, J. (2017). 'Sizing the prize: What's the real value of AI for your business and how can you capitalize?' PwC.

and new jobs are created in areas such as data analysis, AI ethics, and machine learning engineering[1233].

For the Black community, this represents a promising opportunity. As Dr. Anderson underscores, "Black individuals and communities must leverage this AI revolution to create wealth and jobs"[1234]. Developing digital skills will be essential in this process.

- AI and Racial Bias: Challenges and Countermeasures

However, AI is not without its challenges. There are mounting concerns over AI systems perpetuating racial bias, such as facial recognition technologies misidentifying Black individuals at a much higher rate[1235]. As Joy Buolamwini and Timnit Gebru found in their Gender Shades project, commercial gender classification AI systems performed worse on darker-skinned and female faces[1236].

In the face of these challenges, countermeasures are needed. This includes involving Black professionals in the development and oversight of AI systems, ensuring a diverse set of training data, and enforcing stricter regulations and standards for AI bias[1237].

- Advocating for Ethical AI: Ensuring Fair and Equitable AI Systems

A commitment to ethical AI is essential to ensure its benefits reach all, including historically marginalized

---

[1233] Chui, M., Manyika, J., & Miremadi, M. (2016). 'Where machines could replace humans—and where they can't (yet).' McKinsey Quarterly.

[1234] Anderson, C. (2001). 'Black labor, white wealth: The search for power and economic justice.' Powernomics Corporation of America.

[1235] Buolamwini, J., & Gebru, T. (2018). 'Gender shades: Intersectional accuracy disparities in commercial gender classification.' Proceedings of Machine Learning Research.

[1236] Ibid.

[1237] Benjamin, R. (2019). 'Race after technology: Abolitionist tools for the new Jim Code.' Polity.

communities. "This calls for Black communities to not only participate in but also shape the discourse around AI ethics"[1238].

To address bias in AI, initiatives like the Algorithmic Justice League advocate for equitable and accountable AI, and regulatory bodies are increasingly prioritizing AI ethics[1239]. Also, involving Black professionals in AI development can lead to more inclusive and equitable AI systems.

It is critical, however, to recognize that technology alone will not solve deep-rooted social and racial inequalities. As Anderson points out, "Black individuals and communities must continue to strive for broader social, political, and economic justice while leveraging technology to empower themselves"[1240].

Policy Interventions for Tech Inclusion

The need for inclusive tech policy is as urgent as it is critical. Dr. Anderson underscores that "Black communities need to be more than just consumers in the tech sector, they must become participants and creators"[1241]. This can be achieved through effective policy interventions that promote tech inclusion and equity.

Firstly, diversifying the tech workforce should be a priority. Tech companies, often critiqued for their lack of diversity, need to actively recruit and retain more Black professionals. As per a 2018 study, Black professionals

---

[1238] Anderson, C. (2001). 'Black labor, white wealth: The search for power and economic justice.' Powernomics Corporation of America.
[1239] Algorithmic Justice League. (2021). 'About.' Algorithmic Justice League.
[1240] Anderson, C. (2001). 'Black labor, white wealth: The search for power and economic justice.' Powernomics Corporation of America.
[1241] Anderson, C. (2001). 'Black labor, white wealth: The search for power and economic justice.' Powernomics Corporation of America.

make up only 8% of the tech workforce[1242]. Policymakers can incentivize diversity through grants and tax breaks. Further, introducing diversity targets, while controversial, could stimulate change. Detractors argue that such policies could lead to tokenism, but others contend that it provides a necessary push to rectify deeply ingrained biases[1243].

Education policy also has a crucial role to play. Introducing computer science and digital literacy in early education can create a pipeline of tech-savvy individuals ready to enter the tech workforce. As of 2020, only 47% of U.S. high schools offered computer science education, demonstrating a substantial room for growth[1244]. Some critics caution that focusing too heavily on tech education may devalue other subjects, but supporters argue that the rapidly evolving digital economy demands these skills[1245].

Lastly, policies promoting affordable access to broadband are essential. In 2019, around 21% of Black Americans were not using the internet, often due to cost and availability[1246]. This digital divide creates a significant barrier to tech inclusion. Expanded broadband access can bridge this divide and unlock opportunities in the digital economy. Critics argue about the cost of such initiatives, but proponents note the long-term economic benefits and the crucial role of internet access in today's society[1247].

Policy interventions can significantly contribute to tech inclusion for Black communities. As Anderson would affirm, "these interventions must be viewed as part of a broader strategy for empowerment and social equity. The

---

[1242] Ashcraft, C., McLain, B., & Eger, E. (2016). 'Women in tech: The facts.' National Center for Women & Information Technology.
[1243] Ibid.
[1244] Code.org Advocacy Coalition. (2020). '2020 State of Computer Science Education: Illuminating disparities.'
[1245] Rose, K. (2017). 'Are we focusing too much on STEM?' The Atlantic.
[1246] Pew Research Center. (2019). 'Internet/Broadband Fact Sheet.'
[1247] Turner, D. (2019). 'The cost of connectivity 2020.' New America.

technology revolution can be a powerful tool for economic liberation if harnessed effectively"[1248].

Delving Deeper: Policy Strategies for Inclusive Technology

Moving beyond the immediate policy interventions for tech inclusion, it's crucial to explore further the nuances and mechanisms that could facilitate a more inclusive technology landscape.

Firstly, it is essential to foster an environment of entrepreneurship and innovation within the Black community. Incentives such as tax breaks and funding opportunities for Black-owned tech start-ups can aid this[1249]. However, critics may assert that these policies might promote "racial preferences," but advocates maintain that such measures are needed to rectify systemic disparities[1250]. As per Anderson, "Economic self-reliance is an essential component of genuine emancipation. The tech sector provides a potent platform for this self-reliance"[1251].

Secondly, policy initiatives to ensure transparency in Artificial Intelligence (AI) algorithms can significantly combat racial bias in tech. According to a study by MIT, facial recognition software has demonstrated bias, wrongly identifying darker-skinned and female faces more frequently than lighter-skinned and male faces[1252]. Legislation requiring companies to disclose their algorithms

---

[1248] Anderson, C. (2001). 'Black labor, white wealth: The search for power and economic justice.' Powernomics Corporation of America.
[1249] Fairlie, R., & Robb, A. (2008). 'Race and Entrepreneurial Success.' MIT Press.
[1250] Ibid.
[1251] Anderson, C. (2001). 'Black labor, white wealth: The search for power and economic justice.' Powernomics Corporation of America.
[1252] Buolamwini, J., & Gebru, T. (2018). 'Gender Shades: Intersectional Accuracy Disparities in Commercial Gender Classification.' Proceedings of Machine Learning Research.

for public scrutiny could help combat this issue. However, opponents may argue for protecting proprietary information, while proponents claim the need for accountability outweighs this concern[1253].

Thirdly, the government should look into increasing tech accessibility for disadvantaged communities. Public libraries and schools could be equipped with updated technology and high-speed internet to serve as tech hubs[1254]. While critics may contend with the cost, advocates argue that it's an investment in future human capital[1255].

Finally, fostering international collaborations to exchange knowledge and experiences can be beneficial. Initiatives like the African Union's Africa-EU Digital Economy Task Force provide blueprints for such collaboration[1256]. Detractors might warn of intellectual property theft or excessive dependency, but supporters highlight the importance of global solidarity in facing common challenges[1257].

Inclusive tech policy should go beyond surface-level interventions. It should delve into the intricacies of the tech sector and devise multifaceted strategies for inclusion. "Technology inclusion is not a destination but a journey. It requires consistent effort, flexibility, and the courage to confront difficult truths," states Anderson[1258].

[1253] Ibid.
[1254] Mossberger, K., Tolbert, C., & Hamilton, A. (2012). 'Broadband Adoption| The Next Step: From Connectivity to Digital Literacy.' Journal of Information Policy.
[1255] Ibid.
[1256] African Union and European Union. (2019). 'Africa-EU Digital Economy Task Force Report.'
[1257] Ibid.
[1258] Anderson, C. (2001). 'Black labor, white wealth: The search for power and economic justice.' Powernomics Corporation of America.

Sowing the Seeds of Tech Inclusion

In promoting tech inclusion, the policy levers at local and federal levels can yield significant results. Dr. Anderson posits that, "Tech inclusion is a multifaceted issue requiring equally multifaceted policy responses. From the local government offices to the corridors of Congress, there is a need for strategic and concerted efforts"[1259].

At the local level, municipal governments can make impactful changes. They can build partnerships with local tech firms to promote hiring from within the community, offering incentives for companies that demonstrate a commitment to diversity[1260]. However, critics argue such incentives may stifle competition, while proponents contend they help level the playing field in a traditionally unequal industry[1261].

Local educational authorities can also play a pivotal role by incorporating tech-based curriculum in public schools, aiming to foster a culture of innovation from an early age[1262]. Detractors might caution against a one-size-fits-all approach to education, but supporters emphasize the growing importance of tech literacy[1263].

On the federal side, the role of national regulatory bodies is paramount. Legislation that promotes transparency in AI and ensures fair practices in tech sectors is an effective tool for mitigating racial bias[1264]. The Federal Trade Commission's 2019 action against Facebook for

---

[1259] Anderson, C. (2001). 'Black labor, white wealth: The search for power and economic justice.' Powernomics Corporation of America.
[1260] U.S. Equal Employment Opportunity Commission. (2016). 'Diversity in High Tech.'
[1261] Ibid.
[1262] Google. (2019). 'Google for Education: Transformation Report.'
[1263] Ibid.
[1264] Buolamwini, J., & Gebru, T. (2018). 'Gender Shades: Intersectional Accuracy Disparities in Commercial Gender Classification.' Proceedings of Machine Learning Research.

discriminatory ad practices is a case in point[1265]. Critics might raise concerns over regulatory overreach, but proponents argue for the necessity of government oversight in protecting consumers and maintaining fairness[1266].

Federal investment in infrastructure is also a crucial policy measure. In the modern era, internet connectivity is as essential as electricity or water. Ensuring affordable and accessible broadband services for all, particularly in marginalized communities, is key for tech inclusion[1267]. While cost is a concern for detractors, proponents underscore the broader economic benefits, noting that internet access is a necessary public utility in the digital age[1268].

The policy response to tech inclusion must be comprehensive and involve all levels of government. The goal should not be merely to address symptoms but to identify and resolve root causes. As Anderson rightly contends, "True tech inclusion will be realized when technology is no longer a luxury for some but a reality for all"[1269].

Strategies for Advocacy to Increase Black Representation in Tech

Dr. Claud Anderson's work has long emphasized the significance of strategic advocacy to promote systemic

---

[1265] Federal Trade Commission. (2019). 'FTC Charges Facebook With Violating 2012 FTC Order by Deceptively Using Data from Onavo to Identify and Acquire Threats.'
[1266] Ibid.
[1267] Federal Communications Commission. (2020). '2020 Broadband Deployment Report.'
[1268] Ibid.
[1269] Anderson, C. (2001). 'Black labor, white wealth: The search for power and economic justice.' Powernomics Corporation of America.

change[1270]. He contends, "Advocacy has the power to turn aspirations into realities, opening doors for Black participation in the tech sphere"[1271].

A key strategy in this endeavor involves organizing at a grassroots level. Building strong coalitions within communities can provide a powerful platform to effect change. For instance, campaigns promoting digital literacy and access to technology in schools can help foster early interest and competence in tech[1272]. Critics may argue that grassroots movements can lack impact due to fragmented efforts, but supporters highlight their potential to effect local changes which can eventually ripple outward[1273].

Leveraging social media is another potent strategy. Social platforms are invaluable for highlighting the achievements of Black tech professionals, as well as broadcasting the need for more diversity in the tech sector. Critics may question the tangible impact of digital advocacy, but the #BlackTechTwitter movement demonstrates the potential to foster community, inspire young aspirants, and gain attention from industry leaders[1274].

An advocacy strategy cannot overlook the role of litigation. Civil rights organizations can challenge discriminatory practices in the tech industry through legal action, as the NAACP's lawsuit against major tech companies for racial bias in hiring demonstrated[1275]. Critics might argue that such measures can foster animosity within the industry, but proponents argue they are crucial to holding firms accountable[1276].

[1270] Anderson, C. (2001). 'Black labor, white wealth: The search for power and economic justice.' Powernomics Corporation of America.
[1271] Ibid.
[1272] Google. (2019). 'Google for Education: Transformation Report.'
[1273] Ibid.
[1274] Williams, B. (2019, December 6). 'The #BlackTechTwitter Movement Helps Connect Tech Professionals.' Forbes.
[1275] NAACP. (2019). 'NAACP sues major tech companies for racial bias.'
[1276] Ibid.

Finally, influencing policy via lobbying is essential. This strategy involves persuading legislators to enact laws that foster diversity in tech. Critics often decry lobbying as an exercise in elite influence, but advocates argue it is a necessary part of democratic negotiation[1277].

Implementing these strategies is a task of considerable scale and complexity. Yet, as Anderson would argue, "In the pursuit of fairness and equity in the tech industry, no effort is too great. Advocacy serves as a vehicle for change, propelling us toward a future where Black participation in tech is not an exception but the norm"[1278].

The Role of Parents And Educators In Nurturing Interest In Tech Among Black Youth

The influence of parents and educators in shaping young minds is beyond compare, as Dr. Claud Anderson consistently highlights in his writings. "Parents and teachers serve as the first role models for our children, their influence in fostering an interest in technology can be transformative," he states[1279].

Parents can ignite a child's interest in tech through conscious efforts, like exposing them to age-appropriate educational tech games and activities at home. Moreover, fostering an environment that celebrates curiosity and innovation can spur an early fascination with technology[1280]. While critics may voice concerns over excessive screen

---

[1277] Lohr, S. (2019, January 26). 'Tech Companies Spend More on Lobbying as Washington Targets Regulations.' The New York Times.

[1278] Anderson, C. (2001). 'Black labor, white wealth: The search for power and economic justice.' Powernomics Corporation of America.

[1279] Anderson, C. (2001). 'Black labor, white wealth: The search for power and economic justice.' Powernomics Corporation of America.

[1280] Epstein, D. (2019). 'Range: Why Generalists Triumph in a Specialized World.' Riverhead Books.

time, the constructive use of technology, under appropriate supervision, can serve as an impactful learning tool[1281].

Parental engagement also extends to advocating for quality tech education in schools. Parents can lobby for comprehensive computer science curricula and access to modern tech equipment, a crucial aspect of fostering tech literacy and interest from a young age[1282].

Teachers, on the other hand, serve as influential gatekeepers of knowledge and skills. They can encourage tech exploration through engaging lesson plans that incorporate problem-solving and critical thinking, the bedrock of tech-related fields[1283]. However, it's also essential that educators receive continuous training to stay current with tech trends, a point critics stress, considering the fast-paced evolution of the tech industry[1284].

Moreover, educators play a pivotal role in dispelling harmful stereotypes about who can succeed in tech. Research suggests that negative biases and stereotypes can deter Black students from pursuing tech-related fields[1285]. Therefore, educators must intentionally promote a diverse image of who can be a tech professional.

Programs that provide exposure to successful Black tech professionals, like career days or mentorship programs, can also be instrumental. Seeing someone who looks like them succeed in the tech industry can inspire Black students and reassure them that they too belong in this space[1286].

[1281] Ibid.
[1282] Anderson, C. (2001). 'Black labor, white wealth: The search for power and economic justice.' Powernomics Corporation of America.
[1283] Google. (2019). 'Google for Education: Transformation Report.'
[1284] U.S. Department of Education. (2017). 'Reimagining the Role of Technology in Education.'
[1285] Cheryan, S., Ziegler, S. A., Montoya, A. K., & Jiang, L. (2017). 'Why are some STEM fields more gender balanced than others?' Psychological Bulletin, 143(1), 1–35.
[1286] Williams, B. (2019, December 6). 'The #BlackTechTwitter Movement Helps Connect Tech Professionals.' Forbes.

Anderson's sentiment encapsulates this thought, "A sense of belonging can be a powerful motivator. When Black youth can envision themselves as tech leaders, we inch closer to a future where the tech industry is as diverse as the society it serves"[1287].

Final Reflections: Why Tech, Blockchain, and AI are Non-Negotiable for the Future of Black People

In the style of Dr. Claud Anderson's impassioned call to action, it is imperative to acknowledge that the future of Black communities hinges upon their integration and prominence within the technology sector. The changing landscape of our global economy, driven by advances in technology, blockchain, and artificial intelligence (AI), is no longer a distant prospect but an unfolding reality[1288].

It is indisputable that technology pervades every aspect of modern life, driving economic growth, societal change, and global connectivity[1289]. Failing to secure a stake within this sector would render Black communities vulnerable to perpetual economic marginalization. Despite the perceived complexity and challenges of technology, blockchain, and AI, these elements have already begun to reshape industries and job markets. By 2030, AI is expected to generate an additional global economic output of around $13 trillion[1290].

In the face of such rapid progression, remaining mere consumers in this digital revolution is not an option. As Anderson would remind us, "Black communities must

---

[1287] Anderson, C. (2001). 'Black labor, white wealth: The search for power and economic justice.' Powernomics Corporation of America.
[1288] Anderson, C. (2001). 'Black labor, white wealth: The search for power and economic justice.' Powernomics Corporation of America.
[1289] Muro, M., Maxim, R., & Whiton, J. (2019). 'Automation and Artificial Intelligence: How machines are affecting people and places.' Brookings Institution.
[1290] PWC. (2017). 'Sizing the prize: What's the real value of AI for your business and how can you capitalise?'

become creators, innovators, and leaders in the tech industry if they hope to secure economic prosperity and autonomy"[1291].

There are those who argue that the tech sector is but one of many potential routes to economic prosperity, and that overemphasis on technology could overshadow other viable industries[1292]. While there is merit to the argument for a diverse economic portfolio, the pervasive influence of technology in all sectors underscores the urgent need for tech literacy and representation.

The potential for blockchain to disrupt traditional financial systems offers unprecedented opportunities for wealth generation and economic empowerment for Black people. However, such promise will remain unfulfilled without the necessary awareness, education, and participation in this space[1293].

Critics express concerns over the security and regulation of blockchain technologies, and while these concerns are valid, they should serve as motivation for Black people to engage and influence regulatory dialogue, rather than shy away from these emerging opportunities[7].

Similarly, AI is poised to revolutionize how we live and work. The potential for job displacement is a common apprehension related to AI, with some reports suggesting that up to 38% of jobs in the U.S. could be automated by the early 2030s[8]. However, it is crucial to note that AI is also projected to create new industries and millions of jobs that we can't yet fully envision[9]. Therefore, the focus should be on acquiring skills that align with this technological shift.

[1291] Anderson, C. (2001). 'Black labor, white wealth: The search for power and economic justice.' Powernomics Corporation of America.

[1292] Florida, R. (2014). 'The rise of the creative class--revisited.' Basic Books.

[1293] Tapscott, D., & Tapscott, A. (2016). 'Blockchain revolution: how the technology behind bitcoin is changing money, business, and the world.' Penguin.

Dr. Anderson's words echo poignantly here, "Our journey towards technological empowerment is not a luxury for the future, it's a necessity for the now. It's not a choice, it's a charge"[10].

Chapter 11

Comprehensive Solutions for Re-Segregation

In addressing the problem of wealth disparity within the Black community, a multi-pronged approach is necessary, one of which includes strengthening local economies and communities. Claud Anderson asserts the significance of this endeavor in his seminal work, "PowerNomics: The National Plan to Empower Black America," positing that thriving local economies and communities are key drivers of Black wealth creation[1294].

Central to this strategy is the fortification of Black-owned businesses. The failure to develop and maintain Black-owned businesses within local communities contributes significantly to the wealth gap. In 2019, the average net worth of Black households in America was only about 15 percent of White households[1295]. This can be remedied by local governments prioritizing the success of Black-owned businesses, reducing bureaucratic hurdles, and promoting these businesses within the community. Such actions provide resources that enable these businesses to flourish, thereby stimulating local economies and creating jobs[1296].

[1294] Anderson, Claud. PowerNomics: The National Plan to Empower Black America. PowerNomics Corporation of America, 2001.
[1295] Kochhar, Rakesh, and Richard Fry. "Wealth inequality has widened along racial, ethnic lines since end of Great Recession." Pew Research Center, December 12, 2014.
[1296] Fairlie, Robert. "The Impact of COVID-19 on Small Business Owners: Evidence of Early-Stage Losses from the April 2020 Current Population Survey." National Bureau of Economic Research, June 2020.

Critics may argue that focusing on Black-owned businesses may engender a form of economic segregation. However, this view is a misunderstanding of the aim, which is not segregation, but self-sufficiency. It is about fostering a sense of community that encourages wealth circulation within the community[1297].

Investment in community development projects such as infrastructure, affordable housing, and community facilities is another cornerstone in building strong local economies. Infrastructure investments not only provide jobs and stimulate local economies but also have the potential to revitalize neighborhoods. For instance, the revitalization of Black neighborhoods in Harlem and Brooklyn has significantly contributed to the local economies[1298]. Skeptics might point out the danger of gentrification and displacement, which are valid concerns. However, a thoughtful approach to community development can bring about revitalization without displacement, through policies such as affordable housing mandates and protection for long-term residents[1299].

Moreover, cultivating entrepreneurship and investing in education within these communities are also paramount. By initiating entrepreneurship training programs and providing mentorship opportunities, local governments can stimulate innovation and economic growth. Quality education, including financial literacy programs, is necessary to equip the next generation with the skills required for wealth creation. Those skeptical of such programs may raise

---

[1297] Boyd, Michelle D. "Black Bourgeoisie and Black Common Folk: An Analysis of Class-Based Ideological Cleavages in Black Chicago's Community Development Discourse." Journal of Black Studies, vol. 41, no. 1, 2010, pp. 3-26.

[1298] Taylor, Keeanga-Yamahtta. Race for Profit: How Banks and the Real Estate Industry Undermined Black home-ownership. The University of North Carolina Press, 2019.

[1299] Fullilove, Mindy Thompson. Root Shock: How Tearing Up City Neighborhoods Hurts America, and What We Can Do About It. New Village Press, 2004.

concerns about the cost, suggesting it would be better spent on immediate relief measures. Yet, data consistently show that investing in education yields significant long-term economic benefits[1300].

The implementation of these solutions, while not exhaustive, represents a comprehensive road-map towards closing the Black wealth gap. This endeavor necessitates collective effort from all levels of society, including individuals, communities, and government. Despite the inherent challenges, it remains a necessary venture for the prosperity of the Black community and the nation as a whole.

Fortifying Black-owned Businesses

The fortification of Black-owned businesses has never been more critical in the current socio-economic landscape. There is an undeniable importance of nurturing and growing these businesses, as they serve as catalysts for economic growth, community stability, and wealth creation[1301]. The necessity of providing resources, reducing bureaucratic hurdles, and promoting Black-owned businesses within the community emerges as a decisive solution.

Recent data affirms that Black businesses are substantially less likely than white businesses to gain approval for loans, contributing to a landscape in which Black wealth is a mere fraction of white wealth [1302]. Addressing this systemic imbalance can only be achieved

---

[1300] Heckman, James J., and Dimitriy V. Masterov. "The Productivity Argument for Investing in Young Children." Review of Agricultural Economics, vol. 29, no. 3, 2007, pp. 446–493.

[1301] Anderson, Claud. PowerNomics: The National Plan to Empower Black America. PowerNomics Corporation of America, 2001.

[1302] Kochhar, Rakesh, and Richard Fry. "Wealth inequality has widened along racial, ethnic lines since end of Great Recession." Pew Research Center, December 12, 2014.

through targeted interventions and policy adjustments. However, some critics assert that these measures may perpetuate racial divisions. They argue that an equal-opportunity approach—providing equal resources to all businesses, regardless of race—promotes a more harmonious society[1303]. But, as Dr. Claud Anderson rightly asserts, an equal-opportunity approach cannot address systemic imbalances effectively, as it fails to recognize the historical and existing racial economic disparity[1304].

A comprehensive strategy to boost Black-owned businesses would necessitate various programs, ranging from entrepreneur mentorship to financial grants. Offering education and training programs, reducing red tape, and giving these businesses priority in public contracts are concrete actions that would usher in significant improvement[1305]. Furthermore, research has found that providing businesses with access to low-interest loans can catalyze their growth[1306]. Critics, however, often contest these measures. They argue that low-interest loans could be a potential risk to lenders and might inadvertently encourage fiscal irresponsibility[1307]. This critique, while potentially valid in some cases, falls short of considering the fact that appropriate risk assessment and business mentoring can mitigate these potential problems.

[1303] Kochhar, Rakesh, and Richard Fry. "Wealth inequality has widened along racial, ethnic lines since end of Great Recession." Pew Research Center, December 12, 2014.

[1304] Anderson, Claud. PowerNomics: The National Plan to Empower Black America. PowerNomics Corporation of America, 2001.

[1305] Fairlie, Robert. "The Impact of COVID-19 on Small Business Owners: Evidence of Early-Stage Losses from the April 2020 Current Population Survey." National Bureau of Economic Research, June 2020.

[1306] Boyd, Michelle D. "Black Bourgeoisie and Black Common Folk: An Analysis of Class-Based Ideological Cleavages in Black Chicago's Community Development Discourse." Journal of Black Studies, vol. 41, no. 1, 2010, pp. 3-26.

[1307] Taylor, Keeanga-Yamahtta. Race for Profit: How Banks and the Real Estate Industry Undermined Black home-ownership. The University of North Carolina Press, 2019.

Moreover, efforts to promote Black-owned businesses within their communities can be an essential step toward building a more robust local economy. Community-level promotions of Black businesses, as well as advocating for consumer support for these businesses, are necessary strategies. Detractors may argue that this approach encourages racial segregation[1308]. However, this critique does not consider that this form of economic self-reliance has been employed by other racial and ethnic groups in America with positive results. It isn't about racial isolation, but about economic empowerment and self-sufficiency[1309].

As the Black community grapples with the COVID-19 pandemic's devastating economic effects, these strategies' relevance cannot be overstated. The urgency to bridge the racial wealth gap necessitates pragmatic actions that effectively address the economic disparities facing Black communities[1310]. Thus, a comprehensive and targeted approach, one that encourages the development and success of Black-owned businesses, is indispensable to the future of Black wealth creation.

Bearing in mind the considerable challenges, critics should understand that the call to strengthen Black businesses isn't one of division, but one of inclusivity and economic justice. Advocacy for the bolstering of Black businesses is a call for a more equitable America where prosperity is shared, and economic mobility is achievable for all[1311].

[1308] Taylor, Keeanga-Yamahtta. Race for Profit: How Banks and the Real Estate Industry Undermined Black home-ownership. The University of North Carolina Press, 2019.

[1309] Anderson, Claud. PowerNomics: The National Plan to Empower Black America. PowerNomics Corporation of America, 2001.

[1310] Fairlie, Robert. "The Impact of COVID-19 on Small Business Owners: Evidence of Early-Stage Losses from the April 2020 Current Population Survey." National Bureau of Economic Research, June 2020.

[1311] Anderson, Claud. PowerNomics: The National Plan to Empower Black America. PowerNomics Corporation of America, 2001.

Community Development Projects

The potential for community development projects to significantly stimulate local job creation and enhance the quality of life is well recognized within the framework of equitable community growth[1312]. Investing in infrastructure, affordable housing, and community facilities can create a momentum that propels economic revitalization and subsequently leads to wealth creation within the Black community. However, the implementation of these initiatives continues to face a measure of skepticism and opposition[1313].

The correlation between infrastructure investment and job creation is well documented. Upgrading and maintaining infrastructure within Black communities could significantly stimulate job creation and improve the community's overall quality of life. For example, a study by the Economic Policy Institute posits that each billion dollars invested in infrastructure can create up to 13,000 jobs[1314]. However, some critics argue that this approach could exacerbate inequality, as jobs generated by such projects often require specific skill sets and, therefore, might not necessarily be accessible to all community members[1315].

Affordable housing initiatives can also play a crucial role in fostering wealth creation within the Black community. Ownership of property serves as a principal

---

[1312] Anderson, Claud. PowerNomics: The National Plan to Empower Black America. PowerNomics Corporation of America, 2001.

[1313] Boyd, Michelle D. "Black Bourgeoisie and Black Common Folk: An Analysis of Class-Based Ideological Cleavages in Black Chicago's Community Development Discourse." Journal of Black Studies, vol. 41, no. 1, 2010, pp. 3-26.

[1314] Bivens, Josh. "The Short- and Long-Term Impact of Infrastructure Investments on Employment and Economic Activity in the U.S. Economy." Economic Policy Institute, 2014.

[1315] Boyd, Michelle D. "Black Bourgeoisie and Black Common Folk: An Analysis of Class-Based Ideological Cleavages in Black Chicago's Community Development Discourse." Journal of Black Studies, vol. 41, no. 1, 2010, pp. 3-26.

means of wealth accumulation in America[1316]. However, the historical practice of redlining and discriminatory mortgage lending practices have significantly limited Black home-ownership[1317]. As a result, critics argue that affordable housing initiatives may not lead to significant wealth creation, as they do not directly address the broader systemic barriers to Black home-ownership[1318].

Community facilities such as parks, community centers, and libraries can enhance quality of life and stimulate local economies. They can serve as sites for community programs, providing services ranging from education to health, thereby creating jobs and fostering community cohesion. Critics often challenge the idea of investing in community facilities, suggesting that they do not necessarily translate into economic development or wealth creation[1319]. However, numerous studies have shown that such facilities often serve as a cornerstone for community revitalization efforts, leading to improved social outcomes and indirectly contributing to wealth creation[1320].
Overall, while these community development projects face certain criticisms, they present an integrated and comprehensive approach to fostering local economies and creating wealth within the Black community. In Dr. Claud

---

[1316] Taylor, Keeanga-Yamahtta. Race for Profit: How Banks and the Real Estate Industry Undermined Black home-ownership. The University of North Carolina Press, 2019.

[1317] Boyd, Michelle D. "Black Bourgeoisie and Black Common Folk: An Analysis of Class-Based Ideological Cleavages in Black Chicago's Community Development Discourse." Journal of Black Studies, vol. 41, no. 1, 2010, pp. 3-26.

[1318] Boyd, Michelle D. "Black Bourgeoisie and Black Common Folk: An Analysis of Class-Based Ideological Cleavages in Black Chicago's Community Development Discourse." Journal of Black Studies, vol. 41, no. 1, 2010, pp. 3-26.

[1319] Boyd, Michelle D. "Black Bourgeoisie and Black Common Folk: An Analysis of Class-Based Ideological Cleavages in Black Chicago's Community Development Discourse." Journal of Black Studies, vol. 41, no. 1, 2010, pp. 3-26.

[1320] Kuo, Frances E. "The Role of Arboriculture in a Healthy Social Ecology." Journal of Arboriculture, vol. 29, no. 3, 2003, pp. 148-155.

Anderson's words, these strategies are an "important component of an overall plan to empower Black America" by focusing on structural interventions that tackle systemic inequities[1321]. Critics should understand that these initiatives are not a magic bullet but are part of a broader strategy to foster local economic growth and contribute to wealth creation in Black communities.

Cultivating Entrepreneurship

Entrepreneurship serves as a cornerstone of economic development and wealth creation[1322] Local initiatives such as entrepreneurship training programs, start-up incubators, and mentorship opportunities, particularly those aimed at cultivating entrepreneurship within the Black community, can significantly stimulate economic growth and innovation. In the contemporary digital age, particular attention must be given to digitizing Black-owned businesses as a driver of revenue and growth. Despite the immense potential of such initiatives, they are often met with varying degrees of skepticism and opposition[1323].

Entrepreneurship training programs are instrumental in equipping individuals with the necessary skills and knowledge to launch and manage successful businesses. They offer a practical understanding of core business principles such as marketing, financial management, and strategic planning. Critics argue that while such programs are beneficial, they may not directly translate into successful

---

[1321] Anderson, Claud. PowerNomics: The National Plan to Empower Black America. PowerNomics Corporation of America, 2001.

[1322] Anderson, Claud. PowerNomics: The National Plan to Empower Black America. PowerNomics Corporation of America, 2001.

[1323] Taylor, Keeanga-Yamahtta. Race for Profit: How Banks and the Real Estate Industry Undermined Black home-ownership. The University of North Carolina Press, 2019.

entrepreneurship given the complex and multifaceted nature of starting and running a business[1324].

Start-up incubators can provide budding entrepreneurs with resources such as office space, mentoring, and access to financing. They often function as collaborative environments that facilitate learning and networking. These, too, face opposition, with critics pointing to the fact that not all businesses incubated succeed, and some suggest that the resources could be better used elsewhere[1325].

Mentorship opportunities can offer invaluable guidance to new entrepreneurs, providing them with insights drawn from the experiences of those who have previously navigated the entrepreneurial journey. While generally agreed upon as beneficial, some critics note that mentorship alone does not guarantee success and may lead to over-dependence on the mentor[1326].

The digital economy presents an enormous opportunity for Black-owned businesses to drive revenue and growth. Digital technologies can enable businesses to reach larger and more diverse customer bases, streamline operations, and adapt to changing market trends. Nevertheless, critics caution against an over-reliance on digitization, citing concerns around digital literacy, cybersecurity, and the potential for further exacerbating existing digital divides[1327].

These initiatives should be viewed not as isolated interventions but as components of a comprehensive

---

[1324] Taylor, Keeanga-Yamahtta. Race for Profit: How Banks and the Real Estate Industry Undermined Black home-ownership. The University of North Carolina Press, 2019.

[1325] Kochhar, Rakesh, and Richard Fry. "Wealth inequality has widened along racial, ethnic lines since end of Great Recession." Pew Research Center, December 12, 2014.

[1326] Taylor, Keeanga-Yamahtta. Race for Profit: How Banks and the Real Estate Industry Undermined Black home-ownership. The University of North Carolina Press, 2019.

[1327] Taylor, Keeanga-Yamahtta. Race for Profit: How Banks and the Real Estate Industry Undermined Black home-ownership. The University of North Carolina Press, 2019.

strategy for stimulating economic growth and innovation in the Black community. As Dr. Claud Anderson posits in his book, PowerNomics: The National Plan to Empower Black America, such a comprehensive approach is required to overcome the economic disparities faced by the Black community and foster wealth creation[1328].

Utilizing Technology and Global Partnerships

The role of technology in wealth creation, particularly for Black communities, cannot be overstated. As we stand at the cusp of the fourth industrial revolution, technology—from artificial intelligence to fintech solutions—provides potent avenues for wealth creation[1329]. The Digital Divide, however, threatens to leave Black communities behind[1330]. Ensuring that these communities have equal access to internet resources and tech education is, therefore, not only an economic imperative but a social one as well[1331].

Similarly, the power of global economic partnerships in creating wealth and driving economic growth must be acknowledged. International trade, the global Black diaspora, and international policy advocacy are tools that could be effectively leveraged by Black businesses for increased growth[1332]. However, this potential remains

---

[1328] Anderson, Claud. PowerNomics: The National Plan to Empower Black America. PowerNomics Corporation of America, 2001.

[1329] Muro, Mark, Sifan Liu, Jacob Whiton, and Siddharth Kulkarni. "Digitalization and the American workforce." Brookings, November 2017.

[1330] Turner, John. "Bridging the digital divide: Mobile access to personal health records." International Journal of Medical Informatics, vol. 108, 2018, pp. 98-104.

[1331] Mossberger, Karen, Caroline J. Tolbert, and Ramona S. McNeal. "Digital citizenship: Broadband, mobile use, and activities online." Oxford Handbooks Online, 2013.

[1332] Zennaro, Marco, et al. "The Internet: An Opportunity for Wealth Creation in Africa." SciELO Analytics, 2018.

largely untapped due to a variety of barriers, including limited access to global markets and systemic biases.

The cultivation of tech literacy and facilitating participation in technology-related education and careers have the potential to be significant wealth creation drivers. The tech industry is one of the fastest-growing sectors with high-paying jobs and business opportunities[1333]. Yet, there is a distinct underrepresentation of Blacks in this sector due to systemic barriers to tech education and digital resources. Policies aimed at bridging this gap can provide a pathway to wealth creation for the Black community.

Digitizing Black-owned businesses is a promising strategy. A strong online presence could drive revenue and growth[1334]. However, critics argue that the existing Digital Divide might hinder this transition, rendering these strategies less effective. Research suggests that while internet use is nearly universal among young, educated, and affluent Blacks, many others remain disconnected from the digital world[1335].

Similarly, harnessing global economic partnerships is a potent strategy for Black wealth creation. Engaging in international trade opens up new markets and avenues for growth. However, critics argue that this approach overlooks systemic issues, such as unfair trade policies and practices that often disadvantage Black-owned businesses[1336].

Leveraging technology and global partnerships can potentially drive Black wealth creation, but these strategies must be coupled with systemic interventions to be effective. These interventions must address the Digital Divide,

---

[1333] Bureau of Labor Statistics. "Employment Projections: Fastest growing occupations." U.S. Department of Labor, 2020.
[1334] Okazaki, Shintaro, and Ana M. Díaz-Martín. "Digitizing the start-up process: A special issue proposal." Journal of Business Research, vol. 69, no. 11, 2016, pp. 4830-4833.
[1335] Horrigan, John. "Digital readiness gaps." Pew Research Center, 2016.
[1336] Bown, Chad P. "Unfinished business? The WTO's Doha Agenda." The World Bank, 2011.

systemic barriers to tech education, and biases in international trade policies.

Bridging the Digital Divide

Bridging the Digital Divide is a critical step in creating wealth for Black individuals and businesses[1337]. However, despite the advantages of technological access, disparities persist that hinder equal opportunities for wealth creation[1338].

It is indisputable that digital technology opens avenues for wealth creation, ranging from telecommuting and freelancing opportunities to digital marketing and e-commerce. A study by the Brookings Institution highlights that occupations involving higher levels of digital skills tend to pay higher wages[1339]. Yet, a 2019 report by the Pew Research Center reveals that 58% of Black adults in America have home broadband, compared to 73% of Whites[1340]. This disparity, often referred to as the Digital Divide, could undermine wealth creation opportunities for Black individuals and businesses.

Efforts aimed at bridging the Digital Divide, such as improving broadband infrastructure in underserved areas and providing affordable internet access, can be significant catalysts for wealth creation. Internet access has the potential to unleash a plethora of economic opportunities, from expanding job markets to fostering entrepreneurship[1341].

[1337] Muro, Mark, Sifan Liu, Jacob Whiton, and Siddharth Kulkarni. "Digitalization and the American workforce." Brookings, November 2017.
[1338] Anderson, Monica, and Andrew Perrin. "Tech adoption climbs among older adults." Pew Research Center, 2017.
[1339] Muro et al., "Digitalization and the American workforce."
[1340] Pew Research Center. "Internet/Broadband Fact Sheet." 2019.
[1341] Mossberger, Karen, Caroline J. Tolbert, and Ramona S. McNeal. "Digital citizenship: Broadband, mobile use, and activities online." Oxford Handbooks Online, 2013.

However, there are critics who argue that simply providing access to technology does not automatically translate to wealth creation. They cite the lack of digital literacy and necessary skills as significant barriers[1342]. As Mossberger, Tolbert, and McNeal assert, digital citizenship extends beyond mere access to include the ability to use technology effectively[1343].

The lack of access to technology in the Black community also impacts businesses. Black-owned businesses have been slower to adopt online tools for commerce and marketing[1344]. By providing the necessary infrastructure and training, these businesses can better leverage the internet for growth and revenue generation.

However, the detractors argue that digitizing Black-owned businesses, though beneficial, will not necessarily translate into economic parity. They contend that systemic biases in access to capital, unfair competition, and other structural barriers will still remain[1345].

Bridging the Digital Divide has the potential to significantly contribute to wealth creation for Black individuals and businesses. However, this strategy must be accompanied by interventions to develop digital literacy and address systemic barriers to wealth creation.

[1342] Horrigan, John. "Digital readiness gaps." Pew Research Center, 2016.
[1343] Mossberger et al., "Digital citizenship."
[1344] Fairlie, Robert, and Alicia M. Robb. "Race and Entrepreneurial Success: Black-, Asian-, and White-Owned Businesses in the United States." MIT Press, 2008.
[1345] Darity Jr., William, and A. Kirsten Mullen. "From Here to Equality: Reparations for Black Americans in the Twenty-First Century." The University of North Carolina Press, 2020.

Advancing Tech Education

Advancing technological education is a powerful pathway to economic progress for the Black community[1346]. As technology permeates all facets of life, skills related to technology are in high demand, offering high-paying jobs and business opportunities. Yet, despite the potential benefits, Black individuals remain underrepresented in these fields[1347].

Statistics show that STEM (Science, Technology, Engineering, Mathematics) careers tend to provide higher wages[1348]. Yet, Black students are underrepresented in these fields. As per National Science Foundation data, Black students comprise only 9% of STEM degree holders, significantly lower than their representation in the overall population[1349].

There are programs, such as Code.org and Black Girls Code, designed to increase Black representation in tech by providing education and mentorship[1350]. Advocates believe these initiatives not only prepare participants for lucrative jobs but also instill the skills necessary to start their own tech-based businesses.

Contrarily, some critics argue that the focus on tech education does not fully address the systemic disparities and biases present in the tech industry. For instance, a report by the Kapor Center highlights how bias, discrimination, and a

---

[1346] Anderson, Claud. PowerNomics: The National Plan to Empower Black America. PowerNomics Corporation of America, 2001.
[1347] U.S. Equal Employment Opportunity Commission. "Diversity in High Tech." May 2016.
[1348] Langdon, David, George McKittrick, David Beede, Beethika Khan, and Mark Doms. "STEM: Good Jobs Now and For the Future." U.S. Department of Commerce, July 2011.
[1349] National Science Foundation, National Center for Science and Engineering Statistics. "Women, Minorities, and Persons with Disabilities in Science and Engineering." 2019.
[1350] Buchanan, Larry, Quoctrung Bui, and Claire Miller. "Why Tech Degrees Are Not Putting More Blacks and Hispanics Into Tech Jobs." The New York Times, October 25, 2016.

lack of inclusivity contribute to a high attrition rate of Black tech workers[1351].

Despite these challenges, tech education can indeed foster wealth creation for the Black community. This can be further augmented by measures to counter systemic biases, thereby ensuring fair access to opportunities in the tech industry.

As we continue to push for tech education, it is crucial to understand that this strategy should be a part of a larger, multi-pronged approach towards wealth creation. This includes addressing the racial wealth gap, improving access to capital for Black entrepreneurs, and promoting inclusive economic policies[1352].

Even as we advocate for tech education, we must heed the caution of those who argue that an over-reliance on tech as a solution might obscure other economic realities and systemic challenges that require addressing. It is, therefore, necessary to pair tech education with other measures that address systemic and structural barriers to wealth creation[1353].

Fostering Global Economic Partnerships

Cultivating global economic partnerships represents an expansive frontier for Black economic advancement[1354]. As we recognize the importance of small businesses in bolstering local economies, it is equally critical to facilitate their engagement in international trade and relationships

---

[1351] Kapor Center. "Tech Leavers Study." April 2017.
[1352] Darity Jr., William, and A. Kirsten Mullen. "From Here to Equality: Reparations for Black Americans in the Twenty-First Century." The University of North Carolina Press, 2020.
[1353] Taylor, Keeanga-Yamahtta. Race for Profit: How Banks and the Real Estate Industry Undermined Black home-ownership. The University of North Carolina Press, 2019.
[1354] Anderson, Claud. PowerNomics: The National Plan to Empower Black America. PowerNomics Corporation of America, 2001.

with the global Black diaspora. Such partnerships can unlock new markets, stimulate investment, and foster a vital exchange of knowledge.

Consider, for example, the potency of the African Continental Free Trade Area (AfCFTA), an agreement among 54 of the 55 African Union nations that has created the world's largest free trade area[1355]. This agreement could potentially offer Black businesses in the U.S. access to a marketplace of 1.3 billion people, providing significant growth opportunities[1356].

Moreover, there is a noteworthy increase in the number of U.S.-based Black businesses seeking to forge ties with countries in Africa and the Caribbean, part of a broader shift toward reconnecting with the Black diaspora for economic advancement[1357]. Such a transnational network of Black businesses could galvanize a powerful, global economic force.

Nonetheless, there is skepticism and concerns associated with this approach. Critics argue that without a firm domestic foundation, Black businesses might be ill-prepared to navigate international markets[1358]. Additionally, there are concerns about how fluctuations in global economic conditions might disproportionately impact Black businesses[1359].

Others caution that international trade agreements often prioritize large corporations, possibly leaving small

---

[1355] Mfunwa, David Luke and Lily Sommer. "Africa Continental Free Trade Area: Challenges and Opportunities of Tariff Reductions." United Nations Economic Commission for Africa, January 2019.

[1356] United Nations Economic Commission for Africa. "African Continental Free Trade Area: Questions & Answers." March 2018.

[1357] Matthews, Dylan. "The growing movement for a 'United States of Africa'." Vox, February 2020.

[1358] Boyd, Michelle D. "Black Bourgeoisie and Black Common Folk: An Analysis of Class-Based Ideological Cleavages in Black Chicago's Community Development Discourse." Journal of Black Studies, vol. 41, no. 1, 2010, pp. 3-26.

[1359] Horsley, Scott. "How A Trade War Could Backfire On The U.S. Economy." NPR, June 2018.

businesses at a disadvantage. Moreover, the unique challenges faced by Black businesses, such as limited access to capital and the racial wealth gap, might be exacerbated in the global arena[1360].

Despite these valid concerns, the potential benefits of global economic partnerships for Black businesses warrant careful exploration and strategic planning. Dr. Claud Anderson emphasizes that the integration of Black businesses into international markets should not be viewed as an alternative to domestic growth, but rather as an addition to it[1361].

By addressing systemic barriers to access and equity, we can empower Black businesses to thrive both domestically and globally. This dual approach can drive sustainable growth, making significant strides towards rectifying economic disparities and realizing the vision of comprehensive Black wealth creation.

Leveraging State and Federal Government Support

State and federal government support represents a crucial lever in fostering Black wealth creation[1362]. By providing financial resources, technical assistance, and policy reforms, government entities can address systemic barriers that impede Black economic progress. Notwithstanding, the relationship between Black communities and government support is complex and often contentious, calling for a nuanced understanding and strategic engagement.

Federal programs, such as the Small Business Administration's 8(a) Business Development Program, aim to help minority-owned businesses compete in the

---

[1360] Taylor, Keeanga-Yamahtta. Race for Profit: How Banks and the Real Estate Industry Undermined Black home-ownership. The University of North Carolina Press, 2019.

[1361] Anderson, Claud. PowerNomics: The National Plan to Empower Black America. PowerNomics Corporation of America, 2001.

[1362] Anderson, Claud. PowerNomics: The National Plan to Empower Black America. PowerNomics Corporation of America, 2001.

marketplace[1363]. However, bureaucratic complexities and access issues often result in many Black businesses not benefiting from these programs[1364].

State-level initiatives can also play a significant role. For example, enterprise zones, which provide tax incentives and other benefits to businesses in specified areas, have been employed as a strategy to stimulate economic development in marginalized communities[1365]. Yet, some critics argue that these programs often fail to reach the businesses and communities that need them the most[1366].

Furthermore, there are concerns about the role of government in the perpetuation of economic disparities. Historical precedents, such as redlining and discriminatory lending practices, have contributed to a profound mistrust in government interventions, underscoring the importance of transparency, accountability, and community engagement in government-supported initiatives[1367].

Contrarily, it is essential to note that, while there is skepticism, the active engagement of the government is an indispensable element in achieving substantial Black wealth creation. Government resources and policy influence can address deeply entrenched systemic barriers in ways that individual efforts or market forces cannot.

For instance, government policies can directly address the racial wealth gap through progressive taxation and

---

[1363] U.S. Small Business Administration. "8(a) Business Development Program." Accessed on June 2023.

[1364] Bradford, William D. "The 'Myth' that Black Entrepreneurship Can Reduce the Gap in Wealth between Black and White Families." Economic Development Quarterly, vol. 23, no. 3, 2009, pp. 225-231.

[1365] Peters, Alan, and Peter Fisher. "The Failures of Economic Development Incentives." Journal of the American Planning Association, vol. 70, no. 1, 2004, pp. 27-37.

[1366] Bondonio, Daniele, and John Engberg. "Enterprise Zones and Local Employment: Evidence from the States' Programs." Regional Science and Urban Economics, vol. 30, no. 5, 2000, pp. 519-549.

[1367] Taylor, Keeanga-Yamahtta. Race for Profit: How Banks and the Real Estate Industry Undermined Black home-ownership. The University of North Carolina Press, 2019.

wealth redistribution. They can also stimulate Black wealth creation by investing in education, affordable housing, infrastructure, and social services in marginalized communities[1368].

It is in this context that Dr. Claud Anderson emphasizes the need for a collective and strategic approach to leveraging government support, one that advocates for policies and programs that explicitly address the unique economic challenges facing the Black community[1369].

The potential of state and federal government support as a tool for Black wealth creation is substantial, albeit fraught with challenges. Recognizing this complexity, the path forward requires deliberate action, persistent advocacy, and the courage to reimagine existing structures, all geared towards ensuring that government support effectively serves its intended purpose of equitable economic empowerment.

Policy Advocacy

Policy advocacy represents a potent mechanism for advancing equitable economic opportunities for the Black community. At both state and federal levels, policy decisions can shape the economic environment, affecting outcomes ranging from lending practices to access to quality education[1370]. However, the efficacy and fairness of these policies have been subjects of ongoing debate.

Fair lending practices, for example, are crucial for Black wealth creation. The Fair Housing Act and the Equal Credit Opportunity Act were landmark policies enacted to

---

[1368] Fullilove, Mindy Thompson. Root Shock: How Tearing Up City Neighborhoods Hurts America, and What We Can Do About It. One World/Ballantine, 2004.
[1369] Anderson, Claud. PowerNomics: The National Plan to Empower Black America. PowerNomics Corporation of America, 2001.
[1370] Anderson, Claud. PowerNomics: The National Plan to Empower Black America. PowerNomics Corporation of America, 2001.

combat discriminatory lending practices[1371]. However, research has demonstrated that discriminatory practices, such as redlining and subprime lending, have persisted, contributing significantly to the racial wealth gap[1372].

Moreover, access to quality education is another area where policy intervention is paramount. Education has been touted as a means of upward mobility, and policies such as Brown vs. Board of Education have aimed at ensuring racial integration in schools[1373]. Despite these efforts, educational disparities continue to exist, with Black students disproportionately concentrated in under-resourced schools[1374].

Critics argue that such policies do not fully address the systemic barriers entrenched in these systems. According to Dr. Claud Anderson, these shortcomings necessitate a refocusing of policy advocacy towards initiatives that tackle structural barriers head-on, providing not just equal opportunities but also equitable outcomes for Black individuals[1375].

The emphasis should be on developing and advocating for policies that specifically cater to the unique challenges faced by the Black community. These could range from enforcing stricter regulations against discriminatory lending to ensuring the allocation of sufficient resources to schools serving Black students.

[1371] Turner, Margery Austin, et al. "Housing Discrimination Against Racial and Ethnic Minorities 2012: Executive Summary." Urban Institute, June 2013.

[1372] Rugh, Jacob S., and Douglas S. Massey. "Racial Segregation and the American Foreclosure Crisis." American Sociological Review, vol. 75, no. 5, 2010, pp. 629-651.

[1373] Orfield, Gary, and Erica Frankenberg. "Brown at 60: Great Progress, a Long Retreat and an Uncertain Future." Civil Rights Project/Proyecto Derechos Civiles, May 15, 2014.

[1374] Reardon, Sean F., and Ann Owens. "60 Years After Brown: Trends and Consequences of School Segregation." Annual Review of Sociology, vol. 40, 2014, pp. 199-218.

[1375] Anderson, Claud. PowerNomics: The National Plan to Empower Black America. PowerNomics Corporation of America, 2001.

Moreover, policy advocacy needs to be complemented by a comprehensive approach that includes economic empowerment and community engagement[1376]. For example, Black individuals and businesses should be empowered with the knowledge and tools to navigate economic systems effectively. Similarly, the community should be actively involved in policy-making processes to ensure that their voices are heard and their needs are addressed.

Despite the challenges, policy advocacy can serve as a potent tool for promoting Black wealth creation when used strategically and in conjunction with other initiatives. The task at hand is to ensure that policies do not just provide equal opportunities on paper but lead to equitable outcomes in practice.

Strengthening Social Safety Nets

Social safety nets, which include measures such as unemployment benefits, are essential components of any effort to provide economic security and prevent wealth erosion, particularly among marginalized populations. The significance of these policies is often underscored during times of crisis, such as the recent COVID-19 pandemic, where they have served as economic lifelines for millions of people[1377].

Unemployment benefits, in particular, have been proven to mitigate financial hardship among jobless workers, allowing them to maintain their spending and thus their standard of living, even as they search for new

---

[1376] Anderson, Claud. PowerNomics: The National Plan to Empower Black America. PowerNomics Corporation of America, 2001.

[1377] Ganong, Peter, et al. "US Unemployment Insurance Replacement Rates During the Pandemic." Journal of Public Economics, vol. 191, 2021.

employment[1378]. For Black communities, however, the safety net has sometimes proven inadequate.

While unemployment benefits are universally accessible to all eligible unemployed workers, studies indicate that Black workers are often less likely to receive these benefits than their white counterparts[1379]. This discrepancy, attributed in part to systemic barriers such as discriminatory practices in the workforce, can exacerbate the racial wealth gap and contribute to economic instability within the Black community.

From the perspective of Dr. Claud Anderson, policies to strengthen social safety nets should address these disparities head-on[1380]. He calls for a revision of the eligibility criteria and application processes associated with these benefits, to ensure that they are accessible to all who need them, irrespective of their racial or ethnic background.

The advocacy for stronger social safety nets, however, does face some opposition. Critics argue that such benefits can disincentivize work and lead to long-term dependency[1381]. These arguments, while valid, often overlook the systemic barriers that limit economic opportunities, particularly for Black workers. As Anderson suggests, the focus should not only be on strengthening social safety nets but also on addressing the root causes of economic instability, such as discriminatory employment practices and the lack of access to quality education[1382].

[1378] Chetty, Raj. "Moral Hazard vs. Liquidity and Optimal Unemployment Insurance." Journal of Political Economy, vol. 116, no. 2, 2008, pp. 173-234.

[1379] Gabe, Thomas, and Julie M. Whittaker. "Unemployment Insurance: Programs and Benefits." Congressional Research Service, 2012.

[1380] Anderson, Claud. PowerNomics: The National Plan to Empower Black America. PowerNomics Corporation of America, 2001.

[1381] Mulligan, Casey B. The Redistribution Recession: How Labor Market Distortions Contracted the Economy. Oxford University Press, 2012.

[1382] Anderson, Claud. PowerNomics: The National Plan to Empower Black America. PowerNomics Corporation of America, 2001.

Strengthening social safety nets, including unemployment benefits, is a crucial aspect of ensuring economic security for the Black community. However, these efforts must be supplemented by broader initiatives aimed at addressing systemic barriers and promoting equitable economic opportunities.

Affirmative Action

Affirmative action, a set of policies aimed at increasing opportunities for underrepresented groups in education and employment, has long been a topic of heated debate. Its proponents argue it can play a key role in rectifying historical imbalances and aiding wealth creation, particularly for the Black community[1383].

Dr. Claud Anderson, a firm advocate for Black economic empowerment, posits that affirmative action can address the entrenched disparities that the Black community faces, primarily because of America's legacy of racial discrimination [1384]. By promoting diversity in educational institutions and workplaces, affirmative action programs help create a level playing field, offering access to opportunities that can foster wealth generation, including quality education, well-paying jobs, and opportunities for business growth[1385].

Empirical evidence supports these claims. For instance, research demonstrates that affirmative action in college admissions has significantly increased the number of Black

---

[1383] Bowen, William G., and Derek Bok. The Shape of the River: Long-Term Consequences of Considering Race in College and University Admissions. Princeton University Press, 1998.
[1384] Anderson, Claud. PowerNomics: The National Plan to Empower Black America. PowerNomics Corporation of America, 2001.
[1385] Holzer, Harry, and David Neumark. "Affirmative Action: What Do We Know?" Journal of Policy Analysis and Management, vol. 25, no. 2, 2006, pp. 463-490.

students in top-tier universities, subsequently leading to higher lifetime earnings[1386]. Likewise, affirmative action in government contracting has been found to increase the revenue and employment growth of Black-owned firms[1387].

However, the concept of affirmative action has also been met with significant resistance. Critics often argue that it constitutes reverse discrimination, asserting that merit should be the sole determinant for opportunities in education and employment[1388]. Some claim it can even be counterproductive by perpetuating stereotypes and creating stigma associated with beneficiaries of these policies[1389].

While these viewpoints highlight some of the potential adverse effects of affirmative action, it is critical to note that they often overlook the systemic and structural barriers that have hindered Black wealth creation for centuries. Anderson's position suggests that affirmative action isn't about preferential treatment but about addressing historical injustices and facilitating equitable access to opportunities[1390].

While the discourse around affirmative action remains contentious, it is essential to recognize its potential as a tool for fostering Black wealth creation. Its effective implementation, alongside other measures, can help to address the enduring racial wealth gap and promote economic stability within the Black community.

[1386] Long, Mark C. "Affirmative Action and its Alternatives in Public Universities: What Do We Know?" Public Administration Review, vol. 67, no. 1, 2007, pp. 315-330.

[1387] Boston, Thomas D. "Affirmative Action and Black Entrepreneurship." The Review of Black Political Economy, vol. 26, no. 4, 1999, pp. 7-19.

[1388] Sowell, Thomas. "Affirmative Action: A Worldwide Disaster." Commentary, vol. 84, no. 6, 1987, pp. 26-32.

[1389] Heilman, Madeline E., et al. "Has Affirmative Action Reached the Backlash Stage? The Impact of Attributions for the Success of Minority and Female Managers." Academy of Management Journal, vol. 38, no. 2, 1995, pp. 593-611.

[1390] Anderson, Claud. PowerNomics: The National Plan to Empower Black America. PowerNomics Corporation of America, 2001.

Empowering Through Collective Economics and Financial Innovations

The concept of collective economics is critical in the journey towards Black wealth creation, a principle firmly espoused by Dr. Claud Anderson in his book, PowerNomics: The National Plan to Empower Black America[1391]. By emphasizing collective economics, Anderson asserts that the Black community can stimulate economic development, sustain businesses, and foster community cohesion, ultimately aiding in wealth generation[1392].

Collective economics refers to the idea of pooling resources to establish and support businesses, making purchases within the community, and collectively negotiating better prices[1393]. Research indicates that other racial and ethnic groups have successfully employed collective economics to generate wealth and boost economic development[1394].

This strategy also involves using financial innovations such as crowd-funding and peer-to-peer lending platforms, which can provide needed capital to Black-owned businesses that often face difficulties in accessing traditional financing channels[1395]. Moreover, innovations

---

[1391] Anderson, Claud. PowerNomics: The National Plan to Empower Black America. PowerNomics Corporation of America, 2001.
[1392] Boyd, Michelle D. "Black Bourgeoisie and Black Common Folk: An Analysis of Class-Based Ideological Cleavages in Black Chicago's Community Development Discourse." Journal of Black Studies, vol. 41, no. 1, 2010, pp. 3-26.
[1393] Marable, Manning. How Capitalism Underdeveloped Black America: Problems in Race, Political Economy, and Society. Pluto Press, 2000.
[1394] Aldrich, Howard E., and Roger Waldinger. "Ethnicity and Entrepreneurship." Annual Review of Sociology, vol. 16, no. 1, 1990, pp. 111-135.
[1395] Bruton, Garry D., et al. "Bridging the Conceptual Divide: The Role of Entrepreneurship in Black Wealth Creation." Academy of Management Perspectives, vol. 34, no. 3, 2020, pp. 367-384.

such as digital currencies and blockchain technology can create new opportunities for wealth generation by enabling secure, decentralized financial transactions[1396].

Despite the potential of collective economics and financial innovations, some critics argue that such an approach might lead to economic isolation, or even undermine individualism and competitiveness[1397]. Others express skepticism about the efficacy and security of financial technologies, pointing to the volatility of digital currencies and potential for fraudulent activities in crowd-funding platforms[1398].

However, while these concerns are legitimate, they often fail to account for the systemic barriers that impede Black wealth creation. Anderson contends that utilizing collective economics and financial innovations, coupled with proper regulatory measures and financial literacy, can provide a viable path towards Black economic empowerment[1399].

While not a panacea, collective economics, aided by financial innovations, offers a unique tool for Black wealth creation. Embracing this strategy can potentially pave the way towards more equitable economic development, as part of a broader, multifaceted approach to closing the racial wealth gap.

[1396] Tapscott, Don, and Alex Tapscott. Blockchain Revolution: How the Technology Behind Bitcoin Is Changing Money, Business, and the World. Penguin, 2016.

[1397] Sowell, Thomas. Race and Economics: How Much Can Be Blamed on Discrimination? Hoover Institution Press, 2011.

[1398] Mougayar, William. The Business Blockchain: Promise, Practice, and Application of the Next Internet Technology. Wiley, 2016.

[1399] Anderson, Claud. PowerNomics: The National Plan to Empower Black America. PowerNomics Corporation of America, 2001.

Cooperative Economics

In his visionary work, PowerNomics: The National Plan to Empower Black America, Dr. Claud Anderson underscores the role of cooperative economics as a catalyst for Black wealth creation[1400]. In essence, cooperative economics refers to collective ownership and operation models such as cooperatives and mutual aid societies, where profits are equitably distributed amongst members, facilitating wealth retention within the community[1401].

Cooperatives, for instance, are an effective means of circumventing capital access challenges faced by Black-owned businesses. They aggregate resources, knowledge, and power, thereby enabling community members to collectively own and operate businesses[1402]. Research has illustrated the viability of such models in creating jobs, reducing income inequality, and strengthening local economies[1403].

Nonetheless, this concept of shared ownership and income distribution is not without its critics. Some argue that cooperatives may struggle to compete in capitalist markets due to their emphasis on social objectives over profit[1404]. Critics also contend that cooperatives may suffer from inefficiencies related to decision-making, management, and member participation[1405].

[1400] Anderson, Claud. PowerNomics: The National Plan to Empower Black America. PowerNomics Corporation of America, 2001.

[1401] Gordon Nembhard, Jessica. Collective Courage: A History of African American Cooperative Economic Thought and Practice. Penn State Press, 2014.

[1402] Münkner, Hans-H. "Cooperatives: A tool for creating employment and improving the living conditions of the poor." ILO Geneva, 2004.

[1403] Vanek, Jaroslav. The General Theory of Labor-Managed Market Economies. Cornell University Press, 1971.

[1404] Ward, Benjamin. "The Firm in Illyria: Market Syndicalism." The American Economic Review, vol. 48, no. 4, 1958, pp. 566-589.

[1405] Cornforth, Chris. "Why do co-operatives fail? In search of the success factors for co-operatives." Paper presented at ICA Research Conference, Potsdam, 2004.

However, in Dr. Anderson's perspective, these arguments overlook the systemic and historical barriers hindering Black economic empowerment. He maintains that cooperatives can indeed thrive in market economies given their resilience during economic downturns and their propensity to re-invest in local communities[1406].

Moreover, cooperative models can create a sense of collective identity and foster a culture of self-reliance and mutual support within Black communities. This is in line with Dr. Anderson's advocacy for building strong, self-sustaining communities as the bedrock of Black wealth creation[1407].

While there are opposing views to the effectiveness of cooperative economics, the model provides an avenue for self-reliance and wealth accumulation within the Black community. By emphasizing shared ownership, equitable income distribution, and mutual aid, cooperative economics, as proposed by Dr. Claud Anderson, is one of the multiple strategies required for comprehensive Black wealth creation.

Local and Impact Investing

Dr. Claud Anderson, in PowerNomics: The National Plan to Empower Black America, makes a compelling case for the pivotal role local and impact investing can play in the elevation of Black wealth[1408]. Essentially, local investing revolves around directing capital to businesses within one's community, while impact investing refers to investments made with the intention to generate a

---

[1406] Anderson, Claud. PowerNomics: The National Plan to Empower Black America. PowerNomics Corporation of America, 2001.
[1407] Anderson, Claud. PowerNomics: The National Plan to Empower Black America. PowerNomics Corporation of America, 2001.
[1408] Anderson, Claud. PowerNomics: The National Plan to Empower Black America. PowerNomics Corporation of America, 2001.

measurable, beneficial social or environmental impact alongside a financial return[1409].

Local investing ensures that money circulates within the community, thereby stimulating local economies, creating jobs, and fostering a sense of communal pride and ownership[1410]. It serves as an economic multiplier, wherein dollars spent locally get re-spent within the same community[1411]. On the other hand, impact investing directs capital to enterprises addressing social and environmental challenges, aligning wealth creation with community betterment[1412]. Both can contribute significantly to catalyzing Black wealth creation.

However, skeptics voice concerns about the risks involved in local and impact investing. Some critics argue that concentrating investments locally may result in a lack of diversification, potentially exposing investors to higher risks[1413]. Others caution that the emphasis on social impact might lead to compromising financial returns, thereby deterring traditional investors[1414].

Despite these critiques, Anderson maintains that such investments can indeed yield sound financial returns, particularly when the broader socio-economic benefits to

---

[1409] Bugg-Levine, Antony, and Jed Emerson. "Impact investing: Transforming how we make money while making a difference." Innovations: Technology, Governance, Globalization vol. 6, no. 3, 2011, pp. 9-18.

[1410] Stoll, Michael A., and Raphael W. Bostic. "The role of race and ethnicity in job matching." Industrial & Labor Relations Review, vol. 52, no. 3, 1999, pp. 402-415.

[1411] Schneiberg, Marc, Marissa King, and Thomas Smith. "Social movements and organizational form: Cooperative alternatives to corporations in the American insurance, dairy, and grain industries." American Sociological Review, vol. 73, no. 4, 2008, pp. 635-667.

[1412] Freireich, Jessica, and Katherine Fulton. "Investing for social and environmental impact: A design for catalyzing an emerging industry." Monitor Institute, 2009.

[1413] Booth, Laurence D., and Richard L. Smith. "Capital market imperfections and the incentive to lease." Journal of Financial Economics, vol. 30, no. 2, 1991, pp. 271-291.

[1414] Saltuk, Yasemin. "Spotlight on the Market: The Impact Investor Survey." JP Morgan and the Global Impact Investing Network, 2014.

the community are considered[1415]. Furthermore, the evolution of social impact bonds and innovative financial tools are gradually mitigating risks associated with impact investing[1416].

In fact, local and impact investing resonate with Dr. Anderson's philosophy of using economic clout as a tool for racial advancement. He posits that Black wealth creation, in large part, can be achieved by investing in and supporting Black-owned businesses and initiatives that contribute to community empowerment[1417].

While there may be challenges associated with local and impact investing, such strategies, as Dr. Anderson postulates, can serve as powerful vehicles for community revitalization and wealth creation. By harnessing the collective economic power of the community, these investment strategies can help to stimulate economic growth, support local businesses, and ultimately catalyze the creation of Black wealth.

Crowd-funding, Peer-to-Peer Lending and Fintech Solutions

In the realm of wealth creation, Dr. Claud Anderson emphasizes that access to capital and financial services is crucial for the development of Black businesses and property owners[1418]. The growing digital revolution, through fintech solutions, crowd-funding, and peer-to-peer lending

---

[1415] Anderson, Claud. PowerNomics: The National Plan to Empower Black America. PowerNomics Corporation of America, 2001.
[1416] Gustafsson-Wright, Emily, Sophie Gardiner, and Vidya Putcha. "The Potential and Limitations of Impact Bonds: Lessons from the First Five Years of Experience Worldwide." Global Economy & Development, 2015.
[1417] Anderson, Claud. PowerNomics: The National Plan to Empower Black America. PowerNomics Corporation of America, 2001.
[1418] Anderson, Claud. PowerNomics: The National Plan to Empower Black America. PowerNomics Corporation of America, 2001.

platforms, may serve to democratize access to funding and financial services, bridging gaps in conventional systems[1419].

Crowd-funding platforms allow entrepreneurs to raise small amounts of money from a large number of people, bypassing the traditional obstacles to securing funding[1420]. Peer-to-peer lending connects borrowers directly with lenders online, often leading to faster loan decisions and potentially lower rates[1421]. On the other hand, fintech solutions leverage technological innovations to deliver financial services, potentially expanding access and lowering costs[1422].

Opponents, however, warn of risks inherent in these systems, such as fraudulent activities and the lack of investor protection measures in crowd-funding[1423]. Similarly, peer-to-peer lending platforms, critics argue, might be fraught with high default rates and unsecured loans, risking investor funds[1424]. Fintech solutions, while promising, may also inadvertently leave out those without access to digital technology, exacerbating inequality[1425].

Notwithstanding these concerns, Dr. Anderson is unwavering in his stance on the potential benefits these platforms can offer. He maintains that these mechanisms

---

[1419] Ziegler, T., et al. "Expanding Horizons: The 3rd European Alternative Finance Industry Report." Cambridge Centre for Alternative Finance, 2017.

[1420] Macht, Stephanie A., and Jeffrey J. Weatherhead. "The benefits and drawbacks of crowd-funding." Entrepreneurship and Innovation, vol. 14, no. 4, 2013, pp. 273-284.

[1421] Iyer, Rajkamal, et al. "The Democratization of Credit?" American Economic Review, vol. 105, no. 5, 2015, pp. 157-162.

[1422] Schueffel, Patrick. "Taming the Beast: A Scientific Definition of Fintech." Journal of Innovation Management, vol. 4, no. 4, 2016, pp. 32-54.

[1423] Davidson, Roei, et al. "Economics of blockchain-based systems." IEEE Cloud Computing, vol. 4, no. 4, 2017, pp. 12-17.

[1424] Demyanyk, Yuliya, and Daniel Kolliner. "Peer-to-peer lending is poised to grow." Economic Trends, 2014.

[1425] Buku, Mwawi W., and Richard Boateng. "Digital exclusion: A threat to universal access to financial services in sub-Saharan Africa?" African Journal of Science, Technology, Innovation and Development, vol. 11, no. 5, 2019, pp. 637-648.

could provide Black entrepreneurs and property owners with much-needed capital and financial services, facilitating business growth, and property development[1426].

As an example, crowd-funding campaigns have already been successful in raising capital for Black-owned businesses and initiatives. For instance, in 2020, a campaign raised over $2 million for the Tulsa Real Estate Fund, a Black-owned real estate crowd-funding platform focused on rehabilitating urban communities[1427].

Moreover, fintech solutions are making strides in improving access to financial services for underserved communities. Firms such as MoCaFi aim to provide financial services to marginalized communities, helping individuals build credit and save money[1428].

While challenges and concerns need to be addressed, crowd-funding, peer-to-peer lending, and fintech solutions hold considerable potential in democratizing access to funding and financial services. These innovations are congruent with Dr. Anderson's vision of economic empowerment and wealth creation within the Black community.

Strategic Areas for Wealth Creation in Contemporary and Sustainable Economies

As Dr. Claud Anderson has consistently highlighted, wealth creation is a multidimensional endeavor[1429]. In light of contemporary economic trends and sustainability concerns, certain strategic areas can provide pathways to

---

[1426] Anderson, Claud. PowerNomics: The National Plan to Empower Black America. PowerNomics Corporation of America, 2001.
[1427] "Tulsa Real Estate Fund." Tulsa Real Estate Fund, https://www.tulsarealestatefund.com/ (accessed June 24, 2023).
[1428] "MoCaFi." MoCaFi, https://mocafi.com/ (accessed June 24, 2023).
[1429] Anderson, Claud. PowerNomics: The National Plan to Empower Black America. PowerNomics Corporation of America, 2001.

prosperity for Black communities. Here, we discuss three main areas: green entrepreneurship, knowledge economy, and the sharing economy.

Green entrepreneurship involves the development of businesses that generate profit while contributing positively to environmental sustainability[1430]. The global emphasis on climate change and the transition to a low-carbon economy presents an opportunity for Black communities to participate in, and benefit from, the green revolution. However, some critics argue that the green economy can be exclusionary due to high start-up costs, complex regulations, and the need for advanced technical skills[1431].

The knowledge economy, characterized by the use of knowledge and information as primary sources of productivity, is another crucial area for wealth creation. It includes sectors like technology, education, research, and services[1432]. However, it's important to recognize that disparities in access to quality education and digital resources could pose challenges[1433]. Critics argue that the knowledge economy can reinforce socioeconomic inequalities, given its reliance on high levels of education and expertise[1434].

The sharing economy, involving peer-to-peer exchanges through digital platforms, can provide opportunities for income generation and entrepreneurship. This includes companies like Uber and Airbnb that allow

---

[1430] Cohen, Boyd, and Pablo Muñoz. "Towards a Theory and Policy of Eco-Entrepreneurship Promotion." International Journal of Green Economics, vol. 5, no. 2, 2011, pp. 135-153.

[1431] Scorse, Jason, et al. "The Barriers and Opportunities for Environmental Entrepreneurship in Developing Countries." Environmental Management and Sustainable Development, vol. 3, no. 2, 2014, pp. 53-69.

[1432] Drucker, Peter. The Age of Discontinuity: Guidelines to Our Changing Society. Harper & Row, 1969.

[1433] Warschauer, Mark. Technology and Social Inclusion: Rethinking the Digital Divide. MIT press, 2004.

[1434] Kuznetsov, Yuri, and Carl J. Dahlman. "Mexico: Paving the Way for a Knowledge Economy." The World Bank, 2008.

individuals to monetize their assets[1435]. Still, it's vital to address concerns such as job insecurity, absence of benefits, and potential for exploitation in this gig-based model[1436].

In light of these prospects, Dr. Anderson's principles of collective economics, self-empowerment, and strategic planning could provide a road-map for Black communities to navigate these emerging sectors effectively[1437]. For instance, cooperatives could be formed in the green economy, educational initiatives could be launched to boost participation in the knowledge economy, and regulations could be advocated for to protect workers in the sharing economy.

Ultimately, wealth creation is not a single-dimensional process—it encompasses a wide array of areas in contemporary and sustainable economies. While challenges abound, the potential benefits for Black communities are significant and worth the concerted effort.

Real Estate and Green Building

Drawing from Dr. Claud Anderson's approach to wealth generation, the potential value of real estate and green building initiatives cannot be underestimated[1438]. These sectors present dynamic opportunities for Black communities to amass wealth, even amidst criticism and skepticism from some quarters.

Real estate ownership, especially in areas with appreciating property values, can be a potent wealth-building tool. Data from the Federal Reserve's 2019 Survey of Consumer Finances shows that home-ownership can be a

---

[1435] Sundararajan, Arun. The Sharing Economy: The End of Employment and the Rise of Crowd-Based Capitalism. MIT Press, 2016.
[1436] Schor, Juliet. "Debating the Sharing Economy." Journal of Self-
[1437] Anderson, Claud. PowerNomics: The National Plan to Empower Black America. PowerNomics Corporation of America, 2001.
[1438] Anderson, Claud. PowerNomics: The National Plan to Empower Black America. PowerNomics Corporation of America, 2001.

significant wealth generator. The median net worth of homeowners was $255,000, compared to just $6,300 for renters[1439]. Despite these promising numbers, some critics contend that housing market volatility, discriminatory lending practices, and the risk of gentrification may threaten the feasibility of this approach for marginalized communities[1440].

On the other hand, green building projects represent a rapidly growing sector with substantial economic and environmental benefits. The U.S. Green Building Council reports that the green construction industry is projected to contribute 3.3 million jobs in the U.S. and $190.3 billion in labor earnings by 2028[1441]. However, critics argue that green building projects often require substantial upfront investment and technical know-how, potentially hindering participation from disadvantaged groups[1442].

By adopting a strategic approach in line with Dr. Anderson's principles, such as focusing on collective ownership and pursuing targeted educational initiatives, Black communities can effectively navigate these sectors. For instance, pooling resources to invest in real estate can mitigate individual financial risk, while training programs can equip community members with the skills needed to participate in green building projects[1443].

[1439] "Changes in U.S. Family Finances from 2016 to 2019: Evidence from the Survey of Consumer Finances." Federal Reserve Bulletin, vol. 106, no. 5, Sept. 2020.

[1440] Rugh, Jacob S., and Douglas S. Massey. "Racial Segregation and the American Foreclosure Crisis." American Sociological Review, vol. 75, no. 5, 2010, pp. 629-651.

[1441] "U.S. Green Building Council Reports Green Construction Industry to Contribute 3.3 Million Jobs in the U.S." U.S. Green Building Council, 28 Sept. 2021.

[1442] Cole, Raymond J., and Paul C. Kernan. "Life-Cycle Assessment of Existing Buildings." Building Research & Information, vol. 28, no. 5/6, 2000, pp. 338-352.

[1443] Anderson, Claud. PowerNomics: The National Plan to Empower Black America. PowerNomics Corporation of America, 2001.

However, the effectiveness of these strategies hinges on a nuanced understanding of the barriers in these sectors and a proactive stance in addressing them. Continued advocacy for fair lending practices, equitable housing policies, and access to green building resources is crucial. Wealth creation in these areas is not without its challenges, but with the right strategies and supports, it is a real and attainable goal.

Investing in Stock Market and Crypto Assets

Stock market investment and cryptocurrency ownership, as proposed by Dr. Claud Anderson[1444], can become significant tools for wealth generation. However, these investment vehicles are not without their critics and inherent risks, necessitating thoughtful strategies and understanding.

The historical average return of the stock market, measured by the S&P 500 Index, has been approximately 10% per year since its inception[1445]. This suggests a strong potential for long-term wealth accumulation for individuals and communities who are able to maintain consistent investments. However, detractors point out the risks of market volatility, complexity of trading, and potential losses, which could disproportionately affect those without significant financial literacy or cushioning[1446].

Cryptocurrency, on the other hand, represents a new frontier in asset ownership, with Bitcoin, the most prominent cryptocurrency, reaching record highs in 2021, yielding a return of over 300% for that year[1447]. The

---

[1444] Anderson, Claud. PowerNomics: The National Plan to Empower Black America. PowerNomics Corporation of America, 2001.
[1445] "S&P 500 Historical Annual Returns." MacroTrends, accessed June 20, 2023.
[1446] Rawley, Thomas, and David A. Wilson. "From the Margins to Mainstream: The Political Power of the Stock Market." International Interactions, vol. 33, no. 4, 2007, pp. 405-412.
[1447] "Bitcoin Price Index from October 2013 to October 2021 (in U.S. dollars)." Statista, accessed June 20, 2023.

decentralized nature of these digital assets offers a unique appeal to marginalized communities, bypassing traditional financial systems that have often excluded them[1448]. However, critics argue that cryptocurrencies are extremely volatile, lack regulation, and pose potential security risks. It's also a relatively new market that can be manipulated, potentially leading to devastating losses[1449].

Taking these considerations into account, Dr. Anderson's principle of pooling resources could be a sound strategy. By investing collectively in stocks or cryptocurrency, communities could share the financial risk, allowing for more conservative investment strategies and the potential for greater returns over time[1450]. Meanwhile, fostering financial literacy around these investment vehicles is crucial for their successful and responsible utilization.

While the rewards of stock and cryptocurrency investment are potentially substantial, they should not be pursued blindly. Understanding the dynamics of these markets, along with strategic planning and risk management, are vital components of a successful investment strategy. As such, government regulation, financial education, and equitable access to financial services should be advocated for, in line with Dr. Anderson's emphasis on systemic change[1451].

[1448] Tapscott, Don, and Alex Tapscott. "Blockchain Revolution: How the Technology Behind Bitcoin Is Changing Money, Business, and the World." Portfolio, 2016.

[1449] Eichengreen, Barry. "The Last Tango of Dollarization: The Rise of Cryptocurrencies." American Economic Review, vol. 108, no. 5, 2018, pp. 507-511.

[1450] Anderson, Claud. PowerNomics: The National Plan to Empower Black America. PowerNomics Corporation of America, 2001.

[1451] Anderson, Claud. PowerNomics: The National Plan to Empower Black America. PowerNomics Corporation of America, 2001.

Retirement Savings and Clean Energy

In his strategic approach to economic empowerment, Dr. Claud Anderson has always championed the creation of wealth in diverse sectors[1452]. Following his line of thought, retirement savings accounts and the clean energy sector can both serve as effective platforms for long-term wealth accumulation for Black Americans. However, critics often highlight the complexities and uncertainties involved in these areas.

Retirement savings accounts such as 401(k)s and Individual Retirement Accounts (IRAs) offer a means for wealth creation through long-term, tax-advantaged saving and investing. Research indicates that the median retirement savings for Black households is significantly lower than their white counterparts, suggesting a significant opportunity for growth[1453]. Critics, however, argue that such savings vehicles are tied to employment benefits, which can be precarious for many Black workers who disproportionately engage in low-wage, benefit-poor jobs[1454].

The clean energy sector, on the other hand, presents a modern frontier for wealth creation. According to the U.S. Bureau of Labor Statistics, the solar photovoltaic installer and wind turbine technician jobs are the two fastest-growing occupations in the U.S., with projected growth rates of 51% and 96% respectively from 2019 to 2029[1455]. This sector's growth, coupled with the global urgency to transition to

---

[1452] Anderson, Claud. PowerNomics: The National Plan to Empower Black America. PowerNomics Corporation of America, 2001.

[1453] "Retirement Inequality Chartbook." Economic Policy Institute, accessed June 23, 2023.

[1454] Hamilton, Darrick, and William Darity Jr. "The political economy of education, financial literacy, and the racial wealth gap." Federal Reserve Bank of St. Louis Review, 2017.

[1455] "Fastest Growing Occupations." U.S. Bureau of Labor Statistics, accessed June 23, 2023.

clean energy, offers tremendous potential for wealth creation.

Opponents, however, often argue that the clean energy sector's volatility, regulatory uncertainties, and high initial costs present significant barriers to entry[1456]. Additionally, they question the overall sustainability of these industries due to their reliance on government subsidies and market demand fluctuations[1457].

Despite these potential obstacles, integrating these strategies into a broad, collective economic model—emphasized by Dr. Anderson—can potentially alleviate some of these challenges. Collective investments into clean energy initiatives can help mitigate initial costs and spread the risks[1458]. At the same time, advocating for policy changes that incentivize and democratize retirement savings can help bridge the existing wealth gap[1459].

As with any investment, understanding the intricacies of these markets, coupled with strategic planning and risk management, is essential. These wealth-building strategies, grounded in the principles of collective economics and systemic change, can offer significant pathways to economic empowerment if navigated effectively and responsibly.

Sustainable Agriculture

Following the philosophy of Dr. Claud Anderson, there are numerous reasons why investing in sustainable agriculture can provide substantial wealth generation

---

[1456] York, Dan. "Clean Energy's Dirty Secret." Foreign Affairs, 2021.
[1457] Houser, Trevor, et al. "The 'Risky Business' of Busting Climate Myths: The Case of Renewable Energy." Brookings, 2018.
[1458] Anderson, Claud. PowerNomics: The National Plan to Empower Black America. PowerNomics Corporation of America, 2001.
[1459] Hamilton, Darrick, and William Darity Jr. "The political economy of education, financial literacy, and the racial wealth gap." Federal Reserve Bank of St. Louis Review, 2017.

opportunities for Black farmers and food producers, as well as significant societal benefits such as improved food security[1460]. Yet, skeptics raise legitimate concerns about the inherent challenges within the agricultural sector.

Sustainable agriculture, including practices like crop rotation, organic farming, and conservation tillage, can increase long-term productivity and resilience, while reducing environmental impacts[1461]. For Black farmers, who have experienced a sharp decline in farm ownership and who manage less profitable small-scale farms on average, sustainable agriculture can offer a profitable niche[1462].

The potential economic benefits of sustainable farming, however, do not go unchallenged. Critics argue that the higher costs of inputs, the need for specialized knowledge, and the increased labor intensity can be prohibitive, especially for disadvantaged farmers[1463]. Furthermore, skeptics point to the relative lack of institutional support and market barriers as significant obstacles[1464].

Despite these challenges, the demand for locally grown, organic food is on the rise. According to the U.S. Department of Agriculture, sales from organic farms in the U.S. increased from $3.2 billion in 2008 to nearly $8 billion

---

[1460] Anderson, Claud. PowerNomics: The National Plan to Empower Black America. PowerNomics Corporation of America, 2001.

[1461] Horrigan, Leo, Robert S. Lawrence, and Polly Walker. "How sustainable agriculture can address the environmental and human health harms of industrial agriculture." Environmental health perspectives 110, no. 5 (2002): 445-456.

[1462] Gilbert, Jess, Spencer D. Wood, and Gwen Sharp. "Who owns the land? Agricultural land ownership by race/ethnicity." Rural America 17, no. 4 (2002): 55-62.

[1463] McBride, William D., and Catherine Greene. "Characteristics and risk management needs of limited-resource and socially disadvantaged farmers." Risk Management Agency, USDA (2008).

[1464] Galt, Ryan E. "The moral economy is a double-edged sword: Explaining farmers' earnings and self-exploitation in community-supported agriculture." Economic Geography 88, no. 4 (2012): 341-365.

in 2017[1465]. This trend indicates a growing market for sustainable farming practices and products that Black farmers can tap into.

Moreover, sustainable agriculture can contribute to food security, particularly in communities facing food insecurity. A report by the Union of Concerned Scientists emphasizes that local, sustainable farming systems can help make nutritious foods more available and affordable in underserved communities[1466].

Therefore, while sustainable agriculture may not be without challenges, it represents a substantial opportunity for wealth creation in the Black community when strategically incorporated within a broader economic framework that advocates for policy changes, financial support, and technical education. This approach aligns with Dr. Anderson's notion of collective economics and systemic change, highlighting that transformative progress is possible despite adversities[1467].

The Way Forward

As Dr. Claud Anderson notes in his paradigm-shifting work, 'PowerNomics,' the key to empowering marginalized communities lies in the implementation of strategic and comprehensive approaches that address systemic inequities[1468]. This understanding aligns with the concept of employing an array of integrated and innovative strategies to bridge the Black wealth gap.

[1465] "Organic Market Overview." U.S. Department of Agriculture, accessed June 24, 2023.
[1466] Hendrickson, John, and Brett K. Moyer. "Breaking local: Can a city really feed itself?." Civil Eats, March (2017).
[1467] Anderson, Claud. PowerNomics: The National Plan to Empower Black America. PowerNomics Corporation of America, 2001.
[1468] Anderson, Claud. PowerNomics: The National Plan to Empower Black America. PowerNomics Corporation of America, 2001.

These proposed strategies, ranging from technological education and cooperative economics to strategic investments in sustainable economies, offer a robust pathway towards economic upliftment. However, some may challenge their efficacy, arguing that they do not take into account the deeply ingrained systemic and historical barriers to Black wealth accumulation[1469]. This perspective emphasizes the importance of not only devising innovative strategies but also addressing underlying systemic impediments[1470].

Indeed, it is critical to acknowledge the impact of historical and ongoing racial discrimination in shaping the wealth landscape[1471]. Addressing these systemic issues necessitates concerted efforts across all societal levels, involving individuals, communities, and the government. For instance, public policies promoting fair lending practices, equitable education, and social safety nets are crucial in dismantling institutional barriers and paving the way for wealth accumulation[1472].

Simultaneously, individuals and communities play a critical role in driving change from the ground up. The implementation of strategies such as local and impact investing, financial innovations, and collective economics can empower Black communities to retain and grow wealth within their neighborhoods^1^.

[1469] Anderson, Claud. PowerNomics: The National Plan to Empower Black America. PowerNomics Corporation of America, 2001.

[1470] Jones, Trina. "The Predatory Lending Wealth Gap." Geo. Wash. L. Rev. 86 (2018): 800.

[1471] Saez, Emmanuel, and Gabriel Zucman. "Wealth inequality in the United States since 1913: Evidence from capitalized income tax data." The Quarterly Journal of Economics 131, no. 2 (2016): 519-578.

[1472] Asante-Muhammad, Dedrick et al. "The Road to Zero Wealth: How the Racial Wealth Divide is Hollowing Out America's Middle Class." Prosperity Now and Institute for Policy Studies, September 2017.

Furthermore, the exploration of contemporary and sustainable economies, such as green building, clean energy, and sustainable agriculture, can provide new avenues for wealth creation. Though critics might argue that such fields are high risk or necessitate high capital inputs, data suggests the long-term potential for return and community upliftment[1473].

Ultimately, the journey towards closing the Black wealth gap is a shared endeavor that requires commitment and effort from all societal sectors. As Anderson emphasizes, progress is achievable, but it requires a persistent focus on empowering strategies and systemic change, underpinned by collective unity and self-reliance[1474].

Resilience and Persistence

In the sage words of Dr. Claud Anderson, author of 'Black Labor, White Wealth,' one finds a key principle for uplifting Black communities: "The survival of blacks in America depends upon whether they can develop the toughness and resilience of previous generations"[1475]. Embodying these principles of resilience and persistence is paramount in overcoming challenges and setbacks, ultimately building a robust Black economy.

However, the conversation surrounding resilience and persistence can be contentious. Critics might argue that these qualities merely serve to propagate a narrative of 'individual responsibility,' which can overshadow systemic barriers to wealth creation for Black communities[1476].

[1473] Barr, Michael S. "Minority and Women Entrepreneurs: Building Capital, Networks, and Skills." The Hamilton Project, March 2015.

[1474] Anderson, Claud. PowerNomics: The National Plan to Empower Black America. PowerNomics Corporation of America, 2001.

[1475] Anderson, Claud. Black Labor, White Wealth: The Search for Power and Economic Justice. PowerNomics Corporation of America, 1994.

[1476] Shapiro, Thomas. "Race, home-ownership and wealth." Washington University Journal of Law & Policy 20 (2006): 53.

Indeed, individual resilience should not supplant or negate the need for systemic and policy reforms aimed at addressing economic inequalities[1477].

Despite these concerns, the importance of resilience and persistence cannot be overstated. Evidence suggests that perseverance is instrumental in overcoming economic challenges. For instance, data from the U.S. Bureau of Labor Statistics reveal that despite higher unemployment rates among Black Americans, their labor force participation rates consistently match or exceed those of other racial and ethnic groups[1478]. This exemplifies resilience in the face of adversity.

At a macro level, this resilience has been manifested in the resilience of Black-owned businesses. In the face of the COVID-19 pandemic, Black-owned businesses have shown a remarkable ability to pivot and adapt [1479]. While this crisis resulted in a disproportionate number of permanent business closures within Black communities, those that survived exhibited extraordinary resilience, innovating in various ways, such as moving their businesses online or changing their product or service offerings[1480].

Moving forward, it's critical to cultivate this resilience and persistence on both individual and community levels. These qualities will be key drivers in building a resilient Black economy that can withstand not only the test of time

---

[1477] Hamilton, Darrick, and William Darity. "The political economy of education, financial literacy, and the racial wealth gap." Federal Reserve Bank of St. Louis Review 99, no. 1 (2017): 59-76.

[1478] U.S. Bureau of Labor Statistics. "Labor force characteristics by race and ethnicity, 2018." Report 1082, October 2019.

[1479] Fairlie, Robert. "The Impact of Covid-19 on Small Business Owners: Evidence of Early-Stage Losses from the April 2020 Current Population Survey." National Bureau of Economic Research, June 2020.

[1480] Fairlie, Robert. "The Impact of Covid-19 on Small Business Owners: Evidence of Early-Stage Losses from the April 2020 Current Population Survey." National Bureau of Economic Research, June 2020.

but also the inevitable fluctuations and disruptions of the global economy.

While the road to economic equity is steeped with challenges and potential setbacks, the application of resilience and persistence, intertwined with comprehensive and systemic economic strategies, can set the course towards a robust Black economy. It's a vision that is achievable, a narrative that must be written, and a journey that must be taken by all levels of society[1481].

A Call for Bold Action

As Dr. Claud Anderson reminds us in 'Black Labor, White Wealth,' "It is up to the black community to demand that its interests be served"[1482]. Today, it is time to heed this call to bold, innovative action. Across the spectrum of societal roles, everyone has a part to play in crafting a future where wealth creation and sustainability are accessible to all, thereby ensuring an equitable and prosperous future for the Black community, and consequently, the nation as a whole.

Some may argue that such action is unnecessary, asserting that the racial wealth gap is a result of individual choices and behaviors[1483]. However, data indicates that even when controlling for factors such as education and income, a significant wealth gap persists[1484]. Therefore, individual behaviors cannot fully explain this disparity, underscoring the need for bold action.

Firstly, policy-makers have a critical role in designing and implementing policies that directly address systemic

---

[1481] Anderson, Claud. Black Labor, White Wealth: The Search for Power and Economic Justice. PowerNomics Corporation of America, 1994.

[1482] Anderson, Claud. Black Labor, White Wealth: The Search for Power and Economic Justice. PowerNomics Corporation of America, 1994.

[1483] Riley, Jason L. "False Black Power?" The New York Times, June 16, 2017.

[1484] Hamilton, Darrick, and William Darity. "The political economy of education, financial literacy, and the racial wealth gap." Federal Reserve Bank of St. Louis Review 99, no. 1 (2017): 59-76.

racial wealth disparities. Policies that encourage equitable economic opportunities, such as fair lending practices, access to quality education, and strengthened social safety nets, are integral to this effort [1485].

Secondly, the business community, including lenders, investors, and corporations, can also play a significant role. For instance, prioritizing investments in Black-owned businesses and neighborhoods, adopting equitable lending practices, and creating diverse and inclusive work-spaces can make significant strides towards wealth equity[1486].

Furthermore, individuals, regardless of their race or ethnicity, can contribute by becoming more informed about systemic racism and its impact on wealth disparity, and by supporting Black-owned businesses and institutions.

Nonetheless, some argue that focusing on the racial wealth gap reinforces racial divisions[1487]. However, Anderson suggests that confronting racial disparities is not about dividing the nation, but rather about rectifying historical and ongoing injustices to achieve a fairer society^1^.

In summary, the task at hand is both complex and imperative. The challenge of bridging the racial wealth gap calls for bold, innovative action from all corners of society. As we take these steps, we must bear in mind that the ultimate goal is not simply wealth, but the ability for all people to live in a society that values and supports their potential, providing equal opportunities for success^1^.

[1485] Conley, Dalton. "Being Black, Living in the Red: Race, Wealth, and Social Policy in America." University of California Press, 1999.

[1486] Baradaran, Mehrsa. "The Color of Money: Black Banks and the Racial Wealth Gap." The Belknap Press of Harvard University Press, 2017.

[1487] Loury, Glenn. "The Undeserving Poor." National Affairs, no. 11 (1984): 13-30.

Chapter 12

The Antonio T. Smith Jr. Power Matrix

Building upon the foundational economic theories of Dr. Claud Anderson, Antonio T. Smith Jr. has devised a framework known as the "Power Matrix." This plan underscores the value of multidimensional strategies in reshaping the socio-economic trajectory for Black communities. Smith's Power Matrix, a comprehensive masterplan for Black Group Economics and Wealth Creation, focuses on Black collaboration, industry control, and market domination[1488]

The Power Matrix echoes Anderson's sentiment from his work, 'PowerNomics,' where he asserted, "Black Americans must pool their resources and do for self, rather than seek to participate as equal and fair competitors in America's closed system of capitalism"[1489]. By promoting a group economic approach, the Power Matrix offers a way forward that directly responds to Anderson's challenge.

Comprised of seven steps—Economics, Finance, Data Information, Manufacturing, Infrastructure, Communications, and Human Resources—Smith's Power Matrix reflects an ambitious and far-reaching strategy for wealth creation. Each of these steps represents a building block towards a robust, self-sufficient Black economy.

[1488] Smith, Antonio T. Jr. "Re-Segregation: Volume I, The Power Matrix: A Masterplan for Black Group Economics and Wealth Creation," 2023.
[1489] Anderson, Claud. "PowerNomics: The National Plan to Empower Black America." PowerNomics Corporation of America, 2001.

The First Floor

Before delving into Antonio's Power Matrix, it is vital to reiterate Dr. Anderson's five-story building plan for black wealth. The base floor of this structure emphasizes Economy. Anderson insists on creating a competitive economy where money circulates 18 times within the community before moving to the second floor, which is Politics.[1490].

Skeptics may question the feasibility of such a plan, given the entrenched racial disparities in the American economic system. Yet, history has shown us that, given the right conditions and the necessary resources, Black communities can and have built thriving economies, as was the case in Greenwood, Oklahoma, famously known as "Black Wall Street" before it was tragically destroyed in the 1921 Tulsa race massacre[1491].

Moreover, critics might argue that focusing on Black wealth creation might exclude other marginalized communities. However, as Anderson rightly notes, it is essential to address the unique economic disadvantages faced by the Black community due to the historical legacy of slavery and segregation. Anderson's five-story building and Smith's Power Matrix should not be viewed as exclusive, but rather as targeted strategies for addressing systemic racial wealth disparities[1492].

As we look towards the future, the Power Matrix presents a road-map for systemic change. The task ahead is formidable, requiring steadfast commitment, collective action, and a significant shift in socio-economic structures.

[1490] Anderson, Claud. "PowerNomics: The National Plan to Empower Black America." PowerNomics Corporation of America, 2001.
[1491] ohnson, Hannibal B. "Black Wall Street: From Riot to Renaissance in Tulsa's Historic Greenwood District." Eakin Press, 1998.
[1492] Anderson, Claud. "PowerNomics: The National Plan to Empower Black America." PowerNomics Corporation of America, 2001.

However, if we heed the lessons from Anderson's foundational theories and Smith's innovative framework, there is potential for a prosperous and economically resilient future for the Black community.

The Second Floor

The second floor of Anderson's wealth creation model is Politics, a key component in any comprehensive economic strategy. Anderson posits that the acquisition of wealth—achieved through a robust economy, symbolized as the first floor—can be leveraged to influence political outcomes that are beneficial to the Black community[1493].

Contrary to popular belief, Anderson asserts that wealth, not votes, is the primary determinant of political influence. He presents the idea that wealthy individuals and groups do not necessarily need to vote; they can instead 'rent,' buy, or donate to politicians to instigate laws that favor their interests[1494]. Critics may argue this reinforces the belief in the 'power of the vote,' asserting that every vote matters, and wealthy influence on politics could be seen as a form of corruption. Nevertheless, the reality of political lobbying, campaign funding, and special interest groups in American politics supports Anderson's claim, as it undeniably evidences the sway of financial contributions over political decision-making[1495].

Anderson's approach here is not to discredit the importance of voting but rather to emphasize that the wealth acquired from the first floor (Economy) can be utilized to gain political favor on the second floor (Politics).

[1493] Anderson, Claud. "PowerNomics : The National Plan to Empower Black America." Powernomics Corporation of America, 2001.
[1494] Ibid.
[1495] Lessig, Lawrence. "Republic, Lost: How Money Corrupts Congress-- and a Plan to Stop It." Twelve, 2011.

Specifically, these resources can be used to advocate for favorable laws on city, state, and federal levels, especially in banking and loan lending practices[1496].

There are voices of dissent. For instance, some critics argue this approach could entrench the very system of influence that has historically disadvantaged Black communities. They might suggest a more grassroots, democratic approach to political engagement, alongside more stringent campaign finance laws to limit the influence of money in politics. However, proponents of Anderson's model might counter that working within the existing system to create more equitable opportunities is a pragmatic approach to achieving immediate change.

Anderson's goal with the second floor is clear: to level the playing field for Black Americans to compete equitably. This involves taking the money created on the first floor and using it to influence the politicians on the second floor. To be clear, this is they way our current lobbying and political system work today. While this may be a contentious strategy for some, its potential for impact in creating a more equitable society cannot be dismissed lightly.

The Third Floor

Dr. Claud Anderson's third floor of wealth creation targets Courts and Police, which focuses on leveraging the financial power and political influence gained from the first two floors to enact meaningful change in law enforcement and the justice system[1497].

The American legal system, while intended to guarantee justice for all citizens, has historically exhibited

---

[1496] Anderson, Claud. "PowerNomics : The National Plan to Empower Black America." Powernomics Corporation of America, 2001.
[1497] Anderson, Claud. "PowerNomics : The National Plan to Empower Black America." Powernomics Corporation of America, 2001.

discriminatory practices towards Black Americans, manifesting in the forms of police brutality and systemic biases within courts[1498]. Anderson proposes using the financial power attained through his model to counteract these practices, insisting that the ability to influence and hold politicians accountable can extend to transforming these areas.

Anderson argues that once Black communities are financially secure and politically influential, they can effectively combat police misconduct, including the tragic incidents of Black individuals losing their lives in routine traffic stops[1499]. Anderson further asserts that the ability to pursue legal recourse is a critical aspect of societal protection and racial justice.

The disproportionate incarceration of Black Americans, as Anderson highlights, stems from systemic issues such as racially biased laws and the application of the Thirteenth Amendment, which abolished slavery except as punishment for crime[1500]. Some may argue that such a conclusion is controversial, as it suggests that America's current prison system is a form of legalized slavery. Critics might counter that the higher rates of Black incarceration are due to a variety of socio-economic factors rather than intentional racial bias. However, research and statistical data indicate racial disparities in arrests, sentencing, and imprisonment, giving credence to Anderson's claim[1501].

Antonio T. Smith Jr. expands on Anderson's point, suggesting that the country with the most slaves during the Transatlantic Slave Trade—America—now has the most prisons globally. This is not a coincidence, according to

---

[1498] Alexander, Michelle. "The New Jim Crow: Mass Incarceration in the Age of Colorblindness." The New Press, 2010.
[1499] Anderson, Claud. "PowerNomics : The National Plan to Empower Black America." Powernomics Corporation of America, 2001.
[1500] U.S. Constitution. amend. XIII.
[1501] NAACP. "Criminal Justice Fact Sheet." NAACP, www.naacp.org/criminal-justice-fact-sheet.

Smith. He asserts that America, through the use of its legal instruments like the Constitution and the Thirteenth Amendment, has essentially permitted the ongoing enslavement of Black people[1502].

While this viewpoint is provocative and may be disputed by some, the argument holds weight when one considers the persistent racial disparities in American incarceration rates. It is a call for the recognition of these systemic issues and the deployment of wealth, influence, and legislation as tools for social change and justice.

The Fourth Floor

On the fourth floor of his model, Dr. Claud Anderson emphasizes the pivotal role of media in empowering Black communities[1503]. Owning radio stations, television stations, newspapers, and cable systems, as Anderson contends, is not just a matter of representation but a strategic move towards self-reliance, communication, and organization.

Media has immense power in shaping narratives and influencing public opinion. However, the mainstream media landscape has been criticized for its limited diversity and skewed representation of Black communities, often reinforcing harmful stereotypes[1504]. By owning media outlets, Black communities can challenge these narratives, represent themselves authentically, and foster positive self-identification.

Contrarily, skeptics may argue that the digitization of media and the rise of social platforms have already

---

[1502] NAACP. "Criminal Justice Fact Sheet." NAACP, www.naacp.org/criminal-justice-fact-sheet.
[1503] Anderson, Claud. "PowerNomics : The National Plan to Empower Black America." Powernomics Corporation of America, 2001.
[1504] Dixon, Travis L., and Charlotte L. Williams. "The Changing Misrepresentation of Race and Crime on Network and Cable News." Journal of Communication 65, no. 1 (2015): 24-39.

democratized content creation and dissemination, reducing the need for physical ownership of traditional media outlets. Nevertheless, the control of mainstream media remains crucial as it still reaches a wide audience and holds significant sway in shaping societal perceptions.

Furthermore, Black-owned media can also serve as an economic engine. As Anderson notes, an autonomous Black economy can finance these media outlets through advertising, thus supporting their operation and growth. This could also foster a supportive ecosystem for Black businesses, as these outlets can provide affordable advertising opportunities targeted towards the Black community[1505].

Real-world advantages of Black-owned media are manifold. Firstly, they can provide accurate, nuanced coverage of issues affecting the Black community, thereby educating both the community and broader public. Secondly, they can offer platforms for Black voices, contributing to diversity in the media landscape. Thirdly, they can spur economic growth by promoting Black businesses and generating jobs within the community.

Moreover, these outlets can also serve as a counter-narrative to the often monolithic representation of the Black experience in mainstream media. By creating their narratives, Black-owned media can celebrate the diversity and richness of the Black experience, challenge stereotypes, and reinforce positive images of the Black community.

In this vein, Antonio T. Smith Jr.'s Power Matrix complements Anderson's model, reinforcing the importance of Communications — a core aspect of Smith's seven-step

---

[1505] Johnson, Travers. "As Black-Owned Media Faces Advertising Inequities, New Approaches and Solutions Emerge." Forbes. Last modified June 19, 2023.
https://www.forbes.com/sites/traversjohnson/2023/06/19/as-black-owned-media-faces-advertising-inequities-new-approaches-and-solutions-emerge/?sh=20acd9a93484.

approach to Black wealth creation. As with all the steps in both Anderson's and Smith's models, the goal remains the same: to establish a resilient, self-sustaining Black economy that effectively addresses the community's needs and aspirations.

The Fifth Floor

The final floor of Dr. Claud Anderson's five story building plan for black wealth calls for the establishment and control of our own educational institutions[1506]. According to Dr. Anderson, the African American community has an urgent need for schools that teach the comprehensive history and potential of Black people, rather than the redacted and distorted version often found in mainstream education[1507]. Dr. Anderson is clear in his vision: we need more producers of resources in the black community, not simply consumers.

However, this notion is often met with skepticism. Critics argue that establishing separate Black schools could lead to further isolation and even re-segregation[1508]. They caution against the potential for such institutions to create an echo chamber that fails to prepare students for the multicultural and globalized world[1509].

Nonetheless, proponents of this model draw attention to the benefits of a self-determined educational system. For example, according to a 2023 Forbes article, successful black-owned enterprises often attribute their achievements to a foundation of education that emphasizes real history,

---

[1506] Anderson, Claud. Powernomics: The National Plan to Empower Black America. Powernomics Corporation of America, 2001.
[1507] Ibid.
[1508] Orfield, Gary. "School Segregation: The Continuing Tragedy of Segregated Schools." New York Law Review 85, (2010): 2140–2194.
[1509] Ibid.

financial literacy, and entrepreneurship, concepts often absent in traditional schooling models[1510].

Moreover, these schools could serve as catalysts for developing producers in the Black community. By equipping students with the necessary skills and knowledge to innovate and create, we can foster a generation of Black business owners, inventors, and industry leaders. This model posits that such an approach could better align educational outcomes with the economic and social needs of the Black community, ultimately contributing to the broader goal of wealth creation and economic empowerment[1511].

While it's clear that professional athletes contribute significantly to sports and society, Anderson's point is that the overemphasis on athletic careers often comes at the expense of producing more Black leaders in fields like technology, science, entrepreneurship, and the arts. By shifting this focus, we can ensure a more sustainable and diverse pipeline of talent that can help drive economic growth in Black communities[1512].

Admittedly, implementing such a vision is not without challenges. It requires significant investment, collaboration, and commitment from all levels of society, including government, private sector, and the Black community itself. However, the potential rewards – a stronger, more resilient Black economy – make it a goal worth striving for.

[1510] Johnson, Travers. "As Black-Owned Media Faces Advertising Inequities, New Approaches and Solutions Emerge." Forbes. Last modified June 19, 2023. https://www.forbes.com/sites/traversjohnson/2023/06/19/as-black-owned-media-faces-advertising-inequities-new-approaches-and-solutions-emerge/?sh=20acd9a93484.

[1511] Anderson, Claud. Powernomics: The National Plan to Empower Black America. Powernomics Corporation of America, 2001.

[1512] Ibid.

Antonio T Smith Jr's Power Matrix

Economy

The Power Matrix's Economic Empowerment Initiative serves as the first element in his innovative Power Matrix, a masterplan for Black Group Economics and Wealth Creation. Like the foundation of a structure, economic empowerment provides the crucial base for wealth creation and industry domination.

Rooted in the modern tech world, Smith's model represents a new paradigm for black economic development, integrating the latest technological innovations to keep black communities competitive in today's rapidly changing digital landscape. It has a broad focus, spanning from tech and data science to artificial intelligence and banking. This initiative advocates for an increased presence in these fields, recognizing that economic power in the 21st century will largely be driven by those who control and leverage digital technologies.

Critics, however, argue that such a tech-centric approach may exacerbate existing inequalities. They point to the current digital divide and the underrepresentation of black individuals in tech fields as potential hurdles[1513]. Furthermore, they question the practicality of such a broad and tech-heavy approach, citing challenges such as access to quality education and resources[1514].

Despite these criticisms, proponents of Smith's model emphasize its adaptability to current and future economic trends. This model recognizes that industries such as data

---

[1513] Williams, Katina. "Digital Divide: Segregation in the Information Age." Media, Culture & Society 21, no. 2 (1999): 197-211.
[1514] Ibid.

science, artificial intelligence, and cloud services (SAAS, PAAS, IAAS) are not only the present but also the future of the global economy.

By actively participating in these fields, black communities can break the traditional barriers to wealth creation and reshape their economic destiny. It is this potential for systemic change that marks Smith's initiative as a groundbreaking path for economic empowerment.

Moreover, Smith's plan does not ignore the existing challenges; rather, it uses them as a clarion call for resource allocation, education reform, and community involvement to equip the black community with the tools needed to navigate and dominate in these industries.

The Economic Empowerment Initiative is a compelling starting point for Antonio T. Smith Jr.'s Power Matrix. By focusing on the intersection of economic power and technology, this model posits a way forward that is both visionary and firmly grounded in today's digital reality.

In the context of the Power Matrix, it's worth scrutinizing the industries that underpin our modern digital economy and highlight the unfortunate lack of black ownership and control in these areas. Taking Software as a Service (SAAS), Platform as a Service (PAAS), and Infrastructure as a Service (IAAS) as examples, we can see glaring gaps in representation and ownership for the black community.

1. **Software as a Service (SAAS):** This business model delivers software applications over the internet. Well-known examples include Microsoft's Office 365, Adobe's Creative Cloud, and Salesforce's Customer Relationship Management (CRM) software[1515]. While these companies are incredibly successful, black people do not own, control, or

---

[1515] "Software as a Service." Investopedia. Accessed March 25, 2023.

significantly influence these tech giants. According to the U.S. Equal Employment Opportunity Commission, black workers make up only 7.4% of the tech industry[1516]. This lack of representation is also mirrored in the ownership and control of these companies.

2. **Platform as a Service (PAAS):** This cloud computing model allows developers to build, run, and manage applications without worrying about infrastructure. Prominent examples include Google's App Engine, Microsoft's Azure, and IBM's Cloud Foundry[1517]. Again, black people neither own nor control these companies, and black representation in these organizations is disproportionately low. As consumers, black communities use these platforms but do not reap the economic benefits of ownership and control.

3. **Infrastructure as a Service (IAAS):** This is another cloud computing model that provides virtualized computing resources over the internet. Notable examples include Amazon Web Services (AWS), Microsoft Azure, and Google Cloud Platform[1518]. These companies, like those in the SAAS and PAAS sectors, are not owned or controlled by black people. Black communities are significant consumers of these services, but the economic benefits of ownership and control do not flow back to these communities.

In each of these examples, black communities play a significant role as consumers, but they do not enjoy the profits and control that ownership offers. This scenario is

---

[1516] "Diversity in High Tech." U.S. Equal Employment Opportunity Commission. Accessed March 25, 2023.
[1517] "Platform as a Service." Investopedia. Accessed March 25, 2023.
[1518] "Infrastructure as a Service." Investopedia. Accessed March 25, 2023.

precisely what Antonio T. Smith Jr. seeks to rectify with his Power Matrix. By focusing on sectors like Finance, Data Information, Manufacturing, Infrastructure, Communications, and Human Resources, Smith's Matrix aims to shift the balance from consumption to ownership, driving wealth creation for black communities in the process.

Establish Black-Led Economic Think Tanks For Policy Advocacy And Research

In the vein of the Power Matrix and the philosophical underpinnings of Dr. Claud Anderson, the establishment of Black-led economic think tanks for policy advocacy and research could serve as an instrumental lever in accelerating economic progress for Black communities. However, there exists a spectrum of viewpoints on this particular strategy, which can be divided into two broad categories: the proponents and the skeptics.

Proponents argue that Black-led economic think tanks can be potent vehicles for generating innovative, research-driven strategies for economic growth, policy changes, and the rectification of systemic inequities[1519]. A study conducted by the National Bureau of Economic Research underscores the influence of such think tanks in shaping public policy by providing data and knowledge to policymakers[1520]. As such, these institutions could play a critical role in advocating for policies that positively impact Black communities and bridge the racial wealth gap. The think tanks could also serve as platforms for uplifting the

---

[1519] Darity Jr., William A., et al. "Stratification Economics, Identity Economics, and the Role of Public Policy." Journal of Economics, Race, and Policy, vol. 3, no. 2, 2020, pp. 91–100.

[1520] Medvetz, Thomas. "Think Tanks in America." University of Chicago Press, 2012.

voices of Black economists, who, according to the American Economic Association, make up a scant 3% of the profession[1521].

On the other hand, skeptics may question the effectiveness of these think tanks, contending that they might merely become echo chambers of lofty ideals with little real-world impact. They could argue that without broad systemic change, the impact of these think tanks would be constrained. Moreover, the skeptics might assert that these think tanks, regardless of their sound policy recommendations, may struggle to effect change in an economic and political system often resistant to altering the status quo[1522].

However, Antonio T. Smith Jr. and Dr. Claud Anderson would likely counter these points by emphasizing the transformative potential of these Black-led think tanks, not just in policy advocacy, but also in the production of groundbreaking research, fostering strategic partnerships, and harnessing the power of black communities to bring about change. This is not a silver bullet solution but a critical component in the broader array of initiatives needed to address the persistent wealth disparities that disproportionately affect Black Americans. Such a strategy could indeed serve as an important stepping stone in the journey towards equitable wealth creation.

[1521] Bayer, Amanda, and Cecilia Elena Rouse. "Diversity in the Economics Profession: A New Attack on an Old Problem." Journal of Economic Perspectives, vol. 30, no. 4, 2016, pp. 221-42.

[1522] DiMaggio, Paul. "Constructing an Organizational Field as a Professional Project: U.S. Art Museums, 1920-1940." In The New Institutionalism in Organizational Analysis, University of Chicago Press, 1991, pp. 267-92.

Promote Black Entrepreneurship Through Collective Funding, Business Incubators, And Mentorship Programs

The promotion of Black entrepreneurship via collective funding, business incubators, and mentorship programs is another element of the Power Matrix, predicated on Dr. Claud Anderson's philosophy. Notwithstanding, such an approach garners varying opinions that span a range of perspectives.

Proponents of this strategy perceive the potential for exponential growth in Black entrepreneurship, viewing it as a fundamental element for wealth creation within Black communities[1523]. In this context, collective funding can serve as a critical tool for Black entrepreneurs to circumnavigate the prevalent obstacles that impede access to capital, a hurdle that disproportionately affects Black-owned businesses. A 2020 report by the Brookings Institution underscores this issue, revealing that Black-owned businesses are twice as likely to be denied loans than their White counterparts, even after controlling for business performance metrics[1524].

Business incubators and mentorship programs further augment this initiative. They provide a robust support system, nurturing entrepreneurship and reducing the likelihood of early business failure by providing an ecosystem of support, advice, and resources[1525]. The National Business Incubation Association (NBIA) cites that 87% of businesses that have graduated from their programs

---

[1523] Fairlie, Robert W., and Alicia M. Robb. "Race and Entrepreneurial Success: Black-, Asian-, and White-Owned Businesses in the United States." MIT Press, 2008.
[1524] Squires, Gregory D., et al. "Capital and Communities in Black and White: The Intersections of Race, Class, and Uneven Development." State University of New York Press, 1994.
[1525] NBIA. "State of the Business Incubation Industry." 2nd ed., 2012.

are still in operation, illuminating the efficacy of such initiatives[1526].

Conversely, skeptics may critique this approach by positing that entrepreneurship, while important, does not inherently equate to wealth creation. They argue that many businesses do not achieve significant profits or even survive past the first five years, adding to the vulnerability of this strategy[1527].

However, Smith and Anderson would likely rebut these critiques, asserting that the risk associated with entrepreneurship is inherent across all demographics and not exclusive to Black entrepreneurs. They would posit that the amplification of support structures and access to capital could significantly enhance the success rates of Black-owned businesses. Moreover, they would emphasize that Black entrepreneurship is not only about wealth creation but also about fostering community resilience, promoting self-determination, and reducing dependency on external economic structures.

Foster Intra-community Trade, With Black Consumers Supporting Black-owned Businesses

The endorsement of intra-community trade, specifically through Black consumers supporting Black-owned businesses, is another critical aspect of Antonio T. Smith Jr.'s Power Matrix. The proposal, which is consistent with Dr. Claud Anderson's perspective on economic development within the Black community, has been met with both acclaim and opposition.

[1526] Aernoudt, Rudy. "Incubators: Tool for Entrepreneurship?" Small Business Economics, vol. 23, 2004, pp. 127-135.
[1527] Bureau of Labor Statistics. "Business Employment Dynamics." United States Department of Labor, 2020.

Those in favor of intra-community trade view it as a dynamic strategy to recirculate wealth within the Black community, thus spurring economic growth. They highlight the potential for a "multiplier effect," where each dollar spent within the community circulates multiple times before leaving, thereby fostering more local economic activity[1528]. In a study by the Kellogg School of Management, researchers found that a dollar spent at local small businesses generates 50% more economic impact than a dollar spent at a large business, further substantiating this perspective[1529].

Detractors, however, argue that promoting intra-community trade could potentially lead to economic isolation and insularity, potentially hindering the broader market opportunities available to Black-owned businesses[1530]. Critics might also emphasize the potential risk of overlooking quality and value for the sake of supporting Black-owned businesses.

Smith and Anderson, though, would likely counter these critiques by emphasizing that fostering intra-community trade doesn't suggest complete economic isolation or sacrificing quality and value. Instead, it suggests a level of community solidarity to foster local economic growth. Furthermore, it would underscore that the global economy's integration does not preclude the benefits of a robust local economy. Local economic growth can provide a strong foundation for businesses to compete in broader markets.

[1528] Anderson, Claud. "Black Labor, White Wealth: The Search for Power and Economic Justice." PowerNomics Corporation of America, 1994.

[1529] Masiello, Betsy, et al. "The Local Economic Impact of Small Businesses." Kellogg School of Management, Northwestern University, 2012.

[1530] Porter, Michael E. "The Competitive Advantage of Nations." Free Press, 1990.

Fundamentally, fostering intra-community trade is about more than just economics. It's also about self-sufficiency, community resilience, and preserving the cultural integrity of the Black community. These are all vital components to achieving the overarching goal of the Power Matrix: building a sustainable and self-determining Black economy[1531].

Encourage Innovation And Control In Emerging Industries, Like Green Energy And Tech

Promotion of innovation and control in emerging industries like Green Energy and Tech is another key step within the Power Matrix. However, it is necessary to address the current realities of these sectors and the challenges that exist.

Smith's proposition comes with the understanding that the future of global industry will be shaped significantly by technological innovation and sustainable energy. Thus, Black communities should not just participate but lead and innovate in these sectors. Presently, Blacks are underrepresented in both the technology and renewable energy sectors[1532]. A report from the Brookings Institution, for instance, shows that Blacks make up only 9% of STEM workers[1533].

Critics may argue that the barriers to entry in these industries, particularly for marginalized communities, are high due to the need for substantial capital investment and

---

[1531] Thomas, June Manning. "Redevelopment and Race: Planning a Finer City in Postwar Detroit." Johns Hopkins University Press, 1997.

[1532] Hsieh, Chang-Tai, et al. "The Allocation of Talent and U.S. Economic Growth." Econometrica, vol. 87, no. 5, 2019, pp. 1435–1474.

[1533] Fears, D., and Chandra, A. "Advancing Black STEM Students Into Professionals: An Overview of Organizational and Programmatic Opportunities and Challenges." Brookings Institution, 2020.

highly specialized knowledge. Access to quality education and resources is also a significant concern in fostering Black participation in these sectors[1534].

However, proponents, including Smith, maintain that these barriers can be addressed by harnessing the collective economic power of the Black community and investing in education and mentorship programs focused on these areas. Smith's Power Matrix aims at reducing these gaps by promoting Black entrepreneurship and fostering education in these emerging sectors.

Intra-community efforts like Black in Green (BIG), a network promoting Black leadership in the Green Economy, represent real-world efforts that align with Smith's model[1535]. Their work underscores the potential of intra-community initiatives to encourage Black participation and leadership in these industries.

Smith's emphasis on controlling emerging industries is not about monopoly but establishing a substantial presence that allows the Black community to benefit from these burgeoning sectors. In conclusion, the encouragement of innovation and control in emerging industries can lead to a more equitable distribution of wealth and resources within the Black community.

Finance

The dynamism in the financial sector, as encapsulated in the Power Matrix's Financial Dominance Plan, relies

---

[1534] US Department of Education. "STEM Attrition: College Students' Paths Into and Out of STEM Fields." National Center for Education Statistics, 2013.

[1535] US Department of Education. "STEM Attrition: College Students' Paths Into and Out of STEM Fields." National Center for Education Statistics, 2013.

heavily on emerging technologies in accounting and finance. These technologies offer opportunities for Black communities to gain significant economic leverage, albeit the present disparities remain formidable.

Firstly, the role of big data in decision-making cannot be overstated. Big data not only quantifies but also qualifies decision-making processes in finance[1536]. Despite these advancements, there is an underrepresentation of Blacks in big data analytics. For instance, only 3% of data scientists in the US are Black[1537], significantly trailing behind their demographic representation. Yet, it's not a simple matter of participation. Critics argue that it's more about ownership and control of these data sets and systems[1538].

Secondly, increased computing power has revolutionized data storage and utilization. Companies like Amazon, Google, and Microsoft dominate this landscape, and there is scant Black ownership or control in these industries[1539]. Skeptics might propose that leveraging these technologies doesn't require direct ownership. Yet, Smith would argue that ownership of such assets could foster self-sustaining Black economies.

Artificial Intelligence (AI) is also instrumental in improving productivity in accounting and finance. While AI opens up opportunities for Blacks in tech, there is a risk of job displacement due to automation. Critics may highlight this risk, but Smith's model emphasizes retraining and the

---

[1536] Tapscott, D., and Tapscott, A. "Blockchain Revolution: How the Technology Behind Bitcoin Is Changing Money, Business, and the World." Penguin, 2016.

[1537] Venkataramakrishnan, R. "The Lack of Diversity in Tech is a Cultural Issue." Financial Times, 2020.

[1538] Benjamin, R. "Race After Technology: Abolitionist Tools for the New Jim Code." Polity, 2019.

[1539] Solomon, B. "Who Owns The Cloud? These Companies Do." Forbes, 2021.

development of new skills in line with these technological shifts[1540].

The Intelligence of Things (IoT) has made it possible to streamline accounting processes, yet the presence of Black professionals in this sphere is nominal. Critics may question the need for Blacks to control these systems, proposing that participation suffices. Smith's model, however, underscores the importance of controlling resources that drive economic power.

Robotic Process Automation (RPA) is a game-changer in accounting and finance. However, Blacks are grossly underrepresented in this field as well[1541]. Critics may assert that technology isn't race-conscious, but Smith's plan seeks to challenge this disparity and create more opportunities for Black professionals.

Lastly, Blockchain technology is revolutionizing finance by enhancing security and reducing costs. Yet, the Black community's participation in this technology is negligible, reinforcing Smith's call for Black communities to assert control over these emerging technologies[1542].

The importance of these technologies within Power Matrix's Financial Dominance Plan underscores the necessity for Black ownership and control in these emerging sectors.

Establishing Black-Owned Banks: A Sustainable Path to Economic Empowerment

Building Black-owned banks, credit unions, and financial institutions is a critical step towards economic

---

[1540] Bughin, J., et al. "Skill shift: Automation and the future of the workforce." McKinsey Global Institute, 2018.
[1541] Lee, J., et al. "The rise of robots in the German labour market." VoxEU, 2019.
[1542] Niforos, M., et al. "Blockchain and Economic Development: Hype vs. Reality." Center for Global Development, 2017.

empowerment and self-sufficiency for Black communities. This not only encourages wealth creation but also addresses economic inequities deeply embedded in the current financial system. Nonetheless, critics question the feasibility and impact of this strategy.

Data shows that Black-owned businesses often struggle to secure loans compared to their white counterparts[1543]. This financial hurdle is compounded by the existing racial wealth gap, which can limit the pool of personal savings and familial wealth from which Black entrepreneurs can draw for start-up capital. A study by the Brookings Institution found that the net worth of a typical white family was nearly ten times greater than that of a Black family in 2016[1544]. This stark wealth disparity places Black entrepreneurs at a distinct disadvantage when trying to launch or grow businesses.

Establishing Black-owned financial institutions can help bridge this gap by providing accessible financial services and support to Black entrepreneurs. Black-owned banks and credit unions, understanding the unique challenges and systemic barriers faced by their customers, can tailor their services to better support Black businesses and entrepreneurs. This is exemplified by institutions like OneUnited Bank, the largest Black-owned bank in the U.S., which prioritizes financial literacy programs and support for Black businesses in its operations[1545].

Despite this, some critics question the viability of Black-owned banks and their capacity to induce large-scale economic change. They contend that these institutions, often smaller in size and limited in resources, may struggle

---

[1543] Fairlie, Robert W., and Alicia M. Robb. "Race and Entrepreneurial Success: Black-, Asian-, and White-Owned Businesses in the United States." MIT Press, 2008.

[1544] Kochhar, Rakesh, and Richard Fry. "The wealth gap between white and Black families is widening." Pew Research Center, 2016.

[1545] "OneUnited Bank: Largest Black Owned Bank." OneUnited Bank, n.d.

to compete in the broader banking landscape. They also express concern that banking regulations may disproportionately burden these smaller institutions, hampering their growth[1546].

However, these concerns fail to acknowledge the inherent value of Black-owned banks beyond their balance sheets. As posited by Dr. Claud Anderson in his book "A Black History Reader: 101 Questions You Never Thought to Ask", these institutions can play an integral role in fostering community development and providing essential financial services to underserved communities[1547]. The success of Greenwood Bank, a digital Black-owned bank that garnered hundreds of thousands of account requests before its launch, further underscores this potential[1548].

Further, a revitalization of Black-owned banks should be seen as part of a broader strategy to promote racial economic equality, not a silver bullet. Additional efforts could include regulatory reforms to support smaller banks, improved financial education, and strategies to address the racial wealth gap.

In sum, establishing Black-owned banks and financial institutions serves as an effective strategy to empower Black communities economically. While critics may raise legitimate concerns, the potential for these institutions to drive meaningful change and contribute to a more equitable financial system cannot be understated.

[1546] Johnson, Michael. "Can Black-Owned Banks Reverse Racial Disparity?" Colorlines, 2016.

[1547] Anderson, Claud. "A Black History Reader: 101 Questions You Never Thought to Ask." PowerNomics Corporation of America, 2017.

[1548] Togoh, Isabel. "Black-Owned Challenger Greenwood Bank Hits 500,000 Sign-Ups Before Launch." Forbes, 2021.

Actionable Steps Towards the Establishment of Black-Owned Banks and Economic Empowerment

Building on the premise of establishing Black-owned banks as a key to economic empowerment, practical steps need to be considered. For one, the establishment of such banks will need concerted efforts from various stakeholders, including individuals, investors, and policy-makers. Yet, critics question whether such initiatives could achieve significant change in economic outcomes for Black communities.

The first step is to secure start-up capital, which is challenging due to the racial wealth gap[1549]. One potential solution is to mobilize the collective power of Black communities and investors. For instance, the 'Bank Black' movement, which urges depositors to move their money to Black-owned banks, generated an influx of capital into such institutions[1550]. Such initiatives, driven by community investment, can form the cornerstone of a Black banking sector.

Private sector investment could also be mobilized to boost the capital base of Black-owned banks. Wealthy individuals, philanthropists, and corporations could support these initiatives by investing or creating partnership opportunities. For example, Netflix deposited $100 million in Black-owned financial institutions as part of its commitment to racial equity[1551].

Another step is to enact policy reforms that create a conducive environment for the growth of Black-owned banks. For instance, reforms could be made to the Community Reinvestment Act (CRA) to incentivize

---

[1549] Kochhar, Rakesh, and Richard Fry. "The wealth gap between white and Black families is widening." Pew Research Center, 2016.
[1550] "The Bank Black Movement." OneUnited Bank, n.d.
[1551] "Netflix to Invest $100 Million in Black-Owned Banks." The New York Times, 2020.

investment in Black-owned banks[1552]. Regulatory bodies should also provide support in the form of risk management training and technical assistance. Critics, however, worry about the feasibility and effectiveness of such policy interventions[1553].

Despite these concerns, the potential benefits of a vibrant Black banking sector are significant. As argued by Dr. Claud Anderson, such institutions could provide crucial access to capital, foster community development, and aid in narrowing the racial wealth gap[1554].

Moreover, the advent of digital banking offers fresh opportunities. Greenwood Bank is a case in point; their digital-first approach to banking has the potential to overcome the traditional barriers that Black-owned banks face, such as limited physical presence and resources[1555]. However, this would require addressing the digital divide that leaves many in Black communities without reliable internet access.

Educational initiatives are equally essential. Financial literacy programs, such as those provided by OneUnited Bank, can empower individuals and businesses to make informed financial decisions[1556]. Yet, critics argue that such programs alone cannot overcome systemic inequities in the financial sector[1557].

The establishment of Black-owned banks can contribute significantly to economic empowerment.

[1552] Richardson, Jesse. "Reviving Black Banks." The American Prospect, 2021.
[1553] Johnson, Michael. "Can Black-Owned Banks Reverse Racial Disparity?" Colorlines, 2016.
[1554] Anderson, Claud. "A Black History Reader: 101 Questions You Never Thought to Ask." PowerNomics Corporation of America, 2017.
[1555] Togoh, Isabel. "Black-Owned Challenger Greenwood Bank Hits 500,000 Sign-Ups Before Launch." Forbes, 2021.
[1556] OneUnited Bank: Largest Black Owned Bank." OneUnited Bank, n.d.
[1557] Baradaran, Mehrsa. "The Color of Money: Black Banks and the Racial Wealth Gap." Harvard University Press, 2017.

However, this process requires strategic investment, supportive policy reforms, technological advancements, and education. Critics may question the impact of these steps, but their potential to transform the economic landscape for Black communities is undeniable.

The Feasibility and Implications of Starting a Black-Owned Bank: An Overview

The idea of starting a bank, particularly a Black-owned bank, has potential for driving economic empowerment. This holds especially true when considering small businesses banding together to initiate such a venture. The process, although demanding and complex, can reap immense benefits and shape the economic landscape of Black communities. However, critics argue that such a move, while symbolically important, might not address systemic racial wealth disparities[1558].

The initial step towards opening a bank involves a robust business plan that takes into account the capital investment, target market, time to break-even, and business name[1559]. The start-up cost of a bank is significant. Banks generally require between $12 to $20 million as starting capital[1560]. Critics might view this as a major obstacle given the racial wealth gap. Yet, if small Black-owned businesses come together, pooling their resources could potentially amass such capital.

The model suggested, where the bank makes money primarily through taking in deposits and lending to others, has a long-established tradition. The bank earns a profit from the interest spread between the interest rate paid to

---

[1558] Baradaran, Mehrsa. "The Color of Money: Black Banks and the Racial Wealth Gap." Harvard University Press, 2017.
[1559] "How to Start a Bank." TRUiC, 2023.
[1560] "How to Start a Bank." TRUiC, 2023.

depositors and the rate charged to borrowers. Other revenue streams include fees charged for various services such as account maintenance, overdrafts, and wire transfers[1561].

The ongoing expenses for a bank are largely tied to its infrastructure, which includes the physical branches and labor costs. As suggested in the link provided, expenses are about 15% of non-interest expenses, with a median expense across the country of approximately $400,000 per branch[1562]. For a bank launched by Black-owned small businesses, these costs could be mitigated by using digital banking platforms, thereby bypassing the need for numerous physical branches.

The banking industry is one of the most regulated in the country[1563]. Banks need to be approved for federal deposit insurance and need to comply with state-specific permits and licenses. Compliance with all regulatory requirements is essential to avoid penalties, including potentially substantial fines.

The endeavor's success hinges on effective marketing and customer retention strategies. Offering competitive banking products, lower fees, and superior customer service can make the bank stand out[1564]. Critics, however, argue that this could be challenging given the intense competition and presence of well-established banks.

Forming a bank requires strategic planning and an understanding of the financial services industry. Critics argue that establishing a Black-owned bank may be a daunting task, given the complexities and regulatory pressures of the banking industry. However, proponents of

---

[1561] "How to Start a Bank." TRUiC, 2023.
[1562] "How to Start a Bank." TRUiC, 2023.
[1563] "Federal Reserve System Purposes & Functions." Federal Reserve, 2016.
[1564] "How to Start a Bank." TRUiC, 2023.

this idea believe that the potential economic empowerment outweighs these challenges[1565].

Moreover, the advent of technology and digital platforms have revolutionized traditional banking, which could make it easier for Black-owned businesses to establish their own banks. Digital banking can lower start-up costs, reach a wider audience, and provide competitive services. Nevertheless, this necessitates addressing the digital divide, which disproportionately affects Black communities[1566].

The idea of Black-owned businesses banding together to form their own bank is not only possible, but also has the potential to promote economic empowerment. This endeavor requires considerable capital, strategic planning, regulatory compliance, and a robust operational framework. Critics may point to the challenges, but the potential economic and societal benefits for Black communities cannot be dismissed.

A Step-by-Step Practical Guide to Launching a Black-Owned Bank

1. **Assemble a Core Team of Founders and Advisors:** Launching a bank requires significant expertise in both business and banking. Assemble a diverse group of founders and advisors with skills in finance, legal affairs, marketing, IT, and operations. Ideally, these should include individuals with prior banking or financial services experience.
    1.1. **Develop a Business Model and Plan:** Define your bank's purpose, target demographic, and

---

[1565] Anderson, Claud. "PowerNomics : The National Plan to Empower Black America." Powernomics Corporation of America, 2001.
[1566] Pew Research Center. "Digital divide persists even as lower-income Americans make gains in tech adoption." 2019.

service offerings. Your plan should outline strategies for deposit acquisition, loan services, risk management, and growth. Also consider how your bank will differentiate itself from existing banks.

1.2. **Raise Initial Capital:** Once your business plan is in place, you will need to raise the necessary capital. This will typically range from $12-$20 million. You can raise funds from the founding members, community stakeholders, angel investors, or through partnerships with existing financial institutions.

1.3. **File for Incorporation:** Form a legal entity to operate the bank. The entity type will likely be a corporation, and you will need to register with the state's Secretary of State office. This process will involve drafting and submitting articles of incorporation and paying the necessary fees.

1.4. **Apply for a Bank Charter:** The next step is to apply for a bank charter, either a state or national charter, based on your business plan. This involves submitting your business plan and other documentation to the appropriate regulatory agency. This process can take time and involves substantial paperwork.

1.5. **Secure Insurance:** Apply for insurance from the Federal Deposit Insurance Corporation (FDIC). The FDIC provides insurance coverage for depositors, which is crucial for building trust with your future customers.

1.6. **Meet Regulatory Requirements:** Ensure your bank meets all local, state, and federal regulations. You will need to develop comprehensive compliance programs and strategies to manage risks.

1.7. **Set Up Banking Infrastructure:** Set up the physical and technological infrastructure. You will need to either lease or purchase a location for your headquarters, set up branches if necessary, and invest in necessary technology for account management, transaction processing, customer service, and online banking.

1.8. **Hire Staff:** Recruit experienced bankers and support staff to operate your bank. You will need professionals in various roles, including bank tellers, loan officers, customer service representatives, risk managers, and executives.

1.9. **Launch Marketing and Outreach:** Develop a marketing strategy to attract your target customers. This may involve community outreach, digital marketing, partnerships with local businesses, and educational initiatives.

1.10. **Open for Business:** After receiving approval from the relevant regulatory bodies and ensuring all systems are ready, you can officially open your bank for business. Make sure to have a grand opening to attract your target customers.

1.11. **Monitor, Adapt, and Grow:** After launch, the work is not done. You need to continuously monitor your bank's performance, adapt to changes in the market, and look for opportunities to grow. Consider offering new services or expanding to new locations as your bank becomes more established.

This comprehensive plan is not an overnight project; it's a long-term commitment requiring diligence, expertise, and significant resources. However, the potential benefits of providing a much-needed financial institution dedicated to serving and uplifting Black communities can be significant and far-reaching.

Leveraging Fintech Solutions for Economic Empowerment in Black Communities

Fintech, short for financial technology, has brought about a paradigm shift in the financial services industry, particularly in banking. This digital revolution presents a unique opportunity for Black communities to bolster economic empowerment, thereby addressing the racial wealth disparities prevalent in society.

It is noteworthy that the proliferation of fintech solutions, such as peer-to-peer lending, micro-investments, and blockchain-based financial services, has democratized access to financial services. These fintech applications provide a viable alternative to traditional banking systems, characterized by redlining and discrimination, which have historically disadvantaged Black communities[1567].

Peer-to-peer lending, for instance, facilitates borrowing and lending transactions directly between individuals, thus circumventing traditional banking systems. It provides the underbanked and unbanked populations within Black communities an opportunity to access loans, thereby stimulating entrepreneurial activities[1568]. Critics, however, question the validity of this model, asserting that it may

---

[1567] Richardson, Rashad, et al. "Fintech, Regulatory Arbitrage, and the Rise of Shadow Banks." Journal of Financial Economics, 2021.

[1568] Berger, Allen N., et al. "Does Function Follow Organizational Form? Evidence From the Lending Practices of Large and Small Banks." Journal of Financial Economics, 2005.

expose lenders and borrowers to potential fraud and default risks. However, these issues can be mitigated by implementing appropriate regulatory frameworks and risk assessment mechanisms[1569].

Micro-investing platforms offer another avenue for financial inclusion. By allowing individuals to invest small amounts of money, they enable individuals with limited resources to participate in the investment ecosystem. A study revealed that Black investors are less likely to invest in the stock market compared to their white counterparts, largely due to a lack of access and understanding of the investment landscape[1570]. Micro-investing platforms could bridge this gap by offering an accessible and simplified investment platform. However, some pundits argue that the returns from these platforms might not significantly contribute to wealth accumulation. Yet, the potential for financial education and investment habit development these platforms provide could lead to long-term financial well-being[1571].

Blockchain technology also presents exciting prospects. By leveraging decentralized ledger technology, blockchain fosters transparency, security, and efficiency. This technology can facilitate remittances, thereby reducing costs and improving speed for Black communities with strong ties abroad[1572]. Critics suggest that the volatility and regulatory uncertainty surrounding blockchain-based services might impede their adoption. However, proponents highlight the

---

[1569] Macey, Jonathan, et al. "Regulating FinTech." Vanderbilt Law Review, 2018.
[1570] Lusardi, Annamaria, et al. "Financial Literacy and Stock Market Participation." Journal of Financial Economics, 2010.
[1571] Tapscott, Don, and Alex Tapscott. "Blockchain Revolution: How the Technology Behind Bitcoin Is Changing Money, Business, and the World." Penguin, 2016.
[1572] Tapscott, Don, and Alex Tapscott. "Blockchain Revolution: How the Technology Behind Bitcoin Is Changing Money, Business, and the World." Penguin, 2016.

potential for blockchain to democratize financial services and foster financial inclusion[1573].

Fintech solutions are not without their challenges. Digital literacy and internet access are prerequisites for leveraging these solutions. According to Pew Research, the digital divide is prominent within Black communities, primarily due to socioeconomic factors[1574]. Therefore, concerted efforts to address this divide are crucial for the successful implementation of fintech solutions.

While critics raise legitimate concerns, the potential of fintech solutions in empowering Black communities economically should not be overlooked. By fostering financial inclusion and economic participation, these solutions could potentially reshape the economic landscape of Black communities.

Fostering Economic Empowerment: Strategies for Black Communities to Develop Sustainable Fintech Solutions

Currently, the fintech landscape is dominated by a few key players. In the realm of peer-to-peer lending, companies like LendingClub and Prosper have established significant footprints[1575]. Micro-investment is often associated with firms such as Acorns and Stash, while blockchain-based services are spearheaded by the likes of IBM and Ethereum[1576].

As we delve deeper, the question arises: how can Black communities draw inspiration from these dominant firms to develop their own sustainable technologies? The potential

---

[1573] Mougayar, William. "The Business Blockchain: Promise, Practice, and Application of the Next Internet Technology." Wiley, 2016.
[1574] Pew Research Center. "Digital divide persists even as lower-income Americans make gains in tech adoption." 2019.
[1575] "The 10 Best Peer-To-Peer Lending Sites." Investopedia, 2023.
[1576] "The Best Micro Investing Apps." Forbes, 2023.

for empowerment through fintech is immense, but the path to that destination requires strategic navigation.

The first step is fostering financial and digital literacy. These are critical competencies in leveraging fintech. Unfortunately, a 2019 report by the Pew Research Center showed that Black communities are disproportionately affected by the digital divide[1577]. A concerted effort is needed to address this divide through education, training, and access to technology.

Secondly, collaboration is key. The collective pooling of resources and expertise can empower Black communities to develop their own fintech solutions. This might involve small businesses, community leaders, and individuals banding together to invest in sustainable technology development.

A critical part of this is encouraging Black entrepreneurs to venture into the fintech space. For instance, in the peer-to-peer lending sphere, Black entrepreneurs could establish platforms that specifically address the needs of Black borrowers, who are often overlooked or disadvantaged by mainstream banking practices[1578].

Critics may argue that breaking into an industry dominated by entrenched players is a herculean task. However, a counter-argument could highlight how catering to the specific needs of a niche market—like the Black community—can be a viable strategy for creating competitive fintech platforms. Providing tailored financial solutions could be a key differentiator in a crowded market.

For micro-investment platforms, a unique approach might involve incorporating financial literacy training within the platform. By doing so, users are not only given the opportunity to invest but also to learn, thereby

---

[1577] Pew Research Center. "Digital divide persists even as lower-income Americans make gains in tech adoption." 2019.
[1578] Bartlett, Robert, et al. "Consumer-Lending Discrimination in the FinTech Era." NBER, 2019.

addressing the lack of financial understanding that has historically impeded Black participation in the stock market[1579].

Finally, in terms of blockchain technology, the opportunities are vast—from creating blockchain-based remittance services to launching cryptocurrencies. For instance, Black communities could develop blockchain platforms to support Black businesses internationally, facilitating trade and commerce.

While the task is indeed challenging, the potential rewards in terms of economic empowerment for Black communities are significant. The pathway to success involves addressing the digital divide, encouraging collaboration, fostering entrepreneurship, and leveraging niche markets to develop unique, tailored fintech solutions.

Financial Literacy and Investment: Tools for Wealth Building in Black Communities

In today's society, financial literacy and investment acumen are more than just skills - they are critical tools for wealth building. This is particularly pertinent for Black communities, which historically, have faced systemic barriers to financial prosperity. According to a study by the Federal Reserve, the typical Black family in the U.S. has about one-tenth the wealth of the typical white family[1580]. There are critics, however, who argue that financial literacy and investment workshops are not effective ways to bridge the wealth gap.

[1579] Lusardi, Annamaria, et al. "Financial Literacy and Stock Market Participation." Journal of Financial Economics, 2010.
[1580] Federal Reserve. "Survey of Consumer Finances." 2019.

One of the keys to altering this disparity lies in boosting the understanding and participation of Black communities in the stock market. Despite the fact that Black Americans represent 13.4% of the U.S. population, they make up only 1.2% of the nation's stock-owning households[1581]. Initiating financial literacy and investment workshops can empower Black Americans with the knowledge necessary to navigate the complexities of the stock market.

There are those who are skeptical of these endeavors. Critics point out that merely understanding how to invest in stocks does not equate to having the disposable income required to do so[1582]. It's a valid concern, which is why these workshops should also focus on personal finance management, saving strategies, and ways to generate additional income.

Real estate is another sector that, if correctly understood and accessed, can serve as a pathway to wealth generation for Black communities. Studies show that Black home-ownership rates lag behind whites by about 30 percentage points[1583]. Hosting workshops that guide prospective Black homeowners through the processes of buying, managing, and investing in real estate could potentially help bridge this home-ownership gap.

However, critics point to structural barriers such as redlining and discriminatory lending practices as the major impediments to Black home-ownership[1584]. Therefore, while financial education is crucial, these workshops must also focus on understanding and navigating systemic barriers,

---

[1581] Ariel Investments and Charles Schwab. "Black Investor Survey: Saving and Investing Among Higher Income Black and White Americans." 2020.

[1582] Lusardi, Annamaria and Mitchell, Olivia S. "The Economic Importance of Financial Literacy." Journal of Economic Literature, 2014.

[1583] U.S. Census Bureau. "home-ownership Rates by Race and Ethnicity of Householder." 2020.

[1584] Rothstein, Richard. "The Color of Law: A Forgotten History of How Our Government Segregated America." Liveright, 2017.

advocating for policy changes, and leveraging available resources like first-time homebuyer programs and affordable housing initiatives.

Similarly, opportunities exist in other investment vehicles like bonds, mutual funds, and retirement plans, which could be explored during these workshops. However, a Pew Research study found that Black households are less likely to own these types of financial assets[1585]. Opponents argue that this is less about financial literacy and more about the lack of disposable income.

While critics correctly point out that financial literacy alone is insufficient to bridge the racial wealth gap, dismissing its potential benefits is short-sighted. The combination of financial education, improved access to resources, and policy changes could position Black communities to take greater advantage of investment opportunities, ultimately fostering economic growth and wealth generation.

Data Science

The Power Matrix's Information Equity Strategy: Closing the Knowledge Gap in Black Communities

It's clear that economic empowerment within the Black community requires both innovative strategies and strong leadership. The Power Matrix's Information Equity Strategy offers an insightful approach, one that attempts to bridge the knowledge gap and promote equality of access to valuable information. The initiative pivots on the concept that knowledge - specifically, data-driven insights - can fuel economic upliftment. Yet, critics raise concerns about the actual execution and effectiveness of such a strategy.

[1585] Pew Research Center. "Wealth Gaps Rise to Record Highs Between Whites, Blacks and Hispanics." 2011.

The first element of Smith Jr.'s strategy involves harnessing data for decision-making. In a world awash with data, harnessing it effectively is a powerful tool for creating wealth and generating business opportunities. By leveraging data, small Black-owned businesses can optimize their operations, target their marketing more effectively, and make strategic decisions that can improve their profitability.

Skeptics, however, argue that acquiring, analyzing, and implementing data insights can be costly and complex[1586]. They point out that small businesses often lack the necessary resources and expertise. To address this, Smith Jr.'s strategy envisions facilitating access to data science skills, potentially through collaborations with educational institutions or tech companies, which can enable businesses to decode and utilize data effectively.

Smith Jr.'s strategy also advocates for increased Black representation in data science and related fields, facilitated through scholarships, boot camps, and mentorships. As per the Bureau of Labor Statistics, Blacks are underrepresented in the tech sector, making up just 9% of STEM workers[1587]. Enhancing representation not only offers individual career opportunities, but can also lead to more inclusive data practices, ensuring that technology and algorithms are developed with a view towards diversity.

Detractors, however, caution that increasing representation is a long-term goal, and cannot provide immediate relief for communities suffering economic hardships[1588]. Critics also point to systemic barriers, such as

---

[1586] Mims, Christopher. "The High Cost of Taking on Tech Giants." Wall Street Journal, 2022.
[1587] Bureau of Labor Statistics. "Labor Force Statistics from the Current Population Survey." 2021.
[1588] Stout, Robert J., and Jenkins, Richard A. "Blacks in the Tech Industry: The Challenge of Equal Opportunity." Journal of Black Studies, 2021.

lack of access to quality education and bias in hiring practices, as major obstacles[1589].

Lastly, Smith Jr.'s strategy emphasizes the importance of financial literacy and investment workshops. By equipping individuals with knowledge about the stock market, real estate, and other investment opportunities, they can better manage their finances and accumulate wealth. Yet, critics maintain that financial education alone is not a panacea for racial wealth disparities and must be complemented with systemic reforms[1590].

The Power Matrix's Information Equity Strategy represents an optimistic road-map towards economic empowerment in Black communities. Critics rightly highlight the hurdles and complexities involved. Yet, as Smith Jr. suggests, overcoming these challenges requires not just strategic planning, but also a commitment to fostering equality in access to knowledge.

Fostering Black-Owned Data and Research Enterprises: A Step Towards Culturally Relevant Knowledge

Information - its creation, control, and dissemination - stands as a potent force in modern society. Given the racial disparities in economic and educational outcomes, there's a pressing need for Black-owned data and research companies that can deliver accurate, culturally sensitive insights. These enterprises could potentially empower Black communities and dismantle some of the systemic barriers that perpetuate inequality. Critics, however, question the feasibility and impact of this proposition.

[1589] Eubanks, Virginia. "Automating Inequality: How High-Tech Tools Profile, Police, and Punish the Poor." St. Martin's Press, 2018.
[1590] Baradaran, Mehrsa. "The Color of Money: Black Banks and the Racial Wealth Gap." Harvard University Press, 2017.

Advocates for this strategy stress the benefits of Black ownership and control over data and research. Black-owned firms are more likely to employ Black workers, contribute to the wealth within Black communities, and address the community's unique needs[1591]. Such companies could serve as trusted sources of information for Black businesses, helping them to make informed decisions that optimize their performance and profitability.

A significant part of this strategy is the creation of culturally relevant data. Current datasets often lack racial specificity, which can mask disparities and hinder effective policy making[1592]. Black-owned data firms could correct this by developing culturally nuanced datasets and research methodologies that accurately reflect the lived experiences of Black individuals.

However, critics challenge the viability of this strategy, citing obstacles such as the high cost of starting a data company, the intensive skills required, and the competitive market landscape dominated by tech giants[1593]. They also raise concerns about the potential misuse of data, especially in relation to privacy and security[1594].

To counter these criticisms, proponents emphasize the need for comprehensive support systems to help Black entrepreneurs overcome these barriers. This might include mentorship, access to start-up capital, and partnerships with educational institutions to cultivate the necessary skills. They also stress the need for robust data governance frameworks to ensure ethical data practices.

[1591] Fairlie, Robert W., and Robb, Alicia M. "Race and Entrepreneurial Success." MIT Press, 2008.

[1592] "Counting the Black Community: A Review of Current Data Collection Practices." Urban Institute, 2019.

[1593] Mims, Christopher. "The High Cost of Taking on Tech Giants." Wall Street Journal, 2022.

[1594] Zuboff, Shoshana. "The Age of Surveillance Capitalism: The Fight for a Human Future at the New Frontier of Power." PublicAffairs, 2019.

Detractors also caution that the establishment of Black-owned data firms alone won't rectify systemic racial disparities[1595]. They argue that these efforts must be part of a broader strategy that addresses root causes of inequality, including racial discrimination, wealth disparities, and unequal access to quality education and health-care.

Nonetheless, the establishment of Black-owned data and research companies represents a promising step towards economic empowerment and data equity. While the challenges and concerns raised by critics are valid, they do not diminish the potential of this strategy to contribute to systemic change. If executed effectively and ethically, these companies could be a significant asset to the Black community, providing accurate, relevant information and fostering economic growth.

Establishing Black-Controlled Media Platforms: Shaping Narratives and Amplifying Success

In an era where media heavily influences public perception, the development of Black-controlled social media platforms and news outlets holds immense potential for shaping narratives and uplifting the Black community. Such initiatives can aid in showcasing success stories, thus offering inspiration and breaking down stereotypes. Critics, however, question the feasibility of such endeavors, considering the dominance of established media conglomerates and the challenges inherent in creating and sustaining digital platforms[1596].

The creation of Black-controlled media platforms could provide a platform for balanced representation, offering an

---

[1595] Baradaran, Mehrsa. "The Color of Money: Black Banks and the Racial Wealth Gap." Harvard University Press, 2017.
[1596] Napoli, Philip M., and Lukito, Josephine. "Who's Producing the News? Journalism Studies." Taylor & Francis, 2019.

alternative to mainstream media outlets often criticized for perpetuating harmful stereotypes and neglecting the positive narratives in the Black community[1597]. These platforms can showcase Black excellence, inspiring new generations to strive for success in various fields, while simultaneously providing role models that resonate with their own experiences.

However, critics raise questions regarding the viability of Black-controlled social media platforms and news outlets, given the significant resources required to compete with established media entities. Building a successful digital platform demands a robust technological infrastructure, skilled personnel, and considerable capital, factors that critics argue may pose challenges for Black entrepreneurs given systemic barriers to resources and opportunities[1598].

To address these concerns, advocates emphasize the importance of supporting Black tech entrepreneurs through access to capital, mentorship, and education. They point to examples of successful Black-owned media enterprises, such as Oprah Winfrey's OWN Network, as evidence of the potential for such endeavors to thrive[1599]. Furthermore, they note the rapid growth of digital technology, which lowers entry barriers and allows niche platforms to gain traction.

A major concern for critics is the potential for further polarization and echo chambers, where users are only exposed to views that mirror their own[1600]. To this, proponents counter that Black-controlled platforms are not about excluding others, but about inclusion and fair

---

[1597] Dixon, Travis L. "Good Guys Are Still Always in White? Positive Change and Continued Misrepresentation of Race and Crime on Local Television News." Communications Research, 2017.

[1598] Bunz, Mercedes. "The Silent Revolution: How Digitalization Transforms Knowledge, Work, Journalism and Politics Without Making Too Much Noise." Palgrave Macmillan, 2014.

[1599] Peck, Emily. "Oprah Winfrey: one of the world's best neoliberal capitalist thinkers." The Guardian, 2018.

[1600] Pariser, Eli. "The Filter Bubble: What the Internet Is Hiding from You." Penguin Press, 2011.

representation, aiming to provide a space where Black voices can be heard and Black stories accurately portrayed.

Moreover, these media platforms can also serve as conduits for disseminating financial literacy, entrepreneurship, and other valuable educational content, thus playing a role in the broader movement towards economic empowerment in the Black community[1601].

While the creation of Black-controlled social media platforms and news outlets poses significant challenges, the potential benefits, in terms of fair representation, education, and community building, cannot be overlooked. Despite the critics' valid concerns, with the right support, these platforms can become powerful tools in the ongoing quest for equality and economic empowerment.

Fostering Technological Prowess: Encouraging Careers in Data Science and AI

As we embrace the Fourth Industrial Revolution, fostering technological prowess is no longer an option but a necessity. The significance of careers and entrepreneurship in fields such as data science and Artificial Intelligence (AI) is skyrocketing[1602]. Consequently, for the Black community to achieve economic empowerment and counter the systemic racial wealth gap, there is a pressing need to encourage participation in these fields through initiatives such as scholarships, boot camps, and mentorship. Critics, however, point out challenges such as the high cost of education, lack of access to quality training resources, and

---

[1601] Anderson, Claud. "PowerNomics : The National Plan to Empower Black America." Powernomics Corporation of America, 2001.
[1602] "Future of Jobs Report." World Economic Forum, 2020.

the underrepresentation of Black people in these fields, as potential roadblocks[1603].

Data science and AI are transforming the global economy, opening up vast opportunities for those equipped with the relevant skills. These fields are expected to generate millions of jobs in the coming years[1604]. Yet, despite these opportunities, Black individuals are significantly underrepresented, creating a racial disparity that could exacerbate wealth and income inequalities if left unaddressed[1605].

To tackle this underrepresentation, offering scholarships targeted at Black students interested in data science and AI could be instrumental. Scholarships can make education in these fields more accessible and encourage more Black students to pursue careers in them. Critics, however, highlight the prohibitive cost of higher education and the limited reach of scholarships[1606].

In response to this, proponents suggest complementing scholarships with alternative educational models such as boot camps and mentorship programs. Boot camps offer condensed, practical training in data science and AI at a fraction of the cost of traditional education. Moreover, mentorship can provide invaluable guidance, inspire confidence, and offer a sense of belonging in an industry where Black individuals are underrepresented[1607].

Yet, critics argue that these initiatives are insufficient to overcome systemic barriers such as bias in hiring practices

---

[1603] Dastin, Jeffrey. "Amazon scraps secret AI recruiting tool that showed bias against women." Reuters, 2018.

[1604] Chui, Michael, et al. "Jobs lost, jobs gained: What the future of work will mean for jobs, skills, and wages." McKinsey Global Institute, 2017.

[1605] Dastin, Jeffrey. "Amazon scraps secret AI recruiting tool that showed bias against women." Reuters, 2018.

[1606] "Trends in College Pricing." College Board, 2019.

[1607] Dweck, Carol. "Mindset: The New Psychology of Success." Random House, 2006.

and lack of representation in the industry[1608]. Advocates counter this argument by citing the increasing recognition of the value of diversity in tech and the various initiatives being undertaken to address these challenges. They argue that these steps, while not a complete solution, are crucial steps forward.

In essence, promoting careers and entrepreneurship in data science and AI among the Black community can significantly contribute to reducing the racial wealth gap. While critics raise valid concerns, the combination of scholarships, boot camps, and mentorship initiatives presents a promising pathway towards greater representation and economic empowerment in the Black community.

Bridging the Tech Divide: Propelling Black Communities into Data Science, AI, and Related Fields

When one speaks of the fields of data science and artificial intelligence (AI), the names of companies such as Google, Microsoft, and IBM often come to mind[1609]. Despite the ever-growing opportunities in these sectors, representation of Black professionals remains low. According to a 2020 report by the Center for Security and Emerging Technology, Black workers represent only 2.5% of the data and AI workforce in the United States[1610].

One possible avenue to address this underrepresentation and foster economic empowerment in Black communities is through the encouragement of careers and entrepreneurship

---

[1608] Buolamwini, Joy, and Gebru, Timnit. "Gender Shades: Intersectional Accuracy Disparities in Commercial Gender Classification." Proceedings of Machine Learning Research, 2018.
[1609] "The AI Spring: How Artificial Intelligence Might Help Us Live Happier and Healthier Lives." World Economic Forum, 2018.
[1610] Center for Security and Emerging Technology. "AI and Compute." 2020.

in these fields. Scholarships, boot camps, and mentorship programs can play vital roles in cultivating these career paths.

Scholarships can provide the financial means for Black students to pursue degrees in data science and AI. Unfortunately, higher education in these fields can be prohibitively expensive for many, perpetuating a cycle of underrepresentation[1611]. A commitment to fund scholarships specifically targeted at these students can go a long way in leveling the playing field.

Critics may contend that scholarships alone aren't the silver bullet for addressing racial disparities in these fields. A report by the National Center for Education Statistics showed that Black students still graduate with more student loan debt than their white counterparts, even with scholarship support[1612]. Thus, to make the impact of scholarships more substantial, they must be substantial in their offering, covering not just tuition but also living expenses and ancillary costs of education.

Boot camps provide another avenue to teach practical, job-ready skills in a relatively short period. They are particularly suited to individuals seeking to switch careers or enhance their skills. Some critics, however, warn about the uneven quality of boot camps and suggest that they might not provide the in-depth understanding needed to excel in these fields[1613].

On the contrary, others argue that when boot camps are thoughtfully designed and carefully executed, they can effectively provide a springboard for careers in data science and AI. Some boot camps, like the ones run by Flatiron

---

[1611] "Is Graduate School Worth It? A Comprehensive Return on Investment Analysis." Payscale, 2021.
[1612] National Center for Education Statistics. "Status and Trends in the Education of Racial and Ethnic Groups." 2018.
[1613] "Tech's Favorite School Faces Its Biggest Test: the Real World." Bloomberg, 2020.

School and General Assembly, have shown strong job placement rates[1614]. For the Black community, targeted boot camps can serve as a rapid on-ramp into these high-paying tech careers.

Mentorship is a crucial, often overlooked element in this triad. A lack of role models and mentors in the field can discourage potential Black entrants. Initiatives that connect Black students and professionals with experienced mentors in the field can help bridge this gap.

The path to improving Black representation in data science and AI involves a multifaceted strategy. Critics and cynics may point to the challenges and potential limitations of these initiatives, but the potential rewards in terms of diversification of the industry and economic empowerment for the Black community make it a challenge worth taking on.

Manufacturing

Forging Economic Resilience: The Power Matrix's Manufacturing Mastery Blueprint

Understanding the power of manufacturing in creating economic resilience, the Power Matrix's Manufacturing Mastery Blueprint proposes a multifaceted approach to economic empowerment for Black communities through manufacturing. Yet, critics question the feasibility of this vision given the decline of manufacturing in the U.S. and the significant capital requirements involved[1615].

[1614] Flatiron School. "Jobs Report." 2020.
[1615] "The Manufacturing Footprint and the Importance of U.S. Manufacturing Jobs." Economic Policy Institute, 2015.

Manufacturing has been a mainstay of the U.S. economy for decades, contributing $2.3 trillion to the U.S. economy in 2020[1616]. Moreover, each dollar spent in manufacturing adds $1.89 to the business growth, the highest multiplier effect of any economic sector[1617]. Despite this, Black communities have historically been underrepresented in the sector[1618].

Smith's blueprint proposes the creation of Black-owned manufacturing enterprises. Critics argue that the high start-up costs, intense competition, and global outsourcing trends make it challenging for new entrants. They also point out that manufacturing jobs have been on a steady decline due to automation and offshoring[1619].

However, proponents argue that focusing on niche sectors, value-added products, and advanced manufacturing technologies can mitigate these challenges. They suggest that Black entrepreneurs could, for instance, focus on areas such as green manufacturing or the production of culturally specific products to tap into underserved markets[1620].

Furthermore, Smith's blueprint advocates for partnerships with established Black-owned businesses and other stakeholders to pool resources and share risks. Critics, however, highlight potential difficulties in collaboration, including disagreements over strategy and the distribution of profits. They also point out the inherent risks of collaborative ventures, such as the possibility of a partner company failing[1621].

[1616] "U.S. Manufacturing: Output vs. Jobs Since 1975." National Association of Manufacturers, 2021.
[1617] "The Facts About Modern Manufacturing." The Manufacturing Institute, 2020.
[1618] "Racial Inequality in the U.S. Labor Market." Center for Economic and Policy Research, 2020.
[1619] "The Future of Work in Black America." McKinsey & Company, 2019.
[1620] "How Green is U.S. Manufacturing? An Analysis of Energy Use and Greenhouse Gas Emissions." The National Academies Press, 2013.
[1621] "The Dark Side of Collaboration." Harvard Business Review, 2015.

Still, proponents stress that strategic partnerships can provide Black-owned manufacturing start-ups with the much-needed capital, industry know-how, and market access. Such collaborations could facilitate economies of scale, enhance competitive advantage, and foster innovation[1622].

While Smith, Jr's Manufacturing Mastery Blueprint faces challenges and criticism, it offers a promising path towards economic empowerment for Black communities. By creating Black-owned manufacturing enterprises and leveraging strategic partnerships, the blueprint points towards a future of increased wealth and resilience.

Accelerating Industrial Autonomy: Fostering the Growth of Black-Controlled Manufacturing Businesses

In the arena of manufacturing, the Power Matrix's vision distinctly emphasizes the importance of Black-controlled businesses, while also calling for improved access to capital, partnerships, and training. However, skeptics often question the feasibility of this approach, citing economic and systemic challenges that are difficult to overcome[1623].

As per the U.S. Census Bureau, in 2017, Black business owners represented only 2.2% of the nation's employer businesses[1624]. This is starkly disproportionate to the fact that Black individuals constitute about 13.4% of the U.S. population. It is evident that this discrepancy stems from systemic issues such as limited access to start-up capital and

---

[1622] "Strategic Alliances for SME Development." United Nations Industrial Development Organization, 2001.
[1623] "Racial Economic Disparity in the U.S." Brookings Institution, 2020.
[1624] "2017 Annual Business Survey." U.S. Census Bureau, 2017.

business education, as well as ongoing racial discrimination in business dealings[1625].

Smith's strategy for boosting Black-controlled manufacturing includes three key elements: capital, partnerships, and training. Critics argue that the financial barriers to entry in manufacturing are significant, with start-up costs and operational expenses often running into the millions[1626]. They question whether sufficient funds could be made available to Black entrepreneurs, especially given longstanding racial disparities in access to capital.

However, advocates for Smith's blueprint counter that such obstacles can be overcome. They emphasize the role of strategic partnerships with established businesses and governmental agencies to reduce the financial burden on individual entrepreneurs[1627]. These partnerships could also provide Black-owned manufacturing start-ups with invaluable industry expertise, market access, and economies of scale.

The role of training is also crucial in Smith's strategy. Detractors point out the high cost of technical training and the perceived lack of interest among Black youth in manufacturing careers[1628]. However, proponents stress the effectiveness of scholarships, apprenticeships, and mentorship programs in cultivating the necessary skills and enthusiasm for manufacturing among Black communities[1629].

Moreover, it is advocated that the creation of a supportive ecosystem, including Black-controlled banks

---

[1625] "Why Are There So Few Black-Owned Businesses in America?" Forbes, 2020.
[1626] "Start Your Own Manufacturing Business or Make Your Existing Business More Profitable." Manufacturing Business Institute, 2021.
[1627] "Collaboration: The Key to Small Business Success." U.S. Small Business Administration, 2019.
[1628] "Bridging the Skills Gap in the Manufacturing Industry." Deloitte Insights, 2020.
[1629] "Apprenticeship Programs are a Ticket to the Middle Class." Center for American Progress, 2018.

providing loans and investment capital, could help overcome financial barriers and facilitate the growth of Black-controlled manufacturing businesses[1630].

While the hurdles are real, Smith's strategy presents a proactive and achievable approach towards greater representation of Black-controlled businesses in the manufacturing sector. With concerted efforts and strategic implementation, his blueprint could significantly alter the economic landscape for Black communities.

United We Stand: Fostering Collaboration Among Black Manufacturers to Compete Effectively

The U.S. manufacturing sector, the Power Matrix places a strong emphasis on the role of Black manufacturers. Notably, his blueprint advocates for increased collaboration and consortiums among Black manufacturers to compete more effectively with larger corporations. Nevertheless, there are critics who question the viability and effectiveness of this approach[1631].

Today, Black-owned businesses, particularly those in the manufacturing sector, tend to be smaller, both in terms of revenue and employees[1632]. This puts them at a competitive disadvantage when compared to larger corporations that benefit from economies of scale and wider market access. The critics of Smith's strategy argue that smaller manufacturers might struggle to compete even with collaborative efforts, owing to the sheer disparity in resources and market presence.

[1630] "The Role of Black Banks in Reducing the Racial Wealth Gap." Center for Global Policy Solutions, 2016.
[1631] "Collaboration Challenges among Small Businesses." Harvard Business Review, 2019.
[1632] "2017 Annual Business Survey." U.S. Census Bureau, 2017.

However, Smith's supporters argue for the transformative power of collective action and industry consolidation. Collaboration among Black manufacturers can lead to increased collective bargaining power, shared resources, improved innovation, and more competitive pricing[1633]. Sharing of resources and knowledge can significantly mitigate the challenges that Black manufacturers face individually, and in turn, establish a competitive advantage in the market.

Collaboration can also foster innovation, another critical factor in gaining a competitive edge in the manufacturing sector. Consortiums of Black manufacturers can pool resources to fund research and development, thereby overcoming one of the significant hurdles that many smaller companies face in innovating[1634].

Moreover, these consortiums can effectively counter the challenges of market access and distribution. By working together, Black manufacturers can leverage their collective networks to tap into larger markets, bypassing traditional barriers and facilitating direct access to consumers[1635].

Furthermore, Smith's strategy includes a call for strategic partnerships with existing corporations and government entities. These partnerships can not only provide access to capital and markets, but they can also facilitate the sharing of expertise and technology, thus aiding the growth and competitiveness of Black manufacturers[1636].

[1633] "Benefits of Collaboration for Small and Medium-sized Enterprises." Journal of Business Venturing, 2018.
[1634] "Innovation in Manufacturing: From Product Innovation to Innovation Systems and Architectures." Journal of Manufacturing Technology Management, 2020.
[1635] "Cooperatives and Shared Economic Prosperity." Democracy at Work Institute, 2017.
[1636] "The Power of Partnerships: Benefits for Small and Medium-sized Manufacturing Enterprises." Journal of Small Business and Enterprise Development, 2019.

While the path to successful collaboration and competition is complex and laden with challenges, the potential benefits to Black manufacturers and the wider Black community are significant. In the spirit of collective action and economic empowerment, Smith's blueprint for collaboration among Black manufacturers offers a potent strategy for fostering a more equitable and prosperous future.

Charting New Territories: Initiatives for Technological Upgrading and Innovation in Black-Owned Manufacturing Enterprises

In a dynamic global economy, technological innovation is a cornerstone of competitiveness, particularly in the manufacturing sector. Power Matrix's blueprint puts forth the idea of launching initiatives to promote technological upgrading and innovation within Black-owned manufacturing enterprises. This proposition, although welcomed by many, does not escape critique[1637].

The current landscape of manufacturing is increasingly characterized by automation, artificial intelligence, and advanced robotics. Black-owned manufacturing businesses often face significant barriers in embracing these advancements due to limited access to capital and resources, contributing to a digital divide[1638]. Critics argue that such initiatives, while well-intended, might not be sufficient to overcome the technological gap between Black-owned manufacturers and larger corporations.

However, supporters of Smith's plan point out that strategic initiatives can effectively facilitate technological

---

[1637] "The Role of Technology in Small Business Success." Journal of Business Venturing, 2020.
[1638] "Digital Divide and its Implications for Minority-Owned Businesses." Federal Reserve Bank of New York, 2018.

upgrading and foster innovation. Access to funds designated for technological enhancement can help Black-owned manufacturing businesses adopt advanced technologies, streamline processes, and improve productivity[1639].

Smith's proposal includes partnerships with technology firms and academic institutions, which could provide necessary expertise and resources for technological upgrades. Such partnerships can pave the way for technology transfer, collaboration on research and development, and training programs, thus helping Black manufacturers to compete more effectively on the technological front[1640].

Moreover, innovation is an integral part of Smith's initiative. Innovation, whether in the form of product development or process optimization, can significantly enhance a firm's competitiveness. Encouraging an innovation culture within Black-owned manufacturing enterprises could not only improve their productivity but also create a unique selling proposition that sets them apart in the market[1641].

The development of incubators and accelerators focused on Black manufacturers is another critical component of this initiative. These platforms could provide a supportive ecosystem for nurturing technological upgrading and innovation, offering resources such as mentorship, capital, and networking opportunities[1642].

The critics may raise valid concerns, but the potential impact of these initiatives on the competitiveness of Black-

---

[1639] "Technology Adoption in Small and Medium-sized Enterprises: Opportunities and Challenges." Journal of Small Business Management, 2019.

[1640] "Technological Partnerships and Innovation in Manufacturing Firms." Research Policy, 2021.

[1641] "Innovation and Firm Performance in Manufacturing Industries: An Empirical Analysis." Technovation, 2020.

[1642] "Business Incubators and Accelerators: The National Picture." Institute for Small Business and Entrepreneurship, 2017.

owned manufacturing businesses and the economic empowerment of the Black community should not be underestimated. The road to technological upgrading and innovation may be challenging, yet the long-term rewards in terms of economic growth, job creation, and community empowerment are invaluable.

Unleashing Potential: An Urgent Call for Manufacturing Mastery in the Black Community

Through the Power Matrix, a clear road-map has been laid out. This is a road-map that acknowledges the realities and challenges of our current economic system, yet it transcends these challenges by offering a pragmatic, actionable plan: fostering the growth of Black-controlled manufacturing businesses, encouraging collaboration and consortiums among Black manufacturers, and launching initiatives for technological upgrading and innovation[1643].

Undoubtedly, the journey will be strenuous. Manufacturing is a complex sector, characterized by fast-paced technological changes, competitive pressures, and regulatory hurdles. For Black-owned manufacturing businesses, these challenges can be even more formidable, given the systemic obstacles in access to capital and resources[1644].

Yet, the potential rewards are vast. As Dr. Claud Anderson frequently emphasized, ownership is a critical pathway to economic empowerment. In manufacturing, ownership isn't simply about having a piece of the pie; it's about baking the pie itself. It's about controlling the means

---

[1643] Anderson, Claud. "PowerNomics : The National Plan to Empower Black America." Powernomics Corporation of America, 2001.

[1644] "Manufacturing and Minority Business Development." National Minority Business Council, 2020.

of production, setting the direction for technological innovation, and determining the shape and size of economic opportunities for our community[1645].

As we conclude this exploration of the Manufacturing Mastery Blueprint, we must also acknowledge the skepticism and doubts that such a vision often encounters. Critics argue that the barriers are too high, the investment is too risky, or the competitive environment is too challenging for Black-owned manufacturing businesses to thrive[1646]. Yet, the critics miss a crucial point: the power of collective action, the resilience born out of historical adversity, and the untapped potential that lies within our community.

The call to action, therefore, is not just about investing in manufacturing. It's about investing in ourselves, in our capacity to create and innovate, in our ability to challenge the status quo and build a more equitable and empowering economic future[1647]. This call goes out to every member of the Black community: Let us take ownership of our destiny, let us build our manufacturing power, and let us create an economy that truly serves our interests and aspirations.

Let this not just be a blueprint on paper. Let it be a catalyst for action, a testament to our resolve, and a stepping stone towards a future where Black-owned manufacturing businesses are not the exception, but the norm.

[1645] Anderson, Claud. "Black Labor, White Wealth : The Search for Power and Economic Justice." Powernomics Corporation of America, 1994.

[1646] "Barriers to Entry in Industrial Sector for Minority Entrepreneurs." Journal of Industrial Economics, 2019.

[1647] Anderson, Claud. "A Black History Reader: 101 Questions You Never Thought to Ask." Powernomics Corporation of America, 2017.

Infrastructure

Charting the Course: The Power Matrix's Infrastructure Development Framework

The idea of infrastructure is often confined to notions of physical spaces like bridges, roads, or buildings. Yet, Dr. Claud Anderson posits a broader perspective. In his seminal work, "PowerNomics: The National Plan to Empower Black America," he depicts infrastructure not merely as physical constructs but as the systems and structures that support the functioning of an economy and society[1648].

Anderson argues that for Black communities to rise to a position of self-sustainability and economic independence, a robust infrastructure – physical, social, and economic – must be developed[1649]. This perspective forms the core of the Power Matrix's Infrastructure Development Framework, a strategic plan aimed at building and enhancing the critical infrastructural elements within Black communities.

Despite the merits of this approach, there are critics who argue that infrastructure development, while crucial, is not the panacea to the economic challenges faced by Black communities. They point to entrenched systemic issues like racial discrimination, unequal access to education and resources, and a skewed criminal justice system as primary obstacles that impede economic advancement[1650].

However, proponents of the Infrastructure Development Framework counter that an effective and inclusive infrastructure can, in fact, serve as a potent tool to combat these systemic challenges. They assert that a robust

---

[1648] Anderson, Claud. "PowerNomics : The National Plan to Empower Black America." Powernomics Corporation of America, 2001.
[1649] Ibid.
[1650] "The Road to Zero Wealth: How the Racial Wealth Divide is Hollowing Out America's Middle Class." Prosperity Now, 2017.

infrastructure would provide access to essential services, foster economic activities, create jobs, and facilitate the integration of Black communities into the broader economic system[1651].

An integral aspect of this framework is the development of Black-owned businesses, which serve as the backbone of the community's economic infrastructure. By encouraging entrepreneurship and providing support for Black-owned businesses, the framework aims to increase economic activity and generate wealth within the community. This approach also ties in with Anderson's argument that economic power is a prerequisite for achieving political and social power[1652].

Beyond businesses, the infrastructure development plan also encompasses social and cultural infrastructure, such as education and health-care facilities, community centers, and cultural institutions. These entities play a pivotal role in fostering social cohesion, promoting cultural identity, and improving the overall quality of life within Black communities[1653].

The Power Matrix's Infrastructure Development Framework is a bold and holistic plan for infrastructure development within Black communities. It acknowledges the multifaceted nature of infrastructure and seeks to address the diverse needs of the community, thereby paving the way for economic empowerment and self-sustainability.

[1651] "The Color of Wealth in Boston." Federal Reserve Bank of Boston, 2015.//
[1652] Anderson, Claud. "Black Labor, White Wealth : The Search for Power and Economic Justice." Powernomics Corporation of America, 1994.//
[1653] "The Economic Impact of Closing the Racial Wealth Gap." McKinsey & Company, 2019.

Prioritizing Infrastructure Investment in Black Communities

The American Society of Civil Engineers report card for America's infrastructure paints a grim picture, assigning a grade of 'C-', with a large proportion of the country's infrastructure needing significant repairs[1654]. It is within this context that the call for focused infrastructure investment in Black communities becomes crucial, not just for the betterment of these communities, but also for the broader national economy.

Dr. Claud Anderson, in his compelling argument for economic empowerment, underscores the importance of a significant investment in infrastructure projects within Black communities[1655]. He stresses that contracts should be prioritized for Black-owned construction and engineering firms. This strategy could stimulate economic growth, generate employment, and catalyze wealth creation within these communities.

However, critics argue that such prioritization may be perceived as discriminatory or reverse racism. They advocate for a color-blind policy where contracts are awarded based on merit and competitiveness rather than racial considerations[1656].

However, proponents of prioritizing Black-owned firms for infrastructure projects in Black communities point to historical and ongoing racial disparities that have resulted in significant wealth gaps. They argue that a 'race-neutral' approach does not adequately address the historical and systemic disadvantages faced by Black communities.

[1654] "2021 Infrastructure Report Card." American Society of Civil Engineers, 2021.
[1655] Anderson, Claud. "PowerNomics : The National Plan to Empower Black America." Powernomics Corporation of America, 2001.
[1656] "Affirmative Action and Minority Enrollment in Medical and Law Schools: A Pipeline Analysis." American Psychological Association, 2018.

Instead, they believe that affirmative action and targeted policies, such as those proposed by Anderson, are essential for addressing these disparities[1657].

The Brookings Institution, in a 2020 report, highlighted that only 2.2% of the nation's employer-owned businesses are Black-owned[1658]. This figure, critics argue, illustrates the urgent need for strategies like Anderson's that aim to enhance the capacity of Black-owned businesses and foster economic growth within Black communities.

In order for Black-owned construction and engineering firms to effectively compete for and execute these contracts, they would require access to capital, skills training, and mentorship programs. Policymakers, therefore, must adopt a multi-pronged approach that not only prioritizes these firms for contracts but also provides them with the necessary resources and support.

Prioritizing infrastructure investment in Black communities and advocating for contracts to be awarded to Black-owned firms, as proposed by Anderson, can serve as a potent strategy for economic empowerment. While this approach is not without its critics, the potential benefits, including job creation, wealth generation, and infrastructure development, make it a worthy cause for advocacy and action.

Infrastructure Investment and Economic Empowerment for Black Communities under the Antonio T. Smith Jr. Power Matrix Framework

The significance of infrastructure development for economic advancement is universally recognized. Thus,

---

[1657] "The Economic Impact of Closing the Racial Wealth Gap." McKinsey & Company, 2019.

[1658] "Black businesses matter: Supporting Black-owned businesses to narrow racial wealth gap." Brookings Institution, 2020.

Antonio T. Smith Jr. argues passionately for an assertive commitment towards infrastructure investment in Black communities. His strategy promotes preferential allocation of construction and engineering contracts to Black-owned firms in these communities, providing an impetus to economic growth, job creation, and wealth accumulation.

The skepticism towards such race-centric allocation of contracts persists among certain quarters, labeling it as a form of reverse discrimination. They propose a system where contracts are awarded purely on the basis of competitiveness and merit, without any racial bias.

Despite these counterarguments, Smith maintains that the historical context of racial disparities, leading to substantial wealth gaps, necessitates a nuanced approach. He believes that a race-neutral policy fails to redress the systemic disadvantages faced by Black communities. Hence, strategic policies that prioritize Black-owned firms for infrastructure projects become imperative to alleviate these disparities.

According to a recent survey, Black-owned businesses constitute a meager 2.2% of the nation's employer-owned enterprises. This data substantiates the urgent need for proactive strategies like Smith's, designed to bolster the capacity of Black-owned businesses and invigorate economic growth within Black communities.

Successful implementation of Smith's strategy, however, requires more than prioritizing Black-owned firms for contracts. It necessitates a comprehensive approach providing these firms with necessary resources and support, including access to capital, skills training, and mentorship programs.

The Power Matrix's strategy of prioritizing infrastructure investment in Black communities, with a focus on contracting Black-owned firms, is a powerful proposition for economic empowerment. While opposition exists, the projected benefits, such as job creation, wealth generation, and community development, underscore the need for rigorous advocacy and concerted action.

Cooperative Ownership: A Pathway to Infrastructure Sovereignty

As part of his Infrastructure Development Framework, Antonio T. Smith Jr. posits that the development of cooperative models for ownership of utilities and vital infrastructure could provide significant economic benefits for Black communities.

Historically, cooperative models have played a vital role in supporting marginalized communities. The Rochdale Pioneers in England, in 1844, were the first to develop a highly successful cooperative model that combined resources to create mutual benefits[1659]. Smith suggests that a similar model could be instrumental in the empowerment of Black communities.

Critics of cooperative models often argue that these structures lack the competitive edge and efficiency of conventional corporate models[1660]. They express concerns over potential operational inefficiencies and the ability of these models to adapt to rapidly changing market conditions.

However, proponents of cooperative models argue that these structures are designed to prioritize the needs of the community, focusing on long-term communal benefits over short-term individual profits[1661]. Smith emphasizes that the

---

[1659] Rochdale Pioneers Museum. "The Rochdale Pioneers," 2021.
[1660] Münkner, Hans-H. "Cooperatives: In Quest of a New Paradigm," in Cooperatives in a Global Economy: The Challenges of Cooperation Across Borders, edited by Darryl Reed and J.J. McMurtry, 23-46. Newcastle upon Tyne, UK: Cambridge Scholars Publishing, 2009.
[1661] Fairbairn, Brett. "Three Strategic Concepts for the Guidance of Cooperatives: Linkage, Transparency, and Cognition," Saskatoon: University of Saskatchewan, 2003.

benefits of cooperative ownership, such as democratic control, shared profits, and economic stability, could provide a powerful platform for economic advancement in Black communities.

According to a 2020 report by the U.S. Federation of Worker Cooperatives, Black and Latinx workers make up more than 60% of worker-owners[1662]. This data underlines the potential of cooperative models to foster economic empowerment for these groups.

Cooperative ownership of utilities and key infrastructure, as proposed by Smith, offers a distinct path to self-reliance and economic stability for Black communities. This model, while facing resistance from traditionalists, has a solid foundation in historical success and current real-world data.

Hence, the creation and support of cooperative models of ownership should be a key consideration for policymakers and community leaders seeking to build economic resilience within Black communities. The road to infrastructure sovereignty may be challenging, but with a cooperative mindset and strategic action, it is entirely achievable.

Green Infrastructure: The Path Forward with Black-led Innovation

The Power Matrix's Infrastructure Development Framework champions innovation in sustainable, green infrastructure, with Black-led firms taking the lead. This approach not only aligns with the global shift towards environmental sustainability but also provides economic opportunities for Black communities.

[1662] U.S. Federation of Worker Cooperatives. "State of the Sector," 2020.

Historically, Black communities have been disproportionately affected by environmental degradation and poor infrastructure[1663]. Smith's proposition encourages the use of green technology and sustainability practices to address these disparities and foster environmental justice. However, critics may argue that green infrastructure projects require significant upfront capital, posing challenges for Black-led firms which often face systemic hurdles in accessing finance[1664].

In response, Smith advocates for targeted investment and policy initiatives to support Black-led firms. By creating an enabling environment, these firms could be at the forefront of green infrastructure innovation, creating sustainable solutions and job opportunities within their communities.

There are already instances of Black-led firms breaking ground in this sector. BlocPower, a Black-led clean technology start-up in New York, has retrofitted more than 1,000 buildings with green technology, reducing energy costs and creating job opportunities[1665].

Despite these successes, a report by the American Association of Blacks in Energy highlights that Black participation in the energy sector remains disproportionately low[1666]. To overcome this, Smith suggests providing scholarships, training, and mentorship programs in green technology and sustainability to encourage more Black professionals and entrepreneurs to enter this space.

While some critics argue that a 'color-blind' approach should be applied, Smith and others point to historical and ongoing disparities. A targeted approach is deemed

---

[1663] Bullard, Robert D. "Environmental Racism and Invisible Communities," West Virginia Law Review, 1994.
[1664] Bradford, William D. "The Wealth Gap in Black America: Past Trends and Future Prospects," Journal of Black Studies, 2014.
[1665] BlocPower. "About Us," 2023.
[1666] American Association of Blacks in Energy. "Blacks in Energy: Challenges and Opportunities," 2019.

necessary to correct these imbalances and create a more equitable green infrastructure sector.

Smith's proposal for Black-led firms to lead the way in sustainable, green infrastructure is both timely and crucial. It aligns with global sustainability goals while also addressing economic and environmental justice issues within Black communities. The challenge lies in garnering the required investment and policy support, but with strategic planning and concerted effort, this vision can become a reality.

Empowering Black Wealth Creation Through the Power Matrix of Technological Transformation

As McKinsey & Company aptly predicts, the next decade will likely experience more technological progress than the preceding 100 years[1667]. This brings forth vast opportunities for wealth creation, particularly for Black entrepreneurs. In this context, it becomes crucial to comprehend and adapt to the top ten technological trends that will define the future, and harness them to empower Black wealth creation.

1. **Process Automation and Virtualization:** As we move into an era where half of the existing work activities could be automated, Black entrepreneurs stand a chance to enhance productivity and cut costs. However, it's important to remember that not all tasks are suitable for automation. Strategic thinking, emotional intelligence, and tasks requiring human touch remain irreplaceable. Therefore, businesses

---

[1667] McKinsey, "Top 10 tech trends that will shape the coming decade," 2021.

need to find a balance between technology and human talent[1668].

2. **The Future of Connectivity:** Faster digital connections through 5G and IoT open the doors for improved service delivery, enhancing business opportunities, particularly in sectors like mobility, health-care, manufacturing, and retail[1669]. Ensuring digital literacy and access to digital resources in Black communities will be a key enabler.

3. **Distributed Infrastructure:** The use of hybrid-cloud or multi-cloud platforms allows businesses to handle data and processing in the cloud but make them accessible to devices faster. This enhances agility and reduces complexity, leading to cost savings and stronger cybersecurity defenses[1670]. Black-owned businesses can leverage this trend to optimize operations and safeguard their digital assets.

4. **Next-Generation Computing:** Quantum computing and AI have the potential to unlock unprecedented capabilities for businesses. Identifying potential applications of these technologies and staying ahead of the necessary shift from current to quantum cryptography will be a crucial strategic decision for Black entrepreneurs[1671].

5. **Applied Artificial Intelligence (AI):** AI has vast potential in developing tech-based tools like pattern recognition and decision-making processes. Ensuring access to AI training and resources can help Black communities stay at the forefront of this transformation[1672].

[1668] PwC, "Impact of Automation on Jobs," 2022.
[1669] Cisco, "The Power of 5G and IoT," 2022.
[1670] IBM, "Benefits of Hybrid Cloud," 2022
[1671] Google Quantum AI, "Quantum Computing," 2022.
[1672] MIT, "Applications of AI," 2022.

6. **Future of Programming:** The advent of neural networks and machine learning writing code, also known as Software 2.0, allows rapid scaling and diffusion of data-rich, AI-driven applications[1673]. It's critical for Black entrepreneurs to stay updated with these changes and leverage them to innovate and stay competitive.
7. **Trust Architecture:** With data breaches becoming more common, trust architectures and cybersecurity measures will play a key role in maintaining customer trust and business continuity[1674]. Black businesses need to invest in robust cybersecurity measures and training to safeguard their digital assets.
8. **Bio Revolution:** Advances in biological science will significantly impact sectors like health, agriculture, and consumer goods. Businesses will need to assess their biological quotient, integrating necessary resources into existing R&D or partnering with science-based start-ups[1675].
9. **Next-Generation Materials:** With potential to transform industries like pharma, energy, transportation, and manufacturing, Black entrepreneurs can leverage these materials to create innovative products and solutions, driving competitive advantage[1676].
10. **Future of Clean Tech Trends:** As clean technologies become more affordable and widespread, they present opportunities for business-

---

[1673] Stanford University, "Future of Programming and Software 2.0," 2022.
[1674] Norton, "Importance of Cybersecurity in Business," 2022.
[1675] Harvard Business Review, "The Bio Revolution: Innovations transforming economies, societies, and our lives," 2021.
[1676] Material Science and Engineering, "Implications of Next-Generation Materials," 2022.

building and cost reduction[1677]. Black entrepreneurs can tap into this trend by integrating sustainable practices in their operations and offering green solutions to their customers.

While these trends present substantial opportunities for wealth creation, it's important to acknowledge and address the digital divide that could potentially widen as a result of these advancements[1678]. Ensuring equitable access to digital resources, infrastructure, and training is paramount for harnessing these trends for Black wealth creation.

Communications

The Communications Catalyst: The Power Matrix Scheme for Controlling Communications

Communications - an essential cornerstone of any societal structure - wields significant power in shaping socio-economic realities. The Power Matrix Communications Control Scheme, born from my military intelligence and psychological operations experiences, offers a blueprint for self-determined prosperity within marginalized communities, with a specific focus on the Black community in the United States.

The scheme illuminates the potential of communication control as an antidote to the systematic erosion of wealth, unity, cultural heritage, and freedom seen in many Black communities.

[1677] McKinsey, "The future of clean tech trends," 2021.
[1678] Brookings Institution, "The Digital Divide and Economic Disparities," 2023.

Firstly, wealth control is reflected in the establishment of Black-owned telecommunications and internet service providers. This step combats the digital divide and guarantees affordable services, empowering economic growth. History reveals that wealth disparity has played a considerable role in destabilizing Black communities[1679]. By promoting financial self-sufficiency, we are directly confronting and challenging this narrative[1680].

Secondly, the creation of conflict — often used to destabilize power structures - can be addressed by investing in Black-controlled media outlets, including TV stations, radio stations, and online platforms. These platforms allow for a balanced narrative, curbing internal divisions, and fostering unity[1681].

Thirdly, depopulation in this context refers to cultural and ideological dissociation. Encouraging collaboration among Black content creators and influencers amplifies messages and increases reach. This counters the trend of cultural dilution and celebrates heritage, encouraging individuals to connect with their communities, and resist the pull of disillusionment[1682].

Finally, enacting "martial law" in the form of disproportionate incarceration rates and heightened policing can be countered by controlling the narrative through owned communication platforms. By shining a light on these

---

[1679] Hamilton, D., & Darity, W. (2017). "The political economy of education, financial literacy, and the racial wealth gap." Federal Reserve Bank of St. Louis Review, 99(1), 59-76.
[1680] Kochhar, R., & Fry, R. (2014). "Wealth inequality has widened along racial, ethnic lines since end of Great Recession." Pew Research Center.
[1681] Galtung, J. (1964). "An Editorial." Journal of Peace Research, 1(1)
[1682] Shihadeh, E. S., & Flynn, N. (1996). "Segregation and crime: The relationship between black centralization and urban black homicide." Homicide studies, 1(2), 180-193.

injustices, we can begin to dismantle these oppressive structures[1683].

Critics may assert that the Power Matrix scheme is an oversimplification and overlooks the significant strides made in Black entrepreneurship and political representation^7^. However, acknowledging progress does not mean overlooking systemic issues that still exist. It is through the lens of this model that these issues can be critically examined and addressed[1684].

The Power Matrix Communications Control Scheme is a powerful tool for transforming the Black community's socio-economic narrative. Through controlling communication, we can redefine wealth distribution, manage conflict, combat cultural depopulation, and challenge oppressive "martial law." In controlling our narrative, we seize the reins of power, reshaping the dynamics in our favor, and fostering a community that is wealthy, unified, culturally rich, and free[1685].

Leveraging Communications for Socioeconomic Prosperity: A Deeper Examination of the Power Matrix Communications Control Scheme

Understanding the nuances of the Power Matrix Communications Control Scheme and its potential transformative effects on marginalized communities, particularly the Black community in the United States, involves digging deeper into its four integral components.

[1683] Nellis, A. (2016). "The Color of Justice: Racial and Ethnic Disparity in State Prisons." The Sentencing Project.

[1684] Fairlie, R. (2020). "The Impact of COVID-19 on Small Business Owners: Evidence from the First Three Months after Widespread Social-Distancing Restrictions." Journal of Economics & Management Strategy, 29(4), 727-740.

[1685] Anderson, C. (2001). "Black Labor, White Wealth : The Search for Power and Economic Justice." PowerNomics Corporation of America.

In the realm of wealth control, the establishment of Black-owned telecommunications and internet service providers is more than a business endeavor. It's a robust strategy to overcome the digital divide, a pervasive issue affecting marginalized communities. In doing so, it bridges the gap between technological access and economic opportunities, empowering these communities to navigate and prosper in a rapidly digitalizing world[1686]. The move towards digital autonomy forms an integral part of the solution to combat historic and systemic wealth disparity[1687].

Managing conflict through the lens of communications necessitates an investment in Black-controlled media. Such platforms become a conduit for unified narratives, a crucial countermeasure against divisive forces. By facilitating a balanced representation of the community's narrative, these media outlets can foster unity and curb conflict, addressing one of the critical issues in the Power Matrix model[1688].

Addressing cultural and ideological depopulation involves a two-pronged strategy: celebrating heritage and strengthening community bonds. In the Power Matrix model, this is achieved through collaborative efforts amongst Black content creators and influencers, effectively amplifying authentic cultural narratives and encouraging community cohesion[1689]. Through such collaboration, the community can actively counteract cultural dilution and the sense of disillusionment that often leads to a departure from heritage.

[1686] Anderson, C. (2001). "Black Labor, White Wealth: The Search for Power and Economic Justice." PowerNomics Corporation of America.

[1687] Galtung, J. (1964). "An Editorial." Journal of Peace Research, 1(1)

[1688] Shihadeh, E. S., & Flynn, N. (1996). "Segregation and crime: The relationship between black centralization and urban black homicide." Homicide studies, 1(2), 180-193.

[1689] Fairlie, R. (2020). "The Impact of COVID-19 on Small Business Owners: Evidence from the First Three Months after Widespread Social-Distancing Restrictions." Journal of Economics & Management Strategy, 29(4), 727-740.

Finally, addressing the "martial law" equivalent in Black communities - the disproportionate incarceration rates and heightened policing - necessitates the utilization of owned communication platforms to highlight and challenge these injustices. This approach not only exposes oppressive structures but also sets the stage for advocating for systemic change[1690].

Detractors may posit that the Power Matrix model oversimplifies complex issues and underestimates the significance of individual agency and progress made within the community[1691]. However, acknowledging advancements shouldn't preclude the critical examination of systemic issues and their continued impacts[1692].

In essence, the Power Matrix Communications Control Scheme provides a blueprint for comprehensive socio-economic transformation. By effectively controlling and harnessing the power of communication, it's possible to rewrite the socio-economic narrative in marginalized communities. The strategy promotes wealth creation, unity, cultural retention, and social justice - the vital elements for a thriving community[1693].

[1690] Nellis, A. (2016). "The Color of Justice: Racial and Ethnic Disparity in State Prisons." The Sentencing Project.

[1691] Kochhar, R., & Fry, R. (2014). "Wealth inequality has widened along racial, ethnic lines since end of Great Recession." Pew Research Center.

[1692] Kochhar, R., & Fry, R. (2014). "Wealth inequality has widened along racial, ethnic lines since end of Great Recession." Pew Research Center.

[1693] Kochhar, R., & Fry, R. (2014). "Wealth inequality has widened along racial, ethnic lines since end of Great Recession." Pew Research Center.

Seizing Control of the Narrative: The Imperative of Black Ownership in Media and Telecommunications

Ownership in media and telecommunications plays a critical role in shaping the socio-economic realities within communities. For Black communities, this form of ownership is not just a matter of economic independence but also a means to control and shape narratives about their communities, thereby challenging longstanding stereotypes and misrepresentations[1694].

Television and radio stations remain influential platforms that shape public perception. Black-owned stations can provide a balanced representation of Black life, countering mainstream narratives that often emphasize negative aspects or stereotype Black communities. In owning these platforms, Black communities can ensure they are portrayed in a multifaceted and authentic manner, highlighting the diversity within these communities and celebrating their unique cultural heritage[1695].

Critics may argue that in the age of social media and digital platforms, traditional media like TV and radio stations have less influence[1696]. However, this argument fails to recognize that these traditional forms of media continue to have substantial reach, especially among older demographics. Furthermore, traditional media often shapes the news and topics that become trending on social media[1697].

[1694] Anderson, C. (2001). "Black Labor, White Wealth: The Search for Power and Economic Justice." PowerNomics Corporation of America.
[1695] Napoli, P. M. (1999). "Deconstructing the diversity principle." Journal of Communication, 49(4), 7-34.
[1696] Pew Research Center. (2021). "Social Media Use in 2021."
[1697] Newman, N., Fletcher, R., Kalogeropoulos, A., Levy, D. A., & Nielsen, R. K. (2018). "Reuters Institute Digital News Report 2018." Reuters Institute.

Building Black-owned internet service providers (ISPs) is also a significant step towards digital autonomy. Ownership in this sector could provide affordable, reliable internet services to Black communities, a crucial need considering the ever-increasing importance of internet access for education, work, and civic engagement. Affordable internet access can play a significant role in reducing the digital divide, a systemic issue that disproportionately affects Black communities[1698].

Black-owned ISPs could also play a role in addressing the issue of net neutrality. While the concept is designed to ensure all internet traffic is treated equally, without Black-owned ISPs, there's a risk that major corporate providers could prioritize their own content[1699]. This could potentially sideline Black-created content, perpetuating underrepresentation.

Detractors may argue that the entry barriers to the ISP market are too high due to the capital-intensive nature of this industry. While it's true that building an ISP requires substantial investment, the long-term economic and social benefits for Black communities outweigh the initial capital challenges. Efforts can be made to secure funding through various channels, including venture capital, community investments, and public funding[1700].

Owning TV stations, radio stations, and ISPs is crucial for Black communities to control their narratives, improve digital access, and foster economic growth. This form of ownership can be a powerful tool in addressing systemic inequalities while ensuring authentic representation of Black experiences in the media landscape[1701].

[1698] Pew Research Center. (2019). "Digital divide persists even as lower-income Americans make gains in tech adoption."
[1699] Federal Communications Commission. (2015). "Open Internet."
[1700] Molla, R. (2018). "The lack of black-owned media companies is a big problem for media diversity." Vox Media.
[1701] Hamilton, D., & Darity, W. (2017). "The political economy of education, financial literacy, and the racial wealth gap." Federal

An Empowered Future: Black Ownership and Influence in the Telecom Industry

The telecommunications industry, which includes services ranging from voice and broadband to cloud computing and network security, is a critical global economic segment. By owning and controlling businesses within this sphere, Black communities could significantly influence their socio-economic realities[1702].

Owning businesses that provide voice services, such as telephone and VoIP services, could allow for increased representation in the telecom industry, a sector where Black representation has historically been marginal[1703]. Moreover, providing affordable, reliable services could directly combat digital divides that disproportionately affect Black communities[1704].

Critics may argue that establishing Black-owned mobile voice and data services or broadband providers would be challenging due to the capital-intensive nature of the industry and existing monopolies[1705]. However, models like municipal broadband and community-based ISPs demonstrate viable alternatives that could enable Black communities to provide these services[1706].

Reserve Bank of St. Louis Review, Fourth Quarter 2017, 99(1), 59-76.
[1702] Anderson, C. (2001). "Black Labor, White Wealth: The Search for Power and Economic Justice." PowerNomics Corporation of America.
[1703] Federal Communications Commission. (2012). "Report on Ownership of Commercial Broadcast Stations."
[1704] Pew Research Center. (2019). "Digital divide persists even as lower-income Americans make gains in tech adoption."
[1705] National Telecommunications and Information Administration. (2018). "Telecommunications Act of 1996."
[1706] Community Networks. (2020). "Successful Strategies for Broadband Public-Private Partnerships."

Similarly, Black ownership in the cable and streaming media sector could significantly impact the representation and narratives of Black communities in media. Critics often argue that diversity in content creation negates the need for ownership. Nevertheless, ownership ensures a level of control over production and distribution that simply being a content creator cannot provide[1707].

Venturing into the retail side of telecom, such as selling mobile devices, could further enable Black economic independence. The dominance of large telecom corporations in this space may deter such efforts. Yet, through strategic collaborations and leveraging communal resources, this barrier can be overcome[1708].

Business infrastructure services, colocation, cloud services, content delivery networks, and edge computing also present opportunities for Black-owned businesses. These sectors, often overlooked, could be an avenue for innovation and diversification[1709].

Offering network security services and participating in the Internet of Things (IoT) landscape could not only offer economic benefits but also ensure the needs and concerns of Black communities are addressed in these evolving tech spaces[1710]. Critics may highlight the technical expertise required in these areas as a barrier. However, this only underscores the importance of investing in STEM education within Black communities[1711].

[1707] Napoli, P. M. (1999). "Deconstructing the diversity principle." Journal of Communication, 49(4), 7-34.

[1708] Howard, P. N., Busch, L., & Sheets, P. (2010). "Comparing Digital Divides: Internet Access and Social Inequality in Canada and the United States." Canadian Journal of Communication, Vol 35 (1).

[1709] Bughin, J., Chui, M., & Manyika, J. (2013). "Ten IT-enabled business trends for the decade ahead." McKinsey Quarterly.

[1710] Kumar, N., Stern, L. W., & Anderson, J. C. (1993). "Conducting interorganizational research using key informants." Academy of Management Journal, 36(6), 1633-1651.

[1711] Southgate, D. (2011). "The US digital divide: a call for a new philosophy." Chinese Journal of Communication, 4(2), 131-146.

Black ownership in the telecommunications industry is more than an economic opportunity; it's a path towards increased representation, influence, and power. Controlling the narrative isn't just about media ownership; it extends to all facets of communication – from how we connect to what we see. As digital and media convergence blurs the line between telecom, media, and technology companies, there's no better time for Black communities to stake their claim in this ever-evolving landscape[1712].

The Dawn of Prosperity: Seizing Black Wealth Opportunities in Modern Communication Technologies

In the era of rapid technological advances, opportunities abound for wealth generation in Black communities. Recognizing and capitalizing on these opportunities could reshape our socio-economic narrative from consumers to producers[1713].

Artificial Intelligence (AI) is revolutionizing user experiences, enabling more personalized and efficient communication. Black-owned businesses can leverage AI to enhance customer service and create unique customer experiences, thus promoting loyalty and profit growth[1714]. Critics may argue that AI demands significant investments and technical knowledge, which could be barriers for Black entrepreneurs. However, numerous accessible platforms

---

[1712] Jenkins, H. (2006). "Convergence culture: Where old and new media collide." NYU Press.
[1713] Anderson, C. (2001). "Black Labor, White Wealth: The Search for Power and Economic Justice." PowerNomics Corporation of America.
[1714] McKinsey & Company. (2020). "The Future of Customer Experience."

exist today that facilitate AI integration without necessitating a high level of expertise[1715].

Automation in communications can streamline processes, increase efficiency, and reduce costs. By embracing such innovations, Black-owned firms could increase their competitiveness and profitability[1716]. The prevailing argument against this is the fear of job displacement due to automation. However, history shows us that while automation may displace certain roles, it also creates new jobs, often higher-skilled and better-paying ones[1717].

Given the rise of inflation, strategic investments in high-potential technologies are more crucial than ever. Investing in augmented and virtual reality technologies, live-streaming capabilities, and advanced video conferencing could open doors for innovative business models and revenue streams[1718]. Although these technologies might seem out of reach for many Black entrepreneurs, partnerships, grants, and community investments can provide the necessary resources[1719].

Cloud storage solutions, mobile technologies, and smart documents are not just trends; they are the new norms. Businesses that adapt to these norms can streamline their operations and improve their service offerings. However, it's essential that Black businesses not only use these

---

[1715] Davenport, T.H., Guha, A., Grewal, D., & Bressgott, T. (2020). "How AI Will Change the Way We Make Decisions." Harvard Business Review.

[1716] Chui, M., Manyika, J., & Miremadi, M. (2016). "Where machines could replace humans—and where they can't (yet)." McKinsey Quarterly.

[1717] Arntz, M., Gregory, T., & Zierahn, U. (2016). "The Risk of Automation for Jobs in OECD Countries: A Comparative Analysis." OECD Social, Employment and Migration Working Papers, No. 189, OECD Publishing, Paris.

[1718] Faisal, S., Yafi, E., & Pink, S. (2020). "The future of augmented reality across sectors: A systematic review of challenges and solutions." Journal of Business Research, 117, 25-38.

[1719] National Venture Capital Association. (2019). "Venture Forward."

services but also strive to create and control these platforms, thus retaining wealth within our communities[1720].

High-quality content and personalized customer journeys are not just beneficial but expected in today's market. Black entrepreneurs and content creators can leverage this demand to build thriving businesses. Similarly, emerging technologies like SMS.2 (Rich Communication Services) offer improved functionality over traditional SMS, presenting opportunities for innovative communication services[1721].

Finally, in an increasingly cashless society, Black communities must proactively adapt to and pioneer secure, trusted digital payment platforms. This shift not only aids in participating in the digital economy but also in controlling it[1722].

Critics may argue that these technologies require substantial capital and expertise. They may also note that competing with dominant tech corporations is an uphill battle. However, the narrative of impossibility has always been the barrier to Black wealth. By fostering a culture of innovation, education, and entrepreneurship, we can overcome these challenges[1723].

The era of modern communication technologies is an era of immense opportunity for Black wealth generation. It is a call to transition from consumers to producers, from spectators to innovators. As we venture into these spaces,

---

[1720] McKinsey & Company. (2020). "Cloud's trillion-dollar prize is up for grabs."
[1721] GSMA. (2020). "The Future of Messaging: How RCS is transforming business communication."
[1722] Bank for International Settlements. (2020). "Payment and settlement systems in the digital age."
[1723] Anderson, C. (2001). "Black Labor, White Wealth: The Search for Power and Economic Justice." PowerNomics Corporation of America.

we can create prosperous futures for ourselves and generations to come[1724].

Powering Progress: The Communications Control Scheme in the Power Matrix

The African American community has a long-standing history of resourcefulness and innovation[1725]. Yet, there exists a substantial gap in ownership within the telecommunications sector. The Communications Control Scheme in the Power Matrix proposes three potent strategies to transform this narrative: Establishing Black-owned telecom companies and internet service providers; investing in Black-controlled media outlets; and encouraging collaboration among Black content creators and influencers[1726].

Telecommunications — a global multi-trillion dollar industry - is a formidable avenue for wealth generation[1727]. The establishment of Black-owned telecom companies and internet service providers presents a prime opportunity to bridge the racial wealth gap. These enterprises would serve two primary purposes: reducing the prevalent digital divide and providing affordable services. Opponents might argue that the initial capital required to enter this industry is prohibitively high. Nevertheless, Black banks, crowd-funding, community investments, and venture capitalists

---

[1724] Anderson, C. (2001). "Black Labor, White Wealth: The Search for Power and Economic Justice." PowerNomics Corporation of America.
[1725] Anderson, C. (2001). "Black Labor, White Wealth: The Search for Power and Economic Justice." PowerNomics Corporation of America.
[1726] Ibid.
[1727] Statista. (2021). "Telecommunications services global spending forecast 2008-2023."

could provide the necessary financial support[1728]. Additionally, the economic returns and socio-economic impact potential from such ventures justify the initial outlay[1729].

The media, a powerful tool for shaping public opinion, has often underrepresented or misrepresented Black narratives. Investing in Black-controlled media outlets - such as TV stations, radio stations, and online platforms - could change this[1730]. These outlets can provide a platform for balanced narratives, fostering unity within the community and positively influencing external perceptions. Skeptics may express concerns about the viability of these outlets given the dominant position of established media corporations. Yet, the burgeoning success of various Black-owned media initiatives counters this argument, illustrating that with the right strategy and content, these platforms can thrive[1731].

Lastly, collaboration among Black content creators and influencers can be a transformative tool in amplifying messages and increasing reach. Collaborations can foster cultural unity, generate wealth, and increase the visibility of Black narratives in mainstream media[1732]. Detractors might assert that the influence of individual creators is limited. However, unity and collective action have been foundational to every significant societal change. Therefore,

---

[1728] Baradaran, M. (2017). "The Color of Money: Black Banks and the Racial Wealth Gap." Harvard University Press.
[1729] Federal Communications Commission. (2020). "Communications Marketplace Report."
[1730] Napoli, P. M. (2010). "Race and audience measurement in the development of the US broadcast industry: evidence from the historical record." Media History 16.2: 161-180.
[1731] Pew Research Center. (2020). "U.S. Media Polarization and the 2020 Election: A Nation Divided."
[1732] Khamis, S., Ang, L., & Welling, R. (2017). "Self-branding, 'micro-celebrity' and the rise of Social Media Influencers." Celebrity Studies, 8(2), 191-208.

a networked approach among Black creators can indeed shift narratives[1733].

The Communications Control Scheme in the Power Matrix is not a panacea to the complex issue of racial wealth disparity. However, it offers a strategic road-map towards self-determined prosperity. As Dr. Claud Anderson rightly states, "Any group that is a consumer and not a producer is on its way to becoming a dependent, underclass population"[1734]. These proposed strategies represent a shift towards becoming producers, in control of our narratives and our wealth. Embracing these strategies marks a significant step towards a more equitable, prosperous future for the Black community.

Mapping the Future: A Practical Guide to the Power Matrix's Communications Control Scheme

Closing the gap in racial wealth and representation within the communications industry requires a well-structured, practical approach. Dr. Claud Anderson once asserted, "A race without power and wealth at the bottom is a powerless race"[1735]. The Power Matrix's Communications Control Scheme presents a powerful strategy for African Americans to leverage this sector and transform socio-economic realities. Below is an advanced, step-by-step guide to implementing this scheme:

[1733] Shirky, C. (2011). "The Political Power of Social Media: Technology, the Public Sphere, and Political Change." Foreign Affairs.

[1734] Anderson, C. (2001). "Black Labor, White Wealth: The Search for Power and Economic Justice." PowerNomics Corporation of America.

[1735] Anderson, C. (2001). "Black Labor, White Wealth: The Search for Power and Economic Justice." PowerNomics Corporation of America.

Step 1: Establishing Black-Owned Telecom Companies and Internet Service Providers

Breaking into the telecom sector demands substantial initial capital and intricate planning. Identify potential investors within the Black community, such as Black banks, community-focused investment groups, and venture capitalists[1736]. Subsequently, gather a team of professionals experienced in telecom operations, legal compliance, and financial management to draft a comprehensive business plan. Approach regulatory bodies, such as the Federal Communications Commission (FCC), for necessary permissions and licenses. In partnership with technology providers, start with a pilot area before expanding operations[1737].

Critics might argue that the telecom industry is oversaturated, and newcomers may struggle. Nevertheless, the digital divide in many African American communities offers a market opportunity[1738]. Providing affordable and quality services in these areas can ensure sustainable growth and customer loyalty.

Step 2: Investing in Black-Controlled Media Outlets

Start by identifying niches in the media landscape that can be uniquely addressed by Black perspectives. Develop a business model encompassing TV, radio, and online platforms. Crowdsource funding and seek investments from Black entrepreneurs. Hire a diverse workforce to ensure a variety of narratives are explored and presented[1739].

[1736] Anderson, C. (2001). "Black Labor, White Wealth: The Search for Power and Economic Justice." PowerNomics Corporation of America.

[1737] Federal Communications Commission. (2020). "Communications Marketplace Report."

[1738] Pew Research Center. (2019). "Digital gap between rural and nonrural America persists."

[1739] Napoli, P. M. (2010). "Race and audience measurement in the development of the US broadcast industry: evidence from the historical record." Media History 16.2: 161-180.

Opponents may caution about stiff competition from established media corporations. However, the market is gradually becoming more receptive to diverse voices[1740]. Providing content that authentically represents and caters to the Black community can carve out a space in this domain.

Step 3: Encouraging Collaboration Among Black Content Creators and Influencers

Create a network of Black content creators and influencers, possibly through a digital platform dedicated to collaboration. Regularly host events and workshops to enhance skills and foster collaboration[1741]. Provide resources and tools that empower these creators to reach larger audiences.

Skeptics may downplay the impact of individual content creators. Yet, the power of collective action and networked influence cannot be underestimated. As a united front, Black content creators can command significant cultural and economic impact[1742].

To conclude, the Power Matrix's Communications Control Scheme offers a strategic road-map to prosperity. It may be a challenging journey, laden with obstacles and skepticism. However, the fruits of this journey - wealth, representation, and power - make it a worthwhile endeavor for the Black community.

[1740] Pew Research Center. (2020). "U.S. Media Polarization and the 2020 Election: A Nation Divided."

[1741] Khamis, S., Ang, L., & Welling, R. (2017). "Self-branding, 'micro-celebrity' and the rise of Social Media Influencers." Celebrity Studies, 8(2), 191-208.

[1742] Shirky, C. (2011). "The Political Power of Social Media: Technology, the Public Sphere, and Political Change." Foreign Affairs.

Human Resources

Leading the Charge: Power Matrix's Human Capital Cultivation Strategy

Instead of urging established companies for diversity, a more sustainable and empowering approach is to control and direct the narrative through Black ownership and leadership. Dr. Claud Anderson eloquently stated, "You can't beg your way into power. You must build your way into power"[1743]. For African Americans, the focus should be on creating, managing, and diversifying enterprises in order to cultivate Black human capital and fundamentally shift the dynamics of economic power.

Ownership is key to this strategy. Establishing Black-owned businesses allows for the creation of not just jobs, but careers for Black individuals that offer fair wages, professional growth opportunities, and a respectful environment. These companies can control their hiring processes, internal policies, and development programs, ensuring that diversity and inclusivity aren't just buzzwords but integral parts of the corporate cultures[1744]. When Black entrepreneurs own their own businesses, they have the freedom to invest in their communities, creating a cycle of wealth that benefits the Black community in the long term[1745].

It is critical to note that this endeavor requires investment in education and professional development within the Black community. Building a reservoir of skilled

---

[1743] Anderson, Claud. (2000). "PowerNomics: The National Plan to Empower Black America." Powernomics Corporation of America.
[1744] Ruggles, Steven, et al. (2020). "IPUMS USA: Version 10.0 dataset." IPUMS.
[1745] Fairlie, Robert W., & Robb, Alicia M. (2008). "Race and Entrepreneurial Success." MIT Press.

and competent Black professionals who can excel in various industries should be a priority[1746]. To counter disparities in education and access to resources, initiatives should focus on improving educational outcomes, facilitating vocational training, and nurturing entrepreneurial skills.

Critics might argue that this approach isolates the Black community and undermines efforts to create multicultural workplaces. However, it is not a matter of segregation, but rather of empowerment. By owning and leading businesses, Black individuals can contribute to the economy on their terms and from a position of strength, rather than dependence. And while it is essential to have diversity within individual companies, it is equally, if not more, vital to have diversity among the companies themselves.

Dr. Anderson's economic model, as laid out in his book "PowerNomics," states, "No group can empower another group. All any group can do for another is get out of their way and give them an opportunity to empower themselves"[1747]. It is high time for Black communities to shake off the mentality of seeking approval and aid from the dominant culture. Instead, we should focus on utilizing our resources, talents, and potential to create our own thriving enterprises.

In the grand scheme of the universe, there is indeed an unlimited number of "rooms," and there is no need to limit ourselves to seeking a spot in someone else's room. By owning our own rooms, we can ensure that they are diverse, inclusive, and supportive of Black growth and empowerment. The Power Matrix's Human Capital

---

[1746] Hamilton, Darrick, et al. (2015). "Umbrellas Don't Make It Rain: Why Studying and Working Hard Isn't Enough for Black Americans." The New School and Duke Center for Social Equity.

[1747] Anderson, Claud. (2001). "Black Labor, White Wealth: The Search for Power and Economic Justice." PowerNomics Corporation of America.

Cultivation Strategy provides a robust framework for achieving this.

Fitting Into Corporate America Is Not Good Enough

Dr. Claud Anderson, in his exploration of Black economics, emphasized the necessity of Black ownership and economic empowerment as a means to overcome systemic barriers. This perspective aligns with that of Antonio T. Smith Jr., who proposes that rather than merely seeking to fit into the structure of corporate America, the Black community must strive to own and control it[1748].

While Black workers make up 12 percent of the private-sector workforce, totaling 15 million out of the 125 million overall[1749], their representation in leadership and ownership roles is woefully low. It is essential to examine the root of this issue. Traditionally, the narrative of corporate America has not included the Black community as stakeholders but as employees trying to fit into a system that was not designed with their advancement in mind.

The call for diversity and inclusion has been a primary focus in the corporate world. However, the question arises, "Is mere inclusion sufficient?" Arguably, it's not. Inclusion in a system without an equitable share of power and control is akin to tokenism. It is not enough to have a seat at the table if one cannot influence decisions[1750].

Smith Jr. asserts that the goal should not merely be to reform corporate America, but to reframe it, shifting the focus from fitting into corporate America to owning it. This

---

[1748] Anderson, Claud. (2001). "PowerNomics: The National Plan to Empower Black America." Powernomics Corporation of America.

[1749] Bureau of Labor Statistics. (2022). "Labor Force Characteristics by Race and Ethnicity, 2020." BLS Reports.

[1750] Combs, G. M., & Griffith, J. (2007). "An examination of the role of impact on tokenism, perceptions of organizational culture, and employee withdrawal." Journal of Leadership & Organizational Studies.

argument stems from the belief that the Black community has been psychologically conditioned to conform rather than innovate and own.

Critics may argue that the goal of ownership is too ambitious and that the focus should be on improving representation and diversity within existing structures. However, this viewpoint limits the potential of Black individuals to existing structures, rather than challenging and changing those structures to better accommodate their ambitions and potential.

Proponents of this perspective argue that increasing Black ownership and control of businesses can create wealth within the Black community, promote economic self-sufficiency, and contribute to societal change. This is not a negation of the need for corporate reforms; instead, it argues for an expansion of ambition, shifting from mere representation to ownership and control. In essence, it is a call for economic self-determination, which is crucial for the empowerment and advancement of any community[1751].

While the journey towards ownership in corporate America is fraught with challenges, it is a goal worth striving for. As Smith Jr. would argue, it is only through owning and innovating rather than conforming and fitting in that the Black community can effect real, lasting change in corporate America.

Unveiling Systemic Disparities That Cannot Be Overlooked In The Private Sector

The examination of Black participation in the private sector unveils systemic disparities that cannot be overlooked. It has been found that Black workers are not

---

[1751] Boston, T. D. (1999). "Affirmative Action and Black Entrepreneurship." Routledge.

situated in regions where the job market is growing most rapidly[1752]. For instance, less than one in ten Black workers live in the fastest-growing cities, such as Provo, Utah. Instead, Black workers are largely located in areas where job growth ranges from low to slightly above average, with mega-cities like Chicago and urban peripheries such as Clayton County, Georgia, standing as exceptions.

An important aspect to note is that for these areas to experience inclusive growth, there needs to be proper connectivity between workers and job opportunities and alignment of skills with in-demand jobs[1753]. This can involve improving transportation systems between Black neighborhoods and job locations, or enhancing vocational training programs to equip Black workers with the required skills.

The analysis further shows that Black workers are disproportionately represented in certain industries. Almost half of Black workers are employed in three industries—health-care, retail, and accommodation and food service—which are characterized by a significant frontline-service presence and lower wages. For example, in retail, 73 percent of Black workers earn less than $30,000 annually, and this figure jumps to 84 percent in accommodations and food services[1754].

In contrast, Black workers are underrepresented in high-growth, high-wage industries such as information technology, professional services, and financial services. These sectors usually offer higher wages and more opportunities for advancement[1755].

[1752] Kishi, R. (2021). "Race in the Workplace: The Black Experience in the U.S. Private Sector." McKinsey & Company.
[1753] Anderson, C. (2001). "PowerNomics: The National Plan to Empower Black America." Powernomics Corporation of America.
[1754] Kishi, R. (2021). "Race in the Workplace: The Black Experience in the U.S. Private Sector." McKinsey & Company.
[1755] Kishi, R. (2021). "Race in the Workplace: The Black Experience in the U.S. Private Sector." McKinsey & Company.

Moreover, the data reveals a disconcerting reality: 43 percent of Black private-sector workers make less than $30,000 per year compared with 29 percent of the rest of private-sector employees[1756]. Such statistics highlight the pressing issue of economic disparities among Black workers.

Opponents of this perspective may contend that these disparities are not systemic but are simply due to the individual choices of Black workers, leading to their overrepresentation in certain low-wage industries. However, such an argument fails to consider the historical and institutional barriers that have constrained the choices available to Black workers[1757].

The importance of these data is to not merely illustrate the stark economic disparities faced by Black workers but also to underscore the systemic changes needed to address these disparities. It is not sufficient to simply acknowledge these issues, but efforts should be made to facilitate the mobility of Black workers into high-wage industries and to foster inclusive growth in regions where Black workers are predominantly situated.

The Underrepresentation and Automation Threats Facing Black Workers

As we grapple with the evolving landscape of work due to technological advancements, one stark reality is the disproportionate threat automation poses to Black workers. It's estimated that one-third of Black workers are involved in occupational areas such as production work, food service, and office support. These roles are particularly vulnerable to

---

[1756] Kishi, R. (2021). "Race in the Workplace: The Black Experience in the U.S. Private Sector." McKinsey & Company.
[1757] Anderson, C. (2001). "PowerNomics: The National Plan to Empower Black America." Powernomics Corporation of America.

automation and potential job losses[1758]. The silver lining might be the projected job growth in health aides occupations, a field where Black workers are notably represented.

However, critics might contend that such disruptions due to automation are universal and not restricted to any specific racial or ethnic group. While it is true that automation will affect workers across all races, it is essential to recognize that the risk is more profound for Black workers due to their overrepresentation in roles susceptible to automation[1759].

Moreover, disparities are not limited to potential job losses due to automation. The job prospects for Black workers and white workers with comparable backgrounds are significantly different. An example of such disparity is found in the employment rates: Black workers with some college or an associate's degree have similar employment rates to the general population of workers with only a high school diploma[1760]. This shows the disproportionately high barriers Black workers face in gaining meaningful employment.

Critics might argue that such differences are due to individual choices or capabilities, but such viewpoints neglect the systemic and institutional biases present in hiring and employment practices[1761].

In our survey of 24 companies across various sizes and geographies, with a total representation of about 3.7 million U.S employees, it became apparent that Black workers encounter representation gaps at every step. Despite

---

[1758] Manyika, J., et al. (2019). "The Future of Work in Black America." McKinsey & Company.
[1759] Anderson, C. (2001). "PowerNomics: The National Plan to Empower Black America." Powernomics Corporation of America.
[1760] Kishi, R. (2021). "Race in the Workplace: The Black Experience in the U.S. Private Sector." McKinsey & Company.
[1761] Anderson, C. (2001). "PowerNomics: The National Plan to Empower Black America." Powernomics Corporation of America.

successful hiring of Black employees into front-line and entry-level jobs, a significant drop-off in representation is observed at the management levels[1762]. For instance, Black employees make up 14 percent of all employees but only 7 percent at the managerial level, dropping further to 4 to 5 percent at senior manager, VP, and SVP levels.

The need to address these disparities is pressing. They represent a systemic issue that transcends individual company policies and practices. Hence, the imperative for broader, more significant societal and institutional changes in addressing these issues is evident.

Envisioning Ownership as a Pathway to Economic Empowerment

In light of the data and Dr. Claud Anderson's perspective on Black economic empowerment, it is compelling to consider Antonio T. Smith Jr.'s proposal: that the Black community must go beyond simply fitting into the structure of corporate America and aspire to ownership and control. This vision aligns with Anderson's emphasis on Black ownership as a critical stepping stone for overcoming systemic barriers[1763].

The need for this shift in focus becomes evident when we observe the representation of Black workers in corporate America. While making up 12 percent of the private-sector workforce, their presence in leadership roles remains disproportionately low[1764]. Critics may argue that this should be addressed by enhancing diversity and representation. Still, Smith Jr. and Anderson challenge this

---

[1762] Kishi, R. (2021). "Race in the Workplace: The Black Experience in the U.S. Private Sector." McKinsey & Company.
[1763] Anderson, C. (2001). "PowerNomics: The National Plan to Empower Black America." Powernomics Corporation of America.
[1764] Kishi, R. (2021). "Race in the Workplace: The Black Experience in the U.S. Private Sector." McKinsey & Company.

perspective, contending that inclusion without equity is mere tokenism.

Smith Jr. asserts that a reformation of corporate America is necessary but insufficient. Instead, the goal should be to reframe corporate America, placing Black ownership and control at its core. Such a shift would not only benefit the Black community through wealth creation and self-sufficiency, but it would also be a catalyst for societal change.

This notion may seem too ambitious to skeptics who prefer to work within existing structures. Still, Smith Jr. and Anderson argue that the Black community's potential should not be confined to these structures. Instead, they should be reshaped to fully accommodate the ambitions and potential of Black individuals.

Smith Jr. envisions a future where Black individuals do not merely fit into corporate America but own and shape it. He acknowledges the significant challenges that lie ahead but maintains that they are worth confronting for the sake of real, enduring change[1765]. This vision of ownership and control signifies more than just economic success; it symbolizes self-determination, empowerment, and a vital step towards dismantling systemic barriers in corporate America.

My Final Words

It's essential to note that the task at hand is an enduring commitment, not a transient project. However, history has proven that persistent, unified effort can yield substantial changes. This is the spirit we need to nurture and cultivate

---

[1765] Anderson, C. (2001). "PowerNomics: The National Plan to Empower Black America." Powernomics Corporation of America.

as we work towards restructuring the socio-economic landscape for Black communities using The Power Matrix.

We stand at the precipice of a significant cultural and economic shift. The information age has disrupted traditional economic models and created new opportunities for wealth creation and group economics. At the heart of this shift is a movement towards autonomy, innovation, and community control. It is in this context that I invented Power Matrix was born.

It envisions a future where Black communities are not just participants in the global economy, but drivers of it. This involves a transformation on multiple fronts—economics, finance, data information, manufacturing, infrastructure, communications, and human resources. Each of these elements is a gear in the machinery of community transformation, and together, they form the core of a robust, self-sustaining economic ecosystem.

A paradigm shift of this magnitude requires both individual and collective action. Every member of the Black community has a role to play in this grand vision. It is a collective calling to business owners, industry leaders, innovators, educators, parents, and youth. We must all commit to supporting Black businesses, investing in Black talent, promoting Black creativity, and, above all, nurturing Black unity.

However, change on this scale cannot occur overnight. We need to exercise patience, persistence, and resilience in the face of setbacks and challenges. In every failure, there are lessons to learn and strength to gain. As we move forward, it is essential to celebrate our victories, no matter how small, as they are milestones on the path to greater success.

Crucially, the Power Matrix is not just about economic prosperity; it's also about building a strong, vibrant community. Our goal is not only to create wealth but also to ensure that this wealth circulates within the community, promoting prosperity for all. In doing so, we also seek to reduce socio-economic disparities, ensure fair representation, and elevate the collective voice of the Black community.

The Power Matrix is not a rigid blueprint but a living, evolving model. As we progress, we must be willing to adapt and adjust to changing circumstances and emerging opportunities. Innovation, flexibility, and adaptability are as essential as determination and resilience in this journey towards socio-economic transformation.

As we embark on this journey, remember that the Power Matrix is not just Antonio T. Smith Jr.'s plan. It's a masterplan for all of us—for every individual, family, and business within the Black community. It's a road-map towards a future of shared prosperity and economic power, where Black wealth is not the exception but the norm.

As we close this volume, let us reiterate that the Power Matrix is not an endpoint, but a starting point—a spark to ignite the flame of transformation. The real work begins now, with each of us playing our part in making this vision a reality.

To my brothers and sisters in the Black community, let us step into this moment with resolve and conviction. Our time is now. Let us rise, unite, and prosper together. Our future is in our hands. Let us shape it with the power of the Matrix.

Stay Tuned For Volume II
Re-Segregation Vol II: The Facts of Black Oppression And The Unfair Abuse Facing The White Ally

In the forthcoming volume of Re-Segregation, subtitled "The Facts of Black Oppression And The Unfair Abuse Facing The White Ally," we delve further into the racial wealth gap, systemic oppression, and the often-misunderstood role of allies in the fight for equality.

BIBLIOGRAPHY

1. "2017 Annual Business Survey." U.S. Census Bureau, 2017.
2. "2021 Infrastructure Report Card." American Society of Civil Engineers, 2021.
3. "A Preliminary Analysis of Opportunity Zone Implementation." Urban Institute, 2020.
4. "Advancing Black Entrepreneurship: A Guide for Policymakers." Brookings Institution, October 15, 2020.
5. "Affirmative Action and Minority Enrollment in Medical and Law Schools: A Pipeline Analysis." American Psychologica5o2l Association, 2018.
6. "Apprenticeship Programs are a Ticket to the Middle Class." Center for American Progress, 2018.
7. "Bank Enterprise Award Program." CDFI Fund, 2021.
8. "Barriers to Entry in Industrial Sector for Minority Entrepreneurs." Journal of Industrial Economics, 2019.
9. "Bitcoin Price Index from October 2013 to October 2021 (in U.S. dollars)." Statista, accessed June 20, 2023.
10. "Black Americans Are Denied Mortgages At A Rate 80% Higher Than White Americans, Study Shows." Forbes.
11. "Black businesses matter: Supporting Black-owned businesses to narrow racial wealth gap." Brookings Institution, 2020.
12. "Black Entrepreneurs Still Face Hurdles in Securing Financing." The Washington Post, February 23, 2022.
13. "Black in Green (BIG)." Accessed 20 June, 2023. "Black in Green (BIG)." Accessed 20 June, 2023. https://www.blacksingreen.org/home
14. "Black Wall Street: The African American Haven That Burned and Then Rose From the Ashes." The Conversation, 2020.
15. "Black-Owned Blockchain Companies Making Waves." AfroTech, 2021.
16. "Blavity: The Website Made for Black Millennials." The Observer, www.observer.com.
17. "Blockchain for Social Impact: Moving Beyond the Hype." Stanford Center for Social Innovation, 2018.
18. "Breakthrough Innovation and Growth." PwC, www.pwc.com/gx/en/ceo-survey/2013/assets/pwc-16th-annual-global-ceo-survey-breakthrough-innovation-and-growth.pdf.
19. "Bridging the Skills Gap in the Manufacturing Industry." Deloitte Insights, 2020.

20. "Building Wealth Together Through Collective Investment Clubs." Black Enterprise, June 3, 2019.
21. "Changes in U.S. Family Finances from 2016 to 2019: Evidence from the Survey of Consumer Finances." Federal Reserve Bulletin, vol. 106, no. 5, Sept. 2020.
22. "Collaboration: The Key to Small Business Success." U.S. Small Business Administration, 2019.
23. "Collective Investment Models." Shared Capital Cooperative, 2020.
24. "Discrimination in Lending: Implications for Economic Inequality." Brookings Institution.
25. "Diversity in High Tech." U.S. Equal Employment Opportunity Commission. Accessed March 25, 2023.
26. "Does Financial Literacy Contribute to Wealth Equality?" Journal of Consumer Affairs, 2019.
27. "Enforcement of the Community Reinvestment Act Has Been Weak." The Washington Post, February 20, 2022.
28. "Examining the Black-white wealth gap." Brookings Institution. https://www.brookings.edu/blog/up-front/2020/02/27/examining-the-black-white-wealth-gap/
29. "Execution is More Important Than Ideas: What Research Says?" Entrepreneur, www.entrepreneur.com.
30. "Explaining the Black-White home-ownership Gap: A Closer Look at Disparities across Local Markets." Urban Institute.
31. "Fastest Growing Occupations." U.S. Bureau of Labor Statistics, accessed June 23, 2023.
32. "Federal Reserve System Purposes & Functions." Federal Reserve, 2016.
33. "Financial Education and the Keys to Economic Empowerment." Federal Reserve Bank of St. Louis, 2018.
34. "Financial Institutions: Definition, Types, Role, Importance." Corporate Finance Institute.
35. "Financial Literacy and Black-Owned Banks in the Fight Against Racial Wealth Inequality." Urban Institute, 2020.
36. "Financial Literacy and Black-Owned Banks in the Fight Against Racial Wealth Inequality." Urban Institute, 2022.
37. "Financial Literacy and Economic Outcomes." Federal Reserve Bulletin, 2016.
38. "Future of Jobs Report." World Economic Forum, 2020.
39. "Generational Wealth and Why It Matters." Center for American Progress, 2021.

40. "Gentrification, Displacement and the Role of Public Investment." Federal Reserve Bank of San Francisco, 2015.
41. "Green Economy Report." United Nations Environment Programme, www.unep.org/greeneconomy.
42. "How Diverse Leadership Teams Boost Innovation." Boston Consulting Group, www.bcg.com.
43. "How Green is U.S. Manufacturing? An Analysis of Energy Use and Greenhouse Gas Emissions." The National Academies Press, 2013.
44. "How Housing Policy Is Failing America's Poor." The Atlantic, June 25, 2015.
45. "How Investment Clubs Perform." National Association of Investors Corporation, 2006.
46. "How This Real Estate Fund Is Bringing Ownership Back to the Black Community." CNBC, May 27, 2020.
47. "How to Start a Bank." TRUiC, 2023.
48. "How to Start an Investment Club." The Balance, March 2, 2022.
49. "How Tyler Perry Built a Billion-Dollar Empire." The Hollywood Reporter, www.hollywoodreporter.com.
50. "Infrastructure as a Service." Investopedia. Accessed March 25, 2023.
51. "Innovation drives growth." PwC, www.pwc.com/gx/en/ceo-agenda/innovation-drives-growth.html.
52. "Innovation: A Risk Worth Taking?" Deloitte, www.deloitte.com.
53. "Is Graduate School Worth It? A Comprehensive Return on Investment Analysis." Payscale, 2021.
54. "Is Tech Closing the Wealth Gap or Making It Worse?" Fortune, www.fortune.com.
55. "Janice Bryant Howroyd: First African American Woman to Run a $1-Billion Business." Black Enterprise, www.blackenterprise.com.
56. "Lobbying: The Art of Policy Change." Harvard Business Review, 2018.
57. "Manufacturing and Minority Business Development." National Minority Business Council, 2020.
58. "Mented Cosmetics Founders Make History As 15th, 16th Black Women Ever To Raise $1M Capital." Forbes, www.forbes.com.
59. "Minority Banks and Their Primary Local Market Areas." National Community Reinvestment Coalition.
60. "Minority Depository Institutions: Structure, Performance, and Social Impact." Federal Deposit Insurance Corporation.

61. "Minority-Owned Firms' Access to Capital." U.S. Small Business Administration, 2020.
62. "Minority-Owned Firms' Access to Capital." U.S. Small Business Administration, 2021.
63. "Minority-Owned Firms' Access to Capital." U.S. Small Business Administration.
64. "MoCaFi." MoCaFi, https://mocafi.com/ (accessed June 24, 2023).
65. "Netflix to Invest $100 Million in Black-Owned Banks." The New York Times, 2020.
66. "OneUnited Bank: Largest Black Owned Bank." OneUnited Bank, n.d.
67. "Operating Agreement for LLCs: What You Need to Know." Business News Daily, January 21, 2021.
68. "Opportunity Zones." Internal Revenue Service, 2021.
69. "Organic Market Overview." U.S. Department of Agriculture, accessed June 24, 2023.
70. "P&G Acquires Walker & Company, Tristan Walker Will Remain as CEO." Black Enterprise, www.blackenterprise.com.
71. "Performance and Profitability of Minority Depository Institutions, 2001-2019." Federal Deposit Insurance Corporation.
72. "Platform as a Service." Investopedia. Accessed March 25, 2023.
73. "Procurement Policies and Economic Inclusion: A Path to Urban Revitalization." National Urban League, 2019.
74. "Progressive Taxation and Wealth Redistribution: An Argument for Economic Equality." Economic Policy Institute, October 15, 2021.
75. "Public Awareness Campaigns and Policy Outcomes." Journal of Policy Analysis and Management, 2020.
76. "Racial Discrimination in the U.S. Banking Industry." ThoughtCo, 2020.
77. "Racial Economic Disparity in the U.S." Brookings Institution, 2020.
78. "Racial Inequality in the U.S. Labor Market." Center for Economic and Policy Research, 2020.
79. "Regulation of Collective Investment Schemes." IOSCO, 2020.
80. "Retirement Inequality Chartbook." Economic Policy Institute, accessed June 23, 2023.
81. "Robert F. Smith: The Billionaire Who Is Trying to Go His Own Way." The New York Times, www.nytimes.com.
82. "S&P 500 Historical Annual Returns." MacroTrends, accessed June 20, 2023.

83. "Self-Reliance vs. Government Support: A False Choice." Forbes, March 13, 2022.
84. "Shea Moisture's Path To Becoming a Multimillion-Dollar Beauty Brand." Forbes, www.forbes.com.
85. "Software as a Service." Investopedia. Accessed March 25, 2023.
86. "Southern Reparations Loan Fund." Southern Reparations Loan Fund, accessed February 1, 2023.
87. "Start Your Own Manufacturing Business or Make Your Existing Business More Profitable." Manufacturing Business Institute, 2021.
88. "Strategic Alliances for SME Development." United Nations Industrial Development Organization, 2001.
89. "Structural Racism and the Wealth Gap." Center for American Progress, July 15, 2020.
90. "Tax Incentives and the City." Brookings Institute, 2018.
91. "Tax Policy and Economic Inequality in the United States." The Balance, January 20, 2022.
92. "Tech's Favorite School Faces Its Biggest Test: the Real World." Bloomberg, 2020.
93. "The 10 Best Peer-To-Peer Lending Sites." Investopedia, 2023.
94. "The AI Spring: How Artificial Intelligence Might Help Us Live Happier and Healthier Lives." World Economic Forum, 2018.
95. "The Bank Black Movement." OneUnited Bank, n.d.
96. "The Basics of Forming a Limited Liability Company (LLC)." Inc., July 20, 2020.
97. "The Best Micro Investing Apps." Forbes, 2023.
98. "The Challenges and Opportunities of Community Banking." American Bankers Association, 2019.
99. "The Challenges of Grassroots Organizing." Nonprofit Quarterly, 2020.
100. "The Collective Power of Investment Clubs." Black Enterprise, May 23, 2019.
101. "The Color of Wealth in Boston." Federal Reserve Bank of Boston, 2015.
102. "The Community Reinvestment Act and Its Impact on Racial Disparities in Bank Credit." The Journal of Economics and Business, 2020.
103. "The Creative Dividend: How Creativity Impacts Business Results." Adobe, www.adobe.com.
104. "The Dark Side of Collaboration." Harvard Business Review, 2015.
105. "The Dark Side of Lobbying." Brookings Institute, 2005.

106. "The Economic Impact of Black-Owned Businesses." Economic Policy Institute, 2020.
107. "The Economic Impact of Closing the Racial Wealth Gap." McKinsey & Company, 2019.
108. "The Facts About Modern Manufacturing." The Manufacturing Institute, 2020.
109. "The Future of Work in Black America." McKinsey & Company, 2019.
110. "The Importance of Minority Banks." Federal Reserve Bank of Cleveland, 2020.
111. "The Manufacturing Footprint and the Importance of U.S. Manufacturing Jobs." Economic Policy Institute, 2015.
112. "The Potential of Minority Banks." Federal Reserve Bank of Boston, December 1, 2021.
113. "The Power of Advocacy Alliances." The Chronicle of Philanthropy, 2020.
114. "The Power of One in Three: Creating Opportunities for All to Breathe." Association for Enterprise Opportunity, 2019.
115. "The Power of Persistence." American Psychological Association. https://www.apa.org/gradpsych/2012/11/persistence
116. "The Pros and Cons of Collective Economics." Harvard Business Review, 2017.
117. "The Pros and Cons of Investment Clubs." U.S. News & World Report, February 14, 2018.
118. "The Racial Wealth Gap: Addressing America's Most Pressing Epidemic." Brookings Institution, 2020.
119. "The Risks of Investment Clubs." Investopedia, March 25, 2022.
120. "The Road to Zero Wealth: How the Racial Wealth Divide is Hollowing Out America's Middle Class." Prosperity Now, 2017.
121. "The Role of Black Banks in Reducing the Racial Wealth Gap." Center for Global Policy Solutions, 2016.
122. "The Role of Grassroots Organizing in Policy Advocacy." Stanford Social Innovation Review, 2019.
123. "The Trouble with Preference Policies." The Wall Street Journal, March 25, 2015.
124. "The World's Largest Public Companies." Forbes, www.forbes.com/global2000.
125. "Trends in College Pricing." College Board, 2019.
126. "Tulsa Real Estate Fund." Tulsa Real Estate Fund, https://www.tulsarealestatefund.com/ (accessed June 24, 2023).

127. "U.S. Green Building Council Reports Green Construction Industry to Contribute 3.3 Million Jobs in the U.S." U.S. Green Building Council, 28 Sept. 2021.
128. "U.S. Manufacturing: Output vs. Jobs Since 1975." National Association of Manufacturers, 2021.
129. "Uber's Path of Destruction." American Affairs Journal, www.americanaffairsjournal.org.
130. "What Makes a Successful Entrepreneur? Persistence, Persistence, Persistence." The Guardian, www.theguardian.com.
131. "Why Are There So Few Black-Owned Banks?" The Balance, 2020.
132. "Why Are There So Few Black-Owned Banks?" The Balance, 2022.
133. "Why Are There So Few Black-Owned Banks?" The Balance.
134. "Why Are There So Few Black-Owned Businesses in America?" Forbes, 2020.
135. "Why Minority Set-Asides Are Essential for Economic Equality." The Nation, August 11, 2018.
136. "Zoning Policies and Economic Disparity: A Closer Look." Urban Institute, January 15, 2020.
137. Abeyratne, S.A., & Monfared, R.P. (2016). 'Blockchain Ready Manufacturing Supply Chain Using Distributed Ledger.' International Journal of Research in Engineering and Technology, 5(9), 1–10.
138. Adner, Ron. "Ecosystem as Structure: An Actionable Construct for Strategy." Journal of Management, 43(1), 2017.
139. Aernoudt, Rudy. "Incubators: Tool for Entrepreneurship?" Small Business Economics, vol. 23, 2004, pp. 127-135.
140. African Union and European Union. (2019). 'Africa-EU Digital Economy Task Force Report.'
141. Albert Bandura, "Self-Efficacy: Toward a Unifying Theory of Behavioral Change," Psychological Review 84, no. 2 (1977): 191-215.
142. Aldrich, Howard E., and Roger Waldinger. "Ethnicity and Entrepreneurship." Annual Review of Sociology, vol. 16, no. 1, 1990, pp. 111-135.
143. Aldridge, Susan. "The Growth Mindset Debate." Inside Higher Ed, 2019.
144. Alexander, Michelle. "The New Jim Crow: Mass Incarceration in the Age of Colorblindness." The New Press, 2010.
145. Algorithmic Justice League. (2021). 'About.' Algorithmic Justice League.

146. Allegretto, Sylvia A., and Lawrence Mishel. "The Teacher Weekly Wage Penalty Hit 21.4 Percent in 2018, a Record High." Economic Policy Institute, September 2019.
147. Alter, Alexandra. "Amanda Hocking, the Writer Who Made Millions by Self-Publishing Online." The New York Times, www.nytimes.com.
148. Amabile, Teresa. "The Progress Principle: Using Small Wins to Ignite Joy, Engagement, and Creativity at Work." Harvard Business Review Press, 2011.
149. American Association of Blacks in Energy. "Blacks in Energy: Challenges and Opportunities," 2019.
150. American Bar Association. "ABA Profile of the Legal Profession." 2020.
151. Anderson, C. "Collective Investment: The Key to Black Wealth." PowerNomics Corporation of America, 2023.
152. Anderson, C. "The Power of Collective Investment." PowerNomics Corporation of America, 2023.
153. Anderson, C. (2001). "Black Labor, White Wealth: The Search for Power and Economic Justice." PowerNomics Corporation of America.
154. Anderson, C. (2001). "PowerNomics: The National Plan to Empower Black America." Powernomics Corporation of America.
155. Anderson, C. (2001). 'Black labor, white wealth: The search for power and economic justice.' Powernomics Corporation of America.
156. Anderson, C. (2001). PowerNomics: The National Plan to Empower Black America. PowerNomics Corporation of America.
157. Anderson, C. (2005). 'The More Things Change, the More They Stay the Same: A Black Perspective on Information Technology.' Journal of Black Studies, 35(5), 375-386.
158. Anderson, Chris. "The Long Tail: Why the Future of Business is Selling Less of More." Hyperion, 2006.
159. Anderson, Claud. "A Black History Reader: 101 Question You Never Thought to Ask." PowerNomics Corporation of America, 2017.
160. Anderson, Claud. "A Black History Reader: 101 Questions You Never Thought to Ask." Powernomics Corporation of America, 2017.
161. Anderson, Claud. "Black Labor, White Wealth : The Search for Power and Economic Justice." Powernomics Corporation of America, 1994.

162. Anderson, Claud. "Black Labor, White Wealth: The Search for Power and Economic Justice." PowerNomics Corporation of America, 1994.
163. Anderson, Claud. "Dirty Little Secrets About Black History, Its Heroes, and Other Troublemakers." PowerNomics Corporation of America, 2001.
164. Anderson, Claud. "More Dirty Little Secrets About Black History, Its Heroes, and Other Troublemakers." PowerNomics Corporation of America, 2006.
165. Anderson, Claud. "PowerNomics : The National Plan to Empower Black America." Powernomics Corporation of America, 2001.
166. Anderson, Claud. "PowerNomics: The National Plan to Empower Black America." PowerNomics Corporation of America, 2001.
167. Anderson, Claud. "The Role of Public Policy in Economic Empowerment." PowerNomics Corporation of America, 2023.
168. Anderson, Claud. (2001). "PowerNomics: The National Plan to Empower Black America." Powernomics Corporation of America.
169. Anderson, Claud. A Black History Reader: 101 Question You Never Thought to Ask. PowerNomics Corporation of America, 2017.
170. Anderson, Claud. A Black History Reader: 101 Questions You Never Thought to Ask. PowerNomics Corporation of America, 2017.
171. Anderson, Claud. Black Labor, White Wealth: The Search for Power and Economic Justice. PowerNomics Corporation of America, 1994.
172. Anderson, Claud. Black Labor, White Wealth: The Search for Power and Economic Justice. PowerNomics Corporation of America, Inc, 1994.
173. Anderson, Claud. More Dirty Little Secrets About Black History, Its Heroes, and Other Troublemakers. PowerNomics Corporation of America, 2006.
174. Anderson, Claud. PowerNomics : The National Plan to Empower Black America. Powernomics Corporation of America, 2001.
175. Anderson, Claud. PowerNomics: The National Plan to Empower Black America. PowerNomics Corporation of America, 2001.
176. Anderson, PowerNomics.

177. Annamaria Lusardi and Olivia S. Mitchell, "The Economic Importance of Financial Literacy: Theory and Evidence," Journal of Economic Literature 52, no. 1 (2014): 5-44.
178. Arntz, M., Gregory, T., & Zierahn, U. (2016). "The Risk of Automation for Jobs in OECD Countries: A Comparative Analysis." OECD Social, Employment and Migration Working Papers, No. 189, OECD Publishing, Paris.
179. Arntz, M., Gregory, T., & Zierahn, U. (2016). 'The Risk of Automation for Jobs in OECD Countries: A Comparative Analysis.' OECD Social, Employment and Migration Working Papers, No. 189, OECD Publishing, Paris.
180. Arntz, M., Gregory, T., & Zierahn, U. (2016). 'The Risk of Automation for Jobs in OECD Countries: A Comparative Analysis.' OECD Social, Employment and Migration Working Papers.
181. Arthur, W.B. (2009). 'The Nature of Technology: What It Is and How It Evolves.' New York: Free Press.
182. Asante-Muhammad, Dedrick et al. "The Road to Zero Wealth: How the Racial Wealth Divide is Hollowing Out America's Middle Class." Prosperity Now and Institute for Policy Studies, September 2017.
183. Ash, Elliott, Daniel L. Chen, and Arianna Ornaghi. "Stereotypes in High-Performing Professions: A Randomized Study of Economists." Proceedings of the National Academy of Sciences, 2019.
184. Ash, Elliott, Daniel L. Chen, and Arianna Ornaghi. "Stereotypes in High-Performing Professions: A Randomized Study of Economists." Proceedings of the National Academy of Sciences, 2020.
185. Ashcraft, C., & Breitzman, A. (2020). 'Who Invents IT? An Analysis of Women's Participation in Information Technology Patenting.' National Center for Women & Information Technology.
186. Ashcraft, C., McLain, B., & Eger, E. (2016). 'Women in tech: The facts.' National Center for Women & Information Technology.
187. Ashley M. Fox, "The Social Determinants of Health in Poverty," Health Affairs, November 18, 2016, https://www.healthaffairs.org/doi/full/10.1377/hlthaff.2016.1153.
188. Asiedu, E., Freeman, J., & Nti-Addae, A. (2012). Access to Credit by Small Businesses: How Relevant Are Race, Ethnicity, and Gender? American Economic Review.
189. Association for Enterprise Opportunity. "The Tapestry of Black Business Ownership in America." 2017.

190. Association of American Medical Colleges. "Diversity in Medicine: Facts and Figures 2019."
191. Atkinson, Robert D., and Michael Lind. "Big is Beautiful: Debunking the Myth of Small Business." The MIT Press, 2018.
192. Atkinson, Robert D., and Michael Lind. Big Is Beautiful: Debunking the Myth of Small Business. MIT Press, 2018.
193. Bandura, "Self-Efficacy."
194. Bandura, A., & Locke, E. A. (2003). Negative self-efficacy and goal effects revisited. Journal of Applied Psychology, 88(1), 87.
195. Bank for International Settlements. (2020). "Payment and settlement systems in the digital age."
196. Baradaran, M. (2017). "The Color of Money: Black Banks and the Racial Wealth Gap." Harvard University Press.
197. Baradaran, M. (2017). The Color of Money: Black Banks and the Racial Wealth Gap. Belknap Press.
198. Baradaran, M. (2017). The Color of Money: Black Banks and the Racial Wealth Gap. The Belknap Press of Harvard University Press.
199. Baradaran, Mehrsa. "The Color of Money: Black Banks and the Racial Wealth Gap." Harvard University Press, 2017.
200. Baradaran, Mehrsa. "The Color of Money: Black Banks and the Racial Wealth Gap." The Belknap Press of Harvard University Press, 2017.
201. Barr, Michael S. "Minority and Women Entrepreneurs: Building Capital, Networks, and Skills." The Hamilton Project, March 2015.
202. Bartlett, Robert, et al. "Consumer-Lending Discrimination in the FinTech Era." NBER, 2019.
203. Bates, T., & Robb, A. (2013). Greater Access to Capital Is Needed to Unleash the Local Economic Development Potential of Minority-Owned Businesses. Economic Development Quarterly.
204. Bates, T., & Robb, A. (2013). Race, ethnicity, and entrepreneurial success: Evidence from the characteristics of business owners survey. Small Business Economics.
205. Bates, T., & Robb, A. (2014). Has the Community Reinvestment Act Increased Loan Availability among Small Businesses Operating in Minority Neighbourhoods? Urban Studies.
206. Bayer, Amanda, and Cecilia Elena Rouse. "Diversity in the Economics Profession: A New Attack on an Old Problem." Journal of Economic Perspectives 30, no. 4 (2016): 221-42.
207. Bayer, Amanda, and Cecilia Elena Rouse. "Diversity in the Economics Profession: A New Attack on an Old Problem." Journal of Economic Perspectives, vol. 30, no. 4, 2016, pp. 221-42.

208. Benjamin, R. "Race After Technology: Abolitionist Tools for the New Jim Code." Polity, 2019.
209. Benjamin, R. (2019). 'Race after technology: Abolitionist tools for the new Jim Code.' Polity.
210. Bera, Sophia. "The Importance of Saving Money: 7 Reasons to Start Saving Today." Gen Y Planning, 2016.
211. Berger, Allen N., et al. "Does Function Follow Organizational Form? Evidence From the Lending Practices of Large and Small Banks." Journal of Financial Economics, 2005.
212. Berriman, R., & Hawksworth, J. (2017). 'Sizing the prize: What's the real value of AI for your business and how can you capitalize?' PwC.
213. Bertrand, Marianne and Mullainathan, Sendhil. "Are Emily and Greg More Employable Than Lakisha and Jamal? A Field Experiment on Labor Market Discrimination." National Bureau of Economic Research, 2004.
214. Bertrand, Marianne, and Adair Morse. "Trickle-Down Consumption." Review of Economics and Statistics, 2016.
215. Bhattacharya, Utpal, Benjamin Loos, Steffen Meyer, and Andreas Hackethal. "Abusing Financial Advice." The Review of Financial Studies, 2012.
216. Blakely, E. J., & Leigh, N. G. (2010). Planning Local Economic Development: Theory and Practice. SAGE Publications.
217. Blau, Francine D., and Andrea Beller. "Wage inequality among men and women: The role of the workplace." Industrial Relations Section, Princeton University, 1992.
218. BlocPower. "About Us," 2023.
219. Board of Governors of the Federal Reserve System. "Report on the Economic Well-Being of U.S. Households in 2018." 2019.
220. Board of Governors of the Federal Reserve System. "Report on the Economic Well-Being of U.S. Households in 2020."
221. Bogan, R. (2020). The Power of the Black Dollar and The Rise of Black Entrepreneurs. Black Enterprise.
222. Bogan, Vicki L., and William Darity Jr. "Culture and Entrepreneurship? African American and Immigrant Self-Employment in the United States." The Journal of Socio-Economics, vol. 37, no. 5, 2008, pp. 1999-2019.
223. Bondonio, Daniele, and John Engberg. "Enterprise Zones and Local Employment: Evidence from the States' Programs." Regional Science and Urban Economics, vol. 30, no. 5, 2000, pp. 519-549.

224. Bonilla-Silva, Eduardo. Racism without Racists: Color-Blind Racism and the Persistence of Racial Inequality in America. Rowman & Littlefield, 2017.
225. Booth, Laurence D., and Richard L. Smith. "Capital market imperfections and the incentive to lease." Journal of Financial Economics, vol. 30, no. 2, 1991, pp. 271-291.
226. Boston, T. D. (1999). "Affirmative Action and Black Entrepreneurship." Routledge.
227. Boston, Thomas D. "Affirmative Action and Black Entrepreneurship." The Review of Black Political Economy, vol. 26, no. 4, 1999, pp. 7-19.
228. Bostrom, N., & Yudkowsky, E. (2014). 'The ethics of artificial intelligence.' Cambridge Handbook of Artificial Intelligence, 1, 316-334.
229. Bowen, William G., and Derek Bok. The Shape of the River: Long-Term Consequences of Considering Race in College and University Admissions. Princeton University Press, 1998.
230. Boyd, Michelle D. "Black Bourgeoisie and Black Common Folk: An Analysis of Class-Based Ideological Cleavages in Black Chicago's Community Development Discourse." Journal of Black Studies, vol. 41, no. 1, 2010, pp. 3-26.
231. Boyd, R. L. (1998). Race, Labor Market Disadvantage, and Survivalist Entrepreneurship: Black Women in the Urban North during the Great Depression. Sociological Forum.
232. Bradford, W. D. (2003). The Wealth Dynamics of Entrepreneurship for Black and White Families in the U.S. Review of Income and Wealth.
233. Bradford, W. D. (2014). The "Myth" That Black Entrepreneurship Can Reduce the Gap in Wealth Between Black and White Families. Economic Development Quarterly.
234. Bradford, William D. "The 'Myth' that Black Entrepreneurship Can Reduce the Gap in Wealth between Black and White Families." Economic Development Quarterly, vol. 23, no. 3, 2009, pp. 225-231.
235. Bradford, William D. "The Wealth Gap in Black America: Past Trends and Future Prospects," Journal of Black Studies, 2014.
236. Brookings Institution, "The Digital Divide and Economic Disparities," 2023.
237. Brown, N., et al. (2016). 'Investigating the Relationship between High School Preparation, Social Supports, and Academic Outcomes.' Peabody Journal of Education.

238. Bruton, Garry D., et al. "Bridging the Conceptual Divide: The Role of Entrepreneurship in Black Wealth Creation." Academy of Management Perspectives, vol. 34, no. 3, 2020, pp. 367-384.
239. Bryant, Kevin D. "Mentoring, Social Capital, and the Economic Mobility of Young Black Males: Moving from 'Network' to 'Mentor-Set'." Urban Education, 53.5 (2018): 640-661.
240. Brynjolfsson, E. and McAfee, A. (2014). 'The Second Machine Age: Work, Progress, and Prosperity in a Time of Brilliant Technologies.' New York: W. W. Norton & Company.
241. Brynjolfsson, E., & McAfee, A. (2014). 'The Second Machine Age: Work, Progress, and Prosperity in a Time of Brilliant Technologies.' W. W. Norton & Company.
242. Buchanan, Larry, Quoctrung Bui, and Claire Miller. "Why Tech Degrees Are Not Putting More Blacks and Hispanics Into Tech Jobs." The New York Times, October 25, 2016.
243. Bugg-Levine, Antony, and Jed Emerson. "Impact investing: Transforming how we make money while making a difference." Innovations: Technology, Governance, Globalization vol. 6, no. 3, 2011, pp. 9-18.
244. Bughin, J., Chui, M., & Manyika, J. (2013). "Ten IT-enabled business trends for the decade ahead." McKinsey Quarterly.
245. Bughin, J., et al. "Skill shift: Automation and the future of the workforce." McKinsey Global Institute, 2018.
246. Bughin, J., Hazan, E., Ramaswamy, S., Chui, M., Allas, T., Dahlstrom, P., ... & Trench, M. (2017). 'Artificial Intelligence: The Next Digital Frontier?' McKinsey Global Institute.
247. Buku, Mwawi W., and Richard Boateng. "Digital exclusion: A threat to universal access to financial services in sub-Saharan Africa?" African Journal of Science, Technology, Innovation and Development, vol. 11, no. 5, 2019, pp. 637-648.
248. Bullard, Robert D. "Environmental Racism and Invisible Communities," West Virginia Law Review, 1994.
249. Bundles, A'Lelia. "Madam C.J. Walker Biography." Biography.com, 2021. https://www.biography.com/inventor/madam-cj-walker
250. Bundles, A'Lelia. "On Her Own Ground: The Life and Times of Madam C.J. Walker." Simon and Schuster, 2001.
251. Bundles, A'Lelia. On Her Own Ground: The Life and Times of Madam C.J. Walker. Scribner, 2001.
252. Bunz, Mercedes. "The Silent Revolution: How Digitalization Transforms Knowledge, Work, Journalism and Politics Without Making Too Much Noise." Palgrave Macmillan, 2014.

253. Buolamwini, J., & Gebru, T. (2018). 'Gender Shades: Intersectional Accuracy Disparities in Commercial Gender Classification.' Proceedings of Machine Learning Research.
254. Buolamwini, Joy, and Gebru, Timnit. "Gender Shades: Intersectional Accuracy Disparities in Commercial Gender Classification." Proceedings of Machine Learning Research, 2018.
255. Bureau of Labor Statistics, U.S. Department of Labor, "Highlights of Women's Earnings in 2019." BLS Reports, November 2020.
256. Bureau of Labor Statistics, U.S. Department of Labor, "Usual Weekly Earnings of Wage and Salary Workers First Quarter 2020," April 2020.
257. Bureau of Labor Statistics. "Business Employment Dynamics." United States Department of Labor, 2020.
258. Bureau of Labor Statistics. "Labor Force Characteristics by Race and Ethnicity, 2018." 2020.
259. Bureau of Labor Statistics. "Labor Force Statistics from the Current Population Survey." 2021.
260. Bureau of Labor Statistics. "Racial, ethnic, and gender disparities in income and wealth." BLS Reports, 2021.
261. Bureau of Labor Statistics. (2022). "Labor Force Characteristics by Race and Ethnicity, 2020." BLS Reports.
262. Burey, Jeb. "The Danger of Failing Forward: Normalizing Failure Has Its Own Risks." Medium, 2020. https://medium.com/swlh/the-danger-of-failing-forward-8b7e69c9c5ea
263. Buterin, V. (2013). 'Ethereum: A Next-Generation Smart Contract and Decentralized Application Platform.'
264. Buterin, V. (2021). 'A Proof of Stake Design Philosophy.' Ethereum.org.
265. Cardone, Grant. The 10X Rule: The Only Difference Between Success and Failure. John Wiley & Sons, 2011.
266. Center for Security and Emerging Technology. "AI and Compute." 2020.
267. Chaganti, R., & Greene, P. (2002). Who are ethnic entrepreneurs? A study of entrepreneurs' ethnic involvement and business characteristics. Journal of Small Business Management.
268. Chatterji, A., Glaeser, E., & Kerr, W. (2013). Clusters of Entrepreneurship and Innovation. NBER Working Papers.
269. Chen, B.X. (2020). 'Cash App and Venmo may be so easy to use, but are they safe?' The New York Times.

270. Cheryan, S., Ziegler, S. A., Montoya, A. K., & Jiang, L. (2017). 'Why are some STEM fields more gender balanced than others?' Psychological Bulletin, 143(1), 1–35.
271. Chetty, Raj, et al. "Race and Economic Opportunity in the United States: an Intergenerational Perspective." Quarterly Journal of Economics, vol. 135, no. 2, 2020, pp. 711–783.
272. Chetty, Raj, et al. "Race and economic opportunity in the United States: An intergenerational perspective." The Quarterly Journal of Economics 135.2 (2020): 711-783.
273. Chetty, Raj, et al. "The fading American dream: Trends in absolute income mobility since 1940." Science 356.6336 (2017): 398-406.
274. Chetty, Raj, Nathaniel Hendren, Maggie Jones, and Sonya Porter. "Race and Economic Opportunity in the United States: An Intergenerational Perspective." Quarterly Journal of Economics, 2018.
275. Chetty, Raj. "Moral Hazard vs. Liquidity and Optimal Unemployment Insurance." Journal of Political Economy, vol. 116, no. 2, 2008, pp. 173-234.
276. Chicago Community Loan Fund. (2018). Building Black Wealth.
277. Christensen, Clayton M. The Innovator's Dilemma: When New Technologies Cause Great Firms to Fail. Harvard Business School Press, 1997.
278. Christensen, Clayton M., et al. The Innovator's Dilemma: When New Technologies Cause Great Firms to Fail. Harvard Business Review Press, 2016.
279. Christensen, Clayton M., et al. "Disruptive Innovation for Social Change." Harvard Business Review, www.hbr.org.
280. Christopher J. Coyne and Abigail R. Hall, "Four Decades of the War on Drugs and Counting," The Independent Review 18, no. 3 (2014): 456-457.
281. Chui, M., Manyika, J., & Miremadi, M. (2016). "Where machines could replace humans—and where they can't (yet)." McKinsey Quarterly.
282. Chui, M., Manyika, J., & Miremadi, M. (2016). 'Where machines could replace humans—and where they can't (yet).' McKinsey Quarterly.
283. Chui, M., Manyika, J., Miremadi, M., Henke, N., Chung, R., Nel, P., & Malhotra, S. (2018). 'Notes from the AI frontier: Applications and value of deep learning.' McKinsey Global Institute.

284. Chui, Michael, et al. "Jobs lost, jobs gained: What the future of work will mean for jobs, skills, and wages." McKinsey Global Institute, 2017.
285. Cisco, "The Power of 5G and IoT," 2022.
286. Claud Anderson, PowerNomics : The National Plan to Empower Black America (Powernomics Corporation of America, 2001).
287. Code.org Advocacy Coalition. (2020). '2020 State of Computer Science Education: Illuminating disparities.'
288. Cohen, Boyd, and Pablo Muñoz. "Towards a Theory and Policy of Eco-Entrepreneurship Promotion." International Journal of Green Economics, vol. 5, no. 2, 2011, pp. 135-153.
289. Cole, Raymond J., and Paul C. Kernan. "Life-Cycle Assessment of Existing Buildings." Building Research & Information, vol. 28, no. 5/6, 2000, pp. 338-352.
290. Collins, Chuck, Dedrick Asante-Muhammed, Josh Hoxie, and Emanuel Nieves. (2017). The Road to Zero Wealth: How the Racial Wealth Divide is Hollowing Out America's Middle Class. Institute for Policy Studies.
291. Combs, G. M., & Griffith, J. (2007). "An examination of the role of impact on tokenism, perceptions of organizational culture, and employee withdrawal." Journal of Leadership & Organizational Studies.
292. Community Networks. (2020). "Successful Strategies for Broadband Public-Private Partnerships."
293. Conley, Dalton. "Being Black, Living in the Red: Race, Wealth, and Social Policy in America." University of California Press, 1999.
294. Cook, L. D. (2014). 'Violence and economic activity: evidence from African American patents, 1870–1940.' Journal of Economic Growth, 19(2), 221-257.
295. Cook, Lisa D. "Racism Impoverishes the Whole Economy." Foreign Affairs, 2021.
296. Cornforth, Chris. "Why do co-operatives fail? In search of the success factors for co-operatives." Paper presented at ICA Research Conference, Potsdam, 2004.
297. Coursera. (2021). 'Blockchain Basics.'
298. Crawford, E. R., LePine, J. A., & Rich, B. L. (2010). Linking job demands and resources to employee engagement and burnout: A theoretical extension and meta-analytic test. Journal of Applied Psychology, 95(5), 834.
299. Cutcher, Leanne, and David Grant. "Demystifying Diversity in Organizational Culture." Routledge, 2020.

300. Cutrona, Carolyn E. "Social Support in Couples: Marriage as a Resource in Times of Stress." Sage Publications, Inc., 1996.
301. Darity Jr., William A., et al. "Stratification Economics, Identity Economics, and the Role of Public Policy." Journal of Economics, Race, and Policy, vol. 3, no. 2, 2020, pp. 91–100.
302. Darity Jr., William, and A. Kirsten Mullen. "From Here to Equality: Reparations for Black Americans in the Twenty-First Century." The University of North Carolina Press, 2020.
303. Darity, William A., and A. Kirsten Mullen. From Here to Equality: Reparations for Black Americans in the Twenty-First Century. The University of North Carolina Press, 2020.
304. Darity, William Jr., and A. Kirsten Mullen. "What We Get Wrong About Closing the Wealth Gap." Samuel DuBois Cook Center on Social Equity and Insight Center for Community Economic Development, 2018. https://socialequity.duke.edu/wp-content/uploads/2020/01/what-we-get-wrong.pdf
305. Darling-Hammond, L. (2010). 'The flat world and education: How America's commitment to equity will determine our future.' Teachers College Press.
306. Darling-Hammond, Linda. "Unequal Opportunity: Race and Education." Brookings, March 1, 1998.
307. Dastin, Jeffrey. "Amazon scraps secret AI recruiting tool that showed bias against women." Reuters, 2018.
308. Daugherty, P., Carrel-Billiard, M., & Biltz, M. (2016). 'Technology for people.' Accenture Technology Vision 2016.
309. Davenport, T.H., Guha, A., Grewal, D., & Bressgott, T. (2020). "How AI Will Change the Way We Make Decisions." Harvard Business Review.
310. David J. Johns, "The Role of Mentorship in Achieving Equity in Education," Brookings Institution, June 5, 2019, https://www.brookings.edu/blog/brown-center-chalkboard/2019/06/05/the-role-of-mentorship-in-achieving-equity-in-education/.
311. Davidson, L. (2019). 'The Importance of Financial Literacy in the Age of e-Finance.' The Balance. https://www.thebalance.com/financial-literacy-in-age-of-e-finance-4771994
312. Davidson, Roei, et al. "Economics of blockchain-based systems." IEEE Cloud Computing, vol. 4, no. 4, 2017, pp. 12-17.
313. Davis, M. "Racial Discrimination in the U.S. Banking Industry." ThoughtCo, October 20, 2021.

314. Del Rey, J. (2018). 'Procter & Gamble is acquiring Walker & Company, Tristan Walker's five-year-old start-up.' Recode.
315. Demyanyk, Yuliya, and Daniel Kolliner. "Peer-to-peer lending is poised to grow." Economic Trends, 2014.
316. Dennis, Richelieu. "Shea Moisture Founder on Selling Sundial Brands to Unilever." Inc.com, November 27, 2017.
317. Diemer, Matthew A., and Adam M. Voight. "Racial/ethnic disparities in US college students' experience: Discrimination as an impediment to academic performance." Journal of College Student Development 59, no. 5 (2018): 564-577.
318. DiMaggio, P., & Hargittai, E. (2001). 'From the 'digital divide' to 'digital inequality': Studying internet use as penetration increases.' Princeton University Center for Arts and Cultural Policy Studies.
319. DiMaggio, Paul. "Constructing an Organizational Field as a Professional Project: U.S. Art Museums, 1920-1940." In The New Institutionalism in Organizational Analysis, University of Chicago Press, 1991, pp. 267-92.
320. Dingle, R. (2019, Jun 27). Black Tech Founder's Communications start-up Now Worth $62.3 Million. Black Enterprise.
321. Dixon, "A Dangerous Distortion of our Families."
322. Dixon, Travis L. "Good Guys Are Still Always in White? Positive Change and Continued Misrepresentation of Race and Crime on Local Television News." Communications Research, 2017.
323. Dixon, Travis L., and Charlotte L. Williams. "The Changing Misrepresentation of Race and Crime on Network and Cable News." Journal of Communication 65, no. 1 (2015): 24-39.
324. Drucker, Peter. Innovation and Entrepreneurship: Practice and Principles. Harper & Row, 1985.
325. Drucker, Peter. The Age of Discontinuity: Guidelines to Our Changing Society. Harper & Row, 1969.
326. Dua, T. (2015, Oct 27). How Sundial Brands CEO Turned Soap Into A Mission-Driven Business Of 'Economic Freedom'. Forbes.
327. Duckworth, Angela L., et al. "Grit: perseverance and passion for long-term goals." Journal of Personality and Social Psychology 92, no. 6 (2007): 1087.
328. Duckworth, Angela. Grit: The Power of Passion and Perseverance. Scribner, 2016.
329. Dweck, Carol S. Mindset: The new psychology of success. Random House Digital, Inc., 2008.

330. Dweck, Carol S. Mindset: The New Psychology of Success. Random House, 2006.
331. Dweck, Carol. "Mindset: The New Psychology of Success." Random House, 2006.
332. Edelman, P., et al. (2017). 'Unemployment Rates for Black and White College Graduates.' Economic Policy Institute.
333. EEOC. (2018). 'Diversity in High Tech.' U.S. Equal Employment Opportunity Commission.
334. Ehrenberg, Ronald G., and Donna S. Rothstein. "Do Historically Black Institutions of Higher Education Confer Unique Advantages on Black Students: An Initial Analysis." In Choice and Consequence, edited by Tom Schelling. Cambridge, MA: Harvard University Press, 1984.
335. Eichengreen, Barry. "The Last Tango of Dollarization: The Rise of Cryptocurrencies." American Economic Review, vol. 108, no. 5, 2018, pp. 507-511.
336. Ekblaw, A., Azaria, A., Halamka, J.D., & Lippman, A. (2016). 'A Case Study for Blockchain in health-care: "MedRec" prototype for electronic health records and medical research data.' Proceedings of IEEE Open & Big Data Conference.
337. Elliott, R., Friston, K. J., & Dolan, R. J. (2000). Dissociable neural responses in human reward systems. Journal of Neuroscience, 20(16), 6159-6165.
338. Ellsworth, S. (1982). Death in a Promised Land: The Tulsa Race Riot of 1921. Louisiana State University Press.
339. Epstein, D. (2019). 'Range: Why Generalists Triumph in a Specialized World.' Riverhead Books.
340. Eubanks, V. (2018). Automating Inequality: How High-Tech Tools Profile, Police, and Punish the Poor. New York: St. Martin's Press.
341. Eubanks, Virginia. "Automating Inequality: How High-Tech Tools Profile, Police, and Punish the Poor." St. Martin's Press, 2018.
342. Eun, Cheol S., & Resnick, Bruce G. (2015). International Financial Management, 7th Edition. McGraw-Hill Education.
343. Ewing, Paul. "Prosperity Advisory Group." Prosperity Advisory Group, 2023.
344. Fairbairn, Brett. "Three Strategic Concepts for the Guidance of Cooperatives: Linkage, Transparency, and Cognition," Saskatoon: University of Saskatchewan, 2003.
345. Fairlie, R. (2020). "The Impact of COVID-19 on Small Business Owners: Evidence from the First Three Months after Widespread

Social-Distancing Restrictions." Journal of Economics & Management Strategy, 29(4), 727-740.
346. Fairlie, R. (2020). The Impact of Covid-19 on Small Business Owners: Evidence of Early-Stage Losses from the April 2020 Current Population Survey. NBER Working Paper.
347. Fairlie, R. W., & Robb, A. M. (2008). Race and Entrepreneurial Success. MIT Press.
348. Fairlie, R. W., & Robb, A. M. (2008). Race and Entrepreneurial Success: Black-, Asian-, and White-Owned Businesses in the United States. MIT Press.
349. Fairlie, R., & Robb, A. (2008). 'Race and Entrepreneurial Success.' MIT Press.
350. Fairlie, R., & Robb, A. (2008). Race and Entrepreneurial Success. MIT Press.
351. Fairlie, R., & Robb, A. (2008). Race and Entrepreneurial Success: Black-, Asian-, and White-Owned Businesses in the United States. MIT Press.
352. Fairlie, Robert W., & Robb, Alicia M. (2008). "Race and Entrepreneurial Success." MIT Press.
353. Fairlie, Robert W., and Alicia M. Robb. "Race and Entrepreneurial Success: Black-, Asian-, and White-Owned Businesses in the United States." MIT Press, 2008.
354. Fairlie, Robert, and Alicia Robb. "Race and Entrepreneurial Success." MIT Press, 2008.
355. Fairlie, Robert. "Kauffman Index of Entrepreneurial Activity 1996–2010." Ewing Marion Kauffman Foundation, 2011.
356. Fairlie, Robert. "The Impact of COVID-19 on Small Business Owners: Evidence from the First 3 Months After Widespread Social-Distancing Restrictions." Journal of Economics & Management Strategy, 2020.
357. Fairlie, Robert. "The Impact of Covid-19 on Small Business Owners: Evidence of Early-Stage Losses from the April 2020 Current Population Survey." National Bureau of Economic Research, June 2020.
358. Fairlie, Robert. "The Impact of COVID-19 on Small Business Owners: Evidence of Early-Stage Losses from the April 2020 Current Population Survey." National Bureau of Economic Research, June 2020.
359. Faisal, S., Yafi, E., & Pink, S. (2020). "The future of augmented reality across sectors: A systematic review of challenges and solutions." Journal of Business Research, 117, 25-38.

360. Farley, Robert, et al. "The Avenue: The Devaluation of Assets in Black Neighborhoods." The Brookings Institution, November 2018.
361. Fears, D., and Chandra, A. "Advancing Black STEM Students Into Professionals: An Overview of Organizational and Programmatic Opportunities and Challenges." Brookings Institution, 2020.
362. Federal Communications Commission. (2012). "Report on Ownership of Commercial Broadcast Stations."
363. Federal Communications Commission. (2015). "Open Internet."
364. Federal Communications Commission. (2020). "Communications Marketplace Report."
365. Federal Communications Commission. (2020). '2020 Broadband Deployment Report.'
366. Federal Reserve Bank of New York. "Household Debt and Credit Report." 2021.
367. Federal Reserve Bank. "Distributionsal Financial Accounts." 2019.
368. Federal Reserve System. "Survey of Consumer Finances." 2019.
369. Federal Trade Commission. (2019). 'FTC Charges Facebook With Violating 2012 FTC Order by Deceptively Using Data from Onavo to Identify and Acquire Threats.'
370. Financial Industry Regulatory Authority. "Financial Capability in the United States 2016." FINRA Investor Education Foundation, 2016.
371. Fine, Gary Alan, and Brooke Harrington. "The ethnography of resistance: toward a theory of cultural brokerage in contemporary social movements." The handbook of social movements across disciplines (2018): 127-157.
372. Flatiron School. "Jobs Report." 2020.
373. Florida, R. (2014). 'The rise of the creative class--revisited.' Basic Books.
374. Fomichenko, Dmitriy. "Sense Financial Services LLC." Sense Financial Services LLC, 2023.
375. Forbes Finance Council. "Forbes Finance Council." Forbes, 2023.
376. Franklin, J. H., & Moss, A. (2010). From Slavery to Freedom: A History of African Americans. McGraw-Hill Education.
377. Fraser, George. Click: Ten Truths for Building Extraordinary Relationships. McGraw Hill Professional, 2008.
378. Fredrickson, Barbara L. "The Broaden-and-Build Theory of Positive Emotions." Philosophical Transactions of the Royal

Society of London. Series B: Biological Sciences 359, no. 1449 (2004): 1367-1378.
379. Freireich, Jessica, and Katherine Fulton. "Investing for social and environmental impact: A design for catalyzing an emerging industry." Monitor Institute, 2009.
380. Frey, C. B., & Osborne, M. A. (2017). 'The future of employment: how susceptible are jobs to computerization?.' Technological Forecasting and Social Change, 114, 254-280.
381. Friedman, M. (1962). Capitalism and Freedom. University of Chicago Press.
382. Fullilove, Mindy Thompson. Root Shock: How Tearing Up City Neighborhoods Hurts America, and What We Can Do About It. New Village Press, 2004.
383. Fullilove, Mindy Thompson. Root Shock: How Tearing Up City Neighborhoods Hurts America, and What We Can Do About It. One World/Ballantine, 2004.
384. Gabe, Thomas, and Julie M. Whittaker. "Unemployment Insurance: Programs and Benefits." Congressional Research Service, 2012.
385. Gabridge, Rob. "Tarfis Wealth Management." Tarfis Wealth Management, 2023.
386. Galt, Ryan E. "The moral economy is a double-edged sword: Explaining farmers' earnings and self-exploitation in community-supported agriculture." Economic Geography 88, no. 4 (2012): 341-365.
387. Galtung, J. (1964). "An Editorial." Journal of Peace Research, 1(1)
388. Ganong, Peter, et al. "US Unemployment Insurance Replacement Rates During the Pandemic." Journal of Public Economics, vol. 191, 2021.
389. Gardner, Chris, and Mim Eichler Rivas. The Pursuit of Happyness. Harper Collins, 2006.
390. Gilbert, Jess, Spencer D. Wood, and Gwen Sharp. "Who owns the land? Agricultural land ownership by race/ethnicity." Rural America 17, no. 4 (2002): 55-62.
391. Glickman, L. B. (2009). Buying Power: A History of Consumer Activism in America. University of Chicago Press.
392. Goldin, Philippe R., and James J. Gross. "Effects of mindfulness-based stress reduction (MBSR) on emotion regulation in social anxiety disorder." Emotion, 2010.
393. Google Quantum AI, "Quantum Computing," 2022.
394. Google. (2019). 'Google for Education: Transformation Report.'

395. Gordon Nembhard, J. (2014). Collective Courage: A History of African American Cooperative Economic Thought and Practice. Penn State University Press.
396. Gordon Nembhard, Jessica. Collective Courage: A History of African American Cooperative Economic Thought and Practice. Penn State Press, 2014.
397. Gould, Elise. "Black workers endure persistent racial disparities in employment outcomes." Economic Policy Institute, 2019.
398. Government Accountability Office. "Diversity in the Financial Services Industry and Its Impact on Financial Stability." 2017.
399. Grant, A. M., & Shin, J. (2012). Work motivation: Directing, energizing, and maintaining effort (and research). In R. M. Ryan (Ed.), Oxford Handbook of Human Motivation (p. 505–519). Oxford University Press.
400. Greenburg, Zack O'Malley. "Inside The 35-Year-Long Quest To Find A Safe Haven For The Oprah Winfrey Show Tapes." Forbes, www.forbes.com.
401. Greenburg, Zack O'Malley. "Jay-Z's Net Worth Revealed: The Rapper Is Hip-Hop's First Billionaire." Forbes. June 3, 2019.
402. Greenwood. (2021). Greenwood Launches New Phase of Development.
403. GSMA. (2020). "The Future of Messaging: How RCS is transforming business communication."
404. Gustafsson-Wright, Emily, Sophie Gardiner, and Vidya Putcha. "The Potential and Limitations of Impact Bonds: Lessons from the First Five Years of Experience Worldwide." Global Economy & Development, 2015.
405. Guttentag, Dan. "Airbnb: disruptive innovation and the rise of an informal tourism accommodation sector." Current Issues in Tourism, www.tandfonline.com.
406. Gutter, Michael, et al. "Financial Capability and Financial Satisfaction: Financial Literacy, Behavior, and Capability Among African Americans." Journal of Financial Counseling and Planning 29.2 (2018): 265-277.
407. Halweil, B. (2004). Eat Here: Reclaiming Homegrown Pleasures in a Global Supermarket. Norton.
408. Hamilton, Arlan. "It's About Damn Time: How to Turn Being Underestimated into Your Greatest Advantage." Currency, 2020.
409. Hamilton, D., & Darity, W. "The racial wealth gap: Why policy matters." Brookings Institution, 2017.

410. Hamilton, D., & Darity, W. (2017). "The political economy of education, financial literacy, and the racial wealth gap." Federal Reserve Bank of St. Louis Review, 99(1), 59-76.
411. Hamilton, D., & Darity, W. (2017). "The political economy of education, financial literacy, and the racial wealth gap." Federal Reserve Bank of St. Louis Review, Fourth Quarter 2017, 99(1), 59-76.
412. Hamilton, D., & Darity, W. (2017). The political economy of education, financial literacy, and the racial wealth gap. Federal Reserve Bank of St. Louis Review, 99(1), 59-76.
413. Hamilton, D., and Darity, W. "The political economy of education, financial literacy, and the racial wealth gap." Federal Reserve Bank of St. Louis Review, 99.1 (2017): 59-76.
414. Hamilton, Darrick, and William Darity Jr. "The political economy of education, financial literacy, and the racial wealth gap." Federal Reserve Bank of St. Louis Review, 2017.
415. Hamilton, Darrick, and William Darity. "Can 'Baby Bonds' Eliminate the Racial Wealth Gap in Putative Post-Racial America?" The Review of Black Political Economy, 2010.
416. Hamilton, Darrick, and William Darity. "The political economy of education, financial literacy, and the racial wealth gap." Federal Reserve Bank of St. Louis Review 99, no. 1 (2017): 59-76.
417. Hamilton, Darrick, et al. "Umbrellas don't make it rain: Why studying and working hard isn't enough for Black Americans." Review of Black Political Economy 44.2 (2017): 131-167.
418. Hamilton, Darrick, et al. "Umbrellas Don't Make it Rain: Why Studying and Working Hard Isn't Enough for Black Americans." The New School, Duke Center for Social Equity, Insight Center for Community Economic Development, 2015.
419. Hamilton, Darrick, et al. (2015). "Umbrellas Don't Make It Rain: Why Studying and Working Hard Isn't Enough for Black Americans." The New School and Duke Center for Social Equity.
420. Hammond, R. J. (1951). Poverty and Social Progress. McGraw-Hill.
421. Harrison, Joseph, and Donovan X. Ramsey. "Advancing Black Pathways in Technology." The Brookings Institution, September 2020.
422. Harvard Business Review, "The Bio Revolution: Innovations transforming economies, societies, and our lives," 2021.
423. Hayek, F. A. (1945). The Use of Knowledge in Society. The American Economic Review.

424. Heckman, James J., and Dimitriy V. Masterov. "The Productivity Argument for Investing in Young Children." Review of Agricultural Economics, vol. 29, no. 3, 2007, pp. 446–493.
425. Heilman, Madeline E., et al. "Has Affirmative Action Reached the Backlash Stage? The Impact of Attributions for the Success of Minority and Female Managers." Academy of Management Journal, vol. 38, no. 2, 1995, pp. 593-611.
426. Hendrickson, John, and Brett K. Moyer. "Breaking local: Can a city really feed itself?." Civil Eats, March (2017).
427. Henson, Katie. "The Culture of Overwork: Why We Need a Balance." Medium, 2021. https://medium.com/the-innovation/the-culture-of-overwork-why-we-need-a-balance-27a5c04f9c83
428. Heslin, Peter A., et al. "High performance work systems and employee well-being: A two stage study of a rural Australian hospital." Journal of Health Organization and Management (2005).
429. Hewlett, Sylvia Ann, et al. "The Sponsor Dividend." Center for Talent Innovation, 2019.
430. Hicks, M. (2019). 'Overhyping Technology Can Deepen Inequality.' Inside Higher Ed. https://www.insidehighered.com/blogs/higher-ed-gamma/overhyping-technology-can-deepen-inequality
431. Hirsch, J. S. (2002). Riot and Remembrance: The Tulsa Race War and Its Legacy. Houghton Mifflin Harcourt.
432. Holzer, Harry, and David Neumark. "Affirmative Action: What Do We Know?" Journal of Policy Analysis and Management, vol. 25, no. 2, 2006, pp. 463-490.
433. Horrigan, Leo, Robert S. Lawrence, and Polly Walker. "How sustainable agriculture can address the environmental and human health harms of industrial agriculture." Environmental health perspectives 110, no. 5 (2002): 445-456.
434. Horsley, Scott. "How A Trade War Could Backfire On The U.S. Economy." NPR, June 2018.
435. Houser, Trevor, et al. "The 'Risky Business' of Busting Climate Myths: The Case of Renewable Energy." Brookings, 2018.
436. Howard University. (2022). 'Department of Computer Science.'
437. Howard, A. (2020). 'Equity in AI: Why Diversity Is Essential.' Forbes. https://www.forbes.com/sites/abhoward/2020/06/22/equity-in-ai-why-diversity-is-essential/?sh=6fc095633754
438. Howard, P. N., Busch, L., & Sheets, P. (2010). "Comparing Digital Divides: Internet Access and Social Inequality in Canada

and the United States." Canadian Journal of Communication, Vol 35 (1).
439. Howroyd, Janice Bryant. "The Art of Work: How to Make Work, Work for You!" Greenleaf Book Group Press, 2019.
440. Hsieh, Chang-Tai, et al. "The Allocation of Talent and U.S. Economic Growth." Econometrica, vol. 87, no. 5, 2019, pp. 1435–1474.
441. Huang, L., & Meek, W. (2011). A social capital approach to improving the U.S. SBA 7(A) loan program. Journal of Developmental Entrepreneurship.
442. Hunt, V., et al. (2018). 'Delivering through Diversity.' McKinsey & Company.
443. Hunt, Vivian, Sara Prince, Sundiatu Dixon-Fyle, and Lareina Yee. "Delivering through diversity." McKinsey & Company, 2018.
444. Huston, Sandra J. "Measuring Financial Literacy." The Journal of Consumer Affairs, 2010.
445. Ibid.
446. IBM, "Benefits of Hybrid Cloud," 2022.
447. Isaac, Mike. "Uber's C.E.O. Plays With Fire." The New York Times, www.nytimes.com.
448. Isaacson, Walter. The Innovators: How a Group of Hackers, Geniuses, and Geeks Created the Digital Revolution. Simon & Schuster, 2014.
449. Iyer, Rajkamal, et al. "The Democratization of Credit?" American Economic Review, vol. 105, no. 5, 2015, pp. 157-162.
450. Jelks, R. M. (2019). Buying Power: A History of Consumer Activism in America. University of Chicago Press.
451. Jenkins, H. (2006). "Convergence culture: Where old and new media collide." NYU Press.
452. Johnson, Hannibal B. "Black Wall Street: From Riot to Renaissance in Tulsa's Historic Greenwood District." Eakin Press, 1998.
453. Johnson, John H. Succeeding Against the Odds. Warner Books, 1989.
454. Johnson, K. "Minority-Owned Firms' Access to Capital." U.S. Small Business Administration, 2019.
455. Johnson, Michael. "Can Black-Owned Banks Reverse Racial Disparity?" Colorlines, 2016.
456. Johnson, Travers. "As Black-Owned Media Faces Advertising Inequities, New Approaches and Solutions Emerge." Forbes. Last modified June 19, 2023. https://www.forbes.com/sites/traversjohnson/2023/06/19/as-black-

owned-media-faces-advertising-inequities-new-approaches-and-solutions-emerge/?sh=20acd9a93484.
457. Johnson, William R., and Derek Neal. "The Role of Pre-Market Factors in Black-White Wage Differences." Journal of Political Economy, 1998.
458. Jones, R. "The Liquidity Problem in Collective Investments." Financial Times, May 3, 2023.
459. Jones, Trina. "The Predatory Lending Wealth Gap." Geo. Wash. L. Rev. 86 (2018): 800.
460. Kabat-Zinn, Jon. Full Catastrophe Living: Using the Wisdom of Your Body and Mind to Face Stress, Pain, and Illness. Delta Trade Paperbacks, 2005.
461. Kane, L. "The Risks and Rewards of Investment Clubs." Business Insider, November 12, 2020.
462. Kaplan, A., & Haenlein, M. (2019). 'Siri, Siri, in my hand: Who's the fairest in the land? On the interpretations, illustrations, and implications of artificial intelligence.' Business Horizons, 62(1), 15-25.
463. Kapor Center. "Tech Leavers Study." April 2017.
464. Karnani, A. (2007). The Mirage of Marketing to the Bottom of the Pyramid. California Management Review.
465. Kasser, T., & Ryan, R. M. (1996). Further examining the American dream: Differential correlates of intrinsic and extrinsic goals. Personality and Social Psychology Bulletin, 22(3), 280-287.
466. Ke, Wei. "Simon-Kucher & Partners." Simon-Kucher & Partners, 2023.
467. Kelly, M., & McKinley, S. (2015). Cities Building Community Wealth. The Democracy Collaborative.
468. Kennedy, R. (2002). Nigger: The Strange Career of a Troublesome Word. Pantheon Books.
469. Khamis, S., Ang, L., & Welling, R. (2017). "Self-branding, 'micro-celebrity' and the rise of Social Media Influencers." Celebrity Studies, 8(2), 191-208.
470. Khan Academy. (2021). 'About.' Khan Academy.
471. Kharif, O. (2018). 'The Wealthy Are Hoarding $10 Billion of Bitcoin in Bunkers.' Bloomberg. https://www.bloomberg.com/news/articles/2018-05-09/bunkers-for-the-wealthy-are-said-to-hoard-10-billion-of-bitcoin
472. Killewald, Alexandra, and Brielle Bryan. "Falling Behind: The Role of Inter- and Intragenerational Processes in Widening Racial and Ethnic Wealth Gaps through Early and Middle Adulthood." Social Forces, 2018.

473. Killewald, Alexandra, and Fabian T. Pfeffer. "Wealth Inequality and Accumulation." Annual Review of Sociology, 2017.
474. Kimbro, Dennis. The Wealth Choice: Success Secrets of Black Millionaires. Palgrave Macmillan, 2013.
475. King, M. L., Jr. (1967). Where do we go from here: Chaos or community? Beacon Press.
476. Kinniry Jr., Francis M., Colleen M. Jaconetti, Michael A. DiJoseph, and Yan Zilbering. "Putting a value on your value: Quantifying Vanguard Advisor's Alpha." Vanguard Research, 2014.
477. Kirshner, Ben. Youth activism in an era of education inequality. NYU Press, 2015.
478. Kishi, R. (2021). "Race in the Workplace: The Black Experience in the U.S. Private Sector." McKinsey & Company.
479. Klein, H. J., Wesson, M. J., Hollenbeck, J. R., & Alge, B. J. (2006). Goal commitment and the goal-setting process: conceptual clarification and empirical synthesis. Journal of Applied Psychology, 89(6), 885.
480. Kleingeld, A., van Mierlo, H., & Arends, L. (2011). The effect of goal setting on group performance: A meta-analysis. Journal of Applied Psychology, 96(6), 1289.
481. Kochhar, R., & Fry, R. (2014). "Wealth inequality has widened along racial, ethnic lines since end of Great Recession." Pew Research Center.
482. Kochhar, Rakesh, and Richard Fry. "The wealth gap between white and Black families is widening." Pew Research Center, 2016.
483. Kochhar, Rakesh, and Richard Fry. "Wealth inequality has widened along racial, ethnic lines since end of Great Recession." Pew Research Center, December 12, 2014.
484. Krause, M., & Tolaymat, T. (2018). 'Quantification of energy and carbon costs for mining cryptocurrencies.' Nature Sustainability, 1(11), 711–718.
485. Kropotkin, P. (2002). Mutual Aid: A Factor of Evolution. Dover Publications.
486. Krysan, M., & Crowder, K. (2017). Cycle of Segregation: Social Processes and Residential Stratification. Russell Sage Foundation.
487. Kuhn, Moritz, Moritz Schularick, and Ulrike I. Steins. "Income and Wealth Inequality in America, 1949-2016." Quarterly Journal of Economics, 2020.
488. Kumar, N., Stern, L. W., & Anderson, J. C. (1993). "Conducting interorganizational research using key informants." Academy of Management Journal, 36(6), 1633-1651.

489. Kuznetsov, Yuri, and Carl J. Dahlman. "Mexico: Paving the Way for a Knowledge Economy." The World Bank, 2008.
490. Lacy, S. (2018). 'Meet Delane Parnell, whose esports start-up just raised $46 million.' Vanity Fair.
491. Langdon, David, George McKittrick, David Beede, Beethika Khan, and Mark Doms. "STEM: Good Jobs Now and For the Future." U.S. Department of Commerce, July 2011.
492. LeCun, Y., Bengio, Y., & Hinton, G. (2015). 'Deep learning.' nature, 521(7553), 436-444.
493. Lee, J., et al. "The rise of robots in the German labour market." VoxEU, 2019.
494. Leicht, Kevin T. "Getting Serious about Inequality." The Sociological Quarterly 56, no. 3 (2015): 34-51.
495. Lessig, Lawrence. "Republic, Lost: How Money Corrupts Congress--and a Plan to Stop It." Twelve, 2011.
496. Lewis, R. "Digital Technology Propels Black Banks into the 21st Century." Black Enterprise, March 2, 2023.
497. Locke, E. A., & Latham, G. P. (2002). Building a practically useful theory of goal setting and task motivation. American Psychologist, 57(9), 705.
498. Locke, Edwin A., and Gary P. Latham. A Theory of Goal Setting & Task Performance. Prentice-Hall, Inc, 1990.
499. Loewen, James. (2005). Sundown Towns: A Hidden Dimension of American Racism. New York: New Press.
500. Lofstrom, Magnus, and Timothy Bates. "African Americans' pursuit of self-employment." Small Business Economics 31, no. 3 (2008): 323-339.
501. Lohr, S. (2019, January 26). 'Tech Companies Spend More on Lobbying as Washington Targets Regulations.' The New York Times.
502. Long, Mark C. "Affirmative Action and its Alternatives in Public Universities: What Do We Know?" Public Administration Review, vol. 67, no. 1, 2007, pp. 315-330.
503. Loury, Glenn. "The Undeserving Poor." National Affairs, no. 11 (1984): 13-30.
504. Lown, Jean M. "Development and Validation of a Financial Self-Efficacy Scale." Journal of Financial Counseling and Planning, 2011.
505. Lusardi and Mitchell, "The Economic Importance of Financial Literacy."

506. Lusardi, Annamaria, and Peter Tufano. "Debt literacy, financial experiences, and overindebtedness." Journal of Pension Economics & Finance, 2009.
507. Lusardi, Annamaria, et al. "Financial Literacy and Stock Market Participation." Journal of Financial Economics, 2010.
508. Ly, Dan P., and Ichiro Kawachi. "Racial Disparities in Income and Health in the United States: A State-Level Analysis." JAMA Network Open 3, no. 2 (2020): e1920257.
509. Lyons, A.C., Palmer, L., Jayaratne, K.S.U., & Scherpf, E. (2006). Are We Making the Grade? A National Overview of Financial Education and Program Evaluation. Journal of Consumer Affairs.
510. Macey, Jonathan, et al. "Regulating FinTech." Vanderbilt Law Review, 2018.
511. Macht, Stephanie A., and Jeffrey J. Weatherhead. "The benefits and drawbacks of crowd-funding." Entrepreneurship and Innovation, vol. 14, no. 4, 2013, pp. 273-284.
512. Manyika, J., et al. (2019). "The Future of Work in Black America." McKinsey & Company.
513. Marable, M. (2000). How Capitalism Underdeveloped Black America. South End Press.
514. Marable, M. (2000). How capitalism underdeveloped Black America: Problems in race, political economy, and society. Pluto Press.
515. Marable, Manning. How Capitalism Underdeveloped Black America: Problems in Race, Political Economy, and Society. Pluto Press, 2000.
516. Marr, B. (2019). 'The 4 Types Of Artificial Intelligence: From Reactive To Self-Aware.' Forbes.
517. Masiello, Betsy, et al. "The Local Economic Impact of Small Businesses." Kellogg School of Management, Northwestern University, 2012.
518. Material Science and Engineering, "Implications of Next-Generation Materials," 2022.
519. Matthews, Dylan. "The growing movement for a 'United States of Africa'." Vox, February 2020.
520. Maxwell, John C. Failing Forward: Turning Mistakes into Stepping Stones for Success. Thomas Nelson Inc, 2000.
521. Maxwell, John C. Failing Forward: Turning Mistakes into Stepping Stones for Success. Thomas Nelson, 2007.
522. McBride, William D., and Catherine Greene. "Characteristics and risk management needs of limited-resource and socially disadvantaged farmers." Risk Management Agency, USDA (2008).

523. McKernan, S.-M., Ratcliffe, C., Steuerle, E., & Zhang, S. (2013). Less Than Equal: Racial Disparities in Wealth Accumulation. Urban Institute.
524. McKernan, Signe-Mary, et al. "Nine Charts about Wealth Inequality in America." Urban Institute, 2017.
525. McKinsey & Company. "The economic state of Black America: What is and what could be." McKinsey, 2020.
526. McKinsey & Company. (2020). "Cloud's trillion-dollar prize is up for grabs."
527. McKinsey & Company. (2020). "The Future of Customer Experience."
528. McKinsey, "The future of clean tech trends," 2021.
529. McKinsey, "Top 10 tech trends that will shape the coming decade," 2021.
530. McWhorter, L. "Tulsa Real Estate Fund Raises Over $50 Million." Black Enterprise, June 7, 2022.
531. Means, B., et al. (2010). 'Evaluation of Evidence-Based Practices in Online Learning: A Meta-Analysis and Review of Online Learning Studies.' U.S. Department of Education.
532. Medvetz, Thomas. "Think Tanks in America." University of Chicago Press, 2012.
533. Metz, C. (2021). 'We Teach A.I. Systems Everything, Including Our Biases.' The New York Times. https://www.nytimes.com/2021/11/22/technology/artificial-intelligence-bias.html
534. Mfunwa, David Luke and Lily Sommer. "Africa Continental Free Trade Area: Challenges and Opportunities of Tariff Reductions." United Nations Economic Commission for Africa, January 2019.
535. Micheletti, M., & Stolle, D. (2007). Mobilizing Consumers to Take Responsibility for Global Social Justice. The ANNALS of the American Academy of Political and Social Science.
536. Mims, Christopher. "The High Cost of Taking on Tech Giants." Wall Street Journal, 2022.
537. Mistry, I. (2018). 'Blockchain potential applications & disruption: open music initiative.' Blockchain Research Institute.
538. MIT, "Applications of AI," 2022.
539. Mokyr, J., Vickers, C., & Ziebarth, N. L. (2015). 'The History of Technological Anxiety and the Future of Economic Growth: Is This Time Different?' Journal of Economic Perspectives.
540. Molla, R. (2018). "The lack of black-owned media companies is a big problem for media diversity." Vox Media.

541. Morisano, D., Hirsh, J. B., Peterson, J. B., Pihl, R. O., & Shore, B. M. (2010). Setting, elaborating, and reflecting on personal goals improves academic performance. Journal of Applied Psychology, 95(2), 255.
542. Mossberger, K., Tolbert, C., & Hamilton, A. (2012). 'Broadband Adoption| The Next Step: From Connectivity to Digital Literacy.' Journal of Information Policy.
543. Mougayar, W. (2016). 'The Business Blockchain: Promise, Practice, and Application of the Next Internet Technology.' New Jersey: Wiley.
544. Mougayar, W. (2016). 'The Business Blockchain: Promise, Practice, and Application of the Next Internet Technology.' Wiley.
545. Mougayar, William. "The Business Blockchain: Promise, Practice, and Application of the Next Internet Technology." Wiley, 2016.
546. Mougayar, William. The Business Blockchain: Promise, Practice, and Application of the Next Internet Technology. Wiley, 2016.
547. Muhammad, Khalil Gibran. "The Condemnation of Blackness: Race, Crime, and the Making of Modern Urban America." Harvard University Press, 2010.
548. Mulligan, Casey B. The Redistribution Recession: How Labor Market Distortions Contracted the Economy. Oxford University Press, 2012.
549. Muro, M., Maxim, R., & Whiton, J. (2019). 'Automation and Artificial Intelligence: How machines are affecting people and places.' Brookings Institution.
550. Münkner, Hans-H. "Cooperatives: A tool for creating employment and improving the living conditions of the poor." ILO Geneva, 2004.
551. Münkner, Hans-H. "Cooperatives: In Quest of a New Paradigm," in Cooperatives in a Global Economy: The Challenges of Cooperation Across Borders, edited by Darryl Reed and J.J. McMurtry, 23-46. Newcastle upon Tyne, UK: Cambridge Scholars Publishing, 2009.
552. NAACP. "Criminal Justice Fact Sheet." NAACP, https://naacp.org/resources/criminal-justice-fact-sheet
553. NAACP. (2019). 'NAACP sues major tech companies for racial bias.'
554. Nakamoto, S. (2008). 'Bitcoin: A Peer-to-Peer Electronic Cash System.'

555. Napoli, P. M. (1999). "Deconstructing the diversity principle." Journal of Communication, 49(4), 7-34.
556. Napoli, P. M. (2010). "Race and audience measurement in the development of the US broadcast industry: evidence from the historical record." Media History 16.2: 161-180.
557. Napoli, Philip M., and Lukito, Josephine. "Who's Producing the News? Journalism Studies." Taylor & Francis, 2019.
558. National Center for Education Statistics. "Race/Ethnicity of College Faculty." 2019.
559. National Center for Education Statistics. "Status and Trends in the Education of Racial and Ethnic Groups." 2018.
560. National Equity Atlas. "Workforce Race and Ethnicity: United States." 2020.
561. National Science Foundation, National Center for Science and Engineering Statistics. "Women, Minorities, and Persons with Disabilities in Science and Engineering." 2019.
562. National Telecommunications and Information Administration. (2018). "Telecommunications Act of 1996."
563. National Venture Capital Association. (2019). "Venture Forward."
564. NBIA. "State of the Business Incubation Industry." 2nd ed., 2012.
565. Nellis, A. (2016). "The Color of Justice: Racial and Ethnic Disparity in State Prisons." The Sentencing Project.
566. Nembhard, J. G. (2014). Collective Courage: A History of African American Cooperative Economic Thought and Practice. Penn State University Press.
567. Newman, N., Fletcher, R., Kalogeropoulos, A., Levy, D. A., & Nielsen, R. K. (2018). "Reuters Institute Digital News Report 2018." Reuters Institute.
568. Nickerson, Raymond S. "Confirmation bias: A ubiquitous phenomenon in many guises." Review of General Psychology 2.2 (1998): 175-220.
569. Nielsen (2018). From Consumers to Creators: The Digital Lives of Black Consumers. Nielsen Holdings.
570. Niforos, M., et al. "Blockchain and Economic Development: Hype vs. Reality." Center for Global Development, 2017.
571. Noel, N., & Hardcastle, D. (2020). 'The economic impact of closing the racial wealth gap.' McKinsey & Company.
572. Norton, "Importance of Cybersecurity in Business," 2022.
573. O'Neil, C. (2016). 'Weapons of Math Destruction: How Big Data Increases Inequality and Threatens Democracy.' New York: Crown.

574. Oden, M. (2010). The Digital Divide: Where We Are. Routledge.
575. Oishi, Shigehiro, and Ed Diener. "Goals, culture, and subjective well-being." Personality and Social Psychology Bulletin, 29.12 (2003): 1436-1449.
576. Oliver, M. L., & Shapiro, T. M. (2006). Black Wealth, White Wealth: A New Perspective on Racial Inequality. Taylor & Francis.
577. Oliver, Melvin L., and Thomas M. Shapiro. "Black Wealth, White Wealth: A New Perspective on Racial Inequality." Routledge, 1995.
578. Oliver, Melvin, and Thomas Shapiro. "Black Wealth/White Wealth: A New Perspective on Racial Inequality." Routledge, 2006.
579. Oreopoulos, Philip, and Uros Petronijevic. "Making College Worth It: A Review of the Returns to Higher Education." The Future of Children, 2013.
580. Orfield, Gary, and Erica Frankenberg. "Brown at 60: Great Progress, a Long Retreat and an Uncertain Future." Civil Rights Project/Proyecto Derechos Civiles, May 15, 2014.
581. Orfield, Gary. "School Segregation: The Continuing Tragedy of Segregated Schools." New York Law Review 85, (2010): 2140–2194.
582. Padar, Jody. "New Vision CPA Group." New Vision CPA Group, 2023.
583. Pager, Devah and Shepherd, Hana. "The Sociology of Discrimination: Racial Discrimination in Employment, Housing, Credit, and Consumer Markets." Annual Review of Sociology, 2008.
584. Pager, Devah, and Bruce Western. "Race at Work: Realities of Race and Criminal Record in the NYC Job Market." The ANNALS of the American Academy of Political and Social Science, 2009.
585. Pager, Devah, and Hana Shepherd. "The Sociology of Discrimination: Racial Discrimination in Employment, Housing, Credit, and Consumer Markets." Annual Review of Sociology 34 (2008): 181-209.
586. Pager, Devah, and Hana Shepherd. "The Sociology of Discrimination: Racial Discrimination in Employment, Housing, Credit, and Consumer Markets." Annual Review of Sociology, 2008.
587. Pager, Devah, and Shepherd, Hana. "The Sociology of Discrimination: Racial Discrimination in Employment, Housing,

Credit, and Consumer Markets." Annual Review of Sociology, 2008.
588. Pan, Yuhao, et al. "Grit: A predictor of risk-taking behavior and resilience." Personality and Individual Differences 149 (2019): 35-40.
589. Pariser, Eli. "The Filter Bubble: What the Internet Is Hiding from You." Penguin Press, 2011.
590. Park, Young-Hoon, et al. "Abundance mindset, work engagement, and financial success: A cross-national investigation." Journal of Applied Psychology 106.4 (2021): 481-494.
591. Peck, Emily. "Oprah Winfrey: one of the world's best neoliberal capitalist thinkers." The Guardian, 2018.
592. Perez, Carlota. Technological Revolutions and Financial Capital: The Dynamics of Bubbles and Golden Ages. Edward Elgar, 2003.
593. Perry, Andre, et al. "Know Your Price: Valuing Black Lives and Property in America's Black Cities." Brookings Institution Press, May 2020.
594. Perry, Vanessa G., and Marlene D. Morris. "Who Is in Control? The Role of Self-Perception, Knowledge, and Income in Explaining Consumer Financial Behavior." Journal of Consumer Affairs, 2005.
595. Peters, Alan, and Peter Fisher. "The Failures of Economic Development Incentives." Journal of the American Planning Association, vol. 70, no. 1, 2004, pp. 27-37.
596. Pew Research Center. "Digital divide persists even as lower-income Americans make gains in tech adoption." 2019.
597. Pew Research Center. (2019). "Digital divide persists even as lower-income Americans make gains in tech adoption."
598. Pew Research Center. (2019). "Digital gap between rural and nonrural America persists."
599. Pew Research Center. (2019). 'Internet/Broadband Fact Sheet.'
600. Pew Research Center. (2020). "U.S. Media Polarization and the 2020 Election: A Nation Divided."
601. Pew Research Center. (2020). Black Americans Face Systemic Hurdles in Getting Good Jobs.
602. Pew Research Center. (2021). "Social Media Use in 2021."
603. Philpot, Tasha S., Daron R. Shaw, and Ernest B. McGowen. "Winning the Race: Black Voter Turnout in the 2008 Presidential Election." Public Opinion Quarterly, 73.5 (2009): 995-1022.
604. Pink, Daniel H. Drive: The Surprising Truth About What Motivates Us. Riverhead Books, 2009.

605. Porter, Michael E. "The Competitive Advantage of Nations." Free Press, 1990.
606. Prasad, M. (2006). The politics of free markets: the rise of neoliberal economic policies in Britain, France, Germany, and the United States. University of Chicago Press.
607. Prudence L. Carter and Kevin G. Welner, "Closing the Opportunity Gap: What America Must Do to Give Every Child an Even Chance," Oxford University Press (2013).
608. PwC, "Impact of Automation on Jobs," 2022.
609. PWC. (2017). 'Sizing the prize: What's the real value of AI for your business and how can you capitalise?'
610. Quillian, Lincoln, et al. "Meta-analysis of field experiments shows no change in racial discrimination in hiring over time." Proceedings of the National Academy of Sciences 114.41 (2017): 10870-10875.
611. Ramirez, Zachary. "US Business Funding." US Business Funding, 2023.
612. Ransby, B. (2017). "The Class Politics of Black Lives Matter". In Futures of Black Radicalism. Verso Books.
613. Rawley, Thomas, and David A. Wilson. "From the Margins to Mainstream: The Political Power of the Stock Market." International Interactions, vol. 33, no. 4, 2007, pp. 405-412.
614. Reardon, Sean F., and Ann Owens. "60 Years After Brown: Trends and Consequences of School Segregation." Annual Review of Sociology, vol. 40, 2014, pp. 199-218.
615. Reardon, Sean F., et al. "A 'Meta-Analysis of the Relationship between Socioeconomic Status and Academic Achievement." American Educational Research Association 135.2 (2019): 457-473.
616. Richardson, Jesse. "Reviving Black Banks." The American Prospect, 2021.
617. Richardson, R., & Arsenault, C. (2009). Knowing the Past, Facing the Future: Indigenous Education in Canada. UBC Press.
618. Richardson, Rashad, et al. "Fintech, Regulatory Arbitrage, and the Rise of Shadow Banks." Journal of Financial Economics, 2021.
619. Ries, Eric. "The Lean start-up: How Today's Entrepreneurs Use Continuous Innovation to Create Radically Successful Businesses." Crown Publishing Group, 2011.
620. Riley, Jason L. "False Black Power." Templeton Press, 2017.
621. Riley, Jason L. "False Black Power?" Philadelphia: Templeton Press, 2017.

622. Riley, Jason L. "False Black Power?" The New York Times, June 16, 2017.
623. Riley, Jason L. "Please Stop Helping Us: How Liberals Make It Harder for Blacks to Succeed." Encounter Books, 2014.
624. Riley, Jason L. Please Stop Helping Us: How Liberals Make It Harder for Blacks to Succeed. Encounter Books, 2015.
625. Robb, A., & Watson, J. (2012). Gender differences in firm performance: Evidence from new ventures in the United States. Journal of Business Venturing.
626. Robehmed, Natalie. "How Tyler Perry Built a $600 Million Entertainment Empire." Forbes, www.forbes.com.
627. Robert H. Frank, "Does Studying Economics Inhibit Cooperation?," Journal of Economic Perspectives 7, no. 2 (1993): 159-171.
628. Roberts, Laura Morgan, et al. "Being Black in Corporate America: An Intersectional Exploration." U.S. Chamber of Commerce, 2019.
629. Robinson, Bryan. "Tulsa Real Estate Fund Faces Investor Complaints." The Atlanta Journal-Constitution, October 14, 2021.
630. Rochdale Pioneers Museum. "The Rochdale Pioneers," 2021.
631. Rogers, Everett M. Diffusion of Innovations, 5th Edition. Free Press, 2003.
632. Rolnick, D., et al. (2019). 'Tackling Climate Change with Machine Learning.' arXiv preprint.
633. Rose, K. (2017). 'Are we focusing too much on STEM?' The Atlantic.
634. Rothstein, Richard. "Education, economic growth, and social stability: Why the three are inseparable." Progressive Policy Institute, Washington, DC (2004).
635. Rothstein, Richard. "The Color of Law: A Forgotten History of How Our Government Segregated America." Liveright Publishing, 2017.
636. Rothwell, Jonathan. "The Hidden STEM Economy." Brookings Institution, 2013.
637. Ruggles, Steven, et al. (2020). "IPUMS USA: Version 10.0 [dataset]." IPUMS.
638. Rugh, Jacob S., and Douglas S. Massey. "Racial Segregation and the American Foreclosure Crisis." American Sociological Review, vol. 75, no. 5, 2010, pp. 629-651.
639. Russell, S., & Norvig, P. (2016). 'Artificial Intelligence: A Modern Approach.' Malaysia; Pearson Education Limited.

640. Saez, Emmanuel, and Gabriel Zucman. "Wealth inequality in the United States since 1913: Evidence from capitalized income tax data." The Quarterly Journal of Economics 131, no. 2 (2016): 519-578.
641. Saltuk, Yasemin. "Spotlight on the Market: The Impact Investor Survey." JP Morgan and the Global Impact Investing Network, 2014.
642. Samuel, A. L. (1959). 'Some studies in machine learning using the game of checkers.' IBM Journal of research and development, 3(3), 210-229.
643. Sbicca, J. (2012). Growing Food Justice by Planting an Anti-Oppression Foundation: Opportunities and Obstacles for a Budding Social Movement. "Agriculture and Human Values", 29(4), 455–466.
644. Schmarzo, Bill. "The Economics of Data, Analytics, and Digital Transformation." Wiley, 2021.
645. Schmidhuber, J. (2015). 'Deep learning in neural networks: An overview.' Neural networks, 61, 85-117.
646. Schneiberg, Marc, Marissa King, and Thomas Smith. "Social movements and organizational form: Cooperative alternatives to corporations in the American insurance, dairy, and grain industries." American Sociological Review, vol. 73, no. 4, 2008, pp. 635-667.
647. Schor, Juliet. "Debating the Sharing Economy." Journal of Self-Governance and Management Economics, vol. 4, no. 3, 2016, pp. 7-22.
648. Schueffel, Patrick. "Taming the Beast: A Scientific Definition of Fintech." Journal of Innovation Management, vol. 4, no. 4, 2016, pp. 32-54.
649. Schumpeter, Joseph A. Capitalism, Socialism, and Democracy. Harper Perennial, 2008.
650. Schwab, K. (2016). 'The Fourth Industrial Revolution.' Currency.
651. Schwab, K. (2016). 'The Fourth Industrial Revolution.' World Economic Forum.
652. Scorse, Jason, et al. "The Barriers and Opportunities for Environmental Entrepreneurship in Developing Countries." Environmental Management and Sustainable Development, vol. 3, no. 2, 2014, pp. 53-69.
653. Scott, James C. "The Art of Not Being Governed: An Anarchist History of Upland Southeast Asia." Yale University Press, 2009.
654. Selig Center for Economic Growth. (2019). The Multicultural Economy 2019. University of Georgia.

655. Seltzer, Michael. "Verite Group, LLC." Verite Group, LLC, 2023.
656. Shapiro, Thomas M. "The Hidden Cost of Being African American: How Wealth Perpetuates Inequality." Oxford University Press, 2004.
657. Shapiro, Thomas. "Race, home-ownership and wealth." Washington University Journal of Law & Policy 20 (2006): 53.
658. Sherraden, Michael. "Financial Capability: What Is It, and How Can It Be Created?" Center for Social Development, Washington University, 2010.
659. Shihadeh, E. S., & Flynn, N. (1996). "Segregation and crime: The relationship between black centralization and urban black homicide." Homicide studies, 1(2), 180-193.
660. Shiller, Robert. Irrational Exuberance. Princeton University Press, 2015.
661. Shirky, C. (2011). "The Political Power of Social Media: Technology, the Public Sphere, and Political Change." Foreign Affairs.
662. Sibilia, Rebecca. "Why America's Schools Have A Money Problem." NPR, 2016.
663. Siburg, K. F. (2020). Banking on a Revolution: The Financial Sector's Role in Racial Wealth Equality. Journal of Business and Management.
664. Sitkin, S. B., See, K. E., Miller, C. C., Lawless, M. W., & Carton, A. M. (2011). The paradox of stretch goals: Organizations in pursuit of the seemingly impossible. Academy of Management Review, 36(3), 544-566.
665. Smith Jr., Antonio T. "Re-Segregation: Volume I, The Power Matrix: A Masterplan for Black Group Economics and Wealth Creation." Chicago: Self-Published, 2023.
666. Smith Jr., Antonio T. (2023). "The Road to Economic Empowerment." ATSJR Companies International.
667. Smith Jr., Antonio T. (2023). "The Uncomfortable Truth: The Black Experience in Business." ATSJR Companies International.
668. Smith, Antonio T. Jr. "Re-Segregation: Volume I, The Power Matrix: A Masterplan for Black Group Economics and Wealth Creation," 2023.
669. Smith, J. "Understanding Your Rights in Collective Investments." Forbes, July 22, 2022.
670. Smith, J. W. A., & Deng, S. (2019). 'Pipeline or Personal Preference: Women and Computer Science in U.S. States.' Social Forces.

671. Smith, John. "Why Are There So Few Black-Owned Banks?" The Balance, July 15, 2020.
672. Smith, Stacy L., et al. "Inclusion in the Director's Chair? Gender, Race & Age of Film Directors Across 1,000 Films from 2007-2016." USC Annenberg Inclusion Initiative, 2017.
673. Soergel, Andrew. "Robert F. Smith: The richest black man in America." U.S. News & World Report, 2021. https://www.usnews.com/news/the-report/articles/2020-06-12/robert-f-smith-is-the-richest-black-man-in-america
674. Solomon, B. "Who Owns The Cloud? These Companies Do." Forbes, 2021.
675. Southgate, D. (2011). "The US digital divide: a call for a new philosophy." Chinese Journal of Communication, 4(2), 131-146.
676. Sowell, "Wealth, Poverty, and Politics."
677. Sowell, T. (2004). Affirmative Action Around the World: An Empirical Study. Yale University Press.
678. Sowell, Thomas. "Affirmative Action: A Worldwide Disaster." Commentary, vol. 84, no. 6, 1987, pp. 26-32.
679. Sowell, Thomas. "Wealth, Poverty, and Politics." Basic Books, 2015.
680. Sowell, Thomas. Race and Economics: How Much Can Be Blamed on Discrimination? Hoover Institution Press, 2011.
681. Sprenger, Charles D., et al. "The Economic Importance of Financial Literacy: Theory and Evidence." Journal of Economic Literature, 2015.
682. Squires, Gregory D., et al. "Capital and Communities in Black and White: The Intersections of Race, Class, and Uneven Development." State University of New York Press, 1994.
683. Stanford University, "Future of Programming and Software 2.0," 2022.
684. Stankorb, Sarah. "Robert F. Smith: The billionaire who is trying to cleanse his reputation." Bloomberg.com, 2021. https://www.bloomberg.com/news/features/2021-02-18/robert-f-smith-vista-equity-billionaire-seeks-redemption-after-tax-case
685. Statista. (2021). "Telecommunications services global spending forecast 2008-2023."
686. Stoll, Michael A., and Raphael W. Bostic. "The role of race and ethnicity in job matching." Industrial & Labor Relations Review, vol. 52, no. 3, 1999, pp. 402-415.
687. Stone, Brad. The Upstarts: How Uber, Airbnb, and the Killer Companies of the New Silicon Valley Are Changing the World. Little, Brown and Company, 2017.

688. Stout, Robert J., and Jenkins, Richard A. "Blacks in the Tech Industry: The Challenge of Equal Opportunity." Journal of Black Studies, 2021.
689. Sundararajan, Arun. The Sharing Economy: The End of Employment and the Rise of Crowd-Based Capitalism. MIT Press, 2016.
690. Swan, M. (2015). 'Blockchain: Blueprint for a New Economy.' O'Reilly Media, Inc.
691. Sweet, Ken. "Americans face a post-COVID-19 flood of personal debt, NY Fed warns." Fortune, 2021.
692. Taleb, Nassim Nicholas. Antifragile: Things That Gain from Disorder. Random House, 2012.
693. Tapscott, A., & Tapscott, D. (2020). 'Financial Services: Building Blockchain One Block at a Time.' Financial Times.
694. Tapscott, D., & Tapscott, A. (2016). 'Blockchain Revolution: How the Technology Behind Bitcoin Is Changing Money, Business, and the World.' New York: Portfolio.
695. Tapscott, D., & Tapscott, A. (2016). 'Blockchain revolution: how the technology behind bitcoin is changing money, business, and the world.' Penguin.
696. Tapscott, D., and Tapscott, A. "Blockchain Revolution: How the Technology Behind Bitcoin Is Changing Money, Business, and the World." Penguin, 2016.
697. Tapscott, Don, and Alex Tapscott. "Blockchain Revolution: How the Technology Behind Bitcoin Is Changing Money, Business, and the World." Penguin, 2016.
698. Tapscott, Don, and Alex Tapscott. "Blockchain Revolution: How the Technology Behind Bitcoin Is Changing Money, Business, and the World." Portfolio, 2016.
699. Tapscott, Don, and Alex Tapscott. Blockchain Revolution: How the Technology Behind Bitcoin Is Changing Money, Business, and the World. Penguin, 2016.
700. Taylor, Keeanga-Yamahtta. Race for Profit: How Banks and the Real Estate Industry Undermined Black home-ownership. The University of North Carolina Press, 2019.
701. Taylor, Kira Hudson, Margaret T. Hicken, and Kristine Siefert. "Perceived Discrimination, Depression, and Mental Health: The Impact of Multiple Dimensions of Discrimination." The Lancet Psychiatry, 6.12 (2019): 975-981.
702. Thomas Sowell, "Wealth, Poverty, and Politics: An International Perspective," The Hoover Institution (2015).

703. Thomas, June Manning. "Redevelopment and Race: Planning a Finer City in Postwar Detroit." Johns Hopkins University Press, 1997.
704. Togoh, Isabel. "Black-Owned Challenger Greenwood Bank Hits 500,000 Sign-Ups Before Launch." Forbes, 2021.
705. Tomaskovic-Devey, Donald, and Dustin Avent-Holt. "Relational Inequality: Gender Earnings Inequality in U.S. Federal Agencies." American Journal of Sociology 124, no. 4 (2019): 908-949.
706. Tomaskovic-Devey, Donald, and Kevin Stainback. "Discrimination and Desegregation: Equal Opportunity Progress in U.S. Private Sector Workplaces since the Civil Rights Act." The ANNALS of the American Academy of Political and Social Science, 2012.
707. Topol, E. (2019). 'High-performance Medicine: The Convergence of Human and Artificial Intelligence.' Nature Medicine.
708. Topol, E. J. (2019). 'High-performance medicine: the convergence of human and artificial intelligence.' Nature medicine, 25(1), 44-56.
709. Travis L. Dixon, "A Dangerous Distortion of our Families," Color Of Change, January 2017, https://colorofchange.org/dangerousdistortion/.
710. Troy, A. S., Shallcross, A. J., & Mauss, I. B. (2013). A person-by-situation approach to emotion regulation: Cognitive reappraisal can either help or hurt, depending on the context. Psychological Science, 24(12), 2505-2514.
711. Tufekci, Z. (2017). Twitter and Tear Gas: The Power and Fragility of Networked Protest. New Haven: Yale University Press.
712. Turner, D. (2019). 'The cost of connectivity 2020.' New America.
713. Turner, Margery Austin, et al. "Housing Discrimination Against Racial and Ethnic Minorities 2012: Executive Summary." Urban Institute, June 2013.
714. U.S. Bureau of Economic Analysis. (2021). 'Gross Domestic Product by Industry: Fourth Quarter and Year 2020.'
715. U.S. Bureau of Labor Statistics. "Highlights of women's earnings in 2021."
716. U.S. Bureau of Labor Statistics. "Labor Force Characteristics by Race and Ethnicity, 2018."
717. U.S. Bureau of Labor Statistics. "Labor force characteristics by race and ethnicity, 2018." Report 1082, October 2019.
718. U.S. Bureau of Labor Statistics. "Labor Force Statistics from the Current Population Survey." 2020.

719. U.S. Bureau of Labor Statistics. (2021). 'Labor Force Statistics from the Current Population Survey.'
720. U.S. Census Bureau, Current Population Survey/Housing Vacancy Survey, October 2020.
721. U.S. Census Bureau. "Income and Poverty in the United States: 2019." U.S. Census Bureau, September 15, 2020.
722. U.S. Census Bureau. (2016). 2012 Survey of Business Owners. U.S. Department of Commerce.
723. U.S. Constitution. amend. XIII.
724. U.S. Department of Education, National Center for Education Statistics. "The Condition of Education 2020."
725. U.S. Department of Education, Office of Civil Rights. (2018). '2015-16 Civil Rights Data Collection: STEM Course Taking.'
726. U.S. Department of Education. (2017). 'Reimagining the Role of Technology in Education.'
727. U.S. Equal Employment Opportunity Commission. "Diversity in High Tech." May 2016.
728. U.S. Equal Employment Opportunity Commission. (2016). 'Diversity in High Tech.'
729. U.S. Federation of Worker Cooperatives. "State of the Sector," 2020.
730. U.S. Government Accountability Office. "K-12 Education: Better Use of Information Could Help Agencies Identify Disparities and Address Racial Discrimination." April 21, 2016.
731. U.S. Small Business Administration. "8(a) Business Development Program." Accessed on June 2023.
732. U.S. Small Business Administration. "Small Business Facts." 2018.
733. United Nations Economic Commission for Africa. "African Continental Free Trade Area: Questions & Answers." March 2018.
734. US Department of Education. "STEM Attrition: College Students' Paths Into and Out of STEM Fields." National Center for Education Statistics, 2013.
735. Van Dijk, J. A. G. M. (2006). 'Digital Divide Research, Achievements and Shortcomings.' Poetics.
736. Vanek, Jaroslav. The General Theory of Labor-Managed Market Economies. Cornell University Press, 1971.
737. Venkataramakrishnan, R. "The Lack of Diversity in Tech is a Cultural Issue." Financial Times, 2020.
738. Vista Equity Partners. https://www.vistaequitypartners.com/
739. W. K. Kellogg Foundation. (2017). The Business Case for Racial Equity. W. K. Kellogg Foundation.

740. Walker, Tristan. "Our Story." Walker & Company Brands, www.walkerandcompany.com/our-story.
741. Ward, Benjamin. "The Firm in Illyria: Market Syndicalism." The American Economic Review, vol. 48, no. 4, 1958, pp. 566-589.
742. Warschauer, Mark. Technology and Social Inclusion: Rethinking the Digital Divide. MIT press, 2004.
743. Warzel, C. (2019). 'The Tech Industry's Psychological War on Gig Workers.' The New York Times. https://www.nytimes.com/2019/12/04/opinion/uber-lyft-gig-economy.html
744. Webb, A. (2020). 'How Arlan Hamilton went from homeless to founding a multi-million dollar venture capital fund.' Forbes.
745. Werbach, K. (2018). 'Trust, But Verify: Why the Blockchain Needs the Law.' Berkeley Technology Law Journal, 33, 489–548.
746. West, D. M. (2015). 'Digital Divide: Improving Internet Access in the Developing World through Affordable Services and Diverse Content.' Brookings Institution.
747. Whelan, D. (2017, Nov 27). Unilever Buys Sundial Brands To Expand Personal Care Offerings. Forbes.
748. Whyte, W. F., & Whyte, K. K. (1991). Making Mondragon: The Growth and Dynamics of the Worker Cooperative Complex. ILR Press.
749. William A. Darity Jr., A. Kirsten Mullen. "From Here to Equality: Reparations for Black Americans in the Twenty-First Century." The University of North Carolina Press, 2020.
750. William Darity Jr. and Darrick Hamilton, "Bolstering the Business of Blackness," The Nation, June 28, 2017, https://www.thenation.com/article/archive/bolstering-business-blackness/.
751. Williams Shanks, Trina R., and Meschede, Tatjana. "Family assets, postsecondary education, and students with disabilities: Building on progress and overcoming challenges." Children and Youth Services Review, 31.11 (2009): 1131-1137.
752. Williams, B. (2019, December 6). 'The #BlackTechTwitter Movement Helps Connect Tech Professionals.' Forbes.
753. Williams, David R., and Toni D. Rucker. "Understanding and Addressing Racial Disparities in Health Care." Health Care Financing Review 21, no. 4 (2000): 75-90.
754. Williams, Katina. "Digital Divide: Segregation in the Information Age." Media, Culture & Society 21, no. 2 (1999): 197-211.

755. Williams, T. "Banking on the Hard Sell: Low Rates, High Pressure at OneWest Bank." LA Times, January 12, 2020.
756. Wilson, Valerie, and William M. Rodgers III. "Black-White Wage Gaps Expand with Rising Wage Inequality." Economic Policy Institute, 2016.
757. Wilson, Valerie, and William M. Rodgers. "Black-white wage gaps expand with rising wage inequality." Economic Policy Institute, 2016.
758. Wilson, Valerie. "Racial disparities in income and poverty remain largely unchanged amid strong income growth in 2019." Economic Policy Institute, 2020.
759. Wolff, E. N. (2017). A Century of Wealth in America. Harvard University Press.
760. World Economic Forum. (2020). 'The Future of Jobs Report 2020.'
761. Yeager, David S., et al. "Boring but Important: A Self-Transcendent Purpose for Learning Fosters Academic Self-Regulation." Journal of Personality and Social Psychology, vol. 107, no. 4, 2014, pp. 559-580.
762. Yeager, David S., et al. "Boring but Important: A Self-Transcendent Purpose for Learning Fosters Academic Self-Regulation." Journal of Personality and Social Psychology, vol. 107, no. 4, 2014, pp. 559–580.
763. Yeager, David S., et al. "Teaching a lay theory before college narrows achievement gaps at scale." Proceedings of the National Academy of Sciences, vol. 113, no. 24, 2016, pp. E3341–E3348.
764. York, Dan. "Clean Energy's Dirty Secret." Foreign Affairs, 2021.
765. Zaharna, R. S. (2010). Battles to Bridges: U.S. Strategic Communication and Public Diplomacy after 9/11. Palgrave Macmillan.
766. Zetzsche, Dirk A., et al. "Regulating a Revolution: From Regulatory Sandboxes to Smart Regulation." Fordham Journal of Corporate & Financial Law, 23(1), 2017.
767. Zhan, Min, and Michael Sherraden. "Assets, expectations, and children's educational achievement in female-headed households." Social service review 77, no. 2 (2003): 191-211.
768. Ziegler, T., et al. "Expanding Horizons: The 3rd European Alternative Finance Industry Report." Cambridge Centre for Alternative Finance, 2017.
769. Zuboff, S. (2019). 'The Age of Surveillance Capitalism: The Fight for a Human Future at the New Frontier of Power.' New York: PublicAffairs.

770. " Robert F. Smith." Forbes, www.forbes.com/profile/robert-f-smith/.
771. " The World's 100 Largest Companies: Forbes Global 2000 Guide." Forbes, www.forbes.com/global2000/.
772. "A Guide to Green Business Ideas." US Small Business Administration, 2023.
773. "About Us." National Association of Health Services Executives, 2023. "About." Black Wellness Community, 2023.
774. "African American Consumers are More Relevant Than Ever." Nielsen, 2019.
775. "Federal Grants for Green Businesses." Grants.gov, 2023.
776. "Global Wellness Economy Monitor." Global Wellness Institute, 2021.
777. "Green Economy Market Report." Fortune Business Insights, 2021.
778. "Health Equity Considerations and Racial and Ethnic Minority Groups." Centers for Disease Control and Prevention, 2023.
779. "Sustainability: A 'Win-Win' for Small Businesses." US Chamber of Commerce, 2021.
780. "The Sustainable Consumer and the 2020s Holiday Shopping Season." Accenture, 2020.
781. "Top 12 Environmental Leaders of Color to Watch in 2020." GreenBiz, 2020.
782. "Understanding crowd-funding and Its Regulations." Securities and Exchange Commission, 2021.
783. . Akers, Ronald L., and Adam L. Silverman. "Toward a Social Learning Model of Violence and Terrorism." Violence: From Theory to Research, edited by Margaret A. Zahn, Henry H. Brownstein, and Shelly L. Jackson, Anderson, 2004, pp. 19-35.
784. . Anderson, Claud. PowerNomics: The National Plan to Empower Black America, Powernomics Corporation of America, 2001.
785. . Dweck, Carol S. Mindset: The New Psychology of Success, Random House, 2006.
786. . Locke, Edwin A., and Gary P. Latham. A theory of goal setting & task performance, Prentice-Hall, 1990.
787. . MarksJarvis, Gail. "Robert F. Smith: Who is America's richest black man?" Chicago Tribune, 2019.
788. . Smith, Robert F. "The Wealth Gap: A Race or Class Divide?" The New York Times, 2019.

789. 0 Anderson, Claud. "A Black History Reader: 101 Question You Never Thought to Ask." PowerNomics Corporation of America, 2017.
790. 0 Eyal, Amir. "Mylestone Plans LLC." Mylestone Plans LLC, 2023.
791. 0 Katznelson, Ira. "When Affirmative Action Was White: An Untold History of Racial Inequality in Twentieth-Century America." W. W. Norton & Company, 2005.
792. 0 Locke, E. A., & Latham, G. P. (1985). The application of goal setting to sports. Journal of Sport Psychology, 7(3), 205-222.
793. 1 Anderson, Claud. Black Labor, White Wealth: The Search for Power and Economic Justice. Powernomics Corporation of America, Inc, 1994.
794. 1 Bundles, A'Lelia. "On Her Own Ground: The Life and Times of Madam C.J. Walker." Simon and Schuster, 2001.
795. 1 Cardone, Grant. The 10X Rule: The Only Difference Between Success and Failure. John Wiley & Sons, 2011.
796. 1 Lyubomirsky, S., Sheldon, K.M., and Schkade, D. "Pursuing happiness: The architecture of sustainable change." Review of General Psychology, 9 (2005): 111–131.
797. 1 Rothstein, Richard. "The Color of Law: A Forgotten History of How Our Government Segregated America." Liveright Publishing, 2017.
798. 2 Anderson, Claud. "Black Labor, White Wealth: The Search for Power and Economic Justice." PowerNomics Corporation of America, 1994.
799. 2 Federico, Francesca. "Twelve Points." Twelve Points, 2023.
800. 3 Fomichenko, Dmitriy. "Sense Financial Services LLC." Sense Financial Services LLC, 2023.
801. Aaronson, Daniel, et al. "The Effects of the 1930s HOLC 'Redlining' Maps," Federal Reserve Bank of Chicago, 2017.
802. Adler, Paul S., and Seok-Woo Kwon. "Social Capital: Prospects for a New Concept." Academy of Management Review 27, no. 1 (2002): 17-40.
803. Alesina, Alberto, and Dani Rodrik. "Distributive Politics and Economic Growth." Quarterly Journal of Economics 109, no. 2 (1994): 465-490.
804. Anacker, Katrin B., et al. "Black home-ownership: The Role of Temporality and Politics in Housing, Race, and Wealth Inequality in America." Journal of Urban Affairs, 2019.

805. Anderson, Claud. "PowerNomics : The National Plan to Empower Black America." PowerNomics Corporation of America, 2001.
806. Anderson, Claud. A Black History Reader: 101 Questions You Never Thought to Ask. Powernomics Corporation of America, 2017.
807. Anderson, Claud. Black Labor, White Wealth: The Search for Power and Economic Justice. Powernomics Corporation of America, 1994.
808. Anderson, Claud. PowerNomics: The National Plan to Empower Black America. PowerNomics Corporation of America, 2000.
809. Anderson, Claud. Powernomics: The National Plan to Empower Black America. Powernomics Corporation of America, 2001.
810. Anderson, Claud. PowerNomics: The National Plan to Empower Black America. PowerNomics Corporation of America, 2001. 2 3
811. Anderson, Maggie. "Our Black Year: One Family's Quest to Buy Black in America's Racially Divided Economy." HarperCollins, 2013.
812. Ayres, Ian, and Peter Siegelman. "Race and Gender Discrimination in Bargaining for a New Car." American Economic Review, 1995.
813. Badkar, Mamta. "Robert F. Smith: the billionaire paying off black students' debt," Financial Times, 2019.
814. Baptist, Edward E. The Half Has Never Been Told: Slavery and the Making of American Capitalism, 2014.
815. Baradaran, Mehrsa. "The Color of Money: Black Banks and the Racial Wealth Gap." Belknap Press, 2017.
816. Bates, Timothy, and Alicia Robb. "Race, ethnicity and entrepreneurial success: Evidence from the characteristics of business owners survey." Federal Reserve Bank of Kansas City (2008).
817. Bates, Timothy. "Financing Small Business Creation: The Case of Chinese and Korean Immigrant Entrepreneurs." Journal of Business Venturing 12, no. 2 (1997): 109-124.
818. Bates, Timothy. "Minority Business Success: Refocusing on the American Dream." Stanford University Press, 2011.
819. Becker, Gary S. "Human Capital: A Theoretical and Empirical Analysis, with Special Reference to Education." University of Chicago Press, 1994.
820. Bertrand, Marianne and Sendhil Mullainathan. "Are Emily and Greg More Employable Than Lakisha and Jamal? A Field

Experiment on Labor Market Discrimination." American Economic Review, 2004, 94(4): 991-1013.
821. Bertrand, Marianne, and Sendhil Mullainathan. "Are Emily and Greg More Employable Than Lakisha and Jamal? A Field Experiment on Labor Market Discrimination," The American Economic Review, 2004.
822. Bibliography
823. Black Business Network. (n.d.). Our Mission. Black Business Network.
824. Black in AI. "About Us." Black in AI, 2023.
825. Blanchflower, David G., Phillip B. Levine, and David J. Zimmerman. "Discrimination in the Small-Business Credit Market." Review of Economics and Statistics 85, no. 4 (2003): 930-943.
826. Blanchflower, David G., Phillip B. Levine, and David J. Zimmerman. "Discrimination in the Small-Business Credit Market." The Review of Economics and Statistics 85, no. 4 (2003): 930-943.
827. Blanchflower, David G., Phillip B. Levine, and David J. Zimmerman. "Discrimination in the Small-Business Credit Market." The Review of Economics and Statistics, 2003.
828. Bocian, Debbie Gruenstein, Keith S. Ernst, and Wei Li. "Unfair Lending: The Effect of Race and Ethnicity on the Price of Subprime Mortgages." Center for Responsible Lending, 2008.
829. Bonilla-Silva, Eduardo. "Racism without Racists: Color-Blind Racism and the Persistence of Racial Inequality in the United States." Rowman & Littlefield, 2017.
830. Bonner, F. A., Alfred, M. V., James, M., Lewis, P., Nave, F., & St juste, S. (2010). Creating Environments of Success and Resilience: Culturally Responsive Teaching and Learning. Texas Education Review, 1(1).
831. Borjas, George J. "Labor Economics." McGraw-Hill Education, 2016.
832. Borjas, George J. "The Slowdown in the Economic Assimilation of Immigrants: Aging and Cohort Effects Revisited Again," Journal of Human Capital 9, no. 4 (Winter 2015): 483-517.
833. Borjas, George J. 2015. "The Slowdown in the Economic Assimilation of Immigrants: Aging and Cohort Effects Revisited Again." Journal of Human Capital 9, no. 4 (Winter): 483-517.
834. Bradford, William D. "The Wealth Dynamics of Entrepreneurship for Black and White Families in the U.S." Review of Income and Wealth 46, no. 1 (2000): 89-116.

835. Bradford, William D. "The Wealth Dynamics of Entrepreneurship for Black and White Families in the U.S." Review of Income and Wealth 47, no. 1 (2001): 89-116.
836. Bradford, William D. "The Wealth Dynamics of Entrepreneurship for Black and White Families in the U.S." Review of Income and Wealth 56, no. s1 (2010): S65-S81.
837. Brookings Institution, "Five-star reviews, one-star profits: The devaluation of businesses in Black communities," 2020.
838. Brown, Dorothy. "The Whiteness of Wealth: How the Tax System Impoverishes Black Americans--and How We Can Fix It." Crown, 2021.
839. Bundles, A'Lelia. "Madam C.J. Walker: Entrepreneur, Leader, and Self-Made Millionaire," Biography, 2020.
840. Buolamwini, Joy. "How I'm Fighting Bias in Algorithms." TED Talk, 2016.
841. Carson, Clayborne. "The Civil Rights Movement: Past, Present, and Future," Annual Review of Sociology, 1993.
842. Cavalluzzo, Ken S., and John D. Wolken. "Small business loan turndowns, personal wealth and discrimination." The Journal of Business 78, no. 6 (2005): 2153-2178.
843. CBInsights. "The State of Black Tech start-ups in the U.S." CBInsights, 2023.
844. Centers for Disease Control and Prevention. "Risk for COVID-19 Infection, Hospitalization, and Death By Race/Ethnicity." June 2021.
845. Chatterji, Aaron K., Edward L. Glaeser, and William R. Kerr. "Clusters of Entrepreneurship and Innovation." Innovation Policy and the Economy 14, no. 1 (2014): 129-166.
846. Chatterji, Aaron K., Solène Delecourt, Sharique Hasan, and Rembrand Koning. "When does advice impact start-up performance?" Strategic Management Journal 40, no. 3 (2019): 331-356.
847. Chetty, Raj et al. "Race and Economic Opportunity in the United States: An Intergenerational Perspective." The Quarterly Journal of Economics, 2018.
848. Chetty, Raj, Nathaniel Hendren, Maggie R. Jones, and Sonya R. Porter. "Race and Economic Opportunity in the United States: An Intergenerational Perspective." The Quarterly Journal of Economics 135, no. 2 (2020): 711-783.
849. Chetty, Raj, Nathaniel Hendren, Patrick Kline, and Emmanuel Saez. "Where is the Land of Opportunity? The Geography of

Intergenerational Mobility in the United States." The Quarterly Journal of Economics 129, no. 4 (2014): 1553-1623.
850. Chiteji, Ngina, and Darrick Hamilton. "Family Connections and the Black-White Wealth Gap Among Middle-Class Families." Review of Black Political Economy, 2002.
851. Civil Rights Act, 42 U.S.C. § 2000e (1964).
852. Coates, Ta-Nehisi. "The Case for Reparations." The Atlantic, June 2014.
853. Code2040. "About Us." Code2040, 2023.
854. Cohen, Lizabeth. "A Consumers' Republic: The Politics of Mass Consumption in Postwar America." Vintage Books, 2003.
855. Cohen-Cole, Ethan. "Credit Card Redlining." The Review of Economics and Statistics, 2011.
856. Collins, Patricia Hill, and Sirma Bilge. "Intersectionality." Polity, 2016.
857. Comaroff, John L., and Jean Comaroff. Ethnicity, Inc. University of Chicago Press, 2009.
858. Community Reinvestment Act (CRA), Pub. L. 95-128, 91 Stat. 1147, 12 U.S.C. § 2901 et seq.
859. Critics may argue that these efforts amount to favoritism or reverse discrimination. However, supporters contend that they're necessary corrective measures to address historical and systemic racial disparities. It's not enough to make these technologies widely available; they must be made accessible and usable for all, irrespective of racial or socioeconomic status.
860. Cultivating Partnerships: Navigating the digital world can be complex. Seek out partnerships with tech consultants or professionals who have a proven track record in automation and virtualization. They'll provide guidance on effective implementation and tackle any challenges that come your way.
861. Darity, William A., and Patrick L. Mason. "Evidence on Discrimination in Employment: Codes of Color, Codes of Gender." The Journal of Economic Perspectives, 1998.
862. Darity, William, and A. Kirsten Mullen. "From Here to Equality: Reparations for Black Americans in the Twenty-First Century." The University of North Carolina Press, 2020.
863. Deming, David J. "The Growing Importance of Social Skills in the Labor Market," The Quarterly Journal of Economics, 2017.
864. Desmond, Matthew, and Carl Gershenson. "Housing and Black Wealth," The American Journal of Sociology, 2016.

865. Duncan, Greg J., and Richard J. Murnane. Whither Opportunity?: Rising Inequality, Schools, and Children's Life Chances. Russell Sage Foundation, 2011.
866. Dweck, Carol. Mindset: The New Psychology of Success. Ballantine Books, 2008.
867. Economic Policy Institute, "Black-white wage gaps expand with rising wage inequality," 2016.
868. Economic Policy Institute, "Racial disparities in income and poverty remain largely unchanged amid strong income growth in 2019," 2020.
869. Embarking on the Digital Frontier: A Focused Guide for Black Entrepreneurs
870. Epstein, Richard A. "Forbidden Grounds: The Case Against Employment Discrimination Laws," Harvard University Press, 2016.
871. Epstein, Richard A. 2016. "Forbidden Grounds: The Case Against Employment Discrimination Laws." Harvard University Press.
872. Ericsson, K. Anders. Peak: Secrets from the New Science of Expertise. Houghton Mifflin Harcourt, 2016.
873. Eyes on the Horizon: The digital landscape changes rapidly, and it pays to stay ahead of the curve. Regularly peruse tech news sites, online forums, and professional networks to stay informed.
874. Fairlie, Robert W. "Kauffman Index of Entrepreneurial Activity 1996–2013." The Ewing Marion Kauffman Foundation (2014).
875. Fairlie, Robert W., and Alicia M. Robb. "Race and Entrepreneurial Success." MIT Press, 2008.
876. Fairlie, Robert W., and Alicia M. Robb. "Why Are Black-Owned Businesses Less Successful than White-Owned Businesses? The Role of Families, Inheritances, and Business Human Capital," Journal of Labor Economics, 2010.
877. Fairlie, Robert W., and Alicia M. Robb. "Why are black-owned businesses less successful than white-owned businesses? The role of families, inheritances, and business human capital." Journal of Labor Economics 25, no. 2 (2007): 289-323.
878. Fairlie, Robert W., and Alicia M. Robb. Race and Entrepreneurial Success, 2008.
879. Fairlie, Robert W., and Alicia M. Robb. Race and Entrepreneurial Success: Black-, Asian-, and White-Owned Businesses in the United States. MIT Press, 2008.

880. Fairlie, Robert, and Alicia Robb. Race and Entrepreneurial Success: Black-, Asian-, and White-Owned Businesses in the United States. MIT Press, 2008.
881. Fairlie, Robert. "Black and White: Access to Capital among Minority-Owned start-ups," Stanford Institute for Economic Policy Research, 2013.
882. Fairlie, Robert. "Race and the Lifecycle of Entrepreneurial Firms: Evidence from U.S. Census Bureau Data." Stanford Institute for Economic Policy Research, 2008.
883. Fairlie, Robert. "The Impact of COVID-19 on Small Business Owners: Continued Losses and the Partial Rebound by June 2020." National Bureau of Economic Research, 2020.
884. Fairlie, Robert. "The Impact of COVID-19 on Small Business Owners: Evidence of Early-Stage Losses from the April 2020 Current Population Survey." National Bureau of Economic Research, 2020.
885. Federal Reserve Banks. 2020 Small Business Credit Survey: Report on Employer Firms.
886. Federal Reserve Board, "Changes in U.S. Family Finances from 2007 to 2010: Evidence from the Survey of Consumer Finances," 2012.
887. Federal Reserve Board, "Survey of Consumer Finances," 2019.
888. Federal Reserve, 2019 Survey of Consumer Finances
889. Federal Reserve. (2019). Changes in U.S. Family Finances from 2016 to 2019: Evidence from the Survey of Consumer Finances. Federal Reserve Bulletin, 106(5).
890. Federal Reserve. (2020). Changes in U.S. Family Finances from 2016 to 2019: Evidence from the Survey of Consumer Finances.
891. Fernandes, Daniel, John G. Lynch Jr, and Richard G. Netemeyer. "Financial Literacy, Financial Education, and Downstream Financial Behaviors." Management Science 60, no. 8 (2014): 1861-1883.
892. Forbes. "Forbes' Top Earning Musicians." Forbes, 2022.
893. Forbes. "The World's Billionaires: Robert F. Smith." Forbes, 2023.
894. Furnham, Adrian. "The Psychology of Money." Routledge, 2014.
895. Gentry, William M., and R. Glenn Hubbard. "Entrepreneurship and Household Saving." Advances in Economic Analysis & Policy 4, no. 1 (2004).
896. Gerardi, Kristopher, et al. "Race, Ethnicity and High-Cost Mortgage Lending." Federal Reserve Bank of Atlanta, 2015.

897. Gilens, Martin. "Why Americans Hate Welfare: Race, Media, and the Politics of Antipoverty Policy." University of Chicago Press, 1999.
898. Gould, Elise, and Valerie Wilson. "Black workers face two of the most lethal preexisting conditions for coronavirus—racism and economic inequality." Economic Policy Institute, June 2020.
899. Granovetter, Mark. "The strength of weak ties." American Journal of Sociology 78, no. 6 (1973): 1360-1380.
900. Gullah Geechee Cultural Heritage Corridor Commission. "Management Plan." National Park Service, 2013.
901. Hamilton, D., Darity Jr., W., Price, A., Sridharan, V., & Tippett, R. (2015). Umbrellas don't make it rain: Why studying and working hard isn't enough for Black Americans. New York: The New School.
902. Hamilton, Darrick, and William Darity Jr. "The political economy of education, financial literacy, and the racial wealth gap." Federal Reserve Bank of St. Louis Review, 2017, 99(1): 59-76.
903. Hamilton, Darrick, and William Darity Jr. "The racial wealth gap: Why policy matters." Economic Policy Institute, 2017.
904. Hamilton, Darrick, and William Darity. "Race, Wealth, and Intergenerational Poverty." American Prospect, 2009.
905. Hamilton, Darrick, and William Darity. "Race, Wealth, and Intergenerational Poverty." The American Prospect, 2009.
906. Hamilton, Darrick, et al. "Umbrellas don't make it rain: Why studying and working hard isn't enough for Black Americans," The New School, Duke Center for Social Equity, and Insight Center for Community Economic Development, 2015.
907. Hamilton, Darrick, et al. "Umbrellas Don't Make it Rain: Why Studying and Working Hard Isn't Enough for Black Americans." The New School, 2015.
908. Harding, Sandra. "Standpoint Theories: Productively Controversial." Hypatia, 2004.
909. Haskins, Ron. "Work Over Welfare: The Inside Story of the 1996 Welfare Reform Law," Brookings Institution Press, 2006.
910. Haskins, Ron. 2006. "Work Over Welfare: The Inside Story of the 1996 Welfare Reform Law." Brookings Institution Press.
911. Hatcher, Desiree. "Estate Planning for the African American Family." Howard Law Journal 53 (2009): 731.
912. Herbert, Christopher E., Daniel T. McCue, and Rocio Sanchez-Moyano. "Is home-ownership Still an Effective Means of Building Wealth for Low-income and Minority Households? (Was it

Ever?)." Joint Center for Housing Studies, Harvard University (2013).
913. Herbert, Christopher, et al. "The Role of Investors in Acquiring Foreclosed Properties in Low- and Moderate-Income Neighborhoods: A Review of Findings from Four Case Studies," U.S. Department of Housing and Urban Development, 2012.
914. Hoang, Ha, and Bostjan Antoncic. "Network-based Research in Entrepreneurship: A Critical Review." Journal of Business Venturing 18, no. 2 (2003): 165-187.
915. Holohan, Meghan. "Patricia Bath, 76, Who Took On Blindness and Earned a Patent, Dies," The New York Times, 2019.
916. In conclusion, the Power Matrix's focus on digital infrastructure as a tool for Black wealth generation and sustainability is not just timely but also essential. It aligns with global digital trends while also addressing economic and digital equity issues within Black communities.
917. Institute for Policy Studies, "The Ever-Growing Gap: Without Change, African-American and Latino Families Won't Match White Wealth for Centuries," 2017.
918. Investing in the Future: Now, it's time to back your vision with tangible commitment. Equip your enterprise with the tools it needs, whether that be software automation or IoT devices. Remember, this isn't an expense, but an investment that will reap significant long-term rewards.
919. Jackson, C. Kirabo, Rucker C. Johnson, and Claudia Persico. "The effects of school spending on educational and economic outcomes: Evidence from school finance reforms," The Quarterly Journal of Economics, 2016.
920. Katznelson, Ira. "When Affirmative Action Was White: An Untold History of Racial Inequality in Twentieth-Century America." W. W. Norton & Company, 2005.
921. Katznelson, Ira. When Affirmative Action Was White: An Untold History of Racial Inequality in Twentieth-Century America, 2005.
922. Kauffman Foundation. (2017). Race and Entrepreneurial Success.
923. Kendi, Ibram X. "How to Be an Antiracist." One World, 2019.
924. Kendi, Ibram X. "Stamped from the Beginning: The Definitive History of Racist Ideas in America." Nation Books, 2016.
925. King, M. L. (1968). The other America. Speech at Grosse Pointe High School.

926. Kochhar, Rakesh, and Richard Fry. "Wealth inequality has widened along racial, ethnic lines since end of Great Recession," Pew Research Center, 2014.
927. Kochhar, Rakesh. "Black workers face two of the most lethal preexisting conditions for coronavirus—racism and economic inequality," Economic Policy Institute, 2020.
928. Krysan, Maria and Kyle Crowder. "Cycle of Segregation: Social Processes and Residential Stratification." Russell Sage Foundation, 2017.
929. Ladd, Helen F. "Education and Poverty: Confronting the Evidence." Journal of Policy Analysis and Management, 2012, 31(2): 203-227.
930. Laurencin, Cato T., and Aneesah McClinton. "The COVID-19 Pandemic: a Call to Action to Identify and Address Racial and Ethnic Disparities." Journal of Racial and Ethnic Health Disparities, 2020, 7: 398–402.
931. Li, Yue, and John R. Robinson. "Evidence on the Effect of Recognition and Disclosure on Cost of Equity Capital in the Nonprofit Sector." Research in Accounting Regulation 28, no. 2 (2016): 136-145.
932. Lusardi, Annamaria, and Olivia S. Mitchell. "Financial Literacy and Retirement Planning in the United States." Journal of Pension Economics & Finance 10, no. 4 (2011): 509-525.
933. Lusardi, Annamaria, and Olivia S. Mitchell. "Financial literacy and retirement planning in the United States." Journal of Pension Economics & Finance, 2011.
934. Lusardi, Annamaria, and Olivia S. Mitchell. "Financial Literacy and Wealth Accumulation: The Importance of Financial Literacy," National Bureau of Economic Research, 2014.
935. Lusardi, Annamaria, and Olivia S. Mitchell. "The Economic Importance of Financial Literacy: Theory and Evidence." Journal of Economic Literature 52, no. 1 (2014): 5-44.
936. Lusardi, Annamaria, and Olivia S. Mitchell. "The Economic Importance of Financial Literacy: Theory and Evidence." Journal of Economic Literature, 2014, 52(1): 5-44.
937. Lusardi, Annamaria, and Peter Tufano. "Debt Literacy, Financial Experiences, and Overindebtedness." Journal of Pension Economics and Finance 14, no. 4 (2015): 332-368.
938. Mani, Anandi, et al. "Poverty impedes cognitive function." Science 341.6149 (2013): 976-980.

939. Massey, Douglas S., and Nancy A. Denton. "American Apartheid: Segregation and the Making of the Underclass." Harvard University Press, 1993.
940. McKenzie, B. (2021). 'The Color of Tech Can Change.' Scientific American. https://www.scientificamerican.com/article/the-color-of-tech-can-change/
941. McKinsey & Company. "The Economic Impact of Closing the Racial Wealth Gap," McKinsey & Company, August 2019.
942.
943. McKinsey & Company. "The economic impact of closing the racial wealth gap." McKinsey & Company (2019).
944. McKinsey & Company. 2019. "The Economic Impact of Closing the Racial Wealth Gap." McKinsey & Company.
945. McKinsey Global Institute. "Jobs Lost, Jobs Gained: Workforce Transitions in a Time of Automation." McKinsey Global Institute, 2017.
946.
947. Minority Business Development Agency. (2012). Disparities in Capital Access between Minority and Non-Minority Businesses.
948.
949. Mirowski, Philip, and Dieter Plehwe. "The Road from Mont Pelerin: The Making of the Neoliberal Thought Collective." Harvard University Press, 2009.
950. National Bankers Association. "Our History." National Bankers Association; Black Business Investment Fund. "About Us." Black Business Investment Fund.
951.
952. National Bureau of Economic Research. "Minority and Women Entrepreneurs: Building Capital, Networks, and Skills." The Hamilton Project (2015).
953. National Museum of African American History and Culture. "About the Museum." Smithsonian, 2023.
954. Navigating the Legal Maze: With great power comes great responsibility, especially in the realm of data privacy and security. Ensure your business complies with all relevant digital laws.
955. Obschonka, M., et al. "Entrepreneurial Passion and Personality: The Case of Academic Entrepreneurship," Frontiers in Psychology, 2017.
956. Oliver, Melvin L., and Thomas M. Shapiro. Black Wealth/White Wealth: A New Perspective on Racial Inequality. Routledge, 2013.

957. Oliver, Melvin, and Thomas Shapiro. "Black Wealth, White Wealth: A New Perspective on Racial Inequality." Routledge, 2006.
958. Oliver, Melvin, and Thomas Shapiro. Black Wealth/White Wealth: A New Perspective on Racial Inequality. Taylor & Francis, 2006.
959. Outlaw, Lucius. "On Race and Philosophy." Routledge, 1996.
960. Page, Benjamin I., and Martin Gilens. "Democracy and Equality: The Enduring Link between Wealth and Political Power." Perspectives on Politics 18, no. 3 (2020): 690-707.
961. Pappano, Laura. The Year of the MOOC. The New York Times, 2012.
962. Perry, Andre, et al. "The devaluation of assets in black neighborhoods: The case of residential property," Brookings Institution, 2018.
963. Pew Research Center, "Racial, gender wage gaps persist in U.S. despite some progress," 2020.
964. Pew Research Center, "Trends in Income and Wealth Inequality," 2020.
965. Pfeffer, Fabian T., and Alexandra Killewald. "Generations of Advantage. Multigenerational Correlations in Family Wealth." Social Forces, 2018.
966. Piketty, Thomas. "Capital in the Twenty-First Century." Harvard University Press, 2014.
967. Process Automation and Virtualization: McKinsey predicts that nearly half of existing work activities could be automated in the next few decades, and that more than 50 billion devices will be connected to the Industrial Internet of Things (IIoT) by 2025. This rise in automation and virtualization creates an immense opportunity for Black-led businesses to innovate, streamline operations, and tap into the burgeoning data economy. However, it's critical to address the digital divide that disproportionately affects Black communities, ensuring they have the necessary digital literacy and access to technology to participate in and benefit from these trends. Critics might argue that automation could lead to job losses, but proponents contend that it also creates new opportunities in sectors such as AI, data analysis, and digital services.
968. Reardon, Sean F. "The Widening Academic Achievement Gap Between the Rich and the Poor: New Evidence and Possible Explanations," 2011.

969. Reardon, Sean F., and Kendra Bischoff. "Income Inequality and Income Segregation." American Journal of Sociology, 2011, 116(4): 1092-1153.
970. Riley, Jason L. "Black Culture and the Racial Wealth Gap." The Wall Street Journal, 2018.
971. Rivera, Lauren A. "Hiring as Cultural Matching: The Case of Elite Professional Service Firms." American Sociological Review 77, no. 6 (2012): 999-1022.
972. Robb, Alicia. "Access to Capital among Young Firms, Minority-Owned Firms, Women-Owned Firms, and High-Tech Firms." Office of Advocacy, U.S. Small Business Administration (2013).
973. Robert Wood Johnson Foundation. "How COVID-19 Exposes Racial Disparities in Health, Wealth." March 2021.
974. Rothstein, R. (2017). The color of law: A forgotten history of how our government segregated America. Liveright Publishing.
975. Rothstein, Richard. "The Color of Law: A Forgotten History of How Our Government Segregated America," Liveright Publishing, 2017.
976. Rothstein, Richard. 2017. "The Color of Law: A Forgotten History of How Our Government Segregated America." Liveright Publishing.
977. Rothstein, Richard. The Color of Law: A Forgotten History of How Our Government Segregated America, 2017.
978. Rothstein, Richard. The Color of Law: A Forgotten History of How Our Government Segregated America. Liveright Publishing, 2017.
979. Rothwell, Jonathan. "Housing costs, zoning, and access to high-scoring schools," Brookings Institution, 2012.
980. Rugh, Jacob S., and Douglas S. Massey. "Racial Segregation and the American Foreclosure Crisis." American Sociological Review 75, no. 5 (2010): 629-651.
981. Rugh, Jacob S., and Douglas S. Massey. "Racial Segregation and the American Foreclosure Crisis." American Sociological Review, 2010, 75(5): 629-651.
982. Sampson, Robert J., and William Julius Wilson. "Toward a theory of race, crime, and urban inequality." Race, crime, and justice: A reader, 1995: 37-54.
983. Seek and Identify: Rather than merely copying and pasting digital strategies, a more personal approach is needed. Scrutinize every corner of your business operation, identifying areas where automation and virtualization might streamline processes or

improve customer service. Remember, it's not about the tools, but how they can be harnessed to elevate your business to new heights.

984. Self, Charles S. "The Power of Positive Thinking: A Review." The Personnel and Guidance Journal, vol. 46, no. 4, 196
985. Shapiro, Thomas, and Melvin Oliver. "Black Wealth/White Wealth: A New Perspective on Racial Inequality." Routledge, 1995.
986. Shapiro, Thomas, Tatjana Meschede, and Sam Osoro. "The roots of the widening racial wealth gap: Explaining the black-white economic divide." Institute on Assets and Social Policy, 2013.
987. Sibilia, Rebecca. "Why America's Schools Have A Money Problem," National Public Radio, 2016.
988. Smith, Robert F. "Speech at the Morehouse College commencement." 2019.
989. Sourcing Support: Funding can be the make-or-break point for many ventures. Look to organizations like the SBA and the MBDA for grants or low-interest loans, which are specifically designed to support businesses in digital infrastructure.
990. Sowell, Thomas. "Wealth, Poverty and Politics." Basic Books, 2015.
991. Squires, Gregory D., and Chester Hartman. "There's No Such Thing as a Free Market." American Journal of Economics and Sociology 59, no. 2 (2000): 301-317.
992. Strength in Unity: The journey of digital transformation is challenging but shared with many. Collaborate and connect with other businesses. It can foster innovation and build resilience.
993. Tax Policy Center. "Distributional Analysis of the Conference Agreement for the Tax Cuts and Jobs Act," Tax Policy Center, December 2017.
994. Tax Policy Center. 2017. "Distributional Analysis of the Conference Agreement for the Tax Cuts and Jobs Act." Tax Policy Center.
995. Taylor, Dorceta. "The Rise of the American Conservation Movement: Power, Privilege, and Environmental Protection." Duke University Press, 2016.
996. Taylor, Keeanga-Yamahtta. "Race for Profit: How Banks and the Real Estate Industry Undermined Black home-ownership." The University of North Carolina Press, 2019.
997. Taylor, Keeanga-Yamahtta. From #BlackLivesMatter to Black Liberation. Haymarket Books, 2016.
998. The Art of Reflection: As your business evolves, it's crucial to reflect on what's working and what needs improvement. Regular

evaluations will help you adjust your strategy and maintain a trajectory towards your goals.

999. The Future of Connectivity: Faster digital connections, powered by technologies such as 5G and IoT, are set to unlock significant economic activity. It's estimated that implementing these technologies in key sectors could boost global GDP by $1.2 trillion to $2 trillion by 2030. Black-led businesses, particularly in the sectors of mobility, health-care, manufacturing, and retail, can harness these advancements to drive growth and create wealth. However, to do so, there's a need for increased investment in digital infrastructure in Black communities, and targeted programs to build digital skills.

1000. The Power Matrix, as conceptualized by Antonio T. Smith Jr., recognizes the transformative potential of digital technology for Black wealth generation, creation, and sustainability. The World Economic Forum highlights process automation, virtualization, and enhanced connectivity as pivotal tech trends that could reshape the global economy in the coming decade. These trends present an enormous opportunity for Black wealth creation if leveraged appropriately.

1001. The Power Matrix's digital infrastructure plan, therefore, aims to ensure Black communities are at the forefront of these technological revolutions. It calls for increased digital literacy programs, expanded access to high-speed internet, and targeted support for Black entrepreneurs in digital sectors.

1002. The Power of Learning: As your business begins to embrace these new technologies, make sure your team isn't left behind. Ongoing training and workshops are invaluable to ensure everyone is on the same page and working towards the same vision.

1003. The White House. "Fact Sheet: The American Jobs Plan." The White House, 31 Mar. 2021; The White House. "Fact Sheet: The American Families Plan." The White House, 28 Apr. 2021.

1004. Thompson, Cheryl. "Black Women, Beauty, and Hair as a Matter of Being." Women's Studies, vol. 38, no. 8, 2009, pp. 831-856.

1005. U.S. Bureau of Labor Statistics. "Unemployment rates by race and ethnicity, 2019-2020." March 2021.

1006. U.S. Census Bureau, "Annual Business Survey," 2017.

1007. U.S. Census Bureau, "Black-Owned Businesses in the United States," 2012.

1008. U.S. Census Bureau. "Computer and Internet Use in the United States: 2016." U.S. Census Bureau, 2018.

1009. U.S. Census Bureau. (2018). Annual Business Survey: Black or African American-Owned Businesses in the U.S.
1010. U.S. Census Bureau. (2020). Quarterly Residential Vacancies and home-ownership.
1011. Unearthing Knowledge: The foundation of digital success is built on understanding. Submerge yourself in a wealth of resources that are readily available from platforms like Khan Academy or Code.org. Explore the extensive landscapes of process automation, virtualization, and IIoT. Knowledge is power, and in the digital world, it is the key to unlock endless opportunities.
1012. Urban, Carly, Maximilian Schmeiser, J. Michael Collins, and Alexandra Brown. "State Financial Education Mandates: It's All in the Implementation." Insights on Financial Capability from the FINRA Investor Education Foundation (2015).
1013. Webb Hooper, Monica, Anna María Nápoles, and Eliseo J. Pérez-Stable. "COVID-19 and Racial/Ethnic Disparities." Journal of the American Medical Association, 2020, 323(24): 2466–2467.
1014. Western, Bruce and Becky Pettit. "Incarceration & social inequality." Daedalus, 2010, 139(3): 8-19.
1015. Western, Bruce, and Becky Pettit. "Incarceration & Social Inequality," Daedalus, 2010.
1016. Williams Shanks, Trina R., and Mesmin Destin. "Parental Expectations and Educational Outcomes for Young African American Adults: Do Household Assets Matter?" Race and Social Problems 2, no. 3-4 (2010): 81-97.
1017. Williams, David R., and Selina A. Mohammed. "Racism and Health I: Pathways and Scientific Evidence." American Behavioral Scientist, 2013, 57(8): 1152-1173.
1018. Williams, Richard et al. "The Changing Face of Inequality in Home Mortgage Lending." Social Problems, 2005, 52(2): 181-208.
1019. Wilson, Valerie, and William M. Rodgers III. "Black-white wage gaps expand with rising wage inequality." Economic Policy Institute, 2016.
1020. Wilson, William J. "More Than Just Race: Being Black and Poor in the Inner City." W.W. Norton & Company, 2009.
1021. Wilson, William Julius. More Than Just Race: Being Black and Poor in the Inner City. W. W. Norton & Company, 2009.
1022. Woodward, C. Vann. The Strange Career of Jim Crow, 1955.
1023. World Economic Forum. "The Future of Jobs Report 2022." World Economic Forum, 2022.
1024. Your journey to digital mastery may be challenging, but through commitment and strategic planning, Black-owned businesses can

take the reins of digital innovation and transform not just their own futures, but those of their communities.
1025. Zukin, Sharon. The Cultures of Cities. Blackwell, 1995.